T0369820

THEATRE THEORY READER
PRAGUE SCHOOL WRITINGS

EDITED BY
DAVID DROZD,
TOMÁŠ KAČER
AND DON SPARLING

KAROLINUM PRESS
PRAGUE 2016

KAROLINUM PRESS
Karolinum Press is a publishing department of Charles University
Ovocný trh 560/5, 116 36 Prague 1, Czech Republic
www.karolinum.cz

Layout by Jan Šerých
Printed and bound by CPI Group (UK) Ltd, Croydon, CR0 4YY
First English edition

A catalogue record for this book is available from the National Library
of the Czech Republic.

This book is published as part of the research project *Czech Structuralist Thought on Theatre: Context and Potency* (Český divadelní strukturalismus: souvislosti a potenciál; 2011–2015), which is financed with funds from GAČR (the Czech Science Foundation), No. P409/11/1082.

ISBN 978-80-246-3578-1
ISBN 978-80-246-3579-8 (pdf)

The original manuscript was reviewed by Prof. Veronika Ambros (University of Toronto) and Prof. Yana Meerzon (University of Ottawa).

TABLE OF CONTENTS

LIST OF FIGURES

ACKNOWLEDGMENTS

This book owes its existence to the urgings of Veronika Ambros (University of Toronto) and Eva Stehlíková (Masaryk University), both of whom, *firstly*, have always asserted that the intellectual legacy of the Prague School theatre writings is a cultural treasure that ought to be cultivated and promoted world-wide, and *secondly*, stated their conviction that the Department of Theatre Studies at Masaryk University was ideally suited to put together a team capable of undertaking such a project. The book you are holding in your hands proves their latter point; the former is up to you as reader to judge.

We were fortunate to obtain financial support for our research project from the Czech Science Foundation (GAČR). This enabled us to establish a research team, carry out wide-ranging archival research and hold two international conferences. This reader is the final outcome and crowning achievement of the research project. The concept of the book was refined over time in the course of many discussions amongst international scholars and the members of the team, all of whom have contributed generously with their views and findings. The team members were David Drozd (project leader), Martin Bernátek, Barbora Diego Rivera Příhodová, Pavel Drábek, Šárka Havlíčková Kysová, Tomáš Kačer, Radka Kunderová, Martina Musilová, Eva Šlaisová, Jitka Šotkovská, Don Sparling and Eva Stehlíková.

Many thanks go to all those colleagues who attended our two conferences, entitled Prague Semiotic Stage Revisited I (2011) and II (2013), and helped us both to reassess the Prague School in today's theoretical contexts and to discuss the many complicated translation issues. In addition to Veronika Ambros, who has acted as the unacclaimed patron of the project, four specialists have offered constant support: Andrea Jochmanová, Yana Meerzon, Manfred Pfister and Herta Schmid.

Our research would not have been possible without access to archival materials kept in the Museum of Czech Literature (*Památník národního písemnictví*), the National Museum (*Národní muzeum*) and the archives of Charles University and Masaryk University as well as personal family archives. We are grateful for the expert assistance given by all the archival specialists at the above mentioned institutions; special thanks go to Zita Honzlová and Jarmila F. Veltrusky.

Colleagues and friends around the world have helped with the many areas of expertise such a project entails, ranging from linguistic advice through historical and theoretical knowledge to bibliographical assistance: Christian M. Billing, Maria Bochkova, Campbell Edinborough, Francesca Fulton, Elena Khokhlova, Tomáš Kubart, Dita Lánská, Markéta Polochová, Gabriella Reuss, Sergei Tcherkasski, Dmitri Trubotchkin, and James Zborowski.

The results of the research were regularly discussed with students in various seminars held at the Department of Theatre Studies. Their feedback confirmed the continuing relevance of Prague School theory and helped us to shape the selection of texts for the volume.

The whole project lasted five years, throughout which we were fortunate to be able to rely on the administrative (and moral) support of our invaluable departmental Secretary Jitka Kapinusová.

Finally, a symbolic expression of thanks and respect goes to all those scholars who promoted Prague School theory in the 1970s and 1980s. Without their introductions, translations and editions this volume would have scarcely been possible. Among them, foremost respect should go to the memory of Michael L. Quinn (1958–1994), Prague School scholar and enthusiast, editor, translator and author of the seminal book *The Semiotic Stage: Prague School Theater Theory* (1995).

David Drozd
Project Leader
Brno, August 2016

INTRODUCTION

DAVID DROZD and TOMÁŠ KAČER

> *Theory can clarify, not sit in judgment. Moreover, theoretical concepts are abstractions*
> *that cannot be substituted for concrete facts; these never exist in such a pure form.*
> Jiří Veltruský, "Theatre in the Corridor"

This book features thirty-eight texts from nine authors connected to the Prague Linguistic Circle (PLC), sometimes referred to simply as the Prague School. In the 1930s and 1940s members of the Circle created a complex theory of the theatre. Though these dates might suggest something outdated, yet another Theory consigned to the ash heap of history, the following two quotes point to a different conclusion.

> … the most urgent task of theatre studies is to examine all the individual components within the structure of a theatre performance and to learn how each of the components, with its own specific features, affects the structure as a whole … We should not only describe a word, a gesture or the set as signs but also study the characteristics of the theatrical sign as a whole, which is a synthesis of several sign systems represented by its individual components. (Veltruský 1941: 133)

Jiří Veltruský (1919–1994), who was a member of the PLC, wrote these words in the spring of 1941. That same year his tutor Jan Mukařovský (1891–1975), one of the PLC's founding members, formulated the goal of structural theory, as he called their approach, in a different way:

> We have only a single theoretical task: to show through a few remarks and examples that, despite all the material tangibility of its means (the building, machinery, sets, props, a multitude of personnel), the theatre is merely the base for a non-material interplay of forces moving through time and space and sweeping the spectator up in its changing tension, in the interplay of forces we call a stage performance. (Mukařovský 2016 [1941]: 61)

These two short fragments from Veltruský and Mukařovský grasp the core of the Prague School perspective on theatre performance. They include all the "material" elements of a theatre performance and key concepts employed by

the PLC (such as structure, sign and component), providing in fact a structural definition of theatre. Although this may sound simple, it was precisely
such a simple formulation that was the starting point for structurally oriented
theatre studies – and in fact the task outlined by Mukařovský has remained
the point of departure for all subsequent research on the theatre.

Theories of theatre have developed and diversified immensely since the
1930s and 1940s. Fashions changed throughout the twentieth century and
even theory as such has often been neglected. This book provides an opportunity to return to one of the founding moments in the history of theatre
theory.

The texts in the reader you are holding in your hands were written by a group
of critics and scholars, theatre-lovers and theatre practitioners associated
with the Prague Linguistic Circle in the period from the 1920s to the 1940s.
This whole community has become known as **The Prague School**. Most of
its members dealt with language and literature, but those included in this
reader explored **methodological approaches to theatre** (as well as drama
and performance).

Theatre is much more than a play presented on a stage. There are dozens
of professions associated with the theatre, and all of them influence what
a piece will be like, from actors and the directing team to designers and tech
people, to name but a few. But the list of those associated with each theatrical
event ultimately runs all the way through to audiences, without whom the
whole concept of theatre lacks any meaning. Put simply, theatre can come
into existence in a variety of ways and a variety of activities can be understood as theatre. Today the term can be used to cover a funny sketch by a pair
of middle-aged jugglers on monocycles in a piece inspired by *Hamlet*; a local
amateur production of the *Oresteia* in a brutally cut version of this Classical
play that lacks virtually all props and has a minimal cast, with Clytemnestra and Electra being played by one actress; or – from a completely different
context – the Broadway hip-hop musical hit *Hamilton*, which has met with
immense critical and popular acclaim.

When we say "theatre" in this book, we often mean what is now commonly referred to as "performance". The development of **performance studies**
in the 1980s was a scholarly reaction to changes in what was understood as
performance in the previous decades, and the concepts that were developed
then went on to influence performative practices as such. The concept "performance", with its many secondary and implied meanings (all of which are
worth studying), has become commonplace. It distinguishes itself in certain
respects from "theatre", which is often limited to a specific art form. We
would like to do away with this division and return to a broader use of the
term "theatre".

In their heyday the Prague School thinkers made a shift in terminology similar to that employed in performance studies. They did not introduce the term "performance" as a generic label for a wide range of human activities, instead using "theatre" in this sense. Therefore this reader calls for an open mind: in nearly all cases, what the Prague School says about the theatre is also applicable to what is now called performance.

This similarity between the two schools is manifested in two areas. The first is their shared interest in non-artistic activities (the Prague School in "folk culture", "popular culture", "audience"; performance studies in "rituals"; "happenings", "performativity"), with the result that they borrow from sociology and anthropology. The second is the conceptualization of the avant-garde theatre movements of their respective eras by both schools. That is why most ideas of the Prague School are applicable to contemporary theatrical activities and to a variety of performative events, including cultural performance. And the latter concept has an immense scope. Imagine you are walking through town, turn round a corner and find yourself in the middle of a political rally. The people gathered there are applauding the speakers, who are addressing them with hand-held megaphones. A minute later, the protesters set out on a march through the streets, holding signs such as "We are the 99%" and "Occupy!" How cleverly shaped this manifestation of exercising citizens' rights suddenly seems, what a brilliant example of the town as performance itself!

Why, then, should we read the Prague School? Can its rather early investigations of theatre shed any new light on how we see theatre today? We believe so. The reason for this belief lies in the fortunate circumstance that what is referred to as the theory of the Prague School was never theory for theory's sake. Although we refer to them as theorists, Prague School thinkers always kept **close ties with theatre practice**. Instead of inventing rigid systems, they developed a multi-faceted set of analytical distinctions that can be used flexibly and universally. Although all these **analytical "tools"** have their grounding in the theatre of that period, most of them continue to prove useful today and deserve universal application.

Among the most innovative concepts, which have not grown old but on the contrary have become a standard part of the toolbox of any serious analyst of the theatre, are the following: sign, structure, dominant, component, stage figure and dramatic space. These are the most crucial concepts for understanding the Prague School. In what follows we have arranged these concepts into clusters, with brief explanations intended to elucidate the relations between them and the dynamic nature of the system.

Structure is a term that is almost self-explanatory today, but it is important to remember that it was only in the 1920s that it became a key term for aesthetics. Prague School scholars introduced structure as something highly organized yet dynamic, full of inner tension yet unified, energy-charged, yet organized. Only such a concept of structure is then capable of encompassing the variability of avant-garde art, which asks for and provokes such conceptualization. In the early 1930s Mukařovský stated that "the conception of a work of art as a structure – that is, a system of components aesthetically deautomatized and organized into a complex hierarchy that is unified by the prevalence of one component over the others – is accepted in the theory of several arts" (Mukařovský 2016 [1931]: 192), thus providing one of the standard definitions of *structure* in the work of art.

The element that organizes the structure is usually called the **dominant**. It might be anything – in the case of theatre, think of a gesture, a motif in the text, music, the shape of a costume or spatial organization. What counts is the functionality of the dominant element or feature: "The *dominant* is that component of the work that sets in motion, and gives direction to, the relationships of all of the components" (Mukařovský 1983 [1932]: 170). Identifying the dominant is often crucial, because the dominant is what makes a particular work of art specific and unique. This approach was of significant help in overcoming a content-oriented aesthetics focusing merely on expression. Mukařovský's study "An Attempt at a Structural Analysis of an Actor's Figure" is an instructive example of the new approach: all he is doing here is trying to answer the simple question "What holds Chaplin's acting together?" Or to rephrase this in technical terms, "What is the dominant in the structure of Chaplin's acting?"

The term **element** (or **component**) describes any part of a structure that is a work of art – in our case, a theatrical performance. The first serious attempt to discuss the *elements of a theatre performance* is found in Otakar Zich's *The Aesthetics of Dramatic Art* (1931). In this extensive work, Zich provides a detailed analysis of audience perception during a theatre performance and proposes a distinction between its relatively constant elements (such as the setting, costume and actors) and those that are constantly changing (such as facial expressions, gestures and intonation). Prague School scholars took this further. Many different lists of particular elements can be found in their texts; what is striking is their methodological flexibility. When in his *Components of Theatre Expression* (1946) Jaroslav Pokorný sets out to demonstrate the variability of theatre *structure* in the course of history, he makes do with only five *elements* (literary, musical, movement, visual and dramatic), while when Mukařovský analyses Chaplin's acting he offers a much more detailed listing. It is precisely this sensitivity to the material that prevents Prague School scholars from sterile formalism (a fault sometimes attributed to semiotics).

Structure is always more than just a simple summation of its *elements* – what makes it specific is its organization, the internal contradictions of *elements* and the *dominant*. When applied to theatre, this may lead to the following statement:

> Modern art has revealed the positive aesthetic effect of internal contradictions among the components of the work of art too clearly for us to be able to view the interplay of the individual elements of drama as merely complementary to one another. The modern stage work is an extremely complicated structure (more complicated than any other artistic structure) that eagerly sucks up everything that the contemporary development of technology offers and that other arts provide, but as a rule it does so in order to employ this material as a contrastive factor. (Mukařovský 2016 [1937]: 212)

Contemporary theatre is also open to conceptualization in accordance with this concept of theatrical structure.

For example, when discussing directors' approaches to classical drama, whether Shakespeare or Chekhov, we may concern ourselves with differences not only in dramaturgy or rehearsal methods but also in the very structure of productions. It is enough to compare the function of the set and visual design in Robert Wilson's theatre with that of Peter Brook's. Or consider the actor's position: some directors tend to give the actor a prominent, dominant function in the structure of a piece, while in other cases the actor may be subordinated to visually and/or musically organized stylization. A structural approach can also be used on a more subtle level. Think, for example, about different elements of acting (such as facial expression, gesture, posture and movement as well as aspects of voice – intonation, timbre and speech rhythm) in Stanislavsky's system, the Brechtian approach and Jerzy Grotowski's theatre. In each of these "systems" a different dominant element is the organizing principle. Dealing with such issues was present at the very birth of performance analysis when it was becoming established as a field within theatre studies in the early 1980s. The Prague School theory is one of the channels that provided the conceptual tools for developing this approach to the theatre.

The concept of theatre performance as a dynamic event includes the audience. It was Prague School scholars who provided the initial impulse for exploring the interaction between **a performance and its audience**. The audience is part of Mukařovský's definition of a stage performance quoted above. For him the theatre artefact could not exist without the physical presence of an audience. Bogatyrev discusses the audience on many occasions in his explorations of folk and puppet theatre, where it usually plays quite an active role (compared to, for example, its role in the fourth-wall theatre tradition) and can actually intervene in the performers' actions. Such an approach is not limited to folk (and folklore) theatre – many contemporary theatre productions draw on it. Take for example Peter Schumann's world-famous

Bread and Puppet Theatre. Their performances start with sharing bread with the audience in an attempt to create – at least for the duration of the performance – a feeling of real community. Schumann usually employs a mixture of means of expression, combining masks, puppets, clowning and fragments of improvised dialogue in unexpected and innovative ways. The event often takes place in some public space, which is invaded and transformed by the action of the performers. And when a parade of monstrous puppets is part of the show, then theatre has to (almost literary) fight its way through crowds of spectators and passers-by. All of them – the performers, the spectators and the passers-by – then get involved in debates on current political issues. As a result there is a constant interplay between performers and audience and continual shifts in spatial organization.

All discussion about new theatre space arises from a re-thinking of the actual audience and its social status. But the audience is also understood more broadly as the society for which the theatre is made. This perspective is the omnipresent background to many Prague School texts. In their analyses these scholars often focus on the internal structure of a performance or artefact, but the final question is "How does the whole structure relate to its audience?" The materiality of theatre and its everyday reality is never absent from these authors' considerations.

All the concepts mentioned above influence the way the PLC deals with the term *sign*; for us what is most important is how its members use *sign* for conceptualizing theatre. Originally the concept of the **sign** occurred most frequently in connection with linguistics and psychology - that is, in fields dealing primarily with the production of meaning. However, it found its use in theatre analysis in the works of Prague School thinkers. Their principal insight is that, typically, people and things on the stage do not stand there as themselves but rather represent something else (in traditional drama) or create new meanings characteristic of the performing art (in all sorts of performances and happenings). "The whole of stage reality – the dramatist's words, the actors' performances, the stage lighting – all these represent other realities. The theatre performance is a set of signs," says Jindřich Honzl (Honzl 2016 [1940]: 129). But then comes a more difficult question: what is there that is specific about a theatrical sign? "In order to understand the signs correctly, we must recognize them," claims Petr Bogatyrev (Bogatyrev 2016 [1937]: 97). Is there any unique way in which theatre produces meaning? Honzl gives a very simple but somewhat paradoxical answer:

Many other examples could be given to illustrate the special character of the theatrical sign whereby it changes its material and passes from one aspect to another, animates

> an inanimate thing, shifts from an acoustical aspect to a visual one, and so on. ... This variability of the theatrical sign, its ability to "change its garb", is its specific property. It enables us to explain the variability of the theatrical structure. (Honzl 2016 [1940]: 139)

This passage goes a good way towards demonstrating the qualities of structural thinking: the specific feature of the sign is not something material but rather the relation between sign and meanings. Acknowledging the dynamic character of the theatrical sign is a very strong argument against a literary (or text-centred) concept of theatre. The notorious discussion of the relation between drama and theatre, which can be traced back to Aristotle, becomes rather animated – even dialectical – from a structural perspective:

> ... the relationship between the theatre and the drama [is] always tense, and for this reason also subject to change. In essence, however, the theatre is not subordinate to literature, nor is literature subordinate to the theatre. These extremes can only occur in certain periods of development, whereas in others there is equilibrium between the two. (Mukařovský 2016 [1941]: 69)

Drama (that is, a literary genre) becomes only one of the elements of theatre alongside many others. It is no surprise that Honzl formulated his thesis on the **mobility** of the theatre sign based on his avant-garde experiments as a director.

Signs can produce different meanings within one performance, as Honzl shows. A square of white light projected on a backdrop can become a door. The same character can be played by two or more actors – typically, at different stages of life (when young and when old). And a sign can even travel from one performance to another. A good case in point is the well-known melody of the "Wedding March", composed originally by Felix Mendelssohn as incidental music for an 1842 production of *A Midsummer Night's Dream*. In time, the March became a sign of the wedding as such and so it is used in countless contexts – even outside the performing arts— to signify a wedding.

There are endless examples of the mobility of the theatrical sign and many directors who use this quality to produce a special effect on the audience. One particularly notable example is Peter Brook's famous production of *A Midsummer Night's Dream* (1970), which began with an empty white stage littered about with toys and circus props; in the background the sound of Mendelssohn's composition could be heard. In the course of the performance all these things were turned into signs that gained (and changed) meaning according to the actors' actions. This effective use of the ability of the theatrical sign to shift/change its meaning dynamically made a major contribution to the enormous success of the production.

This simple but basic distinction of **sign** and **meaning** can be further refined. The most fruitful distinctions are those that arise when we think about acting and performance space.

In the case of acting, we arrive at a terminological triad: **actor**, **stage figure**, **dramatic character**. The concept of the *stage figure* has proved to be one of the most productive innovations when dealing with a dramatic text, acting and actors. Otakar Zich was the first to apply the term "stage figure" to what an actor creates on the stage: it is not just a product of the actor's inner creativity but is also an amalgam of the actor's body, costumes and actions. It is the actor when acting. More strictly formulated: "The stage figure is the dynamic unity of a whole set of signs, whose vehicle may be the actor's body, voice, movements, but also various things, from parts of the costume to the set" (Veltruský 2016 [1940]: 148). The dramatic character for Zich is then the audience's interpretation of all the signs they can see and hear on the stage produced by the actor.

This distinction had not been made earlier – and often, especially in connection with realist drama and film, it is still not clear to some audiences even today. But it is extremely difficult to analyse acting without it, because such an analysis requires considering the actor, the stage figure and the dramatic character at the same time. Strange as it may seem, it is clear that we perceive an actor as a "real" person and the actor's specific impersonation of a particular fictional person from a play simultaneously. This claim can be illustrated by an example of an internationally famous star playing a character. Let us take Benedict Cumberbatch playing the role of Hamlet. The audience know it is Cumberbatch and they are familiar with his typical features as a star actor in British theatre and film, just as they know and are familiar with Shakespeare's Hamlet (most likely from discussions in English classes). But when watching *Hamlet* with Cumberbatch, the audience are seeing a particular impersonation of the Prince of Denmark by the actor Cumberbatch; they are watching a unique stage figure. They perceive the actor (Benedict Cumberbatch) and his creation on the stage (the stage figure), while being able to imagine Hamlet (the dramatic character) – all at once. To borrow a term from cognitive theory, the spectator can perceive a stage figure and understand that it consists of an actor and represents a character thanks to **conceptual blending**.

The same phenomenon of co-existing layers can be recognized in the case of **space**. Otakar Zich introduced a strict differentiation between the theatre space (an actual theatre building), the stage (an empty space built intentionally for theatre productions), the set (real space, material on stage that represents another space) and finally **dramatic space**, the imagined (and fictional) place of an action. The pair of terms "stage figure" and "dramatic character" is in fact parallel to "set" and "dramatic space". Mukařovský describes the difference as follows:

> Dramatic space is not identical with the stage and not at all with three-dimensional space, for it originates in time through the gradual changes in the spatial relations between the actor and the stage and between the actors themselves. ... Owing to its energy, dramatic space can extend beyond the stage in all directions. This gives rise to the phenomenon referred to as the imaginary stage. (Mukařovský 2016 [1941]: 69–70.)

Note especially the importance Mukařovský accords to "gradual changes" and the "energy" of the dramatic space. He evidently understands the production of meaning as a dynamic process (which of course includes the audience, as we have seen above in his definition of theatre), not as a merely static (or even mechanical) decoding or reading of signs. Zich's idea that dramatic space is not just an imagined place of action but also an energy-charged space that is a reflection of relations between characters was adopted by both Prague School theoreticians and avant-garde theatre practitioners and further developed. When Veltruský touches upon the issue of *dramatic space*, he stresses the spatial character of relations between dramatic characters: "All the relations between stage figures and characters are projected into space. They constitute what is termed dramatic space, a set of immaterial relations that constantly changes in time as these relations themselves change" (Veltruský 2016 [1941]: 250). The same is true of Mukařovský, Honzl and others – they see dramatic space not only as a fictional space but as a manifestation of relations in performances. In such a conceptualization, the *dramatic space* describes the same phenomenon that Eisenstein terms *mise-en-scène*.

This concept of the *dramatic space* has also had a profound impact on modern theatre **directing and stage design**. The dynamic relationship between the set and dramatic space becomes the driving force of artistic creativity. What was quite stable/settled in the realist theatre of the late nineteenth century was viewed as problematic by avant-garde directors and architects. For them, the set should not only represent the place of action but also embody in visual form the structure of the dramatic relations, the inner structure of the dramatic space. The stage and set should be as dynamic as possible. This led to many discussions on the new organization of theatre space, which have become an inseparable part of contemporary stage design.

Experiments with space marked the whole of the twentieth century. The idea that the stage (or any performance space) should reflect the inner structure of the dramatic space found a very explicit manifestation, for example, in the performances of Grotowski (*Cordian, Faust, The Constant Prince* and especially *Apocalypsis cum Figuris*). Each of them had a unique, special organization of the auditorium and the acting space. This is one of the practical results of the modernist and avant-garde projects that were theorized by the Prague School (see especially Veltruský's "Theatre in the Corridor"). Actual practice confirmed that there is a mutual connection between the structure of the (imaginary) dramatic space and the performance space.

The background of the Prague School in **linguistics** meant that great attention was also devoted to the language of theatre and drama. Roman Jakobson and Jan Mukařovský provided some of the most relevant insights into language and its functions (as most of their essays are available in English in existing editions we have not included all the relevant texts in this book).

Structural linguists identified various **functions of language**; these could also be identified in the language of drama. These functions are organized in theatre and drama in a different way than in everyday communication. Speech in drama has two addressees – a fictional person (or persons) in the play and, simultaneously, the audience/reader of the play.

Speech is a system of various signs. Through speech, a speaker expresses his or her state of mind, but at the same time speech is also a sign of the speaker's cultural and social status and so forth. The playwright and the actors employ all of these signs on the stage to express the social and/or cultural status of the characters. These ideas, developed among others by Petr Bogatyrev in "Theatrical Signs" (included in this reader), can be used in drama analysis – for example to describe the style of a particular playwright or for a more cultural studies oriented reading of a play.

Mukařovský paid particular attention to the semantic construction of speech. His analysis showed that the traditional distinction between **dialogue** and **monologue** is not subtle enough to describe the changing characteristics of speech in delivery and the construction of semantic contexts in a spoken or written text. For this reason he introduced the concept of *"dialogic quality*, designating a potential tendency toward the alternation of two or more semantic contexts, a tendency that is manifested not only in dialogue but also in monologue" (Mukařovský 2016 [1940]: 243). To demonstrate the **dialogic quality** (or *potential*) of a monologic text, Mukařovský used a theatre adaptation of a prose text made by the avant-garde director E. F. Burian, concluding that "the monologue has, therefore, actually generated its dialogization from itself, from its structure, not from its subject" (ibid.). He again devotes more attention to construction (or structure) than to the content. Veltruský followed Mukařovský's method. In his *Drama as Literature* (1942) he provided many examples of dramatic monologues with a dialogic internal structure (for example, Iago's speeches in *Othello*), leaving aside superficial distinctions such as the number of speakers in a dialogue and monologue.

This approach is even more inspiring today than it was in the 1930s. In the **post-dramatic theatre**, the function and nature of the dramatic text undergoes a significant change. Starting from Beckett's late experimental plays (*Not I*, *That Time*, *Catastrophe*, *Footfalls* and others), through writings by Heiner

Müller, Elfriede Jelinek and Sarah Kane, we can observe the disappearance of the traditional concept of character and the dissolution of narrative structures and dialogue.

An approach to the theatre that sees it as a complex **structure** of signs enabled the Prague School theorists to arrive at a detailed study of the creation of the sign and of changes and shifts within it. What happens in a performance is not a simple one-directional communication between the stage and the auditorium – or, for that matter, the author(s) and the audience. Complex relations exist between all the signs on the stage. A performance is an organism with only a few fixed features (and that if the analyst is lucky). It works as a structured system of signs and as such it can be "read". Its internal relations are continuously changing and they exist within a certain hierarchy.

The emphasis on this view of theatre as a system of signs (a functional, ordered and meaning-productive model) directly preceded the **semiotic** approach, which dominated the theatre theory of the 1970s and 1980s and as such is familiar to theory-oriented students of theatre. Rather paradoxically, the above-mentioned performance studies tried to incorporate semiotic findings into its framework, but at the same time it was a direct reaction to the course of development of the semiotics of theatre, which had turned into a jargon-littered self-referencing "club".

Semiotics as a discipline has a long tradition (beginning with the work of the Swiss linguist Ferdinand de Saussure and the American philosopher C. S. Peirce around the turn of the twentieth century) and several stages. For a number of historians, the Prague School represents a particular stage of semiotic thinking. Zich's work in particular has been interpreted as a proto-semiotic analysis of traditional (realistic) theatre and opera. A number of Prague School authors included in this reader developed Zich's ideas, applying them to avant-garde theatre and performance in general. It is not surprising, then, that semioticians of the 1970s and 1980s acknowledged the semiotic legacy of the Prague School.

The approach of the Prague School to the concept of the sign inspired others to apply it to the arts as well as to other **cultural activities** in the general sense. Roland Barthes's *Mythologies* (1957) as well as various concepts of cultural studies advanced by many other thinkers treated *culture as text*. This idea can be traced back from Roland Barthes to Claude Lévi-Strauss and further back to the latter's key inspiration, Roman Jakobson, and even to the 1920s, to Jakobson's early collaboration and friendship with Petr Bogatyrev in Moscow and then in Prague. This reader includes several essays by Petr Bogatyrev in which he studies how our daily actions might be intended to signify something or be understood as meaningful. This is something we have all experienced. For instance, imagine you are passing by a four star hotel and see the doormen and porters hurrying back and forth. Their elegant uniforms and smooth, practised movements when opening limousine doors and carrying luggage send a clear message: this is a true four-star performance.

Petr Bogatyrev's analysis of "Clothing as a Sign", for example, offers revealing examples of dress conventions (sign structures) that reflect social situations or social status. This is the exact point that is later developed in Barthes's discussion on fashion, Richard Schechner's concept of "restored behaviour" and Yuri Lotman's semiosphere. In this context, it is then also possible to read the Prague School as a direct precursor of **cultural studies**.

Yet the approach of the Prague School to theories of art and culture was different. While some recent theories (or rather, "Theories" with a capital T) have often tended to be self-obsessed with new concepts and terms, the Prague School focused primarily on the analysis of its material. Here the Prague School's pragmatic approach to theory is clearly evident: the functional strategy of analysis is used when it brings results. Conceptions of the theory are subject to a functional approach as well: when the application of a tool brings no new findings, it is put back in the toolbox or even discarded completely. When Veltruský wrote an essay on Burian's production of *Alladine and Palomides* in 1939 he provided an analysis of an actual theatre event – in fact, what we would today call a **performance analysis**. At the same time he tested the linguistic concept of sign and tried to see to what extent it could be used in understanding specific ways of creating meaning in the theatre. Reading the essay makes this clear: theory follows the material that is to be analysed, not the other way round.

A BRIEF DESCRIPTION OF THE STRUCTURE OF THE READER

This publication consists of two main parts, which follow after this Introduction and the short commentary on editorial issues entitled "Editors' Choices and Guidelines". The first major part is the reader itself, which provides the first comprehensive and critical anthology of texts reflecting the development of Prague School theatre theory from its beginnings in the aesthetics of Otakar Zich. The majority of the thirty-eight texts presented here come from the 1930s and early 1940s, the time when the Prague Linguistic Circle was most active, functioning as a theoretical laboratory as well as a focal point for scholars, artists and intellectuals. A number of the essays presented here date from the postwar period but carry on the original pre-war momentum. This first major part is followed by the second, an afterword entitled "Prague School Theatre Theory and Its Contexts" by Pavel Drábek and a group of authors. This describes the background to the emergence of the Prague School, its aim being to facilitate a better and deeper understanding of these texts.

By its very nature the book is not meant to be read as though it were a novel, from first word to last in a given order. Instead, the reader is invited to explore those parts that are personally relevant at a given time. Just as the Prague School theorists viewed theory as a **toolbox** of approaches to theatre analysis, so this reader should be considered a toolbox of possibilities. For this reason, the eight sections of the anthology cover the most common areas of performance analysis.

The reader is organized thematically and structurally rather than chronologically, focusing on issues and themes in the study of the theatre as an art form and as artistic practice.

I THEATRE IN GENERAL

This section is devoted to the theatre as a specific and unique art form with its own set of theoretical problems. The Prague School was among the first to emancipate the theatre as a discipline worthy of academic and critical reflection, independent of literary studies, sociology and popular culture or ethnographic enquiry.

II SIGN – OBJECT – ACTION

The essays presented here are the first to theorize the concept of the sign in the theatre, doing so in a pre- or proto-semiotic way. Moving outside linguistic systems as set up by Ferdinand de Saussure and C. S. Peirce, the Prague School formulated its own dynamic system of terminology of the sign, drawing heavily on contemporary phenomenology. Its theories developed into discussions of signs within larger systems of relations – structures – that operate in particular hierarchies where some of the components are dominant, others less so. The essays in this section, written by theorists as well as the theatre practitioner Jindřich Honzl, elaborate a terminology that helps articulate what actually happens in the theatre during a performance.

III FIGURES AND PLAY

With Otakar Zich's theory of acting as their starting point, Petr Bogatyrev, Jan Mukařovský and Jindřich Honzl elaborated critical tools for speaking of and analysing the actor and the actor's art. These essays are related not only to theatre studies but also to early play theory (Bogatyrev's first essay). While three of the texts discuss Charlie Chaplin, Honzl's study contextualizes analytical theory in the framework of theatre history and its stock types.

IV FROM PAGE TO STAGE

Jan Mukařovský and Jiří Veltruský devoted systematic attention to dramatic literature and the literary component in the theatre. While Otakar Zich disregarded the special position of the dramatic text within the theatre performance, viewing it as a merely subservient component of the whole, both Mukařovský and Veltruský highlight its unique position as an artefact that exists within the theatrical structure in a certain state of autonomy. Mukařovský also observes – in one of the earliest texts on adaptation and dramatization – that the theatre often makes use of an inner dialogism present in non-dramatic literature.

V LAYERS OF SPACE
The essays in this section are dedicated to innovative and sometimes visionary explorations of the stage space, from implied or imaginary space in drama through performance space and the proxemic relations on stage to early theories of scenography as stage space in the theatre and in film. These essays link the theatre with the visual arts, theorizing the moment when the in house visual artist (the stage designer) became a virtual poet of form, creating spaces that will then be inhabited by characters, action and drama.

VI TOWARDS STRUCTURES OF MODERN ACTING
Advancing general theories of acting, the stage directors Jiří Frejka and Jindřich Honzl contributed not only to modern, avant-garde theatre practice but also to criticism by discussing particular details of the modern actor's art, from mimicry through mimetic signs and signals to a creative engagement with actorly conventions. This section is complemented by a 1976 essay by Jiří Veltruský that further refines the critical tools of acting theory with a view to the current state of the art.

VII ETHNOGRAPHICAL ENCROACHMENTS
The essays in this part focus on the relations between the theatre and society – both civic and folk – discussing performative folk traditions (among them folk ballads, which also had a visual and a performative aspect), folk costumes in relation to their performative, theatre-like qualities, as well as the theatre's function in the public sphere and its role for the formation of a civic society. Rather than being concerned with the artefact of the theatre, these essays focus on the theatre's social dimensions.

VIII ART – MEDIA – SOCIETY
The concluding section of the reader is dedicated to texts that might – somewhat anachronistically – be referred to as intermedial theory. Their focus is on the use of different media in the theatre, the concept of the stage metaphor (both essays on this topic were written by a leading avant-garde theatre director), the active use of puppets in an innovative theatre production, and a far-reaching rethinking of the theatre as a hierarchy of components that

is inherently linked with the norms and values of the society in which it exists.

WORKS CITED

Bogatyrev, Petr (2016 [1937]) "A Contribution to the Study of Theatrical Signs", this reader, pp. 91-98.

Honzl, Jindřich (2016 [1940]) "The Mobility of the Theatrical Sign", this reader, pp. 129-46.

Mukařovský, Jan (1983 [1932]) "Standard Language and Poetic Language" in Josef Vachek and Libuše Dušková (eds) *Praguiana. Some Basic and Less Known Aspects of the Prague Linguistic School. LLSEE*, vol. 12, Amsterdam, Philadelphia: Benjamins, pp. 165-85.

— (2016 [1940]) "Dialogue and Monologue", this reader, pp. 220-46.

— (2016 [1941]) "On the Current State of the Theory of Theatre", this reader, pp. 59-75.

— (2016 [1931]) "An Attempt at a Structural Analysis of an Actor's Figure (Chaplin in *City Lights*)", this reader, pp. 192-98.

— (2016 [1937]) "On Stage Dialogue", this reader, pp. 212-15.

Veltruský, Jiří (1941) "Dramatický tekst jako součást divadla" [Dramatic Text as a Component of Theatre], *Slovo a slovesnost*, vol. 7, no. 3, pp. 132-44.

— (2016 [1940]) "People and Things in the Theatre", this reader, pp. 147-56.

— (2016 [1941]) "Dramatic Text as a Component of Theatre", this reader, pp. 247-67.

EDITORS' CHOICES AND GUIDELINES

Access to Prague School structuralist texts on the theatre has been difficult for readers of English. A number of texts have been translated, but they are scattered among various publications[1] that appeared over time and differed in their focus (literary studies, film studies, collections of a particular author's texts on a variety of subjects). An even larger number of texts has remained untranslated. As editors, we made it our first task to collect all existing texts on the theatre written by Prague School structuralists, disregarding whether they were available in English or not. We then made a representative selection, the aim being to include texts covering the widest scope of topics within the field of theatre studies as well as reaching beyond it; these were subsequently grouped together according to areas. The result is thirty-eight texts divided into eight groups. Within each of these groups the texts are presented in chronological order based on their date of origin (typically, the date of first publication or the date when the paper was given as a lecture). This helps to create a sense of the context of the theoretical debate at the time and, where appropriate, of the development of concepts over the course of time.

To provide the reader with the fullest context, this edition includes previously published footnotes (those of the authors as well as of later editors). Authors' footnotes have been preserved, but when these include references they have been incorporated into the main text; footnotes added by subsequent editors are marked as "editorial notes" with the date of publication of the edition in which they appeared. Newly added notes are marked as "editor's notes".

In the case of cited works, wherever possible references are made to the most recent English translation. Where no English translation exists, we refer to the most recent, or the most standard, edition in the original language.

---

1   Most importantly the following: Garvin, Paul L. (ed.) (1964) *A Prague School Reader in Esthetics, Literary Structure and Style*, Georgetown: Georgetown University Press; Matejka, Ladislav and Titunik, Irwin R. (eds) (1976) *Semiotics of Art: Prague School Contributions*, Cambridge, Mass.: The M.I.T. Press; Matejka, Ladislav (ed.) (1976) *Sound, Sign and Meaning*, Ann Arbor: University of Michigan Press; Mukařovský, Jan (1977) *The Word and Verbal Art*, New Haven and London: Yale University Press; Mukařovský, Jan (1978) *Structure, Sign and Function*, New Haven and London: Yale University Press; Steiner, Peter (ed.) (1981) *The Prague School: Selected Writings, 1929–1946*, Austin: The University of Texas Press.

We include dates of original publication in square brackets after the year of publication of the cited edition. It is hoped that this practice will make it easier for the reader to follow the intellectual context in which the authors were writing, what trends they were reacting to and the chronology of the debate. There is a special case of this referencing: whenever an author cites from a work that is included in this reader we make a cross-reference to this volume (marked as "Author 2016") but also provide the date of the first publication – usually in Czech – of this work so as to give a better idea of the diachronic development of a particular critical issue.

All references and quotes have been double-checked or researched in accordance with current academic standards. The citation style has been updated and unified in all texts. However, it will come as no surprise that, with texts as dated as these and in view of the "open-minded" approach towards standards of academic citations that prevailed at the time when they originated, it proved impossible at times to find exact references. These instances are footnoted.

As this reader is a collection of translations, a specific set of editorial rules relating to English editions had to be adopted. The thirty-eight texts included in this volume break down into three main groups as far as their availability hitherto in English is concerned. Something over a third (14) have appeared earlier in English translation. Slightly under a half (18) are appearing here in English for the first time. Six articles (four by Jiří Veltruský and two by Karel Brušák) were either written in English originally or translated into English by their authors. This situation presented the editors with a number of problems when it came to language editing. Two in particular loomed large.

First, the translations that already existed were the work of a great many different translators. Some had a deep knowledge of Czech, others less; in some cases pairs (one a Czech speaker and the other a native English speaker) worked together to produce the translation. As a result, the quality of the translations varied greatly. This was exacerbated by the varying approaches to translation: some translators favoured a faithful rendering of the original, while others felt free to paraphrase or even edit the original text, leaving out passages or adding bits at will. In addition, there was great diversity in the English terminology, with a number of key terms appearing in three or four guises, thus clouding their meaning for the English-speaking reader.

Second, most of the translations had been made at a fairly late date, when semiotics had come to rule the roost. Hence semiotic terminology was often employed in the translations, in this way distorting the texts in a way that tended to mask their originality and their intellectual origins.

Faced with this situation, the editors agreed on the following guidelines:
- The translations should keep as close to the original as possible, without additions or excisions. In some cases this has resulted in texts that are by current standards repetitive or stylistically odd, even obscure in places, but it was felt that it was more important to present to the reader the texts as they were actually written by the authors in question rather than tidied up versions reflecting some particular editorial bias.
- The vast majority of the texts were written seventy years ago and earlier. Though nowadays they may strike one stylistically as somewhat old-fashioned, even in places archaic, this was not the case when they were written. Thus the translations employ neutral current English, neither colloquial nor overly literary.
- Wherever possible, the effort has been made to unify terminology, the aim being to make it easier to understand the approach of the Prague School and appreciate the links between authors. In a few particular cases, however, authors developed a somewhat personal terminology which, though idiosyncratic, was consistent and is made clear in the texts in question. In these cases the texts were left largely untouched. This relates in particular to texts by Jiří Veltruský and Karel Brušák.
- Where necessary, translations have been "de-semoticized"; that is, terms more appropriate to the period in which the texts were written have been used to replace terms that became current with the rise of semiotic discourse. A typical example can be found in Jindřich Honzl's "Ritual and Theatre". In the original translation of this essay into English, published in 1982, there is the following passage: "A religious interpretation is a special case of a semiotic interpretation of reality, and a religious act is a special case of a semiotic action. We have said that the semioticity of a ritual action makes it analogous to a theatrical action." For the current publication, this passage has been re-formulated as follows: "A religious interpretation is a special case of a sign-based interpretation of reality, and a religious act is a special case of an action that functions as a sign. We have said that the ritual action's nature as a sign makes it analogous to a theatrical action."

One last point. In many places the texts quote passages that have been translated into Czech from some foreign language. Whenever such passages came from texts that have been translated into English, these versions have been used. Where this was not the case, every effort has been made to obtain access to the original text (for example, in French or German or Russian) and use this as a check in determining the final English wording.

I THEATRE IN GENERAL

The texts in this opening section of the reader provide a conceptual framework for the whole volume. Three crucial personalities with their distinctive contributions are introduced here.

Otakar Zich's theoretical work, especially *The Aesthetics of Dramatic Art: A Theoretical Dramaturgy* (1931), is referred to frequently in texts by members of the Prague School. However, the work itself is too complex (and too extensive) to be included in the present volume. We have therefore chosen a different text by Zich – a 1923 lecture entitled "Principles of Theoretical Dramaturgy", which outlines all his key concepts and can serve as a short summary of, and introduction to, concepts that preceded the writings of the Prague School.

"On the Current State of the Theory of Theatre" (1941) is one of Jan Mukařovský's few texts dedicated solely to theatre. His first attempt to systematize a structural approach to theatre, it relies on and appropriates a great deal from Zich's notions. He builds on Zich's idea that in the case of theatre it is the actual theatre performance that is the work of art, and arrives at the quite radical concept of the theatre performance as an interplay of meanings and forces between the actors and the audience. In his definition, Mukařovský captures the processual and interactive nature of theatre. He also stresses the function of the theatre audience in the processes of creation and reception, while reflecting on the constant interest of avant-garde theatre practitioners in the social function of theatre.

The full version of Jiří Veltruský's "Structuralism and Theatre" was only discovered recently (see the note on its publication history), but it demonstrates well the open critical discussions that went on within the Prague Linguistic Circle. Written and delivered in 1941 by a young scholar (Veltruský was only 22 at the time) as the precondition for his admission as a member of the Circle, it is a daring and well-thought-out critical summary of the state of structural theatre theory at the time. It is important to contextualize the text. In the preceding paper, "On the Current State of the Theory of Theatre", Mukařovský (who was Veltruský's teacher) is attempting to sketch out a system, while Veltruský is providing a critical evaluation of the founding theoretical concepts. Both papers were written at the same time, a clear indication that in this period Prague School accounts of theatre did not form a coherent theory but were rather part of a work-in-progress.

PRINCIPLES OF THEORETICAL DRAMATURGY

OTAKAR ZICH

[Zich wrote "Principy teoretické dramaturgie" in Czech before the publication of his 1931 seminal work, *The Aesthetics of Dramatic Art: A Theoretical Dramaturgy*. It remained in manuscript until 1997, when it was published in *Divadelní revue*, vol. 8, no. 1, pp. 12–24.]
Translated by Pavel Drábek

Editor's note: Throughout the text, Zich frequently employs the convention, originating in Greek and Latin usage and continuing down to the present in Czech, of referring to a literary work as a "poem", to literature as "poetry", to an author as a "poet", to something literary as "poetic", and so on. At a few points, this also has some bearing on his argument. As this convention has not held such a prominent place in English-language criticism and critical theory, both in the past as well as, more particularly, in the present, this translation employs instead, in most cases, the standard current terminology.

Some of the numbers and letters dividing the text into units have been adjusted to form a logically organized whole.

There are several instances where Zich makes a reference to a passage elsewhere in his text that cannot be found in his article. However, the manuscript of the text was never properly edited, and such references would appear to be notes Zich made for himself, indicating how he planned to develop the concepts in question; as such they have been deleted and marked with an ellipsis in square brackets.

This article will deal with the aesthetics of drama as a stage or theatrical work. It will also deal with specific theoretical problems stemming from the fact that not only are these works very complex but their components are *heterogeneous*. There exist very complex works of art (architecture, the symphony) whose components are, nevertheless, homogeneous. The complexity that characterizes them when executed arises from a division of labour. But all those involved carry out labour of the same kind, whereas with a theatrical work not only is there the greatest complexity but the performances and contributions of the individuals are of different kinds. Most importantly, the work we perceive has components of quite different natures and we perceive them differently: the actors' acting, dance (if present) and the set through sight, and the actors' speech, and song and music (if present), through hearing.

Nevertheless, a work, if it is a work of art, must form a unified whole. The task then is to examine the mutual *relation* of these components and the *nature* of the individual components as parts of the whole work.

These issues are usually addressed by deductive logic, which leads to dogmatic claims that are at variance with reality. Even superficial observation tells us that some of the components of a dramatic work point to specific disciplines in the arts. The dramatic text may be assigned to literature; opera music to music; the stage set to the visual arts. With a view to the unity of a work, it was felt that one of these arts had to be dominant; hence drama was simply assigned to one discipline or another. But this is too one-sided; the other components are insufficiently valued. A play is defined as "primarily (or wholly) a literary work", an opera as "primarily (or wholly) music". The former definition in particular is commonly accepted (theatre critics, for instance, are mostly literary people). The latter has been challenged, in particular by Wagner's reform, at least to the extent that it is said that "opera is music and literature" (like vocal music).

These views are understandable given that those who express them consider the *printed text* to be the "play" and the *score* to be the "opera". For them the art of acting (which includes the stage set) is no more than a reproductive art, like the arts of recitation or playing an instrument. This view has its critics, especially among actors, who are right in claiming their art to be not only reproductive but also productive; they do not merely carry out what the author directly prescribed for them but also create something new, which the author specifies only indirectly or partially but which is otherwise free.

There is no question that when the text of a play or an opera score is written down this does *not* mean that the dramatic work is finished in the way that a completed novel or painting is finished, or even in the way that a score of, for example, a symphony is to a certain extent finished, where the only remaining task is to perform (or to bring to completion, homogeneously) what is indicated by the notes. A dramatic work must still be brought to completion by heterogeneous creation, that is by the performer's art – not only speaking or singing but also acting – and also the creation of the set in which it is to be acted.

In view of this sequential creation of the dramatic work, it is clear that several arts work together to achieve a common end, and that a dramatic work is thus one that *links up* several arts, arts that are of artistically equal value, though some precede others in time while others follow later.

This realization raises the question of the relation between the arts when sharing in the creation of drama on the one hand, and these arts when operating on their own on the other. For with the exception of acting, which exists only within the dramatic work, all the other arts that are joined together in drama (literature, music, the visual arts) have their own spheres of activity, and it is clear that the laws they comply with when they are independent and when they are linked are not identical.

This circumstance is sometimes expressed by saying that their autonomy (which is the subject of the aesthetics of the individual arts) is forced to make compromises when they are joined together; there is talk of the autonomy of the literary demands, of the demands of the actors, and so on. This does indeed recognize the actual fact (that the laws are not identical in both cases), but the formulation is incorrect, since a work of compromise or full of contradictions – which arise from the *essence* of the dramatic work (as a "combination of arts") and are therefore inherent – could never achieve any unity. The evidence of good dramas and operas does not bear this out. If there are such contradictions in other works, they arise solely from faulty theory, which for example approaches drama as literature and so disregards the actor; however, these are dramatically imperfect works. Often this is no more than ineptitude on the part of the author in asking the impossible of the actor – but the same thing may happen to a composer with respect to the musician. In a good dramatic work (be it spoken or musical) there are *no* antinomies or contradictions.

However, much more often, even when it is realized that several arts of equal value are joined together in the dramatic work, the approach followed is deductive and dogmatic. What is sought is uniformity among the laws valid for the various arts, whether they are on their own or form components of a dramatic work. This has two consequences:

(a) Laws valid for one art are transferred unchanged to the dramatic work. This is very often the case in theatre practice and quite naturally the art of acting suffers most, since in the creation of the dramatic work it comes last. So despite the theory of "arts of equal value", this case coincides with what was mentioned above. The drama is conceived exclusively as a purely literary work with no regard for its being performed by actors; these are termed *closet dramas*. These dramas represent a crux for both actors and stage directors; if they nevertheless decide to perform one, the author's disregard for acting has its revenge and the drama proves to be – undramatic. Likewise in opera: the autonomous efforts of the musical performers are so great that they require the author to provide texts fit "for music". These "librettos" are then of such a nature that literary histories do not even mention them. And an *opera* created in such a way (with arias, duets, choruses, and so on) is, once again, undramatic when performed. One could talk in this respect of *concert opera*. (An error analogous to deductive dogmatism is to impose laws valid in the visual arts as *laws of the theatre stage*.) ... That the audience does not feel this undramatic quality as strongly as with a theatre performance results from their satisfaction with the impressions they have become used to in concert halls, even though they are sitting in a theatre auditorium. Nevertheless, anyone who has at least a little dramatic sense is well aware of this, and it is understandable that playwrights scorn these "operas".

(b) Laws that are valid for a particular art within a *dramatic* work are regarded as its laws *generally*. This view has only been expressed theoretically, by Wagner, who took it *ad absurdum* by denying the individual arts the right to an independent existence at all. It was claimed that such individual egotism on the part of the arts was merely of developmental, so to speak "educational", import. But the actual life of the arts shows clearly enough that this artistic communism of the arts is a theoretical error.

If we are to address the problem we set forth at the start, we have to proceed by a *strictly inductive* method. That is to say, we have to identify the *material* to be examined and induce the laws *from it*. And right away, in demarcating this material, it is necessary to emphasize its nature in order to avoid making a common mistake, which is in fact that of begging the question. "Dramatic works" are not manuscripts or printed texts but works that are performed. That is, they are not Shakespeare's *Hamlet* or Smetana's *The Bartered Bride*[1] as they appear in a book or a score but these works performed on real stages by real artists. What we have just experienced when we are leaving the theatre is the dramatic work. Although this seems almost self-evident, in reality we are so used to substituting for it the abovementioned printed texts or manuscripts that our theoretical reflections continually lead us to an erroneous conception and to incorrect formulations of laws and rules that give the false appearance of being empirical. Please bear this in mind throughout the entire essay.

The dramatic work, then, is what we have perceived in the theatre (and not while reading at home). If we wish to arrive at its laws, we have to *analyse this percept of ours*. And this is the second important thing. This percept forms a unity and there is nothing to indicate that it is "composed" – let alone sequentially – of several arts. We may be aware of how the work was created; however, that is theoretical knowledge. The *psychological analysis of an impression of a theatrical performance* must be our point of departure. We shall certainly recognize the individual heterogeneous artistic aspects but we shall consider them as they are (as components), without any connection to the arts to which they may be related. This is not to say that we shall completely ignore the process through which the dramatic work is created. Once we have resolved the questions posed at the beginning of this essay and turn to the question of the style of dramatic works, we shall have to take into account

---

1   [Editor's note: The opera *The Bartered Bride* (1866), by the composer Bedřich Smetana (1824–1884), probably the best known and most frequently performed work of Czech classical music, considered both a classic and a national treasure.]

the psychological processes of their creation. However, that is another question, one that can only be resolved when questions are precisely formulated with regard to the *essence* of the dramatic work and the *nature of and relation between the components* that are found in it.

Our clear definition of the material has another important consequence: that we must limit our consideration to *the dramatic art of the present*, since it is the only theatre we know in the way required, that is, as produced. From the past we may consider only what is still viable – that is, what is still being produced, and in the form in which it is currently being produced. From earlier periods our only sure knowledge is of what has managed to survive – that is, written (printed) texts and/or music; for even more remote periods, only texts (though we know, for example, that Classical tragedy was accompanied by music). Our information on historical performance practices is very imperfect, and sometimes lacking completely. Hence the historical perspective is irrelevant and of no value for our aesthetic reflections since the objective here is to deduce the laws of today's dramatic art, laws that might be employed in current artistic practice. This is also the broader requirement of aesthetics (and of scholarship generally) – to be living scholarship. And of course there is even less reason to consider "prehistoric" hypotheses of the origins of dramatic art, of some original unity, of some "primeval art" that gave birth to all the others, and so on.

If we look at all the material that can be gathered together in accordance with the above principles, taking into account various types of "dramatic" and "theatrical" and "scenic" art (spoken drama, music drama, mime, ballet, the great variety of mixed forms such as *mélodrame*, concert opera, costume dramas and such like, not to mention those of lower artistic quality), it transpires that *all of them* share one element, which is *acting*. The art of acting is then the *necessary* component of dramatic art, ever-present and therefore *essential*. All the others may be there but they need not be, whether it is a question of an entire work or of its segments or parts. This is immediately obvious with music, but it is also true of the text. There is no text in a mime performance accompanied by music, but in opera and in spoken drama there are sometimes also passages, even very long ones, in which the word is absent. Yet the work remains a piece of dramatic art. This is even true of the stage, at least in the sense that it may be reduced to a mere space, a place (without any further specification) where the actors are acting.

This insight into the essential nature of acting for the dramatic work is of such crucial importance that nothing would change even if we were to extend our material to include other historical periods, relying on the sketchy accounts of the performance of dramatic works in past eras (Classical theatre, medieval plays, folk plays, and so on); here in particular we would meet with numerous genres where the text was completely subordinate or absent altogether. However, only texts, dramatic "poems", have survived from the past and we have therefore become accustomed to looking upon drama as a type of literature. This error, supported by the earliest known theory (Aristotle), which has been misinterpreted (drama and literature then were much closer to each other in all ways), needs to be corrected first before we move on to a positive diagnosis.

Drama is not a type of literature. The objective proof was presented above: a dramatic work may exist without a text, for example mime. Still, it could be objected that the theme of the mime performance, its "storyline" (and also "characters"), is literary, "poetic". However, that would be a mistake resting in an overly broad understanding of the term "poetic". It is not only poems and novels that we call poetic but also anything that evokes a multitude of varied notions and thoughts in our imagination, such as a painting, or even something that puts us in a certain mood. We speak about a poetic landscape, a poetic moment; what is meant by this is a calm, harmonious mood – "poetic" here is almost the same as "beautiful". This is the idiom of everyday life and of popular aesthetics, as used by critics in particular. The *scholarly* sense of the word *poetic* has to be defined accurately so that the word may become the label for a concept. And here it is evident that we can only designate as poetic or literary qualities the qualities of literature proper, that is, the art that uses speech to achieve aesthetic effects. The literary effect, quality, and so on are then the *aesthetic effect* (quality, and so on) *of words*.

This definition indicates that the real (that is, the acted) "storyline" of a mime performance, as well as of any other drama, is characterized not by literary qualities but rather by acting, and the same is true of the real characters of a mime performance and of any drama (that is, the characters represented by the actors). It is only the lines spoken by these characters that have, or may have, literary qualities. It is worth observing what happens to these literary qualities during the performance of a drama. Relatively speaking, they retreat into the background. The effect of specifically literary qualities – nuances of thought and mood, wordplay, allusions, images, and so on – is weakened in performance. Hence the blandness, when we listen to them on the stage, of many closet dramas that, when read, moved us with their exceptional literary quality. This is not always the fault of the acoustics, though this is a well-known phenomenon, referred to as *theatre acoustics*. The cause lies elsewhere, as the opposite case shows: the dialogues of true dramatists (Shakespeare, Molière) have a stronger effect on the stage than when read. This is because they have, in addition to literary qualities, dramatic qualities. Similarly, on stage, unlike in reading, the temporal structure (architecture) of the drama and the coherence and concreteness of characters stand out more clearly. And of course by the same token the deficiencies of these qualities also stand out, since these are not literary qualities, or at least not exclusively literary. Diderot, the first great theorist of dramatic art, claimed that an act is too long if it has too little action (that is, acted, not narrated, action) and too much talking. Otto Ludwig (1871) later wrote that a drama is good when it is comprehensible even without words (as for instance when it is performed in a language we do not understand).

However, one may object to all this that the dramatist first creates the text and this text as a verbal form is a literary creation, even within our strict definition. The performances of the actors as well as the stage set and possibly even the music are then shaped on the basis of the text. So is the literary creation not then the essence of a dramatic work, or even its guiding principle? Mime is in fact a special phenomenon – and after all, its artistic legitimacy may be questioned.

This objection would certainly be a fundamental one if it agreed with the reality. This leads us to the process of the creation of a dramatic text, and this mental process must be subjected to psychological analysis by means of empirical tools, that is, from relevant material. If we do so and study the claims of true dramatists about their work, particularly dramatists who were also theorists of their discipline, we find that their initial impulses were not verbal, that is literary, but were related instead to actors and the stage. Diderot says: "When playwrights conceive of a character, they associate it with a concrete physiognomy. The image of a character acting on the stage must suggest the character's lines to the author" (Diderot 1883). Ludwig gives several examples of how his dramas were created from optical visions (almost hallucinations) of the stage action.[2] Wilhelm von Scholz claims that drama first starts to develop in the author's mind as a sequence of scenes in a certain space and time, and these are filled by the dialogues of the onstage characters only later and piecemeal (1914: 180). If Ludwig says that "the lyric poet delves into himself; the epic poet into his characters; and the dramatic poet into the actors of his characters" (1871),[3] this is also an expression of the priority of the stage vision, and it should be added that in many cases it was quite specific actors who gave rise to the dramatists' conception (for example Coquelin – Cyrano).[4] (Until the present this was the only way of capturing actors' personalities – compare the cinema!) This also confirms the general fact that the artist creating his work does not think abstractly

---

2   See Müller-Freienfels, Richard (1912) *Psychologie der kunst* [Psychology of Art], vol. I, Leipzig and Berlin: A. G. Teubner, p. 219; Binet, Alfred (1886) *La Psychologie du raisonnement* [Psychology of Reasoning], Paris: Germet Baillière, where Ernest Legouvé and Eugène Scribe's claim is to be found, as quoted in Bathe, Johannes (1916) "Leben und Bühne in der dramatischen Dichtung" [Life and the Stage in Dramatic Poetry], *Zeitschrift für Aesthetik u. allgemeine Kunstwissenschaft*, vol. 11, p. 304.

3   [Editor's note: We were not able to locate this quote in Ludwig 1871.]

4   [Editor's note: Benoît-Constant Coquelin (1841–1909), the most prominent French actor of his time. His Cyrano was famous both in its theatre and film versions.]

(in "ideas") but in terms of his material. For the dramatist, this material is actors (on the stage).

We see then that not even a reference to the origin of the dramatic work speaks in favour of literature; on the contrary, it shows that the original conception is related to actors and the stage, and that this guides the literary conception. The actors merely bring this original conception into being. The logical concurrence with the previous finding – that is, that the art of acting is the essential aspect of the dramatic work – is clear. A work of art should evoke in us those mental states (visions, ideas, emotions) that its creator had when creating them (that is as an artist, not as a person). In our case, the work of art is the actual performance, not the dramatic text (as read), and we see that this performance arises at the very start of the long process through which the dramatic work comes into existence. Naturally, the dramatist's vision of the work in performance is not and cannot be identical with the actual performance. Productions of the same work may be very different from each other, and yet all may be good. This is a consequence of the imperfect means available in the dramatic work for prescribing anything. The dramatist can only accomplish this by means of words – that is, only partially. However, this imperfection is not an aesthetic shortcoming, for it is this that offers creative freedom for those who bring the dramatic work into being. Indeed, even in music the score is never completely prescriptive and performing artists (virtuosos, conductors) enjoy the freedom arising from this by right. Thus every performance of a dramatic or musical work is a unique artistic event; herein is found considerable aesthetic appeal and great artistic value (the expression of the individuality of the performing artists). ...

After this analysis we can return to our initial standpoint, on the basis of which we intend to consider the completed dramatic work – that is, one that is performed and is perceived by us – and provide a positively worded formulation of the special position of the art of *acting* (that is, mimesis) within it as the first principle of dramatic art.

The principle of mimetic supremacy (that is, the principle of *dramaticality*). Through a comparison of various (performed) dramatic works we have found that the art of acting forms its necessary and essential part. The disinterested impression gained from every single performance in and of itself shows that the art of acting is the core and the basis of the dramatic work. This principle says that the art of acting is above all a *dramatic* art; the terms *mimetic* (in the broad sense of the word, comprising not only gestures and facial expressions but also speech) and *dramatic* should be considered identical. This will be addressed in the discussion of the essence of the art of acting. However, our principle says something more. This art of acting governs the dramatic work; it rules over all other aspects. All the other artistic aspects must subordinate themselves to the rules that guide the art of acting. The epithet "dramatic" may be accorded them only when they are governed by the rules of the art of acting. Definitions of the "dramatic poem", the "dramatic stage" and "dramatic music" arise from an analysis of these aspects of the dramatic work.

Hence we again find ourselves rejecting the popular aesthetic use of the word "dramatic". In ordinary speech and casual writing the word is employed in a very broad sense; it is used (like the word "poetic") to conjure up a certain emotional impression, as synonymous with "exciting", "thrilling", "electrifying", "tempestuous" and so forth. Even in everyday life we speak of a "dramatic scene" or a "dramatic moment". This captures only one feature of the dramatic – a sensation of tension or excitement (or the release and dissipation of this emotion). This is a use both imprecise and unscholarly. *Too broad:* it comprises not only things that are extra-dramatic (a ballad is dramatic; an electrifying piece of music is dramatic) but also those that are extra-artistic. *Too narrow:* many truly dramatic phenomena (such as a light conversation piece) would not be covered. (And it is by this standard that the "dramatic" talent of an author or a musician is judged!)

A. ACTING

1. Whenever we recall our impressions of a theatre performance and ask ourselves what it was that triggered them first and foremost, we must acknowledge that it was the people represented on the stage and their actions. Both of these were created by the actors. So – to put it simply but exhaustively – the subject of the art of acting is *acting persons*.

These people are *real*; that is, they actually exist – which is what differentiates the art of acting from all other arts that represent people. A statue of a person is stone or bronze; a portrait is a painted canvas. People in a novel exist only in my imagination. Only acting represents people by people. In this case the material with which the artist creates is almost identical with what the artist is creating. I repeat, almost, since they are not identical. An actor is a real person though not, for example, a real king but an *unreal*, false one. This falsity also relates in many ways to the actor's makeup, wig, costume, and so on. There has been much philosophising about this. There is also a certain *artistic illusion* but this illusion – and this has to be borne in mind – is substantially different than in other artistic disciplines. The distance from "reality" is minimal, and this is often reflected in a temptation to view the illusion as reality. (Quite simple naive people in particular are capable of taking the theatre for reality.) This is also the psychological reason for the theatre's propensity for "illusionism", for naturalism.

What is this "acting person" for the audience from the psychological point of view? A phenomenon that is optical (visual), acoustic (auditory) and kinetic (motor); I register it through an inner imitation of the person's movements and bearing, at least implicitly (innervations). The visual component comprises both his appearance (makeup, wig, costume) and his movements (gestures, facial and bodily mimicry, action). In this *double* (or triple) way we come to know the *character* (played by the actor) just as we come to know people in life.

And just as in life, where the determining feature when we think of a certain person is the visual appearance (whenever I think of Mr X, I see him in my mind in the first place), so it is in the theatre. The visual appearance is primary – of course the visual appearance in its temporal variability, in its (optically speaking) *play.*

The auditory manifestation of a character comprises all its acoustic aspects, both those that are inarticulate (laughter, groaning, and so on) and of course those in particular that are articulate, that is its *speech.* Speech is secondary in our perception. It is a rather abstract feature of the character and it only becomes more concrete when we can also see the person speaking; cf. the abstract nature of "a voice offstage".

What is the relation of acting and speech? Both are *complementary,* but in a quite specific way, allowing the exclusion of both as extreme forms.

"Acting" is either an expression of emotions (mimesis in the narrower sense of the word) or a manifestation of the will – that is, action in the narrower sense of the word. On the contrary, speech is either an expression of thoughts (communicating ideas) or an expression of emotions. In the expression of emotions both complement each other; the word demands gestures and vice versa. But rational speech does not require acting, and vice versa, action does not require words. In extreme cases, that is; in fact there is a smooth transition between categories. Hence the following schema:

Acting	0	Emotional gesticulation	Action
Speech	Rational speech	Emotional speech	0

It follows from the primacy of acting that rational speech is the least effective. Ruminations ("philosophizing") and especially narration are least dramatic since they require the least acting. The actors cannot enliven them with forceful acting (gesticulation). These are dead moments in the drama; unfortunately, at the beginning (the exposition), at least, they are almost necessary, but the fewer there are, the better. An absolute requirement for speech is that it be *comprehensible* to the audience (that is, not too faint or too fast or addressed away from it); otherwise it comes across as unnecessary and pointless. Very important for stylization!

In contrast to this, action as the supreme expression of the character is always dramatic, even though at its peak it does not require speech. Overly literary playwrights often trespass against this principle when they assume that everything that is acted needs to be announced ("Die!"). The lyrical mode is situated midway. ...

The character represented by the actor as an "acting person" is a *dramatic character*. For the actor to represent the character as a coherent individual, the *sum of his acting* and naturally of his *speech* (in the sense of the manner of speaking, not the ideas that are expressed!) must form an *incontestable whole*. For us then, psychologically speaking, the *dramatic character* is *the sum of the acting and speech* of the actor representing that character.

In a drama there are several such characters (two at least), since it deals with interaction between people. Every character has its individuality, which is guaranteed by the fact that each is created by a different actor (the prerequisite: a good one!). These dramatic characters can be seen as the basic elements of a dramatic work, and these are, I would say, static, since they pass through the entire work more or less unchanged. That, however, does not preclude partial development or even radical changes in characters' personalities. Naturally the continuity of the character must be maintained; all action and all changes must be psychologically justified. This is the law of *psychological truth*, internal rather than external ("nobody would act like that"). If the law is broken at some point, we are unable to make a synthesis of the character's features; we fail to understand the character, and it comes across as flawed or unclear. Nevertheless the flaw may also be in us – that we are unable to understand, for instance, the strength of some particular motivation. One must therefore be very cautious in these judgements. Nonetheless, we generally understand every (well-performed) character intuitively – through putting ourselves in its place, through empathy. Unity is continuity. ... On the other hand, the *external* truthfulness of a character (that is, whether such a person can exist) is unnecessary: plays also contain supernatural and symbolic characters, personifications, animals, and so on.

2. We also understand the mutual relationships of the dramatic characters in a dual fashion. Visually this relationship is the onstage *situation* – which is a changing one. Acoustically it is the *dialogue*. Both take place in time and create the material for the construction of the *dramatic action*.

Given that we have defined "dramatic character" as an acting person, we may define "*dramatic action*" as (mutual) *human action*. We are therefore dealing not with abstract action, a story that may be recounted (as in the narrative mode), but with a concrete action created through the situations of people and their dialogues. The salient feature of dramatic action is that it occurs *in real time*. However, this time is also "unreal", false, since, for example, the declared "action at the time of the French Revolution" takes place in the present – yet in this "present" lies its full reality. Dramatic action is so bound to time that it cannot be speeded up, slowed down, shortened or transposed (previous for later). In contrast to this, the narrative storyline, for instance in a novel, takes place in a time that is merely notional and can be treated fairly freely. The author may, for instance, provide part of a dialogue and add "and they spent the rest of the day in such talk", or sum up action taking place over a long time in a few words, at the beginning of a chapter narrate what preceded, and so forth.

We may also read a narrative rapidly or slowly, stopping anywhere and proceeding at our leisure – but in taking in dramatic action we are bound quite strictly. This close link with time manifests itself most clearly in dramatic action requiring a very specific tempo (in a specific place) and very specific changes of tempo (dramatic progression), be they sudden or gradual. In this respect it is in complete accord with music, which is also bound to real time in such a close fashion. A poem may be read quickly or slowly without apparent loss, but "reading", for instance, the slow movement of a musical composition quickly would turn it into a caricature. We have to imagine it at its proper tempo if we are to understand it correctly. If we are to understand drama fully when reading, we must also read it in this way, or imagine it being performed. It is only the curtain that breaks up the continuous action of the play as if constructing it in some way, and the intermission is arbitrary – the next act may continue where the previous one left off, or "20 years later".

Dramatic action – human action, visually represented and perceived – is created through the development of situations and dialogues. The glue that gives it continuity is, once again, psychological causality. The motivations of individuals' actions are not only internal but also external – the influence of one person on another. Here too the law of *psychological truth* holds: the progress of the action must be governed by psychological laws, otherwise it would come across as incomprehensible, strained or impossible. It must be emphasized that this truthfulness is grounded in the possibility of our understanding it, that is understanding it noetically, and has nothing to do with any relation to reality, that is, to the question whether this action is "possible" in the light of our experience. For there are also dramatic fairy tales and such like. Therefore it is only psychological truth – with relation to both dramatic characters as well as dramatic action – that is the necessary and *absolute* requirement.

The elements of dramatic action, (changing) situations and dialogues, create the *dynamic* (moving) elements of the dramatic work through their being carried out in real time. These elements evoke in us quite specific moods: excitement and tension, emotional release and relaxation, with different intensities, different manners of proceeding, different lengths and different kinds of alternation. It follows from the above schema of the relation between acting and speech that the peaks of dramatic action are always determined by action, by deeds – and that this does not involve words: the word precedes and follows. We have also noted that narrative passages are passages where dramatic flow comes to a halt. Lyrical passages (corresponding to the combination of emotional gesture and emotional speech) are situated midway, signifying a loosening of dramatic movement. This is not meant as denigration: on the contrary, they are necessary for achieving alternation and contrast in the dynamic effect of the work. However, there should not be too many of them (as in lyrical drama), lest the action become too drawn out (the requirement of dramatic progression, brevity). It is only through contrast that a strong moment stands out, and after a strong moment weaker impressions are required in order to prevent fatigue and insensitivity. These are psychological laws that a dramatic work as a work in real time has to observe, just like music. Not inappropriately, we speak of the *rhythm* of dramatic action, by which is meant this alternation – an alternation that occurs in large temporal blocks, something like temporal waves. However, this is no more than a metaphorical expression and it is better to follow the lead of music (where real "rhythm" is present in the true sense of the word) and speak of the *dynamic architecture* or *structure* of the drama.

Creating dramatic action in its temporal structure (rhythm) cannot be the task of the individual actors, since is the product of their interacting with one another. It is the artistic task of the *director.*

B. LITERATURE

The playwright already has a vision of the dramatic characters and the dramatic action at the time of the conception of the play and while putting it down on paper. He can capture only a modest (though significant) part of his vision through the use of words: the *direct speech of the characters with each other* ("dialogues"). In respect of the two dramatic values mentioned above the creation of the text by the playwright involves two types of synthesis.

a) The playwright captures the dramatic character as the *sum of the lines* delivered by that character in the play. Externally, this sum takes the form of the "role" that the actor receives in written form. The sum of these lines must form a *unified and distinctive whole*. This unity relates both to the psychological (though not logical) coherence of all the lines of dialogue as well as to the unified *nature* of the speech, from which the mentality of the individual may be inferred. This concerns both the contents and the formal side of the speech (the syntax, and so on), which of course cohere in many points. An educated person speaks about certain things, an uneducated person about other things – for example a master and a servant. ... A passionate person speaks differently from someone who is phlegmatic; a frivolous chatterbox talks differently from an introverted eccentric.

From the sum of these lines of dialogue (of a single character) the actor has to intuit its personality. The more distinctive the sum, the easier it is for him, since the actor is creating a specific character and therefore needs very specific (individual) source material – and even so the material provides only part of the features. If on the contrary the lines given by the playwright to the character are no more than schematic, the "person" is also schematic and the actor's task is difficult and unrewarding.

The other part – that is, the character's action, facial expressions, gestures, gait, physiognomy (makeup and hair) – must be provided by the actor; this sum of acting also has to form a whole in itself (as has been already mentioned) and has to be in agreement with the whole presented in the lines by the playwright. But also, as far as the lines found in the text are concerned, the actor has to create their spoken form, that is, the way the text is delivered, and of course this has to be done in agreement with the character presented. So not even in relation to the text is an actor a mere reproductive artist, as is the case of a reciter. A reciter – the author's surrogate – delivers a certain passage according to the nature of its contents and atmosphere. An actor speaks a certain passage according to the *overall* concept of the dramatic *character*; consideration of the contents and the atmosphere of the passage takes second place, or rather they are modified in a particular direction in line with the overall concept.

The characters captured verbally by the author must be not only unified and distinctive but also *different* from one another. This is a difficult task and it depends on the author's ability – which is what makes him a dramatist – to get inside the skin of a character and to transform his self into another. This is also an ability that an actor must have, but whereas an actor here focuses on how to play his role, the dramatist must focus mainly on the character's speech. A special difficulty for the dramatist is that he creates all the characters in the play while the actor creates only one. It is therefore not enough for the author to empathize subjectively with all his characters; he must also objectivize them, rid himself of them, rid them of any connection to his own person. Of course he can only do this to a certain extent. If this is too limited, the drama is too subjective and all the characters are similar to one another and similar to their creator. The author may also project his self onto one of the play's characters, though in a different outer form (Molière: *The Misanthrope*; Goethe: *Torquato Tasso*).

b) The playwright captures the dramatic action through the sum of all the lines of dialogue as they follow one another – that is, through the whole dramatic text. This sum, too, must be unified and consistent (psychologically justified). However, the dramatic action is present in it only *potentially and incompletely* (since a part of the dramatic action is also present in the dialogues!): the other aspect, the acting (the action of the characters), is only suggested by the author in a limited and general manner through stage directions. Fixing the dramatic action in time, and doing this precisely, putting in place its temporal structure, its "rhythm", is the task of the director. Here, too, the playwright provides only incidental instructions regarding the intensity and tempo of the speech and the acting. The exact dynamics has to be intuited from the meaning and the mood of the *dialogues*. Each dialogue contains a certain tension originating from the division into the two characters (a "split" understanding); we apprehend a statement made by either of them as at the same time an *effect* on the other. In addition to a dynamic effect, dialogues also have a static atmospheric effect deriving from the contents of the dialogues (atmospheric words and notions, jokes, and so on) or perhaps the literary style (for example metaphors, word repetition) These atmospheric effects are most evident in lyrical passages, where they compensate for the diminished dynamic effect of such moments. Lyrical drama in particular makes ample use and even excessive use of them (Maeterlinck: word repetition and so on); music, which has a great emotional effect, likes to draw out such lyrical, atmospheric passages ("arias", "duets", in particular love duets). But the dynamic performance of the dramatic action, too, relies on the effect of the content and mood of the dialogues, so both are usually in agreement, though sometimes they are also in contrast, which then creates a particularly strong dramatic moment, for instance serious or even sad things in a light dialogue (tragic humour) or, on the other hand, petty things in a serious dialogue (an effective source of comedy). Certainly it is necessary to distinguish these effects clearly. *Narrative* passages in a dramatic work usually lack even (static) atmospheric effect, and as such are totally dead in the water.

The dramatic action is unified but certainly not simple. Every dramatic character acts in the course of the drama – if the character appears onstage – in his or her particular way; these are *partial dramatic actions* out of which the overall action is composed, as though from interwoven threads. (Partial dramatic action is different from personal action. This is not to draw an explicit distinction between *ideational* or *imagined events*, in which more characters participate, and *personal action*, from both of which the dramatic action is spun. Only the latter actions are visible. This does not affect the following argument.) However, the individual partial dramatic actions are not equally significant but depend on the relative importance of the characters. Also the interrelations of these partial actions are different. Against the *action of the main character* (the "hero" of the piece), which usually runs through the whole dramatic work, there is usually the action of the hero's opponent. These are *opposing* actions and therefore they occasionally intersect (as plotlines) –

forcefully or more mildly. Each of them is associated with the actions of characters who share their intentions – whether coerced or voluntary – and these *parallel actions* may run through the entire piece (especially the actions of go-betweens, plotters) or only function for a certain time. And naturally this parallel action may be independent to a greater or lesser extent, so that at times it even turns into a third basic action, which may perhaps intersect with the other two (for example the action of a cunning servant, carried out to benefit his master but also on his own accord). Alternatively, a "counterplay" may be created by several persons of relatively equal weight so that it is only their sum (of the parallel actions) that acts as a counterweight to the hero's action. Or alongside the main play and counterplay there may arise a secondary play and counterplay, relatively independent and less significant (mostly from the ethical point of view), and so on.

In this respect drama is very similar to music. Only drama and music are capable of presenting us with two actions or two musical ideas completely simultaneously; this is based on the fact that only these two arts take place in real time. We are *forced to perceive simultaneously* both aspects (for example, the play and the counterplay in the dialogue), something that the novel, for instance, does *not* require. We may figuratively call this phenomenon *dramatic polyphony*. ... There is another similarity to voices in music: in parallel (even homophonically, for example in thirds) and in counterpoint. But the specificity of dramatic polyphony is that (1) every partial play has two aspects, in that it also contains speech; (2) the acting and the speech of the same character need not move in the same direction (hypocrisy; a supposed friend!).

To sum up these conclusions, we may say that the attribute "dramatic" belongs in reality to the performances of the actors (together with the input of the director); however, since the text created by the dramatist is the basic component of their work, the attribute may be transferred to the text under the following conditions.

A *dramatic text* (literary work) is one that offers the actors (and the director) the *source material* for the creation of dramatic characters and dramatic action (for the definitions of both terms see above). The better it serves this task, the more dramatic it is.

N. B.: With respect to artistic evaluation, since "dramaticality" proper is an *aesthetic* judgment, the source material should be *original* (that is, the source material for the creation of an original character) and *rich* (that is, offering sufficient freedom for the various actors' interpretations); often the latter requirement is also met by "literary" templates ("types").

Dramaticality is therefore a quality that a given text (literary work) may possess to varying degrees, as reality attests. But there are *necessary* conditions for this, most commonly the form of direct speech itself. That, however, is not enough to ensure dramaticality. It would certainly be possible to stage, for instance, Plato's dialogues, but what we would experience would not be "drama" because there would be little human action. The dialogic form is also popular in the novel, since it stirs our imagination. (Such is also the case, for example, with the ballad. Here there is "dramaticality" in the popular sense, that is excitement provided by the quick pace of the narrative and the sombre material.) It is, however, only one of several available forms (for example the framing story, the epistolary novel, and so on). From the extreme case of such a philosophical dialogue a long series of "closet dramas" leads to proper "theatrical" dramas. The degree of "dramaticality" (in our sense) rises steadily, and in addition with any particular drama it varies *within certain limits* because (by definition) it depends not only on the dramatic abilities of the playwright but also on the creative abilities of the actors and the director in a particular stage production.

C. THE STAGE

The theatre stage is a *space* in which *dramatic characters materialize the dramatic action*. What follows most importantly from this is that the stage is a real space, actual and not just imaginary. The *dramatic characters* are represented by actors, who are of course real, material people whom we also apprehend as such. This is a key point of difference from the visual arts, which also present us – for instance in a historical painting – with people, but these people are not only unreal but also immaterial; their representation is flat, two-dimensional, and an impression of materiality and three-dimensionality is only created in us through illusion, based on certain pictorial devices, in particular perspective and modelling through light and shade. What is closer to the stage in this sense is sculpture, which also presents an unreal human but at least one that is corporeal, three-dimensional; we are also aware of the materiality of the statue: it is not an illusion. However, there are substantial differences between a statue and an actor, which will be discussed below.

The *dramatic action* that takes place between dramatic characters, too, necessarily requires a real, three-dimensional space – only here can actors exist and perform – and the spectators have no choice but to view this space as real and three-dimensional since that is how they perceive the actors. The reality, the realness, of the stage space is not at odds with the fact that the space is not identical to the one being represented; we are of course aware of this distinction in the theatre. We know that the space in which the action takes place is in fact "the stage", for example of the National Theatre, and not "a room in a middle-class flat", "the Old Town Square", "a forest" or whatever else it "represents". The stage is a real space, then, but in view of its specific purpose "false", in the same way that this is true of the actor as a dramatic character.

What has been said of space is equally true of the *light* that fills the stage and in fact creates it for the audience, as it conditions their visual impression. This light too is real, actual and not just painted, as is the case for instance of a painting of a room or a landscape. In this respect the stage approximates another visual art, architecture, which also operates with real light in its spaces. And of course stage light is – like almost everything in the theatre – mostly fake; in our age, the light is almost always electric, "representing" sunshine or moonlight or artificial light, for example the light of a paraffin lamp, a torch, and so on.

A case that might seem to contradict the realness of the stage space – and partly also of the light that creates it – is when the stage is meant to represent a space of endless depth, a distant view. It is obvious that an open space like this cannot be created within the limitations of the stage and therefore illusion has to be employed: distant space, stretching out without end, is painted on the backdrop. This substitute for a real space that cannot be created in practical terms is psychologically justified because even in reality a distant view seems like a flat image. But no objections can be raised against it aesthetically either, since it is not at odds with the above definition of the stage. This seemingly distant space is no longer the stage because no acting takes place – or can take place – there, nor do we consider it part of the stage. (Often dramatists do not realise this obvious fact, for instance by having their characters "move off into the distance" or "appear in the distance", which of course cannot be done.) In this case it only appears that the stage, at other times completely enclosed, is *extended* in depth: the space into which it extends is no longer a part of it, and it is therefore irrelevant whether it is real or is to be so. The visual art of painting is used here – for purely practical reasons, as has been stated – to achieve the illusion of wide open space, but this in no way means that the stage itself is therefore illusionistic or realistic. Spatial illusion must be distinguished from physical illusion; we understand, for example, that the open landscape on a backdrop like this may be rendered in as stylized a fashion as the painter wishes.

A similar principle holds in the case of the materiality of any properties and objects on the stage itself. It is certain that, for instance, a chair that is to be sat on must be – and can be as well – really material. But trees – for instance in a scene representing a wood – may to a certain extent be material, corporeal, but they need not be. It is enough if they are painted so that an illusion of materiality is created in us. This illusion is not only justified but in accordance with the aesthetic law of unity it is necessary: in the three-dimensional stage space, in which three-dimensional, material people operate, all other objects must be three-dimensional, material, or at least create such an impression. There is no need to point out that this material illusion does not mean stage illusionism or realism, and therefore the objects in question, for example trees, may be stylized at will.

To sum up, it may be said that a stage is a real three-dimensional space containing real, material objects (the acting persons in the first place, but others as well); for practical reasons the use of things that create merely an illusion of space or materiality (such as backdrops, flats, and so on) is allowed. Not only is this dual illusion not anti-artistic, but on the contrary it is an imperative that follows from the aesthetic law of the unity of the stage, and it is not even an instance of stage realism or illusionism in the strict sense of the word. (Often theories of painting, too, claim that a painting that creates an illusion of space or materiality is *eo ipso* naturalistic and therefore non-artistic, a view that is incorrect and caused by a lack of clarity with regard to concepts. However, in the visual arts, a painting may be conceived of as existing either in an (apparent) space or on a surface; to recognize only one is a product of unjustified dogmatism. As we have seen, on the stage such an alternative does not exist.)

Having outlined the nature of the theatre stage, we are faced with the task of determining which artistic discipline the stage should be classed with. First and foremost, it is obvious that we perceive the stage through sight. The characters portrayed by the actors as dramatic characters, their action and interaction – all these are purely visual impressions. The stage is therefore a visual form of art and as such is close to the *visual arts*. Earlier we have in fact compared the stage and what fills it with sculpture and then with architecture, though in each case we also pointed out major differences. Finally, we have spoken at some length about the importance of painting for the stage, but here the conclusion was that its relation to the stage is merely ancillary; it only helps out for practical reasons, sometimes substituting illusion for reality. Our task now is to examine systematically the relation between the stage and the visual arts. This issue is of crucial importance as soon as there arises the question of according the stage genuine artistic values. These artistic values must certainly be visual, and it is therefore natural to think of artistic values offered "ready made" by the various visual arts. This explains why the purifying reaction that arose at the turn of the twentieth century against tasteless and wholly unartistic theatrical illusionism declared the stage to be a visual work of art and as a result tried to apply to it the rules of the visual arts. Though in practice this movement has played a major role in improving the stage artistically, its theoretical principles cannot be accepted.

The stage is not a work of visual art. A brief analysis will support this claim. First and foremost the particular *dramatic character* represented on stage by the actor is not, from the visual point of view, a work of art and has no artistic values such as those of, for example, a sculpture or a painting of a person.

The beauty of an actor or an actress is undoubtedly a certain advantage but it is not a condition for the artistry of their performance; besides it is always natural beauty, not artistic beauty. (This physical beauty is not only a social advantage, contributing – sometimes undeservedly – to the popularity of an actor or actress, but also a technical advantage, just like a beautiful voice. In numerous plays the beauty of dramatic characters, in particular women, is the occasion for romantic relations and therefore also the driving force of the action – for example *Romeo and Juliet*.) With most dramatic characters it is a question of a distinctive appearance rather than of beauty; often certain characters – especially in comedies – should even be unattractive to the point of being a source of ridicule (for example Falstaff). But the actor, wishing to create the appearance demanded by the dramatic character he is playing, puts on makeup and a costume and this is certainly an artificial creation. However, the purpose of all this is to capture the distinctive features of the dramatic character, and therefore it has – if successful – dramatic artistic values, not those relating to the visual arts. This also follows from the fact that the makeup and costume are closely connected with the actor's mimicry, in particular his facial expressions, forming no more than a constant component of his changing appearance, and also that the change the makeup and costumes make in the actor's appearance varies greatly, from considerable to virtually none at all. It could be objected that certain aspects of characterization are also present in the above-mentioned works of art (sculptures and paintings of people). But the principal difference is that in the creation of the actor's makeup and costume the characterization of the character is the first requirement while in the visual arts it is the second – that is, it is something that may be in evidence but does not need to be so, because it is the purely visual qualities that are crucial and necessary. To demonstrate this, let us think of an actor representing, for example, King Lear, superbly costumed and made up, and let us imagine that the actor is photographed at a moment when he is expressing some kind of mental turmoil in a spell-binding fashion – a fit of anger or madness. Will this photograph – which on the surface can easily be compared to, for example, an etching, a valuable visual work of art – will this photograph be a visual work of art itself? Certainly not.

It must nevertheless be acknowledged that in this depiction of a person's state of mind there is a point of contact between acting and some works of art. However, it is really no more than a *point*; the above-mentioned works of art – statues and paintings of people (and not even all of them!) – portray only one moment, while acting presents the whole *process* of a certain mental sensation or action, one that develops over the course of time. In this development, in this change, lies the essential quality of the actor's performance. A dramatic character's momentary pose has no qualities of its own, but only as a point of transition between what preceded and what follows, for example as the culmination of a steady or sudden gradation. It is only in the whole process that its meaning and value lie; what we are clearly dealing with here is a purely dramatic quality, which in this case manifests itself visually, that is visibly.

The same holds for the *ensemble of characters* filling the stage. Here, too, the positioning of the characters is not governed by the rules of visual art, as it would be with a painting, but solely by dramatic laws. Through these visible *spatial* relations between individual characters (close to or distant from one another, and so on) as well as between the characters and the stage (downstage, upstage, stage left, and so on), the psychological relationships between dramatic characters are expressed visually, as are the weight and nature of their partial dramatic action within the whole of the dramatic action – moment by moment. The stage is therefore not a "painting", as it is usually perceived and as Diderot was the first to call for. However, Diderot's demand arose in reaction to the way classical French drama was performed in his time. In strict accordance with the view that drama is poetry, all that he sought was for this drama to be declaimed properly (in accordance with the taste of the age, of course) and for all the poetic beauties of the poem to be fully expressed; at most there might also be the individual facial expressions and gestures of the various actors. Diderot called for the ensemble filling the stage to be shaped artistically and he formulated this plea by saying that the stage should, at any given moment, form an image worthy of a painter. This was a very wholesome reform, and what is more, Diderot's demand should be recognized as – completely correct, without its contradicting our former statement that the stage is not an image. The reason for this is that Diderot was a good theorist of drama but not of the visual arts – even though he was the first modern critic of the visual arts. He called for a painting to have poetic and dramatic qualities, passing over purely visual qualities. If we were to accept his ideal of a painting we could fully agree with his demand for staging. But we will not do so because we view a painting somewhat differently. Still it cannot be denied that in a figural painting the painter also seeks to position the figures according to their psychological relationships and the importance they have in the action. However, in a good painting this requirement is secondary, the primary requirement being the effort to arrange the elements of colour and shape in the painting in such a way that the satisfaction they offer is purely visual, with no regard for what they mean. Observing this requirement and in addition fulfilling the aforementioned one – this is the problem that makes the group painting the most difficult genre in the painter's art.

Diderot's problem – as one may call the question of the relation of the theatre stage to the visual arts – was correctly resolved by Diderot himself, but incorrectly formulated. This means that the consequences for the stage that Diderot deduced from his claims are correct; on the contrary, it would be wholly incorrect to deduce consequences for the stage from our conception of the visual image, as happens so often. Diderot also recognized that the stage "image" changes over time; rather interestingly, he considered it a *sequence* of images following one after another, always with a small difference – something that in fact happens in the modern cinema. Diderot was well aware of the dramatic qualities stemming from the nature of this change over time – sometimes gradual, sometimes sudden, and sometimes even coming to a standstill. We say that this is the visible rhythm of the changing stage, visually expressing the dramatic rhythm of the action, and that, like the preceding case, no single point in the stage action has any value in itself, but only as a transitional point between what we have seen before and what we shall see after it. So, for instance, we regard the proximity of two characters to one another or their placement downstage as a result of their convergence or movement to the fore – sometimes speedy, sometimes slow – which gives them a different nature and significance in each case, though the resulting "image" is the same. This rhythm of change on the stage, sometimes gradual, sometimes precipitous, sometimes almost coming to a standstill, at others wildly oscillating, is a dynamic quality and we do in fact experience it in real time. On the contrary, in a painting representing a scene we regard the positioning of the figures as a static impression; and although we may sometimes imagine what has preceded and what would follow after the moment captured in the painting, it is no more than a thought, a mere suggestion – there can be no talk of experiencing any rhythm. If in the case of a painting reference is made to its being "dramatic", this is used in the lay sense of the word, which simply equates with emotion, whether the mere emotional nature of the action represented in the work and the persons participating in it or in addition – in a good work – the visual impact of the colours, the interplay of light and shadow and line present in the painting.

So *the essence of the stage* is that *the dynamic effect of the drama* (the dramatic characters and the dramatic action) *is distributed and ordered spatially* on it, *visually transcribed* onto the stage space, as it were. The dramatic characters represented by the actors are something like shifting *power nodes*, their intensity varying in accordance with both the importance of individual characters and the momentary situation. Their psychological relations, shaped by the plot and the situation, are something like *lines of force* pulsating between them. The stage is filled with the network of these lines of force, is a kind of *force field*, changeable in shape and in the strength of its individual components. The effects of this dynamic field are transmitted to the audience; this is *dramatic tension.*

It is very interesting that we also encounter a quite similar configuration in the visual arts themselves. Every piece of architecture is also a dynamic field, a network of lines of force. Here, however, it is a case of mechanical forces, of the weight of matter manifesting itself as compression and tension, and of the firmness and flexibility of the material resisting this. These forces and counterforces are in complete balance: the weight of a vault lies on a column, but the column lifts it up and supports it. So when looking at architecture (most clearly at a Gothic cathedral) we experience the powerful tension that is present there, but the *resultant* impression is one of calm, not of movement. In contrast, the force field of the theatre stage is mobile, in a constant state of change and flow, and it is first of all a field of psychological, not mechanical, forces. (A mobile field of mechanical forces with an aesthetic charge is also possible; such impressions arise, for example, inside a gigantic engineering plant.) The forces we sense here are not real, actual, but only imagined, symbolic. Indeed, does it not seem to us that, between two lovers who find themselves alone on the stage and free from care, a kind of psychological force clicks into place that drives them irresistibly towards one other? And do we not feel at their parting how hard it is for them to separate and how great an effort they have to make to overcome the power of mutual attraction? And do we not, on the contrary, sense the repellent force between two enemies, a force that drives them apart and is overcome only through the brutal force of their thirst for revenge? (Even in life these symbolic notions are common: some people attract us, others repulse us; the tie of friendship binds us, and so on.)

We have said that the dynamic effect of the drama is not only distributed on the stage but is also *ordered*. This means that it is regulated according to laws in terms of both spatial distribution as well as its development in time. The sole possible basis for this order is the dramatic work itself, conceived as a whole; to achieve this is the primary artistic task of the director. This task is specific to the director, separate from the roles of the individual actors. Actors create their action, the director creates their interaction; it is wrong for one of the parties to usurp the rights of the other. If individual actors wish to decide how to interact with one other, the overall unity of the performance is lost, the whole disintegrates, and soon there is artistic anarchy. And the other way round, if a director prescribes how the individual actors should act, their individuality is limited, the actors turn into puppets and the theatre play, which should be an artistic organism, turns into a mechanism, no matter however skilfully it is operated. (Towards young actors, a director has the obligation – and with it therefore the right – to mentor; however, here too this is more a matter of advising than of dictating.) As an old aesthetic maxim has it: in the former case there is variety without unity; in the latter unity without variety; sooner or later, both lead to the artistic degeneration of the theatre.

Dramatic characters and their relationships – these form the *essence* of what fills the stage; what is on the stage besides this is insignificant, accidental. In some cases all that a play needs is merely the neutral space of a stage (naturally a space delimited by a firm frame). This *scenic frame*, marking off the stage space from below, from above and from the sides as well as from behind, is for the main part *relatively unchanging* (for the entire play, for an entire act or a part of an act) and it is an architectural work. Often, however, the dramatic work requires that the stage space be defined more clearly; this is done either by the choice and design of the movable part of the scenic frame (flats, backdrops) or by objects that are placed on the stage and that may come into actual physical contact with the dramatic characters (furniture, and so on). All these things have, in the first place, a logical significance, helping the spectator to understand the dramatic work. In addition, they also have an aesthetic significance, helping to shape the mood. The very size and shape of the stage space (a small or a large stage, whether it is shallow or deep) have a specific atmospheric quality; all the more so the qualities of colour, light or shapes used in framing and filling the space. These qualities, relatively unchanging (as has been noted above), are qualities of the visual arts and of architecture in particular. The role of architecture is to create spaces, interiors – and the theatre stage is, when all is said and done, always an interior. The mood of these relatively unchanging qualities of the stage must correspond to the *overall* mood of the particular part of the dramatic work for which they are conceived. As against the changing, dynamic effect of the stage, which was discussed earlier, this creates its stable, *static* effect – a constant accompaniment to the changing impression created by the action. Its great importance lies in this synthetic power, which turns an act or part of an act into a distinctive unit. From what has been said it is clear that the task of creating such a relatively unchanging scenic frame lies with the architect, that is, an artist gifted with the creative abilities that are specific to architecture. But of course a specific qualification for working in the theatre must be that he have an understanding of the *dramatic* values of theatrical works, since it is these that he translates into a visual language – or to be more precise, an architectural language. (In contrast, an artist with a talent that is purely painterly cannot be a good stage designer, as he does not comprehend stage space, which is after all the main thing.)

A special role on the theatre stage is reserved for light. Works of architecture, too, use real light to shape their spaces. But theatre light is very fluid; it can be fully controlled and it gives the director the ability to change the illumination and therefore the mood of the stage even when the curtain is up – that is, even when the aforementioned framing of the stage cannot be changed. It follows from this that theatre light not only provides the stage with static atmospheric qualities, lyrical qualities, but that it is also capable of following the rhythm of the action, participating in its temporal development, dramatic progression, culmination, gradual or sudden changes – that is to say, light also creates the dynamic qualities of the stage. This capacity is highly important in that even within the same scenic frame the light follows the stage rhythm in general outline and underscores its significant moments, in this way *structuring*, in broad outline, each segment of the drama. Theatre light, then, transcribes into its visual language both the lyrical and the dramatic qualities of the work, and it is therefore – in principle – for spoken drama what music is for opera.

WORKS CITED

Bathe, Johannes (1916) "Leben und Bühne in der dramatischen Dichtung" [Life and the Stage in Dramatic Poetry], *Zeitschrift für Aesthetik u. allgemeine Kunstwissenschaft*, vol. 11, pp. 286–307.

Diderot, Denis (1883) *The Paradox of Acting*, trans. Walter Herries Pollock, London: Chatto & Windus.

Ludwig, Otto (1871) *Shakespeare-Studien* [Shakespeare Studies], Halle: Gesenius.

Müller-Freienfels, Richard (1912) *Psychologie der Kunst* [Psychology of Art], vol. I, Leipzig and Berlin: A. G. Teubner.

Scholz, Wilhelm von (1914) "Das Schaffen des dramatischen Dichters" [The Creation of the Dramatic Poet], *Zeitschrift für Aesthetik u. allgemeine Kunstwissenschaft*, vol. 9, pp. 176–85.

ON THE CURRENT STATE OF THE THEORY OF THEATRE

JAN MUKAŘOVSKÝ

["K dnešnímu stavu teorie divadla", a lecture given at the Circle of Friends of D 41 – that is, of E. F. Burian's Theatre D, in the 1940-1941 season – and published in 1941 in *Program D 41*, vol. 7, pp. 229-42. The English translation, "On the Current State of the Theory of Theater", was published in Burbank, John and Steiner, Peter (trans. and eds) (1978) *Structure, Sign and Function*, New Haven: Yale University Press, pp. 201-19.]

One of the important problems facing the contemporary theatre, and one that is being approached in various ways, is how to establish active contact between the spectator and the stage. Of course the prime responsibility for dealing with this problem lies with the theatre itself, its directors and its actors. And indeed, these individuals have made many attempts to "draw" the spectator into the play in some fashion. The results have been interesting and artistically valuable, but for the most part they have not been very effective as far as their desired goal has been concerned. There is, however, a second party in the theatre: the auditorium and the spectators sitting in it, that is, those who are supposed to be aroused to activity. They, too, have been considered, but for the most part not as a specific community of people frequenting such and such a theatre but as representatives of a social whole. The problem is then shifted to that of the relationship between the theatre and society. We know well enough the profound but in practical terms largely unproductive reflections on how the necessary precondition for intensive contact and full understanding between the theatre and society is the spontaneous unity of a world view and of religious and ethical feeling. Examples include ancient Greece, the Middle Ages and so forth.

But it is not the entire society of a particular time, of a particular nation, that frequents the theatre, especially the contemporary theatre; rather it is an audience, that is, a community that is often very heterogeneous socially (not only in terms of social strata alone but also profession, age, and so on) but on the other hand linked together by a bond of perceptivity to the art of the theatre. The audience is always a mediator between art and society as a whole: literature, painting, music and the other arts also require an audience, that is, a set of individuals with an inherited or acquired ability to adopt an aesthetic attitude toward the material with which a given art works.[1] The "theatre audience" in general, however, is still too broad and relatively abstract a notion. Every theatre, especially the theatre of a distinctive artistic movement, has its own audience, which is familiar with the artistic complexion of the theatre, follows actors from play to play, from role to role, and so on. And this is an important precondition for the audience to take an active stance toward the theatre, leading to one of the most efficacious paths toward "drawing the spectator into the play". It depends on the director's artistic intentions whether he wishes to remove the physical boundary between the stage and the auditorium. Even when this boundary is preserved, however, the relationship between the theatre and the audience is bilaterally active if the audience accepts spontaneously and in full measure the artistic conventions upon which the theatre, and precisely the particular theatre in question, builds its performance. Only in such a case can we expect the audience's reaction to the stage action to become itself an active force that is tacitly but effectively incorporated into the actual theatrical performance. It is well known how sensitively the stage reacts to the understanding and the mood hovering over a silent auditorium.

The effort by the Circle of Friends of D 41[2] to bring the fundamentals of the theatre closer to the audience through a series of lectures, most of which will be delivered by artists active in D 41, therefore seems to be a good beginning for the audience's path to the theatre. On the stage, artistic intention can only be embodied, not explicitly explained. All the work that brought it to life remains hidden from the spectator, yet awareness of it could substantially facilitate his understanding. The performance itself is already too homogeneous a whole, and it is not easy to penetrate its construction, to see it from within. During a performance it seems quite natural that a particular word in the text is pronounced in a certain way or is accompanied by a certain gesture, that its effect manifests itself in a particular manner in the facial expressions, gestures and movements of the other actors, and so on. But during rehearsals the spectator would see that the connection of a word with a gesture, and so forth, is the result of a deliberate selection from many possibilities, that no component of theatre follows automatically from another, that a theatrical performance is a very complex and dangerously fluid composition. If the spectator is enlightened about the origin of a theatrical performance by those who take an active part in theatre work every day, he too will be able to find

---

1   An affinity for a certain material is not at all general, and it is rare to find an individual, no matter how strong his aesthetic sensibility, who is capable of being part of the audiences of all the arts. A feeling for the aesthetic effect of words is not necessarily connected with a feeling for the artistic effect of colours, tones, and so forth.

2   [Editorial note (1978): D 41 was an avant-garde theatre originally founded by E. F. Burian in 1933. The "D" stands for the Czech word *divadlo* (theatre). The number refers to the calendar year of the second half of a particular theatrical season, in this case 1940–1941.]

a place for himself in the stage performance, which as it unfolds only seems to be limited to the stage: in reality it always pervades the entire theatre.

The organizers of this lecture series have also deemed it appropriate that a few words be devoted to the theory of theatre. By no means, of course, can a systematic exposition of all its problems be presented here, nor is there any need for this. We have only a single theoretical task: to show through a few remarks and examples that despite all the material tangibility of its means (the building, machinery, sets, props, a multitude of personnel), the theatre is merely the base for a non-material interplay of forces moving through time and space and sweeping the spectator up in its changing tension, in the interplay of forces we call a stage performance. The theoretical preconditions for such a view of the theatre are advanced in the contemporary theory of theatre and specifically in the Czech theory of theatre. The Czech theory of theatre is frequently the object of much criticism, justified, to be sure, as far as an enumeration of the tasks that should be fulfilled is concerned, but it would not be fair to criticize its past as well. I have in mind primarily a work that appeared recently, Otakar Zich's *The Aesthetics of Dramatic Art* (1931). In this work the theatre is viewed in its entire breadth and complexity as a dynamic interplay of all its components, as a unity of forces internally differentiated by reciprocal tensions and as a set of signs and meanings. The theoretical works of Petr Bogatyrev, Jindřich Honzl, E. F. Burian and several younger thinkers are based on the same conception of the theatre.

But even the generation before Zich made a substantial contribution to our knowledge of the essence of the theatre. It suffices to mention two recently deceased theatre critics, Jindřich Vodák and Václav Tille. In their formative years they experienced the powerful transformative turbulence – viewed from close at hand, almost chaos – through which the European theatre has passed since the final decades of the last century and which, in fact, has still not ended. In this country the course of theatrical development was even more unsettled, because influences from several countries – especially Germany, France and Russia – burst through and intermingled at the same time. It is certain that this haste also had its negative consequences. Unelaborated and not fully digested conceptions were abandoned for other, newer ones; various conceptions were blended in an artistically "impure" manner; sometimes only the external features of a particular conception of the theatre were adopted rather than its essence, and so forth. On the other hand, however, there was a positive side – a heightened perceptiveness to the multiple complexity of the theatre and the mutual counterbalancing of its components. If we read Václav Tille's *Memories of the Theatre* (1917), we encounter a critic at ease with all forms of theatrical expression, whether he is giving an account of the French, Russian, German or Japanese theatre or finds himself dealing with a form in which the actor predominates or another in which the focal point of the play lies in the stage set or finally a third, where the vehicle is the director. He knows how to distinguish precisely between a system of acting that works mainly with gestures and one dependent on declamation. He grasps the almost imperceptible boundary at which gestures turn into facial expressions, and so on. This cultivated perceptivity had already paved the way for the thinker who was to give the Czech theory of theatre its first example of a systematic and philosophically consistent elaboration of the fundamentals of the theatre, namely Otakar Zich. It is important to realize that the way was paved by the local development of artistic practice and theory, a development shaped both by the disadvantages of its occurring in a small nation inundated by the influences of large nations as well as by its advantages: the overly large number of influences ultimately counterbalanced one another, and practice and theory were consequently liberated from a one-sided indebtedness. If, as the proverb says, a person generally has all the vices that accompany the virtues he is endowed with, the opposite is often true of Czechs: they know how to find the advantages that come with the disadvantages they suffer from.

But let us now turn to our subject proper. We have spoken about the complexity of the theatre, so we must first show what it consists in. We shall proceed from a familiar claim: since Richard Wagner's time it has been said that the theatre is in fact an entire collection of arts. This was the first formulation of the complexity of the theatre; it has the merit of primacy, but it does not capture the essence of the matter. For Wagner the theatre was the sum of several independent arts. Today, however, it is clear that, upon entering the theatre, the individual arts renounce their independence, intertwine with one another, contradict one another, substitute for one another – in brief "dissolve", merging into a new, fully unified art.

Let us look at music, for example. It is not present in the theatre only when it is directly heard, not even when – in opera – it actually takes possession of the stage word. The properties that music shares with theatrical activity (the intonation of the voice in relation to musical melody; the rhythm and agogics of movement, gesture, facial expression and voice) mean that every theatrical event can be projected against the background of music and formed on its model. The musician and director E. F. Burian has shown to what extent stage time can become rhythmically measurable according to the pattern of music even when there is no music on stage, and he has shown how the role of a linguistic intonational motif in the overall structure of a performance is closely related to the function of a melodic motif in a musical composition (Burian 1939). Not only musical drama has its melodic "leitmotifs"; spoken drama has them as well.

We encounter a similar situation with sculpture in the theatre. Sculpture is present on stage if a statue is part of the set. Even in such a case, however, the function of the statue is different from what it is off stage. Off stage, for instance right in the lobby of a theatre, a statue is merely a thing, a depiction, whereas on stage it is a motionless actor, a contrast to a live actor. Proof of this may be found in the numerous theatrical themes in which a statue comes to life on stage.[3] As the opposite of an actor, a statue is constantly present on stage, even when its presence is not materialized: the immobility of a statue and the mobility of a live person form a constant antinomy between whose poles the actor's presence oscillates on stage. And when Gordon Craig put forth his famous demand for the "Übermarionette" actor, whose predecessors were, as he explicitly stated, the statues of gods in temples, he did nothing more than draw attention to this hidden but always present antinomy of the art of acting. What is usually called a "pose" is clearly a sculptural effect. In the medieval theatre "the movements are free and measured and they occur during the pauses in delivery, whereas the actor stands still during the delivery itself" (Golther 1926: 97). The sculptural mask of Classical times, of Japan and of other times and places also links the actor directly to a statue, and the transition between the immobility of a solid mask and the makeup of a modern actor is quite continuous, as is well known.

The other arts, whether literature, painting, architecture, dance or film, have a status in the theatre similar to that of music and sculpture. Each of them is always potentially present in the theatre, but at the same time each of them, when it comes into contact with the theatre, loses its intrinsic character and changes fundamentally. In addition, of course, there is another art that is inescapably bound to the theatre, namely acting, as well as an activity of an artistic nature that struggles to achieve the unity of all the components of theatre, namely directing. The presence of these two artistic components most distinctly characterizes the theatre as an independent and unified artistic form.

The complexity of the theatre is by no means exhausted by an enumeration of the arts that participate in the composition of a stage production. Each of these components breaks down into secondary components, which in turn are internally differentiated into other components. For example, the components of the actor's presence are: voice, facial expressions, gestures, movement, costume, and so on. Each of them is then complex in itself. For example the components of the voice are the articulation of speech sound elements, the pitch of the voice and its changes, its timbre, the intensity of exhalation and tempo. But we have still not come to the end. The individual vocal components can be broken down further. Take, for example, the timbre of the voice: every person has a particular vocal timbre forming part of his

---

3   [Editorial note (1978): For a more detailed discussion of this phenomenon see Jakobson 1975 [1937].]

physical personality. A speaker can be recognized by the timbre of his voice even if the listener does not see him. There are also, however, aspects of timbre that reflect various particular moods ("angrily", "joyfully", "ironically", and so forth) and whose meaning is independent of the personal timbre of the individual. Both these kinds of voice timbre can be exploited artistically. The individual vocal timbre of specific actors employed in a particular play can become a significant factor in the director's "instrumentation" of a stage performance. Temporary vocal timbre caused by a mental state is usually accounted for artistically either in the dramatic text itself (the author's stage directions, a wealth of emotional changes and oppositions in the dialogue) or in the actor's performance (cf. the rich range of vocal timbre that Tille, in *Memories of the Theatre*, ascribes to Eduard Vojan[4] in the latter's interpretation of the writer's neutral text).

So theatre has a rich scale of gradation. But can any one of its components be declared fundamental, absolutely necessary for the theatre? If we regard the theatre not from the standpoint of a certain artistic movement alone but as a constantly developing and changing phenomenon, the answer is "no". Individual developmental stages of the theatre and of particular theatrical movements have, of course, their prevailing components. The dominant component of the theatre at one time is the dramatic text, at another time the actor, at another time the director or even the stage set, and there are even more complicated cases – for example, theatre dominated by a director who nevertheless places the emphasis on the actor (Stanislavski 2008). The situation is similar in more detailed matters as well: sometimes components of facial expression, sometimes vocal components, and so on, prevail in the actor's performance (according to the period, the school, and so on). Even in the voice itself, sometimes articulation prevails, at other times intonation. All of this is extremely changeable, and all the components assume the leading role during the course of development without any of them attaining permanent dominance. And this changeability is made possible only because, as we have said, none of the components is absolutely necessary and fundamental for the theatre. A written text is not necessary, for there are theatrical forms in which the dialogue is largely improvised (for instance *commedia dell'arte* and some kinds of folk theatre) or even completely absent (mime). Even the actor himself, the vehicle of dramatic action, can be missing – at least temporarily – from the stage, his role assumed by another component, for example by light (in E. F. Burian's staging of *The Barber of Seville*,[5] through flickering

---

4   [Editor's note: Eduard Vojan (1853-1920), a leading Czech actor at the end of the nineteenth and beginning of the twentieth century and founder of the modern school of Czech acting.]

5   [Editor's note: E. F. Burian's adaptation of *The Barber of Seville*, which made topical allusions to the Spanish Civil War, premiered at the D 37 in 1936.]

and changes in colour the light connected with the howling of the storm expressed a popular uprising that was supposed to be taking place off stage; the stage itself was empty) or even by an empty, immovable stage, which precisely on account of its emptiness is able to express a decisive plot reversal (the Moscow Art Theatre, for example, favoured such "stage pauses"). Cases of this sort are, of course, rare, but they suffice to prove that the theatre is not inevitably bound to any of its components and that therefore its freedom to reconfigure is inexhaustible.

Nor are the individual components of the theatre bound by anticipated and unchangeable relations, as might often appear to be the case from the standpoint of rigid convention. There is no pair of components, no matter how closely related they may be, whose bond cannot be set into motion. It seems to us, for example, that gestures, facial expressions and speech are necessarily concurrent, but the Moscow Art Theatre has shown that their lack of concurrence can be artistically exploited in the theatre. Here is what Tille has to say about this in his comments on their production of *Uncle Vanya*:

> The Russian director drew on his experience that in life gestures, facial expressions and people's actions are not the logical result of the spoken word, just as words are not the result of external impulses, but that both spring – sometimes proportionately, sometimes disproportionately – from inner life, that both are caused by a hidden driving force that consists, on the one hand, in the characters of people in action, shaped through either their will or their unbridled energy, and, on the other hand, in those external influences that determine people's actions without their volition and often even without their awareness. (Tille 1917: 199)

Voice and gesture were therefore separated for the purpose of artistic effect. By breaking former convention and separating them, the Moscow Art Theatre influenced not only the further development of the theatre but also their audiences' life outside the theatre. After experiencing the Moscow Art Theatre's stage system, the spectator viewed himself and his fellow men with more discrimination; for him a gesture was no longer merely a passive companion of the voice but an independent symptom of a mental state, often more immediate than vocal expression. In all its many diverse variations the theatre always affects the spectator in the same direction: again and again, and from new aspects, it reveals to him the multifaceted correlation of the visible expressions of action.

An important requisite for the theory of theatre follows from this – to make the concept of the theatre as a set of non-material relations the method and goal of its study. In itself an enumeration of the components is a lifeless list. An (internal) history of the theatre proper is also nothing but a study of the changes in the interrelations among its components. None of the periods of development of the theatre can be accepted (from the point of view of theory) as the perfect embodiment of its very essence, nor can any of its individual forms, such as the theatre of one nation or another, folk theatre, primitive theatre, children's theatrical activities, and so on. The richer and more varied the material at the scholar's disposal, the more easily he can distinguish individual components and their relations in the total composition of a stage work. But it is not always easy to distinguish individual components from one another, precisely because of the closeness of the relations that can be established among them. For example, it is sometimes almost impossible to distinguish an actor's movement from a gesture (his walk is both a movement and a gesture), or a costume from the actor's physical appearance.

However, components also substitute for one another. Thus in Shakespeare richly developed verbal descriptions are substituted for the set, which the Shakespearean theatre lacked. Or light can be part of the actor's costume (if it changes its colour). Directors often exploit the substitution of one component for another as a technical device. In *My Life in Art* Stanislavsky says that the director can use the set to "relieve" the actor, for example by employing a striking stage design to mask weak acting.

So the essence of the theatre is a changing stream of non-material and constantly regrouping relations. Not only is development from period to period, from director to director, from one school of acting to another, built on this: so is every individual stage performance. Within a stage performance components also confront and counterbalance one another in constant mutual tension borne along by stage time. Everything, not just moving action but also an apparently motionless pause, sinks into the flow of this time. Systems of directing and acting exist that are based on the exploitation of pauses as a dynamic element. The biographer of the German actor Albert Bassermann says:

> In the fourth act [of Schiller's *Wallenstein's Death*] Bassermann only appears in the scene of the entry into the town of Eger. And here he wonderfully expresses the absent-mindedness of a person of strong spirit, the fading away of a powerful force. He speaks with the mayor while retaining a princely demeanour, that of a ruler lending a sympathetic ear, but he is now disturbingly absent-minded. His attention suddenly falters. Long pauses punctuate his speech. (To achieve this artistic effect he makes radical deletions in Schiller's text.) (Bab 1929: 330)

Bassermann's obvious purpose in employing this method was to heighten the dramatic tension; his means were pauses, hence mere flowing time: non-material time as the riverbed of non-material action. Everything on stage is only the material basis of stage activity, whose actual heroes are constantly alternating and interpenetrating actions and reactions. Every shift in the relations of the components is also at the same time both a reaction with respect to what has preceded it and an action with respect to what will follow it. Both the actors as well as the stage as a whole function as vehicles of both actions and reactions. Like everything in the theatre, the stage is in constant movement between the actor and inanimate objects. In a moment of acute tension the revolver that a character aims at his adversary is much more the "agent" than the actor who is playing the character. Even sets can become actors and, vice versa, an actor a set (see Veltruský 2016 [1940]). The sequence of actions and reactions results in a constantly renewed tension that is not identical with a constantly rising tension of plot (conflict, crisis, peripety, dénouement), which only obtains in certain types of theatre and certain periods in its development. Tension of plot presupposes a plot, and even a unified plot, but there are numerous dramatic forms that do not recognize unity of plot (for example the medieval drama, the revue) or even a plot in the proper sense of the word (for example, separate scenes which, when subsequently linked up, gave rise to the Classical *mimos* and the medieval religious drama).

With the essence of theatre now clarified, we shall now attempt to verify and illustrate the assertions just made by analysing several of its constituents. Let us first look at the dramatic text. There have been periods that believed that the sole purpose of the theatre was to reproduce the work of a dramatic author (for example the French theatre of the nineteenth century, when as a rule the author staged his work himself). At other times, on the contrary, the prevalent view has been that a drama is merely the script for a theatrical performance and not an independent literary work (Zich, for example, expresses this view in *The Aesthetics of Dramatic Art* (1931)). Both of these conceptions are, however, no more than expressions of contemporary views of the theatre, limited to a particular artistic system. If we look at the drama without a bias for any period, we find perforce that it is simultaneously both a literary genre homogenous with and equal to the lyric and the narrative, and one of the components of the theatre. In its artistic orientation it can, of course, incline sometimes toward one pole, at other times toward another. The development of literature would be as unthinkable without the drama, the dialogic literary genre, as the development of the drama without literature: the drama has continually drawn on the resources of the lyric and the narrative, and has itself continually influenced these neighbouring genres. As far as the relation of the drama to the theatre is concerned, we must keep in mind that, requiring the word for its purposes, the theatre can resort to any of the basic literary genres and that it does so. The medieval *plancti* (laments of the Virgin Mary), though lyrical forms, were intended to be performed; the narrative enters into contact with the theatre, for example, through the dramatization of novels. If the theatre nevertheless resorts to the drama more often than to the lyric and the narrative, it is only because drama is the literature of dialogue, and dialogue is action expressed in language: in the theatre the individual lines of dialogue take effect as a chain of actions and reactions.

In becoming a part of the theatre, the drama assumes another function and another aspect than that which it has insofar as it is regarded as a literary work. One and the same drama by Shakespeare is something different if it is read rather than staged (for example descriptions, which, as we have said, become a word-set on stage, function in reading as lyrical passages of the work). In this respect, of course, dramas differ greatly from one another. There are dramatic works that resist staging to a considerable extent (closet dramas), and there are others that have almost no life off the stage.[6] In any case, however, there is a tension between the dramatic text and the theatre. Only rarely does a drama appear on the stage without dramaturgic intervention, and the expression "adapted for the stage" is usually no more than a euphemism masking the tension between the theatre and literature. In "embodying" the drama, the actor and the director of their own free will (and sometimes even against the will of the dramatist) highlight certain aspects of the literary work and tone down others; the actor has the choice of how to treat the "hidden meaning" of the text, the meaning that cannot be explicitly expressed in dialogue but is nevertheless part of the drama. The author is the master of the written word alone, but the actor is the master of a rich set of vocal, visual (facial expressions) and other means of expression. It is not even possible for him to present only what the text contains: we always see on stage the entire man, not just what the dramatist shows us of him. Stanislavsky has captured the tension between the dramatic work and the stage graphically in a chapter of *My Life in Art* called "When You Play a Bad Man Look for the Good in Him", where he says:

Watching from out front, I could clearly see the actors' mistakes and began to explain them to them.

"Look," I said to one of them, "you're playing a misery, who moans all the time and who worries lest, God forbid, he be taken for one. But why worry about that when the author has already taken care of it quite well enough? The result is that you are all one colour. But black only really becomes black when you have a little white here and there in contrast to it. So bring in some white, and play and mix other colours of the spectrum

---

6   Tille on Rostand's *Cyrano de Bergerac*: "Plays such as Rostand's resemble most the well-constructed texts of operas and plays requiring lavish stagings, in which the author gives only accomplished artists the opportunity to develop their art" (1917: 15).

with it. Then you will have contrast, variety and truth. So, when you play a misery look for moments when he is happy and content." (Stanislavski 2008: 106–107)

It is not, of course, always simply a matter of complementing a text with a clear-cut contrast: often a text offers the actor many semantic possibilities. In this respect dramatic literature itself develops in an oscillating fashion. There are periods in which there is an effort to predetermine the theatrical performance as much as possible by means of the text, and there are others in which the text intentionally leaves as much freedom as possible for theatrical realization. Ibsen's dramas, which almost systematically insert a double meaning into the text, are of the latter kind: one meaning is expressed explicitly in words, the other is accessible only through the actor's gestures, the intonation and timbre of his voice, and the tempo and style of delivery of the play. Chekhov is a similar case. The appeal of Chekhov's plays

> is not conveyed by the words themselves, but by what is hidden behind them or in the pauses, or the way the actors look at each other or in the way they radiate inner feeling. Then dead objects come alive, as do the sounds, the sets, the characters the actors have created, the whole atmosphere of the play, the whole performance. It is all a matter of creative intuition and artistic taste. (Stanislavski 2008: 192)

Such, then, is the relationship between the theatre and the drama: always tense, and for this reason also subject to change. In essence, however, the theatre is not subordinate to literature, nor is literature subordinate to the theatre. These extremes can only occur in certain periods of development, whereas in others there is equilibrium between the two.

Having looked at the dramatic text, let us now turn to the second of the basic constituents of the theatre, dramatic space. Dramatic space is not identical with the stage and not at all with three-dimensional space, for it originates in time through the gradual changes in the spatial relations between the actor and the stage and between the actors themselves. Every movement on the part of the actor is perceived and appraised in connection with previous movements and with respect to the anticipated movement that will follow. In the same way, the placement of the characters on the stage is understood as a change in their previous placement and as a transition toward the next placement. This is why Zich speaks about stage space as a set of forces:

> The dramatic characters represented by the actors are something like power nodes, their intensity varying in accordance with the significance of the characters in the given dramatic situation. Their dramatic relations as created by this situation are then something like lines of force pulsating between the characters. The dramatic stage,

filled with the network of these lines of force and the motor pathways they create, is a kind of force field, changeable in shape and in the strength of its individual components. (Zich 1931: 246)

Owing to its energy, dramatic space can extend beyond the stage in all directions. This gives rise to the phenomenon referred to as the imaginary stage, which Klára Pražáková and Ferdinand Stiebitz[7] have written about (the action behind the stage or, in some cases, even above or below it (see Pražáková 1921; see Stiebitz 1937)). Even the main action itself can be temporarily shifted to the imaginary stage, and in its different periods of development the theatre has exploited the manifold possibilities of the imaginary stage in various ways. Sometimes the theatre resorts to the imaginary stage for purely technical reasons (actions that would be difficult to realize on stage, for example races or large gatherings of people, are situated on the imaginary stage), sometimes convention compels its use (in French Classicist tragedy, for example, scenes involving bloodshed are transferred to the imaginary stage); sometimes there are artistic reasons for using it (heightening tension, and so forth). Whether the imaginary stage is used a great deal or is avoided is a characteristic feature of the nature of dramatic space in any given period.

But dramatic space extends beyond the stage in another way, one that is more fundamental than just the use of the imaginary stage. It brings the stage and the auditorium together. Zich established that "the effects deriving from the dynamic field of dramatic space are transferred to the auditorium, to the audience" (Zich 1931: 246). The contemporary theory of theatre conceives of the stage and the auditorium as a single whole from the point of view of dramatic space (see Kouřil and Burian 1938). Even when the stage is separated from the auditorium by footlights, it does not have an independent existence: the position of an actor at the front of the stage, at the rear, on the left or on the right holds true from the perspective of the spectator sitting in front of the stage, and if the viewers surrounded the stage (as is sometimes the case in folk theatre, for example) these designations would, as Zich points out, lose their sense. Dramatic space, then, takes over the entire theatre and forms in the spectator's subconscious during the performance. It is a force that establishes unity among the other components of the theatre, taking on from them in turn concrete significance.

Another important constituent of the theatre, one that also groups others around itself, is the actor. The actor's significance for the composition of

---

7   [Editor's note: Klára Pražáková (1891–1933), Classical philologist and Anglicist and translator; Ferdinand Stiebitz (1894–1961), Classical philologist and a translator from Classical Greek and Latin.]

a theatre performance is that he is the most frequent vehicle of the action. The fact that the actor is a living human being is also important. Hegel speaks about this in his *Aesthetics*:

> The properly perceptible material of dramatic poetry, as we saw, is not merely the human voice and the spoken word but the whole man, who does not merely express feelings, ideas, and thoughts, but is involved with his whole being in a concrete action and works on the ideas, purposes, acts, and behaviour of others, and experiences corresponding reactions or asserts himself against them. (Hegel 1975: 1182)

Thus the actor is the centre of stage activity, and everything else that is on stage apart from him is appraised only in relation to him, as a sign of his mental and physical makeup. Hence the abundance and complexity of theatrical signs, which Zich revealed in his pioneering book and which Bogatyrev, following in his footsteps, has fruitfully explored. Other things apart from the actor are only perceived through the senses, but the actor and his performance appeal directly to the viewer's empathy. The actor is therefore viewed as the realest of the realities on the stage or rather as the only reality of the stage. The closer the actor is to the stage action, the more immediately his reality is experienced, and along with it the many-faceted aspects of his presence and performance. Hence the difference between major and minor characters. Because of its participation in the action, even a thing can be experienced by the spectator as an actor: at this moment even it becomes a reality for the spectator:

> A real fountain on the empty Meyerholdian stage, where a camping tent, a tripod and a thermos bottle are the other objects making up the stage. These general and commonplace realities are not on the stage to create a harmonious effect or to "paint a picture" of the setting. They are here for theatre, for emotion and captivation, they are here as an actor – they have thousands of meanings according to the relations and the moments they encroach upon... They are here for action, which they do not describe but instead create through their spatial rhythm and temporal change. (Honzl 1928: 72)

The relationship between an actor and the character he portrays is special. The question as to whether the actor creates a character from within himself, from his personal emotions and experiences, or separately from his personal life, by cold calculation, has been raised many times. It was first posed by Diderot in his famous *The Paradox of Acting*. The contemporary theory of theatre answers it approximately as follows. Both direct experiencing of character by the actor and emotionally detached creation of character are always present (Honzl 1940). In the course of development of the theatre, however, now one, now the other pole has been stressed (for example, the creation of character from personal experience predominated in the case of some great actors in the period of psychological realism – to take a Czech example, Hana Kvapilová[8]). For that matter, we should not forget that the connection between the person and the artist in an actor is reciprocal. Not only does an actor partially live a play, but he also partially plays life. In *Art and the Actor*, Constant Coquelin recounts the following anecdote about the actor François-Joseph Talma: "It is said that when he learned of the death of his father, he uttered a piercing cry; so piercing, so heartfelt, that the artist, always on the alert within the man, instantly took note of it, and decided to make use of it on the stage later on" (Coquelin 1915: 59). In all the arts there is a tension between the artist's subjectivity and the objectivity of his work, but it is more intensely experienced in the actor because he is his own material, in his entire person, body and soul.

Nevertheless, in any given play the connection between an actor's life and his artistic creation is not immediate. Between them there is a layer comprising a fixed set of formative devices that are a permanent feature of a given actor and that transfer from role to role. For the audience these fixed formative devices are inseparably bound to the actor's real person. They enable the audience to recognize the actor in a new role; they render him emotionally sympathetic or antipathetic; it is against their background that the audience appraises his individual performances. The tension between an individual performance and the fixed set of formative devices is also, however, a factor in the artistic composition of acting. There are periods, kinds of theatre and leading actors in which what is constant in an actor's creation predominates; at other times emphasis is placed on a striking differentiation between individual roles. Especially with comic actors the stable personality of an actor often prevails over the differentiation of roles – Vlasta Burian[9] is an example. For that matter, comic acting goes even further in stabilizing the actor's performance by creating types that are independent of a single actor's personality: Pulcinella, Bajazzo, Harlequin, Hanswurst, Kašpárek[10] and so on. The number of tensions that envelop the actor on stage – like everything else that enters the composition of a stage performance – is by no means exhausted by the contradiction and tension between the personality of the actor and an individual performance. Many other antinomies of the art of acting could be listed, especially if we moved from the actor as an individual to the company of actors and from a single

---

8   [Editor's note: Hana Kvapilová (1860–1907), actress at the National Theatre in Prague, famous for her interpretation of roles in works by Ibsen, Chekhov and contemporary Czech playwrights.]

9   [Editor's note: Vlasta Burian (1891–1962), one of the best-loved Czech actors in the interwar period, particularly popular for his leading roles in a long string of Czech film comedies.]

10   [Editor's note: Kašpárek, a popular character in Czech puppet theatre, best comparable to Punch in the English puppet theatre tradition.]

character to the entire set of characters participating in a given stage performance.

The audience is another basic constituent of the theatre. Like dramatic space and the actor, the audience in the theatre has a centralizing role, in the sense that everything that happens in the theatre is addressed in one way or another to the audience. When the actors speak on stage, the difference between their speech and the conversation of everyday life is that its effect on the silent partner (and the one only rarely addressed) listening beyond the footlights is taken into account. The reactions of the characters on stage to what the speaker is saying are also calculated for this partner. Frequently the dialogue is conducted in such a way that the audience understands it differently than one of the characters; the audience can also know both more or less about the situation at a given moment than the characters. All this reveals with striking force the participation of the audience in the stage action. Not only does the stage action influence the audience, but the audience also influences the stage action, though as a rule only in the sense that in their performance the actors are either buoyed up or held back by the anticipated perceptivity of the audience, its mood during the play, and so forth. But there are also cases in which the spectators' participation becomes apparent, as sometimes happens in folk theatre (when an actor engages in direct conversation with the audience (see Bogatyrev 1940)) or in comic improvisations (for example when an actor interprets the audience's laughter as a positive or negative response to his words and picks up on this response in his next verbal exchange with his partner: "See what the audience thinks about you," and goes on).

The theatre also exhibits a constant effort to make the spectator's participation in the stage performance as direct as possible. This, for example, is the purpose of placing actors among the spectators, of having actors make their entrances from the auditorium, or of designating a certain character as a mediator between the stage and the auditorium (the Hobo in the Čapek brothers' *The Insect Play*[11]). However, even when the theatre does not appeal to the spectator in such a direct way, it solicits his participation. Charles Vildrac cites a very instructive example of this from [Vojta Novák's][12] staging of Georges Duhamel's play *The Light*:

One recalls the scene where the blind man, Bernard, who is standing at a window opening on a mountain lake at sunset, imagines, guesses, poetically describes the beauty of

---

11 [Editor's note: *The Insect Play* was written by the Čapek brothers, Karel and Josef, in 1921. It is an allegorical play in which various kinds of insects represent human qualities. The Hobo is the narrator and guide.]

12 [Editor's note: Vojta Novák (1886–1966), theatre and opera director, and a film actor.]

the scene, which he does not see and has never seen. Well, at the Prague National Theatre, when the blind man approaches the window, the beautiful illuminated landscape
becomes pitch black, and it is before an utterly dark background emphasized by the
window frame, which is strongly lit by an unreal mauve light, that the hero goes into
ecstasies. The spectator is thus invited to take the place of the speaker; in front of this
window he, too, becomes a blind man. (Vildrac 1923: 12–13)

Incidentally, the roles of the actor and the spectator differ far less from one
another than might appear at first glance. To a certain extent even an actor is
a spectator for his partner at the moment when the partner is acting; extras
in particular, who do not intervene actively in the play, are distinctly perceived as spectators. The inclusion of actors among the audience becomes
quite apparent, for example, when a comedian makes co-actors laugh. Even
though we are aware that such laughter can be intentional (in order to establish active contact between the stage and the auditorium), we cannot but
recognize that at such a moment the boundary between the stage and the
auditorium runs across the stage itself: the laughing actors are on the audience's side.

The audience is therefore omnipresent in the composition of a stage
performance: the meaning not only of what is happening on the stage but
also of things on the stage depends on the audience and its understanding.
This is especially true of props, which on the stage have only the meaning,
in some cases only the existence, that the audience attributes to them. An
object on the stage can strike the audience as something quite different
from what it is in reality; indeed, it can be present only in some imaginary
way (the imaginary prop in the Chinese theatre (cf. Brušák 2016 [1939])).
In such a case it is enough for the audience to know (thanks to information
conveyed by an actor's gestures) that, for example, the actor is holding an
oar in his hands.[13]

We have reached the end of our outline of the problems facing the study
of the theatre. This has certainly not been intended as a comprehensive survey of its problems, but rather as a cursory sketch of the perspective from
which the contemporary theory of theatre views its tasks. We have seen
that for the theoretician the composition of the stage work is beginning to
acquire more and more distinctly the appearance of a structure, that is, a dynamic composition permeated with and kept in motion by a multitude of
always active contradictions between individual components and groups of
components – a structure that hovers freely before the spectator's eyes and

---

13   Cf. E. F. Burian's staging of *A Comedy about Františka and Honzíček* [Komedie o Františce
    a Honzíčkovi] in *Second Folk Suite* [Druhá lidová suita], which had its premiere at the D 39 on
    1 May 1939.

consciousness without being bound unequivocally to existential reality by any of its components but thereby figuratively representing all the reality that surrounds and creates the individual in a given period and society.

WORKS CITED

Bab, Julius (1929) *Albert Bassermann, Weg und Werk eines deutschen Schauspielers um die Wende des 20. Jahrhunderts* [Albert Bassermann, the Method and Work of a German Actor at the Turn of the Twentieth Century], Leipzig: Erich Weibezahl.

Bogatyrev, Petr (1940) *Lidové divadlo české a slovenské* [The Czech and Slovak Folk Theatre], Prague: Fr. Borový and Národopisná společnost českoslovanská.

Brušák, Karel (2016 [1939]) "Signs in the Chinese Theatre", this reader, pp. 115–28.

Burian, E. F. (1939) "Příspěvek k problému jevištní mluvy" [A Contribution to the Problem of Stage Speech], *Slovo a slovesnost*, vol. 5, pp. 24–32.

Coquelin, Benoît-Constant (1915) *Art and the Actor*, trans. A. L. Alger, New York: Dramatic Museum of Columbia University.

Diderot, Dennis (1883) *The Paradox of Acting*, trans. Walter Harries Pollock, London: Chatto & Windus.

Golther, Wolfgang (1926) "Der Schauspieler im Mittelalter" [The Actor in the Middle Ages] in Ewald Geissler (ed.) *Der Schauspieler* [The Actor], Berlin: Bühnenvolksbundverlag, pp. 92–104.

Hegel, G. W. F. (1975) *Aesthetics. Lectures on Fine Art*, vol. 2, trans. T. M. Knox, Oxford: Clarendon Press.

Honzl, Jindřich (1928) "Vsevolod Meierchold a revoluční oktjabr divadla" [Vsevolod Meyerhold and the Revolutionary October of Theatre] in *Moderní ruské divadlo* [Modern Russian Theatre], Prague: Odeon, pp. 50–58.

— (1940) "Nad Diderotovým *Paradoxem o herci*" [On Diderot's *The Paradox of Acting*], *Program D 40*, vol. 4, pp. 81–85.

Jakobson, Roman (1975 [1937]) "The Statue in Pushkin's Poetic Mythology" in John Burbank (trans. and ed.) *Pushkin and His Sculptural Myth*, The Hague: Mouton, pp. 1–44.

Kouřil, Miroslav and Burian, E. F. (1938) *Divadlo práce: studie divadelního prostoru* [Theatre of Labour: a Study of Theatre Space], Prague: J. Kohoutek.

Pražáková, Klára (1921) "Pomyslné jeviště" [The Imaginary Stage], *Jeviště*, vol. 2, pp. 390–92.

Stanislavski, Konstantin (2008) *My Life in Art*, trans. and ed. Jean Benedetti, London: Routledge.

Stiebitz, Ferdinand (1937) "Pomyslné jeviště v antickém a moderním divadle" [The Imaginary Stage in Classical and Modern Theatre], *Věda a život*, vol. 3, pp. 229–42.

Tille, Václav (1917) *Divadelní vzpomínky* [Memories of the Theatre], Prague: B. Kočí.

Veltruský, Jiří (2016 [1940]) "People and Things in the Theatre", this reader, pp. 147–56.

Vildrac, Charles (1923) "Notes sur le théâtre à Prague" [Notes on the Theatre in Prague], *Choses de théâtre*, vol. 2, pp. 10–14.

Zich, Otakar (1931) *Estetika dramatického umění: teoretická dramaturgie* [The Aesthetics of Dramatic Art: A Theoretical Dramaturgy], Prague: Melantrich.

STRUCTURALISM AND THEATRE

JIŘÍ VELTRUSKÝ

["Structuralism and Theatre" was first presented in Czech as an introduction to a lecture given by Veltruský at the Prague Linguistic Circle on 5 May 1941. The lecture was published (1941) as "Dramatický tekst jako součást divadla" [Dramatic Text as a Component of Theatre], *Slovo a slovesnost*, vol. 7, no. 3, pp. 132–44 (for the English version, see this reader 247–67). However, the first ten pages of the article were not published owing to censorship. In the 1970s, when he was preparing his studies for Matejka, Ladislav and Titunik, Irwin R. (eds) (1976) *Semiotics of Art: The Prague School Contributions*, Cambridge, Mass.: The M.I.T. Press, Veltruský reworked the previously unpublished part of his manuscript and translated it into English. Unfortunately, the publication had to be reduced in size, so in the end Veltruský decided to withdraw his article. The final version of the manuscript was preserved among Veltruský's papers and is published here for the first time.]

The structural conception has developed in the theory of dramatic art differently than in other fields. In linguistics, literary scholarship, general aesthetics, ethnography, and so on, the starting point was the study of empirical facts. The systematic coverage of each discipline was the result of a gradual process. By contrast, the first appearance of structuralism in the theory of dramatic art was Otakar Zich's attempt to construct a whole system (Zich 1931). This could only be done at the cost of some serious oversimplification. So Zich narrowed down the possible functions of the various components of theatre, taking into account only those functions that each component had in what could be broadly called the realistic theatre. Just one example: "White theatrical light represents sunlight. ... With different shades of colour it represents moonlight, a red sky, fire, and so on" (Zich 1931: 268).

This was particularly disconcerting since at the time theatre had already moved far away from the kind of realism that the author had in mind. Therefore, his work had very little impact. Yet Zich's merits are undeniable. They are mainly due to his sensitive and precise examination of theatrical components and their semantics, not to the general "laws" that he deduced from his own analyses. In other words, Zich's system is objectionable because it was not based on sufficient preliminary studies of details; it is valid to the extent that it is not a true theoretical system but rather a collection of such studies. At the same time, the striving to build up a system led Zich to see that theatre is a coherent and distinctive structure and that its components must be examined in their complex relationships rather than in isolation.

If the theory was to develop further, far broader material had to be analysed. It was to this need that Brušák's study on Chinese theatre responded (Brušák 2016 [1939]). The author gave a minute description of a structure made up of lexicalized signs, the meanings of which are rigorously determined by convention – therefore a structure entirely different from the realistic theatre.

* * *

An entirely different approach has been chosen by Bogatyrev (2016 [1938] and 1940). He, too, studies forms of theatre that had not been considered by Zich but his objective is more ambitious. Like Zich, he wants to arrive at generally applicable conclusions. He rightly quotes a great many facts that are incompatible with the "laws" formulated by Zich. Yet he concentrates so much on these "laws" that he does not see Zich's accurate analyses. Instead of revising and correcting the system that Zich tried to build, he throws it into desperate chaos.

This is particularly clear when the author takes up the elements of theatre one by one in order to describe their respective characteristics. What he really does is to wipe away nearly all that distinguishes them from each other. Here is an example:

> Verbal expression in the theatre is a structure of signs composed not only of speech signs but also of other signs. For instance, theatre speech that is intended to signify the social standing of a character is uttered in accompaniment to the actor's gestures and is complemented by his costume, by the scenery, and so on, which are also signs of this character's social standing. (Bogatyrev 2016 [1938]: 106)

It is of course a mystery how gestures, costume and decoration can be considered as being parts of the linguistic utterance. But more important is the fact that there are differences between the semantic potential of the various components mentioned. Whether or not this or that component can be, for example, "a sign of the social position of the person" is beside the point. Even where different components fulfil the same function, each does it in a particular manner and to a particular degree. These distinctive features of the components must be defined with precision – which in many cases had already been done by Zich.

The differences in the semantic quality of the components have something to do with the structural relations into which they enter with each other. Although emphasizing even more than Zich that all the components of the structure are linked together, Bogatyrev fails to study the ways in which they are linked. Zich did not solve the problem but at least he saw it. His solution relies on the old concepts of artistic realism and idealism and is formulated as "the principle of uniform stylization" (Zich 1931: 383 ff). He was not the first nor the last scholar who tried to simplify the intricate relationships within the theatrical structure by resorting to such concepts as "harmony" or "uniform stylization". Suffice it to say that no less a figure in the modern theory of literature than Ingarden dealt with this issue in a similar spirit (Ingarden 1931). This does not prevent Bogatyrev from simply rejecting Zich's thesis on the basis of a few examples to which this thesis, as it is formulated, does not apply. Unfortunately, in his sweeping attack on Zich he brushes aside one of the most important and most difficult problems of dramatic structure.

Bogatyrev insists as much as Zich on the semantic nature of theatre. But he is less precise than Zich in his description of the way the meaning is conveyed by certain components, including even the stage figure. As Honzl rightly pointed out, he is wrong when he claims – in opposition to Zich, who was aware of the intricacies – that theatrical signs have nothing in common with realities. In fact, many of the things on stage are not mere signs. This is true above all of the actor. The figure that he creates represents the character, the *dramatis persona*, but he is also a real, living person with all his physical qualities – both those that denote the character and those that have nothing to do with the character (Honzl 1940). This is one of the main features that distinguish the semantics of theatre.

On other occasions, Bogatyrev confuses the action performed by the actor with action and behaviour in real life (see Veltruský 1987).[1]

Bogatyrev's positive contribution is his subtle analysis of various details found precisely in those forms of theatre that Zich disregarded: folk, medieval, avant-garde and primitive theatre. However, like Zich, he fails in his striving for universal principles. His strength, too, lies in what he himself – unlike Brušák – takes for no more than a means, that is, in the study of specific facts.

* * *

An immediate reaction to, and continuation of, Bogatyrev's approach is the important theoretical article published in 1940 by Honzl (2016 [1940]). A distinguished stage director and one of the outstanding figures of the avant-garde theatre, Honzl has already published, over a period of nearly

---

1   [Editor's note: In his unpublished 1976 manuscript, Veltruský made a reference to his then-unpublished article "Structure in Folk Theatre: Notes Regarding Bogatyrev's Book on Czech and Slovak Folk Theatre", which was published later, in 1987 (see the Works Cited section).]

twenty years, many articles and several books on theatre. The study to which I refer represents a turning point in his approach: for the first time, his only purpose is research, unmixed with his own artistic conceptions; and he adopts the structural method.

Like Zich and Bogatyrev, Honzl wants to penetrate to the very foundations of dramatic art. As distinct from Bogatyrev's, his attitude towards Zich's work is unprejudiced. This is very remarkable since as a stage director Honzl rejects the realistic theatre on which Zich based his theory. Undoubtedly, due to his artistic sensitivity, he sees beyond this barrier so as to appreciate Zich's penetrating insight. This has helped him to avoid many of the pitfalls into which Bogatyrev slips.

While Bogatyrev claims that the essence of theatricality is "transformation" – a mystical, rather than semantic, notion[2] – Honzl agrees with Zich that it is action (Zich 1931: 68). He conceives action as a continuous semantic series that unfolds in time. The various components of the dramatic structure are seen as continually changing vehicles that keep following one another by turns and entering into the most varied relations both with the action and among themselves. In Honzl's view, all these relations can change without any limitation and are in no way predetermined.

Because he examines broader and more diversified material than Zich, Honzl discovers a greater variety in the semantic potential and mutual relationships of the different components. In this respect, his contribution is comparable to Bogatyrev's. But he differs from Bogatyrev in that his description of the dramatic structure is more consistent; in that sense he is closer to Zich.

Honzl, too, has failed in his endeavour to grasp the actual foundations of the dramatic art. Once he has identified action as the essence of theatricality, his analysis goes no further. But at that point there arises the question of what action is and what objective conditions it requires in order to take place. About this, Honzl speaks only in images:

Action – as the essence of theatrical dramaticality – unifies for us word, actor, costume, scenery and music in the sense that we recognize them as different conductors of a single current that flows through them all, either passing from one to another or flowing through a combination of many. And now that we are at this comparison, let us add that this current – that is, dramatic action – is not carried by the conductor that exerts the least resistance (dramatic action is not always concentrated in the actor's acting alone); instead, theatricality is frequently generated precisely through overcoming the resistance caused by some theatrical devices (special theatrical effects in which action is concentrated, for instance, solely in the words or in the actor's movements or

---

2   See my criticism of this concept in Veltruský 1987.

in offstage sounds, and so on), in the same way that a tungsten filament glows because it is offering resistance to an electric current. (Honzl 2016 [1940]: 145)

Unfortunately, Honzl disregards the fact that the resistance set up by various components to the requirements of the action results from the specific semantic potential of each.

Words cannot be fully translated into gestures, pictures, music; the meaning of a picture cannot be fully conveyed by language, music, the play of facial muscles, and so forth. Each of these types of sign is entirely different, each has its own unique ability to refer to certain kinds and certain aspects of reality and each is deficient in some other respects. Language, for instance, is inferior to painting in indicating colours, the location of objects or people within a certain situation, the distances between them, and so on. Painting is at a disadvantage in comparison with sculpture and architecture in referring to relations in space and with language in referring to time sequences, the flow of time, and so on. Music is superior to any other semantic system in the articulation of the passage of time while it is inferior to all of them, except perhaps architecture, in calling up a concrete reality. If not all, at least several semantic systems combine, complement and conflict with each other in dramatic art. The same reality is referred to, either simultaneously or successively, by signs as different as, for instance, speech, image and music. None of them can denote that reality in its entirety; each has a different meaning even though they all refer to the same thing. In this sense theatre offers an opportunity to study in optimal conditions – almost as in a laboratory – both the common and the distinctive features of different sign systems or, to put it differently, to study comparative semantics.

Honzl has passed over these problems in silence. When he speaks about action and about the different theatrical components through which it is carried out, he stresses merely the dynamic character of action and its predominance over the single components. In fact, however, there is a dialectical opposition between the components of theatre and theatrical action. And this opposition is only a particular case of a general antinomy between semantic statics and semantic dynamics, between the unit of meaning and the context, that can be found in every application of any type of sign (see Mukařovský 1977 [1940]: 46 ff).

Since he has studied the antinomy of the components and of action only from the point of view of action, Honzl, like Bogatyrev, pays no attention to the qualitative differences between the components as units of meaning. So he sees no need to classify them. Such a classification was attempted by Zich when he divided all components into the optical and the acoustic (Zich 1931: 17 and 22). No doubt that classification is oversimplified; already Brušák's description of the Chinese theatre shows that it cannot be used in a semantic analysis. Honzl rightly rejects Zich's classification, but he rejects it on wrong grounds: he claims the unity of action precludes any fundamental differences between the components. He does not seem to notice that it was precisely on the basis of his classification that Zich tried to prove that dramatic art relies on the unity of action.

* * *

Had he used his ample material to study the antinomy of the components and of the action from the angle of the components as well, Honzl could have overcome one of the most serious shortcomings of Zich's conception: the tendency to limit the function of the sign to the "representation" of some reality. Such a restrictive conception, according to which the sign is a thing that in itself represents, stands for or characterizes something else, is explicable in the case of Zich because he is concerned with realistic theatre. But once both Bogatyrev and Honzl analyse forms of theatre that in no way fit into this conception, the result is confusion and chaos. For instance, Honzl speaks about the following scene from a Japanese theatre:

> Yuranosuke leaves the besieged castle. He steps forward from the back of the stage.
>
> Suddenly the backdrop (which depicts a life-size door) is rolled up. We see a second backdrop: a small door. This indicates that the actor has moved away.
>
> Yuranosuke proceeds on his journey. A dark green curtain is lowered over the backdrop. This indicates that Yuranosuke can no longer see the castle.
>
> A few steps more. Yuranosuke enters on the "flower way".[3] To mark this further distancing, the *samisen* (a kind of Japanese mandolin) begins to play its music offstage.

Here is the structural description of this scene as worked out by Honzl:

> The first stage of the journey away from the castle: a *step* in space.
>
> The second stage: a *change of painted scenery*.
>
> The third stage: a conventional sign (the *curtain*), which cancels the visual scenic devices.
>
> The fourth stage: *sound*.

The succession of scenic devices, which take up the same function one after the other, is interpreted here as the gradation of a single action being carried out by the actor: Yuranosuke walking, leaving the castle behind.

---

3   The "flower way", *hanamichi*, is a passageway (and acting area) that connects the rear of the auditorium with the right side of the stage.

However, with equal justification we could in this case interpret the actor's step-ping away from the painted backdrop as a function of spatial localization. The stage artist "paints" either with the actor's step or with the sound of the mandolin. In each case he creates spatial relations by different means. But we can go beyond these two in-terpretations and consider others. We could ask whether the changing of the backdrops depicting the castle doors is not in fact an artistic substitution for the playwright's text, that is to say, for the actor's words "I have stepped out of the castle." Or whether the melancholy sound of the *samisen* is not a substitution for the verbal expression "I have set out on a journey to the distant desert." But even if we were to seek further interpre-tations we would still not get to the heart of the matter. We would not be able to make up our mind as to which of them are fundamental and we would not be able to deny the legitimacy of the others. (Honzl 2016 [1940]: 137–38)

In fact, none of the interpretations suggested by Honzl is pertinent. The basic semantic principle here is that all the components acquire their meanings only in relation to the actor. In themselves, they "represent" either nothing or something else than in connection with the actor. For example, without the link with the actor's step, the lowering of the dark-green curtain could mean many things, depending on the convention – it could indicate for instance that night has come – but certainly not the character's moving away from the castle. Moreover, the meanings they acquire in connection with what the actor does are based on the spectator's contemplating everything that is or that happens on stage from the character's, rather than from his own, point of view.[4] It is for Yuranosuke, not for the spectator looking at the situation from outside, that the door diminishes and finally vanishes as Yuranosuke moves away from the besieged castle. The relation between the spectator and the character is probably the same as regards the sound of the *samisen*. On this point, Honzl's description is not clear. But judging from other devices of the Kabuki theatre in analogous situations, it is quite likely that the musical sound means something that is going on in the mind of the character and that the spectator is to share with him.

None of the substitutions suggested by Honzl would convey an equivalent meaning, because each would thoroughly change the semantic structure of the scene. For instance, the verbal communications "I have stepped out of the castle", "I have started the journey into the desert", and so on, would create an entirely different relation between the actor and the spectator. The spectator would be the addressee of the actor's speech, while in the scene as it is he identifies himself with the character impersonated by the actor.

Because he restricts the semantic functions of the sign to its indepen-dently "representing" some reality, Honzl overlooks the distinctions between

---

4   This is not a general principle of the Japanese theatre.

the different types of signs and between their semantic potentialities. As a result, he tends to disregard the specific hierarchy of components that exists in every single wok of dramatic art.[5] Even more serious consequences follow from the same oversimplification in Bogatyrev's writings. The extreme example is where Bogatyrev in fact fails, in the case of certain components, to realize that they are signs properly so called; that is the true meaning of his attempt to divide the components into those that "represent" and those that are "purely theatrical" (Bogatyrev 1940: 123 ff and 129 ff; see also Veltruský 1987).

* * *

The grave shortcomings of the structural theory of dramatic art cannot be attributed to fortuitous circumstances. Their principal sources are in the art of theatre itself, especially in its uniquely involved structure, in the ephemeral nature of its works and in its particular semantics.

1. Unlike the other arts, theatre uses heterogenous materials. Its structure is therefore much more complicated than the structure of any other art; the obstacles that the theoretical study of theatre must face are formidable. That is the explanation for the frequent tendency to draw general conclusions from a limited historical period or a particular kind of theatre, which offer the advantage of being at least fairly homogenous in style.

2. The ephemeral character of the work of art, too, is a distinctive feature of theatre. This is different from what are referred to as the performing arts. A musical composition, for instance, is a lasting work. A theatrical creation exists only during the performance. As soon as the performance is over, its analysis must depend on the spectator's memory, on the literary text, the costumes, the sets, the photographs or designs of specific situations, and such like. As to the works of the past, especially of the remote past, our knowledge relies to a large extent on indirect evidence. The historiography of theatre is full of factual errors and of unwarranted assumptions and interpretations based chiefly on the historians' own ideas of what theatre is. This is another cause of the tendency to draw general conclusions from limited material. The theoretician spontaneously prefers to examine such forms of theatre as are familiar to him, to avoid studying the fancies of contemporaries or historians.

Therefore, the reservations that must be made with respect to the deductions made by Bogatyrev and Honzl must not conceal their great contribution

---

5   Quite obviously, Honzl eventually became aware of this consequence. He devoted a whole article to the problem of hierarchy – see Honzl 2016 [1943]. Characteristically, even that article did not deal with the semantic differences between the components that make up the hierarchy. [Note added in 1973.]

and the debt that we owe to them, as to Brušák, for this determination to broaden the horizon of the theory.[6]

3. Theatre is a distinctive semantic system. Although it draws on other semantic systems or types of sign – language, painting, sculpture, architecture, music, gesture, and so on – it differs from them all. Within the theatrical structure, each of these contributory systems keeps its own, characteristic way of relating the *signifiant* to the *signifié*. As a result, each type of sign to some extent conflicts with all the others. At the same time, in combination with the others each acquires certain new features and semantic potentialities that it does not have in itself, outside theatre. Unfortunately, for all practical purposes the theory of such semantic systems as, for example, painting or music is still non-existent. Yet the description and definition of the specific semantics of theatre cannot be achieved without comparing the meanings every type of sign is capable of conveying, and the ways in which it conveys them, outside and inside theatre. This is not all. The actor is the key to the semantics of theatre. As already mentioned, the stage figure created by the actor is both a sign and a non-sign, that is, a living person whose reality cannot be reduced to what is relevant to the figure as a sign. This fact has no equivalent in other kinds of art. This twofold intricacy of the dramatic sign is the main reason why the theoreticians tend to oversimplify the semantics of theatre and to narrow it down to "representing".

To overcome the shortcomings of the structural theory of dramatic art, the entire structure of theatre will have to be examined in the light of every component so as to find out how and through which of its features each one intervenes in this structure and what its relations are with the other components. Metaphorically speaking, what is needed first is a phonology, a morphology and a grammar of theatre; then the time will come to work out its semantics. Simultaneously, single works of dramatic art must be analysed in order to develop our knowledge of the global sign, or uniform structure, that each work constitutes in spite of all the diversity and heterogeneity of its components.

WORKS CITED

Bogatyrev, Petr (2016 [1938]) "Theatrical Signs", this reader, pp. 99–114.

— (1940) *Lidové divadlo české a slovenské* [Czech and Slovak Folk Theatre], Prague: F. Borový and Národopisná společnost českoslovanská.

Brušák, Karel (2016 [1939]) "Signs in the Chinese Theatre", this reader, pp. 115–28.

Honzl, Jindřich (1928) *Moderní ruské divadlo* [The Modern Russian Theatre], Prague: Odeon.

---

6   In Honzl's case, this refers not only to his theoretical articles in which he adopted the structural conception but also to his previous writings, such as his 1928 book *The Modern Russian Theatre*.

— (1940) "Objevené divadlo v Lidovém divadle českém a slovenském" [The Theatre Discovered in Czech and Slovak Folk Theatre], *Slovo a slovesnost*, vol. 6, no. 2, pp. 107–11.

— (2016 [1940]) "The Mobility of the Theatrical Sign", this reader, pp. 115–28.

— (2016 [1943]) "The Hierarchy of Theatrical Devices", this reader, pp. 157–64.

Ingarden, Roman (1931) *Das literarische Kunstwerk* [The Literary Work of Art], Halle: Max Niemeyer.

Mukařovský, Jan (1977) [1940] "On Poetic Language" in Burbank, John and Steiner, Peter (trans. and eds), *The Word and Verbal Art: Selected Essays by Jan Mukařovský*, New Haven and London: Yale University Press, pp. 1–64.

Veltruský, Jiří (1987) "Structure in Folk Theater: Notes regarding Bogatyrev's Book on Czech and Slovak Folk Theatre", *Poetics Today*, vol. 8, no. 1, pp. 141–61.

Zich, Otakar (1931) *Estetická dramatického umění: teoretická dramaturgie* [The Aesthetics of Dramatic Art: A Theoretical Dramaturgy], Prague: Melantrich.

II SIGN – OBJECT – ACTION

A fundamental task tackled by the Prague School in the interwar period was that of defining the specifics of the theatrical sign. In fact almost all the texts in this volume contribute to a certain extent to this endeavour. Those in this section are devoted almost entirely to this issue, but it was very common for members of the Prague School, even when writing about specific, more limited topics, to explore as well basic concepts such as the sign, structure, the hierarchy of devices and so on.

For example, Jindřich Honzl's texts on gestures and mimicry and Jiří Veltruský's study on the semiotics of acting (see section VI) deal with this basic issue while working with acting as their particular material. Similarly, in his essay on ritual and theatre (see section VII), when defining distinctive features of these phenomena Honzl has to deal with the process of creating meaning both in theatre and in ritual behaviour. Or, more from a practitioner's perspective, E. F. Burian's short note on the stage metaphor (see section VIII) is a practical example of how the idea of a dynamic theatre structure and the new concept of the sign open up fresh possibilities for theatrical practice, while vice versa, Veltruský's analysis of one of Burian's productions (also section VIII) is a theoretical answer to problems posed by progressive theatre experimentation.

Any discussion of the character of the theatrical sign should of course be viewed against a more general background, that of discussion of the sign as such, with special attention to a linguistic approach to the question. This was being carried out in texts by Roman Jakobson, Jan Mukařovský, Sergei Kartsevsky and others (see the Afterword to the volume for further references) as early as the 1930s, with attention shifting to other arts somewhat later. Mukařovský in particular was trying to develop a structural approach towards a comparative aesthetics (or even semiotics) of art. In all these attempts there is a clear tendency to avoid the simple application of a linguistic concept of the sign to the theatre and other arts.

One of the main criticisms the Prague School had with regard to their precursor, Otakar Zich, was the narrow base of his material, which resulted in his conclusions being limited to the framework of realistic theatre. There was therefore a strong emphasis in the Prague School on non-realistic theatre material (folk theatre, puppet theatre, Asian theatre forms and avant-garde experiments), with the result that the concept of the sign was tested in all varieties of theatre forms.

New material, offered primarily by avant-garde productions, helped to refine distinctions between various elements of the theatre performance. In their analyses, members of the Prague School never worked from a fixed set of particular elements of the theatre production, but instead changed – functionally – their criteria: sometimes they dealt with fundamental distinctions such as those between acting and space or actor and puppet, sometimes they narrowed their focus, concentrating on issues such as tensions between gesture and facial expression or the range of vocal expression. The authors also demonstrated how the hierarchy of elements changed both in the current theatre and in its historical forms. And vice versa, discussion of the (dynamic) nature of the theatre sign helped to support the concept of art as a dynamic structure.

A CONTRIBUTION TO THE STUDY OF THEATRICAL SIGNS
ON THE PERCEPTION OF SIGNS IN PUPPET THEATRE, THEATRE WITH LIVE ACTORS AND ART IN GENERAL

PETR BOGATYREV

["Príspevok ku skúmaniu divadelných znakov. K otázke vnímania znakov bábkového divadla, divadla živých hercov a umenia vôbec" (1937-38) was published in Slovak in *Slovenské smery umelecké a kritické*, vol. 5, pp. 238-46. It was published in Czech as "Příspěvek ke zkoumání divadelních znaků. K otázce vnímání znaků loutkového divadla, divadla živých herců a umění vůbec" in Kolár, Jaroslav (trans. and ed.) (1971) *Souvislosti tvorby: cesty k struktuře lidové kultury a divadla* [The Context of Creation: In Search of the Structure of Folk Culture and Folk Theatre], Prague: Odeon, pp. 139-45. The English translation by John Burbank was published as "A Contribution to the Study of Theatrical Signs. The Perception of the Signs in Puppet Theatre, Theatre with Live Actors, and Art in General" in Steiner, Peter (ed.) (1981) *The Prague School: Selected Writings, 1929-1946*, Austin: The University of Texas Press, pp. 55-64.]

Puppet theatre is one of the forms of theatre that are most strongly based on various conventions. Some puppeteers make a special effort to underscore its puppet nature, whereas others try to bring it as close as possible to the theatre of live actors, often the theatre of live actors of the Naturalist movement. But even when the puppeteers do their utmost to be naturalistic, striving to make their actors resemble live actors and living people as much as possible, this very effort highlights even more strongly (often against their will) the conventions of the puppet theatre. Such is the law of the dialectic. The more naturalistic the intonations of the actor who speaks a puppet's words are and the closer his speech is to everyday speech, the more we sense the difference between the living person and the tiny puppet. The more naturalistic the puppet's movements, the more clearly the conventions of the puppet theatre stand out.

The strings by which puppets are manipulated, the reduced dimensions of the wooden actors, who lack facial expressions, the stiff gestures and the numerous other specific features of puppetry all remind the spectator of the puppet theatre that what is before him is merely theatre, merely a theatrical embodiment of life and not life itself. The strikingly expressed theatricality of puppet theatre has attracted leading theatre people in a wide range of movements in very many different periods.

Puppet theatre has attracted particular attention in periods when the theatre has had to fight for theatricality, for the right to the existence of a distinct theatrical life on the stage, subject to its own laws. Among recent reformers of the theatre, Gordon Craig is one such apologist for puppet theatre. "The actor," Craig says, "should be banished from the theatre and replaced by an Übermarionette that obediently realizes the intention of the creator of the stage action" (Craig in Znosko-Borovsky 1925: 251). Many other contemporary directors are turning to the formal means of expression of puppet theatre, and actors are imitating the economical movements of puppets in their own movements.

The distinctive character of puppet theatre – the many specific artistic and technical devices that it has at its disposal and that distinguish it from theatre with live actors – is immediately apparent to everyone who has studied it. On the other hand, it displays in a particularly striking fashion signs that are common to every theatre performance, and for this reason it offers particularly suitable material for an analysis of both theatrical signs themselves as well as their perception by the audience, for here we see exposed what usually remains concealed in the theatre of live actors.

Otakar Zich, the outstanding Czech theoretician of the theatre, has attempted to analyse how the audience perceives the puppet theatre. Here are his conclusions:

> The reason [for this possible resolution] lies in the fact that the controversy exists in the dual conception of what we perceive: puppets may be either taken for live people, or as un-live puppets. The solution therefore lies in the fact that we take them in only one way of the two – which leaves us with a choice between two possibilities:
>
> 1. Either we take puppets as puppets (i.e. we stress their un-live qualities and their materiality). In this case, the physical puppet is something real for us, and we take it with sincerity. In such a case, however, we cannot take equally seriously their speech and movements, in brief their "manifestations of life"; we thus find them comical or *grotesque*. The fact that puppets are tiny and are partially rigid (in their faces, in their bodies) and that their movements are correspondingly clumsy (they are quite literally "wooden"), in such cases contributes to the comedy of the impression. This is not a crude type of ridiculousness, but merely a mild form of humour that these little figures affect us with, particularly given that they behave seemingly like live people. We take them for puppets but they want us to take them for people, which will surely put us into a good mood! Everyone knows that puppets have such an effect.
>
> The second option is:
>
> 2. Puppets can be taken for live beings in that we put emphasis on their apparent manifestations of life (their movements and speech) and take these shows with sincerity. In such a perceptive mode, the awareness of the factual un-liveness of puppets moves to the background and it is apparent merely as a sensation of something inexplicable, a certain mystery that raises a sense of amazement. In this case, puppets have an *uncanny* effect on us. If they had real human size and their facial expressions were

as perfect as can be, the sensation created in such a conception could accordingly be one of terror.

In presenting just these two options, I am deliberately leaving aside the case of the pan-opticon [i.e. seeing both possibilities simultaneously], wishing to remain in the artistic spheres [of theatre practice and live audience perception]. Legends and literature can provide examples of matter similar to puppets brought to life: such as the Commen-datore's statue (in *Don Juan*), or the Golem. Everyone will accept that these fantasies have much more terrible effects than, for instance, the notion of the resuscitated dead, since this is a case of something wholly unnatural, namely life brought into non-living, inorganic matter, whereas the latter case is life brought back to matter that once used to be alive. Nevertheless, I believe that if our puppets were the size of people, it would bring a feeling of awkwardness; however, the mere diminution of their size prevents this completely, even in the second mode of perception described here, which gives them only a serious sense of uncanniness. (Zich 2015 [1923]: 506–507)

The question that Zich has raised of how puppet theatre is perceived goes beyond the bounds of the puppet theatre. What Zich says about it can be applied to other kinds of theatre as well as to other arts. I consider Zich's remarks unusually important and interesting, and therefore I will take the liberty to dwell on them. But despite the unusual interest of his remarks I regard them as essentially incorrect. Zich's fatal error consists in his failing to perceive puppet theatre as a *distinctive* system of signs, in the absence of which no artistic creation can be understood. Everything that Zich says about the puppet theatre can be fully applied to every other art. Once we fail to perceive a work of art as the sign of a thing but regard it as the thing itself, or once we perceive signs in a work of art, continually comparing them with a real thing, and in our comparison start from the real thing and not from the system of signs that shape the given work of art, we will gain the same impression Zich speaks of in connection with the perception of puppet the-atre. Let me give some concrete examples.

In Prague there is a panorama of the Battle of Lipany.[1] Some real things – weapons and other objects – have been placed not far from the spectator as if they remained on the battlefield, while the painting itself is situated at a relative distance from the spectator, with things similar to the real objects lying on the ground painted on it. The "trick" of the panorama consists in the fact that in some cases, thanks to special lighting effects, the spectator is unable to tell a real object from a painted object, and perceives the painted

---

1   [Editor's note: The Battle of Lipany (1434) marked the end of the Hussite Wars in the Czech lands, which lasted fifteen years and were won by the moderate Hussite faction. The panorama referred to, depicting this historic battle, was painted and composed by Luděk Marold (1865–1898) in 1898. With its 1045 m², it is the largest panoramic painting in the Czech Republic.]

ones as real. In other cases, for example if there is trouble with the lighting, this difference is clear. And then such a painted object in comparison with a real object has a rather comic effect. To paraphrase Zich's words about puppets, "We perceive them [the objects] as painted, but they want us to perceive them as real objects." I stress that here – in perceiving the panorama as its creator wanted us to – we start from the real objects lying on the ground.

To move on, let us imagine someone who does not perceive the painted apples in a painting as signs of painting but as real apples, and in his perception of the painted apples starts from real apples. For example, he puts real apples next to the still life with apples and compares a real apple with the coloured splotches in the painting. The apple in the painting will have a comical effect on him, for in the opinion of someone who compares it to a real apple – not, of course, in the artist's view – the apple "wants us to view it as a real apple."

Another possibility for viewing paintings will be, to paraphrase Zich, the following: "Paintings can be understood as living beings." Then every statue and every painting "affects us mysteriously in this case, producing in us what could amount to a feeling of terror." Such a perception is in fact possible. Let us recall Gogol's short story "The Portrait", in which the painter Nikolai Chartkov believes a portrait to be a living person. This evokes "a feeling of terror" in the artist, and he goes mad. We know other cases in which a man falls in love with the portrait of a woman as though it was a living woman. For him the portrait stops being the sign of woman X but is the woman herself. These are pathological cases. To perceive a painting and a statue in this way is unnatural both from an aesthetic standpoint and from that of common sense. It is not only the perception of the system of signs creating a work of art as a living person or a real thing that leads to the perception of the work of art as something comic or close to what evokes "a feeling of uneasiness" or even "a feeling of terror". The results are the same when a sign of some particular system is perceived as a sign of another system.

We perceive poetic language as a natural and normal sign of poetry. Let us now imagine a man who in normal life suddenly begins to speak in verse. For example, at lunch he orders a bowl of soup in verse, or at a meeting of the botanical society he begins to discuss botany in verse. These two situations, in which poetic language is perceived in the former case as practical and in the latter as scientific, will, of course, produce either a comic effect or the impression of something unnatural, incomprehensible, perhaps even "a feeling of uneasiness".

Or again, the signs of a foreign language, when compared with the signs of our native language, are very often perceived as comical or unnatural, mysterious. Imagine the odd impression that would be produced in Czech society if someone, contrary to all expectations, were to begin speaking Chinese instead of Czech.

And even lesser differences such as dialect speech and jargon, the mistakes of a foreigner speaking our language and children's speech are all perceived as comic if the perceiver starts from the assumption that the only correct language is the standard language. And indeed foreigners' speech, children's language, dialects and jargon are all exploited as comic linguistic devices in anecdotes, comedies, vaudeville, and so forth (see Krejčí 1937). The best evidence that a foreign, unintelligible language creates an impression of something mysterious when we view it seriously is the use of foreign, unintelligible or barely intelligible languages in the services of various religions: Arabic, ancient Hebrew, Latin and others. In magic rituals, conjuring formulae in a foreign language can even arouse "a feeling of terror".

This also pertains to other signs insofar as we perceive them on the basis of signs that are generally valid for us. Let us imagine that an African native begins to pay with the signs of his currency – shells – when purchasing various things in this country. If we viewed his currency signs on the basis of ours, we would regard his action as either "comic, grotesque" or the behaviour of a madman, which would involuntarily arouse "a feeling of uneasiness".

Let us take some examples from religion. If we proceed from our own religious signs, we can view the dances of primitive tribes during their prayers to their gods either as something comical or as something unintelligible, mysterious, abnormal, and as such something that arouses in us "a feeling of uneasiness".

Here is a real case that occurred in Russia. A Russian peasant girl found herself in the city and stepped into a Catholic church. As soon as the organ began to play – that sign of Catholic prayer, accompanied by instrumental music – it was so grotesquely ridiculous to the peasant girl, used to the Orthodox service, in which no instrumental music is admissible in the church, that she burst out laughing and was removed from the church.

We could multiply the examples when unfamiliar signs perceived in comparison with signs familiar to us create either a comical impression or "a feeling of uneasiness".

However, let us now return to the theatre. Otakar Zich's basic error consists in his not understanding the system of signs that is a puppet performance as such, as something *sui generis*, but instead comparing it to a performance of live actors. But if we failed, too, to perceive the sign system of live actors on stage as something *sui generis* – that is, if we perceived it as real life rather than as a system of theatrical signs – then we would gain the same impression that Zich did in the case of the performance of puppets.

If we were to regard the puppet theatre too – like every other theatre and ultimately like every art – solely as a system of signs, not even a puppet would strike us as ridiculous, though its movements do not fully conform to the movements of living people.

The facts themselves contradict Zich's conclusions about the comic impression of puppet performances, particularly in the Czech puppet theatre. If we look at the repertoire of Czech folk puppeteers, we find that both dramatic as well as comic plays occupy an important place.

Moreover, "awkward, wooden movements" are in no way an indication of the comical nature of puppets. If one pays attention to the puppets that represent serious characters in Czech puppet theatre – kings, princesses, and others – one sees that their movements are "more wooden" than those of the comic Kašpárek.[2] The movements of the serious characters are more puppetlike, more schematic; this is because they are manipulated using fewer strings than is the case with Kašpárek. Moreover, the puppets that represent serious characters in Czech folk puppet theatre have thick wires fixed to their heads, and this makes them more conventional than Kašpárek.

The audience, even an adult audience, does not always consider a puppet performance a comic spectacle. Several years ago I attended a performance of *The Death of Jan Žižka* by the Holiday Camp Puppet Theatre in Plzeň. The play was put on as a gala performance on 28 October.[3] The elderly puppeteer Karel Novák[4] played the role of Žižka to an overcrowded house. When, with great passion, he recited the monologue of the dying Žižka, he came very close to bursting into tears. Neither the puppeteer nor the audience viewed this performance as comic.

Nor do the facts support Zich's premise that "even our puppets would cause us to feel uneasy if they were as large as people; the mere reduction of their dimensions, of course, completely precludes this from happening." We know that in the Japanese puppet theatre the puppets are as tall as living persons. This is not a hindrance to comic scenes, and the spectators do not experience any "feeling of uneasiness". Finally, children hardly have "a feeling of uneasiness" in playing with dolls that are as big as a living child.

It is natural for children to respond to puppet theatre more intensely than adults. Their training for interpreting the signs of puppet theatre is more developed than that of adults, who have already forgotten the meaning of many of these signs of puppets and their emotional colouring.

---

2   [Editor's note: Kašpárek, a well-known character in Czech puppet theatre, best comparable to Punch in the English puppet theatre tradition.]

3   [Editor's note: Jan Žižka (1360–1424), the leader of the Czech armies in the fifteenth-century Hussite Wars. October 28 is the Czech national holiday, marking the creation of independent Czechoslovakia in 1918.]

4   [Editor's note: Karel Novák (1862–1940), a puppeteer, director and author of puppet theatre plays. He was a prominent figure of the puppetry tradition in the city of Plzeň and is considered one of the founders of puppetry in Czechoslovakia. He is also known for his puppet versions of dramatic works.]

In our everyday life we have to become familiar with the signs of military uniforms in order to recognize them, to distinguish quickly a captain from a lieutenant-colonel. The same holds true for art. In order to understand the signs of Impressionist painting correctly, we must recognize them.

In art, as in religion – in contrast to the cognitive spheres – every sign is emotionally coloured. This is why we understand the protests of the Russian Old Believers, who utterly refused to accept the signs of ancient Byzantine icon painting being changed into the new signs of Western painting. They would rather have sacrificed their lives than be forced to change the ancient religious/painting signs. When the painting signs of the classical school were superseded, its adherents did not understand the signs of realistic art; these new signs struck them as anti-aesthetic. In precisely the same way a person brought up on realistic painting does not understand the signs of Cubist painting. New signs in art must be learned and then taught to others. In order for someone to comprehend the beauty of Oriental painting, he must want to study it, and he must really learn how to understand the signs of this type of painting. But if we perceive them only in comparison with the signs of our painting, against the background of our kind of painting, they may strike us as ridiculous. This also holds true for Oriental music.

At the beginning I called Otakar Zich's observations unusually interesting. Even now, after I have tried to illustrate the basic errors in his views through various examples, I stand by my assertion as to the value of his remarks.

Indeed, in many cases the facts support Zich's observations about the comicality of puppets. We see, for example, that all popular puppet theatres *for adults* have a tendency to become comic theatre *par excellence* (the audiences at Prof. Skupa's theatre get the most pleasure from the comic characters Hurvínek and Spejbl;[5] the greatest successes in Vittorio Podrecca's Italian theatre and with Sergey Obraztsov were their comic numbers).

This can be explained by the fact that an adult audience, unlike children, responds to puppets as such with difficulty, and constantly perceives the signs of puppet theatre almost entirely against the background of the theatre of live actors. Hence the adult audience often regards all the signs of puppet theatre as something comical.

The mutual convergence and divergence of different arts and the perception of a particular art against the background of real things and people – these are things we encounter in the development of all arts. For example, a dialec-

---

5   [Editor's note: Josef Skupa (1892–1957), a puppeteer who became famous for his performances with the character of Kašpárek. He created the character of Spejbl, who was a caricature of a *petit bourgeois*; later, he added the character of (Spejbl's son) Hurvínek and founded the popular Spejbl and Hurvínek Theatre.]

tical antinomy constantly occurs in the development of literature. On the one hand, literature develops through a continuous divergence away from everyday language; on the other hand, at the same time it attempts to move closer to it. The same can also be observed in painting, in music and especially in theatre, where the antinomy manifests itself particularly distinctly. What matters is for the signs of art to be *predominant* in relation to the extra-aesthetic signs. But in the case of something like the puppet theatre, which the audience perceives against the background of the theatre of live actors, that is, where in the process of perception a tension arises between two kinds of art, the signs intrinsic to the art we are perceiving at the given moment must predominate. But the actual process of the divergence and convergence of these two kinds of theatre is one that is absolutely normal.

When it comes to the perception of puppet theatre, it is with its children's audiences that its signs predominate, and therefore puppet theatre achieves maximum expressiveness with this audience. When adult audiences perceive puppet theatre, not infrequently the signs of the theatre of live actors dominate, with the result that this audience is incapable of understanding all of the puppet theatre's means of expression. Often, for example, this audience fails to understand serious scenes. On more than one occasion it resembles that Russian peasant girl who could not understand the signs of the religious instrumental music in a Catholic service as something serious and took it as a deformation, as something comical.

WORKS CITED

Krejčí, Karel (1937) "Jazyková karikatura v dramatické literatuře" [Linguistic Caricature in Dramatic Literature], *Sborník Matice slovenskej*, vol. 15, no. 3, pp. 387–405.

Zich, Otakar (2015 [1923]) "Puppet Theatre", *Theatralia*, vol. 18, no. 2, pp. 505–13.

Znosko-Borovsky, E. A. (1925) *Russkii teatr nachala XX veka* [Russian Theatre at the Beginning of the Twentieth Century], Prague: Plamia.

THEATRICAL SIGNS

PETR BOGATYREV

["Divadelní znaky" was published in 1938 in *Slovo a slovesnost*, vol. 4, no. 3, pp. 138–49. The English translation by Bruce Kochis was published under the title "Semiotics in the Folk Theatre" in Matejka, Ladislav and Titunik, Irwin R. (eds) (1976) *Semiotics of Art: Prague School Contributions*, Cambridge, Massachusetts: The M.I.T. Press, pp. 33–50.]

An item of clothing is simultaneously a thing and a sign – more exactly, it is the vehicle of a structure of signs. An item of clothing characterizes membership in a certain class, nationality, religion, and so on; it indicates the wearer's financial situation, his age, and so on. Similarly, a house is not only a thing, but also a sign of its owner's nationality, financial circumstances, religion, and so on (see Bogatyrev 2016 [1936]; see Bogatyrev 1937).

What exactly is a theatre costume or a set representing a house? When used on the stage, both a theatre costume and a set representing a house are often signs that point to one of the signs of the costume or the house of a certain character in the play. Let me emphasize this: a sign of a sign and not a sign of a thing.[1] A theatre costume and a set representing a house can sometimes denote several signs. For instance, a theatre costume can denote a wealthy Chinaman, thus indicating both a sign of the nationality of the character and a sign of his financial situation. Boris Godunov's costume indicates that he is a monarch and, simultaneously, his Russian nationality. When Pushkin's "The Tale of the Fisherman and the Fish" is produced in the theatre, the first dwelling, a hut, is a sign of the extreme poverty of the old man and old woman; the second is a sign that the old woman is a member of the aristocracy; the third is a sign of the old woman's becoming the tsarina. But the stage settings for all these structures indicate the Russian nationality of their owners. Similar signs of signs on the stage are the commanding gestures of the actor playing a tsar or king, the unsteady tread of an actor representing an old man, and so on.

---

1   The term *sign of a sign* here means something different than Jakobson's "sign of a sign" in his article "The Statue in Pushkin's Poetic Mythology" (1975 [1937]), where "sign of a sign" means that a sign from one kind of art is transferred into another art: for example a sculpture described in literature.

However, neither a theatre costume nor a set representing a house nor the gestures of actors have as many constitutive signs as a real house or a real item of clothing would have. On the stage, costumes and scenery are usually limited to one, two or three signs. The theatre only uses those signs of costumes and structures that are necessary for the given dramatic situation.

I should like to make the point here that theatre costumes and theatre sets, like other theatrical signs (declamation, gestures, and so on), do not always have a *representational* function. We are familiar with the costume of an actor as an actor's costume *sui generis*; we are familiar with stage signs (the curtain, forestage, and so forth) that are only signs of the stage *sui generis*, representing nothing more than the stage. But on the stage we find not only signs of the sign of a thing but also signs of the thing itself: for instance, on the stage the actor playing the role of a hungry person can indicate that he is eating bread *sui generis*, and not bread as a sign of, for example, poverty. Of course cases in which signs of signs are represented on the stage are more frequent than cases involving the representation of the signs of things.

On the stage use is made not only of costumes and scenery, of theatre props, that are only one sign or the sum of several signs and not a thing *sui generis*, but also real things. But even these real objects are not viewed by the audience as real things, but only as signs of signs, or signs of things. If, for example, an actor playing the role of a millionaire wears a diamond ring, the audience will regard it as a sign of his great wealth and not care whether or not the diamond is real or a fake. A royal ermine robe in the theatre is a sign of regal dignity regardless of whether it is made from a real stoat's fur or rabbit skin. On the stage expensive red wine can be represented by real wine or by raspberry soda.

It is interesting that on the stage a real thing, for example, a real diamond, is often only a sign of a sign of a thing (for example, a sign of the wealth of a character) but not a sign of the thing itself. On the other hand in a theatre performance the most schematic sign of the most primitive scenery can denote the thing itself.

For example,

> Among the Altais, in the yurt that serves as a stage there stands a birch, eternally in leaf, that has nine notches. Symbolically, the notches denote the levels of the celestial world, into which the shaman gradually enters. When, in performing the ceremony, he steps up along these notches, in the eyes of those present he ascends from one level of heaven to the next, acting out a separate scene in each heaven. (Kharuzina 1927: 67)

Thus, each notch denotes not only heaven as a whole but also one of its separate divisions: first heaven, second heaven, third heaven, and so on.

Another example. Among the Aranda people, ceremonies (performances) are held in certain places ordained by tradition: at sacred rocks, trees, ponds. Among the Warumungu a ceremony may be performed anywhere at all, but the place of action is denoted by drawings. These drawings denoting the place are drawn either on the bodies of the participants or on the ground. The images have a specific character: for instance, a small red circle on the back or on the abdomen of the performer denotes a pond, or they paint the earth with vermilion and use white pigment to paint wavy lines on it that denote a stream or a mountain (see Durkheim 1925: 532–53; cf. Kharuzina 1928: 67). Here, too, certain signs on the body of the actor or on the ground denote the things themselves.

Verbal scenery, that is the practice in the theatre of having the actor describe the scene to the audience in words in the absence of stage scenery, may depend on a description either of a thing or of only one or several signs of the thing. We encounter such verbal scenery in the traditional theatre of India, and it also found everywhere in the ceremonial performances of shamans.

According to Zich, all objects that are theatrical signs have a double role. First (and most importantly) they characterize, effectively establishing the characters and the place where the story unfolds; second, they have a functional purpose, that of taking part in the dramatic action (Zich 1931: 232). This characterization of Zich's is applicable not only to things in the theatre, to stage properties, but also to any thing we encounter in everyday life. Thus, a cane characterizes my taste and perhaps even my material circumstances, but at the same time I also carry out various actions with this cane: I lean on it when walking, I can use it in a fight, and so on. In the theatre, however, in distinction from everyday life, each thing changes its signs much more quickly and much more diversely. By means of his cloak Mephistopheles expresses his subservience to Faust, and on Walpurgis night by means of this same cloak he expresses his absolute power over the demonic forces. However, even in real life one and the same item of clothing can be a sign of the most differing moods. For instance, one and the same military shirt can, unbuttoned, express the devil-may-care attitude of the soldier who is wearing it as he sits with his comrades over a glass of wine; buttoned up, it expresses his careful, concentrated and correct attitude as he goes to report to his superior.

But in addition, in the course of the play things on the stage that play the part of theatrical signs acquire special features, qualities and attributes that they do not have in real life. Things in the theatre, like the actor himself, are transformed. Just as an actor on stage changes into another person (a young person into an old one, a woman into a man, and so forth), so too any thing the actor acts with may acquire a new, hitherto alien, function. Charlie Chaplin's famous boots are changed by his acting into food, the laces becoming spaghetti (*The Gold Rush*); in the same film two rolls dance like a pair of lovers. Such transformed things used by the actor while performing are very common in folk theatre. For example, playing with things in *Pakhomushkoi* fills almost the entire performance. Of particular interest are the moments when the actor must demonstrate through his acting that a poker has turned into a horse, a bench into a boat, or that an old jacket strapped round with a belt is, in his arms, an infant (Pisarev and Suslovich 1927: 184).

One very complex system of signs is the *speech of the actor* on the stage. This has almost all the signs of literary speech, and in addition is a constituent of the dramatic action. Later on we will return to the signs of actors' speech, which has the task of characterizing the persons in the play.

   Everyday speech is a system of various signs. Through his speech a speaker not only expresses his state of mind, but at the same time his speech (its dialect features, argot, vocabulary, and so on) is also a sign of his cultural and social status and so forth. The playwright and the actors use all of these signs on the stage as a descriptive means for expressing the social or national status of the characters. And so it is common in the theatre for a special vocabulary and speech melody to be used to denote that a person belongs to one class or another, or for a different choice of words, pronunciation, forms of speech and sentence structure to be used to denote that someone is a foreigner. Or again, a certain speech tempo, and sometime also a certain vocabulary, may denote an old man. In some cases, the dominant function of a character's speech may lie not in the speech content as such but in verbal signs that characterize the nationality, the class, and so forth, of the speaker. The speech content is then expressed by other theatrical signs such as gestures and the like. For instance, the devil in the puppet theatre often utters only certain conventional exclamations that characterize him as the devil; in some puppet plays he almost never speaks but performs a mime show on stage in place of a monologue or dialogue.

   The actor's speech on stage normally has several signs. For instance, speech that is full of mistakes denotes not only a foreigner but usually a comic character as well. Therefore an actor playing the tragic role of a foreigner or a representative of another people, for example Shakespeare's Shylock, and trying to depict the Jewish merchant of Venice as a tragic character, must often do without Jewish intonation or reduce it to a minimum, for a strongly pronounced Jewish intonation would add a comic touch to the tragic passages of the part (see Nemirovich-Danchenko 1936: 180–81).

   In folk theatre we have cases where the participation of Jews deforming ordinary speech in a manner traditional for this kind of theatre lends comedy even to serious scenes. Here is an example from *The Three Kings*.

Herod. Ye, who are of Law skilled knowers
And of Scripture right learned scholars,
Have ye perchance any knowledge
Or be there in Scripture some presage
That the Christ should be born,
Or where he might be found?
Jews. Vat on dat point de Scripture says
Ve shall make known, so pleas Your Grace.
(*They go to the table, open books and leaf through them; then they return to Herod, and the First Jew, bowing to him, speaks.*)
First Jew. Jobakh, impikh, thaich uzmrnack: kolkoye, kolkoshe.
Vich is to say: De little town of Betlehem in Judah...
A godly people vill be born... dis saviour,
redeemer of all de vorld. And also in
anoder passage de prophet says...
Herod. Silence!
Jews (*among themselves*). He don't like dat. Come on, you tell him someting.
(*They again retire to the table, leaf through the books and return to Herod.*)
Second Jew. Kirokh shirockh sykorke sharke
yerobim kormifel, tyberes mones.
Vich is to say: O dou, Betlehem, little town,
Of dee werily it be known
Dat from dee a great king vill come
And he vill judge de Jewish kingdom.
Dis is a true vitness,
God's own prophecy.
Herod. Silence, I say!
Jews (*among themselves*). Vait, I vill tell him someting else.
(*They do the same as before and then say to Herod:*)
Efrata betharir ipfata chayer
Bikhord bokhod brafe yehunda mimika,
Bitse moysil Israel
O matsazano mikodem vlan.
Vich is to say: But dou, Betlehem Ephratah,
Dough dou be small among de tousands of Judah,
yet out of dee shall come fort unto me him
dat is to be a ruler in Israel;
whose goings fort haf been from old,
from everlasting.
Herod. Get ye hence, ye scribes,
Mine exceeding great enemies!
(*Afraid, the Jews flee, and meet the three kings.*)

Melchior. Tell us, Jews, if thou dost know:
Where shall we seek the new king?
Jews. Go to Betlehem, der dou vill find
a young maid, an old man,
a small babe, der dou vill learn
de greatest trut.[2] (Fejfalík, 59–61)

At the end comedy takes over completely. And the scene with the Jews, who previously performed as interpreters of the Holy Scriptures, ends with the following routine: Caspar gives a tip to one of the Jews, the other one wants a half share, and they go off quarrelling with one another.

Here we see a characteristic example of the alternation or close interconnection of tragic and comic elements in folk theatre. The comic figures of the Jews have the same function as that of the fools in Shakespeare and other dramatists, where the fool expresses deeply serious ideas, in some cases the thoughts of the dramatist himself.

As in the case of costume, so in the case of speech the dramatist and actor select only a small part of the system of signs that everyday speech possesses.

In everyday speech various class signs (rustic speech) are closely associated with dialect, which is a regional sign of the speaker. It is often unnecessary in the theatre to pinpoint the region a character comes from, and so the actor only makes use of some of the characteristic features of a given region and sometimes even combines the characteristic features of several dialects together to create peasant speech. Such a mixture of diverse dialects contradicts reality but works effectively to depict the peasant as played by the actor. So in my opinion such an artificially constructed dialect has a perfect right to exist on the stage. We encounter similar phenomena in theatre costumes and scenery. Thus in František Kysela's staging of *The Bartered Bride*[3] folk costumes from any one specific region of Bohemia were deliberately avoided, and instead a folk costume representing a generic Bohemian village was created for the theatre.

In addition, in the theatre there existed in the past and still exist today conventional means for distinguishing the speech of ordinary people from the speech of the upper classes. These include, for instance, a stylistic device

---

2   The language that the Jews read is meant to represent Hebrew. This is a typical case found in folklore of using conventionally stylized language with the intention of having it represent a foreign language. In this case the quotations that the Jews read are perhaps basically Hebrew, but in the form that they take here it is difficult to recognize any Hebrew words.

3   [Editor's note: František Kysela (1881–1941), a painter, visual artist and stage designer. His design for *The Bartered Bride* for the National Theatre in 1923 was innovative in its tendency towards abstraction. *The Bartered Bride*, an opera by the composer Bedřich Smetana (1824–1884), considered a cornerstone of modern Czech culture as it depicts scenes from Czech rural life and its motifs have become popular over time.]

used in certain periods and by certain drama movements of having ordinary people speak in prose and the upper classes in verse.[4] Other conventional theatre dialects fall into this category: for example, the tsar and boyars in Russian plays speaking in a high style with an admixture of Church Slavonic elements, and the peasants employing a low style, that is, simple Russian; or the knights in plays of the Czech puppet theatre speaking in imperfect Czech.

Conventions similar to those relating to language are encountered in theatre gestures, costumes, scenery, and so on. Folk theatre is particularly rich in cases that vividly express the conventionality of costumes and properties. However, the conventionality of theatre speech does not always run parallel with the conventionality of costumes, scenery, and so forth. On the contrary: on the stage conventional theatre costumes are often combined with naturalistic speech of a kind close to everyday speech. For instance, folk puppeteers, working in the highly conventional form of puppet theatre, use many elements of the naturalist theatre. One of the best Czech folk puppeteers, Karel Novák,[5] boasted to me that his puppets spoke like living people.

Were we to test Zich's law concerning uniform stylization in the theatre performances of various periods and styles, we would find that it does not hold up; it applies in part only for certain theatre movements of the period that Zich had in mind. In folk theatre the simultaneous use of the most diverse styles in the same play is a widespread phenomenon, a special theatrical formal device. Besides the case already mentioned (combining naturalistic speech with the acting of the puppets in the puppet theatre), we might also mention folk theatre in which live actors perform alongside puppets. I myself saw a child acting with a puppet on the stage in Munster, Westphalia (see Bogatyrev 1931). In the Chodsko region[6] we can observe an interesting example of people acting alongside puppets in a play about the Three Kings.

"Three kings" from town walk through the villages in Chodsko at the time of the feast of the Three Kings. *Two* are always people; the *third* is a wooden figure mounted on an instrument similar to a horn; while a song is being sung this wooden king must bow and for that purpose it is animated by a handle turned by one of the "three kings", who is holding the horn (see Baar 1892; see Hruša 1897).

---

4 "In the drama of the Middle Ages, for example, the male and female characters were at times distinguished by verse with differing numbers of syllables" (Krejčí 1937: 388).
5 [Editor's note: Karel Novák (1862–1940), a puppeteer, director and author of puppet theatre plays. He was a prominent figure of the puppetry tradition in the city of Plzeň and is considered one of the founders of puppetry in Czechoslovakia. He is also known for his puppet versions of dramatic works.]
6 [Editor's note: Chodsko, a region in southwestern Bohemia on the historical border between the Czech and German lands. Owing to the difficult terrain of the Bohemian Forest mountain range, the locals – the Chods – developed a specific culture, which they preserved little altered for centuries.]

Realism and Symbolism "sometimes exist side by side in the drama productions of one and the same people," asserts V. N. Kharuzina; as we have
already seen, they are mutually intertwined. In one and the same production
the costumes may have realistic features (for example, the tail of an animal
that is being depicted, the colouring of an actor's body corresponding to the
colouring of the feathers of the bird he is playing) while the properties or
stage sets may have striking Symbolist features (Kharuzina 1928: 28).

The folk theatre is not alone in combining different styles; we often find
it in other arts as well. The combination of various styles in architecture is
a common phenomenon. Modern painters such as Picasso and the Futur-
ists combined pieces of real things with their Cubist painting. We often see
a similar use of the montage on the covers of books. In folk art we encounter,
wherever we look, the combination of the most diverse styles in the same
artistic product, in one and the same narrative, in one and the same song.

Verbal expression in the theatre is a structure of signs composed not only
of speech signs but also of other signs. For instance, theatre speech that is
intended to signify the social standing of a character is uttered in accompaniment to the actor's gestures and is complemented by his costume, by
the scenery, and so on, which are also signs of this character's social standing. In the theatre the number of fields from which theatrical signs such as
costumes, scenery, music, and so forth are drawn is sometimes larger and
sometimes smaller, but always multiple.

In addition, everyday speech has other characteristic signs that depend
on the person the character is speaking with or turning to to address. This
plays a significant role in the theatre. And in the theatre changes in the style
of speech are often accompanied by special costuming.

Mention should also be made of special speech signs such as special
word order, syntax, the distribution of pauses and other verbal means that
pervade the whole part and give it a comic or tragic colouring.[7] However,
comic or tragic roles are created not only through verbal means but also by
the costume the actor wears and by his makeup. The means used to denote the
costume of a comic character are often the same as in language, where one
of the most common means is what in Italian is called *lazzi*: oxymoron and
metathesis. We find something similar in the appearance of the costumes of
comic characters and in their makeup. In addition, there have been and are
special conventional theatrical signs regarding costume thanks to which it is
possible to recognize a comic character instantly (the fool's cap, Hans Wurst's
fox tail, and so on).

---

7 It thus differs from everyday speech, in which the comic or tragic coloration is given by the
character speaking.

In almost every drama, and especially in drama focussed on exploring character, the point is to convey the distinguishing features of the character being portrayed – the hypocrite Tartuffe, the miser Harpagon, as well as more complex characters such as Shylock: miserly, sly and a loving father all in one. To this end the theatre uses all its available means. These include, in the first place, the self-characterization of a character. The speech of characters in medieval mystery plays, in morality plays and also in folk plays can serve as a good example of such self-characterization. Less clear cases occur in the tragedies of Shakespeare and Pushkin and in other dramas in which a character delivers a monologue acquainting the audience with intimate aspects of his nature. But it is not the content of the monologue alone that serves as a means of self-characterization; that end is also served by what Zich calls a "specific dialect". It should be pointed out that finding a suitable "specific dialect" for each character in the play is one of the knottiest tasks facing the dramatist and the actor. And it must be acknowledged that in the folk theatre this psychological dialect has been applied with success in many variations of folk plays. In addition to words, the characterization of a character is created by costume (the costume of the hypocrite Tartuffe, of the miser Plyushkin in the staging of *Dead Souls*, and so forth) and still more so by the facial expressions and gestures of the actors. Scenery, too, helps a great deal here: the room of the lazy old bachelor in Gogol's *The Wedding*, the study of the learned Faust, aptly express the character of their occupants. In folk theatre scenery generally has little significance and is not commonly used, not even as a means for the psychological characterization of the characters. The role of scenery here is taken on by props.

Characterization is expressed not only by the means already mentioned, but also by action. The Baron in Pushkin's *The Covetous Knight* not only characterizes himself verbally as a man madly in love with his wealth but also proves it by his actions on stage (his gestures, movements, and so on). Another means of psychological characterization of a character is the conversation of other characters about him. This characterization is aided by the costumes of characters who are closely associated with the individual in question, for example, the shabby clothing of the prisoners in Beethoven's opera *Fidelio* characterizes the brutal and unjust governor.[8]

In addition, various movements in the theatre have had special speech signs for representing the actor as actor – this concerns a special "stage" speech for the actors that is marked not only by highly correct pronunciation but also by special intonation, and so forth. There are also special actors' gestures representing only the actor as actor.

---

8   In the contemporary theatre still another device – one that is literary, not theatrical – helps to characterize roles: the characterization of roles in the printed programme.

An analysis of the system of signs of theatre speech shows that all these signs occur, though infrequently, in other types of literary language (the novel, the short story, and so on). The difference, however, is that in the theatre a speech sign is only one constituent of the structure of a theatre performance, a structure that includes, in addition to language, facial expressions, gestures, costumes, scenery, and so forth.

All this polysemy is further expanded by the fact that the part played by the actor has different signs if the public is acquainted with most or all of the characters in the play. Up to the very last scenes, with each and every movement and intonation of his speech, Tartuffe must appear to Orgon to be a kind man, but to the audience a repulsive hypocrite pretending to be kind. An even more elementary case is the following. In the staging of *Little Red Riding Hood* the wolf, dressed as an old woman, must seem to the granddaughter to be her grandmother, though of course somewhat strange; to the public he must appear as a wolf who has changed his voice. For the whole time, the actor is something like a tightrope walker. He cannot play the wolf in such a way that the audience finds it hard to believe that the granddaughter cannot recognize him as a wolf. On the other hand, for the whole time he must indicate that he *is* a wolf, otherwise the audience might believe, like the granddaughter, that he is an old woman. What the actor who plays Tartuffe must do is essentially the same.

There is a special kind of polysemy in the actors' performances in works by Symbolists, where certain characters are vehicles of a number of signs both for the audience and for the other actors. In Gerhart Hauptmann's *The Assumption of Hannele* there is a character who for Hannele is a teacher, while for the other actors and the audience he is both the teacher Gottwald and a foreigner; the deaconess Marta is at the same time a deaconess and a mother. This same phenomenon occurs in Hauptmann's *The Sunken Bell*, Henrik Ibsen's *Peer Gynt* and other Symbolist plays.

The special character of theatrical signs also determines the distinctive relationship of the audience to them, a relationship quite distinct from the relationship of a person to real things and to a real subject. For instance, in real life an old man's gait and gestures usually evoke sympathy, while the same gait and gestures on the stage more often function comically.

We must acknowledge that theatre productions are distinguished from other works of art and from other things that are also signs by their great abundance of signs. This is understandable: a theatre performance is a structure composed of elements from various arts: from literature, the fine arts, music, choreography, and so on. Each separate element brings a number of signs onto the stage. But of course many of these signs are lost on the stage. Sculpture, for example, loses one of its characteristic features – the variety of forms a work of sculpture takes when viewed from various angles (see Mukařovský 1938), since in the theatre we see a piece of sculpture from only one angle. Similarly, works in other art forms lose some of their signs on the stage. On the other hand, however, in combining with other kinds of art and with technical theatrical devices, some of their elements may take on new signs. For example, different lighting effects can enable a sculpture to express different moods (a colourful festive mood can be enhanced by illuminating a piece of sculpture on stage with bright lights, a dreary mood heightened by the use of dim lights). Music on stage, combined with the gestures and words of the actor playing a dying man, expresses sadness more concretely, and so forth. In this way, certain elements of various kinds of art in combination with others constantly acquire new signs on the stage.

This polysemy of the art of the theatre makes it possible for different spectators to comprehend the same scene differently. Take, for instance, a scene of parting in which the dialogue is accompanied by music: to a musically sensitive spectator the music will be of paramount importance, but for a spectator more strongly attuned to declamation the latter will be the dominant factor and music the subordinate one. This polysemy of the art of the theatre, which distinguishes it from any other art, makes it possible for the theatrical performance to be comprehended simultaneously by spectators of various tastes, of various aesthetic standards.

When we compare the naturalistic and the non-realistic theatre, we see that naturalistic theatre uses the various other arts (music, dance, and so on) less frequently than non-realistic theatre; on the other hand, in the latter, the characters, costumes, scenery and props always have many more signs than in the naturalistic theatre, where costumes and scenery usually have only one sign; in this way an economy of theatrical means is achieved.

The actor's role is a structure of the most diverse signs – signs expressed by his speech, gestures, movements, figure, facial expression, costume, and so forth. At the same time, in order to express the various theatrical signs the actor makes use on the one hand of various things such as costumes, toupees, wigs, and on the other of his own gestures (either affected or natural), his own voice, his own eyes, and so on.

We can carry over the concepts of *langue* and *parole* from the field of language phenomena to art. Just as the listener, in order to comprehend a particular utterance of the speaker, must have command of the language, that is, the language as social fact, in art too the observer must be prepared to be receptive to the individual performance of the actor or of any other artist, his specific idiom, by having command of the language of that art, its social norms. This is where the field of language and the field of art correspond.

But there is also a fundamental difference between the process of comprehending the signs of language and that of comprehending the signs of art. In the domain of language, as far as its communicative function is concerned, the process of reception works approximately this way: if we hear an utterance, we screen from it everything individual and focus solely on what in the phrase we have heard is *langue*, on what is social fact. Were a foreigner to utter a sentence with mistakes, for example "He's a good girl, your daughter," we would process it as "She's a good girl, your daughter" and would not be particularly worried about the mistake the foreigner had made.

The process of perceiving a work of art functions in an entirely different way. We perceive an artistically executed work, an artistically performed role in drama, the performance of a musical work, song, and so forth, as a whole. If a talented actor plays Othello, it seems to us – and this is what he is convincing us of – that everything in his performance and in the role of Othello he is playing is artistically right and just: the costume, the gestures, his figure, vocal timbre, facial expressions, and so on. So if his performance is imitated, everything is imitated – the rhythm of Othello's speech as shaped by the famous actor, the timbre of his voice, his gestures, and so forth, and in the process of copying even the individual shortcomings of the actor are often imitated, since they are inseparable from the total image of the role in our minds.

Stanislavsky relates the following story:

> A certain drama school teacher went backstage after the performance of an excerpt at a student production and made a scene: "You're not moving your head. When people speak, they move their heads." There is a little story behind that nodding of the head. There was an outstanding actor who enjoyed great success and had many imitators, but unfortunately possessed one unpleasant shortcoming – the habit of nodding his head. And all of his followers, forgetting completely that the original was a man of great talent with exceptional abilities and a marvellous technique, instead of acquiring from him his good qualities, which are indeed hard to acquire from someone else, only copied his shortcomings – and so that nodding of the head, which is easily acquired. (Stanislavski 2008: 61)

Stanislavsky's abhorrence of such slavish imitation was completely justified. There is a difference, however, between what he says and what we are saying here: we are speaking only about being receptive to the performance of a role, whereas Stanislavsky is speaking about the actor's creative work. Of course every actor is free to draw on the approach of a famous actor in interpreting a part, but in doing so he must make use of his own body, the timbre of his own voice, his own movements, eyes, and so on in a fresh way.

Now we shall pass on to remarks about folklore. Manifestations of folklore such as songs, tales, magic formulas and other types of folklore approach being drama performances. The oral folklore performance, like the performance of an actor, is inseparable from the person who performs it. The person listening to such a performance, unlike the reader of a poem or novel, cannot analyse the artistic performance *sui generis* apart from the author and narrator. Therefore it is incorrect to fix the text of a tale without regard to *how* it is told. What is more, the personality of the storyteller is more tightly bound up with what he is narrating than the personality of the actor with his role on the stage. In the case of an actor, all that actually interests us in his performance is how he uses the devices at his disposal – that is his voice, body, and so forth – to produce a dramatic impression. We are not interested in whether the actor, when representing an evil villain or a positive hero, is a good or bad person in his private life. However, this is not the case when a folktale is being narrated. Here the narrator often draws on his own personal characteristics, as reflected in his life, as a creative device. The Sokolov brothers mention the example of the narrator Sozon Kuzmich Petrushevich, a target of mockery and teasing, who brought himself into the tale he was telling as Ivan the Fool: "Once upon a time there was a peasant, and he had three sons. Two were clever and one was stupid, like me, Sozon." And he even described the wretched appearance of Ivan the Fool as being just like his own – "snotty, pimply, slobbery" – and with this vivid illustration unwittingly led his audience to burst out in laughter (Sokolov 1915: lxiii–lxix).

Likewise, the audience in folk theatre continually makes comparisons between the role an actor-peasant is playing and his own private life.

In the theatre, as in all other arts, there are signs specific to particular artistic movements. Thus in ancient tragedy there was a special sign that distinguished the main character from the secondary characters – the side of the stage from which the actor made his entrance. The eighteenth-century opera worked as follows:

> All the soloists stand in the foreground in a line parallel with the footlights, the comic characters are situated at midstage, and the chorus at the rear of the stage. The order within the first row is also standardized: the actors with the main roles are situated on the audience's left, ranked according to their importance from left to right. The hero or principal lover – the *prima parte* actor – gets the place of honour, first on the left, just as he usually plays the most important person in the play. (Gvozdev 1924: 119)

Here, then, the places where the actors stood were signs of their parts. In the *commedia dell'arte* the costumes of Dottore, Pantalone and others characterized these characters precisely for the spectator.[9]

Indeed, it is not only a matter of individual periods having their own specific theatrical signs that are replaced by other signs later, in another period,

---

9   For the change of one style of theatre declamation to another in various theatre movements, see Honzl 1937: 178–207.

along with a change of the whole style of theatre. Various actors, too, invest particular roles with signs. These signs are repeated (nor could it be otherwise) by their followers until such a time as talented new actors arrive, who reshape the parts, casting off the old signs of their predecessors and creating new ones; these are then again repeated by their followers.

We are familiar with a whole set of signs that have been deemed characteristic of Hamlet (in costume, grimaces, gesticulations, facial expressions, the method of declaiming certain passages, and so forth). Usually they were created by a certain famous actor and became *de rigueur* for his followers and for the public raised on these signs.

Every creative interpretation of a role, like every independent creation in any other art, struggles against traditional signs and strives to replace them with new signs.

In the theatre, then, all theatre performances are signs of signs or signs of things. The only living subject in the theatre is the actor. Though an actor expresses regal dignity by means of his costume, a sign of age by his gait, a sign that he represents a foreigner by his speech, and so on – despite this, we still we see in him not only a system of signs but also a living person. That this is in fact the case is best seen when a spectator observes someone on the stage who is close to them personally – for example, a mother watching her son performing the role of a king, a brother playing the part of a devil, and so on. This peculiar artistic duality achieves great theatrical effect in the folk theatre where the audience knows the actors well. This same duality is experienced by spectators when they see an actor they have known on the stage for a long time in other roles. To a lesser degree spectators also experience it when they see an actor for the first time.

This dual apprehension of the actor on the part the spectator is very important. In the first place, thanks to it, all signs expressed by the actor are brought to life. Second, at the same time this dual apprehension of the role underscores the fact that the actor as such cannot be identified with the figure who is performing, that no equation can be made between the actor and the character whom he is presenting, that the costume and makeup and gestures of the actor are only a sign of a sign of the figure he is portraying. This duality was clearly highlighted by all types of non-realistic theatre and was an obstacle to the realization of absolute naturalism in the naturalistic theatre. Hence it was perfectly reasonable for a director in the naturalistic theatre to request that a particular actor appear in public as little as possible, for otherwise many people would lose the illusion of reality when they saw him in the role of King Lear or Hamlet; they would never be able to imagine that they were seeing before them the real Lear, the real Hamlet, and not an actor who only played these roles.

As for the actor's acting, there were and still are two aspects. On the one hand, actors clearly take great pains with their makeup, their speech and so forth, so as to be entirely different in each role; on the other hand, the actor quite consciously strives to ensure that in each role he plays it is possible to recognize his voice, his face behind the makeup (which is why it is applied lightly), and so on.

In the puppet theatre the actor does not exist as a living person; there the movements of the puppet-actor are a pure sign of a sign. In the puppet theatre, where the puppets speak, all that remains of a living person is a voice; it is through voice that puppets approximate living persons.

The analysis of signs in the theatre brings us to yet one more interesting observation. The following formal devices is very widespread. An actor employs elements of a certain art for the expression of artistic emotion, and this emotion increasingly heightens (for example, in a dance the tempo quickens). When the actor is no longer able to manage the expressive means of his movements, he begins to complement the heightening emotion with cries. And conversely, when a singer in a crescendo no longer has sufficient vocal means, he begins to complement the rise in his singing by dance or movement. Sometimes the dance or movement is not merely complemented by the song, or the song by the dance, but rather they replace one another. A similar formal device is the omitting of one element hitherto related structurally to other elements of the theatre performance. For instance, at the most emotional moment in his speech, accompanied to this point by gestures, an actor ceases to gesticulate and only speaks or, conversely, ceases to speak and depends solely on gestures to express his emotion. Sometimes the formal devices just mentioned are also used in other situations where it is not a question of the heightening of the emotional tension.

A detailed analysis of theatrical signs thus helps us to explain other theatrical formal devices as well.

WORKS CITED

Baar, Jindřich (1892) "Klenčí na Chodsku" [Klenčí in the Chodsko Region], *Český lid*, vol. 1, p. 505.

Bogatyrev, Petr (1931) "Puppentheater in Münster in Westfalen" [Puppet Theatre in Munster, Westphalia], *Prager Presse*, vol. 11, no. 227 (23 August), pp. i–iii.

— (2016 [1936]) "Clothing as a Sign", this reader, pp. 441–47.

— (1937) *Funkcie kroja na moravskom Slovensku* [The Functions of Folk Costume in Moravian Slovakia], Turčiansky Sv. Martin: Národopisný odbor Matice Slovenskej.

Durkheim, Émile (1925) *Les Formes élémentaires de la vie religieuse. Le système totémique en Australie*. [The Elementary Forms of Religious Life. The Totemic System in Australia], 2nd ed., Paris: Félix Alcan.

Fejfalík, Julius (1864) *Volksschauspiele aus Mähren* [Folk Theatre Plays from Moravia], Olomouc: Eduard Hölzel.

Gvozdev, A. A. (1924) "Itogi i zadachi nauchnoi istorii teatra." [End Results and Aims of the History of the Theatre] in *Zadachi i metody izucheniia iskusstv.* [Aims and Methods of Art Studies], Petersburg: Academia, pp. 83–121.

Honzl, Jindřich (1937) *Sláva a bída divadel: režisérův zápisník* [The Glory and the Misery of Theatres: A Director's Notebook], Prague: Družstevní práce.
Hruša, J. F. (1897) "'Tři' králové na Chodsku" [The "Three" Kings in the Chodsko Region], *Český
lid*, vol. 6, p. 244.
Jakobson, Roman (1975 [1937]) "The Statue in Pushkin's Poetic Mythology" in Burbank, John
(trans. and ed.) (1975) *Puškin and His Sculptural Myth*, The Hague and Paris: Mouton, pp. 1–45.
Kharuzina, V. N. (1927) "Primitivnye formy dramaticheskogo iskusstva" [Primitive Forms of
Dramatic Art], *Etnografiia*, vol. 2.
— (1928) "Primitivnye formy dramaticheskogo iskusstva" [Primitive Forms of Dramatic Art],
Etnografiia, vol. 3, pp. 22–43.
Krejčí, Karel (1937) "Jazyková karikatura v dramatické literatuře" [Linguistic Caricature in Dra-
matic Literature], *Sborník Matice slovenskej*, vol. 15, no. 3, pp. 387–405.
Mukařovský, Jan (1938) "Trojí podoba T. G. Masaryka (Několik poznámek k problematice plas-
tického portrétu)" [Three Different Versions of T. G. Masaryk (Some Comments on the Prob-
lem of the Three-dimensional Portrait)], *Lidové noviny*, 27 February, p. 5.
Nemirovich-Danchenko, V. I. (1936) *Iz proshlogo* [From the Past], Moscow: Academia.
Pisarev, S. S. and Suslovich, R. R. (1927) "Dosyulnaya igra – komediia *Pakhomushkoi*" [A Dosyul-
naya Play – the Comedy *Pakhomushkoi*] in *Khristianskoe iskusstvo SSSR*. Leningrad, pp. 176–85.
Sokolov, Boris and Sokolov, Yuri (1915) *Skazki i pesni Bielozerskogo kraia* [Tales and Songs of the
Bielozerski Region], Moscow: A. I. Snegirevoi.
Stanislavski, Konstantin (2008) *My Life in Art*, trans. and ed. Jean Benedetti, London: Routledge.
Zich, Otakar (1931) *Estetika dramatického umění: teoretická dramaturgie* [The Aesthetics of Dramatic
Art: A Theoretical Dramaturgy], Prague: Melantrich.

SIGNS IN THE CHINESE THEATRE

KAREL BRUŠÁK

["Znaky na čínském divadle" (1939) was first published in Czech in *Slovo a slovesnost*, vol. 5, no. 2, pp. 91–98. An early version of the essay was published as Brušák, Karel (1939) "Čínské divadlo" [The Chinese Theatre] *Program D 39*, vol. 3, 23 February, pp. 97–104. The author later translated it into English for publication as "Signs in the Chinese Theater" in Matejka, Ladislav and Titunik, Irwin R. (eds) (1976) *Semiotics of Art: Prague School Contributions*, Cambridge, Mass: The M.I.T Press, pp. 59–73.]

Editor's note: In the process of translation and revision, Brušák made several changes in the text. He added a paragraph in the introduction to cover issues that had been addressed in the meantime, and he divided his article into numbered sections. In this reader, Brušák's alterations have been preserved.

Chinese theatre has devised a complicated and precise system of signs carrying a large and categorically diverse range of meanings. The emergence of the system was made possible by the nature of the repertoire: the number of plays is relatively small and they are familiar to most of the audience. The Chinese play is of little significance from the literary point of view; stage performance is paramount. The components of Chinese theatre appear simple enough, but individual elements within the structure carry numerous obligatory signs standing for referents that are often very complex.

The stage is a rectangular raised platform flanked on three sides by the audience. The rear is formed by a backcloth with two apertures. These provide the only access to the stage; the opening on the spectators' left is the entrance, that on the right the exit. Where an actor is coming from or going to is shown by his choice of aperture. If he both enters and leaves by "the entrance", the audience knows he is going back to the same place; if two actors enter and depart by different apertures, this shows they have come from different places and are returning thence, and so forth. Court theatres, which presented numerous plays involving the appearance of supernatural beings, had their stages built on two levels, mortals figuring on the lower level and spirits on the upper. Chinese stage sets are not made up of painted scenery or architectural structures as in the West but employ only a small number of separate objects, in particular a table and chairs, which then function as specific signs according to their position on the stage. The set is further elaborated by specific elements in the actor's performance. Thus equipped the Chinese stage has survived for centuries and continues to operate unchanged in the classical Chinese theatre of today.[1]

Until recently the development of the theatre has been examined almost exclusively from the angle of literature; the significance of the text has been overestimated. Nowadays it is generally accepted that the words form only the basis of a complicated structure made up of two interrelated series, one acoustic and one visual. The visual aspect of any dramatic performance experienced by the spectator can be termed dramatic space. We can distinguish two qualities in it. The first is furnished by the mere existence of its members and is therefore static; the second is created and characterized only by their change and movement and is therefore kinetic. Of the static aspects of dramatic space the most permanent is the architectural element – the stage. Upon this is erected from performance to performance a variable space in the narrow sense of the word, formed by the scenery, stage equipment, and so on – the scene. Within this space of arbitrary duration there is formed a non-material and transitory fictitious space, conjured up by the movement of actors, by the movements and changes in colour of light, by the moving images of film, and so forth – the action space. In highly developed theatrical systems the stage had a conventional form. The Greek theatre had its orchestra and proscenium; the humanist, Elizabethan and Chinese theatres had their platform; the nineteenth-century theatre had a hollow cube minus the front wall; in folklore theatre the stage is formed anew for each performance. The scene may be identical with the stage if the acting is without scenery, but usually it is an independent structure built upon it. The stage, in its ideally perfect form, is an inner space, limited by the structure of the theatre, and the scene is a fictitious space depicting or suggesting a real space. In the concept of the scene we must include not only the scenery and stage equipment but also the actors' costumes and masks. The lighting is part of the scene only in so far as it renders it visible, contributes to the definition of place or time, or creates an impression. If it functions dramatically in the performance, emphasizing the movements of the actors or forming an independent action, we may include it in the action space. In the same way a film, if shown as part of the scenery, forms part of the scene. But it may be shown to supplement the actions of the actors, as Piscator used to do in his crowd scenes or as an equal partner to their actions, a method invented by the Czech director E. F. Burian and called by him theatregraph.

---

1   [Editor's note: The following paragraph was added by Brušák to the English translation.]

Consequently, the signs of Chinese theatre may be roughly divided into two groups: visual, that is, those associated with the dramatic space,[2] and acoustic, that is, those associated with the dialogue, music and sound effects.

VISUAL SIGNS

This group comprises on the one hand signs related to the scene, on the other hand signs falling under the concept of action space. Let us deal first with the signification of those elements forming the scene, namely scenic articles, costumes and makeup.

I. THE SCENE

(A) SCENIC ARTICLES

Scenic articles are normally grouped under the general heading of stage properties. This term is, however, too imprecise in the context of the Chinese theatre. In addition to the usual scenic articles – those serving to establish characters' qualities and those of a functional nature (Zich 1931: 232) – we have to deal here with scenic articles that, while resembling these, are nevertheless quite distinct in their own right; they function as elementary signs, standing for referents composing the scene.

The hierarchy of scenic articles can be determined if they are considered in terms of their various functions. The most significant, dramatically active, are those that participate in the actor's performance – for example, swords, goblets, and so forth. They represent a point of transition from scene to action space; they can be termed *scenic articles* in the proper sense of the word. After these come articles not brought into active use; their function is to fill out the scene or a character in a passive manner (for example, boulders, trees, armour and accoutrements, rings, and so on); they particularize the place of action (in time, history, society, and so forth) and are closely allied to the scenery – these are *complementary articles*. As two distinct functions are involved, the borderline between the two types is clear enough. Nevertheless, a scenic article may combine both functions; they may be and usually are complementary articles as well (chairs, and so on) or, alternatively, articles previously considered as merely complementary may enter the play at some point as scenic articles. The latter is a less common occurrence and therefore extremely effective dramatically. The signification of these two types of sce-

---

2   The dramatic space consists of the stage as a solid base, the set as a variable construction, and the action space as a dynamic, permanently changing quality created by the actors' physical action.

nic articles is self-evident. An object may appear on the set either in reality or as represented. If the object itself is displayed, it presents, both as a whole and in its individual qualities, the same series of signs as in real life (for example, a specific piece of furniture may be, in relation to its owner, a sign of his social standing, taste, upbringing, state of health, habits, and so forth). While in real life the utilitarian function of an object is usually more important than its signification, on a theatre set the signification is all important. A sign may substitute for a real object on the set if this sign is able to transfer the object's own signs to itself. To satisfy this condition, it is sufficient for the scenic article to possess only a few of the basic characteristics of the object represented. The scenic article when a theatrical sign of the object itself takes on its obligations as a sign; thus scenic articles are theatrical signs of signs, frequently very complex (Bogatyrev 2016 [1938]).

Chinese theatre, however, possesses articles of a special kind, exceptional in their relationship to the actors and scene. These are *object-signs*, able to represent all aspects of the scene alone and unaided. On a stage without scenery or lighting effects these serve to denote the locale of the play. They are elementary theatrical signs and, as such, distinct from scenic articles and complementary articles, that is to say, they are neither signs of signs nor a structure of signs; they are signs not of particular objects but of objects in general.

The most important of these are a table and chair, which are almost never absent from the Chinese stage. If the table and chair are standing in the usual manner, then this indicates an interior. But a chair placed on the ground on its side or on its back signifies an embankment or earthwork; overturned it signifies a hill or mountain; standing on the table, it signifies a city tower. Apart from the table and chair the Chinese theatre uses articles that, while resembling the scenery of Western theatre, differ in that they remain the same for each play they are required for and are consciously interpreted as theatrical signs. A mountainous or desolate area is sometimes represented by a board with a stylized drawing of a mountain; city battlements are represented by a length of blue material held by theatre assistants; sometimes a gate and wall masonry are depicted on it, and sometimes it is simply a plain rectangular piece of cloth, unadorned by any drawing.

These object-signs are also used in the Chinese theatre to portray natural phenomena. Black pennants waved by theatre assistants are a sign for wind; a hammer and mirror signify a thunderstorm; confetti falling from black pennants that unfurl as the assistants wave them is a sign for a blizzard. Chinese theatre does not alter the brightness or colour of the lighting; the onset of dusk and night is marked by a theatre assistant carrying on a lit lamp or lantern. A pennant or piece of material displaying the stylized drawing of a wave and fish is a sign for water; the actor playing a drowning person leaps between the assistants bearing these signs, and all go off together.

But the Chinese theatre also has objects on the set that we have termed scenic articles; for our purposes we shall distinguish articles that are aids to the actor's performance and articles that are signs characterizing the person he is representing.

The elaborate system of signs that has evolved has enabled the Chinese actor to give a comprehensible portrayal of the most varied actions without having to re-create reality on the stage. He is able to manage with a few articles, relying chiefly on his own performance. For example, to act riding on horseback he uses a whip that represents the horse. The colour of the whip denotes the colour of the horse. Thrown at random on the stage, the whip represents a horse grazing. Riding in a carriage is indicated by an assistant carrying a banner on both sides of the actor, usually a yellow banner marked with a circle, the sign of a wheel; to indicate alighting, the assistant raises the banner. To indicate a trip in a boat, it is enough for the actor to carry an oar with which he performs a great variety of precisely prescribed motions while walking about the stage. If an execution is to be enacted, a packet enwrapped in red silk signifies the severed head; the man executed runs off the stage, and an assistant displays the packet to the audience.

Articles that are worn visibly and continuously by the actor are theatre signs that serve to establish his character; they form a point of transition to costume and generally include banners, coils of silk, pieces of fabric. The use of scenic articles linked to costume delineates the character of the person being represented in a comprehensible way while obviating the necessity for explanatory passages in the dialogue. Spirits are indicated by black or red veils or paper tassels, a sick person is marked by a stripe of yellow material tied round the head and running down onto the back, a captive wears a long silk cord round his neck. The sign for the rank of general is a collection of triangular bannerettes, usually four, embroidered with dragons, flowers and phoenixes, which is fastened on the actor's back; a special banner is reserved for a general in command, another for a general concluding peace. Special coils of yellow silk denote an imperial order or imperial safe-conduct, and its bearer may enter places forbidden to others; a board enwrapped in yellow silk denotes an official seal, and so forth.

(B) COSTUMES

Four types of character appear most frequently on the Chinese stage: i) positive heroes, loyal and honourable men (*shēng*); ii) villains, cruel and treacherous men, coarse soldiers, servants (*jìng*); iii) clowns, dancers and acrobats (*chǒu*); iv) female characters (*dàn*). All these roles admit of many nuances according to age, situation, and so on; the second group (*jìng*) is distinguished from the first (*shēng*) by its actors wearing makeup on their faces.

Religious reasons prevented women playing in the Chinese theatre; female parts were formerly distinguished only by the actor playing a woman wearing a blue tulle band around his head, but later this simple sign was replaced by a more elaborate form of dress, makeup and hairstyle.

Each of these types wears a costume appropriate in material, colour, cut, and design to the character's importance. Chinese theatre costume observes strict conventions, but in contrast to Chinese object-signs, which are elementary signs, it is a complicated structure of signs. It differs from Western theatre costume not only in its plurisignification but also in the nature of the referents. It reveals not merely the wearer's social status, age, and so forth, but his worth, character, and so on. This purely theoretical aspect has its practical consequences: it reveals an interesting interdependence between aesthetic outlook and questions of technique. For the costumes used are always made from high quality, expensive materials painstakingly put together to fulfil to perfection the demands of stern convention, while at the same time upholding the immutability of that same convention by their own unusual durability. Chinese theatre costume, however, has another important task to fulfil – that of creating the scene. The object-signs are very restrained; besides, the Chinese classical theatre is without lighting effects. This gives rise to the magnificence of Chinese theatre costume, whose variegated colours, sophisticated cut and intricate embroidery make it the most splendid theatre costume in the world.

We may distinguish three types of costume according to cut and design: ceremonial garb (*măng*), everyday wear (*diéz*), and military uniform (*kăikào*). Any of these may be worn by either male or female characters, situation being the only determining factor. Alongside these, however, there exists a wide range of separate items of dress that function as distinct autonomous signs. In its function as sign, Chinese theatre costume adopts those elements of ordinary dress that are signs standing for specific referents, but it simplifies or adapts them. Thus, for instance, the beggar's costume stems from its counterpart in everyday reality but is converted into an autonomous theatrical sign; the beggar in the Chinese theatre wears an everyday piece of silk clothing (*diéz*) spangled with multicoloured silk patches. A mandarin is distinguished by his long coat and thick-soled shoes, and so on. Occasionally the meaning of the sign varies according to the situation; a cape worn early in the morning betrays the fact that the character returned home late at night, worn later in the day, however, it indicates the wearer's laziness and slovenliness. A woman's skirt signifies dress that is not too clean and as such is common with women of the lower class; if worn by a wealthy woman, it shows either that the person in question is on a journey and unable therefore to care for her appearance or that we are dealing with a disguise.

(C) MAKEUP

Through his makeup an actor is even more closely identified with the character represented. Makeup in the Chinese theatre is used as a sign that sets apart complex and exceptional characters. Not all actors use makeup, only those acting parts in the second and third groups (*jìng* and *chǒu*); honourable men (*shēng*) and women (*dàn*) are never made up. The makeup used is non-imitative and entirely independent of matters of physiognomy; it forms a self-contained, artificial sign system. It is strikingly similar to the ancient Chinese war mask: the theatrical makeup was evidently derived from it when evil and cruel persons were being represented and the need arose to find some way of clearly marking them apart from other characters. These masks, portraying spirits and demons intended to overawe the enemy in battle, had a long tradition behind them and boasted a suitably strict symbolism, but they were too stiff and rigid to be suitable in themselves for the flexible and constantly changing dramatic space of the Chinese theatre. This most probably gave rise to the idea of painting them directly on the skin of the face, which could then still use its expressive resources beneath the colourful abstract patterns of the makeup. The pattern and colour of the makeup are signs of the character. In the course of time, however, signs that in the original system had universal validity and permitted of random combination grouped themselves into schematic units, ideographs, connected with specific heroes of individual plays; within these schemes, however, the signs retained their original values. The scheme painted on the actor's face is, in fact, a chart of the moral qualities of the character.

The patterns employed are several and diverse in meaning. Most widespread is a form of makeup dividing the actor's face into three sections, roughly in the shape of a Y, consisting of the forehead and both cheeks; the chin is generally covered with a beard and has no special function in this regard. Old men are characterized by evenly painted eyebrows extended to the ears. The wounded have their face covered with irregular drawing and many colours. The parts of clowns are marked by makeup distorting the features, with irregular placing of nose and eyes, or alternatively the forehead is painted with a triangle coming to a point on the bridge of the nose.

Colours fulfil a much more precise sign function. It is comparatively rare to find the whole face made up with one colour, white, black, red, and so forth; these indicate either unambiguous characters or supernatural beings. Black means simplicity, sincerity, courage and steadfastness; red denotes loyalty, honesty and patriotism; crimson is used with old men as a sign for the calm of old age and prudence allied to these qualities; blue expresses obstinacy, cruelty and pride; yellow indicates ruthlessness, slyness and wiliness; white stands for hypocrisy, irascibility, baseness and viciousness. The extent of the coloured area on the actor's face corresponds to the extent to which the character he is playing partakes of the moral quality in question. Thus, for example, there are many degrees in the use of white, from a face totally white except for the eyebrows to a mere white spot on the nose. In the first case the spectator is informed that the character has no other qualities than those having white as their sign: that is, he is an utter villain (usually of noble birth). In the second case the moral qualities signified by the white colour form only a very small part of the character's nature; that is, he is an honest man with a few slight moral blemishes (usually a simple soldier). Makeup also serves alongside costume to set apart supernatural beings: green is reserved for spirits and devils, gold for gods.

The use of false beards and moustaches, of which there are more than a dozen kinds, is also subject to convention. They are unrealistic both in shape and in the way they are worn: they are fastened with wires behind the ears, and their styles, often very bizarre, are signs of age, status and personality.

II. THE ACTION SPACE

The second type of visual sign concerns those pertaining to the action space. All the movements, gestures and facial expressions of the actor are signs that, as in Western theatre, serve both to convey an understanding of the character and to indicate its relationship to others. As well as these, however, the Chinese theatre provides abundant examples of signs realized by means of the action space that have a representative function and stand for referents outside the characters; they substitute for non-existent fixed components of the scene or non-existent scenic articles. Every action, whatever its particular significance, has evolved through long tradition into an obligatory convention. Its present shape has been affected not only by the attempt to devise a sign at once simple and comprehensible but also by constant emphasis on aesthetic function. The actions of the Chinese actor are subject to precise rules that allow no basic deviation. Perfect mastery of technique comes from his being educated in these rules from a tender age, and by having him play the same part throughout his career. The conventional sequences of *action-signs* never aim at imitation of reality. They naturally take this as their starting point, but in most cases they are so constructed as to divorce themselves from realism as much as possible. For example, the actor suggests the action of drinking tea by raising an imaginary cup to his lips, but in order to avoid being realistic, masks the hand executing the gesture with a special movement of the other hand. To illustrate the character sleeping, he does not lie down but sits with his temple resting lightly on the fingers of one hand. An action thus owes its final form to a tension between the aesthetic function and other functions, communicative, expressive, and so on. The relationship of action-signs to reality varies; conventional sequences of movements that relate to the scene, even at their most artificial, are in fact in closer contact with reality than actions expounding thought processes and relationships between characters. The Chinese actor creates the action space from the full gamut of elements of movement, gesture and facial expression at his disposal. Movements are understood here in the narrower sense of body movements. One special mode of expression is that of various motions of pheasants' plumes affixed to the actor's headgear. These are very long; he may make them gyrate or sway by turning or drooping his head or he may move them by hand. The Chinese actor's gestures differ profoundly from those of the Western actor. The primary gestures are made by the hands, which are seldom left free but are generally cloaked in long flowing silk cuffs fastened to the sleeves. The gestures carried out by the actor with these sleeves are rich in signification. Though the facial expressions are not in general distinct from those in the West, they are more diverse and specific. Movements of the facial muscles are conventionalized; binding rules govern which facial expression should be used to express a given emotion relative to character type, age and the nature, intensity and duration of the feeling. Generally, movements and gestures in the wider sense of the words are bearers of signs substituting for the scene, while sleeve gestures and facial expressions together express the thoughts and emotions of the character.

A great proportion of the actor's performance is devoted to producing signs whose chief function is to stand for components of the scene. Through his performance the actor must convey all those actions for which the scene in the Chinese theatre provides no suitable material basis. Drawing on the appropriate sequence of conventional movements, the actor performs such actions as surmounting imaginary obstacles, climbing imaginary stairs, stepping over a high threshold, opening a door. The movement-signs performed inform the onlooker of the nature of these imaginary objects, indicate whether the non-existent ditch is empty or filled with water, whether the non-existent door is the main or an ordinary double door, a single door, and so forth. If a character is entering the dwelling of poor people, the actor carries out the proper motion in a bent position, for the poor live in low-ceilinged basements; if appropriate, the rules allow him the opportunity to show himself hitting his forehead on an imaginary lintel. His acting is particularly complicated when it involves objects or animals; here it is sometimes based on fragments or parts of imaginary objects. When speaking about scenic articles, we have mentioned the use of an oar to represent a trip in a boat; if the actor arrives with his oar on an empty stage by the "exit" doorway, this means the whole stage is water; he may receive other persons on board his imaginary boat and row to the "entrance", which stands for the shore. An unusually complicated sequence of actions is employed by the actor to suggest activities with a horse, mounting, riding, trotting, galloping, dismounting, leading, and so on. The signification of all these movements is so precisely elaborated that it allows the spectator to imagine even the nature of the imaginary horse. In one play the actor representing a servant has eight imaginary horses on stage; the audience can tell from his behaviour that one horse is exceptionally beautiful, another bites, another bucks, another is sick, another is worn out with age, and so forth. The servant saddles the horses, leads them to his master's residence, and announces to the company that they are in readiness. The knights come out, pretend to mount the imaginary horses and ride off at a trot. The same degree of detail marks the rules governing the representation of diverse types of work and activity: weaving, sewing, thread making, writing, and so on; they all dispense with scenic articles.

Other signs are connected with the psychological state of a character; these are usually sleeve gestures, carefully worked out to fit each individual instance. The "raised sleeve gesture", in which the long sleeve is flung upwards and hangs out, expresses despair or revolt. Another sleeve gesture signifies a weighty decision; the "sleeve gesture of decision", in which the right hand circles slowly upward and then quickly downward, signifies that the person has made some fateful decision, sacrificed someone's life, and so forth. To show dejection – for example, if a character's plans are frustrated – the Chinese actor is not permitted to let his arms dangle by the side of his body, since this gesture does not comply with Chinese aesthetics; the actor lowers only one arm, but this he holds in front of him, pressing it slightly to the body and gripping it under the elbow with his other arm, bent. This "gesture of repose", which is in fact a set position, is employed not only by actors expressing fatigue but also by those portraying spirits. Another standard position, used to show the poverty or unreality of a character, is the "drooping sleeves gesture"; the actor playing a poor man or a spirit allows his sleeves to droop from his arms, held somewhat forward from the body. Gestures performed with the hands alone are also used to signify emotions. If the concept cannot be expressed by a sleeve gesture, the actor tucks up his sleeve in order to have his hand free and covers it again after completion of the gesture. Hand gestures may only replace sleeve gestures that are signs representing emotions, but some hand gestures cannot be replaced by sleeve gestures. Hand gestures are signs of illness, feelings of heat, cold, powerlessness, disappointment, pain, pity, contemplation, and so on. The gesture of protest may serve to show their complexity. The hand is partially clenched into a fist, the thumb rests on the middle joint of the middle finger, the index finger is curved across the thumb and at the same time the tip of the little finger is made to touch the third finger, to avoid the shape of an ordinary fist. Whereas gestures never signify joyful emotions, body and feather movements have no other function but to express such cheerful states. Military roles contain many movements expressing strength and ardour. A sign of eagerness is a movement that the actor performs using his left leg while standing erect on his right; he raises his left thigh and bends his leg at the knee into an obtuse angle. The "dragon's turn" at the waist has the same meaning. Arms on hips, the actor rotates his trunk, stretching out to the limit in all directions. In one play the actor in this pose uses his teeth to seize a cup of wine from a tray proffered by a servant on his right, leans back, as if quaffing the cup, and returns the glass to the tray, now held by the servant on his left side. The signs of greatest levity and gaiety are dancing movements with feathers, most often performed by one of the female characters (*dàn*).

Finally, the last – but nevertheless important – theatrical signs relating to the concept of action space are those that reveal the relationship of the character carrying out an action to another character. Here we are dealing with signs revealing the social relations between individuals and with signs that are dramatic in the true sense of the word, for it is through these that conflict is most often expressed. Some came to the Chinese stage straight from the world of social ceremonial, in the process acquiring still greater complexity and codification. They concern greeting and welcoming a guest. The "sleeve gesture of respect" signifies a highly courteous greeting; it is performed by crossing the arms. If the actor wishes to indicate that he is expressing his respect to a character or that he asks to be heard by him, he makes the "sleeve gesture of address"; he raises his left arm to beneath his chin, letting the sleeve dangle, lightly touches the latter with the fingers of his right hand, leaving out the index finger, and greets the character being addressed. This gesture and sign of respect, however, are also performed by an actor when uttering the name of a person not present whom he loves or cherishes. An actor acknowledges a greeting or show of respect by performing the "sleeve gesture of attention": he places his right hand beneath his breast, letting the sleeve drop, and at the same time bowing. These movements are a sign replacing the verbal wish that the other desist from his greetings. Another series of signs concerns the greeting of a guest. Together with the usual salutations, the actor welcoming a guest performs other gestures; he conveys the dusting down of the chair by a movement of the sleeve right, left and right again, first with the right arm, then the left, and lastly the right again. The artificial manner and importance of this ceremony, which is also carried out in a similar way in everyday life, enabled it to be brought with only minor alterations into the action space. Similar codified actions for greeting a guest, including dusting the chair, are also known from some rural areas in the Czech lands, where they had their own important place in a series of ceremonies, for instance matchmaking. The action space of Chinese theatre has also elaborated signs expressing disagreeable feelings. Anger, repugnance and refusal are conveyed by the "sleeve gesture of aversion"; with a circling motion the actor flings his sleeve in the character's direction and simultaneously twists his head the other way. To send a person away, the actor carries out the "sleeve gesture of dismissal": flexing both wrists, he flicks the sleeves away from the body once, twice, thrice, stepping back at the third gesture. The "sleeve gesture of concealment" indicates that the actor is hiding his action or words from other characters on the stage; its meaning is thus close to the aside in Western theatre. If the actor wishes to communicate to the audience some secret that must remain hidden from the other characters, or if he wishes to express a private thought, he raises his right-hand sleeve to the level of his face; this gesture denotes an opaque wall between the other characters and the actor, who points to them frequently with his other hand. The actor may hide himself behind a still more perfect imaginary wall when in a dilemma or afraid of discovery by using the "sleeve gesture of hiding". Here the arm is bent in an obtuse angle to the brow, and the sleeve flows down across the whole face.

ACOUSTIC SIGNS

The second group of signs in the Chinese theatre is formed by the signs of theatre language, song and music. The language in the Chinese theatre has special signs that distinguish it from ordinary speech. The composition of Chinese plays is not in most cases dramatic in the Western sense; it generally lacks the tension that is reflected in dialogue. Chinese drama is a structure made up of verse, prose and music; these elements intermingle and appear in every play. Stage language was formed by an artificial mixing of various dialects and its signification also stems from the special mode of declamation employed. The manner in which individual words are declaimed is founded on a strictly observed system of four tones that prevents possible errors in comprehension owing to the homonymous character of Chinese words and also serves to heighten the musicality of the speech; at the same time, however, each of the tones is a sign and expresses the speaker's inner state of mind. The spoken word, whether in prose or verse, must always suit the rhythm of the movements. Verse dialogue and monologue are composed of quatrains; the first two lines are delivered in a monotone, the third line rises and falls, and the fourth is delivered slowly and quietly. If, on the other hand, the actor raises his voice on the last line, this announces the imminence of music and dance.

Music in the Chinese theatre follows convention. It is played at the beginning of a play, at actors' entries and at certain identical situations in the course of the play. The most important instruments of the theatre orchestra are the two-string spiked fiddle (*èrhú*), the three-stringed guitar (*sānxián*), the reed organ (*shēng*),³ horns, flutes, drums, gongs, cymbals and clappers. For centuries the music, played and written, has been based on a five-note scale derived from the ancient Chinese flute, and the classical Chinese theatre remains faithful to this tradition. Conventional themes are prescribed for the principal situations; they always make their appearance when these points in the play are reached. Otherwise there is no music or simply improvised music. The themes are introduced by either a singer or a solo instrument and are then recapitulated by all instruments in unison. Arias are sung in an archaic, almost incomprehensible form of language; thus certain features are signified by the music alone, which is precisely defined thematically, either in conjunction with the action space or in isolation. Occasions when music functions as a sign include, for example, those marked by emotions such as anger, hatred, horror, surprise, anxiety, sadness, meditation, love, joy, drunkenness and actions such as the toilette, fights, flight, and so on. Often the circumstance in question is conveyed by the music alone, for instance if drunkenness is to be represented; its realistic imitation, common on the Western stage, is forbidden to the Chinese actor on aesthetic grounds.

By examining the signification of individual elements in the Chinese theatre, we find a structure generally homogeneous, a stock of several systems of codified signs, of systems that, though autonomous in their own right, develop spontaneously one from another. The shaping of these systems, the stability of whose entire structure depends on the maintenance of virtually inviolate lexicons, evidently owed something to external, extra-theatrical influences (religion, traditions of social intercourse, and so forth) but the influence of the scene itself was highly important. Scenic articles standing for referents composing the scene developed into special theatrical signs, adopting new functions and bequeathing their original ones to the action space. The latter could only discharge its own role by transferring some of its sign functions to the remaining elements of the structure, chiefly the music. In Chinese theatre, as opposed to that in the West, a dramatic work is not waiting to be staged in accordance with numerous chance factors that will determine how it is shaped, from a director's conception to an actor's diction. The productions of well-known individual plays in the ancient Chinese theatre pre-exist, down to the last component. It is as though they formed an uninterrupted series, already familiar to the entire cast in each and every detail, and are merely brought forth from time to time without any serious structural changes. To a certain degree the structure is sure of itself, so that there is not even any need for a director to see to its unity.

---

3   [Editor's note: The Chinese names for these instruments did not appear in the original text, but have been added here for clarity.]

WORKS CITED

Bogatyrev, Petr (2016 [1938]) "Theatrical Signs", this reader, pp. 99–114.
Zich, Otakar (1931) *Estetika dramatického umění: teoretická dramaturgie* [The Aesthetics of Dramatic Art: A Theoretical Dramaturgy], Prague: Melantrich.

THE MOBILITY OF THE THEATRICAL SIGN

JINDŘICH HONZL

["Pohyb divadelního znaku" (1940) was published in *Slovo a slovesnost*, vol. 6, pp. 177–88. The English translation by Irwin R. Titunik was published under the title "Dynamics of the Sign in the Theater" in Matejka, Ladislav and Titunik, Irwin R. (eds) (1976) *Semiotics of Art: Prague School Contributions*, Cambridge, Mass.: The M.I.T. Press, pp. 74–93.]

Editor's note: The change of the title in Honzl's seminal piece from "Dynamics" to "Mobility" aims to reflect the original use of the Czech word *pohyb*, which simply means "movement", but can also be employed in the sense of "mobility". "Dynamics" is an interpretation that attributes internal agency to the sign, and as such we found it misleading. This new, more literal translation of the original title aims to prevent the possible over-interpretation of Honzl's concept that "dynamics" encourages. This editorial decision was also taken by an anonymous translator, whose translation "The Mobility of Theatre Sign" was published without credit in 1969 in *Interscaena*, vol. 10, no. 1, pp. 37–51; the article also appears in French as "La Mobilité du signe théâtral".

The whole of stage reality – the dramatist's words, the actor's performances, the stage lighting – all these represent other realities. The theatre performance is a set of signs.

Otakar Zich expressed this view in *The Aesthetics of Dramatic Art* when he stated that "dramatic art is an *art of images* and this holds *in absolutely every respect*" (Zich 1931: 234). Thus the actor *represents* a character (Vojan[1] represents Hamlet), the set *represents* the place where the story takes place (a Gothic arch represents a castle), white light *represents* daytime, blue light nighttime, music *represents* some action (the noise of battle), and so forth. Zich explains that though the stage is in fact a piece of architecture, it cannot, in his view, be considered as such because architecture does not serve the function of an image, it does not seek to represent anything. The stage, on the other hand, has the sole function of serving as an image, because it ceases to be a stage if it does not represent something (Zich 1931: 227). To put Zich's assertion another way, we may say that it does not matter whether

---

1   [Editor's note: Eduard Vojan (1853–1920), a leading Czech actor, famous for the psychological depth of his roles. His Hamlet, which he played in three productions at the Czech National Theatre (with premieres in the seasons of 1904–1905, 1915–1916 and 1919–1920), was iconic.]

the stage is a structure or not, that it does not matter whether the stage is a place in the Prague National Theatre or a meadow near a forest or a few planks resting on barrels or part of a market square surrounded by spectators. What does matter is for the stage of the Prague National Theatre to represent satisfactorily a meadow, or for the meadow of an outdoor theatre to clearly represent a town square, or for the part of the square occupied by the marketplace theatre to represent the inside of an inn, and so on. But Zich himself does not contest the idea of the stage as something that is by its very nature constructed. Whenever he speaks of the stage, he always has in mind a stage inside a theatre building. Nevertheless, we may venture to expand Zich's argument and arrive at the conclusion mentioned above, that the figurative function of the stage is independent of its architectural nature.

From this example of *nature of the stage as a sign* we can draw analogies for other aspects of the theatre performance. So although the stage is usually a structure, it is not its nature as a structure that makes it a stage but the fact that it *represents* a dramatic place. The same is true of the actor: the actor is usually a *person* who speaks and moves about the stage, but the essence of the actor does not lie in the fact that he is a *person* speaking and moving about the stage but rather that he *represents* someone, that he *indicates a dramatic character*. Whether or not he is a human being is not important. He could just as easily be a piece of wood. If the wood moves about and someone matches speech to its movements, the piece of wood can represent a dramatic character, the wood can be an actor.

We have freed the concept of "stage" from its being limited to architecture and we can also free the concept of "actor" from the limitation that regards the actor as a human being who represents a character. If the only thing that matters is the representation of the character by something else, then not only can a person be an actor, but so can a figure of wood (a puppet), a machine (for example, the mechanical theatre of El Lissitzky, Oskar Schlemmer and Friedrich Kiesler) or a thing (for example, the theatre advertising of Belgian purchasing cooperatives, where a bolt of material, a spider's leg, a coffee grinder and the like were all characters).

But if a voice in itself is enough to indicate a character well, then a voice heard from the wings of a stage or over the radio is an actor. There is an acoustic actor like this in Goethe's *Faust*, where in productions the role of God in the prologue is usually present as merely a voice. And in radio plays, voice and sound represent not only the characters but also all the rest that constitutes the reality of the theatre: the stage, the scenery, the props and the lighting. In radio there are sonic signs for everything. One speaks of acoustic scenery (an office is indicated by the tapping of typewriters, a coal mine by the racket of pneumatic drills and the rumbling of wagons, and the like). A glass as a prop may be represented by the sound of wine being poured or by the clinking of glasses, and so on.

Zich in fact limits his discussion of character to conventional forms of theatre performance. He speaks solely of "plays and operas ... performed in a theatre" (Zich 1931: 15) and is only concerned with actors that act on the stages of our theatres and singers that sing there. But once he has relieved us of the limitation that restricted the stage to architecture, then all the other elements of the theatre performance jostle their way forward to freedom. The character, heretofore closely associated with the human actor, is liberated, the playwright's message, hitherto the *word*, is liberated, other devices are liberated. Much to our amazement, we discover that the stage space need not always be a space, but that sound can be a stage, music can be an event, scenery can be a message.

To begin with, let us look at the stage and the signs that denote it. One can say that the stage can be represented by any kind of spatial reality or that a structure or a town square surrounded by spectators or a meadow or a hall in an inn are all equally suitable as a stage. But the stage, which is a space, need not be denoted by a space. We have already used examples of the radio stage (an office, a coal mine), which is denoted acoustically, but we can also provide examples of conventional theatre plays where sound is the stage. In the final act of Chekhov's *The Cherry Orchard* the main role is played by the orchard. The cherry orchard is on the stage, but in such a way that we cannot see it. It is not represented spatially, but acoustically; in the last act we hear the blows of axes cutting down the orchard. So the playwright and the director can denote the stage by the reality that best matches their intention, that mediates their communication with the audience in the best and most effective fashion.

The facts that we have mentioned so far have resulted from the observation and evaluation of actual artistic work and are not mere scholarly deductions. As we see in Zich, the scholarly explication – which defines the stage correctly as that reality that denotes the dramatic space – does not venture into any implications that go beyond a conventional understanding of the stage. For Zich, the stage remains always in the theatre, in theatre architecture, "where plays and operas are performed" (Zich 1931: 15). It was actual artistic work that dared to move into areas where theatre studies had not yet ventured, even though they had already pointed in that direction. It was the modern theatre that freed itself from the stage as a permanent structural constant.

Cubo-Futurist theatre experiments directed our attention to stages and theatres other than those built for the tsarist ballet, for self-display by members of high society in their boxes, or for the cultural and educative activities of small-town amateur actors. Along with them we discovered the theatre of the street, became enthralled by the theatricality of playing fields, admired the dramatic action created by the movements of harbour cranes. But we also discovered the stages of the primitive theatre, the stages of barkers at fairs, children's games, circus mimes, the tavern theatres of strolling players, the theatres of costumed revellers at traditional village festivals. Stages could spring up anywhere – any place could be seized upon by the theatrical imagination.

Along with the stage, other devices of the theatre performance were also liberated. Scenery fixed in wooden frames and hidden by painted canvas was released from its spell. The still stylized theatre from the time of the Théâtre d'Art in France, of Georg Fuchs and Adolphe Appia in Germany, of the New Drama Fellowship[2] in Russia and of Jaroslav Kvapil[3] in Bohemia adhered to scenic signs that might be called scenic metonymies. A Gothic arch was used to represent an entire church (Kvapil's staging of Claudel's *The Announcement Made to Mary*), the green surface of the stage floor meant a battlefield (Kvapil's Shakespearean cycle) and the English coat-of-arms on a silk banner was enough for scenes set in royal halls (in the same cycle). A part represented the whole. But a part could also indicate several different wholes: a Venetian column and a flight of stairs sufficed for almost all the scenes in the *Merchant of Venice*, except for those in Portia's or Shylock's rooms and in the garden. The column and the flight of steps served as scenery not only for the street but also for the harbour, the square and the court of justice. The allusive scenery of the stylized stage always sought to employ unambiguous devices whenever possible. True, a Venetian column could be placed on a square or in a street or made part of the architecture of a house. But it always indicated a Venetian building and nothing but that building, of which it could be a part. With the advent of Cubo-Futurist theatre, however, new materials appeared on the stage and things formerly undreamed of acquired various representative functions. Russian Constructivist theatre represented a factory yard, a garden pavilion, a field of rye or a mill room by means of structures made of laths. Which part or which property of these laths carried the representative function? Not colour or coloured shapes, since these constructions were made of raw, unvarnished wood or wood of a single colour. Constructivism (or at least the Constructivism of Lyubov Popova and Vsevolod Meyerhold) banished from the stage every painted, coloured sign. However, in many

---

2   [Editor's note: In Russian, Tovarishchestvo novoi dramy; it has several English translations.]

3   [Editor's note: Jaroslav Kvapil (1868–1950), a director, dramaturge and poet (he authored the libretto for Antonín Dvořák's opera *Rusalka*). He adhered to the psychological-realistic and Symbolist traditions in his work for the theatre, which was mainly connected with the Czech National Theatre and the Vinohrady Theatre in Prague. His production of Claudel's *The Announcement Made to Mary* premiered at the National Theatre in Prague in 1914; his Shakespearean cycle appeared at the National Theatre in 1916.]

cases not even through its form did a construction generate unambiguous theatrical signs. Meyerhold's construction for *Tarelkin's Death* was simply a crate made of slats and another object of the same material which, with its circular end facing the audience, could have suggested any number of things, but none of them unambiguously.[4] Perhaps the most definite idea it conjured up was that of a meat grinder. But it could equally well have indicated a circular window or a round cage or a huge mirror, its circular shape being its most striking feature. But "circularity" is so richly suggestive that one could have interpreted this round object as a sign for a great many things. So which properties of a stage construction can function as signs when neither colour nor shape serve as vehicles for such a function?

More than fifteen years ago I wrote about Alexander Tairov's production of *Giroflé-Girofla* along the following lines. We cannot tell what the contrivance on the stage is supposed to signify until it is used by an actor, until he sits on it or bobs up and down in it or climbs up it. It is only when Giroflé and Marasquin sit down at a certain place that we recognize it as a love seat hidden away in a shadowy corner of a park. But during an aria this same seat bobs up and down like a small boat afloat on a calm lake, rocking to the rhythmic strokes of oars. Or, when a band of fierce pirates jumps on it, we know by the way they stand with their legs apart, shifting the weight of their bodies from one leg to the other, that it is part of a deck – a staircase leading to the stern of the ship with its helmsman. The signifying (representative) functions of the scenery and the contrivance are determined solely by the actor's movements or by the manner in which he uses them, but even then their representative function is not entirely unambiguous.

Let us return to the example of Popova's construction for Meyerhold's staging of *Tarelkin's Death*.[5] It is only when we see an actor rushing about in the cylindrical structure like a prisoner and clutching its slats like bars that we realize the representative function of this scenic element: it is a prison cell. But at the same time we are still aware of all the associations based on its form that came to mind when we first looked at it. The idea of a "meat grinder" in combination with the idea of a "prison cell" takes on new meanings thanks to their mutual polarization.

If we examine other constructions used by Meyerhold in his productions from that period, we frequently see a system of suspended platforms, staircases and contrivances that, as a sign, is completely indecipherable. Critics commenting on these productions and constructions often spoke of

---

4   [Editor's note: Varvara Stepanova (1894–1958), a Russian Constructivist artist, the stage designer for this 1922 production.]

5   [Editor's note: In fact it was Stepanova's construction. Lyubov Popova (1889–1924) was the Constructivist stage designer for Meyerhold's 1922 production of *The Magnificent Cuckold*.]

"abstract scenery". But Meyerhold – and this was something he shared with all the other stage designers – had no interest in abstraction when it came to scenery. His stage constructions had very concrete purposes and functions. Indeterminate in shape and colour, they became signs only when used for the actors' movements. It can be said that *neither form nor colour had a representative function, but only the contours of the actors' movements* on the constructions, on the bare floor, on the suspended platforms, on the staircases, on the raked planes, and so on.

However, this does not bring us to the end of our inquiry into the changes undergone by scenic signs on the stage. The structure of signs that is the theatre performance must retain its equilibrium in every situation, whether favourable or unfavourable.

If the support points of a structure are sturdy, alterations in its complex makeup can be offset without substantial changes. If we remove one of the pillars, however, basic changes must be made to the layout of the whole structure. Evidently one example of structural stability is theatres with traditions going back centuries, among them the traditional Japanese Noh theatre, the somewhat younger Japanese Kabuki theatre, the Classic Chinese theatre, Czech puppet theatre, folk theatres, the theatres of primitive peoples, and so on. The sturdiness of a structure enables theatrical signs to develop complex meanings. The stability of signs promotes a wealth of meanings and associations. In the Chinese theatre every step taken by the actor is imbued with meaning, every way of lifting the arm means something different (see Brušák 2016 [1939]), a step toward the exit on the left indicates "a return" and acquires a different meaning in each particular situation. For example, this step may indicate a battlefield to which a wounded hero is returning, but it can also signal a longing that takes a lover back to past memories.

In a similar way, in Czech folk puppet theatre the ways puppets make their entrances and exits have also come to function as signs. The entrance of a puppet from above the stage indicates "a sudden apparition", its disappearance through the floor symbolizes "death or descent to hell" and so on. If we assess the expressive richness of the theatre performance, we find that the constancy of a structure's support points does not necessarily diminish the expressiveness, for within this traditional structure subtler and more nuanced changes can develop. The audience is sensitive to even the slightest vibrations of a taut warp. Nevertheless, it is still necessary to point out to those who look to historical traditional theatres as models for countering the restless spirits of artists in their never-ending quest that the spectators' impressions are only occasioned by *changes* in the structure. The tighter the warp, the finer the yarn of the woof that weaves patterns and images in the fabric captivating us with their beauty.

Here I should like to quote from Petr Bogatyrev's *Folk Theatre*:[6]

A characteristic feature of folk theatre audiences is that they do not hanker after plays with new contents, but watch the same Christmas and Easter plays, *St Dorothy*, and so on, year after year ... The spectators watch these plays with extraordinary interest, though they know them almost by heart. Here lies the essential difference between the spectator at a folk theatre performance and the average member of the audience at our theatre... Since the spectators of folk theatre are very well acquainted with the contents of the play being performed, it is not possible to surprise them with some innovation in the fully developed subjects – that same innovation that plays such an essential role in our theatrical performances. For this reason, *the focus of a folk theatre performance lies in the treatment of detail*. (Bogatyrev 1940: 62–63; italics J. H.)

The desire for freedom of expression and of devices is a tendency that has always governed art. The theatre exposed to "fresh air" by the Cubo-Futurist revolt introduced new devices and lost many others. Russian Constructivism rid the stage of scenery, flats, drapery, backdrops. As a result the stage lost the possibility of localizing an action in any kind of interior or exterior setting through the use of painted signs. But this was not the only difficulty. Not only did directors forsake scenery, backdrops, flats and drapery; they also abandoned the bare stage that remained in the wake of their revolt. They forsook even the five sides that enclosed the space facing the auditorium, constructed such that every spectator could see it. But the directors who succeeded them (Nikolay Okhlopkov,[7] Walter Gropius with his design for a theatre) did away with the stage altogether or, to be more precise, placed the stage among the spectators so that any free place in front of, above, next to or behind the audience could be a stage. Thus they consigned to oblivion all that costly, extraordinary and easily manipulable stage machinery that, in obedience to a single command by the director, lowered from the flies any piece of scenery, set, construction, prop or actor, rotated stage scenery from back to front, shifted scenery waiting in the wings onstage, raised through traps whole sections of the stage with pre-set scenes, and so on. The theatre wizard was deprived of all the machinery that enabled him to perform his magic. All he was left with was his bare hands. With the destruction of many of the conventional devices linking stage and auditorium that had been sanctioned by long tradition, it became more difficult to represent, to suggest, the spatial localization of a play.

6   [Editor's note: The full title is *Czech and Slovak Folk Theatre*. Sections of the book had been published earlier as separate essays, among them one entitled "Folk Theatre", which appears on pages 448–56 of this reader.]

7   [Editor's note: Nikolay Okhlopkov (1900–1967), the artistic director at Moscow's Realistic Theatre from 1930 to 1937, where he experimented with environmental theatre space.]

Furthermore, when the stage is situated among the spectators it is completely impossible to erect scenic signs. Such a stage cannot even utilize constructions whose representative functions, though far more indeterminate than those of scenery, nevertheless do offer the possibility of localizing and organizing the stage space by means of flights of steps, variously located platforms, raked planes, contrivances, machinery, and so on. In the case of Pavel Tsetnerovich[8] and Okhlopkov, of all the stage machinery the only thing that remained for the theatre was the surface of the floor; besides that there was still the actor, lighting and sound.

When the very foundations of the theatre structure are shaken in this way, it must adapt immediately to the new conditions. If one of the muscles in the set of muscles that moves the forearm in a living organism is paralyzed, then the organism is saved by some other muscle in the set taking over the function of the one that is paralyzed. To take one theatrical function: locating a play spatially, indicating a village square or a taproom, representing a cemetery or banquet hall – this is an essential function of the stage. It can be realized just as well by a stage using constructions as by a stage using scenery, by a stage with a proscenium arch or by a stage located in the midst of the spectators. The signs that the function has selected for the purpose of communicating with the spectators always work towards designating a space. It is precisely this designative function that constitutes their stability. Otherwise the signs retain the greatest possible variability. The fact that the signs are supposed to designate the space where the action takes place in no way necessitates their being spatial signs. We have already shown that space can be designated by an auditory sign as well as by a light sign. On the central stage, the possibilities for the placing of objects, large pieces of furniture or scenic signs are extremely limited. While the Constructivist stage focused on the actors' acting, the central stage often has to rely solely on the actor as such. So in the case of Okhlopkov's theatre we witnessed a number of superb instances of the *actor* becoming a sign of spatial localization. Here there was not only the actor-scenery and actor-set, but even the actor-furniture and the actor-prop.

Okhlopkov created an *actor-sea* by having a young man dressed in a neutral manner (in blue – that is "invisible" – overalls with a blue mask on his face) shake a blue-green sheet attached along one side to the floor in such a way that the rippling waves of the blue-green sheet effectively substituted for the waves of a maritime canal. He created *actor-furniture* by having two "invisibly" dressed actors kneel opposite each other and stretch a tablecloth between them in the quadrilateral shape of a table. An *actor-prop* originated

---

8   [Editor's note: Pavel Tsetnerovich (1894–1963), a director at Meyerhold's theatre and later other theatres, such as the "Red Torch" theatre during WWII.]

by placing next to the actor playing the role of the captain another actor dressed in blue overalls who held the handle of the ship's whistle in preparation for the moment when the captain, pulling the handle, blasted a signal to the sailors.

These are three typical examples of the transfer of scenic functions to those of the actor. But I could list many examples of equal or even greater interest. For example, actors denoting a blizzard. We know that theatres have various devices for producing *sound effects* that denote a storm. But in Okhlopkov's production of *The Aristocrats*, a carnivalesque crowd burst onto the stage. Boys and girls (again, actors in blue overalls) threw confetti at one another, jumping about and making a racket. This metaphor of a storm – this carnivalesque whirlwind – was not an *action*, not part of the actors' performance, but spatial scenery: it served to localize the action, was the sign of the storm.

Every theatre person immediately saw analogies between Okhlopkov's approach to staging and the methods employed by classical Chinese and Japanese theatres. The classical Chinese theatre has a primitive stage, so spatial localization is transferred to other agents on the stage. Here, too, we find "invisible" men (dressed in black) who assist in changing scenes, for instance by covering the bodies of dead warriors with a black cloth. The battlefield disappears and the story can continue elsewhere. Similarly, for spatial localization the Japanese stage uses all the devices of the theatre performance. Here, too, space need not be indicated by a space, sound by a sound, light by light, human action by the movement of actors. And here it also happens that we "see tones" and "hear the open countryside" or learn from observing an actor's costume what in the European theatre we would hear from the actor's lips.

I recall the following illustration of the use of changing devices in Japanese theatre:

Yuranosuke leaves the besieged castle. He steps forward from the back of the stage.

Suddenly the backdrop (which depicts a life-size door) is rolled up. We see a second backdrop: a small door. This indicates that the actor has moved away.

Yuranosuke proceeds on his journey. A dark green curtain is lowered over the backdrop. This indicates that Yuranosuke can no longer see the castle.

A few steps more. Yuranosuke enters on the "flower way".[9] To mark this further distancing, the *samisen* (a kind of Japanese mandolin) begins to play its music offstage.

The first stage of the journey away from the castle: a *step* in space.

The second stage: a *change of painted scenery*.

---

9   The "flower way", *hanamichi*, is a passageway (and acting area) that connects the rear of the auditorium with the right side of the stage.

The third stage: a conventional sign (the *curtain*), which cancels the visual scenic devices.

The fourth stage: *sound*.[10]

The succession of scenic devices, which take up the same function one after the other, is interpreted here as the gradation of a single action being carried out by the actor: Yuranosuke walking, leaving the castle behind.

However, with equal justification we could in this case interpret the actor's stepping away from the painted backdrop as a function of spatial localization. The stage artist "paints" either with the actor's step or with the sound of the mandolin. In each case he creates spatial relations by different means. But we can go beyond these two interpretations and consider others. We could ask whether the changing of the backdrops depicting the castle doors is not in fact an artistic substitution for the playwright's text, that is to say, for the actor's words "I have stepped out of the castle." Or whether the melancholy sound of the *samisen* is not a substitution for the verbal expression "I have set out on a journey to the distant desert." But even if we were to seek further interpretations we would still not get to the heart of the matter. We would not be able to make up our mind as to which of them are fundamental and we would not be able to deny the legitimacy of the others.

It would be wrong, however, to regard this variable method of theatrical expression as a speciality of the Chinese or Japanese theatre or of some Russian innovator in 1935. I can point to a similar method of theatrical creation in many Czech stage productions – for example my own production of Vladislav Vančura's *The Teacher and the Pupil*, produced in cooperation with the artist Jindřich Štyrský at the Municipal Theatre in Brno in 1930.[11]

The fourth scene of *The Teacher and the Pupil* takes place on the outskirts of a town. To indicate this we made use of an *actor's mask*. But we *removed this mask from the face of the actor, relocated it and used it as a spatial sign on the stage.* A face was projected across the whole wide expanse of a circular skyline, its lower part covered with a scarf in the manner of a highwayman. This face, with evil eyes below a forehead covered by a hat, arched above the stage, shading the area where the audience usually sees a sky with floating clouds.

---

10   [Editor's note: This passage is to be found in Eisenstein 2010: 118 with a slightly different wording. We have kept Honzl's rather loose translation from Eisenstein's article "An Unexpected Juncture", originally published in 1928, for the sake of maintaining Honzl's argument. Honzl does not provide a reference to Eisenstein, but merely states that he "recalls" reading an article. This discrepancy was addressed in Kalvodová 1992: 18.]

11   [Editor's note: This production introduced the first drama by Vladislav Vančura (1891–1942), who had been known until then as a fiction writer characterized by a highly poetic style. Jindřich Štyrský (1899–1942) was a regular designer of Honzl's productions; his work was influenced by Surrealism. Honzl was at the National Theatre in Brno as a guest director and dramaturge from 1929; in the 1930–31 season he produced several avant-garde productions there.]

Through relocation, the actor's mask acquired new meaning.

In the same production, however, the actor's mask was also projected on the stage in a magnified form, so carrying out another function. In this case, *the scenic image became an actor*. This occurred in the third scene.

The pupil, Jan, whose home confines him like a musty prison, stubbornly defends his plan – he wants to run away from home. He sticks to his plan despite the remonstrations of his aunt and the threats of his teacher. Through the walls of his home he stares into "the brilliant and glowing abyss of the world that opens up" before his eyes. In a long monologue in the third scene he makes his decision.

By making the stage almost completely dark and thus concealing the presence of the actor on the stage, we allowed his words to be heard in such a way as to create the impression that they were being spoken by the projected enlargement of his face, which gazed out fixedly on its longed-for goal.

In our 1929 production of *The Executioner of Peru*[12] (by Georges Ribemont-Dessaignes) duplication was used: an actor's face was projected and could actually be seen on the stage as well.

In our production of Guillaume Apollinaire's *The Breasts of Tiresias* (1927), the verbal expression of a poet was changed to the images of a painter. We transformed the actors into letters that then moved like figures about the stage. The different combinations of the letters created different lines of verse.

In a production of Yvan Goll's *Methuselah* (1927), *stage props* (bread, a bottle, and so on) appeared in the play as characters rising up in rebellion against Methuselah.

Many other examples could be given to illustrate the special character of the theatrical sign whereby it changes its material and passes from one aspect to another, animates an inanimate thing, shifts from an acoustical aspect to a visual one, and so on.

We have already stated that in the theatre it is not possible to decide once and for all, and in every case, that what is normally called the acting will not be entrusted to the scenery, and that it is impossible to foresee whether a visual phenomenon might not be expressed by music.

This variability of the theatrical sign, its ability to "change its garb", is its specific property. It enables us to explain the variability of the theatrical structure.

It is the variability of the theatrical sign that presents the main difficulty in finding a suitable definition of theatricality. Definitions of this concept

---

12   [Editor's note: This production as well as *The Breasts of Tiresias* and *Methuselah* premiered at the Osvobozené divadlo (The Liberated Theatre) in Prague; the latter two productions followed the dramaturgical line of the Osvobozené's INMODKULT (Institute of Modern Culture), which aimed at educating young theatre enthusiasts.]

either reduce theatricality to what is performed in our conventional theatres and opera houses or expand it so broadly that it becomes meaningless.

This changing of the theatrical sign enable us to explain yet another theoretical confusion that hinders research into the problem of who or what is the central, creative element of the theatre performance. If we say that it is the playwright, this is undoubtedly true in many cases and for many kinds of theatre. However, such an answer would not capture the essence of many examples of theatre in the past and we could not demonstrate that it is the playwright's text that forms the axis of theatricality in all cases. The quite free theme or complete lack of a theme in improvised Italian comedies and similar forms shows that even the dramatist and his text can partake of the changes discussed above. Similarly, we cannot regard as completely true the statement that the main vehicle of theatricality is the actor. As proof of this I have in mind the static positioning of actors on the stage, a feature of many theatre styles both past and present that turn theatre into stiffly recited dialogue (Théâtre d'Art, the stylized German theatre, Meyerhold) and the actor into an anesthetized puppet with prescribed movements, in this way transforming the function of actor into the function of stage prop or the function of stage structure. And if a modern director says that he himself is at the centre of creation in the theatre, we can only agree in those instances where he demonstrates this to us. But we will not nod in agreement if he speaks of the theatricality of past times, when there was no director.

This does not mean that the dramatist, the text, the actor or the director are secondary or dispensable factors determining the balance of the theatrical structure. We only wish to show that every historical period foregrounds a different component of the theatre performance and the creative power of one factor can replace or suppress others without in this way decreasing the strength of the theatrical effect. We could also show that certain periods directly demand such shifts in the balance of the theatrical structure. There are or there have been theatres without authors (or at least without outstanding authors), there are or there have been theatres without actors or without great actors, and there are and there have been theatres without directors. However, if we take a closer look, we find that the function of actor is always present even though it has changed into or appears in the guise of another function. Similarly, we must admit that what we call the organizational force of the director was also present in every historical period of the theatre, even when there was no director as such.

These strange and contradictory statements – that an actor participates in the theatrical production even when it is a case of a theatre without actors, that the word always remains an essential component of theatricality even when it is a case of "wordless" theatre, that the "scenic function" is present even in theatre without scenery – these contradictory statements are justified by the specific nature of the theatrical sign, theatrical structure and dramatic material. I believe that in the preceding explanation we have supplied sufficient evidence of the variability of the theatrical sign, which passes from material to material with a freedom unknown to any other art. Certainly there is no music without tones, no poem without words, no painting without colours and no sculpture without physical matter. Or to be more precise, painting is not painting if words are used instead of colours, music is not music if harmony is composed of matter rather than of tones, and so on. There are, however, cases in which an artist turns to other fields for a device if his own material cannot achieve the desired intensity of expression. For example, Beethoven brought the musical expression of the finale of his Ninth Symphony to such heights that listeners would find tones insufficient and could only be satisfied by *words*. In the field of poetry, we could mention as examples of the change of device Apollinaire's *Calligrams* or "visual poetry", which was invented in Bohemia. We could also seek similar examples in painting (Cubism, which paints fragments of newspapers and inscriptions) and elsewhere. However, such examples are always the exceptions that prove the rule about the non-variable nature of material in the various kinds of art. But in the case of the theatre, as we have found, this variability is the rule and the specific characteristic of theatricality.

This has formed the basis for a number of theories of the theatre that have attempted to regularize or unify the great variety of theatrical material, devices and approaches. The best known of these is undoubtedly Wagner's concept of theatre as *Gesamtkunstwerk* (a "total work of art"; in recent years the director E. F. Burian[13] has also promoted this theory).

The multiplicity of devices is organized by the total work of art (*Gesamtkunstwerk*) in such a way as to produce a unified result, to have a "collective effect". The dramatic character is present not only on the stage but also in the orchestra; we experience his inner state, development and fate not only through the words and the actions we see on the stage but also through the tones we hear. The stream of music, the acting, the words, the scenery, the props, the lighting and all the other factors act in parallel.

In *Parsifal*, Wagner was not content with scenic denotation alone – presenting on the stage, for example, a spring landscape; this spring landscape was also depicted by the orchestra. The composer of *The Ring of the Nibelungs* employs a variety of means to characterize a stage prop. He specifies the location of Siegfried's sword on the stage, he illuminates it with light and he also makes it glitter in the clear musical tones of its leitmotif. Wagner's

---

13   [Editor's note: E. F. Burian (1904–1959), leading Czech avant-garde producer and director in the interwar and post-World War II Czech theatre; see the section with authors' biographies for further details.]

characters always make their entrance on stage not only as actors but also as leitmotifs. A character's gesture is repeated in the orchestra (in *The Mastersingers of Nuremberg*, Beckmesser's soreness from the beating he received is reflected in the limping music), and the magnificence of the costumes and scenery that characterizes the guests' arrival at Wartburg (in *Tannhäuser*) is also reinforced through the music. In every case, one could illustrate the principle of parallelism, which unifies many theatrical devices in the sense that it puts them to work concurrently.

This principle of *Gesamtkunstwerk* assumes that the intensity of theatrical effect, that is, the strength of the spectator's impression, is directly proportional to the *number of percepts* flooding the senses and mind of the spectator at any given moment. The task of the theatre artist (in the Wagnerian sense) is to shape the effects of the various theatrical devices in such a way as to produce impressions of the same impact.

Thus, this theory does not recognize changes of the theatrical sign, continually taking on the guise of different materials for its implementation. On the contrary, Wagner's theory of the *Gesamtkunstwerk* indirectly claims that there is no specific, unitary theatrical material but that there are many kinds of materials and that they must be kept separate and treated side by side. Accordingly, there is no art of the theatre as such, but instead music, the text, the actor, the scenery, props and lighting, which taken together collectively constitute the art of the theatre. Thus the art of the theatre cannot exist by itself but only as a collective manifestation of music, poetry, painting, architecture, acting, and so on. The art of the theatre manifests itself as a result of the sum of other arts.

When it comes to the spectator and to the psychology of perception, I believe that this theory is inadequate. The prime question is whether the spectator, in the act of perception, perceives acoustic and visual signs simultaneously and with the same intensity or whether he concentrates on one aspect only. In trying to answer this, we must also bear in mind that it is a matter of the perception of *artistic signs* and that this is a special case of perception. If the spectator has to concentrate mentally in order to grasp the meaning of a particular reality as a sign, one can certainly assume that he is also concentrating on percepts of a certain kind, percepts that are visual or acoustic. But even if this concentrated attention involved both visual and acoustic perception, it would certainly not even here be a question of the *sum* of impressions but rather of a special relation of one kind of percept to the other, of the *polarization of these percepts*.

We of course encounter spectators who visit a theatre to listen to the music or who go there to listen to the dramatist's text or to enjoy an actor's performance, and so on. However, even people without special interests find themselves, when in a theatre, listening for a while to the music alone or at another moment just focusing on the actor or at some other time being enchanted by the words of the dramatist. I would say that nearly all theatre-goers fall into this category. At the same time, however, the interest of the spectator does not pass from one device to another merely by chance but rather in a controlled fashion. It is enough to observe the members of the audience in a theatre in order to see how they turn their eyes to the same spot on the stage, how they all have the same interest in a single actor at one moment or an interest in observing the set at another. The psychology of the spectators' perception thus prevents us from accepting the assumptions of the Wagnerian theory of "the total work of art".

Moreover, this theory is contradicted by the development of the art of the theatre, which I have already spoken about and from which I have drawn examples. The art of the theatre has existed without music, there have been theatres without scenery, directors have produced theatre without actors, the *commedia dell'arte* was a theatre without authors and without what we would term a plot. Nevertheless, they offered theatrical performances that made spectators' spirits soar. If it were true that the art of the theatre is the sum of various arts (*Gesamtkunstwerk*), then for example no artistic performance whose sole device was the actor – that is, an actor without a theatre, words, music, scenery and so on – would be theatre. Yet the kind of mime that is expressed in an empty circus ring solely through the action of an actor must also be regarded as a theatre performance. There are numerous examples (such as the famous clowns Grock, Fratellini and others) showing that an actor's action is enough to captivate an audience.

I believe that the Wagnerian theory conceals rather than reveals the essence of the art of the theatre: it surrounds the art of the theatre with so many other arts that theatricality is watered down and vanishes. It cannot be found.

However, it is not our intention to revive the debate over *Gesamtkunstwerk*. I chose this matter merely as an example of the lack of clarity that arises as soon as we fail to understand or are unaware of that special nature of the theatre performance's material and devices that I have been speaking about. In addition to the debate over *Gesamtkunstwerk*, I could also mention other theories of theatricality that are similarly confused owing to their progenitors' inability or unwillingness to understand the special character of theatre material and their transferring too thoughtlessly the circumstances affecting literature, painting, music and other arts to the art of the theatre.

I commenced my study with a quotation from Zich and I should like to conclude by returning to Zich's views. It is worth noting that not even Zich, at the beginning of *The Aesthetics of Dramatic Art*, was able to provide a satisfactory definition of the art of the theatre. Although no adherent of *Gesamtkunstwerk,* he was nevertheless not bold enough to claim without reservation that dramatic art is a *"single* art and not a *combination* of several arts". According to Zich the specific character of theatrical unity is the *combination* of "two simultaneous, inseparable and clear-cut components that are *heterogeneous* – that is, visual (optical) components and audible (acoustic) components" (Zich 1931: 22).

However, even this "combination" does not prevent us from seeking and finding a *unity* in the art of the theatre, from declaring that it is a single, integral art. The binary character of the materials, that is, the visual and acoustic character of the theatrical devices, does not invalidate the unity of the essence of theatricality.

For on the stage the acoustic and the visual can change places with each other, and it may even happen that one of the components sinks below the threshold of the audience's conscious awareness. For example, the meaning of a dialogue one is listening to may block out an awareness of the percepts of the actors' gestures and appearance, the scenery, lighting and so on, or conversely it may happen that watching the acting makes it impossible to register acoustic percepts (words, music, murmuring and so forth).

It is worth noting, too, that the silent film was also once called visual *theatre* and that the radio play could be called acoustic *theatre*. So the specific nature of *theatricality* does not lie in a division of devices into those that are acoustic and those that are visual. The essence of theatricality must be sought elsewhere.

I believe that with our analysis of the variability of the theatrical sign we have accomplished a task that can enable us to test the soundness of many definitions of theatricality and see whether they apply to both old and new types of theatre, which have originated in various social structures, in various historical periods, under the influence of various playwrights and actors, as the result of many technical innovations, and so on. I am also of the opinion that we are restoring lustre to that old view of theatricality that sees its essence in *action*.

In the light of this solution, theatricality of character, theatricality of place and theatricality of plot will not appear to us as elements permanently separated from one another. The relationship of these three components of drama will not seem to us to be one of three *separate theatricalities* operating parallel to each other without touching one another and amounting to a "total theatricality" whose success intensifies in proportion to the number of autonomous arts participating in its structure. We recognize as untenable the notion of the "relative nonparticipation of the scenic image" in the theatrical whole, a notion that "could even maintain that the scenic image (dramatic place) is *not* a fundamental component of a dramatic work, since it can be reduced from extreme elaborateness down to the minimum of *mere space*, demarcated only architecturally" (Zich 1931: 45).

Action – as the essence of theatrical dramaticality – unifies for us word, actor, costume, scenery and music in the sense that we recognize them as different conductors of a single current that flows through them all, either passing from one to another or flowing through a combination of many. And while we are at this comparison, let us add that this current – that is, dramatic action – is not carried by the conductor that exerts the least resistance (dramatic action is not always concentrated in the actor's acting alone); instead, theatricality is frequently generated precisely through overcoming the resistance caused by some theatrical devices (special theatrical effects in which action is concentrated, for instance, solely in the words or in the actor's movements or in offstage sounds, and so on), in the same way that a tungsten filament glows because it is offering resistance to an electric current.

Of course it is possible to speak of the relative nonparticipation of place (that is, scenery and sets) in drama and in theatricality, but this nonparticipation should not be regarded as the constant property of *every theatrical place* but as the property of a *certain type of theatre*, a particular play, a particular directorial method, and so forth. The potential of a place for action, that is its theatricality, in the theatre of the Elizabethan dramatists consisted merely in changes indicated by signs hung on the stage: *a platform before the castle; the throne room; a chamber; a graveyard; a battlefield.* The theatrical action of place consisted solely in this disclosure of information. And in fact our theatres have not deviated from this method of indicating dramatic place, since it is basically the same (from the point of view of action as a dramatic element) whether a change of scene is indicated by a sign or by a costly set depicting *a platform, a throne room, a graveyard, a battlefield.*

Modern theatre begins the moment scenery is assessed according to the function it fulfils in actual theatrical action. When the Théâtre d'Art in the 1890s limited its scenery to "a backdrop and a few movable curtains", this is to be interpreted, from our viewpoint, as recognition of the real function of stage scenery in a play and drama whose theatricality and action are created *verbally* (Maeterlinck). If the German Shakespearean stage was limited to a Gothic arch or a column against a blue backdrop, this limitation was the result of an awareness that the stage set only participates in a Shakespearean play as the simplest scenic sign, used to inform the audience of a change of scene.

The new restraints in stage art brought by Russian Constructivism spring from the idea of the theatre performance, which is manifested by *the actors' movements* and everything that serves these movements: acrobatic props and furnishings, movable walls and floors, and so on.

From the viewpoint of dramatic action, the theatricality of music can be assessed solely according to the part it plays in the *dramatic action*. Thus, scenic musical forms are either *musical scenery* or *music-action*. All the difficulties that arise for the modern opera composer and for the theory of opera stem from an inability or incapacity to recognize their division, to define *music-action*.

The examples I have given show clearly that, for the unification of theatrical devices through the flow of theatrical action, there are no permanent laws or unchangeable rules. In the course of its autonomous development, which is a structural constituent of the development of all art, the theatre always foregrounds a different aspect of theatricality. For example, Maeterlinckian Symbolism foregrounds the *word* as the vehicle of theatrical action (Maeterlinck's *The Blind acts* through the dialogue of immobile actors conversing on stage), while Russian Constructivism *acts* through the choreographed and "biomechanical" movements of the actors.

Variability in the hierarchical scale of components of the art of the theatre corresponds to the variability of the theatrical sign. I have thrown light on both. In doing so, my aim has been to demonstrate the variability that makes stage art so multifarious and all-captivating but at the same time so elusive of definition. Its protean metamorphoses have sometimes even led to doubts as to its very existence. Existence as an autonomous art was granted to the dramatic text, to acting, to painting, to music – but not to "the art of the theatre". It was only a combination of separate arts. Theatre was unable to find either its core or its unity. I have shown that it has both, that it is one and many, like St Augustine's Triune God.

WORKS CITED

Bogatyrev, Petr (1940) *Lidové divadlo české a slovenské* [Czech and Slovak Folk Theatre], Prague: F. Borový and Národopisná společnost českoslovanská.

Brušák, Karel (2016 [1939]) "Signs in the Chinese Theatre", this reader, pp. 115–28.

Eisenstein, Sergei (2010) "An Unexpected Juncture" in *Selected Works. Volume 1: Writings, 1922–34*, trans. and ed. Richard Taylor, London and New York: I. B. Tauris & Co., pp. 115–22.

Kalvodová, Dana (1992) *Čínské divadlo* [Chinese Theatre], Prague: Panorama.

Zich, Otakar (1931) *Estetická dramatického umění: teoretická dramaturgie* [The Aesthetics of Dramatic Art: A Theoretical Dramaturgy]. Prague: Melantrich.

PEOPLE AND THINGS IN THE THEATRE

JIŘÍ VELTRUSKÝ

["Člověk a předmět na divadle" (1940) was first published in Czech in *Slovo a sloves-nost*, vol.6, no. 3, pp.153–59. It was translated into English by Paul L. Garvin as "Man and Object in the Theater" and published in Garvin, Paul L.(trans. and ed.) (1955) *A Prague School Reader on Esthetics, Literary Structure, and Style*, Washington, D.C.: Washington Linguistic Club, pp. 83–91.]

The basis of drama is action. Our daily life, of course, and its course, are also shaped by action, our own and that of other people. Action is the active relationship of a subject to some object; it is a teleological fact, governed by a purpose answering the needs of the subject. Therefore whenever an action occurs, our attention is turned to its purpose. The act itself is secondary to us: the important thing is whether it fulfils a given purpose. However, as soon as an act draws the attention of a perceiving subject to itself, its properties become signs. It then enters into our consciousness by means of signs and becomes meaning. It is well known that two people who were witnesses to the same event will often describe it entirely differently. This difference is caused by the fact that this event was reflected in two differently curved mirrors, that is, in two differently attuned consciousnesses; this caused certain signs to be reinforced and others to be suppressed. The properties of an action directed toward a practical objective are determined by this objective, irrespective of the perceiver, unless the objective of the action is communication.

In the theatre, however, action is an end in itself and it lacks an external practical purpose that might determine its properties. Here the action is geared towards being understood by the audience as a coherent semantic series. This is why it is formed of various signs that only become reflected as properties in the awareness of the audience; the properties of the action are thus pure meanings, just as its purpose is a semiological matter and not a matter of practical life. Action in the theatre differs, however, from action whose practical purpose is communication. Though the latter is also constructed of signs designed for the perceiving subject and its purpose, too, has only semiological value, its final purpose lies outside the action itself and not within it, as is the case in the theatre.

It follows from the teleological character of action that it is the result of the intent of a subject. However it is necessary to differentiate different senses of the concept of the subject. Most importantly there is the basic subject, who is the source of the intent; then there is the subject who is manifestly performing the action, who may be identical with the basic subject but may also be merely his instrument and thus only a partial subject. The borderline between them cannot of course be drawn exactly. Later we shall see that in the theatre the differentiation can go even further: precisely because action here is removed from a practical context and lacks an external purpose, the audience's awareness of the subject – that is, of the being actively performing the action – arises more from the course of events itself than from anywhere else.

In the period when theorists only had in mind the realist theatre, the view arose that the only possible subject was a human being, just as in everyday life. All other components were considered mere instruments or objects of human action. The development of the modern theatre and increasing familiarity with the theatre of non-European cultural spheres, however, led to this view being demolished; subsequently it has been shown that it is not wholly true even for the realist theatre. The purpose of this study is to show that the existence of the subject in the theatre is dependent on the participation of some particular component in the action and not on its actual spontaneity, so that even a lifeless thing may be perceived as the active subject and a living human being may be perceived as an element completely without will.

FROM ACTOR TO THING

The most common example of the subject in the drama is the *stage figure.*

The stage figure is the dynamic unity of a whole set of signs, whose vehicle may be the actor's body, voice, movements, but also various things, from parts of the costume to the set. What is important, however, is that the actor draws their meanings to himself, and to such an extent that through his action he can replace all the carriers of the signs; this can be demonstrated through the example of the Chinese theatre:

> Through his performance the actor must convey all those actions for which the scene in the Chinese theatre provides no suitable material basis. Drawing on the appropriate sequence of conventional movements, the actor performs such actions as surmounting imaginary obstacles, climbing imaginary stairs, stepping over a high threshold, opening a door. (Brušák 2016 [1939]: 123)

The question arises as to the means available to the actor for uniting all these meanings through his action. On the whole the answer is very simple: all that is on the stage is a sign.

However, neither a theatre costume nor a set representing a house nor the gestures of actors have as many constitutive signs as a real house or a real item of clothing would have. On the stage, costumes and scenery are usually limited to one, two or three signs. The theatre only uses those signs of costumes and structures that are necessary for the given dramatic situation. (Bogatyrev 2016 [1938]: 100)

The actor's body, on the other hand, enters into the dramatic situation with all of its properties. Quite understandably, a living human being cannot shed some of them and retain only those he needs for the given situation. This is why not all the components of the actor's performance are purposive; some of them are simply determined by physiological necessity (for instance, various automatic reflexes). The spectator of course understands even these non-purposive components of the actor's performance as signs. This is what makes the stage figure more complex and richer – we are tempted to say more concrete – as compared to the other carriers of signs. In addition to its sign character it also has the character of reality. And the latter is precisely the force that attracts all the meanings towards the actor.

The more complex the actions of the stage figure, the greater the number not only of its purposive signs, but also, and this is important here, of those that are non-purposive, so that the realness of the figure comes to the fore. A figure whose actions are less complex is of course more schematic. In this way a hierarchy of parts is created. The figure at the peak of this hierarchy, the lead, attracts most of the attention of the audience and only at times allows room for attention to be given to the supporting cast. By providing a stimulus to action, the lead also affects the performances of the rest of the cast, at times even having a direct bearing on them. The spectator may still perceive the other figures as active subjects, but their subordination is evident. Usually, however, situations also arise in the course of the play when someone other than the lead becomes the main pillar of the action. In some structures[1] even in these situations the hierarchy of parts remains unaffected; in others the hierarchy may regroup from situation to situation. Quite definitely, however, all of the figures in the play, from the lead to the smallest bit part, form an absolutely coherent line according to their varying degrees of activity, the cohesion of which is maintained precisely by their interaction.

If we follow this line, we can see that it is not even possible to establish a borderline beyond which the action of a figure ceases to be perceived as spontaneous. Without any break, the line leads to figures whose actions are

---

1   [Editor's note: Veltruský uses the word "structure" to mean the whole set of elements and conventions making up the distinctive nature of theatre and theatrical production in a particular historical era or particular culture.]

limited to a few stereotypical patterns of behaviour repeated with minute differences. Such figures carry very few signs beyond those absolutely needed for the given situation. They are quite schematic; the sense that they are real is very weak. For the spectator, such a figure is often linked automatically to a certain action. Thus, for instance, it may happen that the stage represents a sitting room; as soon as a certain servant enters we know that it is to announce the arrival of some visitor. We shall see later that this connection to a certain action is characteristic of *props.* And indeed, such figures appear to the spectator to be more like props than like active performers. We could see human props in E. F. Burian's production of V. K. Klicpera's comedy *Everybody Does His Bit for His Country* [Každý něco pro vlast]: they were the silent figures of servants.[2] Such figures can be found in the theatre in great numbers and are nothing unusual.

Human props do not, however, end the line that begins with the stage figure. The action may fall to "zero level"; the figure then becomes a part of the *set.* Soldiers flanking the entrance to a building, for instance, are examples of this. They serve to indicate that the building is a military barracks. Naturally, humans as parts of the set can no longer in any way be considered active performers. Their realness is likewise reduced to the "zero level", since their constituent signs are limited to the minimum. If we consider what the carrier of these signs is, we see that it is usually their carriage, physique, makeup and costume. It follows, then, that people in these roles can be replaced by lifeless dummies. Thus people as parts of the set form a *transition between the human sphere and that of things.* They are, however, not the only bridge between these two spheres. Otakar Zich, for instance, points out that between the makeup, which is still part of the organic body of the actor, and the costume, which is not part of his body, there are other things such as wigs that we cannot definitely assign to one or the other sphere (Zich 1931: 136 ff). The costume, incidentally, although not part of the physical body, merges with it to a considerable extent. Thus where individual human actions are concerned it is not possible to decide precisely to what extent they are predetermined by the properties of the body, and to what extent by those of the clothing. For

there is a form of gesture and movement that is not merely appropriate to each style of dress, but really conditioned by it. The extravagant use of the arms in the eighteenth

---

2   [Editor's note: E. F Burian (1904–1959), leading Czech avant-garde producer and director in the interwar and post-World War II Czech theatre; see the section with authors' biographies for further details. Václav Kliment Klicpera (1792–1859), pioneering Czech author and playwright in the period of the Czech National Revival. Klicpera wrote *Everybody Does His Bit for His Country* [Každý něco pro vlast] (c. 1829) as a comedy of manners set in an anonymous Czech village. Burian's adapted staging opened in 1937.]

century, for instance, was the necessary result of the large hoop, and the solemn dignity of Burleigh owed as much to his ruff as to his reason. (Wilde 1997: 1036)

As can be seen, the sphere of the living human being and that of the lifeless thing are intertwined, and no exact borderline can be drawn between them. The sequence beginning with the stage figure thus moves without interruption into the sphere of things.

FROM THING TO ACTOR

The human being as part of the set has taken us into the sphere of the *set* in general. The general purpose of the set is "to define effectively the characters and the place of the action" (Zich 1931: 232). Its sphere too is differentiated internally. The lowest level is that of the painted set, which is a pure sign. A three-dimensional set is richer by having real depth, and is thus one step closer to the actual thing that it stands for. On the same level with three-dimensional sets are dummies replacing human parts of the set. Finally, many real things may be part of the set, such as chairs, vases, and so on. They are on the same level with human beings as parts of the set.

The *costume* shares many similar properties with the set. Its purpose too is to convey the distinguishing features of characters and settings. Its main difference from the set is that the latter mainly characterizes the setting, whereas the costume chiefly characterizes the figures. The costume is on the same level as three-dimensional sets and real things that are connected with the set.

The fact that the parts of the set do not act in any evident way might give rise to the impression that the set lies outside the action and has no effect on its course. In that case, it would also constitute a self-contained and clearly delimited sphere. But such an impression would be completely erroneous. It is enough to point out, for instance, how a dispute between two characters when the set represents an inn will take an entirely different course from a dispute between the same two characters in a royal palace. Even if the evident action of the set is at the zero level, it still plays a part in determining the course of the action. That is also why it cannot be delimited as a closed sphere, nor can a point be distinguished at which things begin to take a visible part in the action and become *props*. It often seems that a particular thing is part of the set or costume in one situation, and in the next becomes a prop. In reality, however, its function is determined by the antinomy of two opposing forces contained within it – the dynamic forces of action and the static forces of characterization. Their relationship is not stable: in certain situations one predominates, in others the other, sometimes they are in balance. Let us, for instance, take a *sword* in the following situations:

1. Figure A with a sword. The sword here is part of the costume and shows the wearer's noble or military status. The characterizing force of the sword here clearly outweighs its action force, which is pushed completely into the background.

2. Figure B insults figure A, draws his sword and stabs B to death. Here, in the context of a certain action, the action force of the sword suddenly comes completely to the fore: it becomes a prop and takes part in the action as an instrument of the character. The characterizing force is reduced, but not completely eliminated, because in the following situation it comes immediately into play.

3. Figure A flees holding a bloody sword. The sword here is a sign of murder, but at the same time is closely connected with the flight, that is, with the action. Here both forces of the thing are in balance.

The prop is usually called a passive instrument of the actor's active action. This does not, however, do full justice to its nature. The prop is not always passive. It has a force (which we have termed the action force) that attracts a certain action. As soon as a certain prop appears on the stage, this force within it induces in us the expectation of a certain action. It is so closely linked to this action that its use for another purpose is perceived as a scenic metonymy. This link is shown even more clearly in the case of what are termed *mimed props*. What is a mimed prop? The actor performs an action for which a certain prop is usually required, but without using any props; the spectator feels its presence although in reality it is not present. For example, there is this scene from Vsevolod Meyerhold's production of Alexander Ostrovsky's *The Forest*:

> ... the comedian gives a virtuoso mime performance. He sits down on the step, holding a rod, and pretends to be casting into the wings to the left; there is of course no line on the rod... the comic actor "catches a fish", unhooks it – although he has nothing in his hand – grabs for it on the ground, finally puts it away. (Tille 1929: 40)

An analogous procedure can be found in everyday life – gestures imitating the use of a certain object, in order to designate it. For example, such gestures are used by foreigners when, for instance, they ask for a drink by imitating drinking movements. In the theatre, of course, the purpose is different.

The link between a prop and a certain action is demonstrated in the opposite way *when the subject is not present in the play*. This occurs when there is no actor on stage. Even then, the action does not stop. The action force of the thing comes to the fore in all its strength. The things on the stage, including perhaps their mechanical movements, for example that of the pendulum of a clock, exploit our awareness of the uninterrupted nature of the course of events and evoke in us a sense of action. Without any intervention on the part of the actor, the props shape the action. They are no longer instruments of the actor: we view them as spontaneous subjects equivalent to the stage figure. For this process to occur, one condition must be met: the prop must not be a mere suggestion of the thing to which it is linked by a factual relationship, because only if it preserves its real character can it radiate its action force and suggest action to the spectator. If Honzl claims that "tables may become beings whom we hate more passionately than our enemies" (Honzl 1937: 218), then this principle is certainly connected to his statement that

> Stockmann's torn coat is one of those things that were the forte of the realist theatre and the naturalist stage. For them alone, the Moscow Art Theatre will be dear to us, for they built real doors that squeaked, they set out real furniture and a genuine billiard table with two white balls and one black, and Andrei Sergeyevich Prozorov pushed a real pram about the stage. Genuine things, a table, a coat, a tear, the distant sounds of the marching band, are perhaps the only legacy of theirs that we shall be able to adopt. (Honzl 1937: 56)

The absence of the subject in the play, however, is not the only mode of *personification*. And what exactly is personification? It is

> a force, indefinite but powerful, that reinforces the impression of the spontaneity of the action by emphasizing the participation of the active subject. In terms of spontaneity, action in general can be divided into three categories. At the lowest level there is natural mechanical action, lacking in any kind of spontaneity, its course determined by pre-existing laws that allow no exceptions; one step higher are those kinds of behaviour of living beings which, though not subject to laws that allow no exceptions, are directed by habit and whose course is thus predictable (for instance, our daily activities when getting up, eating, going to sleep, and many of our professional activities); finally the third group includes action in the proper sense of the word, based on the unrestricted initiative of the subject and therefore unpredictable, different in each case. The purpose of personification is to raise the first two levels of action to the third. This does not mean that things have to be "turned into persons" in the true sense of the word, as is the case, for instance, in the fable: that is merely a special case of personification [for instance, in Maeterlinck's *The Blue Bird* – J. V.]. It is enough if things that in reality are passive objects of the action behave as active subjects, even while retaining their usual shape. (Mukařovský 1938: 7)

Such personification occurs, for instance, in Reinhardt's production of August Strindberg's *The Pelican*. The scene after the burial of the husband, in which his wife, who has caused his death, is on stage, is described by Tille as follows:

The overall impression is as though the shadow of the dead man were pacing the house; the woman is constantly afraid of being alone, the door opened by the wind frightens her. ... The only room used in all three acts, filled to overflowing with dark furniture, is plunged in gloom. Throughout all three acts, with only brief interruptions, the wind whistles and whines behind the stage, rattling the open window and swaying the white curtains, becoming a strong draft whenever the door opens and blowing the papers from the desk, where the book leaves flutter and the lamp flame flickers. At first this naturalistic virtuosity makes a terrifying impression, especially when the leaves of the open door swing mysteriously to no purpose whenever the script requires it. (Tille 1917: 170)

Another, less evident, personification is found in the Japanese drama *Terakoya; or, The Village School*, by Takeda Izumo. Genzo, a teacher, is hiding the young son of the exiled minister Sugawara in his house. Chiyo has brought her child to school, a boy who is the exact likeness of the minister's son. She leaves, and soon after the retainers of the new ruler arrive and demand the boy's head. The teacher goes behind the stage and kills Chiyo's son. The retainers exit. Suddenly Chiyo returns.

Chiyo (*visibly excited*). Oh, is that you, Takebe Genzo, esteemed teacher? Today I brought my little son to you. Where is he? He hasn't by any chance given you trouble?
Genzo. Oh no – he's back there... in the back room... playing with the others. Do you want to see him... Perhaps you want to take him home?
Chiyo. Yes, bring him in please... I want to take him home...
Genzo (*stands up*). He'll be right here. Come in please...
(*Chiyo turns to the rear door; behind her back Genzo pulls out his sword and raises his arm to strike her a terrible blow, but as though warned by something Chiyo turns around and avoids the blow. Jumping quickly between the desks, she seizes her son's box and uses it to ward off another blow from Genzo.*)
Chiyo. Stop! Stop!
Genzo (*taking another swing*). Devilish thing!
(*The blow shatters the box, scattering a little white garment, pieces of paper with prayers written on them, a small burial flag, and some other small things used in burials.*)
Genzo (*horrified*). In the devil's name, what is this?
(*He lowers the arm holding the sword.*) (Izumo 1911: 37–38)[3]

The situation gives the impression that it is a spontaneous intervention of the props that saves Chiyo's life.

---

3   [Editor's note: We are translating into English from a Czech translation by František Sekanina and Emanuel Lešehrad.]

THE RELATIONSHIP BETWEEN PEOPLE AND THINGS

We have followed the different degrees of participation in the action by the various components, degrees that differ from one another by the extent to which they are active. It has been shown that the transition between them is quite gradual, so that they cannot be considered self-contained spheres. The function of each component in the individual situations (and in the drama as a whole) is the result of the constant tension between activity and passivity in terms of the action, which manifests itself in a constant flow back and forth between the individual components, people and things. It is therefore impossible to draw a line between subject and object, since each component is potentially either. We have seen various examples of how things and people can change places, how a person can become a thing and a thing a living being. So we cannot speak of two mutually delimited spheres; the relationship between people and things in the theatre can be characterized as a *dialectic antinomy*. We have seen in the above examples that the dialectic tension between people and things occurs in the most varied structures and is thus not the exclusive property of the modern theatre. In some structures, of course, it is emphasized, and in others reduced to the minimum.

The view that in the theatre people are exclusively the active subject and things the passive object or an instrument of the action arose, as has already been stated, at a time when theorists had in mind only the realist theatre. But not even in the realist theatre was the fluctuation between humans and things eliminated completely: it was only suppressed to such an extent that it was easy to make the mistake we have spoken of. The realist theatre at-tempted (although never successfully) to be a reflection of reality not only in its individual components but also in their linkage. And in daily life we are of course used to differentiating very precisely between people and things when it comes to spontaneous activity – but only in terms of our present-day noetic perspective as shaped by civilized life. From other perspectives, for instance the mythical world views of primitive peoples or children, personification and the linkage between people and things play a very important role indeed. Although civilization is progress as compared to the primitive way of life, it cannot be denied that owing to a wide range of varied conventions its forms so far have broken the direct relationship between man and his environment. Through the example of the absence of the subject in the play we have seen how these particular conventions can be used to link together individual realities in an unconventional way. We are perhaps not exaggerating if we claim that this is one of the most important social objectives of the theatre. This is precisely where the theatre can point to new ways of understanding the world.

WORKS CITED

Bogatyrev, Petr (2016 [1938]) "Theatrical Signs", this reader, pp. 99–114.

Brušák, Karel (2016 [1939]) "Signs in the Chinese Theatre", this reader, pp. 115–28.

Honzl, Jindřich (1937) *Sláva a bída divadel: režisérův zápisník* [The Glory and the Misery of The-atres: A Director's Notebook], Prague: Družstevní práce.

Izumo, Takeda (1911) *Terakoya čili Vesnická škola* [Terakoya; or, The Village School] in Takeda Izumo and Yamada Kakashi, *Dvě japonská dramata* [Two Japanese Dramas], trans. František Sekanina and Emanuel Lešehrad, Prague: Alois Hynek, pp. 1–47.

Mukařovský, Jan (1938) "Semantický rozbor básnického díla" [A Semantic Analysis of a Work of Poetry], *Slovo a slovesnost*, vol. 4, no. 1, pp. 1–15.

Tille, Václav (1917) *Divadelní vzpomínky* [Memories of the Theatre], Prague: B. Kočí.

— (1929) *Moskva v listopadu* [Moscow in November], Prague: Aventinum.

Wilde, Oscar (1997) "The Truth of Masks: A Note on Illusion" in *Collected Works of Oscar Wilde*, Ware: Wordsworth, pp. 1017–37.

Zich, Otakar (1931) *Estetika dramatického umění: teoretická dramaturgie* [The Aesthetics of Dra-matic Art: A Theoretical Dramaturgy], Prague: Melantrich.

THE HIERARCHY OF THEATRICAL DEVICES

JINDŘICH HONZL

["Hierarchie divadelních prostředků" (1943) was published in *Slovo a Slovesnost*, vol. 9, pp. 187–93. The English translation by Susan Larson was published under the title "The Hierarchy of Dramatic Devices" in Matejka, Ladislav and Titunik, Irwin R. (eds) (1976) *Semiotics of Art: Prague School Contributions*, Cambridge, Mass.: The M.I.T Press, pp. 118–27.]

It has become commonplace – and this will continue to be the case – for ancient Greek plays to appear on the stage of the modern theatre stripped of their essence, distorted in terms of the principal device through which this was expressed: the relationship between the ancient Greek theatre and the poet's words. The test of how well the essential nature of ancient Greek drama is reflected when it comes to staging is the way in which the hierarchy of theatrical means of expression is composed. Every accommodation of the language of ancient Greek plays to the patterns and practices that shape dialogue in the contemporary play inevitably destroys their integrity and balance. What is termed action in the modern play, what today's directors consider stage action, is changing fundamentally: in the modern play and modern theatre not only have the means of expression changed (song, music and dance have acquired a different function, the chorus has been abandoned, the acting style has been transformed) but so have their mutual relationships. Every handbook on the art of drama, following Aristotle, says that Greek tragedy emerged from the Dionysian dithyramb and the innovation made by Aeschylus when he added a second reciter (a second actor) to the chorus and single reciter. Aeschylus "diminished the importance of the Chorus, and assigned the leading part to the dialogue" (Aristotle 2009: 1.4). The introduction of new devices (for example, the second actor) did not in itself transform the dithyramb into drama. These new devices paved the way leading to drama, but the dithyramb only set out along this path when the forefather of tragedy *assigned the leading part to dialogue*. The supremacy of *dialogue* over *narration* meant the supremacy of *action* over *reported information* and it meant directing the original and familiar devices towards a new end. But with this new end the traditional devices also acquired a new meaning. Although the poetic devices taken over by drama from the dithyramb appeared to remain unchanged, they altered their essential nature by assuming new functions. And even though Aeschylus had to shift the emphasis from the chorus (the choral chant) to dialogue in order to establish the foundations for the development of dramatic poetry, the chorus still remained an indispensable component of ancient Greek plays. And it was the chorus that preserved most clearly the traces of drama's dithyrambic origin. But even though we recognize the dithyramb in choral passages, the shift in emphasis to *action* is a fundamental shift of function.

> My stave the faltering tread of leaden feet sustains;
> My voice is plaintive like the aged swan's.
> What am I but the merest murmuring of feeble lips,
> The sheerest phantom of a dream? (Euripides: *Heracles Mad*)[1]

This lyrical sigh of the chorus, which both informs and describes ("My stave the faltering tread of leaden feet sustains"), is a component of the play by virtue of its function. The tragic dramatist uses this choral dithyrambic part, which is incorporated into the story-line and conforms to the specific practice of staging tragedy in Athens, as a device for indicating what is being performed by the actors. In choosing his devices, the ancient Greek dramatist enjoyed a freedom similar to that exercised by modern dramatists, who are unwilling to let anything on the stage go unnoticed and who make everything that is perceptible to the audience a vehicle for their thoughts and ideas. Though for the ancient Greek poet the verbal expression of the dithyramb was fixed and predetermined by the dithyrambic tradition, this did not preclude the option of other functions and applications. A modern dramatist would wonder whether it is necessary to verbally express the "faltering tread of leaden feet" of old men walking with the support of staves, when this is in fact the action being performed by the actors, which the audience can see on the stage. In the specific context of the ancient Greek stage and acting style, and owing to the particular compositional demands of tragedy, it was necessary to provide the audience with an auditory percept of what was in essence a visual percept. But the modern dramatist, too, is quite willing to employ auditory deixis (for this is all we are talking about here) for a visual percept when he considers it necessary. So on the modern stage an actress is a "devastating beauty" only because the dramatist indicates this in the dialogue, and we observe "an enigmatic quality in the way she walks" only because the dramatic text states that this is so. It is equally true of both the ancient

---

1   [Editor's note: Honzl used a 1924 translation of *Heracles Mad* by the Classical philologist and Anglicist Klára Pražáková. The excerpts in this edition have been translated into English from the Czech, keeping Pražáková's alterations to the original whenever this was necessary for Honzl's argument.]

Greek and the modern stage that for the audience the only things that exist on the stage are those that are indicated by the action of the dramatist or the action of those involved in the production. Moreover, only those things exist that the audience's interpretative activity apprehends under the influence of the dramatic action. Everything else that might be seen on the stage or heard from it remains "below the threshold" of the audience's awareness. *It is not there, it does not exist!* The audience's mental capacity to focus its attention on some particular thing also means the possibility of not becoming aware of anything that lies beyond it – of being blind to the cheap costume of an actress whose neck is looped round with gaudy strands glittering gold, red and blue on her young bosom and conjuring up the figure of Semiramis or Cleopatra; of being blind to the reality of a torn peasant shirt and focusing all one's visual capacities instead on its dazzling whiteness, which transforms anyone attired in it into a messenger from heaven, into the Archangel Gabriel or any other equally benign and powerful member of the heavenly host. Being blind in this way is not due to some deficiency in the ordinary spectator or a sign of naiveté, but a mark of mental concentration, of an intense focusing of attention, along lines determined by the play and by the spectator's own imaginative capacity for interpretation. We must therefore regard the ability to concentrate one's attention and the ability to exclude elements from it as polar attributes of a single perceptual capacity on the part of the spectator. From the standpoint of the theatre and the dramatist, this particular state of attention and perception is normal and necessary: it is implied in all the basic types of performance and play, whether in an ancient Greek amphitheatre or on the stage of a village theatre. On the contrary, the quality assumed in the spectator by the realist theatre of the nineteenth century – an *incapacity to see and interpret reality* through the prism of the imagination, an incapacity whose implication for production was the need to create *stark* reality – only reality, whole and complete (a need that was doomed to fail inasmuch as it was a task beyond human capacity and the capabilities of the stage) – this quality is one of non-theatrical perception. The dramatist's verbal deixis – employed and cultivated in particular by the ancient Greek play, whose dithyrambic origin led to the lyrical and narrative word becoming a device of dramatic action – is a semantic filter that enables the dramatist to create an image of the world and of people based on the limited repertoire of things and the few artificial phenomena that the ancient Greek actor and ancient Greek stage technology were able to offer. The actor's frozen mask of tragic grief and the fixed structure of the royal palace on stage are changed dramatically by the word, which – like a sun at the centre of the poet's universe – either illuminates the stage, actors and events or hides them in the shadows of darkness. This semantic filter, which blocks the emergence of images the dramatist considers undesirable, transforms the contours of this reality, thus creating the image of the individual and his deeds in the play. Action and behaviour only become visible on the ancient Greek stage through verbal reference to them.

> Do not let your limbs grow weary,
> Like an overburdened horse, climbing a rocky hill,
> Trying to pull some heavy cart!
> Whose foot is feeble, let him hold
> Another by the robe or by the hand.
> Let the old give help to the old. (Euripides: *Heracles Mad*)

This second excerpt from *Heracles Mad* offers an example of the bidirectional alternation of the dithyramb and the drama. If the first excerpt, in and of itself, can be considered a lyrico-narrative dithyramb transformed into dramatic action through functional incorporation into the entirety of the tragedy, the second excerpt – again, in and of itself – takes the shape of a dramatic apostrophe, that is a part of the stage dialogue, but one that plays the role of narrative deixis in the drama. Were it not for the use of the imperative, the entire excerpt would belong within parentheses as part of the "stage directions" or form part of the *description* of an action ascribed to the actor by the dramatist. Yet even without parentheses, the words of the chorus remain *reported information* on the actors' action. But within the entirety of the ancient Greek play, which also means within the entirety of its production on stage, the words acquire dramatic justification through *verbal deixis with reference to action on the stage*, a type of deixis that served as the basic method of composition for Aeschylus, Sophocles and Euripides.

It was not action itself that was dramatic for the Greek dramatist. A turn of events or action on stage only becomes dramatic through the poet's verbal reference; in the ancient Greek play this was an essential prerequisite for awareness and interpretation on the part of the audience.

> Behold him: see how at the start he tosses his head about wildly,
> And rolls his frenzied eyes without a word.
> Nor can he control his panting breath, but like a bull about to charge
> He bellows fearfully, calling on the deathly spirits of Tartarus. (Euripides: *Heracles Mad*)

This is how Euripides has the goddess Lyssa describe Heracles as he leaves his home in a state of madness.

If this passage in Euripides' play were staged in the manner that has now become customary here, every effort would be exerted to ensure that the actor playing Heracles exhibited the changes that the author ascribes to him. An attempt would be made to enable the audience to see the tossing of the head, the fiercely rolling eyes, the laboured breathing and snorting – the actor might even try to produce a fearful bellow that would rock the stage and the whole theatre. We have witnessed stagings here that have interpreted the function of the verbal expression of the ancient Greek dramatist by actually having the actor act out on the stage reported information about events, changes and actions by other actors in such a way that they completely disrupted the unity of the text, chopping it up with the shouts, roars, hisses and facial expressions of the realistic and expressionistic styles of acting, or by the use of stage machinery and lighting and sound effects. Such stagings were clear proof that the hierarchical order of theatrical devices in the ancient Greek play remained a mystery and that the difference in this respect between ancient Greek and contemporary drama and theatre had not been grasped. The poem (which is what ancient Greek tragedy always was) was transformed from dithyramb into drama through a focusing on what Aristotle characterised as "action, not [mere] narration". But the devices of this "action" remained within the domain of the dithyramb, and the word retained its dominance within the hierarchy of devices. It was through the word that the dramatic action unfolded and changes in situations were revealed. In this way, it was possible for the word in the ancient Greek play to become a device that we in some cases regard as action on the part of the actor and at other times as a change of setting. It is precisely this mobility of the theatrical sign that enables the word to become actor or setting, to assume the functions of other poetic theatrical devices.

The Greek poet's words did not refer to what was being performed or what was visible on the stage. He did not describe stage action – that is, he did not duplicate it in words. The deixes we have spoken about were not meant to draw a parallel between reality and reported information about it. Duplication that seeks to achieve as close a parallel as possible in fact diminishes the impression precisely because it never achieves an exact parallel. Imperfections in parallelism are more disturbing than complete disagreement or total contrast. Reality on its own would have a more forceful impact on the audience than it would if accompanied by some incomplete or imperfectly parallel verbal element – just as the word itself evokes a mental impression more intensively than reality related to the word in some distorted fashion. Greek theatre did not deal in parallels, but in a polarity of impressions. Hence the ancient Greek actor's immobile mask with its unchanging face was a fitting accompaniment for Euripides' text, with its description of rolling eyes, frenzied looks, laboured breathing and changes in facial expression as manifestations of Heracles' murderous frenzy. The pleasure of theatrical perception is always based on the discrepancy between a mental impression and reality. This discrepancy is a prerequisite. It is not a result, but rather a *synthesis* of the opposition. Theatrical perception occurs when the discrepancy is overcome, when the opposition of the mental impression and reality is synthesized in the spectator's act of interpretation, which transforms both the reality and the mental impression in a flash of emotionally charged vision.[2] Just as Euripides refers to what is *not* there in the actor, Aeschylus, for example, refers to what is *not* there on the stage but nevertheless present in the mental impressions of the audience, mesmerized by the poet's words:

Prometheus. The time has passed for words: now deeds.
Ah! The earth trembles.
A rumble of thunder resounds from the sea
And fiery flashes leap throughout the sky.
Dust swirls in the raging tempests.
Winds battle winds.
Sea and sky have merged together
And all this terror, sent by Zeus, comes upon me.
O holy Mother, O holy Ethor,
Who sends light into the world,
See how I am wronged! (Aeschylus: *Prometheus Bound*)

The poet's reference to what is *not* on the stage can be called *phantasm-oriented deixis*, since it refers to a stage action that is realized solely in the audience's imagination.

That this phantasm-oriented deixis is one of the fundamental features of the Greek drama can be seen from the fact that deeds of supreme horror in

---

2   Limiting our critical inquiry to examples from Greek tragedy does not imply that different laws of theatrical creation and perception are to be found in other periods in the course of development of the theatre. On the contrary, we are aware that our proposition could be demonstrated equally well by medieval plays (for example mystery plays), by the Symbolist theatre at the turn of the twentieth century or by the theatre of other periods and other theatre movements.

   To prove that the medieval actor did not seek parallelism of the verbal message and his expression, it is enough to quote from an essay by Wolfgang Golther: "Every player steps to the centre [of the stage], turns to all sides, even to the rear of the stage where Christ stands… [During the course of the play] the movements are free and measured and they *occur during the pauses, whereas the actor stands still when singing and speaking*" (Golther 1926: 100 – emphasis J. H.).

   There is no need to offer examples of the Symbolist theatre. They are, I trust, sufficiently familiar. Indeed the very labelling of the Symbolist theatre as "*static theatre*" substantiates the thesis regarding a conscious deployment of theatrical devices involving the deliberate restriction of movement and facial expression on the part of the actor.

   And lastly, to prove that even theatre based on the unity and integrity of the actor's style achieved its best results from the dazzling polarity of the opposition between the mental impression evoked by the text and the actor's performance, one can invoke the work of the best director of the realist theatre and his method. The specific term he coined for describing the disparity between the verbal message and the actor's performance – to act out the subtext – shows that this disparity was viewed as one of the bases of the method of expression of the realist theatre. Thus our findings about the essence of theatrical perception, which we view as a synthesis of the opposition between the mental impression evoked by the word and the stage reality as expressed by the actor or the stage scenery, are a constant law of theatrical creativity and perception.

tragedy do not, as a rule, take place on the stage but are evoked by deixis or represented by auditory signs (calling offstage). Agamemnon's murder and the slaying of Aegisthus and Clytemnestra (in Aeschylus's *Oresteia*) are "hidden" in this manner from the view of the audience. Sophocles' self-blinding Oedipus (*Oedipus Rex*) and his Haemon (*Antigone*); Euripides' Heracles, slaying his own children, and Phaedra (*Hippolytus*) – all of them, too, "act" through the word, through the lamentations of the chorus telling us of their deaths. This of course accords with Greek attitudes and morals, but that is not the only point here.

Actions realized on stage before the audience have a multiplicity of meanings. The tragedy, comedy or meaningless indifference of a particular deed, no matter how horrible or pointless, is not an inherent aspect of its existence, an objective and fixed quality, but rather a matter of subjective interpretation. The audience witnessing Shylock as he sharpens a knife on the sole of his shoe in order to cut a pound of flesh from Antonio's body "nearest his heart", bursts out laughing at the sight of Shylock's bloodthirsty preparations and Antonio's anxiety. Shakespeare's characters did not exclude contradictory interpretations on the part of the audience. Greek drama did. All classicising periods in the evolution of the theatre have concurred with ancient Greek drama in this respect. When a tragedy is performed, nothing but a tragic interpretation of stage reality is acceptable. In a tragedy like this, the actions do not matter: the author sites the actions themselves outside what can be seen on the stage or in such a way as to be hidden from the audience. The actions are replaced by verbal *commentary*, for this, like all acts of naming, is no longer a reality with multiple meanings but instead belongs within a domain of *semantic* fields and *evaluative* systems rigorously differentiated according to a set of poetic, ethical and aesthetic norms.

Acting – and especially, perhaps, acting in the ancient Greek theatre – is a composition made up of artificial vocal and gestural signs. No doubt the actors' techniques were also differentiated depending on whether they were used in tragedy or comedy. But the fact that the Greek dramatist prioritizes the word over other devices in connection with some stage action or another is evidence of the hierarchical superiority of the word, which is employed because it directs the mental impression more strictly and more explicitly to the sphere of tragedy.

It might seem that the aim of our explication has been to do away with the conceptual distinction between "action" and "narration", and that we are trying to construe something that is a narrative report as being an action-focused dramatic element. Not at all. We know that in Greek drama, and in Euripides' plays in particular, plain narration is a frequent compositional device. But that is not the point here. Our aim is to demonstrate that reported information – while still remaining reported information – may become dramatic action when we view it from within the play, from the point of view of the play as a whole, when we keep in mind the specific hierarchy of theatrical devices, *both those relating to language and those relating to the stage*. It is this mobility of the theatrical sign (see Honzl 2016 [1940]) that enables the dramatic text to be connected with the stage realization (in both the positive and the negative sense) in ancient Greek tragedy and leads to our faulty understanding of the function of the verbal and scenic devices when we forcibly separate into two structures what originally formed a single structure. If we do not wish to find ourselves caught up in meaningless theoretical schemes and if we do not wish to use words stripped of reality by abstract deductions, we must link Aristotle with the Greek dramatists in order to grasp the real meaning of what they considered "action, not [mere] narration". A terminological schema of the theory of drama and theatre is not a reality on its own; theory and practice mutually influence and determine each other. Definitions can only be instructive when we have in mind a particular instance of artistic practice.

We wish to conclude this critical analysis by pointing to the fact that contemporary stagings of ancient Greek plays will not be more effective or achieve greater dramaticality through forcible destruction of the given hierarchy of the devices of stage action or by its replacement with today's hierarchy. This will only be achieved by striving to grasp the point of the original hierarchy in such a way that the poem – which is what Greek tragedy will always remain – remains the primary consideration of every staging.

WORKS CITED

Aristotle (2009) *Poetics*, trans. S. H. Butcher, *The Internet Classics Archive*, M.I.T, Web, <http://classics .mit.edu/Aristotle/poetics.html>.

Golther, Wolfgang (1926) "Der Schauspieler im Mittelalter" [The Actor in the Middle Ages] in Geissler, Ewald (ed.) *Der Schauspieler* [The Actor], Berlin: Bühnenvolksbundverlag, pp. 92–104.

Honzl, Jindřich (2016 [1940]) "The Mobility of the Theatrical Sign", this reader, pp. 129–46.

III FIGURES AND PLAY

This section includes early attempts to approach acting from a structuralist perspective. The earliest (such as Petr Bogatyrev's writings on Charlie Chaplin from 1923) are still strongly rooted in Russian Formalism. It is significant how much space is devoted to film acting, especially to Chaplin. Film acting in silent film is evidently highly suited to a sign-oriented approach, as it is easy to divide into segments and sequences. On the other hand, comparing Chaplin's methods with traditional artistic genres (such as *commedia dell'arte*) helps to acknowledge Chaplin's film as art. This strong focus on Chaplin is a good example of the appreciation of popular art by members of the Prague School and avant-garde artists.

In analysing acting, the authors appropriate Otakar Zich's conceptual distinction (dramatic character – stage figure), but at the same time they move the concept beyond the framework of realistic theatre in the direction of modernist anti-illusionist approaches. They provide examples of the concept of the dynamic stage figure, which represents a more complex relationship between the actor, the stage figure and the dramatic character. While in Zich's view the actor was limited to the presentation of a dramatic character, analyses of avant-garde theatre functions that the actor can take on show that these are much more diverse (this theme is summarized in Jindřich Honzl's two texts on the theatre sign – see section II). The concept of play (playing and inter-play) could be interpreted as another way to conceptualize the changing nature of acting in the given time period. At the same time, it is another way to describe the dynamic structure of theatre.

PLAYING AND THE THEATRE

PETR BOGATYREV

["Hra a divadlo" (1937) was first published in Czech in *Listy pro umění a kritiku*, vol. 5, no. 9 and 10, pp. 232–35.]

Translated by Ivan Kolman

Editor's note: The title of this article in the original is "Hra a divadlo". The Czech word *hra* covers a very wide semantic field. Its three main senses are "acting"; "play", in the sense of a stage play, and "game", in the sense of some group activity played for sport or amusement, for example by children. Less commonly, it can also be used in the sense of "performance". All four of these senses occur in Bogatyrev's article, and have been translated in each case by the most appropriate equivalent in English. The title of the article in English is meant to be inclusive of these various meanings while at the same time reflecting the concept of "play" that links them together and permeates the text.

We have to accept as an obvious fact that an actor creates together with the audience. Not only does the actor lead the audience, but the audience leads the actor and practically directs his performance. These are facts that no longer raise doubts. Examples that confirm this can be found more and more often in literature about the theatre. However, theatre researchers pay little attention to another essential factor of actors' work: an actor creates together with other actors.

An actor is firmly restrained by the acting of his partners. Their acting is reflected in his acting just as his acting is reflected in theirs. Just as an individual musician playing in an orchestra cannot differ in tempo from the others, so an actor cannot break the tempo of the whole cast of the play. A dynamic ensemble forces the individual actor to perform in a dynamic fashion. On the other hand, the effort not to step outside the framework of the whole performance forces the individual actor, dependent on the others' acting, to rein back his dynamism during the performance.

Stanislavsky characterizes this dependence of one actor on the other beautifully when he describes performing with the brilliant Maria Ermolova:

You had to be onstage with her to appreciate the force and infectiousness of her presence. I had that joy, honour and happiness when I played Paratov with her in Nizhni Novgorod in [Alexander Ostrovsky's] *The Girl Without a Dowry*. It was an unforgettable performance in which I was, for a moment, a genius. Not surprisingly, since you couldn't help being infected by Ermolova's talent when you were on stage with her. (Stanislavski 2008: 33)

In another passage he describes the acting of experienced actors when performing with amateurs: Stanislavsky says that these experienced actors "dragged us along behind them, as though we had been roped" (Stanislavski 2008: 83).

During the performance not only does a great and experienced actor influence less talented or less experienced actors, but extras too can influence the actor playing the main role. A provincial Russian actress told me the following story. Robert Adelheim, a very accomplished actor, was playing the role of Uriel Acosta in Gutzkow's play of the same name in a provincial theatre. Uriel gives a speech to a crowd of Jews in the last act. The actress who told me the story was among the extras in the crowd. When the act was over Adelheim came to her and thanked her because she was the only one of the extras who had reacted to his monologue with facial expressions and movements. Her reaction to Uriel Acosta's speech helped Adelheim to render it with dynamism.

Everyone who acts on the stage knows how important a successful first scene is for the entire performance and for all its participants.

We could present an endless number of examples when one actor's unsuccessful performance ruined the acting of all the others or when an excellent performance by one of them stimulated all the others to perform better.

Often the acting of the other actors serves as a bridge for a particular actor, connecting him with the audience. Here is an example. Mark Antony in Shakespeare's tragedy *Julius Caesar* gives his brilliant speech over Caesar's corpse. The speech gradually incites the Romans (extras) against Brutus. The crowd of Romans (extras) reacts to Mark Antony's speech and this reaction is transferred to the audience in the auditorium. It is *through the extras* that Mark Antony rouses approval of his speech in the auditorium.

This is one of the simple cases when the reaction of other actors helps evoke a similar reaction in the audience.

However, things may also be more complicated. Here is an example.

A criminal (in a play) turns to a crowd of other criminals (actors) on the stage and evokes excitement among them. The audience in the auditorium does not share the criminals' excitement. The opposite reaction develops. While the speech evokes excitement among the actors (the crowd of criminals), in the auditorium it evokes disgust. In this case the actor responds to two conflicting reactions.

What is more, very often within his role an actor knows less than the audience. In Molière's *Tartuffe* Orgon reacts to Tartuffe's words and deeds without knowing his real character, while the spectators react differently because they have come to know Tartuffe's real character much earlier in the course of the development of the comedy.

In many plays we meet with the opposite situation. A hero is engaged in a struggle with a criminal, while the audience, not knowing the real character of the criminal, accepts him as a positive type. This differing behaviour of the audience and the actor is usually prolonged until the last scene, where the real character of the criminal is revealed (see Mukařovský 2016 [1937]).

When an actor plays a criminal he is aware of two different reactions throughout the play: the sympathy of the other actors playing criminals and the antipathy of the auditorium and the actors playing positive characters. However, both reactions must support him in his role, because both of them prove that he is playing the criminal properly and that his acting is evoking the proper reaction.[1]

Thus we can see that an actor's creative cooperation with other actors has a great impact on how he plays his part, perhaps even greater than his cooperation with the audience. While the reactions of his partners on the stage are clear and the actors clearly understand them – these may be of different degrees and can be achieved through various means (facial expressions, intonation, the movement of the actors, and so forth) – the reactions from the auditorium, which become apparent only at certain moments (clapping, shouts of praise, and so on), cannot be perceived by the actor so strongly and in such detail. For example, in our theatre, where the auditorium is always darkened, the actor can only try to sound out the audience's reactions.

So there are two parallel types of collective creation in today's theatre: that of the actor with the other actors and that of the actor with the audience.

However, both types of collective creation can exist separately, one without the other. The collective creation of actors without any audience whatsoever can be found in children's games, for example when they play

---

1   If an actor feels he has not evoked the reaction he wished to achieve by his role, he has two possibilities: he can either change the way he plays it or remain "misunderstood", fail to achieve the desired effect, and only in subsequent performances train the audience to react to his acting in the proper way. The acting of any great actor – like the work of any creative artist – does not depend on cooperation with the other actors and the audience alone: he must lead his fellow actors and the audience along new paths, he must make them change their tastes and understand and feel along with him the role as he understands it.

We know quite well how a great actor changes the acting style of the whole group and how the audience, which did not react to the actor's acting at first, not understanding his interpretation, becomes accustomed to his style and finally rejects any other kind of acting that is not similar to his. All this can sometimes become complicated when the actor manages to influence the other actors and have a positive response from them, but fails to do so with the audience. This happens when the group of actors is closer than the audience to this actor's style. And on the contrary, an actor can meet with a positive response from the audience, while his colleagues, trained in a different theatre tradition, do not react appropriately to his acting.

at being "mummy and daddy", "a passenger and a conductor", and so on. The children are playing with children and not only is an audience not needed here, it would actually be in the way.[2] The same type of collective creation of actors without an audience can be found in many folk plays.

On the other hand we are also familiar with the pure collective creation of an actor and the audience where collective cooperation with fellow actors is absent. Examples of this are monologues and even entire monologic plays.

From here on, for the sake of brevity, we will call the collective creation of an actor with other actors *pure play* and the collective creation of actors and the audience *play with the participation of the public*.

In the earliest forms of theatre we meet with *pure play*. In ritual performances with scenes where people imitate animals, natural phenomena, and so on, almost all of those present are usually participants. There is no division between actors and audience. We also meet with religio-magical performances that are performed by cult servants – priests. But even here all the people present often participate in certain moments of the performance.

In the medieval theatre we can see how the relationship between the stage and the audience differs depending on the content of the play. This distinction also depends on the individual characters in the play. Serious characters do not have direct contact with the audience in the course of the play. The spectators look on in silence as they play their role, rarely expressing praise or disapproval. However, as soon as a comic character appears on the stage or when a comic interlude is presented, there is a direct connection between the stage and the audience. The actors turn to the audience, speak to it, the audience replies... And from being a play with an audience the performance becomes *pure play,* in which both actors and audience participate.

In the theatre of the eighteenth century, whose traditions have been preserved in some theatres and in some types of plays until today, actors paid considerable attention to the audience. Actors did not allow themselves to stand with their backs to the audience, even when the logic of the play would have required it. Some of the actors' replies were directed to the audience; monologues were addressed to the audience as well. This contact with the auditorium often occurred at the expense of the natural development of the dramatic plot, at the expense of the *pure play* of actors with other actors. For example, when the audience applauded, the actors came downstage in the middle of the act to bow, thus interrupting the natural progress of the play. Sometimes this practice of actors coming forward when called upon by the audience ran directly counter to the very sense of the play: even characters

---

2   All or almost all the elements of the theatre – with the exception of the audience – can often be found in children's games: gestures, monologues, dialogues, costumes, props, and so on.

who had died or who (in the context of the play) had left the stage for good returned for a bow.

Realist theatre and later naturalist theatre, which continued in its style, receded more and more from collective creation with the audience and approached the *pure acting* of actors among themselves.

While pre-realist theatre forbade the actors to stand with their backs to the audience, this often happens in realist and naturalist theatre depending on how the scene is directed. However, actors are strictly forbidden to address individual lines of dialogue to the audience, to appeal to them with words or gestures. The actors in the naturalist theatre act with each other, as though they were completely separated from the audience. However, this separation from the auditorium is merely apparent: in reality an actor in the naturalist theatre senses the audience behind him all the time. It recedes from him, but at the same time he always ensures that this complete separation of the acting from the auditorium makes an even greater impression on the audience through its lifelike quality.

Naturalist theatre was replaced by the Symbolist theatre, which, in contrast to the separation of the stage and the auditorium, placed emphasis on the shared "group" performance of both the actor and the audience.

"Away with the forestage, that cursed barrier between the actor and the audience," exclaimed Vyacheslav Ivanov, the theoretician of the new theatre, "the stage must move out beyond the forestage and involve everybody, or everybody must seize the stage. Enough of auditoriums! We want to work together and not only to watch."[3] This merging of the stage and the auditorium was accomplished differently by other theatre theoreticians and practitioners. For example, at one stage of his activities, with theatrical aims in mind, Meyerhold attempted to remove the audience's passivity in the following way: the forestage was removed and a staircase was built that led from the stage to the auditorium. This was with a small theatre company led by Meyerhold that lasted less than one season (1910–1911); it was located in the House of Interludes. The actors entered and left through the auditorium. They sat on the steps, and in one of the plays, when an actress was dancing on the stage in a tavern scene, the enthusiastic shouts of the actors on stage were joined by shouts from the auditorium. This led to a pre-arranged row that ended in a second dancer-actress starting to dance on one of the tables in the audito-

---

3   [Editor's note: We were not able to locate this quotation from Ivanov in any of his works that are available to us. Bogatyrev may be recalling a public lecture he had attended or an article by Ivanov that he had read. Ivanov's idea of the "collective performance" in the contemporary theatre, which would involve the audience and "cross over" the forestage to unite everyone, is expressed elsewhere, although with different wording (cf. Ivanov, Vyacheslav (1994 [1905]) "Wagner i Dionisovo deistvo" [Wagner and the Dionysiac performance] in *Rodnoe i vselenskoe* [The Native and the Ecumenical], Moscow: Respublica, p. 34.)]

rium in order to show her superiority over her rival dancing on the stage. The same piece included yet another moment that provided an opportunity for a different means of drawing the audience into the play on the stage. A brutal, bloody fight was simulated. The scenery, painted by Sergei Sudeikin in blazing colours, red contending with gold, gave the audience an impression of orgies of blood and fire, strengthened by terrible peals of thunder emanating from the background.

An actor dressed as a soldier stepped forward from the scenery (so at the same time emphasizing that theatre merely represents a fight but is not at all interested in suggesting that a real fight is indeed taking place) and started to speak; a whole stormy scene of the clash of enormous masses of opposing troops took place in his monologue. He spoke, gun shots rang out, cannonballs flew, until finally, frightened, he ran down the stairs and crept under the first table he came to. When he had had a rest, he said: "It seems I can feel fairly safe here." However, the continuing shooting forced him to leave this shelter and finally he fled from the auditorium shouting: "Every man for himself!"

This performance achieved the most extreme form of the *external* merging of the stage and the auditorium.

When we look at these examples from various periods and styles in the history of the theatre, we can see that the dialectical relationship between the stage and the auditorium is one of the basic concerns in the history of the theatre as well as in the development of contemporary theatre.

It is interesting that in the kind of theatre where actors try to distance themselves as much as possible from the audience (for example in the naturalist theatre), where they try to build an insurmountable barrier between the stage and the auditorium, they simultaneously emphasize the presence of the spectator as an element *sui generis*. On the contrary, in the kind of theatre that removes the barrier between the stage and the auditorium, the theatre where actors make a continuous effort to connect with the spectators, address them, react to their applause and ultimately carry out a dialogue with them, transfer a part of the action from the stage to the auditorium – through all these approaches they reject the audience as an element *sui generis*, draw it into the action, make it a participant in *pure play*.

However, in both the first and the second case we can see the actors trying to achieve – often, perhaps, subconsciously – *pure play*. In the naturalist theatre this takes the form of the actors, having separated themselves from the auditorium, dedicating themselves more and more to interaction with each other. In the theatre where the audience is drawn into the performance, the result is interaction between the actors and the spectators, in this way moving closer to the *pure play* we can observe among children or towards the performances of primitive peoples, where all the participants take part as a group.

It is necessary to rouse the interest of theatre researchers in *pure play* as one of the essential factors in the world of the theatre in both the past and the present.

WORKS CITED

Mukařovský, Jan (2016 [1937]) "On Stage Dialogue", this reader, pp. 212–15.
Stanislavski, Konstantin (2008) *My Life in Art*, trans. and ed. Jean Benedetti, London: Routledge.

CHAPLIN AND *THE KID*

PETR BOGATYREV

["Chaplin i 'Kid'" was first published in Russian in Shklovsky, Viktor (ed.) (1923) *Chap-lin. Sbornik statej* [Chaplin. A Collection of Essays], Berlin: Izdatelstvo zhurnala "Kino", pp. 57–80. It was published in Czech as "Chaplin a Kid" [Chaplin and *The Kid*] in Kolár, Jaroslav (ed.) (1971) *Souvislosti tvorby. Cesty k struktuře lidové kultury a divadla* [The Context of Creation: In Search of the Structure of Folk Culture and Folk Theatre], Prague: Odeon, pp. 5–13. The Czech version was authorized by Bogatyrev and served as the source text for the present English translation.]

Translated by Ivan Kolman

Editor's note: Bogatyrev sometimes quotes *The Kid* incorrectly. Clearly he was writing from his memory of having seen the film, not from viewing it and making notes on the spot. We have altered inaccurate details in the text and placed the correct version within square brackets; for example "magazine" was substituted for the mistaken "book". Wherever a more extensive comment was necessary to bring Bogatyrev's argument in line with the actual events of the film, a note was added.

One of the most interesting films recently released is *The Kid*. The script was written by Charlie Chaplin, who also plays the main character – the tramp.

I am going to present briefly the plot of this tragicomic film and explain some of the methods Chaplin used.

A girl is renounced by her lover – an artist. Their child is born. Poverty forces the mother to abandon her beloved child: she puts him into an empty car. The chauffeur finds the child in the car and leaves the little boy on the street.[1] This is the beginning of the melodramatic film.

Chaplin's figure appears in the distance in the street. When he appears on the screen, his peculiar gait arouses Homeric laughter in the audience.

Many people find it strange that Chaplin walks in the same way and makes the same movements in all his films. They discontentedly say: Chaplin repeats himself.

However, this sameness of techniques, the same traditional Chaplinesque makeup, suit and cane, to which Chaplin himself attaches great importance – all this is used deliberately. If Chaplin changed his gait, makeup and clothing

---

1   [Editor's note: Two thieves steal the car and they leave the little boy on the street.]

in every film, there would not have emerged that distinctive type, that stylized costume, that evokes a number of old associations as soon as it appears. This feature has been used in theatre more than once. When a particular costume appeared in the *comedia dell'arte*, it offered the audience a certain characterization as a signal. If Scapino was beating a soldier, the audience was always on Scapino's side. Therefore the author never needed to tell the audience who Scapino was and who the Spanish soldier was. As soon as the audience saw Scapino's costume they knew from tradition he was a cheerful, good, skilful fellow, while the Spaniard's costume signified a braggart, coward and rowdy. Therefore the costume must be familiar; its very appearance must repel or attract the audience's favour.

The audiences in remote provincial theatres divided all the actors into the popular and the unpopular. The popular ones included heroic lovers, heroines and comedians, while the unpopular ones included aggressive characters playing the parts of fiends. One decrepit provincial actor complained to me about the actor-manager who cast him as Savitch in Leonid Andreyev's *Professor Storitzyn* while he himself took the role of Storitzyn: "Is it possible for me to be successful when I must play such a rogue?" Chaplin created a fascinating guise. He plays the role of a noble-minded hero in many of his films (*The Vagabond, The Immigrant*), *The Kid* included. It is interesting that in one of his early films, *Mabel at the Wheel,* when Chaplin was still searching for the most distinctive guise (he changed makeup and costume in every film), he played the part of a thief. And it must be admitted that he played even this role with success. He convincingly parodies the movements of a melodramatic thief.

Chaplin played this part very well, but it was a damaging role for a guise that was meant to be attractive and aimed at becoming popular.

Chaplin apparently understood this and he renounced the role of thief in his subsequent films. He left this role to his permanent partner, who was large. The mere appearance of big actors on the scene evoked certain associations and expectations in the audience. When the voice of a coarse-grained actor such as Varlamov, Sadovskaya or Davydov[2] was heard offstage, their familiar vocal timbre (even before the audience could understand the words) aroused endless laughter. Or another example: in a certain play Varlamov did not appear on the stage for a long time. Finally the audience saw only the tip of his enormous foot sticking out of the door. This brought peals of laughter. The audience saw neither the costume nor the actor's figure. What was evoking laughter then? The tip of Varlamov's foot replaced the actor's traditional

---

2   [Editor's note: Konstantin Alexandrovich Varlamov (1849–1915), Olga Sadovskaya (1849–1919), Vladimir Nikolaevich Davydov (1849–1925): leading figures in the Russian theatre at the turn of the twentieth century.]

costume, just as Chaplin's cane did. The tip of Varlamov's foot evoked a number of happy, comic memories. It is interesting that today Russian theatre is inclined to use stylized costumes. In Foregger's[3] theatre the same unchanged types with the same costumes and makeup appear. These include a blabbering "Commissar", a "young Soviet lady", a "street vendour selling pirozhki", and so on.

I do not think that this was influenced by Chaplin. When these stylized costumes appeared in Foregger's theatre, nobody knew anything about Chaplin in Russia. No, a number of identical forms was created under the pressure of identical artistic tendencies.

But let us return to *The Kid*.

Chaplin comes closer and closer towards the audience. People in the upper floors of buildings throw out old boxes with garbage. Chaplin parries the falling boxes with his cane in an elegant, calm way. He comes to the spot where the little baby is lying. When he sees the baby, he lifts him up placidly and looks around to see how he could make provision for him. Finally he notices a pram with another baby. He quickly comes and puts the foundling in the pram facing the baby. The baby's mother notices this and, furious, returns the foundling to Chaplin. Chaplin wants to put the little boy back on the street but as soon as he leans over to do so, a constable appears behind him. After several unsuccessful attempts to get rid of the child, Chaplin takes the foundling home. On the way home he finds a slip of paper with the child saying: "Please love and care for this orphan child."

Chaplin is with the child at home – in an attic room. The child must be put somewhere. Chaplin ties ropes to four corners of a piece of cloth and hangs it from the ceiling. It is used as a cradle. Chaplin attaches a small kettle with water to the side, which replaces a dummy. Thus Chaplin's hands are free, and with a serious expression he sets about making nappies and furniture for the child.

Chaplin takes on the role of a nanny. Everybody is used to seeing Chaplin as a light-hearted loafer, a skilful brawler – and suddenly such an unexpected change.

This is a pure playing about with contrasts.

Several years pass.

The child has grown up.

Chaplin sits with his foster child at lunch. It is time to go to work.

---

3   [Editor's note: The avant-garde director Nikolai Foregger (1892–1939), known for his experimental agitprop productions in the years following the Russian Revolution.]

The boy whispers to Chaplin where they will be working and runs away.[4] Chaplin loads panes of window glass on his back and leaves. What kind of work is this?

The boy, lurking around a corner, throws stones at windows so that they break the glass, and then runs away. Immediately afterwards Chaplin – as a glazier – follows him. Landlords have no choice but to turn to him right away. Chaplin has found a job. – All this is repeated at every corner. Finally a constable notices Chaplin and his foster son's systematic and "well-planned" job and lies in wait for the boy. The boy raises his arm to throw a stone, when suddenly he notices the constable standing behind him. The constable asks the boy where he wanted to throw the stone. The boy points, the constable stares in that direction and the boy runs away.

Chaplin himself often uses the same trick. In one of his films a constable arrests Chaplin and won't let him budge an inch. Chaplin introduces the constable to a nice girl and while the constable is shaking her hand, Chaplin runs away.

The part of the boy is especially interesting because the child uses the same tricks that Chaplin himself uses in this and other films.

The boy is a miniature version of Chaplin. His acting is immensely interesting for actors and audiences who would like to penetrate the mystery of the techniques Chaplin uses to achieve such enormous comic effect. In the boy's acting all these techniques are much more transparent and it is much easier to split them into their individual components.

Let us follow the plot of the film further.

The boy escapes from the constable and runs to Chaplin. A chase follows – the boy in the lead, followed by Chaplin with the panes of glass and the constable pursuing them in the rear. Chaplin and the boy win, enter their house and hide themselves inside.

A new scene.

Chaplin and the boy are at home. Chaplin lies in bed reading a [magazine]. The boy is preparing pancakes on the stove. Chaplin does not have the role of a nanny any more but is tenderly looked after by his foster child. The pancakes are ready. The boy invites Chaplin to breakfast. Chaplin gets up, sticking his head and arms through holes in his bedspread. The bedspread becomes a dressing gown. After saying grace, Chaplin and the boy start eating. Chaplin carefully makes sure that his foster child does not hurt his mouth and teaches him to eat, although only with a knife (they have no forks), making sure he is not using the sharp but the blunt side of the knife.

Plot parallelism is a typical feature in this film.

---

4   [Editor's note: They talk and plan aloud. Then, the boy puts his head up and gives Chaplin a kiss on the side of his face, which Bogatyrev interpreted as a whisper.]

We move from Chaplin's poor home to a famous actress's rich boudoir.[5] She is the boy's mother. The whole room is full of flowers sent to her by admirers of her talent. The star goes to a great ball where a distinguished artist is introduced to her. It is her former lover, the boy's father. They recognize each other. He courts her but she rejects his love and complains to him that nobody can ever make up for the loss of her own son, whom she had to leave on the street when her lover betrayed her. The boy's mother's only pleasure is to give toys to poor children in the street. She takes a whole load of toys and hands them out to children in the street. She also meets her son and gives him a toy but she does not recognize him. The boy plays with the new toy.[6] A street urchin comes and seizes it. The boy fights him and although he is much smaller he wins.

People gather. Chaplin is also in the crowd. He is excited by his foster son's skilfulness and bravery. However, the street urchin's [older brother] suddenly appears, comes up to Chaplin and suggests the boy fight with his [younger brother] again; he warns Chaplin, though, that if the boy wins, he himself, the beaten boy's [brother], will beat Charlie to death.[7]

The two boys start fighting. And the boy wins again. The time for reprisal comes. Chaplin is afraid. The defeated boy's [brother] raises his arm but Chaplin skilfully dodges. The muscleman punches his fist into a wall.[8] The [brick] wall collapses. [A constable] comes to Charlie's help but falls under the muscleman's blows. He again attacks Chaplin, but Charlie manages to slip through his legs.[9] The muscleman raises his arm again and punches the iron pole of a streetlamp. The pole bends. Finally he manages to get hold of Chaplin, raises his arm again – but a beautiful lady grasps his arm. It is the boy's mother. She implores him not to hit Charlie. The muscleman lets Charlie go. However, Chaplin himself starts fighting again.[10] At the beginning he adroitly escapes the muscleman but then he takes a brick, skilfully dodges his blows and beats him with the brick. Finally the muscleman falls exhausted.[11] Chaplin has won.

It is interesting to pause at these two fist fights: the street urchin's with the boy and the strong boxer – the street urchin's [brother] – with Charlie. Actually, the winners should be the street urchin, who is almost twice as big as the boy, and the boxer, with his destructive strength; his blows demolished

5 [Editor's note: All this actually comes before the scene just described.]
6 [Editor's note: This scene follows the end of the scene with Chaplin and the boy eating.]
7 [Editor's note: The intertitle simply states: "Then I'm going to beat you." Beating to death is Bogatyrev's interpretation.]
8 [Editor's note: This paragraph gives a wrong sequencing of events. The business with punching the wall comes after the constable appears.]
9 [Editor's note: This does not happen in the film.]
10 [Editor's note: The muscleman asks Charlie to hit him.]
11 [Editor's note: He walks away groggily.]

[a wall] and bent [a lamp pole]. However, the winners are the small boy and feeble Charlie. This unexpected victory of the weak over the strong always has a strong effect on audiences. Remember how much the audience always appreciates it when a lightweight wrestler manages to beat a heavyweight wrestler in a Greco-Roman wrestling match.

Chaplin is well aware that such a trick is very successful with the audience. In an autobiographical sketch he says:

> If I am being treated harshly, it is always a big man who is doing it; so that, by the contrast between big and little, I get the sympathy of the audience... It is my luck, of course, that I am short, and so am able to make these contrasts without much difficulty. Everyone knows that the little fellow in trouble always gets the sympathy of the mob. Knowing that it is part of human nature to sympathize with the underdog, I always accentuate my helplessness by drawing my shoulders in, drooping my lip pathetically and looking frightened. It is all part of the art of pantomime, of course. But if I were three inches taller it would be much more difficult to get the sympathy of the audience. I should then look big enough to take care of myself. As it is, the audience even while laughing at me is inclined to sympathize with me. (Chaplin 1918: 136)

We may note that the actor who plays Chaplin's rival is almost always fat and a big man to emphasize the contrast.

Let us follow the story of the film.

The boy falls ill after the fight. A doctor examines him. A comic scene is developed at the patient's bed. The doctor asks Chaplin to pass a thermometer to the patient.[12] Instead of measuring the patient's temperature, Charlie puts the thermometer into his own mouth. The doctor is annoyed and loses his temper. He orders the patient to rest and leaves.

Chaplin does not abandon comic tricks even at the ill boy's bedside. The contrast between the comic and the dramatic is obvious. People who are brought up on contemporary dramas and comedies may not like such "craziness" in dramatic scenes; it is true that comic elements are subdued in contemporary drama so as not to weaken dramatic tension. However, it was not like that with old dramas. In those days sharp contrasts were appreciated. Just remember the old mystery plays. There it was possible to show frivolous and amusing interludes after such deep and tragic scenes as Christ's Passion. In the Czech medieval play *The Ointment Seller*[13] comic scenes are mixed with the monologues and dialogues of the pious women carrying ointments. A play

---

12 [Editor's note: The doctor walks into the room, does not ask who is ill, and he himself sticks the thermometer in Charlie's mouth.]

13 [Editor's note: This play (the Czech title: *Mastičkář*) is also known as *The Apothecary*. For a Czech-English bilingual edition by Jarmila F. Veltrusky, see Veltrusky 1985.]

based on the Biblical story of the young men in the fiery furnace, which was often performed in churches in old Russia, included executioners – "Chaldeans" – who uttered comic comments about Hananiah, Mishael and Azariah, the young men who were entering the furnace to be burnt to death.

Russian folk theatre uses contrasting structure in the play *Tsar Maximilian*. The scene of the heroes' death is immediately followed by an extremely comic scene with deaf gravediggers.

So Chaplin's flexible device of mixing tensely dramatic and strongly comic scenes has its history and in its time it was considered one of the most common methods. The future will show whether it will be recognized as a device acceptable for the majority of contemporary spectators.

Let us return to the storyline of the film.

The boy recovers quickly and finally gets completely well. At that moment [an agent] from the Society for the Protection of Children arrives in a van and notifies Chaplin that the boy will be taken away from him.[14] Chaplin gives [them] the piece of paper he found with the boy[15] ("Please love and care for this orphan child"), and adamantly refuses to submit to the agent's orders. The agent wants to take away the boy by force. A skirmish follows. Chaplin and the boy win but suddenly a constable appears and he and the agent and the driver of the van manage to wrench the boy from Chaplin.[16] They put him in the van and take him away. Chaplin runs from roof to roof trying to catch the van. He jumps into the van from a roof. He appears suddenly and throws the agent for the "protection of children" out. Chaplin and the boy are together again. The van has stopped and they escape.

The boy's mother receives the piece of paper with the words "Please love and care for this orphan child," which she herself wrote, and she immediately realises that the small imp that lives with the itinerant glazier is her son. She does all she can to get the boy back as soon as possible.

Chaplin comes to a flophouse, pays for the night and goes to his bed. There is a window next to the bed; Chaplin opens the window and the boy crawls in. The manager of the flophouse suspects Chaplin is not alone but for a long time he fails to find the other overnighter. The boy cleverly hides himself under the blanket. Finally the manager discovers the illegal overnighter and Chaplin has to pay for the boy as well. Everybody is asleep; only the manager is up, reading a newspaper. He notices the news about a rich lady searching for her child, who lives with a poor tramp. Whoever finds the child will receive a large award. The manager suspects that the tramp and the boy are in his

---

14   [Editor's note: Bogatyrev deduces the name of the agency from a sign, "County Orphan Asylum", written on the car.]

15   [Editor's note: This happened earlier in the scene with the doctor.]

16   [Editor's note: The agent's driver had gone up with him to get the child, and the driver runs downstairs to get a constable.]

flophouse – they are Chaplin and his ward. He takes the sleeping boy from Chaplin's bed and brings him to the police. Chaplin wakes up and discovers that the boy is not with him. He searches the entire flophouse but he can't find the child. He runs about the town, but all in vain. Exhausted from all the running, he sits down by the entrance to his former home and falls asleep.

He has a dream. The whole street is covered with festoons of white flowers. All the people have white robes over their ordinary clothes and white wings like angels. The muscleman who harassed Chaplin because the boy defeated his [brother] makes an appearance. He looks like [an angel] and starts harassing Chaplin—as he did in reality.[17] Chaplin escapes... There is an interesting detail here. In the real fight with the muscleman, as was mentioned above, Chaplin evades the man's blows by slipping through his legs, while in the dream it is the other way round.[18] When [a policeman] catches up with him Chaplin rises on his wings and the [policeman] finds himself between Chaplin's legs.

Finally Chaplin manages to escape the muscleman's harassment. The boy walks out of the house towards him.[19] Like the rest he too has a white robe and wings. The boy flings his arms around his friend and foster father's neck.

The dream fades away and Chaplin sees a constable beside him who is trying to wake him up. He takes Chaplin to a big rich house. The tramp meets the boy and as the film says "he finds his happiness at last"...[20]

Among the many methods by which Chaplin achieves certain dramatic effects at particular points we have on more than one occasion pointed to the use of contrasts. Chaplin himself attached great importance to this kind of composition. As he says in his autobiographical sketch:

Another point about the human being that I use a great deal is the liking of the average person for contrast and surprise in his entertainment. It is a matter of simple knowledge, of course, that the human likes to see the struggle between the good and the bad, the rich and the poor, the successful and the unsuccessful. He likes to cry and he likes to laugh, all within the space of a very few moments. (Chaplin 1918: 135–36)

The whole of *The Kid* is based on the contrast of melodramatic scenes and buffoonery. There is the drama of a mother who is forced to abandon her child

---

17   [Editor's note: In fact, first the strong man is very pleasant to Chaplin, but when the strong man's girlfriend starts flirting with Chaplin he gets angry, being incited by the devil.]

18   [Editor's note: This comparison does not hold, as Chaplin did not slip between his legs earlier in the film.]

19   [Editor's note: This happens at the beginning of the dream sequence. Here he appears from the crowd that has been watching the fight, the policeman then shooting him.]

20   [Editor's note: Not an actual intertitle. The film ends with him and the boy going into the house with the mother.]

on one hand and Charlie's comic scenes on the other. The idea of connecting these two elements in one play is not new. It was quite common in old plays. For example, Shakespeare placed a scene with a comic dialogue between two gravediggers before the scene of Ophelia's funeral.

However, playing with contrast goes further in the film. The dramatic hero is a comic character. But even this is not new. A comic character in the role of a positive hero is quite common in French melodrama,[21] for example *Les Pauvres de Paris* or *La grâce de Dieu*.[22] We might mention in this context that Chaplin had already appeared in the role of the noble hero and the protector of an oppressed girl in *The Vagabond* and *The Immigrant*.

Let us conclude these notes about *The Kid* by summarizing our findings about how the parts of the film were composed into a single whole.

There are various principles according to which the individual scenes of a work of drama are constructed and connected. Storyline composition is most common. One scene is closely connected with another, the following one emerges from the previous one. Greek tragedy was built up this way and the majority of European plays are built up the same way. Something different is composition based on a variety of individual scenes that become the constituents of the entire piece. This is the compositional type found in revues and music hall programmes. In the beginning there is dancing, followed by monologic declamation, dialogue, solo singing, choral singing. All these scenes are arranged so as to avoid monotony – dances are followed by solo singing, then comes a dialogue followed by choral singing, and so on.

Several variants of the folk play *Tsar Maximilian* are built up this way.

In addition to these compositional methods we encounter composition based on the contrast and parallelism of individual scenes. Only storyline composition or composition of this third type can be used in films. Composition of the revue type is out of the question since the film is based on visual perception alone. It is clear from my description of the film that the storyline composition is rather weak. The film has a number of scenes that do not move the story forward. Most of the scenes are built on contrast or on the principle of parallelism. We have already mentioned the alternation of melodramatic and comic scenes. I will just mention a few scenes built on the principle of parallelism. Chaplin prepares a lunch for the boy in one scene and the boy prepares pancakes for Chaplin in another scene. The scene of Chaplin's dream is the slightly changed scene of Chaplin's fight with the muscleman. Here Chaplin applies the rule that he explains when he says that "when one inci-

---

21   [Editor's note: Bogatyrev has in mind French sentimental social dramas from around the middle of the nineteenth century, in particular the plays of Félix Pyat (1810–1899).]

22   [Editor's note: *Les Pauvres de Paris* (1856), by Eugène Nus (1816–1894); *A la grâce de Dieu* (1841, often appearing in translation as *The Mother's Blessing*), by Adolphe Philippe d'Ennery (1811–1899) and Gustave Lemoine (1802–1885).]

dent can get two big, separate laughs, it is much better than two individual incidents" (Chaplin 1918: 134). Besides this, every repetition is usually a variation at the same time; therefore it gives the impression of unexpectedness.

For example we expect that Chaplin will slip between the [policeman's] legs but he flies up in the air and lets the [policeman] pass between his own legs.

In [*The Vagabond*] a big man plunges Chaplin into water and pulls him out again several times. The audience gets used to this and the laughter becomes quieter, the sequence is repeated again but this time it is the big man who ends up in the water and Chaplin walks away majestically – and the auditorium shakes with laughter.

Everybody who is interested in film art should be aware that Chaplin's acting is based on a very rich tradition, one that is in no way inferior to, for example, the tradition of the Moscow Art Theatre.

Great works have been created on the path that Chaplin is now following with his cane.

And it is the true path of the art of the film.

WORKS CITED

Chaplin, Charlie (1918) "What People Laugh At", *American Magazine*, vol. 86, no. 34, November, pp. 134–37.

Veltrusky, Jarmila F. (trans. and ed.) (1985) *Mastičkář: A Sacred Farce from Medieval Bohemia*, Ann Arbor: The University of Michigan Press.

CHAPLIN, THE FAKE COUNT

PETR BOGATYREV

["Chaplin – mnimy graf" [Chaplin – the Fake Count] was first published in Russian in Shklovsky, Viktor (ed.) (1923) *Chaplin. Sbornik statei* [Chaplin. A Collection of Essays], Berlin: Izdatelstvo zhurnala "Kino", pp. 81–94. It was published in Czech as "Chaplin falešným hrabětem" [Chaplin, the Fake Count] in Kolár, Jaroslav (ed.) (1971) *Souvislosti tvorby. Cesty k struktuře lidové kultury a divadla* [The Context of Creation: In Search of the Structure of Folk Culture and Folk Theatre], Prague: Odeon, pp. 14–19. The Czech edition was authorized by the author and represents the latest version; as such, it served as the source text of this translation.]

Translated by Ivan Kolman

Editor's note: At a number of points in his description of *The Count* and *The Immigrant*, Bogatyrev makes factual mistakes. Clearly he was writing from his memory of having seen the film, not from viewing it and making notes on the spot. We have altered inaccurate details in the text and placed the correct version within square brackets; for example "waiters" was substituted for the mistaken "servants". Whenever a more extensive comment was necessary, a note was added. However, it must be pointed out that these inaccuracies do not affect Bogatyrev's argument.

There are two main streams in the world of theatre. One attempts to build an impenetrable wall between the auditorium and the forestage. Actors should not be aware they are acting in front of the audience; the audience does not exist for them. An actor is strictly prohibited from speaking "to the spectators", from reacting to their clapping. Recently another stream has become more prominent. It tries to remove this wall and build a bridge between the auditorium and the forestage, to draw the audience, too, into participation in the performance. Actors in the productions of the Austrian director Max Reinhardt move among the spectators, often speaking "to the audience", something that was common in older forms of theatre and that is still found in Russian folk theatre, for example in the play *Tsar Maximilian*.

A whole series of productions created in the Reinhardtean spirit appeared in Russia. One of the most recent productions at The Bat theatre[1] was

---

1   [Editor's note: The Bat, a cabaret-style theatre, founded in 1908 as an offshoot of the Moscow Arts Theatre.]

of Carlo Gozzi's *The Serpent Woman*. The actors left the stage at certain points and continued their performance among the audience. Quite recently the Semperante Studio was opened in Moscow. It has no stage at all. The actors perform among the audience, where there are tables and chairs that also serve as the set. In the background there is a white wall that is lit in various colours by a magic lantern. The lighting illuminates both the actors and the audience sitting next to them in a special way.

Nothing new under the sun. Villagers in the Arkhangelsk Governorate performed a folk play called *Barin* in almost the same way as that employed at the Semperante. Actors with scourges burst into a room full of villagers who had come to watch the performance and started whipping them. The audience "drew back" so that an empty space was created in the middle of the room. The actors entered this space and the performance started. During performances of Russian folk plays the actors "upset" the spectators, mocking them and so drawing them into the play. Something similar to a cabaret session is created, where a Master of Ceremonies argues with the audience, asks questions and himself answers questions from the audience.

One more step and we will have arrived at the "theatre of congregate action" conceived by Vyacheslav Ivanov.[2] Ivanov claimed that everyone should participate in the theatre performance, just as they did in Classical religious festivals. As can be seen, "theatricality" is an elastic term. In the name of "theatricality" an actor is forced to walk about among the spectators and get involved in arguments and dialogues with them, yet at the same time, in the name of "theatricality", actors pay no attention to the audience. A theatre with an impervious wall between the forestage and the audience requires actors to give up their individuality and take on their role completely. It is considered a great success of theatre technique if an actor changes beyond recognition from role to role. People do not have to know it is Kachalov.[3] They see only Hamlet, Julius Caesar or Chatsky on stage. The *New Journal of Foreign Literature*, a quite serious periodical, published an article by the theatre critic Stanislavsky (not the director of the Art Theatre). Stanislavsky recommended that in their private lives actors should not appear often in public, should not be seen often by theatregoers – and all this for a theatrical effect, so people would be unable to recognize a well-known actor, whom they had been drinking tea with at their friends' place the day before, in the role of King Lear of old.

---

2   [Editor's note: Vyacheslav Ivanov (1866–1949), Russian poet, playwright, philosopher and literary critic, associated with the Russian Symbolist movement.]

3   [Editor's note: Vassily Kachalov (1875–1948), one of the leading actors at the Moscow Art Theatre. Among his most famous roles was that of Chatsky, the protagonist of Aleksander Griboyedov's (1795–1829) *Woe from Wit*, a classic of Russian drama.]

However, there is another, different theatrical effect. Spectators are especially interested when a person they know very well, a close friend, dresses in some kind of clothing that is not usual for him and enters into an entirely atypical situation. Gogol's *Marriage* was performed in a particular village and what interested the local country people was to see their nearest and dearest, sons and brothers, suddenly appearing on stage dressed up in fine clothes and enjoying a comfortable life very distant from that of both the actors and the audience. Here what was required – as in every theatre of costumes – was that the actor, while playing the widest possibility variety of roles, should at the same time remain himself. In some comedies Scapin played the role of a merchant, in others a courtier, but in every role the spectators recognized the well-known Scapin who was familiar to them.

A character called Kašpárek (Kasper in German) appears in various roles in the Czech puppet theatre: Kašpárek the miller, Kašpárek the policeman (an interesting coincidence: Chaplin the policeman, in *Easy Street*!), Kašpárek the Futurist, Kašpárek the speculator, and so on. Always, in every role, Kašpárek wears the same fixed, traditional costume, has the same face and the same squeaky voice. Children, who know Kašpárek very well, wonder how he will behave in a new, unusual situation.

When people see Chaplin in a number of films they also get to know him well. He, too, is close to the public, like Kašpárek for children, like the fellow villagers – who themselves have no rights – playing the notables in Gogol's *Marriage* for the local audience. In these cases it is easier for the audience to understand the actors' experiences; according to Chaplin there is "the tendency of the human being to experience within himself the emotions he sees on the stage or screen" (Chaplin 1918: 134). And the more unusual the situation Chaplin appears in, the more interesting the film and the more likely it will appeal to audiences. Chaplin has been a policeman, has been a fireman, but now he finds himself in what is for him a completely unfamiliar situation: he is a bogus count.

Let us have a look at this film.

Chaplin has become an assistant to a tailor. A lady arrives. Chaplin takes her measurements. He measures her neck, then measures the size of her ear and mouth and waistline and notes everything down. His master comes, looks at Chaplin's notes and finds the measurements for the neck, ear, mouth and waistline (which Chaplin measured as [five feet]). The master drives Chaplin away.[4] Chaplin goes to the next room and puts an iron on clothes ready to be ironed. A rag falls from the iron to the floor.[5] Chaplin doesn't know what to do to remove the iron from the clothes; he cannot touch the

---

4   [Editor's note: First he kicks him out, and only then does he check the measurements.]
5   [Editor's note: Chaplin actually throws it away by mistake.]

hot iron without the rag. The master comes in and sees that Chaplin has left the iron on the clothes ready to be ironed and the iron has burnt a hole in the press cloth as well as in the tailcoat that was under it. The master throws Charlie out immediately. Charlie goes for a rendezvous with a cook who works for some very rich members of high society. She treats him to cheese. The cheese stinks but hungry Charlie manages to deal with this embarrassing situation. He pinches his nose with one hand and stuffs the cheese into his mouth with the other. The cook's husband[6] approaches the kitchen door. The cook hides Chaplin in a basket and hands him the cheese. The cheese stinks in the basket so much that Chaplin throws it out. The cook trembles with fear and puts the cheese back in the basket. But Chaplin throws it out again. The situation escalates – the husband is on the point of discovering Chaplin hidden in the basket and the whole thing almost comes to light but then the cook's husband is called away ... and the atmosphere brightens up. All of a sudden a policeman appears at the door – the cook's second sweetheart. Chaplin hides himself in a little window that turns out to be a dumbwaiter. The cook's husband comes into the kitchen again and the policeman himself must hide in the same basket where Chaplin had been sitting earlier. The policeman can hardly bear the smell of the remaining bits of cheese. A bell rings again – and the cook's husband leaves. The policeman comes out of the basket. Chaplin, afraid that he might fall into the police-man's hands, presses a button and the dumbwaiter goes up.[7] The scene with the lovers, Chaplin and the policeman, who were hidden in the basket by the clever wife, and the agitated behaviour of the hidden lovers, is one of the most widely occurring comic situations in the world. It is found in nearly all nations and in virtually every period. The most recent work to analyse this comic situation is a major study by Yuri M. Sokolov, *The Tale of Karp Sutulov*.[8] It can be found in the *One Thousand and One Nights*, in the *Decameron*, in Russian folk tales and old Russian stories. Nikolai Gogol treats it in his story "Christmas Eve".

Chaplin is very fond of storylines based on delayed action. The audience sees that the dénouement is approaching, that the husband will find the care-less lover and scandal will follow. This device is especially obvious in a scene in Chaplin's film *The Immigrant*. Chaplin arrives at a restaurant and orders [a meal]. The time comes to pay, but he has no money. Chaplin's former girl-friend arrives.[9] He postpones the payment and orders breakfast for her. The

---

6   [Editor's note: Bogatyrev mistakenly takes the butler for the cook's husband; he interprets a com-ic plot based on stealing an employer's property for a love triangle situation.]

7   [Editor's note: There is no business about pressing a button in the film.]

8   See *Trudy Slavianskoi arkhivnoi komissii B V*, Moscow: 1914.

9   [Editor's note: In fact, Chaplin notices a young woman he had met on the immigrant ship, who is sitting at a nearby table, and he then leads her to his table.]

situation gets worse. Chaplin sees some [waiters] giving a thrashing to one of the customers and he asks one of them why they beat him. He learns that it is because he has not paid his bill. Chaplin trembles as he watches the waiters leaving triumphantly after they have beaten the non-paying customer.[10] The audience expects Chaplin will end up in the same way. A man is sitting opposite Chaplin. The waiter receives some money from him but a coin slips down on the floor. Chaplin promptly steps on the coin and wants to pick it up. The audience is riveted by what will happen. If Chaplin picks up the coin unnoticed, he will be saved. If he doesn't succeed, they will knock the living daylights out of him. Hurrah! … Chaplin picks the coin up unnoticed. He calls the waiter over and pays his bill with the coin. The waiter bites the coin and discovers that it is a fake. The situation looks hopeless again. At this moment a film producer comes over to Chaplin and his girlfriend, orders something and sits down next to Chaplin. The waiter leaves for the time being. The producer calls the waiter and wants to pay for himself and for Chaplin and his girlfriend. But Chaplin keeps on objecting. The producer pays only for himself. Chaplin's situation is hopeless again. Nevertheless, Chaplin – against the audience's expectations – wins in the end. The producer has left a small coin as a tip for the waiter. After the producer leaves, Chaplin uses the coin to pay for his modest bill.[11] All ends well.

This is the artistic technique of delayed action. Throughout, the audience keeps expecting a bad ending, but the hero manages to avoid it and then he gets into a difficult situation again. This is repeated several times until the hero gets away unharmed and all ends well. This structure is very frequent in literature found round the world. It is enough to think of folk tales. The hero is usually given three very hard tasks. The tasks are increasingly difficult. The third and last task is almost impossible to fulfil. The listeners are on tenterhooks. The hero nearly perishes. However, at the last moment he unexpectedly emerges as the winner. The same "delaying" technique is often found in melodramas. The noble hero gets into the most difficult situations. At the end of the piece there is no hope he will be saved. Suddenly his innocence is proved by some lucky chance and both the hero and virtue triumph.

This technique, borrowed from literature, was highly suitable for film. In fast-changing scenes it is possible to present the most implausible difficulties of the hero in a brief span of time and then to get him out of the difficult situation equally rapidly.

Let us return to the analysis of *The Count*.

---

10   [Editor's note: When the waiters rush out following the man they have kicked out, we cannot actually see Chaplin—he is hidden by them.]

11   [Editor's note: Chaplin pays with the coin while the producer is talking to the woman, and then they all leave together.]

We left the tailor when he had expelled Chaplin from his shop. The tailor looks sadly at the tailcoat burnt through by the iron and finds in it an invitation to a count to attend a fancy dress party. The tailor puts on a tailcoat and goes to the party, taking with him the invitation.[12] The party is being held in the house where Chaplin's sweetheart works as a cook. The tailor presents the invitation he has found in the tailcoat[13] and is shown into the entrance hall. He notices Chaplin in the dumbwaiter: when Chaplin pressed the button to escape the cook's other lover – the policeman – it rose up and stopped in the entrance hall. The tailor explains to Chaplin how he got to the party and suggests he go with him into the dining room as his secretary. Chaplin goes into the dining room but he is faster than the tailor and introduces himself as the count; then he introduces the tailor as his secretary. The tailor is furious but it is too late to change anything. He has no choice but to accept the situation. It is a fancy dress party so Chaplin's clothes do not raise suspicion. Everybody sits down at the table. It becomes obvious that Chaplin and the tailor have no table manners. For example, the guests unfold their serviettes. Chaplin puts his in his breast pocket as if it were a handkerchief. A watermelon slice is served; Chaplin takes the whole piece and bites the pulp out. As he bites deeper the rind gets into his ears... He wipes his ears with the serviette and finally he discovers how to stop the rind from getting into his ears. He wraps the serviette under his chin and across his cheeks and then ties it on the top of his head as people do when they have a toothache. So he doesn't put the serviette under his chin, but on his head. This is a technique traditionally used by clowns: one particular circus clown used to perform with starched cuffs on his legs. In addition there is another comic effect here. With the serviette around his cheeks Chaplin looks like a man who has a toothache. However, at the same time the audience knows that Chaplin has a different goal in mind. It is as funny as if somebody went for a walk and leaned on a fork or a poker. A fork and a poker evoke in us associations with the kitchen and when they are taken out of their usual setting and used for ends that are totally untypical for them, this raises a laugh. Chaplin with his cheeks wrapped up so as not to soil his ears is as funny as a man who goes for a walk with a poker instead of a cane. Chaplin often uses this method, for example when he cleans his nails with the tip of his cane (which he does in this film) or when he wants to attract a passer-by's attention and hooks him with his cane by the shoulder and draws him closer.

Chaplin's cheeks wrapped in the serviette so as not to soil his ears lead to a third effect. Chaplin doesn't cut up or break the big piece of melon into

---

12 [Editor's note: There is no invitation in the film; the letter is the count's apology for not being able to attend the "dance".]
13 [Editor's note: Rather, he tips the butler.]

smaller bits but protects his face against the wet melon rind, which is much more complicated. This comic construction brings to mind a story about the people in Kocourkov,[14] who hauled a cow up to the roof instead of taking the straw off the roof and using it to bed the cow down.

Let us continue with the plot of the film.

The lunch has finished. Chaplin dances the shimmy with his lady. Chaplin parodies this dance very well. He emphasizes all the dance steps, exaggerates and thus achieves a comic effect.

The real count appears in the entrance hall. He is surprised to learn from the butler that the count is already there. He regards the self-proclaimed count as a criminal and calls the police. [A policeman] rushes in and chases Chaplin around the house. He escapes skilfully and defends himself when the policeman comes closer. He stands on his hands and kicks the policeman with his feet.

In his first films Chaplin jumped and fell just as frequently as in his new, latest films. However, there is a difference: these actions in his first films were only used for the acrobatic effect itself (Chaplin fell and rolled around for the entertainment of the audience), while in his latest films they all have an aim and serve a purpose.

The film ends with Chaplin running away. He has won and escaped from [those] who have been chasing him.

By analysing Chaplin's film *The Count* I have attempted to show that both in his acting methods and in the very plot of the film Chaplin owes a great deal to the old masters of words and mime. Many of the comic tricks used in the film have a very honourable tradition. However, one must acknowledge that Chaplin has combined these old literary and mime techniques very skilfully.

WORKS CITED

Chaplin, Charlie (1918) "What People Laugh At", *American Magazine*, vol. 86, no. 34, November, pp. 134–37.
Trudy Slavienskoi arkhivnoi komissii B V, Moscow: 1914.

---

14   [Editor's note: A proverbial town said to be inhabited by simpletons noted for their illogical and foolish behaviour, something like Gotham in English folklore.]

AN ATTEMPT AT A STRUCTURAL ANALYSIS OF AN ACTOR'S FIGURE (CHAPLIN IN *CITY LIGHTS*)

JAN MUKAŘOVSKÝ

["Chaplin ve *Světlech velkoměsta*. Pokus o strukturní rozbor hereckého zjevu" was first published in Czech in 1931 in *Literární noviny*, vol. 5, no. 3, pp. 2–3. It was translated into English by John Burbank and Peter Steiner and published as "An Attempt at a Structural Analysis of a Dramatic Figure" in Burbank, John and Steiner, Peter (trans. and eds) (1978) *Structure, Sign and Function: Selected Essays by Jan Mukařovský*, New Haven and London: Yale University Press, pp. 171–77. The translation was re-edited and published in 2008 as "An Attempt at a Structural Analysis of an Actor's Figure (Chaplin in *City Lights*)" in Szczepanik, Petr and Anděl, Jaroslav (eds), *Cinema All the Time: An Anthology of Czech Film Theory and Criticism,1908–1939*. Prague: National Film Archive, pp. 245–50.]

Editor's note: The concept "actor's figure" (in Czech, *herecký zjev*) encompasses both the appearance and the physical presence of an actor. Veltruský, for example, uses "stage figure" for the same theoretical concept in the context of theatre; some translations of Zich's terminology use "actor-in-role" (for example, Quinn 1995); Ambros (2014) suggests translating the concept as "actor's appearance". In this early study by Mukařovský, we keep Szczepanik's (2008) editorial alteration of the earlier translation of the study by Steiner (1978), who used "dramatic figure".

Today, the conception of a work of art as a structure – that is, a system of components aesthetically deautomatized and organized into a complex hierarchy that is unified by the prevalence of one component over the others – is accepted in the theory of several arts. It is clear to theorists and historians of music and the visual arts that, in the analysis of a certain work, or even in the history of a given art, we cannot either substitute the psychology of the artist's personality for a structural analysis or confuse the development of a given art with the history of culture or with that of an ideology. Much of this is clear in the theory of literature as well, though certainly not everywhere nor for everyone. Nevertheless, it is quite risky to use the method of structural analysis for the art of acting, especially if it concerns a film actor who uses his real name for his performances and even goes through all of his roles in the same distinctive costume. The theorist who tries to separate the outer appearance from the man and to study the structural organization of the actor's figure regardless of the actor's psyche and ethos is in danger of being considered a scandalous cynic who denies the artist his human value.

Permit him, therefore, in defence and for the sake of a clear visual explanation, to appeal to a recent photomontage in the *Prager Presse*[1] that juxtaposed a man with greying hair and a lively physiognomy and the simple-minded face of a black-haired young man in a bowler hat… Despite its disadvantages, a structural analysis of the actor's figure has a certain small advantage: the equality of even quite different aesthetic canons is generally admitted in the dramatic arts more than in other arts. The Hamlets of Jaroslav Kvapil and Karel Hugo Hilar, Eduard Vojan and Eduard Kohout,[2] are evaluated from a historical perspective without one being depreciated at the expense of another. Perhaps this study, then, will also escape criticism for lacking an evaluative perspective.

The first thing that must be pointed out is that the structure of the actor's figure is merely a partial structure. It only becomes unambiguous in the overall structure of the dramatic work, where it is found in multiple relations; for example, the actor and the stage space, the actor and the dramatic text, the actor and the other actors. We shall consider only one of these relations: the hierarchy of characters in the dramatic work. This hierarchy differs according to period and milieu and, in part, in relation to the dramatic text. Sometimes actors do create a structurally bound whole, but it is one in which no one has a dominant position and no one is the focal point of all the relations among the characters of the work. Sometimes one character (or several) becomes a focal point, dominating the others, who seem to be there only to provide a background, to accompany the dominant character (or characters). Sometimes all the characters appear equal and lacking structural relations: the relations between them are merely composed for their ornamental effect. In other words, the tasks and rights of the director are evaluated differently in different periods and different milieus. Chaplin's case clearly belongs in the second category. Chaplin is an axis around which the other characters gather, the reason why they are there. They emerge from the shadows only insofar as they are necessary for the dominant character. This assertion will be developed and proven later.

Let us now turn our attention to the internal structure of the actor's figure itself. The components of this structure are many and varied; nevertheless, we can divide them into three distinct groups. First, there is the

---

1   [Editorial note (2008): *Prager Presse* (1921–1939), a German-language Prague daily that voiced official government politics.]

2   [Editorial note (2008): Jaroslav Kvapil (1868–1950), progressive theatre director, neo-romantic symbolist; Karel Hugo Hilar (1885–1935), theatre director and actor, expressionist and "civilist" ("Civilism" was the second stage of Expressionism, one that embraced realist elements, developed in Czechoslovakia in the 1920s); Eduard Vojan (1853–1920), psychological-realist actor; Eduard Kohout (1889–1976), actor and colleague of Vojan's whose acting style developed from impressionism and expressionism toward "civilism". All of them worked mainly at the National Theatre in Prague.]

set of vocal components. This group is quite complex (the pitch of the voice and its melodic undulation, the intensity and timbre of the voice, tempo, and so on), but, in the given case, this is of no importance. Chaplin's films are "pantomimes" (Chaplin uses this term himself to distinguish his latest motion picture from sound film). Later, we shall explain why they cannot but be silent. The second group of components can only be identified with a triple designation: facial expressions, gestures, carriage. Both from an objective and a structural standpoint these are three different components. They can parallel one another, but they can also diverge so that their inter-relation is felt to be an interference (an effective comic device). Moreover, one of them can subordinate the others to itself or, conversely, all of them can be in equilibrium. What is common to all three of these components, however, is that they are experienced as expressive, as an expression of the character's mental state, especially his emotions. This property binds them into a unified group. The third group is composed of those movements of the body that express and serve as a vehicle of the actor's relation to the stage space.[3] Frequently the components of this group cannot be objectively distinguished from those of the preceding group (for example the actor's walk can simultaneously be a gesture, that is, an expression of a mental state, and can cause a change in his relation to the stage space); functionally, as we have suggested, they are quite distinct from the previous group and together form an independent category.

There is certainly no need to provide extensive proof in propounding the thesis that with Chaplin the components of the second group hold the dominant position. For the sake of simplicity we will simply term these gestures and thus extend this term to facial expressions and carriage, without undue distortion. As we have already said, the first group (vocal components) is completely suppressed in Chaplin, while the third group (movements) occupies a distinctly subordinate position. Even though movements that change the actor's relation to space do occur, they are charged to the utmost with the function of gestures (Chaplin's walk sensitively reflects every change in his mental state). Hence the dominant position falls to gestures (expressive elements), constituting an uninterrupted series full of interferences and unexpected visual punch lines that carries the entire dynamics not only of Chaplin's performance but also of the whole film. Chaplin's gestures are not subordinated to any other component; on the contrary, all the other com-

---

3   Even with Chaplin, though he is a typical film actor, we can speak about the stage in the theatrical sense, that is, a static stage, because here the camera is almost passive. Even if it moves, it has only an auxiliary role—for the purpose of close-ups. As proof and elucidation of this assertion, let me recall the active role of the camera in Russian films where the changeability of stand-points and perspectives plays the dominant role in the structure of the work, whereas the actor's figure is structurally subordinated.

ponents are subordinated to the gestures. In this, Chaplin's acting differs distinctly from the standard, normal practice. Even when an actor differentiates and emphasizes gestures, they usually serve a word, a movement or the action. They are a passive series whose peripeteia is motivated by other series. And with Chaplin? The word, which is most able to influence gestures, must be completely suppressed if the gestures are to be the dominant component. In a Chaplin film, every distinct word would be a blotch: it would turn the hierarchy of components upside down. For this reason, neither Chaplin himself nor the other characters speak. Typical in this respect is the introductory scene of *City Lights*, the unveiling of a monument, in which distinct words are replaced by sounds having only intonation and timbre in common with words. As far as movements in the stage space are concerned, I have said that they are charged with the function of gestures; as a matter of fact, they are gestures. Moreover, the actor's figure created by Chaplin is rather immobile (the immobility is even stressed by a physical defect in his feet). And now for the plot. The plot lacks any dynamism of its own: it is merely a series of events linked by a weak thread. Its function is to be the substratum of the dynamic sequence of gestures. The divisions between individual events serve only to provide pauses in the sequence of gestures and to render it coherent through this articulation. Even the incompleteness of the plot is an expression of its atomization. Chaplin's film does not end in a plot conclusion but in a gesture-visual point – a gesture by Chaplin (a look and a smile). This holds only for the European version of the film, but it is characteristic that such a way of concluding the film is possible.

If we posit the line of gestures as the dominant of the actor's figure created by Chaplin, we must now define the character of this line. In a negative sense, we can say that none of the three elements (facial expressions, gestures proper, carriage) prevails over the others but that they assert themselves equally. A positive definition of the very essence of this line is: its dynamics are carried by the interference (whether simultaneous or successive) of two types of gestures, gesture-signs and gesture-expressions. Here we must engage in a brief discussion of the function of gestures in general. We have already said that this function is essentially expressive in *all* gestures. But this expressiveness has its nuances: it can be immediate and individual, but it can also acquire supra-individual validity. In this case the gesture becomes a conventional sign, universally comprehensible (either in general or in a certain milieu). This is true, for example, of ritual gestures (a typical case: the gestures employed in religious ceremonies) and especially social gestures. Social gestures are signs that, in a conventional way – just like words – signal certain emotions or mental states; for instance sincere emotional involvement, willingness, respect. But there is no guarantee that the mental state of the person who uses the gesture corresponds to the mood of which the gesture is a sign. That is why all the Alcestes of the world rage against the insincerity of social conventions.

The individual expressiveness ("sincerity") of a social gesture can be reliably recognized only if it is involuntarily accompanied by some nuance that alters its conventional course. It can happen that a particular emotion coincides with the mental state of which the gesture is the sign. In such a case, the gesture-sign will be exaggerated beyond the conventional degree of its intensity (too deep a bow or too broad a smile). But the opposite can also occur: the particular mental state is different from the mood that is supposed to be feigned by the gesture-sign. In this case an interference will occur, either *successive*, that is, such that the coordination of the series of gestures unfolding in time will be disturbed (the sudden invasion of an individually expressive, involuntary gesture into the series of gesture-signs), or *simultaneous*, that is, such that the gesture-sign provided, for example, by a facial expression will at the same time be negated by a contradictory gesticulation of the hand based on individual expression, or vice versa. Chaplin's case is a typical example of the interference of social gesture-signs with individually expressive gestures. Everything in Chaplin's acting is aimed at heightening and sharpening this interference, even his special costume: ragged formal attire, gloves without fingers, but a cane and a black bowler hat. What serves to sharpen the interference of gestures in particular, however, is the social paradox of Chaplin encapsulated by the very theme: the beggar with social aspirations. This provides the basis for the interference. The integrating emotional feature of social gestures is the feeling of self-assurance and superiority, whereas the expressive gestures of Chaplin-the-beggar revolve around the emotional complex of inferiority. These two levels of gestures interweave through the entire performance in constant catachreses. To characterize this interweaving in detail would entail an endless enumeration of verbal paraphrases of the individual moments of the performance, which would be monotonous and useless. Much more interesting is the fact that the double level of gestures is also reflected in the differentiation of the supporting characters in Chaplin's performance. There are two supporting characters: the blind flower girl and the drunken millionaire. All the others are demoted to the level of extras, either partially (the old woman) or completely (all the others). Each of the two supporting characters is modified so that he or she can perceive only one level, one of the interfering series of Chaplin's gestures. Such one-sided perception is motivated by blindness in the girl and by intoxication in the millionaire. The girl perceives only the social gesture-signs. The deformed image she has formed of Chaplin is shown toward the end of the film through an interesting process of realization. A man, a nondescript social type, comes to the shop of the girl, whose sight is now restored, to buy some flowers. His departure is accompanied by the intertitle "I thought that it was *him*." All the scenes in which Chaplin meets the girl – they are always alone so that the presence of a third, normally sighted person may not shatter the girl's illusion – are founded upon the polar oscillation between the two levels of Chaplin's gestures: social and individually expressive gestures. Whenever Chaplin draws close to the girl in these scenes, the social gestures gain the upper hand, but as soon as he takes a few steps away from her, the expressive gestures suddenly prevail. This is especially evident in the scene in which Chaplin brings some gifts to the girl and moves back and forth from the table where the bag of presents is lying to the chair on which the girl is sitting. Here the sudden changes in gestures, the transition from level to level, function almost like the witty points of epigrams. Given this context, it is understandable why Chaplin's film cannot have the usual "happy ending". A happy ending would entail the complete negation of the dramatic contradiction between the two levels of gestures upon which the film is based, rather than its resolution. If it concluded by the beggar's marrying the girl, the film would appear trivial in retrospect, because its dramatic contradiction would be devalued.

Now to the relationship between the beggar and the millionaire. The millionaire, as we have said, also has access to only one of the two interfering series of gestures, those that are individually expressive. For this deformation of vision to be operative he must, of course, be drunk. As soon as he becomes sober, he sees, like all the rest, the comical interference of the two series, and treats Chaplin with the same disdain as everyone else. But whereas the girl's deformation of perception (her ability to see only one series of gestures) is permanent, and the resolution occurs only at the very end of the film, the millionaire's state of deformed vision alternates with states of normal vision. This, of course, determines the hierarchy of the two supporting characters. The girl comes more to the fore, because her permanent deformation of perception provides a broader and stronger basis for the interference of the two levels of gestures than the millionaire's intermittent intoxication. The millionaire is, however, necessary as the girl's opposite. From the first meeting with Chaplin, when, employing his expressive gestures, the beggar sings an impassioned hymn to the beauty of life ("Tomorrow the birds will sing") before the millionaire, their relationship is full of outpourings of friendship, from one embrace to another. And so we have proceeded quite imperceptibly from the structural analysis of the actor's figure to the structure of the entire film. This is another proof of the extent to which the interference of the two levels of gestures is the axis of Chaplin's acting.

I will end here, for I believe everything essential has been said. In conclusion, though, let me make a few evaluative comments. What astonishes the spectator in Chaplin's figure is the immense discrepancy between the intensity of the effect that he achieves and the simplicity of his formative devices. He embraces as the dominant of his structure one that usually occupies (in film) an ancillary position: gestures in the broad sense of the term (facial expressions, gestures proper, carriage). And to this fragile dominant with its limited capacity to carry the story, he manages to subordinate not only the structure of his own actor's figure but even that of the entire film. This presupposes an almost unbelievable economy in all the other components. If any one of them were stressed a little more, called only a little more attention to itself, the entire structure would collapse. The structure of Chaplin's acting resembles a three-dimensional shape that rests on the sharpest of its edges but is in perfect equilibrium. Hence the illusion of dematerialization: the pure lyricism of gestures freed from dependence on a corporeal/physical substratum.

WORKS CITED

Ambrus, Veronika (2014) "Prague Linguistic Circle in English: Semantic Shifts in Selected Texts and their Consequences", *Theatralia*, vol. 17, no. 2, pp. 148–61

Burbank, John and Steiner, Peter (trans. and eds) (1978) *Structure, Sign and Function: Selected Essays by Jan Mukařovský*, New Haven and London: Yale University Press.

Quinn, Michael L. (1995) *The Semiotic Stage: Prague School Theatre Theory*, New York: Peter Lang.

Szczepanik, Petr and Anděl, Jaroslav (eds) (2008) *Cinema All the Time: An Anthology of Czech Film Theory and Criticism, 1908–1939*, Prague: National Film Archive.

THE DRAMATIC CHARACTER

JINDŘICH HONZL

["Herecká postava" was first published in Czech in 1939 in *Slovo a slovesnost*, vol. 5, no. 3, pp. 145–50.]

Translated by Marta Filipová

Editor's note: The Czech title of the article makes use of a concept of Otakar Zich's that has been translated in a number of different ways into English, among them "actor's figure" and "actor-in-role". In his "Principles of Theoretical Dramaturgy" (published on pages 34–58 of this reader), Zich does not use this term, while Veltruský in translations of his own works uses the term "stage figure" as his own idiosyncratic choice, which we have kept in this reader. Honzl does not use the concept strictly in Zich's sense (as the counterpart to an audience's psychological construct of a character and the actor as such), but in a sense that is closest to dramatic character. We have therefore decided to translate the essay, including its title, with this term, as it is most useful for Honzl's argument in this article.

Harlequin. Il Dottore. Pantalone. Brighella. Truffaldino. Scaramouche. Sganarelle. Pierrot. The characters in *commedia dell'arte*.

It is tempting to compare these unchanging characters to the strain, refraction and pressure indexes used by engineers in making their calculations when designing a bridge. This way we recognize in them fixed "rules of the game". The plays themselves were endlessly new permutations in the relations between these typical characters. For an actor in the seventeenth and eighteenth centuries to create a new character would therefore have meant changing the rules and establishing new ones. In order to make this comparison clearer, think about the pieces in a game of chess.

A person who has a smattering of the imagination of an artist is fond of the queen, the bishops, the king, the pawns and eagerly suggests "Since we have a queen and bishops, a king and knights, why don't we – so as to increase the number of permutations – have ... for instance ... an odalisque?" A chess player immediately rejects the beautiful odalisque and asserts that no one has ever exhausted all the permutations of a single chess opening – for example, the queen's gambit. Why is there a need for an odalisque?

The champion of the odalisque and the chess player can never understand each other. It seems to us that we, too, are unable to understand the characters in *commedia dell'arte* and the laws they follow on the stage. Time has brought towers taller than the Tower of Babel, and it has also altered the planets that rule over the arts.

We cannot capture the essence of the *commedia dell'arte* "characters" even when we compare them with the characters of some of today's comic actors – Charlie Chaplin, Buster Keaton, Harold Lloyd, Laurel and Hardy – because the latter are characters of contemporary art. Chaplin is not a typical character, he is simply a single, very specific figure: a failure and a gentleman, a tramp and a dandy, a waddler and a good-looker, happy and melancholy, a contented man and an eternal dreamer, who moves from film to film in the same way d'Artagnan moves from book to book in Alexandre Dumas's *The Three Musketeers*.[1] The costume marks Chaplin off from every social class and job, and every film becomes a new proof of how impossible it is for this society to accept him. This figure cannot come to terms with the principles of any social class or any job.

Harlequin, however, was never a Chaplinesque revolutionary. Nor was he ever such an anarchist. On the contrary, he was at home in all trades and in all social classes. Even though his boundless vitality went beyond the common norms of social discipline (and after all, which dramatic character can be a model of social order and obedience?), it was possible for Harlequin to represent all classes on the stage. It was enough for him to announce that he was a count and the spectator immediately interpreted his colourful clothes as an embroidered coat, richly decorated in gold and lace. Yet Harlequin's multi-coloured garment served just as well for the character of an "innkeeper" who wormed out of his guests the secrets of their loves as well as their money.

Harlequin is not an individual: he is a conventional character who can be adopted by any actor in the same way that an author can adopt the conventions of an adventure novel or a sonnet.

The comparison of a dramatic character with a chess piece was only useful to the extent that it enabled us to realize that the *permanence* of chess rules is for a game of chess what the constant *changeability* of the rules is for a play.

In art, the rules, regulations and laws have an opposite tendency to those in life. It seems as though art only respects laws that have not been discovered and named by anyone, that no one has classified, that no one has managed to turn into ten commandments. The moment a reader or spectator starts to get a clear sense of the rules of the play or novel, the moment we discover the structure of the composition in a painting instead of having an impression – that moment the work of art is transformed into a mechanism of cogwheels and springs that falls apart before our eyes, leaving nothing. Reading Viktor

---

1   [Editor's note: Honzl obviously means all the books from the d'Artagnan Romances series.]

Shklovsky's *Theory of Prose*, we have a feeling that the author listed the rules for the construction of novels and novellas by Cervantes, Dickens and Sterne so as to prevent authors from writing works by following Cervantes's formulae, Dickens's equations with several unknowns, Sterne's rules of "cheating at cards".[2] In this sense, we could say that formalist aestheticians are the true enemies of formalist authors.

Let us recall Gozzi's and Goldoni's struggle with the improvised Italian theatre and with the conventions of characters and situations in *commedia dell'arte*. This paradox is the logical result of how things had developed: the two authors who represent the tradition of Italian comedy at its peak are at the same time its true enemies and gravediggers. In their work the written *commedia erudita* wins out over the improvisation of *commedia dell'arte*. The conventions of the old *commedia dell'arte* had fossilized into a series of static comic situations, typical jokes and puns: the entire play had taken on the dead weight of a structure lacking movement and the pulse of life.

This is why not only authors and actors but the audience as well turned their back on *commedia dell'arte*. Gozzi and Goldoni rescued the characters of the old comedy by giving them new names, by clothing them in new costumes, by writing new dialogues for them. Plays that had previously been a series of situations held together only by the familiar characters were transformed into plays whose parts were linked together by the unity of cause and effect, the unity of plot.

Lessing, coming after Gozzi and Goldoni, swept away the stale theatrical structure of the Harlequin play. He sought help in Shakespeare and his barbaric boisterousness, which defied the rules of balance and proportionality. It is true that the hybridity of Shakespeare's dramatic structure could not serve as a model for any of his German imitators – Lessing, Goethe and Schiller – yet its characters, living their powerful individual lives, which none of the imitators could make conventional, swept the Italian comedians and their characters from the stage. The conventional Harlequin plays only survived in cheap theatres on the outskirts of cities and in street performances of questionable taste.

The eighteenth and nineteenth centuries were marked by the struggle waged by English and French dramaturgy against the empty conventionality of the Italian theatre, with its comic actors and pastoral and chivalric dramas, but *in spite of this*, theatre – that is, dramatic practice (the practice of actors) – retained the conventional typology of characters. The rules of

2 [Editor's note: Honzl speaks of cheating at the card-game "mariáš", which is a typical Czech card-game, unknown in Russia. Honzl most probably interprets Shklovsky's observations regarding Sterne's playing with literary devices, and compares them to cheating at a card-game. The concepts of Cervantes's "formulae" and Dickens's "equations with several unknowns" are also Honzl's inventions.]

tried-and-true theatricality continued to apply, although in a new way and under new names.

At the end of the nineteenth century, at the time of the Provisional Theatre in Prague (1862–1883)[3] and later, actors were taken on and roles assigned according to the strict rules of *stock characters*, which are simply the ancient types and characters in a new guise. Thus the ensemble of the Provisional Theatre was protected from both backstage intrigues and artistic chaos through the system of stock characters, which provided a firm structure for distributing the roles. So the roles of fashionable lovers went to Mr Bittner, the roles of fathers to Mr Chramosta, comic character parts to Mr Chvalkovský, the roles of heroes and villains to Mr J. J. Kolár, roles that involved singing comic songs to Mr Mošna, "lovers" to Mr Seifert and heroes to Mr Šimanovský.[4]

The character as created by the actor– as can be seen – survived epochs of artistic revolution and defeat; it had a lifetime longer than that of the character as created by the playwright. The latter sometimes dies with the author and must wait a long time for its resurrection. Shakespeare's Hamlet was buried for a hundred years – only then did Garrick rediscover him for his country, for Voltaire, Diderot and the French, for Lessing and the Germans and for the entire world. *That aspect of the actor's performance that is craftsmanship* – the rules governing the actor's movement, his speech, the conventions he employs in creating the character – resists changes in art. Until the end of the nineteenth century, the actor's character – as can be seen from the strict categorization of stock characters – was basically considered the product of craftsmanship. The more specialized a craftsman was, the more often he repeated what he did, the better he was.

The act of artistic creation, which is a unique act of inspiration and spontaneity, stands in dialectic opposition to rules of theatre practice and acting.

The dramaturgy of the kind practised by Diderot and Lessing and the dramaturgy of the Romantics was adverse to Harlequin, Trufaldino, Hanswurst and others, yet it came to terms with the stock characters – with the lovers, villains, comic actors who could sing, comic character parts, fathers, heroes, and so on. In their dramas Schiller and Kleist make no effort to prevent the actor or the spectator from recognizing a "villain" in Franz Moor and a "hero" in Hermann. On the contrary – the dramatist provides this knowledge from the first scene and the detailed exposition only reinforces the heroism, villainy, love, and so on for the spectator.

---

3   [Editor's note: A predecessor of the Czech National Theatre; its premiser now form part of the current National Theatre building.]
4   [Editor's note: Jiří Bittner (1846–1903), Josef Karel Chramosta (1829–1895), Edmund Chvalkovský (1839–1934), Josef Jiří Kolár (1812–1896), Jindřich Mošna (1837–1911), Jakub Seifert (1846–1919) and Karel Šimanovský (1826–1904), iconic actors of the period.]

However, the play from the end of the nineteenth century, what is called the realist play, rejects stock characters, does not want to make it easy for the spectator to recognize the characters of a villain, comic character, hero, lover, and so on. Quite the reverse – it aims to place as many obstacles as possible in the way of the spectator so as to prevent him from being able to categorize the character and guess the structure and calculation on which the writer's fiction is based. This kind of play presents the spectator and listener with constant riddles. The character itself is a complex combination, a "dramatic plot". Getting to know and "unravelling" the character is the aim of the play, its conclusion, the end of the performance. What was formerly the beginning of a play is now its ending. Older plays, Classical dramas, folk theatre, Chinese and Japanese plays started with the character explaining his family, his life, his unhappiness, his goal and the obstacles he was facing:

Mandarin Li-Yen. I am the mandarin Li-Yen; my wife passed away eighteen years ago when giving birth to our daughter Peach Blossom. The snow of old age did not turn my hair white – adversity and gossip led me to fall from grace with my Emperor, the noble ruler of the heavens. Thrown down from the heights of honour, I must now set out as the accused and go to the imperial city to restore my honour. I shall wait for the abbess on this bench. (Anon., *The Blanket of Love*, act I)[5]

Anton Chekhov, the late nineteenth century author and Russia's greatest realist playwright, ended his drama *Ivanov* as follows:

Ivanov. I used to be young, eager, sincere, intelligent. I loved, hated and believed differently from other people, I worked hard enough – I had hope enough – for ten men. … I was in a hurry to expend all my youthful energy, drank too much, got over-excited, worked, never did things by halves. But tell me, what else could you expect? We're so few, after all, and there's such a lot to be done, God knows. And now look how cruelly life, the life I challenged, is taking its revenge. I broke under the strain. I woke up to myself at the age of thirty… Heavy-headed, dull-witted, worn out… I moon around, more dead than alive… Love's a fraud, or so I think, and any show of affection's just sloppy sentimentality, there's no point in working, songs and fiery speeches are cheap and stale. (Chekhov 1998: 61).

On the following page, Ivanov shoots himself and the play ends.

---

5   [Editor's note: Honzl quotes from an unpublished manuscript of a Czech translation of a German version by Rudelsberger of the traditional 13th century Chinese comic play *Yuan Yang Pei* [The Blanket of Love] by an anonymous author. It was "translated by F. Spitzer for the Czech Workers' Amateur Theatre" (Kalvodová 1992: 17). Spitzer was also the director of the performance in 1938.]

It has to be added, however, that Ivanov was just as "dull-witted, worn out" in Act 1 as in Act 4 and that the time when he worked and thought so hard is of no concern to the playwright, that he left it in the past, long before the play even started. There is no "dramatic conflict, action, peripety, dénouement" that the play develops; rather, "coming to know the character" is the subject of dramatic interest. Ivanov himself is the plot: the contradictory complexity of his spirit is the dramatic "conflict".

Pierrot's white cotton blouse could clothe Ivanov's deep-seated melancholy beautifully, and his moon-pale countenance could speak eloquently of his continuous longing for four full acts, until he shoots himself.

But the Ivanov who appeared dressed like Pierrot might recite no more than the monologue from Act 4 in the Lebedevs' salon, then shoot himself – and that would suffice.

To prevent us from recognizing the ancient comedian's costume or his character for four whole acts, to constantly feed our interest with hints and riddles, it was necessary for the actor – who after all still carries within himself the ancient Italian comedian – to disguise himself as an ordinary, quite inconspicuous character who gets lost in the crowd, as the character of a certain assistant judge, Nikolai Alekseevich Ivanov. We have to become interested in this assistant judge.

Ivanov often visits Lebedev, the chairman of the district council. And here we see that he is a "man of mystery". Everyone has a different opinion of him. His doctor has proof that his visits are aimed at systematically and slowly killing his wife. But it is during these visits that Lebedev's daughter Sasha comes to understand him as the only person in the district who is honourable and affectionate, while her mother Zinaida is convinced that Ivanov tricked his wife for her dowry and his estate manager Borkin knows he is a good man who is being cheated by his friends and relatives.

Who is Ivanov? We still know nothing in Act 3.

> No, Doctor, we all have too many wheels, screws and valves to judge each other on first impressions or one or two pointers. I don't understand you, you don't understand me and we don't understand ourselves. (Chekhov 1998: 44)

And so the suspicion that Ivanov's wife is slowly dying as a result of "criminal machinations" spreads to everyone else, to "the entire society".

We become interested not only in Ivanov but also in all the other characters. We need to *know each one of these characters well* in order to "disentangle the plot" and the "guilty secret".

We become interested in this story without incidents, in the action, which we might term getting to know a person. – "To know that I love" (Masha speaking of her love for Vershinin in *The Three Sisters*)... in this there is found the whole of Chekhov's drama.

The drama and the dramaturgy of the nineteenth century (realist dramaturgy) resisted classifying a character as a type because this would have meant not only the individual being watered down into a type but also the collapse of the dramatic axis of the realist play, which is built on the tension that exists between the emotional and volitional tendencies of the individual, a tension that is released, that finds its expression, in conflicts within the human personality, in *crises of the complex individual*.

The theatre and the actors' craftsmanship resisted this new, realist dramaturgy for a long time and as best it could. Chekhov's plays were failures even on the best stages and with the best actors. The virtuosity of the *stock characters*, the perfect craftsmanship of the lovers and the comic actors, were of no help. From the historical point of view, one would have to say that the *actors' stock characters* fought off their enemy, who sought their demise. Where *stock characters* remained undisturbed, Chekhov's plays disintegrated, becoming a series of untheatrical and undramatic situations.

However, if Chekhov's plays were to be saved, it was necessary to do away with stock characters, to break down the unity of a character so as to reveal many acting parts, many personalities, many "stock characters", within it. These "partial characters" carry on a dramatic dialogue and are in dramatic conflict. It was necessary to distribute the field of force of the character's personality among several different fields of force, acting together to maintain the unity of the character as the resultant of many centrifugal and centripetal pressures. It was necessary for the actor to master not just one but all the stock characters in order to represent – as the critical jargon of realism would have it – the whole person.

Therefore the first attack launched by the Chekhovian theatre – that is, the theatre of Stanislavsky and Nemirovich-Danchenko – was an attack against the actors' "craftsmanship", which had created firm conventions for depicting a person on the stage.

Prior to Stanislavsky, acting had been divided into different types of stock characters, the aim being to achieve the utmost perfection in the depiction of people. Acting created its own specializations in the same way that doctors, shoemakers, philologists and thieves became specialized.

Stanislavsky saw acting based on perfect craftsmanship as an *obstacle* to the art of acting, to creative acting. It was only designed for those who are not and who cannot be artists. It was designed for those who lack creativity.

For those who cannot believe, religion has ceremonies. For those who elicit no respect for their personality, etiquette is necessary. For those who do not know how to dress, fashion is needed, for those who are not capable of being creative (in acting), there is the craft (of acting). (Stanislavsky 1921)

Stanislavsky and the realist dramaturgy of the late nineteenth century wished to do away with the certainties of craftsmanship, which had led to the situation in which an actor came to the read-through with a fully formed character – precise, clear and comprehensible to the audience. It was enough for an actor to read the name and description of a character in order to know what tone of voice to use, how to articulate, how to declaim sentences and dialogues, how to walk, sit down – everything.

> Without fail, soldiers on the stage speak in a bass voice, barking out words as though giving military orders, fops clear their throats and draw out some consonants, peasants speak haltingly, in a deep voice, clerics speak with an "o",[6] clerks use flat, disjointed speech, and so on. – Craftsmanship has developed a conventional type of speech for all ages and characters. For example young people, especially women, who are naïve, use a very high register that sometimes becomes a screech, while serious men and ladies employ low, firm voices. (Stanislavsky 1921)

Stanislavsky's system concentrated totally on the task of *creating a character*. In order to free the character from any signs of the traditional craftsmanship in acting, he removed it from the play, excised it from the stage image and sought to breathe into it the life of a real being. The character was meant to literally live outside the work: the actor was supposed to know what the character had done before entering into the play and what was going to happen to it after the play. In Stanislavsky's system not only does the way the character moves and how he speaks on the stage become a problem, but also how he sits down to eat, how he amuses himself, what books he reads, whether he puts on his coat by sticking his arm into the right or left sleeve first or if he pulls it on over his head sticking both arms in simultaneously...

The character lives regardless of the author, regardless of the drama, comedy or music-hall entertainment he is supposed to appear in that evening. It is of no importance to him whether the audience that evening laughs or is moved to tears. The comic or tragic quality is a question of theatrical craftsmanship, not of life. Stanislavsky's system creates (manufactures) "real characters, real people".

Chekhov himself also discovered this. The characters in his plays were stronger than the power of their creator, who wished to control them. A true "revolt of the characters on the stage".

---

6   [Editor's note: That is, they do not pronounce the unstressed "o" in Russian in the standard fashion as "ah".]

Chekhov wrote *The Cherry Orchard* as a *comic play*, as music-hall. Yet the characters in *The Cherry Orchard* acted out a *drama*. Although Chekhov was angry that the director had no idea what *The Cherry Orchard* was about, that he did not read a single line of the script – no one took the author's complaints seriously. Stanislavsky's characters "came alive" like "real people" and existed even in defiance of what the author wished.

We have reached the interesting moment in the development of theatre when the stage character is the central question of the drama and the dramatic conception. The rules of dramatic construction (conflict, plot, episodes...) and the rules of characters no longer exist independently of each other.

The character is the drama. The characters are the story, the plot, the conflict...

However, at the same time, their value crumbles, for characters take on the greatest intensity through the static unity of their nature breaking down. The character becomes an energy field of dramatic forces.

At this moment, acting takes on a new meaning. Although it has lost the certainties of its tried and tested craftsmanship, it has acquired a new power over the dramatic work and the stage. No longer are there heroes, lovers and so on – but at the same time there are no longer title characters, main and minor roles, as Stanislavsky says. The play is not "the dramatic struggle of an individual with fate," it is not even the story of the main character. Here there are characters gifted with dramatic life, each of them capable of creating its own play, its own dramatic fate.

The actor can be a creator.

Nevertheless, this moment is just a starting point, a turning point and the ground for new, chaotic changes.

It is a springboard for a leap into the dark and into the future.

WORKS CITED

Kalvodová, Dana (1992) *Čínské divadlo* [Chinese Theatre], Prague: Panorama.

Chekhov, Anton (1998) *Five Plays: Ivanov, The Seagull, Uncle Vanya, Three Sisters, and The Cherry Orchard.* Trans. Ronald Hingley. Oxford: Oxford University Press.

Stanislavsky, Konstantin (1921) "O remesle" [On Craftsmanship], *Kultura teatra*, vol. 5, pp. 10–14; vol. 6, pp. 23–24.

IV   FROM PAGE TO STAGE

Approaching drama in the context of the Prague School is inevitably influenced by linguistics. This explains why Jan Mukařovský, whose texts form the majority of this section, only discusses drama as a specific structure of language. His studies on dialogue and speech presented here form only a part of his many works devoted to issues of language in the novel and fictional prose (for example "Karel Čapek's Prose as Lyrical Melody and as Dialogue" 1964 [1939] or his studies on the novelist Vladislav Vančura, which have not been translated into English).

Mukařovský's preliminary observations about dialogue (and monologue) were systematically developed by Jiří Veltruský. Veltruský based his theory on his recognition of the double nature of the dramatic text – that it can function both as literature and as part of a theatre performance. In his *Drama as Literature* (1977 [1942]) he focused on the literary perspective; owing to its length this comprehensive study is not included in this reader, but it is readily available elsewhere. In other texts, he analysed the functions of the dramatic text in performance, understanding drama as a structure amongst other structures forming a theatre performance. This approach could be traced back to Mukařovský and Petr Bogatyrev and, in particular, to Otakar Zich. The relationship between text and performance is a crucial issue in the Prague School's discussions; Veltruský dealt with it frequently (and further developed it) in his work from the 1970s on. We cannot cover here the development of his ideas in detail; however, his treatment of the acoustic features of dramatic dialogue in the early study "Dramatic Text as a Component of Theatre" and the later study "A Contribution to the Semiotics of Acting", both included in the present volume, can be seen as instructive for the purpose of comparison. But it is important to know that following his initial study "Dramatic Text as a Component of Theatre" he provided other accounts of the issue ("Drama as Literature and Performance" (1985), "Sound Qualities of Text and the Actor's Delivery" (1991)) and summarized his findings in the posthumously published *An Approach to the Semiotics of Theatre* (2012).

ON STAGE DIALOGUE

JAN MUKAŘOVSKÝ

["O jevištním dialogu" was published in Czech in 1937 in *Program D 37*, 31 March, pp. 232–34. It was republished in 1941 as "K jevištnímu dialogu" [On Stage Dialogue] in *Kapitoly z české poetiky* [Chapters on Czech Poetics], vol. 1, pp. 176–79, where it appeared together with the 1940 article "Dialog a monolog" [Dialogue and Monologue], under the joint title "Dvě studie o dialogu" [Two Studies on Dialogue]. It was published in English in Burbank, John and Steiner, Peter (trans. and eds) (1978) *The Word and Verbal Art. Selected Essays by Jan Mukařovský*, New Haven and London: Yale University Press, pp. 112–15, as the second part of "Two Studies of Dialogue", ibid., pp. 81–115.]

Editor's note: We are publishing this article separately from the study "Dialogue and Monologue" (published on pages 220-46 of this anthology) because it was written independently and earlier. This helps to illustrate the development in Mukařovský's thoughts about dialogue and theatrical speech and reveals which issues he managed to study more deeply and which were not developed further.

E. F. Burian is right in saying that the Wagnerian conception of theatre as a synthesis of several arts is coming alive again in the contemporary theatre (1937: 87–88). The difference between the Wagnerian conception and the present state - or rather the present orientation - of the theatre is, of course, likewise evident: modern art has revealed the positive aesthetic effect of internal contradictions among the components of the work of art too clearly for us to be able to view the interplay of the individual elements of drama as merely complementary to one another. The modern stage work is an extremely complicated structure (more complicated than any other artistic structure) that eagerly sucks up everything that the contemporary development of technology offers and that other arts provide, but as a rule it does so in order to employ this material as a contrastive factor. It seizes upon the film in order to juxtapose physical reality and an immaterial image; the megaphone, in order to confront natural sound with reproduced sound; the spotlight, in order to cleave the continuity of three-dimensional space with its sword of light; the statue, in order to heighten the antithesis of a fleeting and a petrified gesture. All of this results in the artistic structure of the contemporary stage work being a protean, fluid process that consists in a constant regrouping of components, in the restless replacement of the dominant element, in the obliteration of the boundaries between drama and kindred forms (the revue, dance, acrobatics, and so on). Of course for the theory of theatre this situation is more interesting than ever before, but it is also consequently more difficult, for the old certainties have vanished, and so far there are no new ones. Today it is even difficult to find the actual point of easiest access into the labyrinth of the theatrical structure. Whenever we attempt to declare some component of the drama to be basic and indispensable, a dramatic expert, a historian of the theatre or an ethnographer can always point his finger at some dramatic form that lacks this element. There are nevertheless certain components that are more characteristic of the theatre than others and that therefore serve to unify a stage work. One of the most basic is dialogue; the following remarks are devoted to it and to its function in the theatre.

First, what is dialogue? From the linguistic viewpoint it is one of the two basic aspects of speech, the opposite of monologue – not, of course, dramatic monologue but an act of speaking that, even if addressed to a listener, is in its uninterrupted flow largely freed from a consideration for his immediate reaction and from a close bond with the actual temporal and spatial context in which the participants in the conversation are situated. Monologue can either express the speaker's subjective mental state (in literature, the lyric poem) or narrate events severed from the actual context by a temporal distance (in literature, the narrative poem). On the other hand, dialogue is closely bound to the "here" and "now" pertaining to the participants in the talk, and the speaker counts on the listener's immediate reaction. As a result, in a split second the listener becomes the speaker, and the function of the vehicle for the act of speaking constantly jumps back and forth from participant to participant. Naturally this also applies to stage dialogue, where there is yet another participant: the audience. This means that in addition to all the direct participants in the dialogue there is added another participant, silent but important, for everything that is said in a dramatic dialogue is oriented toward him, toward affecting his consciousness. We can even speak about well or poorly performed theatre or acting in ordinary speech outside the theatrical sphere, if it happens that the interest of all the participants but one is concentrated – on the basis of a secret agreement – on influencing the consciousness of precisely this individual so that every word of what is said has a different meaning for the conspiring participants than for him. Stage dialogue is hence much more complicated semantically than ordinary talk. If character *A* utters a certain sentence, the meaning of this sentence for him is determined (as is the case, after all, in every conversation) with a view to character *B*. But it is not at all certain that character *B* will understand this meaning as character *A* would wish. At the same time, the audience can be subjected to the same uncertainty as character *A*, but it is also possible that the audience has been informed of character *B*'s state of mind in the course of some previous conversation that character *A* need not be aware of, so that character *A*'s surprise at his partner's unexpected reaction will not be a surprise to the audience. The opposite case can also occur: the characters onstage will know something of which the audience is still ignorant. The semantic context that makes sense of the words that are being spoken can be shared by the audience with only some of the characters; this complicity with the audience can shift alternately from character to character; and finally the audience can understand the semantic orientation of all the characters, even though these characters do not understand one another. Moreover, the audience is always conscious of the entire preceding semantic context of the play, though far from all of the characters need be aware of it. There can also occur cases in which the audience is more extensively informed about the situation onstage than the characters of the drama (for example when the audience sees a spy eavesdropping on characters talking on the stage, while they themselves remain unaware of him). Finally, everything that is said onstage can collide in the audience's consciousness or subconscious with its system of values, its attitude toward reality. All of these circumstances make possible an immensely complex interplay of meanings, and it is precisely this complicated interplay taking place on several levels that constitutes the essence of the dramatic dialogue.

As dialogue is incorporated into the whole of the dramatic work, it need not, of course, be free to the extent that it could develop all its infinite possibilities for change, but can be limited in its flexibility by some other component. Thus, for example, the realist theatre, whose conception of dialogue has still not been completely abandoned even today, bound dialogue closely to the basic fabric of the play, that is, to the interrelations of the dramatis personae as fixed, unchanging characters. Here dialogue serves to reveal the characters' relations with one another with increasing clarity over the course of the play, in this way defining each character more and more sharply through his relationships with others. Unexpected semantic reversals are therefore permissible only insofar as they do not interfere with this main purpose but on the contrary actually serve it. Another possible restriction on dialogue can be found, for example, in medieval plays where dialogue serves to illustrate the plot. In opposition to these two kinds of servitude there is the trend in contemporary stage practice toward dialogue freed of all bonds, dialogue as a continuous play of semantic reversals. Dialogue freed from servitude becomes stage poetry: at any given moment it both comes to an end and begins. Again and again, without an obligation – though, of course, not without a latent relationship – to what has preceded, the word seeks a relation to the characters, the actual situation and the audience's consciousness and subconscious. There is no semantic context that dialogue conceived in this way cannot arrive at from any direction, but neither is there any to which it must adhere. The Aristotelian law of steadily increasing tension cannot be valid for free stage dialogue; on the other hand, it is not impossible that precisely this form is capable of renewing the sense of the tragic that emanates from Classical tragedies, which indeed terminate in a conflict forcibly concluded but actually unresolved and potentially continuing ad infinitum.

WORKS CITED

Burian, E. F. (1937) "Divadelní synthesa" [Theatrical Synthesis], *Život, list pro výtvarnou práci a uměleckou kulturu*, vol. 15, no. 3-4, pp. 87-88.

STAGE SPEECH IN THE AVANT-GARDE THEATRE

JAN MUKAŘOVSKÝ

[This text was originally delivered by Mukařovský at the Conference of Avant-Garde Theatre Practioners, organized by D 37 in Prague in May 1937. It was first published in Czech in Mukařovský, Jan (1966) *Studie z estetiky* [Studies in Aesthetics], Prague: Odeon, pp. 220–23.]

Translated by Eva Daníčková

Today the avant-garde theatre is ceasing – has indeed ceased – to be a kind of wild offshoot of the "official" theatre,[1] a fleeting exception from the rule without its own coherent development; rather, it is a whole series of experiments each of which has blended into the established theatre once it has served its purpose. Today's gathering of avant-garde theatres is the expression of a desire to consolidate avant-garde theatre as an independent artistic form, a form that is permanent and based on laws, with its own historical continuity. If avant-garde theatre today looks to various older and neglected forms of theatrical practice, if it brings to light whole historical periods of theatre that have been entirely forgotten, it does so solely from a desire to seek out tradition, to establish a connection with it. It has been said at the conference that if the avant-garde theatre turns against those who falsify tradition, it does so in order for tradition to be understood properly. So – the avant-garde theatre has its own specific character, its distinctiveness and its specific tasks, which it can only carry out if it becomes a permanent form. One of the most serious problems facing today's theatre in general is the relationship between the stage and the audience. Well, the avant-garde theatre, which is marked by a different relationship between the stage and the spectators than that in the established theatre, is best qualified to solve this problem. Whilst audience attendance in the major theatres is merely ensured mechanically, through the system of season subscriptions, in the avant-garde theatre there is a community of interest between the stage and the audience (shared generational, ideological and artistic interests). It is precisely this certain degree of exclusivity of the avant-garde theatre that makes it a suitable environment for the

---

1   [Editor's note: We have added the inverted commas to indicate that Mukařovský uses the word *official* in opposition to *avant-garde*; "official" theatres include those receiving public subsidies as well as those that conform to the majority taste in general.]

integration of theatre into the life of the society. The avant-garde theatre, then, is beginning to create an entirely distinctive form, one with its own methods, its own artistic possibilities and problems and its own mission. No matter what problem is being propounded, this distinctiveness means that the avant-garde theatre must approach it both theoretically and practically. That is what I wanted to say by way of introduction – partly as an apology for choosing a rather specialized subject.

This subject is stage speech, whose place in the structure of avant-garde stage production has become a concern of renewed and substantial complexity and interest in today's theatre. This is not because speech has been elevated to the forefront of all theatre action but, on the contrary, because language has been put on an equal footing with the other components, brought into dialectical tension with each of them individually and directly.

In the canon of the realist theatre the language component was linked together with gestures and facial expressions. In the canon of the expressionist theatre the language component attempted to dominate on its own, to relegate the other components to the background. Well, today it is not a question of one or the other: all the theatre components have been freed from their mutual relationships of inferiority and superiority, none of them either dominates or is dominated and the tension between them has free play. Several compositional systems are at work simultaneously in the performance, each with its own inner consistency and coherence. Speech, gesture, movement, light, music, film – all these components (and each of them in itself) assume the function of compositional principles; the compositional systems determined by these principles can overlap at one point and separate at another point, intersect or run in parallel. None of the components is connected to the other by historical necessity or common origin; they can form relationships between one another that are quite fleeting and changing. Nor is there here either content or form: everything, every component is – in its independence from the others – at the same time both content and form. Arguments between supporters and opponents of formalism cease to be relevant when it comes to the new theatre. Likewise, the antithesis of the servitude and the independence of the theatre leads to a synthesis in the new theatre: the more the theatre has its centre within itself, in its internal complexity and the mastery of this complexity, the more capable it is of becoming the prefiguration and the model of a new ordering of reality. It serves precisely by remaining itself.

What does all this mean for stage speech? It would be too complicated and difficult here to extrapolate a whole theory of stage speech from the premises of the new theatre, so allow me to limit myself to a brief outline. The form language takes on stage is dialogue, that is, speech constantly being interrupted, skipping from one character to another, issuing forth time and time again from the extra-linguistic situation. Where the dialogue is interrupted, speech on the stage comes into contact with other components of the stage production. But simultaneously, in its sequential flow dialogue continues to be firmly bound by a semantic relationship between what has come before and what will follow after. Statement and response, question and answer, are closely linked and always pick up the thread that has been dropped. In the new theatre – where, as has been mentioned, every component maintains its inner consistency and its independence from the other components at every moment – maximum emphasis is placed on not interrupting the dialogue. Nor does dialogue today see its ideal in charging ahead to reach a certain end, a conclusion that it is driven to by the plot. At any given moment the liberated, internally uninterrupted dialogue is both completed and not completed; it reaches beyond the bounds of the play, potentially continuing ad infinitum. The endings of *The Executioner* and *Hamlet*[2] – or rather the way they faded away – clearly revealed this attribute of the new stage dialogue. Dialogue constructed in this way has direct access to the spectators' own deepest experience: they do not leave the theatre thinking that they have been present at some kind of story that will be irrelevant to them in the future. Such dialogue continues to resonate within them. Of course the vocal element, so important for acting, has a special place in this type of dialogue. There is no absolute reason for liberated dialogue to resemble the sound patterns of everyday speech, just as there is no imperative reason for it to distance itself from them absolutely and strictly. Both extremes and all the nuanced transitions and shades between these two poles are available to the stage artist in maintaining the inner dialogic tension we have already mentioned. These extremes and the transitions between them come into close and immediate contact in the interaction of the actors and the way they play against each other as well as in the speech of the actor when alone. Thus between stage speech and everyday speech there is a steady, uninterrupted tension in which everyday, non-stage speech serves as the yardstick for measuring the degree to which the two diverge from and approximate one other. If we understand the role of pronunciation on stage in this way, then the argument as to whether the basic requirement for stage speech is deformation of or realistic adherence to the canon of everyday speech ceases to make any sense. Both – deviating from everyday speech and "speaking naturally" – are equally valid approaches for the actor. The only thing that must be avoided is stylization, a rigid ornamentalism adhering pedantically to a single principle.

---

2   [Editor's note: *The Executioner* [Kat], E. F. Burian's adaptation of Karel Hynek Mácha's (1810–1836) story "Křivoklad", premiered at D 36 on 22 June 1936 (dir. E. F. Burian), with Mácha, the greatest Czech Romantic poet, being stated as the author of the production; E. F. Burian, *Hamlet III, or To be or Not to Be, or Thrones Good for Wood* [Hamlet III., aneb Být či nebýt, čili Trůny dobré na dřevo], premiered at D 37 on 31 March 1937 (dir. and music E. F. Burian).]

I would like to finish with an explanatory note. Stage speech thus freed in liberated dialogue insofar as sound and semantics are concerned in no way means anarchy but on the contrary a desire for order, though order that is more complicated and dynamic than has previously been the case. It is of course true that all the possibilities of language, the whole range of dialect and argot, all the pathological corruptions of speech – all this becomes a tool that may and should be used by the director and the actor. But it is precisely this utter complexity that requires of both the actor and the spectator absolute assurance in the evaluation of all these various possibilities and devices, in the hierarchical gradation of the language's nuances, layers and dialects. Theatre practitioners used to seek a stage standard, especially in this country, where this was lacking. A stage standard was viewed (and still is in some quarters) as a certain set of rules: this is how X should be pronounced and this is how it should not. But today a different view of what is standard seems to be beginning to take shape: any way of speaking on stage is permissible, but under one condition – that the actor and the audience have a clear awareness of the social, linguistic and artistic range of every way of speaking and that they be capable of clearly identifying the place of every linguistic form in the whole body of the national language. From being a question of linguistic rules, the stage standard has become one of artistic and linguistic culture.

DIALOGUE AND MONOLOGUE

JAN MUKAŘOVSKÝ

["Dialog a monolog" was first published in 1940 in *Listy filologické*, vol. 67, pp. 139–60. It was republished in 1941 in *Kapitoly z české poetiky* [Chapters on Czech Poetics], vol. 1, pp. 145–75, where it appeared together with the 1940 article "On Stage Dialogue" (see pp. 212–15 of this anthology) under the joint title "Dvě studie o dialogu" [Two Studies on Dialogue]. It was published in English in Burbank, John and Steiner, Peter (trans. and eds) (1978) *The Word and Verbal Art. Selected Essays by Jan Mukařovský*, New Haven and London: Yale University Press, pp. 81–112, as the first part of "Two Studies on Dialogue", ibid., pp. 81–115.]

Editor's note: In this edition of the translation, we have omitted examples of a dialogue that lacks a common ground between the participants and a dialogue where one of the participants is hard of hearing. As both examples were based on wordplay from the Czech vernacular tradition that is untranslatable and were merely used as humorous illustrations, their omission does not alter Mukařovský's argument (see footnote 3 below).

I INTRODUCTORY REMARKS

The problem of the relationship between monologue and dialogue is one of the pressing questions facing contemporary poetics and the theory of drama, but it also concerns – in fact, it primarily concerns – linguistics itself. In particular, until the relationship between dialogue and monologue[1] has been examined, we cannot bring the consideration of speech as an actual application of a linguistic sign to a successful conclusion, as will become clear later in this essay. Heretofore linguists dealing with speech have generally had in mind a monologic act. There are, in fact, only two extensive studies dealing with the interconnection of monologue and dialogue (as well as other questions of dialogue). One of these is Gabriel Tarde's "Opinion and Conversation", a long chapter in his *Opinion and the Crowd* devoted to questions of dialogue.

---

1   Here, of course, we construe the term *monologue* in the linguistic sense, not in the sense given to it in the theatre, where it in fact means a dialogue with an absent or imaginary partner. For linguistics, however, "monologue" means an act of speaking on the part of a single active participant regardless of the presence or absence of other, passive participants. Hence narration, for example, is a typical monologue in the linguistic sense.

The other is Lev P. Yakubinsky's "On Dialogic Speech". Methodologically these studies differ in that Tarde's reflections are sociologically oriented, proceeding from the extralinguistic circumstances under which dialogue occurs and which influence its development, whereas Yakubinsky as a linguist proceeds from the internal structure of dialogue even though he does not neglect the relation of speech to the external world, especially to the material context in which it takes place. In the next few paragraphs we shall attempt a critical analysis of those theses of Yakubinsky and Tarde that touch closely on our subject.

Yakubinsky views the "dialogue – monologue" pair as one of the functional linguistic oppositions, similar, for example, to literary and colloquial language or intellectual and emotional language. Within this pair Yakubinsky views dialogue as the basic (or "unmarked", to use a later term introduced by Nikolai Trubetskoy) member, whereas monologue is the "artificial" superstructure of dialogue. In its time, Yakubinsky's classification of dialogue and monologue as functional languages represented a decisive shift in the methodological approach of linguistics toward these two phenomena. If until then it might have appeared that the choice between monologue and dialogue was a matter of accidental and linguistically irrelevant circumstances accompanying the application of a linguistic sign, Yakubinsky's thesis showed that this application is a *linguistic* act of choice between two fixed and rule-bound sets of linguistic conventions. It is to the great merit of Yakubinsky, one of the pioneers of the functional view of linguistic phenomena, that he made the difference between monologue and dialogue a subject of linguistic interest and study. Today, however, when the functional conception of language has become a methodological given, the need for a more detailed conceptual differentiation has become apparent.

The term *functional language* pertains to the relationship between the objective of a statement and the linguistic means appropriate for attaining this objective. In each given case a speaking individual determines the choice of a certain set of means ("a functional language") for the particular speech. The choice between monologue and dialogue does not, however, depend on the intention and decision of the speaker alone, but on the relationship between *both* the parties taking part in the act of speaking, the speaking and the listening participant, the active and the passive subject. An act begun as a monologue can change as it progresses into a dialogue through the interventions of "passive" participants (this happens, for example, in parliamentary speeches) and, on the contrary, a discussion can shift into a monologue – either for a long time or for its duration – through one participant's predominating over the others. Nor is it just one participant who determines the choice of the linguistic means in a dialogue. Proof of this is the fact that each of the participants in a dialogue can use a different func-

222 FROM PAGE TO STAGE

tional language: for example, one can use emotional language and the other intellectual language, one literary language and the other colloquial language. We know what effects can be achieved by such a juxtaposition of functional styles in, for example, dramatic dialogue. In this way the difference between monologue and dialogue manifests itself as something more profound than the differentiation of language into functional styles, although monologue and dialogue are *also* made manifest as canonized sets of particular linguistic devices. But this is more than a mere functional orientation: monologue and dialogue are two mutually opposed elementary approaches; every time language is connected with external reality it does so via one of them with inevitable necessity.

We must still deal with the second of Yakubinsky's theses that concern us: his claim concerning the priority of dialogue over monologue. Let us point out first that Tarde defends quite the opposite thesis: according to him monologue has the priority. We shall cite statements by him first:

> Long before it [language] became usable in conversation, it could only be a means of expressing the orders or warnings of chieftains or the maxims of moralistic poets. In brief, it was first, and necessarily, a monologue. Dialogue only came afterwards, in accordance with the law whereby the unilateral always precedes the reciprocal. (Tarde 1922: 91)

And elsewhere:

> To begin with, it is probable that at the first dawn of speech, in the first family or tribe that heard its earliest stages, it was one individual more gifted than the rest who had the monopoly of speech. The others listened, already able to understand him with effort, but not yet able to imitate him. This special gift must have helped elevate one man above the others. From this one can conclude that the monologue of the father speaking to his slaves or his children, of the chieftain giving orders to his soldiers, preceded the dialogue of the slaves, of the children, of the soldiers among themselves or with their master. (Tarde 1922: 92)

And finally:

> In contrast to the Classical epics as well as the *chansons de geste*, where conversations are so sparse, modern novels, beginning with those of Mlle de Scudéry, are characterized by an ever increasing wealth of dialogues. (Tarde 1922: 99)

Yakubinsky, on the contrary, convinced of the priority of dialogue, quotes Lev Shcherba's assertion about linguistic practice with respect to dialects in his *An Eastern Sorbian Dialect*:

Recalling the time I spent among these half-peasants, half-workers, I realize with surprise that I *never* heard monologues but only *fragmentary* dialogues. On occasion people rode with me to Leipzig to an exhibition or to their work in surrounding cities, and so on, but *no one ever* spoke about their impressions; usually they limited themselves to dialogue, sometimes lively, sometimes less so. And this was not because of a lack of culture but perhaps rather, on the contrary, a result of their ordinary cultivated manners, a constant quest for new, superficial impressions and a certain haste that distinguishes workers from true peasants. ... All these observations show that monologue is to a considerable degree an *artificial* linguistic form and that *language reveals its genuine essence only in dialogue.* (Yakubinsky 1923: 131–32)

Yakubinsky himself then provides an even more emphatic formulation:

There is no linguistic interaction *in general* where there is not a dialogue, but there do exist interacting groups of people who know *only* the dialogic form and not the monologic. ... By its very essence, every *inter*-action strives to avoid the unilateral, seeks to be bilateral, "dialogic", and avoids "monologue". Every unilateral action, insofar as it is perceived by other people, evokes in them a number of reactions, some stronger, some weaker, that strive to be visibly expressed. The same is true of the effect of monologue on the listeners: the reactions arising in the process of perception (the relation to what is being said, evaluation, and so forth) force them to action, to speech. Not without reason is it said that one must *know how* to listen to someone else, that one must *learn* to lend him an ear, whereas one does not have to know how to interrupt him, for this is an inborn tendency ... In order for people to listen to a monologue certain favourable conditions are usually necessary, for example the organization of a meeting with the order of the speakers, yielding of the floor, a chairman – but even so, voices "from the floor" are always heard. ... Dialogue, though undoubtedly a cultural phenomenon, is at the same time – and to a greater degree than monologue – a natural phenomenon as well. (Yakubinsky 1923: 133–39)

So we are faced with two opposing views, one granting primacy to monologue (Tarde), the other to dialogue (Yakubinsky). Which should we agree with? Clearly each of them is partly true. We can, however, object that the orders of fathers and chiefs to which Tarde refers can hardly be considered monologues: they are dialogues in which the replies are extralinguistic acts – compliance with the commands. We can also raise an objection to Yakubinsky by pointing out that milieus where the basic form of speech is monologue are familiar from everyday experience. This is the case, for example, with the school milieu, where monologue prevails in the teacher's presentation. And even the pupils' answers when being examined tend toward a monologic reproduction of the teacher's presentation: if the examinee is interrupted – that is, if the examiner makes an effort to substitute dialogue for monologue – the pupil feels that the exam is being made more difficult. It is therefore impossible either to assume the priority of monologue or to prove the general priority of dialogue. The relation between monologue and dialogue can be characterized rather as a dynamic polarity in which, depending on the milieu and the age, sometimes dialogue, sometimes monologue gains the upper hand. In the following sections of our study we shall attempt to show that the bond between them is even closer than it might appear to be on the basis of the preceding citations and reflections.

II ON THE BASIC ASPECTS AND TYPES OF DIALOGUE

Some of the rather paradoxical differences between Tarde's and Yakubinsky's views follow from the fact that each of these scholars has in mind a different nuance of dialogue. Whereas Yakubinsky, as is evident from his explanations, is thinking primarily about the dialogue of everyday life merging directly and closely with individuals' activities,[2] Tarde has in mind primarily "conversation", that is artificial dialogue deprived of immediate dependency on experience, carried out as a rule under circumstances specially accommodated to talking (such as a social gathering for the *sole* purpose of talk). Such differing conceptions, of course, lead necessarily to disagreement in research results. It is therefore not good to use the term "dialogue" without being aware in advance of the entire scope and variety of forms of the phenomenon it denotes. So this study, too, although its aim is to define the relation between monologue and dialogue, cannot avoid an attempt to list those aspects of dialogue that derive of necessity from its essence. Only in this way can we hope to arrive at a complete and undistorted perception of dialogue.

What, then, are the necessary and therefore omnipresent aspects of the linguistic phenomenon commonly called dialogue? There are *three*.

1. The first of these aspects is fixed by the relationship between the two participants, which from the standpoint of the person speaking can be designated as the relationship between "I" and "you". Even in a monologue, of course, two parties participate in the act of speaking, but a monologue does not have to be "addressed" by the speaker in any marked fashion. Indeed, if such an "addressing" of a monologue (through the use of apostrophe, the second person personal pronoun, and so forth) occurs, it actually colours the monologue dialogically. So the polarity between "I" and "you" is emphasized to such an extent in a dialogue that the roles of the speaker and the listener

---

2   See his reference to the incorporation of dialogue into the context of everyday life (1923: 174–94).

are constantly alternating. Hence the interrelation of the two people talking is felt as a tension not bound to either of them but actually existing "between" them; it is thus objectified as the "psychological situation" of the dialogue. This is reflected in the well-known fact that a particular mood, even if it originated in the mental state of a single participant in the dialogue, often takes rapid hold of all the other participants and sets the overall tone of the emotional coloration of the dialogue.

2. The relationship between the participants in a talk on the one hand and the real, material context surrounding them at the moment they are talking on the other forms the second basic aspect of dialogue. The material context can penetrate the talk both indirectly, when it becomes its theme, and directly, when changes in context influence the direction of the talk (for example, the subject of their talk changes as a result of an event that attracts the speakers' attention – a shout overheard from the street, and so on), or even when a reference to the material context replaces individual words or even sentences and entire responses (for example, someone enters a room but does not see there is a dead man lying there, and is not informed of his fate; he asks the other person present: "Where is X?", and this second person answers without speaking but merely by making an indicative gesture). The influence of the material context upon the conversation can, of course, be extremely limited. This happens, for example, when those involved in the conversation are gathered in a room specially designated for talking or when they are isolated from the surrounding material context owing to the subject of the conversation being very remote from it. Even in such cases, however, a negligible impulse arising from the material context is often enough to exert its influence on the conversation. The material context, then, is omnipresent in a dialogue, if not always actually, then at least potentially.

3. The specific character of the semantic structure of dialogue constitutes its third necessary aspect. If both of the preceding aspects are fixed by the external circumstances accompanying the act of speaking, this third aspect lies within the act of speaking itself, for it pertains to its internal coherence. Unlike monologic speech, which has a single and continuous context, several or at least two contexts interpenetrate and alternate in dialogic speech. Not even dialogue, of course, can do without semantic unity, but this is furnished primarily by the subject of the conversation, the theme, which at any given moment must be the same for all the participants. Dialogue is impossible without unity of theme.

[...][3]

---

3   [Editor's note: At this point Mukařovský gives two examples of kinds of dialogues in which a lack of common ground between the participants makes communication impossible. The first is based on them speaking about quite different things, similar to the situation in English when

Something different from the theme is the context provided by the meaning that the person speaking ascribes to the theme – that is, by the point of view he adopts toward it and the way in which he evaluates it. Because there is more than one participant in a dialogue, there are also several kinds of context: each person's utterances, although they alternate with those of the other person or persons, create a certain unity of meaning. Because the contexts that interpenetrate in this way in a dialogue are different, often even contradictory, sharp semantic reversals occur on the boundaries of the individual dialogue turns. The more vivid the talk, the shorter the individual dialogue turns, the more distinct the collision of the contexts. This gives rise to a special semantic effect, for which stylistics has even created a term: stichomythia.

Such are the three main and essential aspects of dialogue. Dialogue is impossible without all of them, for two of them follow from the necessary real premises of a conversation, and the third constitutes the semantic difference between dialogue and monologue. Each of them also manifests itself in its own way in the linguistic structure of dialogue.

1. The opposition between "I" and "you" has its linguistic correlate in the semantic opposition between the first and second person pronouns – personal and possessive; in the opposition between the first and second person of the verb; and in the imperative, in the vocative and to a certain extent in the interrogative sentence. It can also be projected into the opposition between affirmation and negation (yes – no) and into certain syntactic relations between sentences, especially the adversative (however, but) and the concessive (despite, nevertheless) relation. All of these linguistic means are capable of emphasizing the mutual demarcation of the speaking subjects of a dialogue from one another and of highlighting the variety of their opinions, feelings and intentions.

2. The speaking subjects' relation to the actual situation in which the talk takes place, to the "here and now", finds its linguistic expression through spatial and temporal deixis, represented by demonstrative pronouns (this, that, and so forth), adverbs and adverbials of place and time (here, there, now, in the morning, in the evening, today, tomorrow, and so forth) and verbal tenses (the present in opposition to the past and the future).

3. The semantic reversals, which, as we have said, occur on the boundaries of the individual turns in a dialogue as a result of the interpenetration of several kinds of context, have their linguistic correlate in lexical oppositions of an evaluative character such as good – bad, beautiful – ugly, noble – base,

---

someone says "We're talking apples and oranges here." The second results in confusion because one of the participants is deaf, and mishears what the other says. Neither of these examples can be translated usefully into English.]

important – insignificant, useful – harmful. An evaluation can, of course, be projected into qualitative oppositions, for example big – small, young – old. The nuances of semantic reversals possible on the boundary of dialogue turns are, of course, much richer than these strict contrasts; often they are based on a mere play with meaning, as, for example, in the exploitation of ambiguity and in various kinds of paradox. Phonologically, semantic reversals in dialogue find their expression through differences of intonation (for example, a contrast of intonational height between two contiguous dialogue turns), intensity, tone of voice (for example, the ironic repetition of a partner's words) and tempo. Of course these phonological means, too, have semantic implications, often expressing semantic shifts beyond the reach of verbal expression. The more a dialogue is based on semantic reversals, the greater demands it makes on the speakers' ability to control their voices with respect to these qualities. For this reason, too, conversation can attain real cultivation only in those milieus where a highly accomplished vocal culture prevails, and vice versa, the development of social conversation promotes the development of subtle nuances of intonation, intensity and tempo.

The three basic aspects of dialogue we have just enumerated and characterized are, as was said, necessary and therefore omnipresent: no dialogue completely lacks any one of them. In spite of this there are cases in which one of them predominates and thus colours the talk with its characteristics. In this way mere aspects of dialogue become *types*. In the following few paragraphs we shall attempt to characterize these distinctive forms of dialogue corresponding to its individual basic aspects.

A dialogue of the first type emphasizes the opposition between "I" and "you". When oriented in this way, its emotional and volitional elements come to the fore especially distinctly. Its most extreme case is therefore the *quarrel*, from which it is only a step to physical blows. The more cultivated the community, the more strongly this extreme outcome of "personal" dialogue is suppressed. But as Tarde shrewdly demonstrates, this "personal" aspect of dialogue nevertheless has an elementary significance: "The pleasure of arguing corresponds to a childish instinct, identical to that of kittens, of all young animals... But in the dialogues of mature men, the proportion of argument to conversation diminishes" (1922: 108). Hence from the ontogenetic standpoint Tarde sees argument as the primal form of dialogue. But according to Tarde philogenetic development also follows the same course. He explains that a gradual diminishing of the impulses for disputes and hence of disputes themselves occurs in the development of society. Bargaining in commerce was eliminated by fixed prices; the collective vanity of corporations, families and Churches, which had frequently provided the impulse for disputes, disappeared; knowledge of foreign lands, the vagueness of which had often provoked disputes, became more precise.

It is true that, if the progress of clear and certain information has solved many problems that were once hotly debated, it has on the other hand also raised new questions
and provoked new disputes, but these are of a less personal and less harsh nature. All
abrasiveness has been excluded from them – philosophical, literary, aesthetic, moral
discussions, which stimulate adversaries without injuring them. (Tarde 1922: 109)[4]

Let us now take a look at the second basic aspect of dialogue, the relation between the persons speaking and the actual material context. How and
when does this aspect manifest itself in a pure form? It occurs most distinctly
when talking about "business". Let us imagine, for example, two engineers
speaking to one another in the countryside, or even just over a map of the
countryside, about building roads or making rivers navigable. As long as
their talk does not turn into a discussion, it will be full of deictic references
to the individual details of the countryside, its overall configuration, and so
forth. Many substantives will be replaced by demonstrative pronouns; sentence parts or even entire sentences will often be replaced in the course of
the talk by indicative gestures; the talk will also be bound to the countryside
itself by numerous adverbs of place. A talk conducted in this way will be as
pure a representative as possible of dialogue bound to the material context.
Similarly, other talks carried out at work will also come close to "situational"
talk; sometimes in the case of manual work the talking will become no more
than a fragmentary accompaniment of the work itself. Talking of this kind
lacks strong emotional coloration; there is no tension between the speakers;
they do not lead to physical blows but to action with respect to the situation.
We must also add that the context to which they are related can even be remote from the actual "here and now", can be located elsewhere in space and
time. Take, for example, a foreman talking with a worker in a workshop about
a job that has to be done in another place known to both or about a job that
has already been done there.

Let us now turn to the third aspect of dialogue and so of course to its third
type. We shall focus our attention on dialogues based predominantly on semantic reversals arising from the interpenetration and alternation of several
contexts. The boundary that we are crossing here is more significant than
that between the first type (the "personal") and the second (the "situational").
This is because dialogue of the third type is removed to a quite considerable
degree from direct dependence on external circumstances, both the mutual
emotional and volitional relation of the interlocutors and the material context. The pure play of meanings is both its aim and its extreme limit. What

---

4   We must add to Tarde's remark that, in our conception, discussion constitutes a linking member
between predominantly "personal" dialogue (type 1) and dialogue based on the opposition of
semantic contexts (type 3).

is required is a concentration of attention on the dialogue itself as a chain of semantic reversals. External circumstances, too, are adapted to this requirement: people gather for the sole purpose of talking, often in special rooms, and if there are more than two people conversing, one of them (the host) usually sees to it that a distance is kept both from mutual emotional and volitional relations among the individuals as well as from the actual material context. Under these conditions, a *conversation* occurs – talk for the sake of simply talking, to a certain extent an end in itself and hence quite strongly coloured aesthetically, as Tarde has correctly understood:

> By "conversation" I mean every dialogue without direct and immediate usefulness, in which one talks primarily in order to talk, for pleasure, for play, out of politeness. This definition excludes from our concern judicial inquiries and diplomatic and commercial negotiations and Church Councils, and even scholarly conferences, even though they abound in superfluous talk. It does not exclude fashionable flirting or in general amorous chats, despite the frequent transparency of their objective, which does not prevent them from being pleasing in themselves. ... If I were to restrict myself to polite and cultivated conversation as a special art, I should hardly be able to date it to earlier – at least since the end of Classical antiquity – than the fifteenth century in Italy, the sixteenth or seventeenth centuries in France, then in England, the eighteenth century in Germany. But long before the full bloom of this aesthetic flower of civilization its first buds began to appear on the tree of languages; and though less fertile in visible results than the discussions of an elite, the matter-of-fact talking of primitive peoples does not lack great social importance. (Tarde 1922: 83–84)

Conversation, then, unlike the first two types of dialogue, is not something self-evident in life but a cultural achievement, and as a result it entails a great deal of artificiality, even in the very choice of subject. In the first two types of dialogue, the "personal" and the "situational", the subject is generally predetermined to a considerable extent or even determined completely from outside by the psychological or material context, whereas in a conversation the subject is a matter of the speakers' free choice. It is well known how often it requires several shared attempts to settle on the subject of an informal discussion before one suitable for all the participants is found. Concern that the subject should be kept as far as possible from the actual psychological and material context plays a very important negative role in this search. Sometimes a conversation, or at least the semblance of it, is even intentionally used to divert attention from this dual context, to "talk around" it.

It is, of course, impossible to disregard the ambient external and internal reality completely. Rather, it is a question of a tendency toward talk that is pleasing in itself, and this tendency only reaches its goal as fully as possible in extreme cases of "subject-free" talk. As a rule such cases are only created artificially for the purpose of a special effect, most often comic – here we have in mind especially the "subject-free" dialogues of comic clowns on stage (see Jakobson 1987 [1937]). Sometimes, of course, it happens that even a "real" conversation comes quite close to the very boundary of being without a subject, as, for example, in the talk of strangers who, forced by some external circumstance to remain in each other's company for a long while, talk only in order to avoid an "awkward silence". In such cases this consists almost entirely of formal "synsemantic" phrases that could only mean something in connection with a particular subject but mean almost nothing without it ("I'm of the same opinion as you, but still I think that..." – "Of course, this has to be considered from a broad perspective" – "But it'll work out somehow", and so on). But even these cases are merely marginal. The relation to reality, as we have already said, cannot be completely suppressed, but the main emphasis in conversation is not placed there. Hence the tendency in conversation toward the variability of the subject, in contrast to dialogues of the first two types, which usually stick to the original subject or at least keep coming back to it.

But if conversation is thus disengaged – though not completely detached – from an immediate relation to actual reality, the question arises whether we may attribute to conversation "great social importance", as Tarde does in the above citation. Well, despite all its independence from the actual context or perhaps rather precisely because of it, conversation is very closely incorporated into the general social context. The very influence that the social context, in the broad sense of the word, exerts upon conversation is evidence of this, as Tarde points out (1922: 99). Thus in certain periods *religion* limits conversation by forbidding particular subjects, by imposing silence upon particular groups (monastic orders), while on the other hand it may furnish certain subjects. In a democracy *politics* leads to talking about public affairs, while in an absolute monarchy by necessity it favours literary subjects and psychological observations. *Economic conditions* influence conversation in the sense that when they are favourable they create enough free time for talking and facilitate its cultivation, if only by satisfying at least the most urgent material needs. Such is the passive connection between conversation and social reality. As far as the active creation of a general consensus in a wide variety of matters of public concern is concerned, there is no need for an extensive discussion because this is so obvious. Just as an example, let us recall the influence of conversation upon the creation of a broadly-shared outlook in literary matters: "In particular, wherever literature has been much talked about in a certain milieu, without being aware of it people as a group have been elaborating a poetics, a literary code accepted by all and capable of supplying ready-made opinions, always consistent with one another, on all kinds of creations of the mind" (Tarde 1922: 147). The relation of conversation to reality is therefore of a special kind: even when conversation concerns some concrete case, what "is meant" by it is a generality. In this respect conversation resembles – *mutatis mutandis*, of course – the work of art, whose objective impact also goes beyond a concrete subject (see Mukařovský 1941).

We should add that conversation is not the only kind of dialogue based on the interpenetration of several semantic contexts and the semantic reversals deriving from this. Forms of dialogue akin to conversation but not identical with it can often be found in literature, especially in drama – for example, the "lyrical" dialogue. Incidentally, though drama exploits all three aspects of dialogue and all the types based upon them for its own purposes, it always – by virtue of its artistic nature – focuses the audience's attention more sharply on the semantic aspect of the talking than is the case in everyday dialogues.

We have analysed in some detail the three characteristic types of dialogue, types that are quite distinct from one another: "personal" dialogue, "situational" dialogue and conversation. We must not, of course, forget the basic unity of dialogue: the types we have analysed are only the extreme limits to which the prevalence of one of the three basic aspects of this fundamentally homogeneous linguistic phenomenon may reach. There is, however, a vast, almost endless number of nuances of dialogue arising from different combinations and different "dosages" of its basic aspects. In this study we cannot attempt a more detailed enumeration and typology of the nuances of dialogue; nevertheless, we would like to point out the transitional types forming links between the third type (dialogue of a conversational character) and each of the first two types ("personal" and "situational" dialogue). We believe this is necessary in order to show that the seemingly very deep divide separating conversation from the other two distinctive types of dialogue does not affect the essence of the phenomenon called dialogue.

The first of the transitional types that we wish to analyse mediates between conversation and "personal" dialogue based on the opposition "I" and "you"; this is *discussion*. We have already quoted Tarde's observation that discussion largely replaced arguments in the course of civilization, being less personal than them; the transition from "personal" dialogue to dialogue based on the interpenetration and alternation of contexts is also illustrated historically in this way. We may also recall that there was a much stronger element of personal emotion in the relations between participants in medieval disputations than is usual in modern scholarly discussions. Gradually an opposition of *persons* gave way to an opposition of *theses*, that is, of semantic contexts, and thus discussion moved closer to conversation without ever merging with it completely. The surprising semantic reversals on the boundary of contiguous dialogue turns, which sometimes lead us, indeed even tempt us, to paradoxes sharply elucidating differences of opinion, also bring discussion closer to conversation.

The transition from "situational" dialogue to dialogue with a predominant semantic aspect, that is to conversation, is even more interesting. In speaking about conversation, we emphasized that the influence of the material context upon it is usually carefully removed by the very nature of the place where it is taking place. It might therefore seem that we are dealing with an uncrossable boundary. But Tarde's observation shows that there has long been a close connection between situational and purely semantic dialogue:

> Quite often, and much more often the closer one is to primitive life, men and women, particularly women, only talk among themselves while doing something else, whether it be performing some easy task, like the peasants who, during evening get-togethers, shell legumes while their wives spin, sew or knit. (Tarde 1922: 101–102)

The transitional type of dialogue between situational and purely semantic dialogue is therefore the kind of talk that is usually referred to as a *chat*. It is connected with conversation by a purely semantic (most often associative) linking of the dialogue turns, and with situational dialogue by an obligatory, though only formal, bond with the material context.

So the divide between talk that is purely semantic and the remaining two types of dialogue, though very significant epistemologically, can be bridged very easily in practice precisely because dialogue by its very essence is a single and indivisible phenomenon. But even dialogue as a whole must not be viewed as an isolated fact. In our introductory remarks we explained that monologue is its indispensable companion and constant competitor. In the following sections we shall attempt to prove that their interconnection is even closer and more substantial than might appear at first glance, that monologue and dialogue are simultaneously present in the speaker's awareness in every act of speaking, already struggling for dominance in the very course of this act. In order to prove this we must first look at the psychology of language.

III THE QUESTION OF THE MENTAL SUBJECT IN DIALOGUE AND MONOLOGUE

Every act of speaking presupposes at least two subjects between whom the linguistic sign mediates: the subject from whom the linguistic sign proceeds (the speaker) and the subject to whom this sign is addressed (the listener). We have already indicated that in monologue one of these subjects is constantly active, the second constantly passive, whereas in dialogue the roles constantly change: each of the two subjects is alternately active and passive. At first glance it seems that the notion "subject" here is necessarily a synonym of the concept "concrete psychophysical individual", but this is not so. The phenomenon termed "soliloquy", in which an individual addresses an act of speaking (whether mentally or even out loud) to himself, is familiar from the most ordinary linguistic experience. In a soliloquy, therefore, a single psychophysical individual is the vehicle of *both* subjects necessary for an act of speaking, the active and the passive. If the act is of a dialogic nature, the two subjects realized by the voice of a single individual can alternately address one another as "I" and "you". The origin of the medieval literary theme called "A Dispute between the Body and the Soul" is to be found in such a splitting of one and the same individual consciousness into the two subjects of an act of speaking. Here the duality of the subject in a single psychophysical individual is projected into a biune bond of the body with the soul. The relation between "I" and "you" in a soliloquy is naturally very fluid. Thus we find, for example, in Otokar Březina's lyric poems several examples in which it appears as if the first and second person pronouns have changed places. This is the case, for instance, in a poem characteristically called "I Hear in my Soul" [Slyším v duši], whose first and last stanzas are as follows:

> When the sun was singing, *you* touched not your instrument,
> only under *my* piercing did the blood of *your* tones gush forth!
> *your* hand in convulsions only thundered on the keys
> as anxieties at night on the door of weary ones.
>
> And the audacious swarm of *your* bees, which flew away from *my* hive,
> I chased back from a hollow tree with smoke;
> I imprisoned *your* days and through the suggestiveness of my will
> I made the sap, breath and blossom of *your* songs bitter.[5]

Who is speaking here? The one who addresses the other by the pronouns "you" and "your" or the other who is thus addressed? This is left in uncertainty, for nothing would be easier than to reverse their interrelation by interchanging the pronouns ("When the sun was singing, I did not touch my instrument, only under your piercing did the blood of my tones gush forth," and so on). Here the inversion of the grammatical persons is used as a technique that is simultaneously poetic and epistemological.

---

5   [Editor's note: The italicization is Mukařovský's. The poem "I Hear in my Soul" was published in *Daybreak in the West* [Svítání na západě], 1896. Otokar Březina (1868–1929), the most prominent Czech Symbolist poet. His books of poetry are regarded as a high point in the Czech Modernist literary movement, as he combines various aesthetic and religious symbols and uses a highly imaginative and inventive language.]

234 IV FROM PAGE TO STAGE

These considerations alone suffice to indicate the complexity of the question of the subject in the act of speaking in general. However, our concern is testing the hypothesis that the oscillation between an orientation toward "I" and an orientation toward "you", and hence the oscillation between dialogue and monologue as well, manifests itself at the very origin of an act of speaking. Let us therefore see what Victor Egger says in his famous treatise *The Interior Word*: "... tormented by insomnia, we cannot silence our thought; we hear it, for it has a voice...; not only do we hear it, but we listen to it, for it goes against our wishes..., it astonishes us, it troubles us; it is unexpected and hostile..." (Egger 1881: 4). Elsewhere in the same work the author says, "Moreover, it happens sometimes in the hypnagogic state [that is, on the boundary between the waking state and sleep, J. M.] that we do not attribute the words that we hear either to ourselves or to others" (Egger 1881: 77–78). In such cases, therefore, "I" remains completely undistinguished from "you". I myself remember an event I experienced when I was tired after a long journey. A friend said a few words to me that stuck in my memory; however, to this day I do not know whether these words were actually spoken or whether I only imagined them myself at the time. The story of a dream that Georg Christoph Lichtenberg recounts offers very striking evidence of the oscillation between "I" and "you" in the individual's consciousness:

It was at the end of September 1798 when I told someone in a dream the story of the young and beautiful Countess Hardenberg, which I and everyone else found deeply moving. She died in September 1797 at the time of her confinement, in fact during childbirth, which went wrong. She was cut open, and her child was put next to her in the coffin, and in this way they were brought by torchlight at night, accompanied by an enormous crowd, to a nearby town where the family tomb was situated. This was accomplished by means of the Gottingen hearse, a very unwieldy vehicle, with the result that the corpses were tossed about a great deal. At the end, before she was put into the crypt, several people once more wanted to see her. The coffin was opened, and she was found lying on her face in a heap with her child. ... At that time my mind was often preoccupied by this scene, because I knew her husband, who was one of my most diligent students, quite well. Now in the dream I was telling this sad story to someone in the presence of a third person who also knew the story, but I forgot (strangely enough) the circumstance with the child, which was, after all, the major point. After I had finished my story - narrated, so I believed, very forcefully and leaving the listener greatly moved - the third person said: "Yes, and the child was lying next to her, all in a heap." "Yes," I almost blurted out, "and her child was lying in the coffin with her." That was the dream. What I find strange is the following: who reminded me of the child in the dream? After all, I was the one who recollected this circumstance. Why didn't I myself recall it as a memory in the dream? Why did my imagination create a third person who surprised and almost embarrassed me? Had I told this story while awake, this interesting detail would certainly not have escaped me. In the dream I had to omit it to let myself be surprised. ... A story I found very astonishing was dramatized here. However, it is not at all unusual for me to be instructed in a dream by a third person. Yet it is nothing more than dramatized recollection. (Lichtenberg 1949: 112–14)

We have cited this rather extensive passage virtually in its entirety because it is so instructive. The story that the dream reproduced in the form of a narrative was evidently retained in the author's mind as a monologue bound to a single narrator. However, the dream leads the narrator to omit an important detail and attributes it to another person. It is interesting that in the story itself the unexpected semantic reversal, the point of the story, occurs where the subject of the narration is split from the person of the main narrator. We have said above that semantic reversals at the boundaries of contiguous dialogue turns are a characteristic feature of dialogue as a semantic structure of a particular kind. Therefore it may be supposed that to a certain extent the dialogization was already present latently in the monologic version of the story and that the dream only revealed the potential dialogic quality hidden in the aforementioned place of the monologue. This finding is important for the further development of our deliberations.

The problem of the interior monologue, which has been a concern of both the practice and theory of narrative prose for the last few decades, beginning with the 1880s, provides us with an even more detailed insight into the mental event that gives rise to the act of speaking. The aim of writers who employ interior monologue for artistic ends is to render an equivalent of the mental event in the actual form in which it takes place in the deep strata of mental life, on the boundary between consciousness and the subconscious. Several successive art movements, beginning with the Symbolists and ending for the time being with the Surrealists, have dealt with this problem. The Surrealists have even given it a new name: "automatic writing" (*écriture automatique*). The difficulty of artistically mastering interior monologue consists – as Jean Cazaux (1939) has correctly recognized – in the fact that a precise record of the individual phases of a mental event is not enough to evoke the illusion of a direct insight into the inner life. This requires a different mode of presentation than that which presents itself spontaneously to the author during self-observation: here too, as always and everywhere, the necessity for an artistic reshaping lies between reality and art. This is the source of the theoretical interest of artists themselves in the problems of interior monologue. Their reflections concern us insofar as we find in them mention of the psychological connection between monologue and dialogue. In the following paragraphs we shall cite several passages from the most comprehensive discussion of interior monologue, *Le Monologue intérieur*, by the poet (and historian) Edouard Dujardin.[6]

The author's conception of monologue itself is of interest to us. We would have expected the author to view "interior" monologue as involving only a *single* subject, the one who experiences the mental event. Instead, however, Dujardin links his conception of interior monologue to dramatic monologue, which is essentially a dialogic act. Charles Le Goffic, whom Dujardin quotes, says that "an exact description of all the feelings, ideas and sensations that pass through a human brain from seven o'clock till ten in the evening would be a monologue worthy of such a great [comic] actor as Coquelin the younger" (Dujardin 1931: 98). And Dujardin himself dedicated his novel to the memory of the dramatist Racine. In a characteristic manner, he explains in his book on the interior monologue how this dedication came about:

> This dedication was not only a reaction against the unfairness of the Romantics, not only an expression of my supreme admiration for classical beauty; it indicated my determination, against winds and tides, to connect my attempt to tradition; it signified above all my ambition ... to continue Racine's poetic achievement by other means and on another level.
>
> But this was not understood. There was too great a distance between the rational order within which the seventeenth century had evolved and the irrational order that I was trying to penetrate into. Most of my friends asked why I had dedicated my book to Racine. (Dujardin 1931: 104-105)

So the young Dujardin, creator of the technique of interior *monologue*, was consciously following in the tradition of *drama*, a dialogic literary genre, and wished to transfer this tradition to "another level" and continue in it "by other means". Like all the Symbolists, he yielded to the paradoxical temptation to express what is hidden and inexpressible in human mental life, but unlike his fellow poets he had a keen sense of the potential *dialogic nature* of mental activity; this is where his discovery lies. From the linguistic standpoint the

---

6   By way of introduction to these quotations we should mention that in 1887 Dujardin, one of the Symbolists, published *Les lauriers sont coupés* [The Laurels Are Cut Down], a novel considered by many – and of course by the author himself – to be the first attempt to exploit the interior monologue artistically. Following its publication the novel went virtually unnoticed; memory of it revived only at the beginning of the 1920s with the resounding success of Joyce's *Ulysses*, whose author referred to Dujardin as his precursor. At the same time, however, there were some, such as for example André Gide, who denied Dujardin's priority by claiming that older authors, in particular Dostoyevsky, had already been familiar with the technique of interior monologue. Thus, in order to defend himself, Dujardin was compelled to come up with a theory of interior monologue, especially a definition of the difference between this technique and earlier "indirect" descriptions of the inner life of characters in novels. Like every serious polemic, this one, too, led to a series of shrewd observations.

objective that Dujardin had in mind can be formulated as the transposition of dialogue into monologic speech.

At the same time it was also a matter of another transposition, equally instructive for us. Dujardin, again as a good Symbolist, yearned to transfer the artistic techniques of Richard Wagner's music into literature:

> I undertook the novel *Les Lauriers sont coupés* [The Laurels Are Cut Down] with the foolish ambition of transposing into literature Wagner's technique, which I defined as follows: the expression of mental life by means of an uninterrupted stream of musical motifs, which come to express one after the other, indefinitely and successively, "states" of thought, feeling and perception; one realizes or rather attempts to realize this technique by means of an indefinite succession of short sentences, each of which presents one of these states of thought and which follow one another without logical order, rising from the depths of being or, as one would say today, from the unconscious and the subconscious. ... (Dujardin 1931: 97)

It begins to become clear to us why Dujardin views mental life as dialogue: the "randomness" of succession in which its individual elements follow one another causes a constant semantic changeability resembling the changeability of dialogue. This will become even clearer from the following passage:

> ... a psychologist would, I think, say that not only do we think on several levels at once, but our thought continually races from one level to another with a rapidity that may later seem to be simultaneity but is really not; interior monologue gives the impression of precisely this racing "in fits and starts"; Joyce's "continuous line" is actually a broken line. (Dujardin 1931: 61–62)

Here Dujardin describes what we have called one of the basic aspects of dialogue, the interpenetration and alternation of several contexts. As the author shows, this essential feature of dialogue is already contained in the mental event from which the act of speaking originates and which therefore has priority over the latter. Now the source of the oscillation between the unity and the multiplicity of the subject in the individual's consciousness that is spoken of in the above quotations from Egger and Lichtenberg also becomes clear: the variety of semantic contexts into which mental events fit can be very easily attributed to a variety of subjects. What follows from these considerations is that the monologic and dialogic qualities are already simultaneously and inseparably present in the mental event from which the act of speaking originates and that monologue and dialogue must not be conceived as two mutually alien and hierarchically gradated forms of the act of speaking, but as two forces that are always struggling with one another for predominance, even in the very course of speaking. In our next and final section we shall attempt to prove this thesis on the basis of the act of speaking itself.

IV DIALOGUE IN MONOLOGUE AND MONOLOGUE IN DIALOGUE

Let us first attempt to reveal the dialogic quality potentially contained in monologue. For our purposes the most suitable material, with the persuasive force of a scientific experiment, is the dramatization of Viktor Dyk's story "The Ratcatcher" [Krysař][7] undertaken by E. F. Burian and presented in January 1940 at the D 40 theatre. In dramatizing the story, Burian proceeded in a manner that differed fundamentally from the usual procedure. He did not limit himself to the extraction and dramaturgical adaptation of the dialogues present in the author's text, but instead dramatized the entire text, even its monologic sections, while maintaining the precise original wording wherever possible. This modus operandi is more suitable than any other for revealing the potential dialogic quality concealed in the monologic parts of Dyk's story.

Let us begin with an example.

Viktor Dyk:

On Sunday after high mass it was lively and busy in the pub called "The Thirsty Fellow".

"The Thirsty Fellow" was the most famous and most popular attraction in the Hanseatic Town of Hamelin. No better wine could be drunk anywhere else for miles around, and the cook at the tavern, Black Liza, could measure up to any cook anywhere. Nor did the leading figures in the community disdain to enter the vaulted hall of the pub; they had their own table, carefully guarded against intruders. They were the first to taste the newly arrived barrels; they uttered the important and decisive word in matters of cuisine and public opinion.

Business deals were made at "The Thirsty Fellow" because it was only here that the cautious and prudent citizens of the Town of Hamelin livened up. Marriages were contracted here because it was only here that the cautious and prudent citizens of the Town of Hamelin started thinking about something that might resemble love, perhaps in the same way that a sparrow resembles an eagle. If sadness afflicted a citizen of the Town of Hamelin, he went to drink at Konrad Röger's (this was the name of the stocky proprietor, a good fellow who didn't shun the treasures of his own cellar!). But if there was some joyful occasion, that also called for drinks at Konrad Röger's. No one else

---

7   [Editor's note: "The Ratcatcher" (1915), by Viktor Dyk (1877–1931), is inspired by the old German story of the Pied Piper of Hamelin, but in Dyk's version the Ratcatcher leads away the whole town because of his disappointment in love.]

knew how to share joy so exuberantly: christenings were celebrated, and it seemed that the baptism was taking place in Röger's family; name-days were celebrated, and it was like Röger himself was celebrating.[8]

E. F. Burian:

First guest. And it's liveliest and busiest at "The Thirsty Fellow" on Sunday after high mass, stranger.

Second guest. "The Thirsty Fellow" has always been the most famous and most popular attraction in the town of Hamelin.

Stranger *(indifferently)*. Hmm...

First guest. You can't drink better wine anywhere else for miles around. ...

Second guest. And the cook, Black Liza, can measure up to any other cook anywhere. *(Röger serves them another glass of wine.)*

First guest. It's true, friend ... nor do the leading figures in the community disdain to enter your pub. ...

Röger *(grandly)*. Over there – they have their own table, carefully guarded against intruders. And they taste the newly arrived barrels. ... They utter the important and decisive word in matters of cuisine and public opinion. ... Over there – at their table. ... *(He hurries off.)*

Second guest. Business deals are made at "The Thirsty Fellow" ...

First guest. ... because it's only here that the cautious and prudent citizens of Hamelin liven up. ...

Second guest. Marriages are contracted here!

Stranger. Even marriages!

First guest. ... because it's only here that the cautious and prudent citizens of the Town of Hamelin start thinking about something that might resemble love, perhaps in the same way that a sparrow resembles an eagle. ... *(He starts laughing and the others join in.)*

Second guest. Yes... that's the way it is at "The Thirsty Fellow", stranger. ... You have to know all of this if you're coming to Hamelin.

First guest. If sadness afflicts a citizen of the Town of Hamelin, he comes to drink at Konrad Röger's.

Stranger. Röger's the name of that stocky proprietor?

First guest. Oh, he's a good fellow! He never shuns the treasures of his own cellar.

Second guest. But if there's some joyful occasion, that also calls for drinks at Konrad Röger's.

First guest. No one else knows how to share joy so exuberantly!

---

8   [Editor's note: This is a literal translation of the Czech original, employed for the sake of supporting Mukařovský's argument concerning the use of the original text in Burian's dramatization. Dyk's *The Ratcatcher* was published in English, in a translation by Roman Kostovski, in 2014 (Washington, D.C.: Plamen Press).]

Second guest. No one else knows how to celebrate christenings in such a way.

First guest. Many times it's seemed that the baptism was taking place in Röger's family.

Second guest. Name-days have been celebrated, and it was like Röger himself was celebrating.

Monologue has been transformed into dialogue here with virtually no change in the wording, and not monologue that is itself dramatic, but rather smooth narrative monologue. The narrator of the monologue was the author himself. The participants in the dialogue are characters arising from an actualization of the material context that the monologue merely recounts; these characters are the customers at "The Thirsty Fellow". But in the actual text of the monologue itself they are not present in any way. The monologue has, therefore, actually generated its dialogization from itself, from its structure, not from its subject. How did this come about? First, there was Dyk's predilection for using main clauses, linked to each other paratactically. These clauses are usually joined to form compound sentences copulatively, even though their real semantic relation is not copulative ("christenings were celebrated, and it seemed" instead of "if christenings were celebrated, it seemed" or "whenever christenings were celebrated, it seemed"). Thus even in its original state the monologue is divided into independent semantic segments, each of which can stand alone to a considerable extent regardless of the fact that the polyfunctionality of the copulative connection renders their syntactic and hence their semantic interrelation as well potentially ambiguous. The possibility of semantic reversals at the boundaries of the individual lines of dialogue is indicated in this way, even though in the passage just quoted the lines of dialogue follow after one another smoothly without striking semantic shifts.

Another aspect of the original monologue that facilitated the future dialogization is the multitude of words and phrases that are overtly or at least implicitly of an evaluative nature. These include the superlative ("the most famous and most popular"); the conjunction "nor" in a comparative sense ("nor do the leading figures in the community disdain"); words whose very meaning contains an evaluative nuance (for example "important and decisive", "cautious and prudent"); and finally the evaluative simile "that might resemble love, perhaps in the same way that a sparrow resembles an eagle". With few exceptions the evaluations in the text are uniformly positive, and they thus lack the contradictory quality that would seem to be desirable for dialogue. This is, however, made possible by the fact that some of these evaluations are obviously intended to be ironic ("the cautious and prudent citizens"), while others at least admit an ironic interpretation. These two circumstances – the predominantly copulative character of the sentence linkages and the multitude of partly positive, partly ironic evaluations – enabled the dramaturge to loosen up the continuous structure of the monologue at a single stroke, transforming it into successive lines of dialogue. The dialogic quality was already potentially present in the monologic text, which only substantiates the thesis we presented in the preceding section. What is important here is that the means by which this dialogic quality was attained are *linguistic* in nature and that hence the linguistic aspect of the text itself appears here as an oscillation between monologue and dialogue.

The dialogic nature of the passage cited was even more distinct in the stage presentation than in the written dialogue, for the director was able to draw on differences in sound properties – in intonation, tone of voice, intensity and tempo. And as director, Burian made rich use of these properties. This is also evident in the script of *The Ratcatcher*, which contains a strikingly large number of stage directions that, either directly or indirectly, require the actor to change his voice with respect to one of these sound properties. For example, in the brief first scene (corresponding to the first chapter of Dyk's text) there is a stage direction of this kind accompanying almost every line, sometimes even several in the course of a single line. We shall cite them in order to make apparent, at least from their wording, how wide a range they cover, which of course in vocal reality is far richer. *Agnes*: with a slight laugh; laughing; a tone of laughter, urgently in a feminine manner; laughing lightly; sighing, enraptured; barely breathing; very seriously; whispering; laughing in a caressingly child-like manner; after a while sighing quietly, very deeply. *The Ratcatcher*: ardently; with passion; quietly; hollowly, but sharply. Nuances like these are already contained in the original monologue, too, but they are unwritten: they are provided by the content of sentences, by meanings of words, by their emotional coloration, by sentence structure.[9] And thus sound changes as well constitute a component of the latent dialogic nature of Dyk's monologue.

The "dialogic nature" of an act of speaking does not, therefore, begin only with its division into individual lines of dialogue. We can even find – again in Burian's dramatization of *The Ratcatcher* – evidence that directly proves the secondary nature of this division in dialogue itself. Dyk's text, in this case dialogic, reads:

---

9   Burian as director often takes expressive intonational motifs from literary texts and then uses them to create a lexicon of acoustic signs for certain dramatic situations that are independent of the original texts. Anecdotal evidence for this assertion can be seen in a comment overheard at a rehearsal. An actress was supposed to utter the word "Ratcatcher!", the tone of which is described clearly in Dyk's text: "'Ratcatcher,' whispered Agnes in a soothing and imploring manner." Burian pronounced the word himself and added: "This is how it must be spoken; [the poet Fráňa] Šrámek discovered this intonation once and for all for the Czech theatre" – in other words, a poet in a written text.

"Yes," laughed the woman in the doorway. "A huge rat appeared at Katherine's wedding. The groom was as white as a sheet, and Katherine fell into a swoon. People don't find anything more off-putting than something that spoils their appetite; then they decide to call in a ratcatcher."

"Are you preparing a wedding or a christening?" asked the ratcatcher suddenly, without any transition.

Burian takes over this dialogue word for word but shifts the division between the two parts:

Agnes (*laughing*). A huge rat appeared at Katherine's wedding. The groom was as white as a sheet, and Katherine fell into a swoon.
The Ratcatcher. People don't find anything more off-putting than something that spoils their appetite. Are you preparing a wedding or a christening?

One of the sentences that Agnes utters in Dyk's text has been allotted to the Ratcatcher in Burian's play. So a dialogic reversal was found *within* the first of the original utterances that struck the dramaturge as a more desirable boundary between the two than the boundary that was chosen by the author. But this has in no way suppressed the semantic reversal between the sentence "There's nothing more off-putting for people..." and the following question "Are you preparing a wedding..." – even though the dramaturge has shifted it to the response. Rather, this reversal has been highlighted, for in a live performance it will necessarily manifest itself by a sudden change in tone of the Ratcatcher's voice.

What does this example tell us? The fact that the "dialogic quality" of even dialogic speech itself is not concentrated only at the boundaries between the individual dialogue turns but, just as in a monologue, uniformly saturates it throughout. In order to verify this assertion even more unequivocally, we shall provide one last example from *The Ratcatcher*. This time the dramaturgic adaptation alone will suffice, with no need for recourse to the author's text. It concerns a scene between Agnes and the Ratcatcher: the setting is Agnes's room, the time the morning after a night of love. The Ratcatcher paces back and forth restlessly on the stage, while Agnes sits on the bed:

Agnes (*quietly, after a moment of anxious observation*). How handsome he is in his anger! His eyes are burning with ominous fire. All his movements have become beautiful. It's as if he grew up. ... (*She huddles fearfully in the corner of the bed.*) Grow, Ratcatcher, beautiful Agnes is waiting. ... I'm afraid, Ratcatcher, of your unknown power. I don't understand it very well, but from time to time I yield to it. I'm afraid, and I love my fear. I also love you, Ratcatcher. ... (*She rushes to him and embraces him. Beseechingly.*) Ratcatcher. ...

What we read here is certainly a rather long continuous speech, but it has been wedged into a dialogue and addressed to a partner, and as such is dialogic. In three places there are stage directions that prescribe changes in facial expressions and gestures and also, of course, changes in voice. Possibly there will be even more vocal changes in a performance. But since these changes are signals of semantic reversals – also obvious in this case from the changes in the emotional coloration of the text (admiration, fear, love) – their presence proves that even the inner semantic structure of the passage is in a state of constant motion. The more "dialogic" the dialogue, the more densely it is saturated with semantic reversals regardless of the boundaries of the individual dialogue turns. So from the thesis concerning the potential dialogic nature of every act of speaking there follows as a result a second thesis, concerning dialogue as a special kind of semantic structure oriented toward a maximum of semantic reversals. In this light the breaking up of the dialogue into individual lines is of secondary importance.[10] Therefore from this aspect, too, functional linguistics was right in introducing the term *dialogic speech*, meaning a special kind of linguistic (and thus, of course, semantic) structure alongside the term *dialogue*, meaning a certain external form of an act of speaking. It is only necessary to add the term *dialogic quality*, designating a potential tendency toward the alternation of two or more semantic contexts, a tendency that is manifested not only in dialogue but also in monologue.

We must now reverse the problem by posing the question of the *monologic quality* in dialogue. The presence of the monologic element in dialogue is most evident when monologue (a speech delivered without the interventions of a second participant in the talk, even if he is present, hence not a "dramatic" monologue) is inserted into dialogue. This is the case of old Petr Dubský's narration in Ladislav Stroupežnický's *Our Proud Peasants* [Naši furianti], when he explains how he acquired his memorable ducats.[11] In such cases, however,

---

10 The tendency of dialogue toward maximal and continual semantic changeability helps explain the imperishable affinity of drama for verse, an affinity that has even been able to withstand the crushing blows of Realism and Naturalism. At first glance it might seem that drama, which depends on a performance in a material setting with the help of real people (actors), has the fewest reasons for maintaining a literary convention as remote from real speech as poetic rhythm. But instead drama has maintained the option of verse presentation right up to the present time, whereas the narrative mode has largely abandoned it. The explanation for this is to be found in the fact that a line of verse is not only a rhythmic but also a semantic unit and through this property it increases the possibility of semantic reversals, which are so desirable for dialogue. Every verse boundary in a versified dialogue is a potential location of a semantic reversal. In any particular case the text itself can exploit or disregard this possibility. Thus there arises a certain syncopative relation between the rhythm and the semantic structure of a text, making possible an unusual wealth of nuances.

11 [Editor's note: *Our Proud Peasants* (1887), set in a small Bohemian village, is regarded as the quintessential Czech realist play. In the passage referred to by Mukařovský, Dubský recounts at length

it is a question of the encounter of two distinctive linguistic forms. We are concerned rather with the *monologic tendency* penetrating dialogue without violating its specific character.

We can observe this tendency in almost every conversation. It is enough to recall the well-known fact that as a rule one of the speakers makes an effort to dominate the talk: "... between two speakers, very seldom are the roles perfectly equal. Most often, one speaks much more than the other. Plato's dialogues are an example of this" (Tarde 1922: 93). The predominance of one speaker over the others happens for various reasons: because he is better informed, because of his intellectual or social superiority, because of his seniority. But whomever this predominance falls to always embodies the tendency toward the monologization of dialogue, and this tendency also acquires linguistic expression (in the sentence structure, in the choice of words, and so on). It also, of course, affects semantic structure, which, in the speech of the individual who predominates in the dialogue, begins to display a tendency toward an uninterrupted logical continuity without semantic reversals. There are still other cases of the monologization of dialogue. It also occurs, for example, in a quiet chat between participants who are close and equal to one another when one of the speakers forgets his partner and speaks "to himself" by indulging in recollection or by becoming self-absorbed. Larger numbers of participants talking together almost necessarily leads to monologization, for the division of roles here can hardly be equal. In such cases, as a rule, one of the participants automatically becomes the main speaker, the others virtually passive listeners. Sometimes it also happens that a chain of monologues arises instead of a dialogue: the individual speakers take the floor in turn for uninterrupted utterances. This mode of "talking through monologues" is, as is well known, a favourite and very old compositional scheme of short story cycles.

A special kind of monologization occurs when the interlocutors reach such a degree of consensus that the multiplicity of contexts necessary for a dialogue completely vanishes. In such a case the dialogue as a whole turns into a monologue carried by the speakers in turn. A fragment of a dialogue from Maeterlinck's drama *Interior* can serve as an example. In this scene two people, an old man and a stranger, are standing outdoors and observing a family in a room through a window. The dialogue goes as follows:

The Stranger. See, they are smiling in the silence of the room. ...
The Old Man. They are not at all anxious – they did not expect her this evening.

how, as a young man, he once had the honour of driving the Emperor Francis I and the Russian Tsar Alexander I in a coach-and-four; as a mark of thanks, Francis presented him with two gold ducats.]

The Stranger. They sit motionless and smiling. But see, the father puts his finger to his lips. ...
The Old Man. He points to the child asleep on its mother's breast. ...
The Stranger. She dares not raise her head for fear of disturbing it. ...
The Old Man. They are not sewing anymore. There is a dead silence. (Maeterlinck 1969: 181)

Thus the degree and the nuance of monologic quality in a dialogue can be extremely varied, and only the analysis of a number of specific cases could show the significance of the monologic quality for dialogue in its entire import and scope. However, such an analysis would have to be preceded by a detailed linguistic differentiation of monologic from dialogic speech. Both these tasks exceed the limits of our essay, the purpose of which is to present the noetic premises of such research. As a provisional characterization of the variety of the possible combinations of dialogue with monologue, let us cite Dujardin's words, which were of course intended to apply to dramatic dialogue alone, but are essentially valid for dialogue in general:

If so many authors have been attracted by the dramatic form, it is not because this form offers them the rather crude (and generally dearly paid for) delight of embodying their conceptions in an atmosphere of painted cardboard but because it enables them to let the voices that they hear in the depths of their hearts speak. Such is, in fact, the interest not only of those rather rare monologues that we encounter in the theatre but also of sections of dialogue in which a character speaks as if he were speaking to himself, whether in a reply that seems to be but actually is not addressed to his interlocutor, whether in a sentence uttered in the middle of the speech or in a simple syntactic member where the cry of the subconscious rises like a puff of smoke, and which are nothing but fragments of concealed monologues. In this sense, the true dramatic dialogue is a continual combination of concealed monologues expressing the character's soul and dialogues in the proper sense of the word. (Dujardin 1931: 35)[12]

We have reached the end of our deliberations about monologue and dialogue. Our aim has been to demonstrate the thesis that the monologic and dialogic qualities comprise the basic polarity of linguistic activity, a polarity that reaches a temporary and always renewed equilibrium in *every* utterance, whether monologic or dialogic from the formal point of view. It was not, however, our intention to answer the question of monologue and dialogue by means of this assertion. The aim was simply to pose it.

---

12 Of course it must be added, as has been said above, that the hidden monologic quality is not always an "expression of the soul" but often the result of the external circumstances of the conversation.

WORKS CITED

Cazaux, Jean (1939) *Surréalisme et psychologie. Endophasie et écriture automatique* [Surrealism and Psychology. Endophasia and Automatic Writing], Paris: Corti.

Dujardin, Edouard (1931) *Le Monologue intérieur: Son apparition, ses origines, sa place dans l'oeuvre de James Joyce et dans le roman contemporain* [Interior Monologue: Its Appearance, Origins and Place in the Works of James Joyce and the Contemporary Novel], Paris: Messein.

Egger, Victor (1881) *La Parole intérieure: Essai de psychologie descriptive* [Interior Speech: An Essay on Descriptive Psychology], Paris: Librairie Germer Baillière.

Jakobson, Roman (1987 [1937]) "An Open Letter to Voskovec and Werich on the Epistemology and Semantics of Fun" trans. Michael L. Quinn, *Stanford Slavic Studies* 1, pp. 153–55.

Lichtenberg, Georg Christoph (1949) "Die 'Bemerkungen'" ["Notes"] in *Gesammelte Werke* I, Frankfurt am Main: Holle.

Maeterlinck, Maurice (1969) *Interior*, in John and Mollie Gassner (eds) *Fifteen International One-Act Plays*, New York: Washington Square Press.

Mukařovský, Jan (1941) "Básnické pojmenování a estetická funkce jazyka" [Poetic Designation and the Aesthetic Function of Language] in *Kapitoly z české poetiky* [Chapters on Czech Poetics], vol. 1, Prague: Melantrich, pp. 157–63.

Tarde, Gabriel (1922) *L'Opinion et la foule* [Opinion and the Crowd], 4th ed., Paris: F. Alcan.

Yakubinsky, L. V. (1923) "O dialicheskoi rechi" [On Dialogic Speech] in L. V. Shcherba (ed.), *Russkaya rech*, vol. 1, St Petersburg: Izd. Foneticheskogo Instituta Iazykov, pp. 96–194.

DRAMATIC TEXT AS A COMPONENT OF THEATRE

JIŘÍ VELTRUSKÝ

[First published in Czech as "Dramatický tekst jako součást divada" in 1941, *Slovo a slovesnost*, vol. 7, no. 3, pp. 132–44. The article was translated by the author into English and published in 1976 as "Dramatic Text as Component of Theater" in Matejka, Ladislav and Titunik, Irwin R. (eds) (1976) *Semiotics of Art: Prague School Contributions*, Cambridge, Mass.: The M.I.T. Press, pp. 94–118.]

Editor's note: In the process of translation, Veltruský made several changes to the original 1941 Czech version, among them adding several paragraphs to ensure a better understanding of the context, updating sources and adding footnotes. He used the specialized vocabulary of semiotics, which he championed at the time, to translate various structuralist concepts. We have kept Veltruský's "semiotized" translation of his own text.

This paper proposes to analyse one of the fundamental components of theatrical structure, the dramatic text. It does not seek to examine all the aspects of its theatricality – that would be impossible within the limited space of a single article – but rather to focus on those features of the play which in a general way determine its place in the structure of theatre.

The fact that at present many stage directors take great liberties with the written text will be disregarded here. Theory can derive little benefit from the polemics provoked by this practice, which have centred especially around the so-called avant-garde directors. It is too often forgotten that Stanislavsky, too, used to interfere with the work produced by the dramatist (Stanislavski 2008: 276–79). And we just do not know how the problem was dealt with in the past – not even how Shakespeare the actor treated his own plays.

In any event, the theoretical implications of those practices we do know about are so enormous that they would require a special study. Suffice it to say that sometimes by tampering with the text the stage director and the actors reveal points that the author himself then perceives as defects in his drama, even as a literary work. The present form of Karel Čapek's *R.U.R.*, for instance – established in its second edition – differs in many respects from the first edition because Čapek adopted all the changes made in the first theatrical performance. Only two factors are relevant for the present study.

On the one hand, the dramatic text performed in the theatre belongs to the dramatic genre, whether it is or is not identical in its direct speech with what the dramatist wrote (if the stage director's changes have replaced its dramatic structure by a narrative or lyric structure, it no longer falls within the scope of what is to be examined here). On the other hand, the text exists with all its structural features before the other components of the theatrical structure are created; the fact that it may undergo further modifications in the course of their creation is of minor importance.

DRAMA AS LITERATURE AND ITS PERFORMANCE IN THE THEATRE

The unending quarrel about the nature of drama, whether it is a literary genre or a theatrical piece, is perfectly futile. One does not exclude the other. Drama is a work of literature in its own right; it does not need anything but simple reading to enter the consciousness of the public. At the same time, it is a text that can, and mostly is intended to, be used as the verbal component of theatrical performance. But some forms of theatre prefer lyric or narrative texts to drama; theatre enters into relation with literature as a whole, not just with the dramatic genre.

DRAMATIC DIALOGUE AND THE PLURALITY OF ACTORS

The primary distinctive feature of drama as a literary genre is that its language is rooted in dialogue, while lyric and narrative derive from monologue. As a result, the semantic construction of a play relies on a plurality of contexts that unfold simultaneously, take turns, interpenetrate and vainly strive to subjugate and absorb one another. Each one of them is associated with a different character.

The theatrical counterpart of the complicated relationship between the semantic contexts is very simple: each character is usually enacted by a different actor. It may seem that this goes without saying and is due to simple technical reasons. But this is not so. Much more often than not, only one character speaks at any given moment because in dialogue the speakers alternate. It would be feasible for one actor to enact them all. That is what actually happens in some forms of theatre. For instance, in folklore certain tellers of traditional tales put on a solo theatrical performance, impersonating the characters of the tale, miming their gestures and even complicated actions, constantly moving from spot to spot and changing the pitch, the loudness, and the speed of the delivery in the course of the dialogue in accordance with the alternation of speakers.[1]

---

1   See I. V. Karnaukhova's description of a performance by Russian folktale teller P. J. Belkov, as reproduced in Bogatyrev 1940: 17 ff.

When a separate actor stands for every character, the spectator continuously perceives all the participants in a dialogue, not just the one who says something at a given moment. This leads him to project each semantic unit into all the competing contexts immediately, without waiting until the other characters react one way or the other to what is being said. Yet this is precisely what distinguishes dramatic dialogue from the ordinary kind. The mere presence of the actors representing all the participants signals the co-existence of several contexts. Moreover, in this arrangement, dramatic action is rarely limited to the momentary speaker. Significantly, the simultaneous representation of more than one character by a single actor can usually be found in the performance of a narrative, rather than a dramatic, text. Narrative dialogue differs from dramatic dialogue chiefly in that it emphasizes the succession of speeches rather than the simultaneous unfolding and interplay of the contexts from which they spring.

DIRECT SPEECH, AUTHORIAL NOTES AND THEIR TRANSPOSITION

One of the fundamental oppositions within drama as a literary genre is between direct speech and authorial notes and remarks, usually though somewhat misleadingly called the stage directions. In theatrical performance, these notes are eliminated, and the resulting gaps in the unity of the text are filled in by signs other than linguistic ones. This is not an arbitrary process but essentially a matter of transposing linguistic meanings into other semiotic systems. Yet even where it endeavours to be as faithful as possible it necessarily brings about important modifications in the meanings themselves. The whole semantic structure of the work is recast. The extent of the change depends mainly on the number and weight of authorial notes in the text, that is to say, on the importance of the gaps created by their deletion.

In so far as such gaps disrupt the continuous flow of meanings, the play tends to disintegrate into separate roles or parts and to abandon those parts to the actors as mere components of the stage figures they are to create. The less pronounced such gaps are, the more the language tends to keep its unity. If this tendency gets the upper hand, the creative freedom of the actor is confined within fairly narrow limits; the stage figure he constructs is much more absorbed by the language of the play than his lines are absorbed by the stage figure. Maeterlinck's plays, especially his early ones, are an outstanding case in point. Significantly, it was in his production of Maeterlinck's *The Death of Tintagiles* that Meyerhold for the first time achieved, to his own satisfaction, the "stylized theatre" of which he had been dreaming; incidentally, in the whole of the first two acts of *The Death of Tintagiles*, not a single speech is interrupted by a stage direction.

The relative weight of direct speech and of authorial notes in the dramatic text is also reflected in various types of relations among stage figures (and characters) that arise on stage. Where the deletion of the notes does not open really important gaps, these relations tend to remain chiefly on the plane of pure meanings, characteristic of language as a semiotic system: the simultaneous and successive interplay of semantic contexts, their reciprocal tensions, their striving to decompose each other's unity of sense. All variable relations between characters are more or less perceived against the background of constant relations, which give them a broader perspective; that, of course, does not prevent such constant relations from drawing their own concreteness from the variable ones as the play unfolds. More important gaps open the way for what might be called material relations, that is, for action in the narrow sense of the word. When such relations among stage figures prevail over the purely semantic ones, all that is variable in them becomes more important than what is constant. Single physical acts multiply and attract so much attention that they overshadow the basic, less variable but immaterial relations between semantic contexts. The momentary superiority of one character over another, which shifts from one situation to the next, almost totally obscures the general hierarchy of all the characters, which remains constant for the whole play.

DRAMATIC TEXT AND THEATRICAL SPACE

All the relations between stage figures and characters are projected into space. They constitute what is termed dramatic space, a set of immaterial relations that constantly changes in time as these relations themselves change (Zich 1931: 246). Of course variability is possible only against the background of something constant. Where the purely semantic, immaterial relations between whole contexts are veiled by the variable material relations between stage figures or, to put it differently, where the balance of dramatic space is not maintained by the constant forces deriving from the linguistic component of the performance, dramatic space must draw its stable forces from somewhere else. That is the function of the set or scenic objects, which are semantically independent signs – the set does not substantially change during a given situation. Wherever the dramatic space contains a constant element of this kind, it may itself expand, through its variable components, beyond the limits of the stage (I am referring here to the interplay between the actor and the spectator on the one hand and the "imaginary stage", that is, the audible off-stage action, on the other). It can also restrict itself at given moments to small parts of the stage.

So the existence and importance of the set, too, depend on the structure of the dramatic text or, more precisely, on the extent to which the continuity of meaning is disrupted by the deletion of authorial remarks. The more suitable the constant relations between semantic contexts are as a background to the variability of the dramatic space, the more semantically vague the set can become. In an extreme case, it may even lose all independent meaning of its own, receiving different meanings as they are bestowed upon it by other theatrical components (compare the localization through dialogue in Elizabethan theatre). The meanings the set receives in this way are not of course as constant as its own, independent meaning. The set merges with the stage, a delimited, semantically unspecified playing area.

The construction of the stage, its shape and location, is determined by the needs of the performance. Like all other components of theatre, the stage depends, though to a variable degree, on the structure of the dramatic text; since the auditorium is inseparably connected with the stage, we can say that the arrangement of the entire theatrical space depends to some extent on the structure of the dramatic text. In the Elizabethan theatre, for example, the use of the upper stage, not radically different, it seems, from certain spectators' "rooms",[2] corresponded to the intimate relationship the plays tended to set up with the audience. The presence of some spectators on stage – as well as the strict separation of the "rooms" from the galleries, and especially from the pit – corresponded to the same tendency, since it turned the spectators on stage and in the "rooms" into something like performers in relation to the other spectators, especially those standing in the pit. Similarly, the immense dimensions of the auditorium in Classical Greek theatre satisfied two concerns of tragedy: for language to predominate over the actor and for the stage figure created by the actor to be so abstract as to remain below the threshold of consciousness as merely a fairly irrelevant carrier of a function.

The idea that the stage and the entire theatrical space are partly dependent on the dramatic structure would seem to conflict with the experience of many avant-garde stage directors. They condemn the picture-frame stage because they feel the relations between actors and audience need to be thoroughly recast. Yet in most cases this condemnation remains purely theoretical; buildings with a different stage and auditorium are not available. With very few exceptions, however convincingly he may write about the need to reorganize the whole theatrical space, the stage director must, in practice, use the traditional picture-frame stage. Even detailed projects for a new theatre, such as the total theatre designed by Walter Gropius for Erwin Piscator (Piscator 1980: 180–83) or E. F. Burian and Miroslav Kouřil's

---

2   [Editor's note: Often termed "gentlemen's rooms", these were portioned-off seating areas for the higher class of spectator, situated immediately to left and right of the main stage level, something akin to boxes in later theatres.]

"The Theatre of Labour" (Kouřil and Burian 1938: *passim*), remain on paper for lack of financing. However, the contradiction may be more apparent than real. A theatre performance is ephemeral by its very nature, while the construction of a theatre building is, usually, a long-term venture. Therefore it takes time for the theatrical space to adjust to the requirements of the dramatic structure. Such a time lag must often have occurred in the history of theatre, especially when a new dramatic structure emerged gradually. And as regards avant-garde theatre, nobody could claim that it is a new structure that has already acquired a shape; by its very mission it is experimental and widely diversified, each initiator pushing his experiments in a different direction.

Moreover, a negative proof that theatrical space is more dependent on dramatic structure than the other way round was provided when a new theatre that could have satisfied all the ambitions of Vsevolod Meyerhold, Alexander Tairov, Evgeny Vakhtangov, Erwin Piscator, Oskar Schlemmer, Jindřich Honzl, E. F. Burian and all the others was constructed in Paris in the hope that it would give rise to work comparable to theirs. It did not stimulate the development of a new structure, nor did it attract stage directors, and in the end it had to be converted into a cinema (Honzl 2016 [1937]: 298).

DRAMATIC TEXT AND MUSIC

So far, little attention has been paid to the intricate problems of the semiotics of music. Therefore I must limit myself to a few observations.

As a component of theatre, music has its starting point in the dramatic text. This applies both to vocal music and to musical accompaniment of the spoken word. In both functions, the musical structure is connected with the sound structure of the text. The possibilities of setting a dramatic text to music or of composing music to be played during its declamation are delimited by the phonic line – *ligne phonique* – of the text itself.

The manner and the degree of that delimitation are variable, depending on the nature of the phonic line. For instance, the text may necessitate being set to music and at the same time impose few limitations upon the musical creation. Such is especially the case of a text written in what is called sung verse.[3] But the phonic line of a text can also be of such a nature and intensity that a composer attempting to set the text to music must make a strenuous search within the repertory of musical resources in order to discover those that come closest to the phonic line concerned. He may even be obliged to infringe certain canonized musical norms, for instance consonance (cf. Leoš

---

3   See the analysis of sung verse in Old Czech in Jakobson 1985 [1934]. Some remarks on what was clearly sung verse in modern Czech can be found in Veltruský 1940.

Janáček's transcriptions of the intonations of speech into musical tones). There are also cases where the phonic line of the text resists being set to music.

Therefore the possibilities of theatrical music are, one way or another, determined by the language of drama. That is also attested by the special difficulties that arise when the libretto of an opera is translated into another language, as well as by the many textual modifications that some composers make. On the other hand, even if the dramatic text is its starting point, music, especially operatic music, often tends to eliminate it from the theatrical structure altogether. The observation Meyerhold made in connection with his staging of Wagner's *Tristan and Isolde*, namely that opera is much closer to mime than to the performance of drama, is relevant here. Theatrical music where that is true is outside the scope of the present study.

In any event, theatrical music is not as closely bound up with the dramatic text as the actor's performance. Even when they sound the most alike, the components of music and the sound components of the text belong to two entirely different semiotic systems. By contrast, the same sound components of the text enter right into the stage figure, becoming part of the actor's voice performance.

PREDETERMINATION OF THE STAGE FIGURE BY THE TEXT

INDEPENDENT MOVEMENTS

Semantically independent movements are transpositions of the meanings conveyed by authorial notes, remarks and comments. Apart from that, they are often directly called for, therefore predetermined, by the dialogue that refers to them while they are being carried out, for example:

Hamlet. Come on, sir.
Laertes. Come on, my lord.
(They play.)
Hamlet. *One.*
Laertes. No.
Hamlet. Judgment!
Osric. A hit, a very palpable hit.
Laertes. Well, *again!*
King. *Stay, give me drink.* Hamlet this pearl is thine,
Here's to thy health. Give him the cup.
Hamlet. I'll play this bout first; *set by awhile. Come. Another hit. What say you?*
(Trumpets sound, and shot goes off.)
Laertes. A touch, a touch; I do confess.

King. Our son shall win.
Queen. *He's fat and scant of breath. Here, Hamlet, take my napkin, rub thy brows. The queen carouses to thy fortune, Hamlet.* (William Shakespeare, *Hamlet* 5.2 – italics J. V.)

Elsewhere, there is a gap in verbal communication, and the speech following it reacts to the physical action that occurred in the meantime. In the following example, the last line reacts to the movement ordered in the stage direction, which is itself really redundant.

Laertes. ... Hold off the earth awhile,
Till I have caught her once more in mine arms.
(Leaps in the grave.)
Now pile your dust upon the quick and dead ... (*Hamlet* 5.1)

Whether a movement is determined by the dialogue or by the author's notes, the actor is given considerable leeway in his choice of the specific means by which to carry out the movement, since only its global sense, never exactly transposable from language into the action of the muscles, is imposed on him.

ATTENDANT MOVEMENTS

The actor also complements the dramatic text by the kind of movements that help to shape the meaning of what is being spoken. Movements falling into this second category are often numerous and important even when a play with few authorial notes is performed. They, too, are far from being completely at the actor's discretion. They are there to convey meanings that, though contained in the written text, are difficult to convey by the vocal resources on which spoken language relies:

1. The emphasis marked by italics in the following speech from Ibsen's *John Gabriel Borkman*: "You betrayed the woman you *loved!* Me, me, me!" cannot be created by intensity, since the loudest point is reached at the end of the triple exclamation that follows. The meaning of the graphic sign will almost automatically be transposed into a gesture.

2. The ironic meaning of a word, which may be signalled by quotation marks, cannot be adequately expressed by voice colouring when the phonic line of the speech is dominated by the continuous undulation of intonation, because an abrupt change in voice colouring would break up the continuity of the intonation; so the irony must be signified by a gesture, a grimace, and so forth.

3. Gestures are also quite often used to mark the articulation of a syntactically complicated sentence, signalled by punctuation in the text but perhaps beyond the scope of the actor's vocal resources.

4. Some meanings have no signifier of their own in the written text because they derive from the sense of the whole context, as, for instance, when a speech is addressed to a specific character who is not explicitly indicated in any way. The reader recognizes the addressee because of the overall sense of the speech concerned, though perhaps only at the end of the speech or when the addressee responds. In the theatre, the actor must usually face his addressee from the very beginning of the speech. All this comes out more clearly in the frequent cases where a character first replies to what another said and then immediately, within the same speech, speaks to a third.

5. Deictic gestures also fall into to this category, especially when they accompany deictic pronouns or adverbs that reveal the reality to which they refer only in conjunction with the context of the speech or with the extra-linguistic situation. What I have in mind here is sentences like: "He was the one." In the written play, this needs no authorial note, since the reader already knows who the culprit is. In a theatrical performance, this declaration would strike us as very odd – indeed as a striking artistic device behind which we would perceive the hand of the stage director – if it were not accompanied by a deictic gesture.

6. Lexicalized gestures often accompany linguistic clichés, as when a glass is lifted to the words "To your health".

7. Instinctive movements that in fact are physiologically conditioned but function for the audience as signs underlining the meaning of the speech they accompany (distortion of the face in a scream, and so on). Since the attendant movements receive their meanings from the speech that they accompany, and since they mostly have little or no independent meaning of their own, their specific form adapts itself to the speech, especially to its phonic line.

MOVEMENTS AND VOCAL EXPRESSION

The dominant position of any given sound component manifests itself through its free variability, which is independent of the intrinsic tendencies of the others. Three sound components – intonation, voice colouring, and intensity – are in this respect particularly important for the construction of dramatic dialogue because they correspond to the three fundamental types of dialogue:

1. *Intonation* in the dominant position tends to undulate continuously. It also tends to loosen the direct relation of single language units to the realities they refer to, to make speech flow smoothly; this enables the meanings to enter into complicated mutual relations. In dialogue, the undulation of intonation freely crosses the borders between successive passages. This reveals unexpected semantic shifts and brings into play scarcely perceptible connotations, because such shifts throw the usual meaning of the words out

of balance. It generates all kinds of faint and fleeting connections between the words (see Mukařovský 1955 [1948]). The author interrupts the continuity of intonation as little as possible by his notes. Indeed, dramatists as different from each other as, for example, Maurice Maeterlinck, Oscar Wilde and Karel Čapek, the outstanding common aspect of whose plays is the dominance of intonation, all make exceptionally sparing use of authorial notes. Finally, intonation aims to restrict semantically independent movements – actions in the physical sense – because they disturb its free and smooth undulation. It mainly allows such movements as acquiesce in its dominance, without usurping attention either by the wealth of their own meanings or by their striking materiality – in other words, to movements that are highly stylized (see Mukařovský 1955 [1948]), to more or less lexicalized conventional gestures and to deictic gestures.

2. *Voice colouring* or *timbre* tends, by its frequent and abrupt changes, to break up speech into a multitude of independent segments that are separated from each other by what might be called semantic hiatuses. Every line of dialogue is hermetically sealed off, as it were, from those before and after it. Moreover, it is generally divided into separate segments, each of which points directly to some psychological feature or momentary state of mind of the character who says it. The cohesion of each semantic context is relegated to the background by a rapid sequence of emotional responses.

The dialogue frequently turns into physical activity, which is largely arbitrary and unforeseeable, since it is motivated by purely emotive causes. Authorial notes are numerous because the concrete changes in voice colouring cannot be predetermined by the construction of the speech alone and so must be explicitly indicated by the notes. But this means that it is not the sound components of the literary text that give rise to the specific voice components of the stage figure. These spring rather from elements transposed from a different material: the emotive qualities of direct speech on the one hand and the directions given in the authorial notes on the other.

3. *Intensity* in a dominant position markedly divides the speech into segments ordered in a clear hierarchy of expiratory stresses. The borders between successive passages of dialogue are underlined by striking intonational cadences, which end nearly all of them. The distinctions between individual contexts tend to be very pronounced and every individual line of dialogue is formulated in such a way as to recall the context to which it belongs.

In theatrical performance, the relationship between language and physical movement varies, as does language itself, depending on the combinations into which intensity enters with the other sound components of the text. The movements may be numerous, in which case they tend to be semantically independent of the speech, or they may be extremely limited in scope and number. Especially important in this connection is whether it is voice colouring or on the contrary intonation that comes closest to the dominant intensity in the hierarchy of sound components. But as a rule physical movements tend to be strongly typified. In periods when intensity dominates the sound structure, the actor's movements are frequently subjected to convention and even to a certain degree of lexicalization.

CONSTANT COMPONENTS AND FEATURES

The sound structure of the dramatic text also tends to predetermine the set of what are termed constant components or features of the stage figure, such as the name of the character, the actor's physical constitution and characteristics, the costume, the actor's face or guise, the general pitch, loudness, and colour of his voice, and so forth, as well as certain more or less permanent features of the variable components, for instance a given actor's characteristic gestures or voice inflections, the way he articulates certain words, and so on. They have the double function of unifying all the variable components of the same stage figure and distinguishing it from all the others. In fact, it is this double function, not the constancy, that characterizes them. Not all of them need be really constant. Indeed, certain theatrical structures facilitate their maximum variability and reduce the opposition between constant and variable components to an opposition between components that vary occasionally and those that vary all the time.

The semiotics of these components has not yet been properly studied, so here I can give just a few indications.

1. The name of the character, which comes from the text, may be semantically poor, serving merely to indicate the character's sex (Mary, Charles); or it may not even do that, as is often the case in Maeterlinck. However, the name can also be used to convey a variety of meanings, such as the nationality of the character (a foreign name), the main features of his personality (Sir Toby Belch and Sir Andrew Aguecheek in *Twelfth Night*, the conventional characters in *commedia dell'arte*), and so on. It can even assume a whole cluster of precise meanings and shades of meaning (the name of a real person intimately known to the audience or the name of a famous and much discussed character like Electra, Antigone, Faustus, St Joan).

2. The physical constitution and characteristics can best develop their semiotic potential in the performance of difficult and exacting movements and when the body is partly or wholly stripped. If these elements are to assume a heavy load of meanings, the costume takes a subordinate position: it must not hamper the actor's movement nor distract attention from his body. Many illustrations of this principle can be found in Tairov's work. But the costume can also have the contrary function, to conceal the actor's body. It may serve, for instance, to prevent the body from attracting undue attention when it is

the text that is to dominate the whole dramatic structure (Classical Greek tragedy).

3. When it is subject to strong convention, the costume can convey very rich and diversified meanings. Convention may link a specific costume with a traditional or famous character. Harlequin's or Pierrot's costumes have perpetuated that link far beyond the *commedia dell'arte*.

Another, though in many respects different, case in point is Hamlet's black costume; certain modern stage directors deliberately produced a shock by the mere fact of dressing him otherwise. However, convention may also operate in an entirely different way, as in the Chinese theatre, where costume is composed of a great number of lexicalized signs (see Brušák 2016 [1939]).

Costume can also acquire a great semantic charge without the help of any convention whatever. An interesting case is reported by Stanislavsky. After watching a performance of *The Seagull*, Chekhov asked him to play Trigorin in torn shoes and check trousers. Here is Stanislavsky's comment:

> Trigorin is a fashionable writer, a ladies' man, and suddenly we have check trousers and cracked shoes. I, on the other hand, had worn a very elegant suit, white trousers, town shoes, white waistcoat, white hat and made up to look handsome.
>
> A year or more passed. I played Trigorin again and, suddenly, in the middle of one performance, it came to me:
>
> Of course, check trousers, cracked shoes and not handsome at all! Therein lies the drama, that for young women it is important for a man to be a writer who publishes romantic fiction and then Nina, like other girls, throws herself at him without realising that he is not a handsome man, but has check trousers and cracked shoes. (Stanislavski 2008: 199)

4. As one of the constant components of the stage figure, the face presents certain problems that distinguish it from all the others. This is mainly due to its inherent semiotic quality, which is very strong, in both its variable and its constant features. The movement of facial muscles is one of a person's most effective resources in expressing his personality and state of mind. At the same time, the face is by far the most important of the characteristics by which we recognize an individual. Its features are more often than not interpreted as signs of a person's mentality, personality, intelligence, temperament, even his way of life, background, and so forth. Finally, what a speaker does with his facial muscles significantly complements his speech. None of these semiotic qualities of the face can be ignored in theatre. They must be either exploited or neutralized. Since they draw on the variable features of the face as much as on its constant ones, there are certain problems inherent in using it as one of the constant components of the stage figure, as may be illustrated by the effects obtained by "sculpting" the actor's face with a kind of putty: this

may increase the constant semiotic potential of the face but it immobilizes certain facial muscles and therefore reduces the expressive potential of their movement.

To neutralize the semiotic qualities of the face, an immobile mask is used in some forms of theatre. That was probably the main function of the mask in Classical Greek tragedy; it was the dramatist's word rather than the play of facial muscles that gave the face its specific meanings. But in other dramatic structures, the mask is used to increase the role of the face among the constant components. On the other hand, in the many periods when makeup is systematically used, the fact of leaving the face bare may be a means of reducing or even neutralizing its semiotic potential because it signals that no importance is to be attached to the face and its movements; bareness produces the opposite effect in the case of the actor's face as it does in the case of his body.

Through theatrical convention, the face can be made to convey an enormous variety of meanings, some of which are entirely unrelated to its semiotic qualities in everyday life. Particularly rich material of this kind can be found in the Chinese theatre, where highly complicated makeup, uniform coloration of the face and a lack of makeup, all three lexicalized, are combined with the play of facial muscles (see Brušák 2016 [1939]). It would not be altogether surprising if further study revealed that here the semiotic function of the dynamic play of the muscles has been dissociated from that of the face as one of the constant components.

5. As regards the constant voice features, the particular relationship that exists between timbre and intonation is especially important. Wherever intonation prevails, the timbre of the voice is relegated to the lowest place in the hierarchy of sound components and vice versa. In this most subordinate position intonation asserts itself mainly as the general pitch of the voice, timbre as its constant, characteristic colour. The sound structure of the text determines the component that will take this position but it does not determine the specific quality of that component. It determines, for instance, that the pitch of each stage figure will be relatively immobile but not that one figure or another will have a high, low or medium pitch, let alone a specific register; it determines that each figure's voice will keep approximately the same colour during the whole performance but not whose voice should be raucous, whose squeaky, whose melodious, and so on; that may, however, be indicated by the nature of the parts.

The general colour of the voice is capable of carrying a considerable semantic load; it can denote the character's sex, age, some features of his mentality (for example, tenderness, rudeness, shyness), and so forth. Therefore, in a play dominated by intonation, even the set of constant components can be dominated to a large extent by linguistic means. By contrast, since the pitch has a very low semantic potential, the dominant position of voice colouring in the text makes it necessary to draw heavily on extralinguistic components in constructing the constant features of the stage figure.

THE STAGE FIGURE AS A STRUCTURE OF SIGNS

The stage figure is a complicated structure of signs that includes all the components, whether linguistic or extralinguistic, whether constant or variable, and so on. But though integrated, it is a structure of structures. All the movements of a figure also compose a structure of signs whose parts are all interrelated and hierarchically arranged. So do its constant components and features. And so do its vocal components. They are structures within the structure. The whole structure of the stage figure is made up of links by which they are connected. But there is a fundamental difference between the structure of the vocal expression and the others. In its general outline, the vocal expression is a direct translation of the sound contour of the text, which exists before any theatrical performance. This enables the text to predetermine, though to a variable degree, the stage figure in all its aspects.

The fundamental relationship just mentioned exists even where the actors improvise, as for instance in folk theatre, the Chinese theatre, *commedia dell'arte*, and so forth. Improvisation is only a different way of performing a play. As a rule, the actor's freedom in the choice of both the verbal and the nonverbal means he may use in his improvisation is restricted by stringent norms (see Veltruský 1987 [1940]; and Brušák 2016 [1939]).

The actor's creation can never fully escape the obligations imposed on him by the dramatic text. It is true that he alone creates all the extralinguistic components of the stage figure. But even here, his scope is not unlimited. He is very restricted in his creative freedom when the vocal expression is strongly dominated by a component such as intonation, which is already so concretely shaped in the text that relatively little can be added in the performance. The actor must adapt himself and mould the extralinguistic resources accordingly, so that they do not disrupt the dominant sound component. In practice, this means that he must limit them as much as possible, so that they do not deflect attention, because of their striking materiality, from the subtle meanings conveyed by the movements of the dominant sound component. On the contrary, when the sound structure is dominated by a component such as timbre, the movements and specific shape of which are only predetermined by the text in a very general way, the actor's freedom to choose his resources increases. Language is subordinated to the extralinguistic resources at his disposal. An infinite variety of combinations can be found between these two extremes.

As a structure of signs, the stage figure is not only a structure of structures but also an integral part of that broader structure of signs, the whole performance. There lies another source of its predetermination by the dramatic text.

THE DRAMATIST, THE STAGE DIRECTOR AND THE ACTOR

Because of the unity it presents despite its great diversity, every artistic structure is not only an object but also the act of a subject.[4] This problem is far from simple at the best of times. But it is particularly complicated with regard to theatrical structure. It cannot be fully adumbrated, let alone analysed, within the scope of this paper. I shall limit myself to a few, rather sketchy, remarks concerning the way in which the characteristics of the dramatic text affect the position of the subject in theatrical performance.

The characters engaged in the dialogue are subjects, let us say operative subjects. But they are subjects only to a certain degree because there is also the author. He, too, is a subject – and indeed an operative subject as well – albeit on a different level. In contrast to the characters, the author is the central subject – the subject behind the characters, the maker of all the semantic contexts to which they are respectively linked, of all the situations, of all the speeches, and so on. So we have a double complication in drama as regards the subject of its structure: on the one hand, there is a plurality of subjects, let us say partial subjects, linked to the plurality of semantic contexts; on the other hand, there is a definite antinomy between these partial subjects and the author, who is the central subject.

However, drama is not only dialogue but also plot. In the plot, all the intrinsic contradictions, reversals and modifications of the dramatic conflict are unified into a single whole. Just as the interpenetration of the semantic contexts gives rise to semantic shifts and reversals, so the plot provides all those semantic changes with a single motivation.

---

4   The concept of subject is used here in the same sense as in modern philosophy (for example, in Ernst Cassirer's *Philosophy of Symbolic Forms*, particularly in its third volume), that is to say, as a member of the antinomy object-subject. In this sense, the subject perceives the object, acts upon the object, makes the object, and so on. The subject in this sense is that to which all mental representations or all operations and actions are attributed. Unfortunately, in the English language there is a danger of confusion. Although such derivatives as "subjective" and "subjectivity" are found in common usage, the term "subject" is most frequently used, when it is a question of art, semiotics, and so forth, in the sense of "subject matter". This danger of confusion cannot be avoided. The concept is too important to be replaced by circumlocutions or by terms that are only partly synonymous. For instance, it would be tempting to avoid the language difficulty by replacing the antinomy object-subject by the antinomy "it" – "I". But that would be misleading because it would conceal the antinomy inherent in the concept of subject itself: the subject can be not only "I" but also "thou"; it can be not only the first person subject but also the second person subject. Because of its psychological connotations and its intrinsic paradoxicalness, the antinomy "Ego" – "other Ego" cannot help either.

When they are viewed in the light of the plot, all the semantic shifts that abound in drama converge to a single point from which the whole structure can be seen in perspective, so to speak. It is on this spot that we find the one central operative subject of the dramatic structure. Though it remains in the background, this central subject always makes its presence and its operation felt as the conveyor of the plot and the source of its "proportionality", pace and unity.

When it comes to the theatrical performance of the text, the dramatist may or may not retain this key position. That will be determined mainly by the structure of the text itself. Naturally, much will depend on whether, in theatrical performance, this structure makes the linguistic components predominate over the extralinguistic or the other way round. But the problem has other aspects as well.

The dramatist will, for instance, be perceived as the principal originator of the theatrical structure when the way the dialogue unfolds appears necessary, inevitable. This happens particularly where the spontaneity of the characters is restricted while the differences in their basic attitudes are emphasized: in such cases fortuitous elements are generally eliminated from the dialogue and each segment of the dialogue contributes to the progression of the plot. The lack of spontaneous decisions on the part of the characters points to the dramatist as an invisible force above them, as a subject whose intention manifests itself in the orderliness of both dialogue and plot. Sophocles' tragedies provide a typical example. The operation of the dramatist may also be emphasized when characters in specific, unique situations make statements of more general application than their immediate setting warrants. This tends to project whatever is said and done on stage onto a different plane and to relate it to certain general "truths". The dialogue conveys a kind of wisdom to be expected from somebody observing the action from a distance, rather than from persons directly involved, with the result that they are, to some extent, perceived as being formulated, and put into the characters' mouths, by the central subject. Many examples can be found in Shakespeare's plays.[5]

In plays that bring the emotions of the characters to the forefront, the situation of the dramatist is different. The single, partial, subjects appear to be more or less emancipated from their immediate dependence on the central subject and the dialogue looks like a chain of spontaneous reactions that reveal the characters' minds and dispositions much more than their attitude to reality. Dialogue based on momentary moods appears to progress in an ex-

---

5   In order to avoid any possible misunderstanding, it should be pointed out that what is discussed here is an artistic device, not the question whether or not maxims used by Shakespeare's characters reflect the sentiments, the ideas or even the *Weltanschauung* of the dramatist himself.

tremely haphazard and tortuous manner, so that the audience largely ceases to be aware of its being organized; consequently the operation of the central subject tends to sink beneath the threshold of consciousness. Naturally, in drama as literature, the author makes his presence felt in such plays through frequent notes and comments. But these are absent in the performance.

The sound structure of the text is also relevant to the problem under discussion. In the performance of a text dominated by intonation, individual characters tend to become blurred in the flow of the dialogue and the author remains continuously present in the minds of the audience.

His presence also tends to be strongly felt where intensity predominates, though here he remains more in the background and tends to manifest himself through the characters. Since every line of dialogue is quite clearly related to the specific context to which it belongs, emphasis is put on the distinctive philosophy of the character, his goal or permanent psychological profile. Shaw's *The Devil's Disciple* provides a good illustration. The plot is organized in such a way as to give prominence to two reversals in the hero's situation: the first comes when, at the most critical moment, he acts in a manner contrary to what all the characters expect of him, the second when the devil's disciple turns into a minister of the gospel. But since the phonic line of the play is dominated by intensity (though in certain scenes the changes in voice colouring come fairly close to taking the upper hand), there are no reversals in the semantic context created by Richard Dudgeon's lines. In his confrontations with the other characters, the hero reacts very clearly from first to last as "a Puritan of the Puritans", to use Shaw's description (Shaw 1906: xxiv).

The situation is entirely different when abrupt changes in timbre dominate the vocal expression of the actors: the characters are in the forefront and the dramatist remains more or less hidden behind them. Moreover, to perform this kind of drama also raises numerous problems that are not solved in the text; the text merely indicates the direction in which the solution should be looked for.

This is where the stage director takes over from the dramatist. In the first place, he must choose actors whose constitution, physical qualities and voice correspond to the requirements of the parts. He must also participate in the choice and moulding of semantically independent movements, which are numerous and very important here, while the text determines them only in a very general way. He must influence and consolidate the intentions of individual actors in their choice of specific timbres and gestures so as to create an integrated "psychological situation". Finally, he must shape their interplay and coordination, because the relationships between the characters keep shifting, and create the "proportionality" of the whole performance, because the proportionality of the plot tends to recede into the background under the impact of the emotionally charged dialogue and the materiality of physical action.

In the performance of a text relying mainly on timbre, the actor's freedom increases as well. The many semantic gaps in the direct speech enable him to shape his independent movements as he sees fit. The text only predetermines their global meaning, the starting point and the outcome of every movement, not the specific means by which it is to be carried out. However, when the emancipation of the actor's performance goes beyond a certain limit, a qualitative change sets in. The stage figure becomes an independent sign and tends to clash with the semantic requirements of the text. Various inhibitions begin to afflict the actor; for instance, he keeps forgetting his lines. That is why a tendency on the part of an actor to develop his own creativity to the maximum may call for the constant intervention of a strong stage director. The decisive contribution of Stanislavsky, as stage director, to the dominant position of the actor in the Moscow Art Theatre is a classic case in point.

Some texts also seem to give the actor a considerable degree of freedom in the selection of linguistic as well as extralinguistic means, confining themselves only to predetermining the global sense of the dialogue and action. Yet even in such an extreme case as *commedia dell'arte*, the theatrical structure was predetermined by the text. In fact, in addition to the general sense, the text also prescribed the whole set of specific means that the actor had at his disposal. It did so in two different fashions. First, the name of each character designated a standard type that by convention was associated with a fixed set of devices. Second, each situation, as indicated by the text, was marked by a certain set of specific devices that were also governed by convention. Only within these repertoires was the actor free to exercise choice. Finally, the relations between the standard characters were fixed by convention as well, so that the name of a character, as given in the text, also predetermined his relation to all of the other characters. All this goes to show that even when the actor predominates over the other operative subjects of the theatrical structure to the highest possible degree, he does so not in defiance of the text but in conformity with it.

CONCLUSION

Drama brings intense pressure to bear upon all the other components of theatre. But none of these yields to that pressure entirely or ceases to maintain a certain degree of resistance. This is so because each one is an integral part of an independent art: acting, music, architecture, and so on. At each moment of its development, an art can break new ground in more than one direction. But the number and the nature of these openings are not infinite. Therefore any single component of theatre can respond to the requirements of drama only up to a certain point; if it went beyond this point, it would cut itself off from the art to which it belongs.

Consequently, the individual arts in their turn influence the development of dramatic literature through the intermediary of theatre. Indeed, when he writes a play, the dramatist is not unaware of the existing theatrical structure and of the various openings it presents to new developments. This is true even though the play is a self-sufficient work of literature that does not necessarily require theatrical performance; the creating subject usually senses, though often unconsciously, the possible applications of his work.

We have seen, however, that the dramatist can assign certain components of theatre such a place in the dramatic structure that they will become pure meanings, deprived of their specific material – as, for instance, in the verbal localization of the action, where it eliminates the use of material scenery. Even then theatre is a synthesis of all the arts because the contribution of a given art to its structure is noticeable even when that art is present only potentially (see Mukařovský 2016 [1941]).

There is only one art whose participation in the theatrical structure cannot be reduced to the degree of mere potentiality. That art is acting, for, as far as we know, without acting there is no theatre, at least no drama-performing theatre. Gordon Craig's dream of a theatre without actors remained confined to his programmatic writings, while as stage director he did not go beyond reforming the actor's style. He actually anticipated that difference between programme and practice in his famous essay "The Actor and the Übermarionette" (originally published in 1907).

In theatre, the linguistic sign system, which intervenes through the dramatic text, always combines and conflicts with acting, which belongs to an entirely different sign system. All the other components, such as music, scenic sets, and so forth, can be eliminated by the text itself; thus the intervention of the sign systems to which these components belong can be reduced to "zero degree" – unless they reenter the theatrical structure through the intermediary of the actor. Therefore the general function of drama in the shaping of the semiotics of theatre can be brought out only by means of confronting the two sign systems that are invariably present, that is, language and acting.

Of all the characteristics of the semiotics of language, the most important in this connection is that meaning is so tenuously tied to sensory material – the sound components on which the linguistic meaning relies are to a large extent predetermined by the meaning itself. This enables the linguistic meaning to create the most complicated combinations and relationships. The exact opposite is true of the semiotics of acting. Here, the material signifier – the actor's body in the most general sense—absolutely predominates over the immaterial meaning. In theatre, the sign created by the actor tends, because of its overwhelming reality, to monopolize the attention of the audience at the expense of the immaterial meanings conveyed by the linguistic sign; it tends to divert attention from the text to the vocal expression, from dialogue to physical actions and even to the physical appearance of the stage figure, and so on.

None of the other semiotic systems intervening in theatre attains either of these extremes. Let us take the signs that make up the stage space. No matter how they are chosen and treated, they have neither the same semantic potential as speech nor the same degree of reality as the actor. The meanings they convey are limited in their free play by being bound to the material that bears them. In its turn, this material does not display the same degree of reality as the actor because it is an artefact.

Since the semiotics of language and the semiotics of acting are diametrically opposed in their fundamental characteristics, there is a dialectical tension between the dramatic text and the actor, based primarily on the fact that the sound components of the linguistic sign are an integral part of the vocal resources the actor draws on. The relative weight of the two poles of this antinomy varies. If the linguistic sign prevails, there emerges a tendency to strip the sign embodied by the actor of its materiality, or at least some of it; that explains why Maeterlinck, Craig and many others were so fascinated by puppets. If, on the contrary, the linguistic sign is outweighed, its semantic potential diminishes. However, both sign systems not only check but also enrich each other. The actor gives more weight and punch to the language he uses and in return receives from it the gift of extremely flexible and variable meanings.

These characteristics of the sign systems that combine in theatre determine what may be called the basic, and in a sense constant, structure of the components. This basic hierarchy may never materialize in its pure form. But it is perceived by the audience as the background of a specific structure into which the components may be grouped in a given performance or in a given period or style. Therefore the variability of the theatrical sign, which Honzl regards as its distinctive feature (Honzl 2016 [1940]), must be seen in its dialectical unity with its opposite, the stability of that sign. Though extremely variable, the theatrical sign is at the same time extraordinarily stable in that its basic, "unmarked", structure is strongly pronounced.

WORKS CITED

Bogatyrev, Petr (1940) *Lidové divadlo české a slovenské* [Czech and Slovak Folk Theatre], Prague: Fr. Borový and Národopisná společnost českoslovanská.

Brušák, Karel (2016 [1939]) "Signs in the Chinese Theatre" in this reader, pp. 115–28.

Honzl, Jindřich (2016 [1937]) "Spatial Concers in Theatre" in this reader, pp. 290–302.

— (2016 [1940]) "The Mobility of the Theatrical Sign" in this reader, pp. 129–48.

Jakobson, Roman (1985 [1934]) "Old Czech Verse" in *Selected Writings*, vol. 6: *Early Slavic Paths and Crossroads*, Part 2: Medieval Slavic Studies, ed. Stephen Rudy, trans. S. Fusso, The Haque: Mouton, pp. 417–65.

Kouřil, Miroslav and Burian, E. F. (1938) *Divadlo práce* [The Theatre of Labour], Prague: Jaroslav Kohoutek.

Mukařovský, Jan (1955 [1948]) "K. Čapek's Prose as Lyrical Melody and as Dialogue" in Garvin, Paul L. (ed.) *A Prague School Reader on Esthetics, Literary Structure, and Style*, Washington: Washington Linguistic Club, pp. 133–49.

— (2016 [1941]) "On the Current State of the Theory of Theatre" in this reader, pp. 59–75.

Piscator, Erwin (1980) *The Political Theatre: A History 1917–1929*, trans. Hugh Rorrison, London: Methuen.

Shaw, Bernard (1906) *Three Plays for Puritans*, New York: Brentano's.

Stanislavski, Konstantin (2008) *My Life in Art*, trans. Jean Benedetti, New York: Routledge.

Veltruský, Jiří (1940) "Zpěvní kultura obrozenské doby" [The Song Culture of the Period of the National Revival], *Slovo a slovesnost*, vol. 6, pp. 231–33.

— (1987 [1940]) "Structure in Folk Theatre: Notes Regarding Bogatyrev's Book on Czech and Slovak Folk Theatre", *Poetics Today*, vol. 8, no. 1, pp. 141–61.

Zich, Otakar (1931) *Estetika dramatického umění: teoretická dramaturgie* [The Aesthetics of Dramatic Art: A Theoretical Dramaturgy], Prague: Melantrich.

Otakar Zich's concept of "dramatic space" was a source of great inspiration for the Prague School. Jan Mukařovský devoted several paragraphs to it in his review of Zich's *The Aesthetics of Dramatic Art* and he also appropriated the concept as part of a structural discourse of theatre in his overview of the Prague School (see "On the Current State of the Theory of Theatre" in section I).

Mukařovský also drew on the concept of "dramatic space" in his short text "A Note on the Aesthetics of Film" (1933). Not only is this a preliminary exploration of the youngest art at the time, it is also a comparative study of the differences between theatre and film, in particular of the differences in the way "dramatic spaces" are created in these arts.

Zich's concept of the dramatic space, which is not a mere representation of the place of action but rather a dynamic complex of spatial relations between characters developing over time, resonates both in the theory of the Prague School and in avant-garde theatre practice. This explains the presence in this section of both texts on theory as well as essays on the theatre space and proposals for a new theatre space that would be appropriate for the new, avant-garde theatre.

A NOTE ON THE AESTHETICS OF FILM

JAN MUKAŘOVSKÝ

[First published in Czech as "K estetice filmu" (1933) *Listy pro umění a kritiku* I: 100–108. This translation by John Burbank and Petr Steiner was published under the present title in Burbank, John and Steiner, Petr (trans. and eds) (1978) *Structure, Sign, and Function: Selected Essays by Jan Mukařovský*, New Haven: Yale University Press, pp. 178–90. A recent edition of this translation can be found in Szczepanik, Petr and Anděl, Jaroslav (eds) (2008) *Cinema All the Time. An Anthology of Czech Film Theory and Criticism, 1908–1939*, Prague: Národní filmový archiv, pp. 251–61.]

(1)

It is no longer necessary, as it was only a few years ago, to begin a study of the aesthetics of film with the argument that film is an art. Nevertheless, the question of the relation between aesthetics and film has not yet lost its immediacy, for this young art, whose development is still being constantly unsettled by changes in its technological ("mechanical") basis, has a much stronger need than traditional arts for a norm, both in a positive sense (something to observe) and in a negative sense (something to violate). Film artists are at a disadvantage because they face possibilities in their work that are too broad and undiversified. Arts with a long tradition always have at hand a wide range of devices that have gained a definite, stabilized form and conventional meanings through a lengthy development. For example, comparative studies of literary topics show that there are in fact no new themes in literature: the development of almost any theme can be traced back thousands of years. In his *Theory of Prose*, Viktor Shklovsky cites the example of Maupassant's story "The Return" [Le Retour], which is based on an adaptation of the very old theme of "a husband at the wedding of his wife" (Shklovsky 1991: 20), and counts on the reader knowing it from elsewhere. The same holds true for poetry, for example with metrical patterns. Every body of poetry has a certain repertoire of traditional verse patterns that have acquired, through long years of use, a fixed rhythmical (not only metrical) organization and semantic nuances under the influence of the poetic genres in which they have been used. The genres themselves can be characterized as mere canonized sets of particular devices. This does not, however, mean that the artist cannot alter traditional norms and conventions; on the contrary, they are frequently violated (the contemporary theory of genres is based on the knowledge that the development of genres results from the constant violation of generic norms), and this violation is perceived as an intentional artistic method.

What seems to be a limitation is thus, in essence, an enrichment of artistic possibilities – and until recently film had almost no truly distinct norms and conventions; even now there are only a few. Film artists are therefore seeking norms. The word "norm", however, brings to mind aesthetics, which used to be, and sometimes still is, considered a normative discipline. But modern aesthetics, which has given up the metaphysical notion of beauty no matter what form it takes and views artistic structure as a developmental fact, should not be expected to prescribe what should be. A norm can only be the product of the development of art itself, a petrified impression of the developmental process. If aesthetics cannot be the logic of art, judging what is correct and what is not, it can nevertheless be something else: the epistemology of art. Every art has certain basic possibilities provided by the character of its material and the way in which the given art masters it. These possibilities imply a limitation, although not a normative one in the sense promoted by, for example, G. E. Lessing and Gottfried Semper,[1] who presumed that art does not have the right to overstep its boundaries, but a factual limitation, in that a particular art does not cease to be itself even if it extends into the territory of another art. *Si duo faciunt idem, non est idem*; fast motion in film is thus understood as a deformation of temporal duration, whereas the acceleration of an actor's gestures in theatre would be perceived as a deformation of his personality, for dramatic time and film time are epistemologically different.

The transgression of boundaries between the arts is a very frequent phenomenon in the history of art. For example, literary symbolism has often characterized itself as the *music* of the word, while Surrealist painting, which works with poetic tropes (with the "transfer" of meaning), claims for itself the name of *poetry*. After all, this is just a return of the visits poetry made to painting in the period of what is termed *descriptive poetry* (the eighteenth century) and the period of Parnassianism (the nineteenth century). The developmental significance of such transgressions of boundaries lies in the fact that art learns to perceive its formative devices in a new way and to view its material from an unusual perspective. At the same time, the given art remains itself, does not merge with the adjacent art, but attains different effects through the same device or attains the same effect through different devices. If, however, the approximation of another art is to be incorporated into the developmental order of the art that is striving for this approximation, one condition must be fulfilled: the developmental order and tradition

---

1   [Editor's note: Gottfried Semper (1803–1879), German architect and theorist of art.]

must already exist. The basic condition for this is certainty in handling the material (which does not mean a blind subordination to the material).

Film has already been in close contact with several arts: drama, narrative literature, painting, music. However, this was in the days when film had not yet fully mastered its material and it was more a matter of seeking support than a matter of natural development. The effort to master the material is connected with the tendency toward the purely filmic. This is the beginning of natural development. New approximations to other arts will surely come with time, but by then as developmental stages. The striving for pure film is paralleled in film theory by an epistemological inquiry into the conditions provided by the material of film. This is the responsibility of the aesthetics of film: its task is not to set the norm but to reinforce the intentional shaping of its development by revealing its latent preconditions. This study is an outline of a particular chapter in the epistemology of film: the epistemology of film space.

(2)

Film space used to be confused with theatrical space, especially in the beginning. However, this does not correspond with the reality, not even if the camera were simply to photograph the action on a theatre theatrical stage without changing its position, as the nature of theatrical space requires (Zich 1931). Theatrical space is three-dimensional, and three-dimensional people move within it. This does not apply in film, which does allow the possibility of movement, but movement projected onto a two-dimensional plane and into illusory space. The actor's attitude toward space, as has been pointed out many times, is also quite different in film than in theatre. The theatre actor is a living and integral person clearly distinguished from the inanimate surroundings (the stage and its contents), whereas the consecutive images of the actor (sometimes only partial ones) on the screen are mere parts of the overall projected picture, just as, for example, in painting. Hence Russian theorists of film coined the term *naturshchik* ("model") for the film actor, in order to capture the analogy between the position of the actor and that of the model in painting.[2]

What is the relationship now between film space and illusionistic pictorial space? It is clear that this pictorial space does exist in film, and with all the means of painterly illusionism (disregarding more profound basic differences between perspective as a formative device in painting and perspective

---

2   There are, however, nuances in film practice; the actor's individuality can be emphasized in film or, on the other hand, suppressed. Compare the differences between Chaplin's films and Russian films.

in photography). This illusionistic quality can be considerably enhanced by certain means, but these are generally available to painting as well. One of them consists in a reversal of the usual treatment of depth in illusionistic pictorial space: the viewer's attention, which is usually directed toward the background, is instead drawn outward from the picture. This device was often used, for example, in Baroque painting. In film it is found in such things as the direction of a gesture (the person standing in the foreground of the image aims a revolver at the audience) or the direction of movement (a train moves off as though at right angles to the pictorial plane). Another means of intensifying spatial illusion is the high-angle and low-angle shot; for example, looking down from a high floor of a building into a deep courtyard. In such cases, the illusion is strengthened by the change in the position of the axis of the perceiver's eyes. In reality this position is horizontal (for the perceiver viewing the image); however, the position presupposed by the image is almost vertical. Film shares both of these devices with painting.

Another possibility is the following. The camera is mounted on a moving vehicle, with the lens aimed forward. Movement then takes place in a street or an avenue of trees, in other words, along a path lined on both sides by a continuous series of objects. We do not see the vehicle in the image; we see only the street (the path) leading into the background of the image but speeding rapidly in the opposite direction, outward from the image. Because of the motion it might seem that this is a specifically filmic device, but in fact it is only a modification of the aforementioned case (the reversal of the conception of spatial depth), which is wholly amenable, in some of its variants, to painting.

The basis for film space is thus illusionistic pictorial space. In addition, the art of film has at its disposal another form of space that is unavailable to other arts. This is the space determined by the technique of the shot. Whenever a change from one shot to another occurs, whether smoothly or abruptly, the angle of the lens or the placement of the entire camera in space changes as well. This spatial shift is reflected in the spectator's consciousness through a peculiar feeling that has often been described as the illusionistic displacement of the spectator himself. René Clair explains: "Thus the spectator who sees some faraway automobile race on the screen is suddenly thrown under the huge wheels of one of the cars, scans the speedometer, takes the steering wheel in hand. He becomes an actor and sees, in the turns of the road, rushing trees swallowed up before his eyes" (Clair 1993: 369). This presentation of space from "inside" is a specifically filmic device; it was the discovery of the shot that made it possible for the film to cease being an animated picture.

The technique of the shot, moreover, has also had a reverse influence upon the technique of photography itself. It has called attention to the interesting possibilities of the high-angle and low-angle shot obtained by circling the object from all sides; still more importantly, it has created the technique of the close-up. The visual effectiveness of the close-up consists in the unusual way in which an object is brought nearer the viewer (Epstein says: "I tilted my head and to my right I saw only the square root of a gesture, but to the left, this gesture was raised to the eighth power" (Epstein 2012: 291)), while its spatial effectiveness is achieved by our impression of the incompleteness of the image, which we experience as a section of three-dimensional space felt to exist in front of the image and on both its sides. Let us imagine, for example, a hand in a close-up. Where is the person to whom this hand belongs? In the space outside the image. Or let us envisage the image of a revolver lying on a table. This creates the expectation that at any moment a hand will appear and pick up the revolver, and this hand will emerge from a space situated outside the image, where we have only an inkling that something exists. And finally another example. Two people are fighting and rolling on the floor; a knife lies near them. The scene is presented in such a way that we see alternately the pair who are fighting and the knife in close-up. Every time the knife appears, there is suspense. When will the hand that will grab it finally appear? When the hand finally appears in a close-up, there is new suspense. Which one of the pair has taken hold of the knife? Only where we have an intense awareness of the space outside the image may we speak of a dynamic close-up. Otherwise it would be a matter of a static section of a normal visual field. It should be noted, however, that the awareness of its "pictorialness" does not disappear during the close-up; we do not transfer the size of the close-up into off-screen space, and we do not take the magnified hand to be that of a giant.

In shots, film space is presented successively through a series of images; we feel it in passing from one image to another. Sound film has introduced the additional possibility of the simultaneous presence of film space. Let us imagine a situation quite common in film today. We see an image, and at the same time we hear a sound whose source must be placed somewhere outside the image rather than inside it. For example, we see a person's face and hear speech that is not uttered by the person in the image; or we see the legs of people who are dancing and hear them speaking; or on the screen a street rushes by, seen from a moving vehicle that itself remains hidden, while we hear the hoofbeats of horses drawing a carriage; and so on. This produces a consciousness of a space "between" the image and the sound.

Let us now pose the question of the essence of this specifically film space and its relation to pictorial space. I have named three means through which filmic space can be achieved: the shot transition, the close-up and the off-screen localization of sound. I will start from the one that is fundamental, without which film space would not exist at all: the shot. Let us imagine any scene occurring in a particular space (for example a room). This space does not have to be shown in a full shot; it can be presented by means of hints, a sequence of partial shots. Even then we will feel its unity; that is, we will perceive the individual pictorial (illusionistic) spaces shown consecutively on the surface of the screen as images of individual sections of a unified three-dimensional space. How will this total unity of space be presented to us? To answer this question, let us recall the *sentence* as a semantic whole in language. The sentence is composed of words, none of which contains its total meaning. That meaning becomes fully known to us only when we have heard the entire sentence. Nevertheless, as soon as we hear the first word we evaluate it in accordance with the potential meaning of the sentence, of which it will be a component. The sense, the meaning of the whole sentence is thus not contained in any of its words but exists potentially in the speaker's and the listener's consciousness in every word from first to last, and we can observe the successive unfolding of meaning from the beginning of the sentence to its end. All of this can also be said about film space. It is not fully there in any of the images, but each image is accompanied by an awareness of the unity of the total space, and the notion of this space gains definition with the progression of the sequence of images. Thus we may suppose that specifically film space, which is neither a real nor an illusionistic space, is space-as-meaning. Illusionistic spatial segments presented in consecutive images are partial signs of this space-as-meaning, the entirety of which "signifies" the total space.

We can deduce the semantic nature of film space from a concrete example. In a study on the poetics of film, Yury Tynyanov cites this pair of shots: (1) a meadow where a herd of pigs is running around; (2) the same meadow, trampled down, but now without the herd, where a man is walking (Tynyanov 1927:67). Here Tynyanov sees an example of filmic comparison: man – pig. But if we imagine these two scenes in one shot (whereby the intervention of specifically film space would be eliminated), we discover that the awareness of the semantic link between the two phenomena gives place to an awareness of the mere temporal successiveness of the two scenes. Film space thus operates only through a change in shot and does so as a semantic factor. The semantic energy of the close-up, one of the means of creating film space, is also well known. Epstein says: "Another form of the power of the cinematograph is its animism. An inanimate object – for example, a revolver – is merely a prop in the theatre. In film, however, it can be magnified. The Browning that a hand pulls slowly from a half-open drawer... suddenly becomes alive. It becomes a symbol of a thousand possibilities."[3] This polysemic quality of the close-up is facilitated by the very fact that the space into which the revolver will be aimed and into which it will disgorge its bullet is, at the moment of the pro-

---

[3]   [Editorial note (2008): This passage is a very loose quotation from Epstein (2012: 289–90).]

jection of this close-up, a space-meaning of which we have a mere inkling, concealing precisely these "thousand possibilities".

Because of its semantic character, film space is much closer to space in literature than to theatrical space. In literature, too, space is meaning: what else could it be if it is rendered by the word? Many narrative sentences can be transcribed into film space without a change in their structure. Let us take this one as an example: "They embrace slowly, then abruptly break apart, savagely snatch up their knives and throw themselves forward, weapons raised." This sentence, with its present tense, could serve as an expression of a moment of suspense in a novel; in reality it has been excerpted from the screenplay by Louis Delluc for *Spanish Fiesta* (1920) and broken down into shots as follows:

shot 175—It's a deal. They embrace slowly, then abruptly break apart, savagely snatch up
shot 176—their knives
shot 177—and throw themselves forward, weapons raised... (Delluc 1923. 14)

It should also be remembered that narrative has at its disposal, and has had for a long time, a means of presenting space similar to that of film, especially the close-up and panning (a smooth transition between one camera position and another). As proof let me cite a few traditional stylistic clichés: "I lowered my gaze toward...", "his eyes were riveted upon..." – close-ups; "X. looked around the room: On the right side of the door stood an étagère, next to it a closet..." – panning; "here two people were standing in animated conversation, over there a whole group of people who ... elsewhere a small crowd was hurrying somewhere..." – straight cut.

The resemblance between film and book illustration is instructive as an example of the proximity between the filmic and the literary treatments of space. Let me mention only one instance. Certain movements in the art of illustration specializing in marginalia to the text frequently work with the close-up. There is, for example, Svatopluk Čech's illustrator, Viktor Oliva;[4] when Čech's text speaks about Mr. Brouček lighting one match after another, there is a marginal illustration next to the printed text – a half-open box from which a few matches have fallen. This is a close-up; however, it is not quite the same as in film, because the standard frame size is not maintained; that is, the real film close-up fills the same space on the screen as, for example, the

---

4   [Editorial note (2008): The painter Viktor Oliva (1861–1928) illustrated *The True Excursion of Mr. Brouček to the Moon* (1889), a famous satirical novel by Svatopluk Čech (1846–1908) about a petit-bourgeois philistine undertaking an imaginary journey to the moon.
Editor's note: The novel is well-known in the international context as the inspiration for the opera *The Excursions of Mr. Brouček to the Moon and to the 15th Century* (1920), by Leoš Janáček (1854–1928).]

long shot. Therefore we could only speak of the equivalence of illustration and film (with the exception of movement) if all the illustrations in a given work, close-ups as well as long shots, took up whole pages. However, Oliva consistently avoids any spatial scale in his illustrations, letting the images, which are not framed, project irregularly over the surface of the pages. In this his particular technique is a reflection of literary space, which is such pure meaning that it has no dimension; this is because the sign of literary space is the word, whereas the sign of film space is the shot. Film space thus has dimension, at least in its signs (actual filmic space-as-meaning does not, of course, have dimension, as we saw when we dealt with the close-up). So despite their considerable similarities, literary space is distinguished from film space by a higher degree of sheer semantic quality. This is related to the fact that we may abstract from space in literature, whereas space is always inevitably present in film. Moreover, literary space has all the centralizing power of the word. Hence the impossibility of a mechanical transposition of a literary description into film. Gus Bofa has caught this vividly: "The poet wrote that a horse cab trotted by. The director will show it to us; it's an authentic cab, decked out with a coachman in a white hat whose horse trots for a few metres of film. You're not given the option to imagine it – it's a bonus for the spectator's laziness" (Bofa 1925: 53).[5]

So far we have treated the subject as if the overall space that is gradually built up by contextualization were unique and unchanging in every film. However, we must also take into account that space can change in the course of the same film, and can even do so several times. In terms of the semantic character of this space, each time there is such a change it involves a transition from one semantic context to another. A change in *setting* is something quite different from the transition from shot to shot in the same space. Even if there is considerable disparity between shots, this transition is not an interruption of the continuous succession, whereas a change in setting (a change in the overall space) does constitute such an interruption. We must therefore examine changes in setting.

These changes in scene can occur in several ways: by means of a jump, a gradual shift or bridging. In the first case (a jump), the last shot of the preceding setting and the first shot of the following one are simply juxtaposed. This is a considerable interruption of the spatial context, the extreme limit of which is complete disorientation, so it is natural that this kind of transition is charged with meaning (is semanticized); for example, it can mean a condensed summation of the action. In the second case (a shift) a slow fade-out and fade-in are inserted between the two settings, or the last shot of the first

---

5   [Editorial note (2008): Gus Bofa (Gustave Blanchot, 1883–1968), a French caricaturist and book illustrator.]

setting dissolves into the first shot of the second. Each of these devices has its specific meanings. The fade-out can signify, for example, the temporal distancing of consecutive sequences; the dissolve can mean a dream, a vision, a memory; in both cases, of course, many other meanings are possible. In the third case (bridging), the transition is accomplished through a purely semantic process, for example a filmic metaphor (a motion occurring in one scene is repeated with a different meaning in the following one: for instance we see young men tossing their leader, whom they like, into the air —then a change in setting —and a quite analogous motion, which is, however, the tossing of earth that has been dug up) or an anacoluthon ("a dislocation in syntactic construction"; a policeman's gesture meaning "the way is clear"— then a change in setting: we see the metal roller shutter of a shop flying up as if in response to the sign given by the policeman).

We should add that sound film has multiplied the possibilities of film transition. On the one hand, it has made possible new variations in transition by bridging (a sound occurring in one setting is repeated in another with a different meaning); on the other, it has provided the possibility of linking by means of speech (it is mentioned in one scene that the characters will be going to the theatre; in the following sequence, presented without visual transition, we see a theatre auditorium). Each of the methods of transition we have mentioned has a specific character, which is exploited in various ways according to the structure of the given film. In general, we can only say that the more film comprehends its own essence, the more we see the gradual shift and bridging becoming its basic mode of transition. The introduction of sound film in particular has begun a new stage. As long as film worked with intertitles, transition by means of a jump was always possible, so that it was not felt as something exceptional, even in sequences with no intertitles. Since intertitles have disappeared, the feeling of the continuity of space has become increasingly strong. And so even the transition from setting to setting is not exempt from the general character of film space: its sequential unfolding is oriented toward continuity.

Of course the sequential nature of film space, whether this concerns a change in shot or a change in setting, does not automatically entail a smooth flow; on the contrary, the tension arising from these changes creates the dynamics of this unfolding of space. It is precisely at these places in a film that the spectator must make some effort to understand the spatial semantic relation between contiguous shots. The degree of this tension varies from case to case, but it can be stepped up to such an intensity that it alone suffices to carry the dynamics of the whole film, especially if frequent transitions from setting to setting are used, since they are more dynamic and striking than transitions between shots. An example of a film constructed solely upon this specifically filmic tension is Dziga Vertov's *The Man with a Movie Camera*, in which the theme is almost entirely suppressed and could be expressed by a single caption: a day in the city streets.

This case is exceptional. Usually a film has a theme, and one that takes the shape of a story. If we ask about the essence of this theme, we find – just as in the case of film space – that a specific meaning is involved here: despite the fact that the "models" of film are concrete people and objectively real things (the actors and the scenery), the story itself is nevertheless provided by someone (the scriptwriter) and is constructed during the shooting and montage (by the director) so that the audience will understand it in a certain way, will interpret it in a certain way. These circumstances give the story meaning. But the similarity between filmic story and filmic space-as-meaning goes even further. Filmic story, like literary story, is sequentially realized meaning: in other words, the story is provided not only by the quality of the motifs but also by their succession; if the succession of motifs is changed, the story changes, too. As evidence, let me quote from a daily newspaper:

> This happened some time ago in Sweden. The censor did not pass... the Russian movie *The Battleship Potemkin*. As is well known, the film begins with a sequence depicting the maltreatment of sailors, after which the malcontents are to be shot, but a revolt and uprising take place on the ship. There is fighting in the city as well. Odessa in 1905! A fleet of battleships appears, but it lets the mutineers sail away. This plot was too revolutionary for the censor. The distribution company presented the film to the censor once more. There were no changes in the images and intertitles. The film was simply "re-montaged" and the scenes scrambled. The result: the film edited in this way begins with the middle part. With the mutiny (that is, after the scene in which the execution is interrupted) – Odessa 1905! The Russian fleet, with which the original version ends, appears, but the first part of the film follows immediately after this. After the mutiny the sailors are now stand in a row; they are bound and put it front of the muzzles of guns. The film ends![6]

If, however, story is meaning and moreover successively realized meaning, then in a film with a story line there are two sequential semantic series that run simultaneously, but not parallel to one another, through the whole film: space and story. Their interrelation is felt regardless of whether the director takes them into account or not. If this relationship is treated as a positive value, its artistic exploitation is guided in every particular case by the structure of the film in question. In general, one can only say that of these two semantic series the story is felt to be basic, whereas sequentially realized space is a differentiating factor. This is because space is, after all,

---

6   [Editorial note (2008): We were unable to identify this quote. A similar event is described in almost the same way by Balázs (1930: 48–49).]

predetermined by action. But this is not to say that this hierarchy could not be reversed by subordinating story to space, only that such a reversal is felt to be a deliberate deformation. A complete reversal of this kind is quite possible in film because this does not violate its specific character; rather, it enhances it. Proof of this could be the above-mentioned film *The Man with a Movie Camera*. The opposite extreme is the suppression of sequential space in favour of the action; however, to achieve this completely would mean to nullify the specifically filmic space by immobilizing the camera during shooting. What would remain would be only pictorial space as a shadow of the real space in which the action took place during shooting. Hence we could find cases of such a radical "defilmization" of film in the initial stage of development of this art.

Between these two extremes there is a wide range of possibilities. General rules for selection cannot be found theoretically because selection is determined not only by the character of the story chosen but also by the director's intention. Without risk of dogmatism we can only say that the more weakly the plot is connected through motivation (that is, the more it works with mere temporal and causal continuity), the more easily the dynamics of space can be brought to bear in the plot, although this does not mean that it would not be possible to attempt to link strong motivation with strong dynamization of space. After all, the dynamization of space in film is not a simple concept, as has been shown: shots function in the structure of film in one way, changes of setting in another. We can therefore distinguish between story lines that yield easily to considerable disparity between individual shots (those in which motivation is transmitted primarily to the inner selves of the characters, so that unusual transitions between shots can be viewed as shifts in the fields of vision of the characters themselves) and story lines easily reconciled with frequent changes in setting (those based on the external acts of the characters). But here, too, we are not expressing a rule but simply describing the path of least resistance; certainly the path of greatest resistance can also be taken in a specific case.

All that has been said in this article about the epistemological conditions of film space claims only a very limited validity. As early as tomorrow, a revolutionary change in the technology of this art may provide it with new, quite unexpected conditions.

WORKS CITED

Balázs, Béla (1930) *Der Geist des Films* [The Spirit of Film], Halle: Wilhelm Knapp.
Bofa, Gus (1925) "Du dessin animé, et plus généralement du cinéma envisagé comme une mobilisation de l'absurde" [On the Cartoon; and More Generally on Cinema Understood as a Mobilization of the Absurd], *Les Cahiers du mois*, vols 16–17 (special issue "Cinéma").

Clair, René (1993) "Rhythm" in Abel, Richard (ed.) *French Film Theory and Criticism: A History/ Anthology 1907-1939*, vol. 1: 1907-1929, Princeton: Princeton University Press, 368-69.

Delluc, Louis (1923) *Drames de cinéma* [Cinema Dramas], Paris: Éditions du Monde Nouveau.

Epstein, Jean (2012) "The Cinema Seen from Etna", trans. Stuart Liebman in Keller, Sarah and Paul, J. N. (eds) *Critical Essays and New Translations*, Amsterdam: Amsterdam University Press, pp. 287-92.

Shklovsky, Viktor (1991) *Theory of Prose*, trans. Benjamin Sher, Champaign and London: Dalkey Archive Press.

Tynyanov, Yury (1927) "Ob osnovakh kino" [On the Foundations of Cinema], ed. Boris Eikhenbaum, *Poetika kino* [The Poetics of Cinema], Moscow: Kinopechat.

Zich, Otakar (1931) *Estetika dramatického umění: teoretická dramaturgie* [The Aesthetics of Dramatic Art: A Theoretical Dramaturgy], Prague: Melantrich.

THE NEW THEATRE SPACE

E. F. BURIAN

[First published in Czech in 1936 as "O nový divadelní prostor", *Stavba*, vol. 13, pp. 75–77.]
Translated by Eva Daníčková

The role of the contemporary theatre director remains an enigma for many theatre theoreticians and practitioners. Some believe, mistakenly, that to make theatre all that is needed is a playwright and an actor, that the director's role is to arrange the actors on the stage and serve as a kind of dispatcher for the playwright. Others believe that the director is something like a glorified stage manager who makes sure "everything falls into place" and who supervises the technical staff to ensure they make it possible for the actors to perform. And still others view the director as the lord and master holding the power of life and death over the play: they see his main function as casting the roles and seeing to the set and costumes. But few people understand that the longer the period of development the theatre goes through, the more it needs a centralized functional authority. Today this is still represented by the director but in the future, if theatre keeps up with the times and with the discoveries and the progress this will entail, there may have to be a whole board of directors. In the past, when theatre was simply the performance of a play by a famous playwright, it was quite possible to manage without this functional centre embodied in the figure of the director. The main concern was for the various people involved to keep out of each other's way, for the play to be in good taste, and for it to have decent sets and costumes. As we well know, the terminology of theatre reviews even today is limited to an account of the play, how richly it was staged and what the performances were like. "The play is directed by so and so. X and Y appear in the leading roles. The sets and costumes were bad / excellent." Sentences like these are now relics of the past, welcomed by theatre managers for dissemination as blurbs and for inclusion in advertising posters. Meanwhile, theatre has undergone a development diametrically different from all the engrained notions of traditional theatre. Theatre, as a typical social institution, has moved in step with all the various trends in society, experienced its crises, reflected its positive and negative aspects and, by simply existing, has served as a stimulus for endless new innovations. The theatre form has become richer and more complex and has moved into what had previously seemed very distant fields. As a highly sensitive and delicate mechanism, theatre has reacted to every technical innovation, even the slightest.

If this has not been particularly evident in actual theatre productions, that is the fault not so much of the theatre form itself as of the people who possessed it and who were deaf and blind to anything new that made it impossible for them to carry on with their customary simple theatre-making. If technology was not introduced into the theatre, this was not because it was not available but because there were not enough people who understood it, who had mastered it and who were willing to use it to create extraordinary new productions. And then the old-style system of work in the theatre also prevented the old-style theatre boards from being ripped out because then it would become necessary to find new people, creative individuals who would know exactly *what* should replace the old boards and who would be sufficiently familiar with the modern technology given us by science and brought into the world by the whole modern age. Faced by the wasteland created by the shortcomings of new people, the old theatre practitioners think up various phrases for saving the old-style boards. They fight tooth and nail against anything that might threaten reputations based on questionable theatrical genius. They wrap their fear of new prospects in the romantic cloak of "mastery". They seek refuge in cardboard tales that they call life. They pump intense emotion into all manner of trivial stories that are no more than kitschy versions of classical plots. They cover up their artistic shortcomings with cheap effects that have been seen a thousand times. They call upon the playwright to inject poetry and metaphor into long lost values so that theatre can once again be what it was in the good old days, when everything was better, worthier, more honest. In reality, theatre in that golden age was in a wretched state: the stage was lit by oil lamps, cheap comedies rather than great theatrical works were the usual fare, discipline and wit were absent, the audiences were stupid and the actors worked under conditions that were not even admissible for prostitution. Today, when theatre is once again approaching its classical ideal – to be a platform of public opinion – no one gives a thought to that golden age of travelling players and bohemians. It is no exaggeration to say that our theatre began when the oil lamp was replaced by the light bulb and the first spotlights made their appearance in the wooden sheds of our famous past.[1]

Wagner, or still further in the past, Monteverdi, or further still, the ancient Greeks, all dreamed of the kind of theatre that is only today starting to become a reality. They dreamed of creating a form neither music nor speech, neither sculpture nor dance, neither poem nor image, but all of these together. They dreamed of a synthetic form that was only revealed to us when the

---

1   [Editor's note: Burian here alludes to "the Shed" (1786–1789), the first purely Czech theatre and the predecessor of the Czech National Theatre.]

first electric ray of light struck a backdrop and that is presented to us directly by every new technical invention. Today, for the first time, we are able to create theatre that breaks down the barriers of misunderstanding between the different arts. Today, for the first time, we are amazed by a concurrence of elements that people in the past rightly anticipated, but which they lacked the technical capacities to combine. Architecture, which has taken upon itself the task of working with space to achieve a new social, healthier life, finds in the theatre a genial colleague. Painting, which had become fixed in static surfaces, discovers in the theatre its mobility. Sculpture, with its dynamic matter and its flair for filling space with material, comes together with the theatre at the very moment of its most radical experiments with new materials and with the message these materials convey. Music – this art of unknown dimensions, the art that through its rhythm speaks directly to the rhythm of the heart and the muscles – moves from the orchestra pit onto the stage, just as dancers abandon the pointe technique and place their feet firmly on the floor. Poetry ceases to be something merely visual, linked with facial expressions, it takes over space the way music does, just as music "from nowhere" becomes wordless poetry. If we understand the word as a totality of rhythmic signs, then even prose takes on the quality of spatial poetry on stage, and in the colouring of its words and the syntax of its sentences stage speech can be compared to colour and its composition. We can speak of a whole palette of speech, which careful analysis shows to correspond literally to the palette of a painter. And if we understand sound to be a delicate composition of matter, we can find the same laws for sound as for sculpture. And what is a muscle? Matter in rhythmic motion. If a muscle moves in direct response to light, this means that three elements are cooperating rhythmically in space – sculpture, painting and music. But this muscle is alive. It has its centre in the heart and brain of a person. Through the movement of his muscles, this person-actor mimes either the state of his body or the situation in which he came to this state. The totality of states and the totality of situations, if not left to chance, is the best image of theatrical poetry, which is based on the construction created by these elements. All these components move rhythmically in time and space, so their connection to music is incontestable. The components of the classical arts partaking in the construction of the new synthetic theatrical form are being joined by new, contemporary components such as film and slide projection, radio music and sound montage, new devices and new musical instruments (electronic music). However, none of these exist without mutual dependence. Everything is intimately connected, guided by the laws of music regarding rhythm and dynamics, homophony and polyphony, harmony and discord. The space the stage architect has at his disposal is no longer the illusive space of the old stages. It should encompass within itself all the prerequisites necessary for putting into play all the synthetic components of the new theatre. But where is the functional centre that determines the course of the compositional process of this theatre? Is it the actor? No, because he is only one of many components of this spectacular collective theatrical form. Is it the playwright? No, because, like the actor, he only plays his particular part in the creation of the theatre. It is the director, but a director who stands above all these components, who controls them, weaves them together and composes them, or rather arranges the theatre score, giving it an exact rhythm, tempo, colour, tone, harmony and polytonal action.

The correlation of arts that we have discovered in the new theatrical creation presupposes, as we have observed, a new space designed in such a way as to facilitate the development of all the components simultaneously – that is, homophonically and polyphonically. In the old opera or in the *mélodrame*, one component dominates over another in the sense that one always serves as accompaniment to the other, to which everything is sacrificed.

Either the text fell by the wayside (as in the old Italian and old French opera) or the music suffered this fate (as we see in Wagner and his epigones). Either music became literature or literature became music. In the case of ballet, as the saying goes, the ballet danced the music into the orchestra pit. As we see it, the individual components of the theatrical synthesis must either function simultaneously – that is, in such a way that they are not hidden and serve to enhance each other – or, counterbalanced, relate to each other in a marked counterpoint fashion such that, without losing their own character, they nevertheless merge inseparably in a polyphonic form. For this kind of theatre, the old stage and the old auditorium are completely unsuitable. The material of drama, which still continues to suffer from the unsuitable dimensions of stages, will thus reach undreamt-of proportions. Already today, if we rid ourselves of the normally proportioned stage we can reveal the actor to the spectator in full shot and close-up, make sound part of spatial dramatic action; with a little invention we can stroll with the actor from place to place without employing dusty treadmills or revolving stages – but when it comes to bringing the actor closer to today's spectator, all the above devices pale in comparison with an easily transferrable space shared by both actors and audience. Drama must take place all around us as an intense, sensational experience in order for the climax – the climax we need if we are to experience the drama deeply – to build up within us. We cannot simply *observe* the catastrophes[2] from which the drama of human existence is composed. It is essential to integrate the spectator directly into these catastrophes in such

---

2   [Editor's note: Burian here is employing a scheme derived ultimately from Aristotle's *Poetics*, the "climax" being the turning point, the point of highest tension, when the protagonist's fate is sealed, and the "catastrophe" being the dénouement, the final resolution during which the intrigue is unravelled and the piece comes to an end.]

a way that they shake him and draw him out of his overly critical composure. The spectator who is surrounded by noise resonating somewhere in space rather than in the orchestra pit, the spectator who is looking through a film strip at an actor negotiating the obstacles life has put in his path, both explicably and by chance, such that he is unable to overcome them and free himself, the spectator who sees himself in the midst of all these real phenomena – such a spectator cannot remain unshaken.

The principle of mazes, haunted houses, the music hall and market fairs, the principle of sports grounds and meetings – this is the principle of creation in the new theatre. Only the theatre where the stage is the auditorium; only the theatre that is wholly a stage for even the most intimate as well as the most social phenomena; only the theatre that is already *in terms of space* in itself *dramatic,* that is, dynamic – only this theatre has the possibility of becoming a place where people will come together, an artistic and cultural assembly where people will not listen impassively but rather *speak out and take an active part in deciding* on life and death questions of socio-economic, and therefore cultural, import. That is why the abyss between the spectator and the actor must disappear. This does not mean that spectators should become actors, should shout out to the actors or interact with them to produce superficial effects. However, the new disposition of the theatre space will allow the audience to observe the actor's face from close up, and through gestures and words the spectator will be able to glimpse the inner depths of the person-actor, whom he will then interact with as a person-spectator. The play must become truth in the retina of the spectator's perception, and not otherwise. We want to put an end to the falsity that made possible a distance between the stage and the auditorium. There is a great deal of sloppiness and skulduggery hidden behind the curtain of today's theatre. We want to put into effect what is expressed in this quatrain from the opening of our production of *The Beggar's Opera:*[3]

The worst thievery
Goes on behind the scenes;
That's why, 'cause we want this to be clear,
We're throwing out the set.

The new theatre space must be capable of complex projection, of moving spectators and actors rapidly from place to place, of having the space filled with music, of transmitting the sounds of the natural world as well as of games and playgrounds. It must be built in such a way that the action will not

---

3   [Editor's note: Version of *Three-penny Opera,* by Bertolt Brecht, translated and directed by E. F. Burian. The premiere took place at theatre D 35 on 20 November 1934.]

be interrupted by an interval, and by applying the methods of the film studio it should lend theatre the magic of surprise where seemingly minor things become important, where worlds can disappear as if by the stroke of a wizard's wand, where people appear and disappear magically, almost as they do in life or even better. In short, the new theatre space must be variable, like the whole theatrical form.

SPATIAL CONCERNS IN THEATRE

JINDŘICH HONZL

["Prostorové problémy divadla" was first published in Czech (divided into two parts) in *Volné směry*, vol. 30 (1933/34), pp. 59–63 and 84–88.]

Translated by Eva Daníčková

At a time when civilization is advancing so rapidly that we are constantly being surprised by new inventions that expand the artistic possibilities of production and reproduction such that art based on old technologies is flagging and dying – at this point in industrial civilization, which is asserting its mastery over all the matter of the earth and the ether above, it is the task of the director, architect and painter to take stage devices, often decades or centuries old, and use them to create new and surprising combinations of surfaces, colours, spaces and artificial and rhythmically constituted compositions. It would be difficult to enumerate everything that has already been represented or depicted on the stage. However, we are not concerned primarily with what the stage represents but *what it is*. This is not a question of the painterly style of depiction in their stage work for which Léon Bakst, Aleksandr Golovin and Natalia Goncharova were famous, or the Impressionist designs of Max Slevogt, Ernst Stern and César Klein[1] or the Futurism of Enrico Prampolini or the Cubism of Fernand Léger. It concerns the stage as place, as physical substance, as space, and the fundamental laws of these elements. The stage has long been all sorts of things; for a while we should let it be and allow it to remain a stage – *a place of dramatic action given material form in such a way as to be perceptible to the spectator*. But this very simple and basic definition of the stage has become incomprehensible to us because theatre development from the theatre of the ancient world to our types of theatres has so fixed the idea of the stage in Europe that it is almost impossible for us to grasp the rudimentary beginnings of the stage – the dramaticality of place and the dramatic impact of things. But only by looking at these can we determine the fundamental laws of the stage as such. For it is fundamentals and basic premises that concern modern art.

To begin with, I feel I must emphasise this disparity between the premises of the art of the theatre in the past and today. This fundamental difference

---

1   [Editor's note: Stern and Klein are nowadays regarded more as Expressionist stage designers.]

is similar to the difference between modern painting and earlier painting. The painting of El Greco, Velázquez, Rubens and Ingres – in short all painting until Picasso – aims at *depiction* as its primary function. The aesthetic of earlier theatre (like the aesthetic of earlier painting) stems from the task of the stage, and indeed of all dramatic art, to depict [as reflected in these quotes from Zich 1931].

> Dramatic art is the art of depiction. (54)
> A characterizing stage object must *have an appearance* that will evoke in us the desired mental image. (236)
> The stage is a space *representing* the place of the dramatic action. (227)
> Through their interplay the actors depict a certain dramatic action. (57)

These definitions from the aesthetician Otakar Zich accord the stage, stage structures, things (that is, props), painted flats and even light no more than a depictive function. White light must not be used as *white light,* but rather, according to Zich, "White theatrical light *represents* sunlight in the full light of day; nuances of colour *represent* moonlight, fire ... and so on" (1931: 268 – emphasis J. H.). Zich is so rigorous in his definitions that he begins to doubt *whether the stage exists at all at times when it does not represent anything* – that is, when along with the actors and scenery it is not depicting, not representing, a street or a room.

In short, the stage, scenery, surfaces, colours, lights, props – all this only exists for the old theatre as an image, as an instrument for depicting the real world. For the old aesthetic, the stage does not possess its own reality; its technical equipment, physical substance and machinery do not merit attention or use on the part of the artist until they *lose* their *material* essence and authenticity, until they *are deprived of* their direct effects and substitute for them a representation of something they are not and cannot be.

But the modern stage does not explore ways of creating picturesque representations of a street, a forest or a room: it does not explore how the stage should cease to be a stage, but seeks methods of artistic work as well as new technologies that will enable the stage to become a space for the greatest possible dramatic action, to evoke the most intense dramatic emotions. Modern scenography is thus based on the study of material, which for the theatre is the physical substance of the stage and the complex structure of its technology. While for the director the actor is the central object of study, for the stage designer he is the fundamental measure of all the proportions of the stage structures, distances and relationships. All stage forms, lighting and movements are organized round the actor and with him in mind. In film there is no boundary between large and small, between what is enlarged as though seen through a microscope and what is extremely reduced. While film does not respect the usual boundaries of human vision, distorting spatially (zooming in and out) and temporally (slowing down and speeding up the action) at will, the theatre designer must conform everything to a single height, width and depth, which is fixed by the height and bodily proportions of the actor, and enclose the action within the sole viewpoint of the spectator. It is necessary to apply this measure to all the dimensions of the stage and the auditorium. The figure of the actor determines the dimensions of the stage structure, establishes the distance from the spectator, limits the size of the auditorium and becomes the guiding principle in the non-realistic organization of the stage space. The possibilities of movement open to the actor, his rhythm as he walks about and the area he covers, his leap when dancing – that is, the actor's biomechanics, defying gravity in the most astonishing way – are limited by the horizontal and vertical axes of the stage. The possibilities, dimensions and speed of the actor's movements are the prerequisite for the movements of stage machinery, which must conform to the movements of the actor.

But our theatres and stages often lack the human dimension. An age that has become accustomed to evoking astonishment through quantity builds the Grosses Schauspielhaus in Berlin – a theatre that is non-functional acoustically. It is a theatre not for actors but for mass spectacle.

Large opera houses and state theatres prevent the staging of a great many plays that depend for their effect on the visibility of the actor's face and the audibility of subtle nuances in the actor's voice. Or they prevent a large portion of the audience from actually perceiving such a performance.

The extensive dimensions of all these stages and theatres result from architects' solutions to the problem of size that are not based on fundamentals. The need for such size, bulk and height does not derive from the needs of stage and theatre work but is forced on the architect from the outside in the form of a requirement that the theatre be imposing and commercially successful. These theatres could be compared to interiors with chairs so large that it would be impossible to climb up onto them. If we compare these theatres with any primitive theatre or the ancestor of all mass theatres, the Greek amphitheatre, we can discern the intense artistic logic behind those ancient theatre models. The ancient Greek theatre added to its huge structure devices appropriate to mass theatre: exaggerated masks, chanted song in place of speech, an amplifier in the mouth of the mask, enlargement of the proportions of the body through the use of buskins, the chorus. In *commedia dell'arte* the mastery and freedom of improvisation in the actor's humour and its punchlines bring the actors and the audience very close to one another. This form of theatricality suits small theatres performing in marketplaces, town squares and halls, theatres employing rudimentary devices, yet so satisfying and so intensely theatrical that they cannot be matched by our most lavishly decked out stages.

If we wish to find a form of stage so basic that it could serve as a starting point for new discoveries, we cannot look to our theatre and our stages. But the stage is not just the richly-developed form a European has in mind when he speaks of the theatre; rather it is the material of theatricality and dramaticality, which takes on physical form. The function – that is the theatricality, the dramaticality – organizes the matter, and the matter (the instrument) in turn predetermines the form of the theatricality. *The stage is a place of dramatic action given material form in such a way as to be perceptible to the spectator.* Dramaticality and theatricality does not arise from the representation of some story transferred onto the stage. The stage does not become a dramatic agent when actors *begin* to act nor is it a space that is theatrically meaningless and neutral *before* the actors enter. Anyone who knows anything about the relationship of the primitive theatre to its stage knows that the place where the stage is located is in itself a place of theatrical and dramatic power. It is not only the physical substance of the stage and its complex, ordered structure, organized naturally or artificially, that is capable of dramatic impact: the location of the stage – where it is situated, its relationship to the community in which it is found – and its socially real or religiously symbolic significance can also have dramatic impact. It is said that performance and theatre have a religious origin. Every such account points to the fact that the stage itself is a dramatic and dramatizing place: the origin of the ancient Greek theatre lies in Dionysian revels. It can be shown that it was most likely the dramatic emotions associated with place that gave rise to drama.

> The Dionysia took place four times a year before the god's temple. A member of the chorus, which had raised its voice in the dithyramb, stepped forth from the temple, dressed as Dionysus, into the porch and to the chorus gathered around the sacrificial altar, which was surrounded by a crowd of people in a large circle, and with a few words induced the dancers to sing.[2]

And as in the case of ancient Greek theatre, so too in the theatre of primitive peoples, in Japanese and Chinese theatre and in the original medieval mysteries as well, a sacred place – that is, a space characterized by emotion and drama – served as the first stage in the evolution of the theatre and the place (in a certain period of historical development) that made it possible for performance, tragedy, theatre to develop.

European theatre of the modern age has lost this emotional relationship to places of tragedy and performance, despite the many theatre reformers who have striven to bring about its rebirth and renewal. It was Richard Wag-

---

2   [Editor's note: We have not been able to identify this citation.]

ner who attempted to *sacramentalize* the stage with his Bayreuth Festival and *Parsifal*. But the emotional relationship of the spectator to the stage or, as defined above, *a place of dramatic and theatrical action,* was misunderstood by Wagner. People in the nineteenth and twentieth centuries cannot be moulded along the lines of ancient Greeks or the spectators of medieval mystery plays. We have no need of either religious or artistic mysticism in order to be affected by the stage as a place. It is a matter of the stage, through its complex, ordered structure, which is both supranatural and artificial, becoming a place of miracles, capable of bringing the modern spectator to the point of ecstasy. Let the emotional values of the stage be generated by more than the presence of the actors alone. As in the primitive theatre, let the stage exist as a place of emotions, let it be dramatic before seeing to its tasks of depiction and representation – let it be a dramatic agent in its essence and its complex, ordered structure.

The concern of modern theatre is to show that the physical substance and complex, ordered structure of the stage can be used for the direct impact of the drama, relationships, tension and action. The illusionist, depictive stage was not able to become dramatically evocative because, feigning a reality other than its own (for example that of a flat or a military camp), it lost its own reality. The stage did not have its own colours but was painted, did not have its own light but was lit, did not have its own space but was given artificial perspective, did not have its own time but was a storage space for a series of time segments.

Our stage, whose form took shape as a result of the technical requirements and difficulties posed by depictive functions, is an example of a task that has been badly framed and badly executed. If the stage had tackled its problems with a view to the changes in and dynamics of the dramatic theatricality of space, it would have dealt with the task by going back to fundamentals, as is demanded in modern art.

To overcome the technical difficulties that hindered rapid changes of illusionist sets depicting interiors, Karl Lautenschläger invented the revolving stage, which was used for the first time at the Residence Theatre in Munich in 1896 for Mozart's operas.[3] But revolving motion is spatial action – and since the invention of the revolving stage thirty-six years ago, the spatial dynamics and dramaticality it affords has remained virtually unutilized. Perhaps some of Meyerhold's productions (for example Nikolai Erdman's *The Mandate*) formed an exception, in that they based the theatricality (that is, the humour) of several scenes on the movement of the stage turning on its axis.

---

3   Though it should be pointed out that the revolving stage was known in the classical Japanese theatre.

A number of technicians and theatre specialists have been instrumental in making the stage mobile – Fritz Brandt, a theatre technician from Berlin, the architect Max Littman, who designed the Staatstheater in Stuttgart (1912), and the architect Adolf Linnenbach, whose designs put the stage into motion through the use of moveable platforms that could slide sideways and to the rear and be lowered below the floor level. The movement was controlled either by electric power or by hydraulic pressure. Despite all these designs, the problem of how to stage a classic drama – a play by Shakespeare or Goethe's *Faust* – remained. To stage the thirty-three scenes of the first part of *Faust* in such a way as to adequately depict Faust's study, a space outside the town gate, Martha's and Gretchen's rooms, the cathedral, a street, the Walpurgis Night celebration and heaven – that was the task facing the old theatre. The task was badly framed by theatre art but well executed by technology. This was certainly not the first time technology had served a bad master, in this case theatre illusionism. So often it serves empty, wrong or even evil human needs.

The old stage freed itself from illusionism thanks to the stylization of Gordon Craig, Georg Fuchs and Meyerhold; in France by the creations of the Théâtre d'Art, founded by Paul Fort. The anti-realism of the stylized stage was at the same time a denial of the thee-dimensional nature of the stage. The stage had changed into a bas-relief (Munich's Künstlertheater from 1908) or a painting (Meyerhold's production of *Sister Beatrice* at the Komissarzhevskaya Theatre in 1906).

But a conflict with the laws of stylization developed at the very heart of the stylized theatre. An example of this dialectical development is the work of the theatre director Alexander Tairov. In contrast to Meyerhold's immobile stylization from 1906, Tairov's stylization set things into motion; instead of the stylization of the surface of a painting, he introduced a rhythmic element into the stage space. Space was rediscovered on the stage, brought to the spectators' attention through a three-dimensional non-realistic set (which was still non-dynamic and visually static) and the free, unfettered, choreographed movement of the actor. In short, the stage here served as a solid, reliable instrument for the actor's virtuosity of movement.

To give the actor the opportunity to express himself through movement, to organize and divide up the stage space so that the division of the stage floor both horizontally and vertically would dramatize the spatial relationship between actor and actor, between actor and group and between groups – these were the formal tasks facing both Tairov's stage and the Expressionist stage. The spatial premises for stage structures and scenery remained unchanged. With regard to our major stages, even today we cannot talk of any fundamental changes because so far only the terminology of painted stage designs has changed: Expressionism, Cubism (but only in painting), Constructivism,

Neorealism – these are simply various momentarily fashionable labels for these painted stage designs, adding to their interest. The only exception is that our stages are now equipping themselves with an invention that is almost 40 years old – revolving stages.

A turning point vis-à-vis the static nature of decorative structures came with several of Meyerhold's productions (and along with him Tairov, too, started to treat the stage with a view to its spatial dramaticality): moveable, suspended platforms in Ernst Toller's *Masses Man,* sliding stage walls in Ilya Ehrenburg's *D.E.*, a circular mobile floor in Nikolai Erdman's *The Mandate.* At the same time Tairov distanced himself from the decorative spatial stylization that had dominated the stage of his Chamber Theatre from Oscar Wilde's *Salome* in 1917 through Paul Claudel's *The Exchange* and *The Annunciation* to Racine's *Phèdre.* In *Giroflé-Girofla,* the stage lost its decorative nature, its entrances and the painted and architectural intersection of surfaces and spaces. Instead the stage was filled with structures and furniture that had no meaning; their only purpose was to serve as a prop for the movements of the actors. One and the same folding wall was a house gate and the side of a ship, poles could be interior columns or masts, through movement benches were transformed into a canoe. Alexander Vesnin's design proposal for *The Man Who Was Thursday* dealt with the stage in a completely radical way: it envisaged a structure that would have to be made of iron, as bridges, stairs, moving lifts, collapsible planes, and so on were to be suspended from two central towers and massive structures to the sides. Vesnin's design depicted a structure that would rise to a great height: it no longer envisaged the stage as a hollow opening in a theatre auditorium but instead situated the theatre technology in a space that was meant to be surrounded by the spectators. Of course the design never became a reality, since Tairov's Chamber Theatre was a theatre with a stage of the old type.

In 1927, Europe linked up with the Russian stage innovations: Erwin Piscator's theatre in Berlin organized the stage space with no regard whatsoever for stylization or painting styles, in the same way that it had little interest in architecture with aesthetic pretensions. With regard to style, Piscator said:

> Never in any of my productions did I allow myself to be governed by a particular style in the aesthetic sense of the concept. Style was always a secondary consideration for me at any given moment, and I was always concerned to get the most – that is, the optimum objective impact – out of any effect that the subject seemed to offer. (Piscator 1980: 290)

Piscator is not aesthetically selective in his devices and it is thanks to this unbounded theatricality that he has unleashed so many new theatre effects – discovered, admittedly, by the Russian Constructivist stage but introduced successfully by him for the first time in Europe. He employed new materials, using iron in his towering and spherical stage structures (*Hoppla, We're Alive!* and *Rasputin*) and he utilized older inventions such as the sliding platform stage and revolving stage in new ways, giving rise to a new term in the field of directing – the technical style. For the inventions of Littmann and Brandt, when it came to the circular and horizontal movement of the stage floor, were used by the old stage only to facilitate fast scene changes that would otherwise have been impossible for the stage hands to master. Piscator's technology is not concerned with scenery. In his 1928 *Schweik*,[4] it was used to produce horizontal movement of the stage floor: two moving conveyor belts on the right and the left side brought Schweik's adventures before the spectators. The achievements of technology freed from the burden of providing pictorial illustration, technology disrupting the illusionist unity of time, place and space, are astonishing. Kurt Kersten saw in Piscator a director who had "a technical imagination the like of which we have never seen before; he releases all the power of the stage, he wheedles out all its secrets" (Kurt Kersten in Piscator 1980: 257-58). Technology enchants the spectator, affects him emotionally.

It is also important to mention the new communicative and emotive devices Piscator employs in his theatre – film and the projection of images and melodies. All of this was known to Meyerhold, for example in *D.E.* (1924). Piscator added new elements to the projection of film and its inclusion in the stage action. However, film did not replace theatre – Piscator cannot be accused of mixing different types of dramatic art. For him, film is a device for achieving dramaticality, just like music. He did not funnel the stage action into the film but offered an interesting contrast: on the one hand stage action, treating the story of an ordinary man, and on the other film action, showing important events affecting governments, armies and revolutions in the same time period in newsreels and period news reports. The specific story of an individual person was thus integrated socially into the collective course of events in the world. Film of this kind – or news reports – projected simultaneously with the action on stage gave the hero's story genuine meaning: it informed the spectator of the causes and results of the fates of individuals, it educated, advised, guided, took on the role of the ancient chorus. Four film projectors and one projector showing news reports linked the current of stage action to the great stream of history and social upheavals.

Circumstances that prevented Piscator from making ideal use of technology to achieve a dramatic effect made him realize the technical shortcom-

---

4   [Editor's note: Full title *Adventures of the Good Soldier Schweik* [Die Abenteuer des braven Soldaten Schweik], by Piscator with Bertolt Brecht and Leo Lania. An adaptation of the novel of the same title by the Czech writer Jaroslav Hašek published in 1921. Its German translation by Greta Reiner was published in 1926.]

ings of today's stage, even when newly equipped. Next to the Staatstheater, Piscator's Theatre on Nollendorfplatz is the best equipped theatre in Berlin technically. But this well-equipped stage, with the proscenium opening designed so as to allow several sets to be replaced in succession, cannot deal with a structure of any great height, depth or width. The whole stage must be used for the acting in order for the upstage area to contrast with the forestage in its spatial dynamism, for the film screen to be used to highlight contrasts in action and emotion. This is what led Walter Gropius, at Piscator's request, to design a new theatre building that would seek to achieve the maximum freedom possible for the stage and link together three major forms of theatre space: 1) the arena, with a central stage; 2) the amphitheatre, with a semi-circular stage area and a forestage; 3) the classic proscenium theatre. In his design Gropius drew on the experiences and inventions of theatre architects such as Henry Van de Velde and the tripartite stage of his Werkbund Theatre in Cologne (1914), Auguste Perret's three-part theatre from the 1925 Decorative Arts Exhibition in Paris and Hans Poelzig's Grosses Schauspielhaus in Berlin (1919), which boasts a proscenium stage projecting in front with a rear stage behind. Gropius was concerned with embodying in material form Piscator's demand for maximum changeability in the stage space, which would be capable of being rotated, elevated, extended and divided into individual moveable parts so as not to limit the director's imagination but rather stimulate it to attempt new technical marvels. Naturally, film projection would play a major role in this theatre. Gropius's design is most successful when it comes to the shape of the auditorium, whose oval space can be transformed from a circus arena to an amphitheatre auditorium or even an auditorium resembling the best types of old theatres (Bayreuth). Gropius achieves these changes through moveable stalls and a forestage that can be lowered and replaced by a stage surface. In the frontal stage opening, Gropius installed three stages, as Van de Velde and Perret had done. Another stage is created on the encircling passageway behind the uppermost rows of seats. Gropius called this theatre the Total Theatre, because the spectator is surrounded by the action and the stage, especially when the film projection turns even the spaces above the audience into a stage.

Owing to Piscator's going bankrupt, Gropius's theatre was never built.

It was left to a man named Rothschild, hiding his love for theatre behind the name André Pascal, to build a modern stage in Paris, the same Paris known for its antiquity and the simplicity of the theatre machinery in all its theatres. Rothschild's theatre, Théâtre Pigalle, was opened on 18 June 1929; especially where its stage machinery is concerned it is truly the last word in what stage engineers can achieve in the area of technology. The stage consists of the moveable iron structures of the front and the rear stage, with the construction at the front in fact being three stages, one on top of another. When the middle stage is in operation, the upper and lower stages are hidden in the fly and underneath the stage. The rear stage can be moved in such a way that its two stages can join up with the front stages, and in addition this rear stage can be moved to the front so that it replaces the front construction, which can be lowered into the trap room space. The ease with which the stages can be moved is unique: they are operated by technicians, and mechanical relays block any mistaken command that might lead to a collision of moving parts; these relays also correct any oversight on the part of the technician in control such as forgetting to stop them at the edges of the stage areas or in places where the constructions meet. Another speciality of the Pigalle is the mechanically controlled cables with their unusual weight-bearing capacity, making it possible to support suspended stages, sets and risers. Admittedly, this machinery is missing something – the creative imagination of a director and an author who could develop its technical beauty. And for the moment, among its authors and directors, France lacks individuals with *an artistic technical mind,* like Piscator in Germany. In spite of its worldwide appeal, ordinary French theatre has a provincial character, either not understanding technology or avoiding it altogether. So today the most modern French theatre is closed, its beautiful and wonderfully functional stage structures lying idle, while before this superbly equipped stage a screen has been erected. On it are projected films, those successors to and highest embodiments of a technology that has learned to serve theatricality and dramaticality.

Piscator's example well illustrates the way stage space regained its miraculous quality and theatricality through the exposure of the technical innovations that the illusionist stage had carefully hidden behind its stage scenery. The functioning machinery itself, the complex movement of the stage and its parts, possess theatricality and dramaticality. Littman's stage with its moveable platforms hid movement in darkness and behind the curtain; Piscator uses movement to make the spatial action more theatrical. Before the eyes of theatre directors who have been denied access to sophisticated stage machinery owing to chance or the poverty of their theatres, Piscator paints visions of the dramatic performance that only require material means in order to be made a reality. For these visions have already been dreamt of, formulated and longed for on many occasions, in the form of ideas and designs. In his *Notes of a Director*, Alexander Tairov, left unsatisfied by the many resounding triumphs of his static stage, dreams of a dynamic and dramatic stage:

> If you have ever been in a theatre during the so-called mounting rehearsals, or after the performance when in the weak illumination of the work lights the stage hands are dismantling the set, then you have no doubt experienced that somewhat strange,

peculiar feeling which unconsciously and imperceptibly comes over us in those moments. You sit in the dark and empty auditorium and look at the stage. Suddenly the
backdrop which is hanging in front of you drops swiftly to the floor, and the undulating rays of ropes hang poised in mid-air. They interlace with other rays, trailing after
the fallen backdrop. On the ghostly skeletons of the frames and on the toppled, now
useless forms fantastic ships and masts rise up. Virgin, impenetrable forests fall to
the ground, and secret, undulating corridors extend in endless windings and beckon
to you.

The work continues.

In various places canvases and cloths float, now quietly, now soaring up with
a rush, and in their capricious movement ever newer mirages loom up, powerfully
drawing you into their orgiastic phantasmagoria.

O! This is theatre! you exclaim, joyfully excited by the unexpected explosion of the
usually quiet and static scenic atmosphere. (Tairov 1969: 118–19)

So everything that has been done so far with the help of stage technology
to enhance the theatricality of stage space is nothing in comparison with
what *could* be accomplished by directors and playwrights familiar with stage
technology. So far only small experimental theatres, for example at the Bauhaus (the efforts of Oskar Schlemmer and his *Triadic Ballet* and Kurt Schmidt
with his *Mechanical Ballet*), have filled the stage with moveable machinery,
though in this case it would be more accurate to speak of puppets or only
of puppet costumes, worn by performers whose movements were limited
by their stiff, mechanical construction. The idea and its implementation
were anticipated in the mechanical figures of Picasso and Mikhail Larionov
and in Léger's costumes for the ballet *The Creation of the World* (1923). Stage
machinery in the true sense of the word was not present. The logic of en-
hancing the theatricality and dramaticality of the stage space was carried
further by El Lissitzky in his unrealized design for the *theatre machine*, that
is a stage entirely liberated from the fixed form of our theatres, creating its
spatial, acrobatic structures freely in three dimensions, without regard for
any auditorium structure. Inspired by the Bauhaus and Lissitzky, Friedrich
Kiesler implemented his idea of spatial theatre in Berlin in 1923; its visual
action consisted in the movement of stage surfaces, in the midst of which
there struggled the lone hero, a human being. These designs and the projects that were carried out served to create a sort of alphabet or grammar
of spatial action. Like all grammars, this stage grammar too was grounded
in the elements of space and dealt with its role in the abstract. This was not
a weakness, for it is through these examples dealing with fundamentals that
the modern theatre learns to think and to imagine forms in new ways. As
László Moholy-Nagy says: "Abstract objects are not here because they are
particularly liked – there is nothing likeable about them – abstract objects

are here like test tubes and flasks, which are transparent so we can observe the chemical changes occurring inside."[5]

So we conclude our discussion and thoughts on the theatricality of space by rejecting the idea of the fixed stage to the extent that no existing theatre stage is a necessary precondition for theatrical space. Axioms and unchanging principles are not to be found in richly-developed forms. Only man and his needs persist. The need for theatricality. Ours is a classic example of the non-dramatic stage, because its emotional impact lasts for a few seconds at most after the curtain goes up – until the stage image takes effect.

So let us reject the idea of the stage as something fixed and given: simply put, the problem of the stage is that it must be the embodiment of some dramatic theme or another in physical material and in space. Let the stage – like all primitive stages, whether of medieval mystery plays or the ancient Japanese theatre – be built for performance and drama, for a special theatricality, or, as in the early ancient Greek theatre, determined by the dramaticality of the place where the theatre originates.

The stage is not an image. Let the stage depict or represent, perhaps, nothing before the start of the performance. Let it be perhaps a neutral place. For theatricality lies in action, in becoming.

Let the stage be a place of dramatic and poetic thinking. Poetic thinking is thinking in metaphors. Let the technical engineers create poems in space and transform the stage through metaphors.

The theatrical emotional quality of the stage and its dramaticality are similar to the fear and joy children experience when faced with unfamiliar things or places.

It is also the anxiety and inquisitiveness of primitive man, for whom physical matter and distances are not abstractions but beings that act, change and are in the process of becoming. A miracle is the ever-unattainable measure of all stage magicians.

Light, which is the fourth dimension of stage poetry in space, is the most mobile and therefore the most theatrical of all material elements. Observe throngs gathered to watch fireworks. Recall how signal fires have galvanized armies and crowds. The invasive force of neon signs, affecting even the most apathetic passer-by in the city streets. The invasion of light, reflections, refractions. Mirroring. And, finally, film.

And let all these dimensions be dramatized and theatricalized by constant movement, by the succession of changes that is the performance, the drama, the poem.

---

5 [Editor's note: We were not able to identify this quotation.]

WORKS CITED

Piscator, Erwin (1980) *The Political Theatre*, trans. Hugh Rorrison, London: Methuen.

Tairov, Alexander (1969) *Notes of a Director*, trans. and introd. by William Kuhlke, Coral Gables, Florida: University of Miami Press.

Zich, Otakar (1931) *Estetika dramatického umění: teoretická dramaturgie* [The Aesthetics of Dramatic Art: A Theoretical Dramaturgy], Prague: Melantrich.

IMAGINARY ACTION SPACE IN DRAMA

KAREL BRUŠÁK

[First published in Schmid, Herta and Král, Hedwig (eds) (1991) *Drama und Theater: Theorie – Methode – Geschichte* [Drama and Theatre: Theory – Method – History], München: Otto Sagner, pp. 144–62.]

Editor's note: Although the above publication dates this article to 1991, research in the literary remains of both Karel Brušák and his close friend Jiří Veltruský, including correspondence between the two, indicates a different date for its origin. From the 1970s on, Brušák had clearly worked on various versions of this paper (he often discussed his drafts with Jiří Veltruský). Originally, his article was to be included in the 1976 volume edited by Ladislav Matejka and Irwin R. Titunik, *Semiotics of Art: Prague School Contributions*. Unfortunately, however, Brušák was not able to meet the deadline so it was omitted. Only in the late 1980s did he present it at a conference; eventually Herta Schmid succeeded in obtaining the final version for publication. But the testimony of Jiří Veltruský (see his comment on "Theatre in the Corridor", this volume, pp. 499–500) suggests that the first draft of Brušák's concept emerged during the author's seminars with Jan Mukařovský before 1939. Veltruský even states that the first version was published in the monthly journal of Theatre D (where an early version of Brušák's study "Signs in the Chinese Theatre" appeared in 1939 as "The Chinese Theatre"), but this was probably no more than Brušák's intention. Yet it is reasonable to suggest that when Brušák was working on the piece in the 1970s he might have been drawing on a draft version from the 1930s (a supposition strengthened by references included in the article and several examples of theatre productions).

Although Brušák wrote the initial version (or versions) in Czech in the 1930s, he then moved to Great Britain, where he started translating his older works and writing new ones in English. The present article is thus not a translation but rather an original contribution of Brušák's. In it, he employs his own idiosyncratic terminology, which partly departs from standard usage, as well as specialized structuralist vocabulary. However, he is absolutely consistent in using his own terminology in both his essays (see his "Signs in Chinese Theatre", this anthology, pp. 115–28), so we have retained his terminology and vocabulary. Brušák employs the following three terms: stage – scene – imaginary action space. He understands as "stage" only the static, physical architecture of a performance space. "Scene" is a variable space, formed by the actual scenery, stage equipment, and so on. Brušák defines "imaginary action space" as "a space where action indispensable for the development of drama takes place", which lies beyond the physical limitations of the stage and is only fully formed in the mind's eye of the spectator.

Drama, a complex art form composed of elements from many other arts – literature, oratory, mimicry, choreography, music, architecture, sculpture, painting, and so on – draws on other semantic systems but constitutes a distinctive structure with its own semiotics. Within this structure, however, each element appropriated from other systems retains its own way of relating the signifier to the signified. As a result, each type of sign is, to some extent, in conflict with all the others, yet, combined in a syntagma, they acquire potentialities that they do not have outside drama (see Veltruský 2016 [1976]). In order to arrive at the structural theory of drama, the system has to be examined in the light of every component so as to establish its relations with the other components. I propose to deal with one component of this complex and specialized semiotic system, to which little attention has been paid by theoreticians so far (see Pražáková 1921 and Stiebitz 1937).

As an introduction I shall quote a scene from a farce performed in the thirties. At that time there was intensive campaigning for the abolition of so-called theatrical illusion, and for so-called alienation and suppression of the barrier between the stage and the auditorium. There are two characters on the stage, representing – or rather deputizing for – two soldiers, waiting for a messenger from their army. Soldier One is lying on the floor, Soldier Two is looking into the wings or, more correctly, into a gloomy corridor, as there is no décor.

Soldier One. Is he coming?
Soldier Two. I don't know.
Soldier One. What do you mean? Do you see him or not?
Soldier Two. I don't know.
Soldier One. Well, what do you see there?
Soldier Two. Well, there are some stage hands playing cards and the stage manageress is necking with the fireman.
Messenger (*rushing in*). Sorry, mate, that bitch of a stage manageress didn't call me.

Now the dramatist, the producer and the actors were fooling themselves if they believed that they had destroyed what they considered theatrical illusion. The notion in the minds of the spectators that somewhere beyond the visible stage there was an imaginary army was certainly not destroyed, but what is more, another notion, that somewhere beyond the visible stage some sort of imaginary hanky-panky was going on, was superimposed on it.

According to a theory proposed first by Hippolyte Taine and later elaborated by others, from Tairov to Bogatyrev, the basic condition for the perception of a theatrical performance as art, that is aesthetically, is the varying apprehension on the part of both the actor and the spectator. At a certain moment the spectator is able to perceive the performance not as a simulation but as a unique and unrepeatable reality and, similarly, the actor can have the feeling of complete metamorphosis into a real individual in a specific situation. These, as Diderot observed long ago, do not need to coincide.

But the view that the spectator alternates between feeling that he is perceiving reality and cognizance that he is in a theatre completely disregards the semiological character of drama. The spectator never imagines that he is perceiving a reality and consequently it never occurs to him that what he perceives is not reality. He is aware that he perceives a reality different from his own reality, but he is also aware that he gradually construes this reality for himself. The reality of the drama, or the dramatic world (W_d), to use the term of Keir Elam, is alien to the reality of the spectator, or the spectator's world (W_s), by the very fact that it unfolds in time and space that are not those of the spectator's reality (Elam 1980). He is, however, able to construe it to a certain degree through the elements recognizable to him and contained in the signs perceived, from the spoken word to the facial expression of the actors, the sum of which constitutes the structure. Thus an observer unacquainted with Chinese theatre would not be able to decode its semiotic system, because for him the signs would be devoid of their referential function. They might, however, appeal to him through their aesthetic function, which a spectator acquainted with the code would consider subdominant. Drama, as an autonomous semiotic system, is very resilient and it can withstand an astonishing amount of deformation before it is nullified. Thus, when speaking of the theatre of the absurd one has to realize that this term is something of a misnomer. All drama is absurd vis-à-vis the spectator's reality and it would be a mistake to call a certain type of drama absurd because it seems to deviate from what is wrongly considered to be a norm.

Drama is brought into existence by being realized into a complex structure that, for the sake of brevity, we may call the dramatic space. It is built up of three basic constituents: the stage, the scene and the action space. The action space consists almost entirely of signs originated by the actors, emphasized or complemented by signs supplied by sounds and lighting. It is the kinetic quality of the action space that gives drama its specific character; yet it does not depend only on its inner tension but also on its confrontation with the spectator.

The correlation between the spectator and the action space is a very special one. The action space and the audience are parts of one totality in which the former is a dynamic, developing component, which is actualized from a latent state and expends itself through its actualization, while the latter is assembled on an *ad hoc* basis and remains static. This does not mean that the audience remains psychologically inert; a funny episode would lose its meaning if it was not accepted with laughter and a tragic one if it was not accepted with silence. But the involvement of the spectator must not overstep the psychological area; involving the spectator in direct action would destroy the whole structure. The action space and the audience have, at the same time, a common and autonomous existence, influencing each other within the structure, yet remaining separated in whatever type of arrangement they are placed.

Basically, there are only two types of arrangement on which the action space can evolve: first, the full or central stage, with the audience all around it, and secondly, the partial stage, with the audience either in front of it or also along its sides. There may be different combinations in various theatrical systems, but in all cases the audience must remain separated from the action space by an imaginary line. In some systems this separation may be stressed by placing a physical barrier between the action space and the spectator. What is not realized by the advocates of the so-called involvement of the spectator is that the abolition of this physical barrier does not annul the imaginary line that separates the action space from the spectator. The very existence of action space is based on this special correlation, on this dialectical contradiction between itself and the audience.

As we have noticed, dramatic space constitutes a kind of field of forces with a considerable kinetic energy. The interplay of these forces results in what is commonly understood as dramatic tension. Yet the energy thus created is severely restricted within a circumscribed space-time continuum. Limitation both to the spread and the duration is a general feature of dramatic space. This has been expressed by one of the greatest of dramatic practitioners and theoreticians:

> ... But pardon, gentles all,
> The flat unraised spirits that hath dared
> On this unworthy scaffold to bring forth
> So great an object. Can this cockpit hold
> The vasty fields of France? Or may we cram
> Within this wooden O the very casques
> That did affright the air at Agincourt? (Shakespeare, *Henry V*, Prologue)

The passage also indicates what seems to be a spontaneous tendency on the part of the structure to break out of its boundaries. It appears to expand outwards and form a kind of twin to the dramatic space. This twin is, however, not identical. It only exists in the imagination of the spectator, and it does not possess all the elements of the dramatic space. But it is a space where action indispensable for the development of drama takes place. In relation to the dramatic space it can be called secondary, indirect, outer, remote or

IMAGINARY ACTION SPACE IN DRAMA **307**

oblique; but since its main function is to carry action, it may be called imaginary action space.

In examining the use of the imaginary action space throughout the history of theatre, one might be led to suppose that it is no more than a spatial extension of the stage. Indeed, it is argued that it is entirely dependent on the type of stage. Stiebitz[1] sees its origin in the Greek theatre, which introduced a permanent architectural stage; Bogatyrev denies its existence in the folk theatre, which has no conventional stage (Bogatyrev 1940: 95). Arnuf Perger, who divides dramas into "*Einortsdramen*", that is, those that take place in one locality, either throughout the whole play or throughout the individual acts, and "*Bewegungsdramen*", those that move from one locality to another within sight of the spectator, such as the medieval mysteries, attributes imaginary action space, or what he calls "*idealische Bühne*", to the "*Einortsdrama*" alone (Perger 1929).

It is argued that the strict delineation of the stage has preconditioned the spectator to presume its continuation beyond its limits. If a scene represents a forest, the spectator automatically imagines the forest continuing at the sides of the stage or behind; if a room, he imagines further rooms, and so on. The relationship of the outer to the dramatic space proper can remain dormant but they can enter into active relationship when the action from the imaginary space invades the stage, when it overflows from the latter to the former or when it is completely relegated to beyond the boundaries of the stage. In these cases the imaginary action space has to be actualized for the spectator by signs. The first requirement is its localization, not only in space but also in time.

As far as place is concerned, there are two types of localization. In the first case the imaginary action space may be situated at the side or at the back of the stage – behind a window as in Hebbel's *Maria Magdalena* or behind a closed door as in de Vigny's *Chatterton*, Gogol's *The Government Inspector*, Ibsen's *The Wild Duck*, Chekhov's *The Seagull* and Buero Vallejo's *Story of a Stairway* – or it may be freely accessible as in the Chinese theatre. It may be under the stage as in Schiller's *Mary Stuart* or above as in Shaw's *Misalliance*. It may flank part of the stage as in Ibsen's *The Master Builder*, Chekhov's *Three Sisters* and Synge's *Riders to the Sea*, or it may envelop the whole stage as in Sheriff's *Journey's End* and Langer's *The Mounted Patrol*.[2] In

---

1   [Editor's note: Ferdinand Stiebitz (1894–1961), Czech Classical philologist, historian of ancient Greek and Roman literatures and translator from these languages. His comprehensive textbook for secondary schools was a standard reference source for Classical literature (including drama and theatre).]

2   [Editorial note (1991): František Langer (1888–1965), Czech dramatist. In his *The Mounted Patrol* [Jízdní hlídka] (1935) the action takes place in a hut where a patrol is beleaguered by partisans and in the surrounding countryside.]

the second case the imaginary action space may be located far away from the stage as in Greek tragedies, Chinese operas, Japanese Noh plays, French classical drama, several of Shakespeare's plays, Pirandello's *Right You Are (If You Think So)*, Cocteau's *The Human Voice*, Sartre's *No Exit*, and so on. When the imaginary action space is in the close vicinity of the stage it is actualized either directly by auditory or visual signs coming from the outside or by signs originated by the actors. Auditory signs can be provided by music, such as the sounds of a lyre from Hermes' underground cave in Sophocles' *Ichneutae*, dance music from the adjoining room in Strindberg's *The Father*, drums from the jungle in O'Neill's *The Emperor Jones*, ships' sirens in his *Long Day's Journey into Night*, the sound of axes in Chekhov's [*The Cherry Orchard*], the flushing of a lavatory in Graham Greene's *The Living Room*, incomprehensible speech and shouting in Ibsen's *The Wild Duck*, and so on. Optical means are semiotically less productive; they are restricted to changes in the intensity and colour of lighting or to intermittent flashes of light such as in Shaw's *The Doctor's Dilemma* and Claudel's *The Break of Noon*. Indirect actualization of the imaginary action space close to the stage depends on the speech or extra-linguistic sounds of the actors and on their physical reactions. In Gogol's *The Government Inspector* the mayor with his "psst, psst!" accompanied by anxious gestures evokes the illusion that the drunken Khlestakov is asleep in the next room.

When the imaginary action space is distant from the stage, the onus of its actualization falls entirely on the actor. The Greek and French classical drama used the figure of the messenger. Some modern dramatists and producers have introduced technical aids. But these prove successful only if the rule is observed that the imaginary action space must be actualized by signs. Such is the case in Cocteau's *The Human Voice* and in Genet's *The Maids*, where the imaginary action space on the other end of the telephone line is actualized by the signs provided by the actresses making or answering the call, or in Čapek's *R.U.R.*, where the sudden failure of the electric light suggests that the robots have taken over the power station. On the other hand, Piscator's use of film projections and Shaw's introduction of the video-telephone in his *Back to Methuselah* are failures, because their authors did not understand the semiotics of the imaginary action space. The disadvantage of film projection – now so fashionable as a means of shortcutting dramatic action – lies in the fact that in practice it cancels the action by transference into another medium, that is, film, which is governed by entirely different structural rules.[3]

---

3   In this short survey it was not possible to deal with systems allied to some extent to the theatre, that is film, television and radio drama. Of these, paradoxically yet understandably, radio drama, relying as it does exclusively on the imaginary dramatic space, remains closest to theatre.

But paradoxically, the imaginary action space may also be placed on the stage, in which case it will cause a partial or complete suppression of some or all of the other constituents of the dramatic space. The partial suppression of action space and its replacement by imaginary action space occurs for instance in Marlowe's tragedy *Edward II*, if the scene in which Edward is murdered by stamping on his chest and belly is played out of sight of the spectators. An example of the complete suppression of action space by darkening the stage is provided in the hospital scene of the mass administration of enemas in E. F. Burian's version of *The Good Soldier Švejk*.[4] An opposite treatment is prescribed by Maeterlinck in his play *Ariadne and Bluebeard*. Immediately after the scene showing the attempt of Ariadne and the other girls to escape from the castle, the author actualizes the imaginary action space on the stage, which is sunk in darkness, by introducing what he calls a flood of intolerable light. This effect, technically impossible in his time, could easily be achieved today by dazzling the spectators with psychedelic effects. An example of two imaginary action spaces, one on the stage and one very distant, is found in Maeterlinck's *Interior*. The scene represents a garden with a house in the background. Its three windows are lit and through them both the actors in the garden and the spectators see a family. Maeterlinck writes in his stage directions: "When one of them rises, walks or makes a gesture, the movements appear grave, slow, apart, and as though spiritualized by the distance, the light and the transparent film of the window-panes" (Maeterlinck 1915: 65).

At the same time, both the actors in the garden and the spectators are aware of a no less important imaginary action space in the form of a distant river, in which one of the girls from the house had been found drowned. The whole drama is based on the conflict between these three constituents – the imaginary space where the tragedy occurred, the dramatic space from which it will be announced, and the imaginary space it will shatter at the end of the play. An interesting and novel attempt at the introduction of imaginary action space onto the stage occurs in a comedy called *The Complete Guide to Sex*.[5] It has only two actors who, supported by a pianist and a dancer, perform a series of sketches satirizing bedroom manners in history and fairy tale. In one of these sketches the stage is left empty and the imaginary action, although invisible and inaudible, is so effective that it causes the audience to laugh and applaud.

There is one area, however, where the imaginary action space cannot arise and that is in the auditorium. The reason is simple: it is filled with spectators,

---

4   [Editorial note (1991): E. F. Burian (1904–1959), Czech producer, founder of the Prague D 34–41 theatre. His dramatization of *The Good Soldier* Švejk was performed there in May 1935.]

5   [Editorial note (1991): By Patrick Barlow and Jim Broadbent; produced at the National Theatre of Brent and put on at the Lyric Hammersmith (London) in April 1984.]

who must remain the addressees and not the originators of the signs within the structure. When the spectators are envisaged as representing something other than themselves, as in Jerzy Grotowski's productions, for example the descendants of Cain in Byron's *Cain*, the inmates of a lunatic asylum in Słowacki's *Kordian* or Indian monks and courtesans in Kalidasa's *Shakuntala*, the device succeeds only in the mind of the producer (Roose-Evans 1973: 131). From the spectators' point of view they remain what they are – Mr White, Mrs Green and Miss Blue, sitting in the theatre and watching a play.

As far as its localization in time is concerned, imaginary action space usually progresses in the present or in the past. But there are also instances in which it is envisaged in the future. Such is the case in the witches' scene in *Macbeth*, but an even more striking example occurs in Pirandello's *Six Characters in Search of an Author*, where the action, which allegedly took place in the past, is supposed to materialize in the future. Nevertheless, it remains imaginary. As the Stepdaughter says in the second act:

> Oh, darling, darling, what a horrid comedy you've got to play! What a wretched part they've found for you! A garden... a fountain... look... just suppose, kiddie, it's here. Where, you say? Why, right here in the middle. It's all presence, you know. That's the trouble, my pet: it's all make-believe here. It's better to imagine it, though, because if they fix it up for you, it'll only be painted cardboard, painted cardboard for the rockery, the water, the plants... (Pirandello 1998: 21)

As has already been said, the imaginary action space is actualized by various devices that are derived from the action space proper and that are usually combined. This process of the sign being followed by its explanation by another sign, which combines with it to form a new sign, requiring an additional explanation in the form of a further sign, which Peirce calls "development", is more important in drama than in other semiotic systems. It makes it different from others, in particular from language, as it places the stress not on the result, that is the final *signatum*, but on the process of interpretation. This is important both for the action space proper and for the imaginary action space, actualized through signs originated in the former. These signs do not appear one by one but in clusters: speech plus facial movement plus gesture; a change of lighting plus a gesture; an off-stage sound plus a change of bodily position plus an extra-linguistic sound and so on. Jakobson's principle that combination works not only in sequence but also in concurrence is evident both in the action space and in the imaginary action space. Yet it has to be emphasized that we do not necessarily arrive at a *signatum*, as is proved by several plays by Pirandello, Beckett, Genet and others.

Although many signs actualizing the imaginary action space are produced through mechanical means, their main source is the actor. In some dramatic systems he conveys them by mime, without speech. Thus in the Noh play *Sanemori* a single actor, representing the ghost of the knight Sanemori, conveys the progression of the imaginary action space as it were backwards. He conveys the actions of another knight picking up Sanemori's severed head and washing it, the emotions of their knights on recognizing the head, and then the preceding event, the battle in which Sanemori was decapitated. Western drama relies much more on verbal actualization. In Greek tragedy, where the imaginary action space is usually revealed after a lapse of time, the induction itself is impressive but far from concise. In Sophocles' *Oedipus Rex* the messenger depicts the suicide of Jocasta and the blinding of Oedipus in seventy-eight lines of the most gruesome detail, which are only interrupted twice by irrelevant questions from the Chorus. On the other hand, one could hardly find a more concise yet no less expressive verbal actualization of the imaginary action space than in the Czech fourteenth-century comedy *The Ointment Seller*.[6] It consists of a short sentence. In this case the sudden emergence of the imaginary action space is more or less accidental but dramatically important. At one point the Quack's assistant, Pustrpalk, disappears, probably behind the backcloth. His master calls him, using debased German, obviously for comic effect. Here is a polite translation without any attempt at the obscene rhyme of the original:

The Quack. Pustrpalk, wo bistu?
Pustrpalk. Here I am, Master, squeezing a nice furry pussy.

The imaginary action space springs into existence in all its complexity as if revealed by lightning.

Shakespeare is a master of verbal actualization, combining signs with referential, expressive, conative and aesthetic functions, and his various techniques provide masses of material for the theses industry. Some of them rely on *topoi* but many are very original:

Full fathom five thy father lies;
Of his bones are coral made;
These are pearls that were his eyes;
Nothing of him that doth fade,
But doth suffer a sea-change
Into something rich and strange.
Sea-nymphs hourly ring his knell:
Hark! now I hear them – ding-dong bell. (*The Tempest*, 1.2)

---

6   [Editor's note: This play (the Czech title: *Mastičkář*) is also known as *The Apothecary*. For a Czech-English bilingual edition by Jarmila Veltrusky, see Veltrusky 1985.]

The authors of the French classical tragedies, on the other hand, are rather heavy-handed in this respect and Molière is only slightly better. English Restoration comedy and the Romantic drama use more direct methods, but it is only in modern drama that the potentialities of the verbal actualization of the imaginary action space are pitifully underutilized, by authors such as Ibsen, Strindberg, Chekhov and Maeterlinck. Of the twentieth-century dramatists, Shaw was among the most lacking in this skill. In the contemporary theatre Ionesco is among the authors who best understand the rule about the concurrent working of signs from different categories. In one of his plays there is a scene during which we hear the noise of a beast panting in headlong course and a prolonged trumpeting. The characters on the stage continue their conversation, paying no attention. Then the noise is heard again very close.

Jean. Whatever is it?
Waitress. Whatever is it?

Another man continues speaking as before but Jean bounds to his feet, knocking his chair over, and looks off left pointing.

Jean. Oh, a rhinoceros!
Waitress. Oh, a rhinoceros!

Ionesco adds in his stage directions:

The noise made by the animal dies away swiftly and one can already hear the following words. The whole of this scene must be played very fast, each repeating in swift succession: 'Oh, a rhinoceros!' (Ionesco 1960: 8)

Perhaps the most striking verbal actualization of the imaginary action space in contemporary drama is achieved by Sartre in *No Exit*. The semantic situation in Sartre's play is very complex, because the constituents of the dramatic space, that is the scene and the action space proper, as well as several imaginary action spaces exist independently both in place and time, yet merge intermittently and cannot be distinguished from each other. First, there is an imaginary action space closely associated with the stage. One of the three main characters is taken to a room by a valet.

Garcin. ... Is it daytime now?
Valet. Can't you see? The lights are on.
Garcin. Ah yes, I've got it. It's *your* daytime. And outside?
Valet. Outside?
Garcin. Damn it, you know what I mean. Beyond that wall.

Valet. There's a passage.
Garcin. And the end of the passage?
Valet. More rooms, more passages and stairs.
Garcin. And beyond them?
Valet. That's all. (Sartre 1989: 6)

This verbal actualization of imaginary space, situated outside our experience, that is in a static, eternal and infinite continuum, works perfectly, because Sartre chooses signs that refer to our conception of such a continuum. A claustrophobic room, the scenic constituent of the dramatic space of *No Exit*, is itself a polysemic sign, open to various interpretations, but gradually we arrive at a definite *signatum*, as we are made to realize that the room is only one unit in an infinite series.

No less satisfying is the actualization of the distinctive imaginary action spaces pertaining to each of the three characters. They remain separated both in place and time not only mutually but also vis-à-vis the action space. To quote an example: Garcin, who has been executed, describes, as if it were happening in the present, how his wife is waiting in front of the military barracks where he is being held. Only a few moments later he speaks of her, again as if in the present, sitting at home with his coat riddled with twelve bullet-holes on her knees. Yet this episode took place some six months after the first. And finally, he remarks shortly afterwards: "She [my wife] died just now. About two months ago" (Sartre 1989: 38). The sequence of signs establishes for the spectator the temporal polarity between the imaginary action space relating to Earth, where time rushes on, and the action space relating to Hell, where it stands still.

This complexity of the imaginary action space and of its relation to the whole dramatic space arises whenever the imaginary space plays an important or even dominant part in the play. In Cocteau's *The Human Voice* the imaginary action space, created entirely by the voice, gestures and facial expressions of the single actress, suddenly undergoes a dramatic change. In Beckett's *Krapp's Last Tape* there is the imaginary action space behind the scene into which Krapp retires from time to time, and several partly defined imaginary action spaces, actualized by his voice on the tapes.

As has already been mentioned, some authors assert that what they call the illusory stage, that is the imaginary action space, was introduced by the Greeks after the adoption of the permanent scene. Exceptional actions, actions technically impossible on the stage or actions unacceptable on social, religious or moral grounds, had to take place off stage, and finally this became a source of dramatic effect. This, however, is not a valid explanation. Approaching the question, as it were, from the point of view of *langue* and not *parole*, we find that the principle of the imaginary action space applies to the whole corpus of drama. We find it in systems unconnected with Greek drama, not only in Oriental drama but also in medieval liturgical plays. In several of these the Resurrection of Christ is not represented directly but by the three Marys' reaction to it. Indeed, the main function of the imaginary action space is to raise tension within the structure. The suicide of Hedwig in *The Wild Duck*, of Voynitsky in *The Wood Demon*, of Treplev in *The Seagull*, the death of Baron Tuzenbach in a duel in *Three Sisters*, Oswald's attempt at rape in *Ghosts* and so on, are much more dramatic off stage.

But as a constituent of the dramatic structure the imaginary action space has yet another specific quality. As a rule, all signifiers connected with it are polysemic. This admits a binary opposition – propitious versus ominous, good versus evil, and so on. There is always a certain disquieting ambiguity and mysteriousness. This is felt even in such a relatively simple case as in the opening scene of Wedekind's *Earth Spirit*, where the circus behind the stage conceals something quite different from what the spectator imagines from the Ringmaster's speech. In Strindberg's *The Dance of Death* the music behind the stage functions either as a signifier for the enjoyment of the guests or for the isolation of those who were not invited. In the two episodes with the boy in *Waiting for Godot* we can never be sure whether there is only one or two imaginary action spaces pertaining to the boy or whether they both or only one or none of them constitute the imaginary action space pertaining to Godot. As Genet says in his notes "How to Perform *The Balcony*": "The existence of the rebels – is this *inside* the brothel or outside? It is necessary to maintain this ambiguity right until the end" (Genet 1962: 9).

As in many other art forms, in drama the stress is rather on the signifier and not on the signified and in the imaginary action space the signifiers have free play. There is no automatic reference to signifieds, which causes conflicting interpretation by the audience on the one hand and the characters of the drama on the other. In the old Chinese play *What Price Life?* [*Cho Fang Ts'ao*] the tyrant Ts'ao Ts'au, on whose head a reward is offered, takes refuge in the house of Lu, who is a friend of his father. Lu orders his servants to kill a pig and goes to the market to buy wine. After he has left, Ts'ao comes on the stage and finds that Lu is not at home. Both Ts'ao and the audience hear the sound of knives being sharpened. Ts'ao suspects that Lu has gone to denounce him and that the servants are sharpening their weapons preparing to kill him. He rushes behind the stage; there is a din of gongs and weapons on the imaginary stage. Ts'ao appears and sings that he has murdered the whole family, only to realize later that his suspicion was unfounded. A similar conflicting interpretation occurs in an even more complicated form in Chekhov's *The Seagull*. When they hear the shot from the imaginary stage the audience guesses that Treplev has killed himself, then for a moment they are deceived by the doctor and finally they learn that they were right.

We have observed that the action space proper and the imaginary action space remain separate and are brought into confrontation. It is this confrontation that enhances the tension within the structure. There are, however, examples of their being mixed in an arbitrary way. This was quite common in the Greek theatre, where the result of an episode that took place on the imaginary stage, such as a suicide or murder, was shown in the form of a tableau on a platform, the *ekkyklema*, pushed onto the stage. Aristophanes satirized this practice in *The Acharnians*. Dikaiopolis comes to Euripides to borrow a costume but Euripides is busy composing poetry. Finally the *ekkyklema* with a costume on it is pushed onto the stage from the imaginary action space. In Pirandello's *Finding Oneself* the actress, brooding in her dressing room, imagines her triumph on the stage. Suddenly the dressing room is changed into a stage as the back-cloth is lifted and a fictitious auditorium with spectators appears. The imaginary action space is shattered, the tension is diminished and paradoxically, the verisimilitude of the scene is destroyed. Another example proving that mixing the action space with the imaginary action space is not only counter-dramatic but ridiculous is the revelation of Hedda Gabler's corpse in Ibsen's play.

The prerequisites of the separation of the imaginary action space and of its ambiguity are convincingly demonstrated by [the Baroque artist and architect Gian Lorenzo] Bernini. In one of his plays he placed on the stage two theatres complete with two auditoria. Two actors, one with his face towards what was supposed to be the real audience, the other facing what was supposed to be the fictitious audience, entered into conversation and came to the conclusion that the group that each of them beheld was deemed illusory by the other. Then they pulled a curtain across the stage, separating the two audiences, and said that each would stage a performance for his audience alone. One of the actors disappeared behind the curtain in the imaginary action space, while the other arranged a performance in the visible theatre. But the performance was frequently interrupted by laughter from the imaginary action space, giving the impression that the comedy taking place on the imaginary stage was much funnier. At the end the two actors reappeared and asked each other how they had fared. The actor from the imaginary theatre said that he had never shown anything more than the audience itself, preparing to leave with its carriages and horses and accompanied by a great number of lights and torches (Bernheimer 1956: 243).[7]

At present many producers disregard the semiotics of the imaginary action space and transfer to the stage many scenes originally relegated to the

---

7   [Editor's note: The text of this play has not survived, but we possess a detailed description of the production in a letter by an eye-witness as well as a second-hand account based on Bernini's own recollections some years later.]

imaginary action space by the dramatist, not realizing that rape and violence on the imaginary stage are more dramatic and sinister than their simulation before the spectator. But the producer can also improve on the dramatist. In Duhamel's *The Light* a blind man stands before an open window through which the spectators see a mountain lake at sunset. The blind man raves about the beauty of the scene though he has never seen it. In Hilar's production at the Prague National Theatre,[8] as soon as the blind man approached the window, the vista turned into total darkness, stressed by the sharply lit window frame. Charles Vildrac, who saw this production, wrote: "The spectator is invited to put himself in the speaker's place; the spectator too, turns into a blind man in front of this window" (qtd. in Mukařovský 2016 [1941]: 73–74).

We have observed that the dramatic structure, restricted in space and time, tends to break outwards. A similar process takes place in painting, where the imaginary space is also actualized by polysemantic signifiers. Yet, unlike drama, painting can also actualize the imaginary space in front of the picture, abolishing, as it were, the spectator. One of the most common devices used is the mirror. Perhaps the earliest and at the same time the most complex example is Jan van Eyck's painting *The Arnolfini Portrait*. There is a mirror behind the couple that reflects not the observer but, besides the Arnolfini couple, two additional figures. Moreover, there appear in it two additional imaginary spaces, one suggested by a window, another by a half-open door. This picture has a counterpart in Magritte's *The False Mirror*. The eye on the canvas obviously reflects space in front of it, but all we see is a sky interspersed with clouds. A mirror abolishing the spectator was also used by Velasquez in his picture *Christ in the House of Martha and Mary*, and most effectively by him in *Las Meninas*, where the painter at his easel is apparently looking at the observer but is in fact facing the Spanish royal couple, whose reflection appears in the mirror on the wall in the background. A mirror adds several new signifiers to the scene in Manet's *A Bar at the Folies-Bergère*. Holman Hunt's painting *The Awakening Conscience* is exceptionally interesting. The lady, probably the kept mistress of the reprobate playing the piano, is looking out from the picture towards the observer, but what she sees is the garden reflected in the mirror behind her. This is obviously a symbol of the freedom, purity and various other things she has lost. But we may also presume that the imaginary space in front of the picture includes the painter himself, who eyes the lady reproachfully, and any other observer ready to condemn her. Incidentally, this picture is literally loaded with symbols – the cheap lamp on the piano, the wall paper, the pretentious bindings of the

---

8   [Editor's note: *Světlo* [The Light], actually directed by Vojta Novák (1886-1966), premiere on 26 February 1921. Karel Hugo Hilar (1885-1935), a writer, stage and costume designer, and director, was the head of the drama division at the Czech National Theatre the season the play was produced.]

books, the cat eating the bird, and so on. Another device used in painting to suggest imaginary space is the door. It can be half-open as in Fragonard's *The Stolen Kiss*; an even more dangerous imaginary space is suggested by the door being bolted by the lover or pursuer in the same painter's *The Bolt*. Finally, even in such a frivolous scene as Fragonard's *The Swing* imaginary space is cleverly used to conceal the elusive truth. The incidence of imaginary space in painting is as plenteous and manifold as that of the imaginary action space in drama. This proves that, just as the imaginary action space is an inseparable part of dramatic structure, it is also an inherent component of the structure of painting and that both drama and painting have a metaphoric essence in common.

But in addition to being an indivisible component of the structure, imaginary action space is also the space-time continuum from which the play emerges, in which it continues (if there are intervals between the acts) and into which it finally retreats. It is therefore a permanent entity and in seeking its origin as a permanent constituent of the structure we must turn to what Preuss calls *"der Unterbau des Dramas"* [the foundation of drama], those magic rites from the dawn of civilization, which survived until recently amongst so-called primitive peoples (Preuss 1930). Broadly speaking, these were of two kinds: first, those concerning the deities or spirits of ancestors and second, those connected with sympathetic or analogous magic. In these ritual performances and dances there was a complete metamorphosis of humans, not into real ancestors, real demons or real animals but into their spirits, that is into their ideas. The shaman left the village, entered another dimension where he took upon himself the substance of the spirit, appeared amongst the villagers and after performing the rite disappeared. Then after having deposited the substance of the spirit he returned as the shaman. In Polynesia, men connected with these magic rites had to be members of a secret society. Secretly made masks were kept in a special hut, which women and uninitiated youths were not allowed to approach. Similar secrecy was observed in performing the rites themselves. Catlin (1851) describes the fertility rite of the [Mandan Indians of North Dakota] in which *O-kee-hee-de*, the demon of the buffaloes, suddenly appeared among the villagers during the festival and danced. At night he escaped to the prairie pursued by one of the women. At dawn she returned with the phallus of the demon, showed it to the villagers and announced that she was holding the power of creation.

The Baffinland Eskimos used to perform yearly a rite of the fight with Sedna, the mother of sea animals. The success of the hunting season depended on her being killed. The goddess was never seen; she entered the village secretly and hid in one of the igloos. Her fight with the shaman took place in the igloo and could only be imagined by the villagers from the terrible din. Finally the shaman appeared and showed a harpoon stained with blood. One could quote literally hundreds of such examples (Boas 1888: 605). When the belief in the complete metamorphosis of humans into spirits begins to wane, the mask loses its magical power. It changes into a mere disguise and the idea of the spirit of the animal becomes man-animal. Rasmussen reports that in his time the adult Eskimos in King William Land watched the shaman's performance with amusement (Rasmussen 1926). The substratum of magic disappears and the spectators witness a theatrical performance. Nevertheless, the residuum of magic survives even if the performance acquires other than magical functions. In the Middle Ages and up to the beginning of the nineteenth century a peculiar ceremony was performed in northern Bohemia before Midnight Mass on Christmas Eve. All the children disappeared from the church and started running round it outside, bleating like sheep. The village shepherd ran after them but not in his normal role – he acted like a ram. This custom, allegedly connected with the Christian religion, was called "the sheep of Bethlehem" (Dostál 1896: 585). But it is not difficult to discern in it a remnant of sympathetic magic, designed to ensure big flocks of sheep the following spring. Even in its debased form it retains the important factor of magic rites – only a fraction is enacted; the sheep come from and return to some imaginary pasture where they graze, copulate and multiply. Most of their ideal life remains a mystery, only vaguely imagined by the spectator.

When a sufficiently large sample from the vast amount of ethnographical material concerning magic rites and ceremonies is analysed for common denominators, one arrives at a model that shows a complete parallelism with the dramatic structure. The main constituents – the stage, the scene, the action space, the imaginary action space and the spectators – are common to both, even if the structures differ semiologically and functionally. In both it is the action space and the imaginary action space that are the main sources of energy, generating tension within the structure. The only difference is that in the magic rite structure, the amount of energy engendered in each of them is rigidly fixed, while in the dramatic structure it fluctuates between them. They are seldom in balance; more often one or the other is preponderant. Their interrelation changes from one theatrical system to another, from age to age, from author to author, from play to play.

When one remembers the identity of energy with matter, the action space might be compared to a contracting star that draws outside matter into its interior by its own gravity and on reaching its maximum density shoots it forth again into outer space.

WORKS CITED

Bernheimer, Richard (1956) "Theatrum mundi", *The Art Bulletin* vol. 38, no. 4, pp. 225–47.

Boas, Franz (1888) *The Central Eskimo*, Smithsonian Institution – Bureau of Ethnology 6th Annual Report, Washington: Government Printing Office, pp. 399–670.

Bogatyrev, Peter (1940) *Lidové divadlo české a slovenské* [Czech and Slovak Folk Theatre], Prague: Fr. Borový and Národopisná společnost českoslovanská.

Catlin, George (1851) *Illustrations of the Manners, Customs and Condition of the North American Indians*, 8th edition, London: Henry G. Bohn.

Dostál, Alois (1896) "Betlémské ovčičky" [The Sheep of Bethlehem], *Český lid*, vol. 5, p. 585.

Elam, Keir (1980) *The Semiotics of Theatre and Drama*, London: Methuen.

Genet, Jean (1962) "Comment jouer Le Balcon" [How to Perform *The Balcony*], introduction to *Le Balcon*, Lyon: l'Arbalète.

Ionesco, Eugène (1960) *Rhinoceros*, trans. Derek Prouse, in *Rhinoceros and Other Plays*, New York: Grove Press, pp. 3–108.

Maeterlinck, Maurice (1915) *Interior*, trans. Alfred Sutro, in *Three Little Dramas*, New York: Brentano's, pp. 65–88.

Perger, Arnulf (1929) *Einortsdrama und Bewegungsdrama* [Single-Place Drama and On-the-Move Drama], Schriften der philosophischen Fakultät der Deutschen Universität in Prag, vol. 3, Brünn: Rudolf M. Rohrer.

Pirandello, Luigi (1998) *Six Characters in Search of an Author*, trans. Edward Storer, New York: Dover Publications.

Pražáková, Klára (1921) "Pomyslné jeviště" [The Imaginary Stage] in *Jeviště*, vol. 2, pp. 390–92.

Preuss, Konrad Theodor (1930) "Der Unterbau des Dramas" [The Foundation of Drama] in *Vorträge der Bibliothek Warburg 1927–1928* vol. 7, Leipzig: Teubner, pp. 1–88.

Rasmussen, Knud (1926) *Rasmussens Thulefahrt* [Rasmussen's Thule Expedition], Frankfurt a. Main: Frankfurter Societäts-Druckerei.

Roose-Evans, James (1973) *Experimental Theatre*, London: Studio Vista.

Sartre, Jean-Paul (1989) *No Exit*, trans. Stuart Gilbert, in *No Exit, And Three Other Plays*, New York: Vintage, pp. 1–46.

Stiebitz, Ferdinand (1937) "Pomyslné jeviště v antickém a v moderním dramatě" [The Imaginary Stage in Classical and Modern Drama], *Věda a život*, vol. 3, pp. 229–242.

Veltrusky, Jarmila F. (trans. and ed.) (1985) *Mastičkář: A Sacred Farce from Medieval Bohemia*, Ann Arbor: The University of Michigan Press.

Veltruský, Jiří (2016 [1976]) "A Contribution to the Semiotics of Acting" in this reader, pp. 376–424.

THEATRE SPACE AND A VISUAL ARTIST'S PARTICIPATION IN THEATRE

MIROSLAV KOUŘIL

[First delivered in Czech as part of a lecture at Sdružení pro divadelní tvorbu při Umělecké besedě v Praze [The Association for Theatrical Creation within The Artistic Society in Prague] on 23 November, 1943. It was published in Kouřil's 1945 book *Divadelní prostor* [Theatre Space], introd. Jan Mukařovský, along with shorter texts by Antonín Dvořák and Jaroslav Pokorný, Prague: Ústav pro učebné pomůcky průmyslových a odborných škol, pp. 21–72.]

Translated by Eva Daníčková

Editor's note: The following text consists of chapters 4–7 of the published version of Miroslav Kouřil's series of lectures of the same title (pp. 35–50 in Kouřil 1945). The series of lectures is accompanied by an introduction and two postscripts. A brief summary of these texts and the missing parts of the series (chapters 1–3 and 8–9) is presented here so as to provide a better understanding of the text, its context and the overall argument.

The essay "Structuralism in Aesthetics and Literary Studies" (pp. 5–16) by Jan Mukařovský is a programmatic study serving as an introduction to the book. Kouřil's text itself begins with an opening chapter in which he declares the grounds of his method – structuralism and Otakar Zich's theory of theatre. He adopts Zich's concept of "dramatic art", seen as a complicated structure comprising various means of theatrical expression, which he develops further. Where Zich only makes a few distinctions between the sign and meaning in a theatre production (such as stage / dramatic space; stage figure (the actor on stage) / dramatic character), Kouřil introduces other distinctions and elaborates them into a whole system (see the fig. in Quinn 1995: 59 – note: some translations of Zich's and Kouřil's concepts differ from the standard forms used in this anthology). At the same time, he conceptualizes theatre production as a dynamic structure with a changing hierarchy of devices. He provides samples both from history and from his own avant-garde theatre productions.

Chapters 4–7 deal in particular with theatre space and its function in theatre structure – hence their inclusion in this anthology.

The final chapters (8–9) briefly discuss the relation of a dramatic text and a theatre production, compare avant-garde theatre methods with historical styles (such as psychological realism and naturalism) and show how theatre conventions/norms change. In the final paragraph, Kouřil quotes Mukařovský's definition of structuralism as "a noetic perspective", that is, not an ideology or a normative artistic style. He then states he has shown that a theatre structure is ever-changing and that "for the development of theatre it would be inappropriate to take one particular experience as a norm; each discovery is to be negated by the following development of theatre praxis" (Kouřil 1945: 66).

Kouřil's text is then followed by short postscripts further applying the structural method (referring especially to Mukařovský and Veltruský) by Jaroslav Pokorný ("On Drama" (83–92) and "On Reviewing" (117–18)) and Antonín Dvořák ("On Directing" (93–103) and "On the Dramatic Character" (104–16)).

(4)

Let us now move on to the problem itself and shed light on the term "theatre space". Earlier we established that everything in the theatre creates a structure and comes together in a synthesis; let us add that this applies not only to the whole but also to the parts. One of those parts is the theatre space, which, as we know, is a synthesis of the auditorium space and the stage space; at the same time we see that it is qualitatively subordinate to the dramatic space, which for us is the set, the auditorium with its spectators, the actions of the characters, light and sound, all of them functioning simultaneously. This theatre space is filled with the action of the production but not yet with dramatic life and time; nevertheless, it is in antagonistic tension with the dramatic text, to which the actors' delivery and inner experience are inseparably linked.

Our task is limited – we are to concern ourselves with the theatre space alone – yet we must not forget the whole context; we are examining only one of the forces of a complex interplay of components and a rich structure. We must also remember that this is but one pole of the synthesis, which we can study separately *from a theoretical point of view* but which we can never treat on its own without doing damage to the whole.

There are two ways to analyse theatre space, either as a product of the ground plan, vertical stratification, materials and light employed statically, or as the static part of the dramatic space.

In making the first type of analysis, we start from the beginning of the method through which the theatre space is to be created. At the beginning there is a model of the stage that shows the main details of the ground plan and vertical stratification as well as the relationship of this stage space to the auditorium and indicates the materials that will be used; this model can be replaced by a perspective drawing or orthogonal projections, should the parties involved have sufficient spatial imagination. I mention this because the presence of a model does not always serve as a guarantee of this method; often the designer offers a model as proof of his ability to work with "space" on the stage, while later the actual stage space fails to connect up adequately with the rest of the life of the production. Further work leads to the set itself, where physical materials come into play, and finally to the first rehearsals, when we add light, which not only illuminates the set but acts simultaneously as a means of shaping space. In this connection, we must deal later with the concept of perspective as the means by which the spectator perceives space in general and theatre space in particular.

The essential characteristic feature of a theatre space is determined by the way that it is organized; it is characterized by the relationship between the stage and the auditorium. One other thing should be considered. It is natural that the relationship of the spectator to the stage is individual, determined by where he is seated in the auditorium; because this is different for every spectator (each of whose seat is uniquely angled to the set), there arise different views of the stage space, delimited by the physical structure of the set and the light. With regard to sculpture, Benvenuto Cellini formulated the principle that every work should be created with a view to eight points of observation (two opposite one another in each of the four main axes). This principle applies in a similar fashion to free-standing structures (and to architectural works in particular), where viewpoints from all sides should be taken into account. In the same spirit, let us apply this principle to the work of visual art that is the set. It is immediately clear that the degree of synthesis between the stage and the auditorium is directly indicated by the number of possible viewpoints offered by the particular theatre space.

We can see that the full eight points of observation can be achieved with the circular arrangement. (As an example, take the folk tradition in Czech

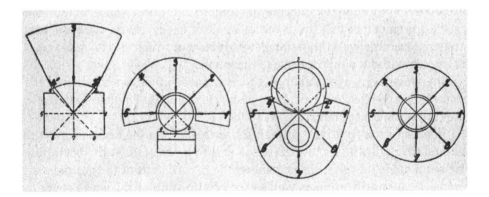

Fig. 1

villages of "three kings" going from house to house, in particular the part that is played out on the village square, where the spectators surround the performers and create a primitive circus-like form or, at the sophisticated end of the scale, Norman Bel Geddes's plan for an "intimate theatre"[1]). Seven points of observation can be achieved by a theatre where the proscenium has an extreme forward thrust (such as the Grosses Schauspielhaus in Berlin, Meyerhold's theatre and other similar theatres). The ancient Greek theatre had five points of observation (a piece of evidence for the conjecture that a *sculptural* disposition of the characters on stage played an important role there). The proscenium theatre has three points of observation. (We must not be misled by cases where the curtain or the forestage may be missing, for example in folk plays like *St Dorothy*, which were performed in the main room of a farmhouse and where the relationship of stage to auditorium was similar to that of the theatre space in the proscenium theatre; or Bel Geddes's plan for a chamber theatre where the curtain and the proscenium are absent but otherwise the way the rest of the space is organized remains unchanged.)

This all leads to the conclusion that the ground plan and the vertical stratification will take on a different perspective for each individual spectator and for each type of theatre space in accordance with differing distances (and therefore the differing extent of fields of vision), differing positions of the projection plane (that is, the imaginary frontal plane between the spectator and the set), and sometimes differing heights of the vanishing point (a spectator in the stalls views the set from the perspective of a frog while a spectator in the gallery has a bird's-eye view). Let me make a minor preliminary comment here: one must not confuse this kind of perspective with the perspective *represented* by the actual physical set and the stage space, which is an illusion of perspective and which we will speak about later. In this instance we are talking about real perspective, in other words, basic perspective, upon which the perspective of the physical set is then built, and further still the dramatic illusion of perspective, which, like everything in the theatre, becomes part of the whole of the production. Finally, I would like to forestall the criticism that allowing for eight points of observation in the composition of the production is something impossible or superfluous. We have to differentiate between two ways of looking at the production, that of those who have created it and that of the spectators. The creative artist must see all the points of observation and work with them in mind (good directors and good designers do not remain seated at a table in the middle of the auditorium); the spectator has the opportunity to experience the different points of observation progressively by going to several performances, or, in a variable theatre space, will experience changes in the perspective itself thanks to changes in acting areas and where they are positioned.

---

1 [Editor's note: Norman Bel Geddes (1893–1958) worked on plans for Theatre Number 20, a project he called "The Intimate Theatre", in 1925–1926. The theatre building was to be a theatre-in-the-round and have 322 seats, but it was never built.]

In making the second type of analysis, we start from the dynamic form of dramatic space. Analysis of the first type might give the impression that theatre space is something static, which is why we also mention the second point of view, one on a higher qualitative level, where the theatre space is seen as an inseparable static component of the dramatic space, a space filled with dramatic life and time (if, for the sake of simplicity, we go directly to the whole of the production). Theoretically, we can imagine a space filled with no more than the dynamics and rhythm of light and the action of the characters being represented by the actors and dancers (that is, only with what has to do with the director's spatial concept), but in practice this abstract concept is inseparable from the delivery and inner experience of the performers, which affects their gestures and movement. This examination only serves to remind us that the theatre space is not something in itself independent, but merely one force in a complicated structure.

(5)

Let us now return to the relationship between the concept of theatre space and purpose. So far we have only talked about purpose in its relationship to the whole, seeing in it the link that connects the theatre to society, to its ideology. But if the theatre as a whole is a synthesis, then each of its components must have some kind of relationship to purpose. At the same time, this relationship is a fresh answer to the question of why a medley of arts is not enough if we wish to achieve perfection in theatre. In the course of the dramatic action the dramatic emphasis shifts in turn from one component of the theatre structure to another; the great majority of the dramatic action is invested in the action of the dramatic characters and the dramatic text. These two components join forces with the set, the lighting and music to create further action, either parallel or contrasting. However, there may also arise dramatic situations in which the characters and the text step back from their dominant position, in which the set (as a whole or a part, that is, a prop) or light or sound move to the fore. I mention all this merely to indicate that during the dramatic action any intended objective attracts whichever component of the structure that it needs at the moment in order to function. Herein lies an answer that applies particularly to the question of the style of the set and everything that is good and bad in it. The set must also comply with the function that follows from the conception of the production. It must evoke all the things and spaces that the production needs for its action and must strip away everything that has no function during the action and is there purely for the sake of making a visual effect. This applies as much as possible both to the creative devices as well as to the technical equipment. Nor should technology override the functionality of the set; the revolving stage should not be present on the stage simply for the effect it creates by rotating if it has no dramatic function during the dramatic action and its motion is merely a distraction. Finally, there is an answer here to the question of the style of the set as well. It too must be functional; it must correspond to the style of the other parts of the production and to the direction of the whole. Unity of style is the primary and most important unity of the production; the other unities are subordinate to it and, in the new avant-garde context, different. Unity of time is determined by the length of the performance, unity of place by the unity of theatre space and unity of plot by the unity of the dramatic action. For us, the issue of the unities and their number has changed, since we take as our starting point the production, not just the drama. Finally, we must also realize that there are qualitative unities imparting order to the creative work: unity of work (with respect to its organization), unity of skill (concerning theatre craftsmanship), unity of the method of theatre work and unity of style, which is determined from the opposite direction by the production's above-mentioned unities of place, time and plot.

In this constellation of forces, if an equilibrium is achieved a synthesis arises. All other states lead to forms that may well be interesting, but are determined by other considerations than that of serving some purpose. This is how we should understand theatrical functionalism, which is a characteristic feature of the synthetic theatre: *Nothing that lacks purpose belongs on the stage!*

(6)

We have touched upon the issue of perspective in theatre and so far have dealt with it only in the wider context of the relationship between the auditorium and the stage. Now we must also analyse its purely scenic form, which we call *the illusion of perspective.*

The stage space with the physical set is a three-dimensional configuration, all its parts – whether solid, concave or convex – conceived so as to serve the needs of the text, the acting and the sound. The question of sound must not be forgotten. I recall the use of thin fibreboard sheets in a production of *Men Don't Love Angels,*[2] which served the formal function of suggesting the sloping ceiling of an attic room. This detail played a major role acoustically, as the surface of the board allowed the actress sitting beneath it to whisper in the course of the increasingly dramatic scene. I mention this because the

---

2   [Editor's note: For details of all productions quoted in this article, see the endnote.]

purpose of the text and the acting are generally recognized but so far the purpose of sound has not been considered.

Such a stage space – like a structure, sculpture or painting that demarcates part of the stage space by certain signs – has its own basic perspective, created by its extension in depth and breadth and by its vertical stratification. This, however, is real perspective, which assumes that the stage structure, sculpture or image will be fully lit by diffused light coming from one direction. It is certainly possible and sometimes even necessary to represent the set this way in the design proposal, but the spectator (and in the actual production it is *his* view that is paramount) will never see it in this form.

It is light that creates the physical set's illusion of perspective. Its role is not only to light the set but above all to help shape the space: it should mould the set so as to enhance the actual space (as fixed by the ground plan, vertical stratification and materials). In stage light the spatial order is thus multiplied formally as a structure and made more dynamic; the set takes on life simply with the mere vibration of light waves pulsating according to the inherent laws of lighting composition and then through the rhythm of the lighting shifts (dimming the light) and changes (alternating spotlights). Light, then, is an essential component of the physical set; it is the technological foundation of the set similar to the way in which the muscles and nervous system are the foundation of the dramatic character. We cannot consider lighting an independent artistic component of theatre because it is firmly and inextricably linked to the other details of the visual artistic side of the production and because it lacks dramatic independence. In a similar fashion, we do not consider the structure of a painting (brush strokes and the treatment of the surface) to be an independent artistic activity.

Like everything in the theatre structure, the degree of illusion of perspective has its qualitative limits. Or to put it another way, the degree of illusion is not the same for every production and it results from the quantitative relations of the basic components of the structure of the theatre performance.

Basically we can differentiate between three groups, which I will illustrate with examples. For greater precision, analysis of the historical development of the theatre is useful. Here we find that the set has been either *an image* or *a relief* or *a construction*. We must not imagine, however, that these groups somehow divide up the development of the theatre into three periods; they alternate and return in new shapes, in more sophisticated theatre technology and technology in general. An analysis of the developmental stages according to this principle would be interesting but it is beyond the scope of this study.

Let us remain with these three groups, for which I will provide examples that I will attempt to analyse. To do so, let us return to the problem of perspective and first determine its relationship to reality. In the theatre this is conditioned by the spectator. An awareness of perspective is created by the combination of memories and thoughts in the spectator's mind (for instance the impression of one-point perspective evokes the experience of viewing a long, straight street or an avenue of trees). Theatre perspective here is a sign of real perspective; it stands for a whole series of phenomena relating to perspective from which it selects some typical detail (in our case the central convergence of two parallel lines in a vanishing point). This understanding enables us to construct a system of three different kinds of theatre perspective. In this scheme, theatre perspective is first an idealised derivative of real perspective represented by the pictorial type. Second, it is merely a hint, a suggestion, of perspective, employing a kind of pictorial and plastic shorthand, which allows details to be combined even when these run counter to the laws of reality. And third, there is absolute stage perspective, created by a painting or a sculpture whose only bridge to reality is through the spectator's imagination. As examples of the first group, there is my stage design for *A Great Guy*, where I set out to create a structure on the stage whose effect would depend solely on an idealization of the real perspective of the main hall of a house, as well as the set design for a production of *Cloudy with Bright Intervals*, where a similar effect was achieved by a stylization of the real perspective of the painter's study and the main hall of his house; here there was a departure from reality in that two different spaces were combined into one on stage. Finally, there is the set I designed in collaboration with Josef Raban[3] for a production of *The Canterville Ghost*, with a stylized perspective of the hall of a country house. This type of perspective becomes more complicated when it transitions to a second type, where the designer breaks the reality down into a series of phenomena, selects certain signs from them and then reassembles them to create a new stage reality serving dramatic life. Examples here are my set for *Charles III and Anne of Austria* and Raban's for *Everyone Plays Two Parts*. In both cases, it was a question of creating a new stage reality from elements that in real life would not be linked together in such a fashion. In Raban's case, this phenomenon was heightened through the use of an organdie backdrop for the set of an amateur theatre group, which made possible simultaneous action on the "stage" and in the "backstage" area of the amateur theatre being depicted.

The second group, in which real perspective is suggested by a kind of shorthand, is typified by relief. For this type, too, the theatre form allows for changes that bring us a new form of relief; we must not imagine that this term is limited to pictorial and plastic relief. In my work on *Merry Wandering of Souls* I experimented with the Renaissance relief technique, a technique that formed the basis of Sebastiano Serlio's "stage in relief". I regard this type as

---

3   [Editor's note: Josef Raban (1912–1986), a prolific Czech architect and stage designer, who worked
      for various theatres.]

the simplest in this group. This technique proves more complicated if we draw on the principle of a painted backdrop employing some image (as I tried out in a production of *Manon*) or if we replace the painted image by a blown-up, larger than life size photograph. This is because on the stage, which is always constructed for acting and not just for being looked at, this image is never enough; we must complement it with three-dimensional objects, and this is where connections emerge, connections that have their counterpart in painting in dioramas. In addition to the above-mentioned *Manon*, we could refer to the set of *Loretka*, especially the scene in the pub ("At the Sign of the Spider"), where interesting relationships were created between the characters in the play and a photographic image of Prague's Old Town. The next degree, when stage reality frees itself from the real world and merely hints at it, offers examples in the set for *Kátinka*, where pictorial relief composed of hints such as this was used; Raban's stage design for a production of *Beauty Does Not Bring Happiness*, where these hints were distorted by being comical; my set for *Trunda and Lajda*, which used the principle of the kind of set used by travelling theatre companies (a circular stage with a single exit at the back) and hinted at reality; a set for *The Bride of Messina*, which I created with depictions of Ancient Greek theatre found on vases in mind; and finally the set for a production of *Everybody Does His Bit for His Country*, situated on the borderline between where the set is composed of signs of reality and where to a certain extent it also creates a new reality, a purely stage reality. Moving on from these examples we arrive at the next group, the relief sculpture form, which enables relief to emerge, as seen from the viewpoint of pictorial and sculptural relief, without the basic signs of relief perspective. Examples here are the sets for *The Village of Stepanchikovo*, *Věra Lukášová* and *Passengers*. Finally we arrive at the last type of stage relief, which we can call montage relief. The difference between this and the previous type is mainly in the use of details as building blocks of the theatre perspective. Whereas relief is created from real details, distorted at the most by a demand for comedy (for example the furniture used in *Everybody Does His Bit for His Country* and *Trunda and Lajda*) or stylization (for example in *Turandot*), montage relief is created from signs of reality, from representatives of forms and things from which it is the spectator's imagination that creates real things and forms within the structure of the complicated life of the production. Examples of this are the sets of *The Executioner, Paris Plays First Fiddle* and *May*.[4] All the forms of the first two groups dealt with so far are linked to a greater or lesser degree to the proscenium-type theatre space or a very similar space (for example the above-mentioned space of Bel Geddes's proposed chamber theatre).

---

4   [Editor's note: Kouřil was responsible for the stage design for *May* together with Novotný and Raban.]

The third group, however, is characterised by its synthetic form, a form that no longer needs the proscenium-type theatre space, even though up until now it has been forced to use it. It is typified by freedom of principle and includes pictorial, relief and structural examples. Its main feature is absolute stage perspective; this does not mean, however, that the divide and the precise distinction between the perspective of the set and the illusion of perspective created by light disappear. Examples of such a set using a construction include the set designed by Jiří Novotný,[5] Raban and myself for *Aristocrats* and *The Beggar's Opera* and my set for *The Barber of Seville*. Examples of the sculptural approach are Raban's set for *Figaro's Divorce* and mine for *Lover and Husband; Leonce and Lena; School, The Foundation for Life*; and *Lovers from the Kiosk.*[6]

This overview would not be complete without pointing out that perspective qualities are not always due to the effect of the lighting alone. Although this effect plays the basic and major role, we must acknowledge the great contribution of the dramatic artistic work, that is the work of the director and the actors. Only in connection with them does the correct *raison d'être* of forms and things emerge on the stage. Without them, without dramatic life, the physical set, no matter how architecturally, sculpturally or pictorially beautiful, is nothing but a pictorial or sculptural object with no purpose. And thus our discussion of one individual aspect brings us back to the realization that theatre is a synthetic structure that we must consider in all its breadth, even though for the sake of simplicity we may observe just one of its parts separately.

We should also discuss this particular individual problem from the point of view of the theatre that makes use of projections, in which light is also a material of the set (slide or film images). We would come to the same conclusion as in the previous analysis. But this would go beyond the scope of this study, because it concerns a subject that is very broad and, in addition, rather specific, which must be studied separately.

(7)

... We live in an age that will be referred to one day as a turning point in the history of theatre in the development of theatre space. The old theatre space represented by the proscenium arch is on its last legs and has been the subject of attacks and efforts at improvement for the past twenty years. So far no new theatre space has actually been built, but we will now show that it has been born and has revealed its capacity to flourish.

By "the old theatre space" we have in mind the form based on the proscenium arch, which was fixed in the seventeenth century by Joseph Furttenbach. Its distinctive sign is the divide created between the audience and the stage by the proscenium, curtain and forestage. Naturally this form has undergone extensive development in the three hundred years since it emerged; it has been reformed and adapted. However, this has only affected details: the basic stratification of the theatre space has remained the same. Development was first seen in connection with the stage, in line with general technical progress, and alongside this there was development of the auditorium, reflecting progress from an aristocratic to a bourgeois society (the idea of popular theatre was born, and ways were sought for attracting corresponding audiences).

In recent decades a revolution has broken out against the proscenium arch. A number of individuals have attempted to tear it down and replace it with a new space. These attempts have been marked by an effort to make use of all the inventions of technology but even more by an intensification of the idea of a popular theatre and the construction of "mass theatres";[7] here too we again observe the connection between theatre and society. But these attempts themselves came to nought, or failed to move beyond the realm of theory.

Like others, we have attempted to devise a new principle of theatre space, characterised by *variability* on one hand and *linkage with the preceding development* on the other. This was reflected in the projects of *The Theatre of Labour* (1936, 1938, 1939). These efforts also remained within the realm of theory.

However, I must note a production that showed the possibility and the feasibility of a new theatre space and that also documented its artistic values. This was a 1939 production of Maeterlinck's puppet drama *Alladine and Palomides* put on [at the theatre D, then situated on] Na Poříčí, with E. F. Burian as director. ... The following spaces corresponded to the five acts of the play:

The first space: in front of a glass-brick wall, with an armchair and a length of ruffled silk on the floor (figure 2).

The second space: a corridor in front of a staircase adjoining a wall of the auditorium; the space was dominated by three massive columns painted with a green lacquer (figure 3).

The third space: between the two glass walls of the main staircase, framed at the front by a low marble wall, and with two sculptures and an armchair (figure 4).

---

7   [Editor's note: That is, theatres able to accommodate huge audiences.]

Fig. 2

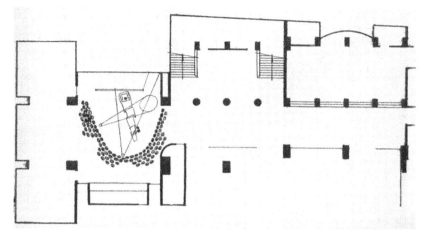

Fig. 3

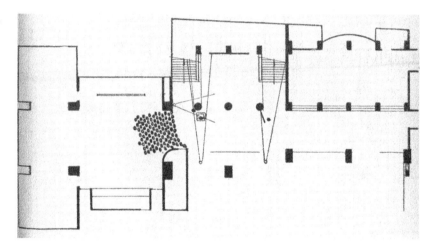

Fig. 4

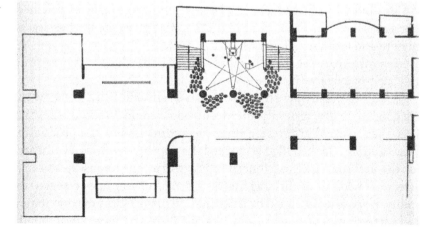

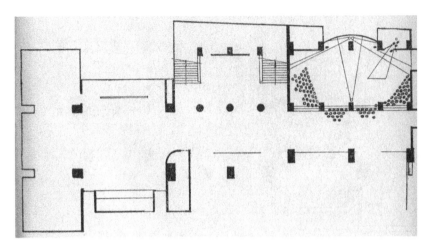

Fig. 5

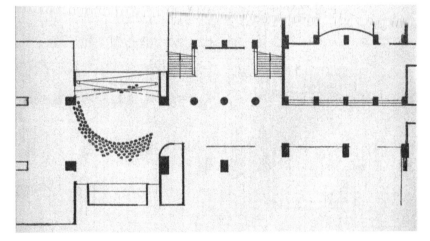

Fig. 6

The fourth space: the rehearsal room, with walls made of polished maple and a massive column, a space that otherwise gives the impression of being austere and ordinary (figure 5).

The fifth space: again at the glass-brick wall, which this time functioned as a back-lit surface (figure 6).

The audience always stood around in a semi-circle; with a view to ensuring good visibility, around a hundred people could attend the performance. This, then, was what the stage and the auditorium of the production – the theatre space – looked like: it marked the appearance of a new theatre form. For the first time we experienced in practice a continuous theatre space, the direct connection of the stage with the auditorium in one space, the variability of space determined by its structural form. Of course this achievement had some shortcomings (its temporary nature and improvised quality), the spectators had to stand and move about, it was simply a higher form of staging akin to the principle by which the medieval mysteries were staged. From here to a perfect form is probably just as far as from the medieval mysteries to Serlio's first productions. A year later, reading the translation of *My Life in Art*, we learned of a similar experiment that had been made by Mme. Georgette Leblanc-Maeterlinck in the poet's house, the former Abbey of St. Wandrille in Normandy. This was a staging of *Pelléas and Mélisande*.

> There were many picturesque spots in the abbey that seemed ready-made for Maeterlinck's plays: here a medieval fountain, hidden in thick foliage for the scene when Pelléas meets Mélisande meet, elsewhere, the entrance to a cave for the scene between Pelléas and Golaud, etc. We decided to mount a production in which the audience and the actors would move from one place in the abbey to another to see the open-air staging of the play. If I am not mistaken, this idea was later carried out by Madame Maeterlinck-Leblanc. (Stanislavski 2008: 279)

This attempt was thus the precursor of the experiment at the Na Poříčí theatre, only in the form of theatre in the open air, where the surroundings themselves created the poetry of the space.

The form in which the production of *Alladine and Palomides* was staged was an eloquent practical demonstration of the new principle of theatre, which had previously been treated theoretically three times in three different ways.[8] It showed that it is possible to abolish the space of the proscenium arch theatre and that the obstacles are not insurmountable. It showed that doing away with the divide between the stage and the spectator does not destroy the dramatic effect or the dramatic illusion. This is confirmed by Josef Träger in an introductory comment to his study "On the Birth of Theatre Convention, or Twenty Years of Growth: 1923–1943" (Träger 1945: 5)[9]. For those who saw that production, its dramatic effect is still powerfully alive.

---

8 [Editor's note: Kouřil is referring here to his three projects in *The Theatre of Labour* (see above).]

9 [Editor's note: The lecture was delivered on 18 October 1943 at the Association for Theatrical Production of The Artistic Forum in Prague. It was published under a slightly different title in 1945; see the Works cited section below.]

ENDNOTE

The list below includes productions mentioned by Kouřil in his article in the order in which they appear in this text. It gives details concerning the productions that are important for understanding the historical context of Kouřil's stage designs. It does not include productions whose details are clear from the main text.

Men Don't Love Angels [Muži nemilují andělů] – a dramatization by Milena Nováková (1888–1970) of her short story (published in a 1939 collection of short stories under the same title), directed by E. F. Burian, premiere at the D 41 on 5 March 1941; this was Burian's last production before he was taken into custody by the Gestapo.

A Great Guy [Chlapík] – the German original *Ein Ganzer Kerl*, a comedy by Fritz Peter Buch, produced at the Na Poříčí theatre, directed by Antonín Kadert, premiere on 12 August 1942.

Cloudy with Bright Intervals [Střídavě oblačno] – a comedy by Vlasta Petrovičová (1903–1980); produced at the Na Poříčí theatre, directed by Karel Konstantin, premiere on 30 October 1942.

The Canterville Ghost [Strašidlo cantervilleské] – by Dalibor C. Faltis (1906–1984); directed by E. F. Burian, premiere at the D 41 on 9 October 1940.

Charles III and Anne of Austria [Karel III. a Anna Rakouská] – the German original *Karl III. und Anna v. Oesterreich* by Manfried Roessner, translated by Rudolf Kautský (1888–1962), produced at the Na Poříčí theatre, directed by Karel Konstantin, premiere on 12 December 1942.

Everyone Plays Two Parts [Každý má dvě úlohy] – a farce by Josef Trojan (1905–1965); directed by E. F. Burian, premiere at the D 41 on 4 September 1940.

Merry Wandering of Souls [Veselé putování duší] – the German original by Emanuel Geibel; directed by Bohuš Stejskal, produced at the Na Poříčí theatre in Prague, premiere on 1 May 1942.

Manon (full title: *Manon Lescaut*) – a drama in verse by Vítězslav Nezval (see below); directed by E. F. Burian, premiere at the D 40 on 7 May 1940. This is an adaptation of a story by Antoine François Prévost (1697–1763) about the love of Des Grieux and the beautiful Manon. This production was considered a crucial artistic achievement of Czech culture at the time of its oppression under the Nazi German occupation, especially thanks to the high aesthetic quality of the verse. Des Grieux's love confessions for Manon were often interpreted as confessions of love for the Czech nation. The author, Vítězslav Nezval (1900–1958), was a progressive Surrealist poet and an author of Social Realist prose and poetry after WWII. There are clear anti-Nazi themes in his work from the late 1930s and early 1940s; hence his *Manon*, as the play has come to be familiarly called, became a symbol of cultural resistance.

Loretka – by Vítězslav Nezval (see the note above); directed by E. F. Burian, premiere at the D 41 on 15 January 1941. Unlike *Manon*, this poetic play full of nostalgia for the Prague of the past did not prove to be a success.

Kátinka – a ballad by Zdeněk Němeček (1894–1957); directed by E. F. Burian, premiere at the D 40 on 7 March 1940.

Beauty Does Not Bring Happiness [Krása neblaží] – by Václav Kliment Klicpera (1792–1859); directed by Jan Port, premiere at the Na Poříčí theatre in Prague on 9 September 1942.

Trunda and Lajda [Trunda a Lajda] – the German original *Schluck und Jau* by Gerhardt Hauptmann; translated by František Vrba, produced at the Na Poříčí theatre, directed by Bohuš Stejskal, premiere on 12 November 1942.

The Bride of Messina [Nevěsta messinská] – based on the German original *Die Braut von Messina* by Friedrich Schiller, produced at the Na Poříčí theatre, directed by František Salzer, premiere on 7 October 1942.

Everybody Does His Bit for His Country [Každý něco pro vlast] – a comedy by Václav Kliment Klicpera; directed by E. F. Burian, premiere at the D 37 on 24 November 1936.

The Village of Stepanchikovo [Ves Štěpančikovo] – a dramatization by Karel Poláček (1892–1945) of the story by Fyodor Dostoyevsky; directed by E. F. Burian, premiere at the D 40 on 26 November 1939.

Věra Lukášová – by Božena Benešová (1873–1936); directed by E. F. Burian, premiere at the D 39 on 29 November 1938.

Passengers [Plavci] – by Jaroslav Pokorný (1899–1940); directed by E. F. Burian, premiere at the D 41 on 13 November 1940.

Turandot – by Carlo Gozzi, produced at the Na Poříčí theatre, directed by František Salzer, premiere on 19 June 1941.

The Executioner [Kat] – E. F. Burian's adaptation of Karel Hynek Mácha's (1810–1836) story "Křivoklad", directed by E. F. Burian, premiered at the D 36 on 22 June 1936. Mácha, the greatest Czech Romantic poet, was stated as the author of the production.

Paris Plays First Fiddle [Paříž hraje prim] – based on poems by François Villon, translated by Otokar Fischer (1883–1938); adapted for an opera libretto and directed by E. F. Burian, premiere at the D 38 on 22 February 1938.

May [Máj] – a dramatized version of Karel Hynek Mácha's *May*, which is considered the greatest Romantic poem in Czech literature. The production, directed by E. F. Burian, premiered at the D 35 on 16 April 1935. A new version of the production reopened in 1939, that is, under the Nazi occupation.

Aristocrats [Aristokrati] – a comedy by Nikolai Pogodin; directed by E. F. Burian, premiere at the D 36 on 26 September 1935.

The Beggar's Opera [Žebrácká opera] – version of *Three-penny Opera* by Bertolt Brecht; directed by E. F. Burian, premiere at the D 35 on 20 November 1934.

The Barber of Seville [Lazebník sevillský] – by Pierre Beaumarchais, translated by Otto Jirsák (1907–1940); directed by E. F. Burian, premiere at the D 37 on 22 September 1936.

Figaro's Divorce [Figarův rozvod] – an original comedy by Otakar Štětka, directed by E. F. Burian, premiere at the D 41 in November 1940.

Lover and Husband [Milenec manželem] – a comedy by Jan Vtelenský; directed by E. F. Burian, premiere at the D 41 on 25 September 1940.

Leonce and Lena [Leonce a Lena] – the German original of the comedy *Leonce und Lena* by Georg Büchner; directed by E. F. Burian, premiere at the D 38 on 25 January 1938.

School, The Foundation for Life [Škola základ života] – by Jaroslav Žák (1906–1960), based on his feuilletons; directed by E. F. Burian, premiere at the D 38 on 31 August 1937. A comedy about secondary school students, it was turned into a hit film in 1938.

Lovers from the Kiosk [Milenci z kiosku] – a lyrical comedy by Vítězslav Nezval (see the note above); E. F. Burian composed music for it in 1932 and thus co-created the popular version of the play. The production referred to by Kouřil was directed by E. F. Burian, premiere at the D 36 on 13 November 1935.

WORKS CITED

Kouřil, Miroslav (1945) *Divadelní prostor* [Theatre Space], introd. Jan Mukařovský, Prague: Ústav pro učebné pomůcky průmyslových a odborných škol.

Quinn, Michael L. (1995) *The Semiotic Stage: Prague School Theater Theory*, New York: Peter Lang.

Stanislavski, Konstantin (2008) *My Life in Art*, trans. Jean Benedetti, London: Routledge.

Träger, Josef (1945) "Ke zrodu dnešní divadelní konvence u nás" [On the Birth of Today's Theatrical Convention in This Country] in *Dvě přednášky z války o divadle* [Two Wartime Lectures on Theatre], Prague: Umělecká beseda, pp. 5–51.

VI TOWARDS STRUCTURES OF MODERN ACTING

This section includes texts reflecting avant-garde theatre practices. Both Jiří Frejka and Jindřich Honzl were directors with highly individual styles: in their essays and programmatic pamphlets they provide insights into their own artistic intentions as well as observations that are more generally valid. (It is important to note that in the 1940s both Honzl and Frejka became teachers – though often informally – of the younger generation; this may have motivated them to approach their experience critically and share it.) It is difficult to draw a strict line between "subjective" reflection and "objective" interpretation in their writings – and perhaps this is not even worth trying. It is more interesting to follow how certain concepts such as gesture, convention and motivation are elaborated against the background of the authors' theatre practice and Prague School theories.

Jindřich Honzl, the most explicit theorist among Czech avant-garde directors, was particularly noted for a number of studies dealing with Czech actors from the first half of the twentieth century. For a non-Czech reader, lacking an awareness of the historical context, these texts are very difficult to understand, but it is crucial to mention them. These occasional studies (from the 1920s and 1930s) served as preparatory material for Honzl's generalizations in his later studies. But it can already be seen in these early studies that Honzl was influenced by a late formalist and early structuralist approach: in his analysis of actors' personal styles he paid great attention to picking out the characteristic details of the particular styles and conceptualized acting as a composition of particular elements or layers, while showing little to no interest in the actors' inner psychological motivation. (This method is very similar to the structuralist approach to the author and his subjectivity employed by Mukařovský and Jakobson in their structural analyses of literary texts.)

The section is closed by Jiří Veltruský's extensive study "A Contribution to the Semiotics of Acting" (1976). This is the only text in this volume that was written well after the "classical" period of the Prague School, which is usually considered to have come to an end by 1948. There are two reasons for its inclusion. First, it is the most complex attempt to theorize acting using a structuralist methodology while at the same time considering diverse historical and local styles. Second, even though written in the context of 1970s theatre semiotics, the study is based on the Prague School (Mukařovský, Jakobson, Karl Bühler and Otakar Zich are the key references) and should therefore be understood as a continuation of the writings of the Prague School rather than as part of the French or German theatre semiotics of the period when it appeared (Veltruský quite deliberately avoids these schools in his texts).

THE CONCEPT OF CONVENTION

JIŘÍ FREJKA

[First published as a chapter titled "Divadlo roste z konvence a přece proti ní bojuje" [Theatre Grows From Convention and Yet Fights against It] in Frejka's 1929 book *Člověk, který se stal hercem* [How People Became Actors], Prague: Melantrich, pp. 85–89. Frejka continued his work on the text. This edition is based on a version found in Frejka's papers, which was published in 2004 under the present title "Pojem konvence" [The Concept of Convention] in a collection of Frejka's studies entitled *Divadlo je vesmír* [Theatre Is a Universe], Petišková, Ladislava (ed.), Prague: Divadelní ústav, pp. 445–48.]
Translated by Eva Daníčková

Theatre, like every other art, is something functional. The actor's task and objective is to appeal to the human mind and imagination. To create a series of stimuli now aggressive, now subdued, that flow round the calm pools and troubled waters of the human spirit, at times causing excitement, at other times bringing peace and quiet. The whole seemingly objective mechanism of the theatre is nothing but counterpoint, composed by the artist on the theme of the life and the mind of the spectator. We are possessed by the idea that every art has been conceived, composed and created for the greater enrichment of its nameless spectator and listener – that the spectator is really like a simple melody, yet one that is the truest of all, harmonized and brought to full-blooded multivocal sonority on the stage. The stage resembles an amplifier; through the stage and its strange, imaginative order there arises the possibility of highlighting, analysing, choosing from the chaotic richness of the human spirit, from this rich store of resources rooted in the public. Humanity is the reservoir of the art of the theatre; every person in the audience holds immanently within him all future tragedies, all future comedies. The theatre is merely a system for bringing them into existence. And this is the melody that will be harmonized by the stage. The theatrical impression, theatre itself, plays with human experience, which, stirred and roiled by the theatre piece and the actor, builds from out of itself a new world that is a new reality, yet one that is at the same time the spectator's own, incorporated in him through his response and close to him.

The theatrical impression does not consist in imitating life. Imitation is not an artistic matter – on the contrary, it is anti-artistic and provokes resistance. "Imitative" realistic art did not work its magic owing to its ability to imitate but by the way it gave intensity and depth to each character. As we have already pointed out elsewhere, the greatest contribution of this era lies in its discovery of the human spirit and in the development of the actor's ability to react to impulses from within as well as from without. In a similar way, a landscape is not beautiful in itself; beauty is ascribed to it by the observer. As the old saying has it, a landscape is a state of the spirit. What we are speaking of here is a new, creative world, a world that goes against convention but at the same time is built upon convention.

Acting consists in the actor as its vehicle being divided, differentiated, mentally; his richness is the richness of performance. He holds the audience under his spell not through his power of thought but through his ability to be a vehicle, a representative, of life and thought. His job is not to know things in the usual sense of the word but rather to reincarnate himself and to objectivize this reincarnation. The actor has disengaged himself from and violated his own conventionalized movements so as to be able at any moment to enter into, to embody, the conventions of movement of the character, and by doing so to communicate something. In a similar fashion, he captivates us through this disengagement and the richness of the art of speech, of facial expressions and of gestures. A drunkard we meet on the street is marked by certain conventions of movement, speech and thought that are characteristic of a drunkard. His whole bearing is shaped, normalized, standardized, by his drunkenness. Fine – for the actor this convention precedes any experience of his own, and so if he is to play a drunkard he must shape his own individual reactions in accordance with this image of the drunkard, no matter how he may then go on to stylize them as he wishes. And so convention, the polar opposite of creativity, is the cornerstone of creative acting. It is its subject and the basis of its language.

Convention: a time-tested causal relationship, a causative nexus that helps the spectator to understand that certain movements indicate a drunkard, just as he has previously observed them in people who were drunk. But it need not be this kind of example. For instance, you are accustomed to the dignified sight of top hats perched on heads at formal events. Fine – but a clown who shows you that a hat like this may serve all kinds of other purposes turns the conventional function on its head. You find him interesting because you know the hat's function before it was used for the purposes of art – in fact for you this is its primary function. Thus it is the reverse of the first example.

The everyday world of a cobbler or an office worker is seen through the eyes of a certain job or profession. Everything, the whole chaos of the civilized world, can at one point be reduced to its weights and measures, at another to the ability to pay one's taxes. But there is also the possibility (and what is more, the direct necessity) of a synthetic vision, and this is an artistic vision; this also where the magic of perceiving art resides. The spectator is drawn out of himself by a series of characters and the way they are brought to life, made part of the crowd in the auditorium, moulded as a member of the collective, in order to experience completely new sensations through this reincarnation.

Any element serving to characterize something evokes a certain idea. But almost immediately, and as it develops, it evokes many other associations linked to the idea. So at one point a red curtain plays the role of fire, at another it is the fatal danger of fiery passion, at other times again an uprising or the depressing crimson shade of a bar. These associational elements, which are highlighted, are much more important for the actor's work and the spectator's perception than the first impression and the first idea, for it is not the idea of red cloth but its symbolic, associational meaning that has moved us. Associations share in the basis of artistic emotional thinking; stage symbolism rests on them.

The symbol. A symbol, as defined by Ermatinger, is a "meaning-image" (Ermatinger 1921: 98) – meaning as an image, the image as a vehicle for meaning or an idea. For the author, a symbol is a means that enables us, through his work, to see and sense life, so that the work is a mental analogue to reality. The world shaped by man.

The stage symbol thus takes shape before the actor's eyes as the result of this work of discovery. The entire stage is a symbol. The stage seen clearly, especially in terms of its dynamics. A character with its various typical features is also a symbol, as is a well-chosen tone of voice, the trembling of a body, makeup or a costume. A complicated construction, articulated by the actor's language. The very smallest symbolic expression is a building block from which the structure of the play, the structure of a new world, is erected.

We have already mentioned that nature is divided from the stage creation by a certain enhancement, that the actor, by as it were recasting the character within his own body, adds something to nature here and takes something away there in order to achieve greater expressiveness. The more finished the work, the more obvious it becomes that the auditorium and the stage are separated by a mystical abyss that gives the stage the sanction of universality, of universal meaning. But it is better to call this enhancement by its real name – exaltation. It is exaltation that raises the stage above the greyness of the everyday, and the mystical abyss between the auditorium and the stage can only be bridged in one way, by the atmosphere on the stage being mirrored by that in the auditorium. Let us call it the exaltation of the auditorium. And just as the basis of the theatre lies in the spectator, the basis of his role as a spectator lies in his (restrained) exaltation.

The art of the stage symbol consists in playing with the spectator (that is, characterization, facial expressions, gestures, tone of voice – the acting symbol), but all this must be marked by a firm, accentuated stage "morality", some stage objective. But those facial expressions and gestures, that tone of voice? These are nothing more than the opening up of a path by which the spectator enters into the synthetic work on the stage, into its objective, into its atmosphere – above all through internal imitation.

WORKS CITED

Ermatinger, Emil (1921) *Das dichterische Kunstwerk* [The Poetic Work of Art], Leipzig – Berlin: B. G. Teubner.

EXAMPLE IN ACTING AND THE STAGE AS THE SUPERSTRUCTURE OF LIFE

JIŘÍ FREJKA

[First published as a chapter titled "Jevištní imitace není jevištní iluze ani jevištní pravda" [Stage Imitation Is neither Stage Illusion nor Stage Truth] in Frejka's 1929 book *Člověk, který se stal hercem* [How People Became Actors], Prague: Melantrich, pp. 90–95. Frejka continued his work on the text. This edition is based on a version found in Frejka's papers, which was published in 2004 under the present title "Příklad v herectví a jevišti jako životní nadstavbě" [Example in Acting and the Stage as the Superstructure of Life] in a collection of Frejka's studies entitled *Divadlo je vesmír* [Theatre Is a Universe], Petišková, Ladislava (ed.), Prague: Divadelní ústav, pp. 448–50.]

Translated by Eva Daníčková

The circus, the music hall, film and most of all theatre are superstructures rising upon the base of everyday reality for the sake of a captivating... lie? No – for the sake of a new reality. The principle of causality, or better still the laws of association, are highly distorted. The laws of association – that is, the basis of convention; that is, the automatisation of our life through our thinking. A door that is opening raises the expectation of a person standing behind it; where there is a throne we look for a king; where there is a battered old shoe we look for its mate. Even the most striking alogism in fact builds most effectively upon these foundations. If books could fly from one place to another on their own, if doors were not normally opened by people, we would scarcely be interested in such special effects in films as flying books or magic carpets. The essence of the impression here is precisely this inversion of the causal chain, linking up to it.

The actor, like any other artist, works with the associational norms of the spectator's consciousness. By "norm" here we mean, for example, the above-mentioned connection linking a door that is opening with the expectation of a person behind it, or the drunken staggering of someone who is very drunk. *Post hoc, ergo propter hoc.* The difference between the stage and life is that in life these norms result from the automatization of our perceptions and awareness, whereas on the stage some of them are chosen as building blocks from which the artist constructs a new world. The "alogism" of a new work of art may lie either in a new arrangement of these building blocks or in a completely new, symbolic interpretation of them. But the norm is always something that catches the spectator's attention. The failure of the

"Abstractionists"[1] results from the fact that only very few people with the capacity to grasp formal structures are capable of taking an interest in their art. Everyone else requires a means of entering into the imaginative flow of the work of art, everyone else seeks in art not exactly imitation, but certainly a powerful personal impact, and this impact will be strongest when it captures not only the spectator's formalist feelings but when it builds upon his whole manner of thought and perception in everyday life.

A theatre performance is a series of symbols, a series of markers, a series of magical formulae that, like the vibration of the tuning fork in the ear, mean nothing in themselves: the audience, that chaotic collective, only makes the theatre something real at the moment when it understands these markers, when it is guided by them, when bits of its collective heart are selected from out of its chaos and dragged onto the stage in the form of its norm of perception, its experience. This means that theatre plays to certain norms in its audience and only then is it able to pull them along wherever it pleases in its imaginative flow.

For instance, stage illusion does not consist in imitating a certain milieu and the people found there but only in selecting sufficiently explicit norms of perception. Only with the discovery of these norms does art begin. Its ground and creation is where it takes off from them into associations and the creation of characters for the stage, where, building on their logic, it attains "alogism", where, building on their explicitness, it radiates an emotional force.

The dramatic text is not divided into scenes but into units that are determined objectively and subjectively. Objectively: a certain passage in the play has its props, its vocal intonation, its pattern of movements and verbal gradation, its lighting. And subjectively it is all connected in the person of the actor, who evokes a whole range of associations that are materialized for the spectator by a gesture of the actor's or a new prop. And so a whole broad stream of poetry is induced, one that is not determined solely by the words of the play but driven by all of the spectator's senses through a host of associations.

Thus we arrive at a kind of stage materialism, if we may call it that. Words, movements, are ideas taking on material form. All this is transposed and shaped for the stage by the director, compressed into pure stage truth and effectiveness. Dialogue is not accompanied, but actually materializes in the props. The props then have their own lyricism, which is both dynamic (a lyricism of the word, borne by the actor, and of movement, present in every spectator, who would fall down from a similar thing) and static (material). What occurs is an activation of the whole stage, which from being an

---

1   [Editor's note: Abstractionism, a school derived from German Expressionism; it emphasized abstract and formal artistic devices.]

image documenting and underlining the action becomes true theatre and moves us in more than an intellectual way. The dualism of older approaches to directing, which often meant no more than documenting a work of literature, is gone. Ideas, imagination, materialize on the stage as theatre, for the theatrical performance has a perfectly self-sufficient formal expressive side.

Every artistic symbol is a material analogue to the reality of life, acquired by a process of creative differentiation.

Theatre is not words (that is, literary symbols) but stage action, fixed by word, movement, space, colour and so on. It is a perfect, non-reproducing expression, a new reality from which analogies flare out to the reality of life.

Realism wished to achieve the stage impression through the artistic imitation of symbols from real life, or more precisely through the identification of the law of causality on stage and in life.

But the actor must not stick to mere reincarnation, nor the director to simple imitation. Once the actor has reincarnated himself in a character, he must objectify his experience in the performance, in a synthetic and concentrated image, in a stage metaphor, a symbol, an exclamation mark.

DEFINING MIMICRY

JINDŘICH HONZL

["Definice mimiky" (1946–47) was first published in two parts in *Otázky divadla a filmu*, vol. 2, no. 4, pp. 154–58, vol. 2, no. 6, pp. 209–13.]

Translated by Marta Filipová

Editor's note: The key words employed by Honzl in this article, *mimika* (a noun) and *mimický* (its corresponding adjective), are commonly used in Czech, echoing similar usage in French (*le mimique, mimique*) and German (*die Mimik, mimisch*). Unfortunately they have no real equivalents in English. *Mimika*, for example, may mean facial expressions or even imitative or expressive gestures in a broader context. In order to enable the reader to appreciate the main line of Honzl's argument, which would be lost if the Czech terms were translated into English in different ways in different contexts, it was decided to use the English words "mimicry" and "mimetic", both of which convey clearly the core sense of "imitation".

If we examine how physiologists and psychologists define mimicry, we find that they do not identify mimetic movements with what is usually understood as mimicry, for they do not regard all the movements of the facial muscles as mimetic movements. Physiologists and psychologists study the movements of the facial muscles based on their origin and the stimuli that produced them. These stimuli can be very diverse and this diversity leads to the movements being classified in various ways and to only some of them being termed mimetic movements. The movements of the facial muscles and the movement of the muscles in general can be instinctive, automatic, habitual or even volitional. Nevertheless it should be admitted that a strict isolation of the individual kinds of movements from one another is uncommon. Many volitional movements betray the presence of instinctive stimuli, while the participation of the will cannot be completely excluded from many automatic movements.

A physiological and psychological definition would be impossible if one were not able to distinguish each kind of movement separately: otherwise its origin and traits could not be discovered. On the other hand, however, it is true that we would be mistaken if we restricted ourselves solely to an understanding that tried to define a physiological and psychological fact as something completely isolated. That is because it would be impossible to understand the function of such a fact if it were not associated with those other physiological and psychological facts that are most closely related to it.

Different kinds of stimuli can therefore be found in specific examples of mimetic expressions, and if we wish to categorize movements we have to note which of these stimuli predominate.

Since some facial expressions – or rather, in more general terms, some movements of the facial muscles – are movements that are performed spontaneously and non-consciously, without our volitional involvement, physiological psychologists are unwilling to call them mimetic movements. They justify this by invoking the meaning of the Greek word *mimesis*, which means the imitation, accommodation or adaptation of one thing on the part of another. They say that only a facial expression controlled by our volition can be termed an imitated facial expression, so that all movements that *do not originate* as consciously imitated movements are non-mimetic and therefore do not fall into the category of mimicry. The concept of mimicry and its definition is thus limited to cases of the facial movements that we make for the purpose of imitating, representing, indicating facial movements that we observe in others and that we are familiar with from experience. However, we can imitate – insofar as our physical body and mind allow this – many movements and expressions. We can imitate instinctive, reflexive, automatic, habitual and volitional movements. If we cannot imitate some spontaneous movements – that is, represent them faithfully – we can at least *indicate* them. Still, none of these imitated movements – if we stick to the above definition of mimicry – will possess spontaneity, which is characteristic of non-imitated, that is non-mimicked, movements.

So the physiologist says that if the muscles of the forehead and eyelids contract when a person experiences anger, if the nostrils enlarge and the teeth clench, the face takes on an expression of anger.

Yet when, in the course of conversation, we speak about anger that we have detected in someone or that we have experienced ourselves, and when, while doing this, to illustrate our words we consciously repeat one of the movements in a weakened or an exaggerated fashion, then *we are engaged in mimicry*. This can be said of both facial mimicry as well as vocal mimicry. (Dumas 1933: 295)[1]

According to this view, mimicry is imitation, imitation not only of facial expression but also of vocal expression. If Dumas had been even more con-

---

1 [Editor's note: In Honzl's original this quotation is attributed to Georges Dumas and André Ombredane. Though the two scientists did collaborate on vol. 3 of *A New Treatise on Psychology*, from which the quotation is taken, each wrote separate sections, with Dumas being responsible for the one on mimicry (see Works Cited).]

sistent in his premises, he would have said that mimicry is also imitation of behaviour, imitation of a way of dressing, imitation of a way of life. But mimicry would have to be seen in every example of imitation: every work of art, which cannot exist without depicting or representing some fact taken from reality (an artist's painting cannot exist without a subject – a landscape, person, still-life arrangement, and so on – that the painting depicts; a narrative work of literature cannot exist without the illusion of life – without a story and characters – making its presence felt, and so on), would have to be considered the result of and an example of such mimicry.

On the one hand, Dumas narrowed down the concept of mimicry in order to be able to simplify the classification of facial movements. On the other hand, however, the principle that led to a narrowing of the classification of facial movements broadened the concept of mimicry and opened it up to other areas not related to facial movements. So what Dumas studies in people is not only facial mimicry but also vocal mimicry, mimicry of posture, mimicry of walking, mimicry of writing, and so on, in the sense that people, in addition to their own *spontaneous* facial movements, in addition to their own spontaneous posture, in addition to their spontaneous manner of walking and their own spontaneous style of writing, also perform volitional movements, imitated movements, whose aim is to express certain features of a particular carriage, the certain character of a gait, certain characteristics of a way of writing that they like, that they themselves accept.

Such a definition of mimicry creates the difficult obligation of distinguishing clearly between non-spontaneous movement, whose intention is to *imitate* someone else's or one's own movement, and spontaneous movement. As we said at the start and as Dumas also admits, it is not always easy to single out, clearly and with no exceptions, those of our movements that were performed spontaneously and to separate them from those that were prompted by the intention to imitate. To clarify this, we should recall the non-conscious imitative movements of children. Mimicry in children is completely spontaneous (and also non-conscious). The volitional movement that produces such imitation in children originates in the non-conscious (subconscious) part of the mind. Yet a child's imitative movement cannot be called instinctive or reflexive or automatic or habitual. It is unconscious mimicry and *it is completely spontaneous mimicry.*

Yet even in adults we cannot rule out such spontaneous mimicry. Here, too, unintentional imitation of the movements of facial muscles and the hands, of gait, and so on, which people adopt from others, becomes operative. Thus many mimetic features are adopted by members of the same family or members of a specific social circle or members of a community that has a common interest or has been brought together by some shared way of life. These mimetic features often create the characteristic trait of the social group in the same way that a common language is the most important characteristic of a national whole, and certain peculiarities of accent, pronunciation and word forms are the characteristic traits of people from a specific region or from a specific place or even from a specific family.

The volitional stimulus for such imitation – for such mimicry – can sometimes be conscious but is in most cases non-conscious. What enters the consciousness during the imitation of behaviour or speech is not the fact of imitation itself, not the way the imitation is done; rather, it is *the need to imitate. The need to share* with others compels a member of a specific social group to acquire their language and their ways of expressing themselves through imitation. A member of a social group is very conscious of this need, and this need to communicate and share in the communication of the others makes itself felt very urgently. The urgency of this need forces, for instance, a foreigner to concentrate his mind and his will completely on "imitating speech" – so as not to perish. The less urgently this need is felt and the longer it lasts, the less conscious the adaptive aim and the more non-conscious the mimicry. Just as we learn a foreign tongue by concentrating our will and our other mental abilities, so in contrast we acquire our mother tongue involuntarily, unintentionally, without conscious volitional intent, without a precise knowledge of language forms and without an awareness of the rules of syntax. Mimicry becomes automatic, unintentional, involuntary, spontaneous in all the ways in which it is practised. It must be admitted that a large portion of mimetic movements, especially those that we use for communication,[2] arose through *imitation,* for these communicative movements are instinctive or reflexive manifestations of inner states, yet they *are also signs* just as, and in the same sense as, words or phrases are signs of our expression of a certain reality.

It can be said that all mimetic movements that have a social function (especially a communicative function) arise from conscious, non-conscious or subconscious imitation.

Once an individual acquires the ability to perform these communicative mimetic movements, they become habitual and automatized and they are carried out spontaneously, without a *conscious impulse to imitate.*

The division of facial movements into imitated and spontaneous movements should be replaced by a division into those on the one hand that have their origin in the principles of the physiological system of *every* human being and that are expressions of a specific state and those on the other hand that have their origin in the social needs of communicating, expressing emotions, warning, encouraging, giving orders and asking questions – that is, the

---

2   For instance winking, sneering, frowning in refusal and so on are examples of mimetic communicative signs.

needs of social intercourse, which are indispensable for every individual who lives in society.

This would be a division of mimetic movements similar to Descartes' division in his *Passions of the Soul* (1649) and to that of Buffon in his *Natural History, General and Particular* (1749). The same distinction concerning mimetic expressions as that of Descartes and Buffon was also made by the German Enlightenment thinker Johann Jakob Engel, a follower of Lessing's, in his *Ideen zu einer Mimik* (1785).

All these authors agree that there are mimetic movements and expressions that are "the physical (that is, physiological, direct) results of inner changes of the spirit" (Engel)[3] and that they can be considered natural (a term also used by Descartes), that is, that they originate naturally and necessarily as the result of physiological and psychological causes that our conscious will does not control.

We would call such uncontrolled, spontaneous, natural mimetic expressions mimetic signals. If we do not call them signs nor attribute to them the functions of signs, it is not because these expressions do not convey to us a certain meaning or because they do not enable us to guess or know the inner state of a person in whom some natural mimetic expression of one kind or another is being observed. Crying – that is real tears, which no one or only very few people can shed as the result of a deliberate, consciously volitional stimulus without experiencing the appropriate mental state – is a sign for anyone who sees a person crying that enables him to infer that individual's sadness, grief or pain.

But even if these tears fulfil, in this certain way, a communicative function, in the study of mimicry we do not regard crying and tears as a mimetic sign but rather as a mimetic *signal*.

A signal, then, is an expression of those "natural", spontaneous, nonconscious and often uncontrollable inner states whose origins did not require imitation or the influence of society on the individual, where the needs of social contact played no role.

In theory this criterion for distinguishing between signals and signs of mimicry should lead to the clarity that is needed in any scholarly classification of a particular subject, which would otherwise become unmanageable.

In practice, however, employing this criterion only simplifies the difficulty of dividing the subject of mimetic expressions to a minimal degree. Moreover, it could be said that the principle on which this division is based only creates a new difficulty for the study of mimicry.

This is because a person has the ability to become aware – for example, in hindsight – of the spontaneous, unintentional, non-conscious and natural

---

3   [Editor's note: Honzl's paraphrase of Engel, not a citation.]

expressions of his own face and body and he also has the ability to learn by observing these expressions not only in himself but in others. But what is more, a person can *repeat* these spontaneous, natural signals of mental and physiological states, that is, he can *imitate* himself, as Dumas would put it. He can also notice mimetic signals in others and can himself adapt to them in situations where he needs to or where he finds these expressions suitable (for instance, if someone else's expressions appeal to him, if he finds them "good", "refined", "ethical", and so on).

A perceptive, trained spectator can sometimes distinguish between these imitated or repeated signals and spontaneous signals, but often even an expert *cannot distinguish* natural and spontaneous signals from those that are imitated and consciously repeated.

A signal, which is basically always the result of the state or an action of a *specific individual*, which is necessarily (naturally) reflected in certain physical changes and which is also reflected in the movements and in the behaviour of the individual, is a fact so independent of other people and society that it would be manifested just as necessarily and naturally even if the individual were isolated from other people. Such expressions therefore occur of necessity in the presence of other people as well, in company, unless – and this is a very important condition, which shows that even quite individual states depend on the company of others in a certain way – the expression of this certain individual signal is hampered or suppressed by non-conscious or conscious social censorship, which is present in every individual brought up and living in society.

We can all, for example, suppress our spontaneous laughter or spontaneous tears, even though both these expressions function as signals whose physiological mechanism – considered solely from the physiological point of view – is not accessible to our will, since a special kind of spasm in the throat, which triggers the discontinuous series of exhalations and sounds we call laughter, is the result of the action of muscular reflexes that cannot be directly controlled by our will. In the same way the shedding of tears from the lacrimal sacs cannot be controlled directly. We can suppress our laughter and sometimes even our tears when we feel it is not appropriate to cry or to laugh, or when we follow social conventions that forbid laughter or crying in some situations just as firmly and irrevocably as they demand them in other situations.

However, social censorship intervenes in the spontaneous expressions of the individual, in the realm of mimetic signals, not only in a negative, suppressive sense. Social censorship, or rather social conventions, also force spontaneous signals (such as crying and laughter) to change their nature, to become signs, to adopt the functions of social communication. We see a communicative function of this kind (that is, one acting as a sign) in a face marked by suffering and in the tears that we see in someone shaking the hand of the bereaved at a funeral. The smiling face and joyful burst of laughter that greet a surprise visitor also have such a communicative function.

It was in this sense that, already in the eighteenth century, Buffon pointed out the difficulties of a scientific classification of mimetic expressions and the difficulty in some instances of determining precisely whether a particular mimetic expression is unintentional, spontaneous ("natural"), or whether it is deliberate. In his *Natural History*, Buffon claims the following:

> These expressions of the passions are involuntary. But there is another species of expression, which consists in an agitation of the eyes, head, arms, and body; and these motions seem, at the same time, to be the effect of reflection, and to depend on the will. They appear to be efforts of the mind to defend the body, and may be regarded as secondary symptoms,[4] by which particular passions may be distinguished. (Buffon 1785: 150)

For instance, when looking at an object of desire,

> we stretch forward the head to make a nearer approach; and we extend the arms and open the hands, in order to seize and embrace the beloved object. On the other hand, in fear, hatred, and horror, we push the arms forward with precipitation, to repel the object of our aversion; we turn back the head and the eyes; we recoil, and at last fly, in order to avoid it. These motions are so sudden, that they appear to be involuntary: But this deception is the effect of habit; for these motions are produced by reflection, and, by their alacrity, discover the perfection of those qualities of the body which enable it to obey, with such amazing promptitude, the commands of the mind. (Buffon 1785: 450)

Buffon shows here quite correctly that natural, non-conscious, spontaneous movements can be repeated – indeed that we often do repeat them, either with a conscious intention or because we have become so used to their repetition that they come into play not only when a stimulus comes directly from conscious volitional intention but also when it is created in some indirect way.

I believe that these studies, quotations and references have provided sufficient support for the claim that mimetic expressions must be considered to include not only expressions of conscious and non-conscious imitation but also all expressions that are in any way visible in the face. These expressions can be divided into those that are signals and those that are signs, but such a division is merely genetic: it tells us how each expression originated, but is

---

4   [Editor's note: The word "symptom" is used by Buffon's translator into English, William Smellie, to convey the concept here translated (from the Czech) as "signal".]

not a functional distinction. The transition from signal to sign is easily made and in fact it must be said that the same mimetic expression can be regarded simultaneously as both signal and sign if we consider the mimetic expression from the point of view of the person who perceives and is observing it.

The definition of mimicry just presented only seems to cover a large range of expressions and movements, because even in the case of the narrow definition of mimicry offered by Dumas, one that restricts mimetic expressions to imitated expressions, *all* possible facial movements can be taken into account, because *all movements, including those that are non-conscious and spontaneous, can be repeated, imitated.* And if any particular mimetic movement cannot be imitated, it can, at least, be indicated. And so it becomes, either as an imitated expression or one that is indicated, the subject of mimicry, whether this is defined in a narrow or a broad fashion.

WORKS CITED

Buffon, Georges Louis Leclerc, comte de (1785) *Natural History: General and Particular,* vol. 2, William Smellie (trans.), London: printed for A. Strahan and T. Cadell.

Dumas, Georges (1933) "Les mimiques" [Mimetic Expressions] in Dumas and Ombredane (1933), 293–360.

Dumas, Georges and Ombredane, André (1933) *Nouveau traité* de psychologie [A New Treatise on Psychology], vol. 3, Paris: Alcan.

Engel, Johann Jakob (1785) *Ideen zu einer Mimik* [Ideas About Mimicry], Berlin.

MIMETIC SIGN AND MIMETIC SIGNAL

JINDŘICH HONZL

["Mimický znak a mimický příznak" was published in two parts. The first part under the current title in *Otázky divadla a filmu* (1947–1948), vol. 3, no. 1, pp. 29–35 and the second part under the title "Herecká inspirace" [Actor's Inspiration] in *Otázky divadla a filmu* (1947–1948), vol. 3, no. 2, pp. 81–94.]

Translated by Marta Filipová

Editor's note: The original title plays upon the shared stem of the words *znak* ("sign") and *příznak* ("signal"), the primary meaning of the latter being "symptom"; an equivalent pair is the German *das Zeichen* and *das Anzeichen*. "Signal" suggests more intentionality on the part of the agent than "symptom", but it at least lacks the medical implications of the latter.

The theory and practice of acting requires an answer to two key questions: the question of mimetic spontaneity and the question of the norm of mimetic expression. Both the theory and the practice of acting develop through overcoming their opposition.

Spontaneity is based on organic stimuli, on the instinctive, subconscious or non-conscious automatic nature of mimetic expression.

In mimicry, the norm involves putting a mimetic mask on an individual's face – the mask that people wear during social intercourse or the one needed by an actor communicating with an audience. It is not, naturally, a static mask but rather a machine, a motor mechanism that is set so as to perform certain sets of movements and that cannot or may not move in any other way.

An *organism* participates in spontaneous movement by means of its impulses, with all the complexity of the mysterious relationship between human physics, physiology and the mind reacting to the world. Spontaneous movement is the individual and unpredictable result of many complex impulses and processes, a result that reflects a *necessity* arising from *random* external and internal preconditions. Spontaneous movement is the movement of a person aiming to preserve or intensify life, as determined by the instinct for life, the instinct for self-preservation, the sexual instinct, the instinct for self-realization and so on. The aim or result of such a movement is to gain mastery over things that threaten the person's life.

At this point we can point to how the opposition between mimetic spontaneity and the mimetic norm developed historically, how science and at the same time art became conscious of it and – what we consider especially important – how they formulated this opposition or how they ignored its existence. The question of mimicry cannot be treated unless one takes into account the historical change in the terms that science and the arts have used; the concept of mimetic spontaneity has changed through the advancement of physiological and psychological research in the area of motor reactions (Pavlov's reflexology), in the area of the emotional centres of the brain and the activity of the sympathetic nervous system (the findings of Walter Bradford Cannon, Vladimir Bekhterev and others) and in the findings of psychoanalysis. Research in modern linguistics and aesthetics (Mukařovský 1970 [1936]) has established a new understanding of norms and signs. Discussion of the antinomy of spontaneous mimicry and mimicry governed by specific norms is not possible without taking these scientific findings into account. Consideration of the history of this issue will help us to formulate the concepts precisely.

Let us turn first to the natural scientist whose views dominated the second half of the nineteenth century and who proved to have the subtlest insight into spontaneity in the life of the individual. This is Charles Darwin. In *The Expression of the Emotions in Man and Animals* (1872) he is concerned with only one type of mimicry, that of its spontaneous expression. What is Darwin's understanding of mimetic expression? For him an expression is a "conserved habit",[1] that is a retained, habitual movement made by an individual or a historical succession of individuals that have found themselves time and time again in similar situations evoking love, hatred or fear. Where does the habit of holding the head erect, expanding the chest, planting one's feet firmly on the ground, clenching the fists, furrowing the brows in anger and so on come from? From the fact that "an indignant man unconsciously throws himself into a fitting attitude ready for attacking or striking his opponent, whom he will perhaps scan from head to foot in defiance" (Darwin 2009: 257). What is the origin of the habit of baring a canine tooth on one side of the mouth in anger? There is no straightforward answer, but one can assume with a large degree of probability, claims Darwin, that

from our affinity with the anthropomorphic apes our male semi-human progenitors possessed great canine teeth, and men are now occasionally born having them of un-

---

1   [Editor's note: "Conserved habit" appears in Honzl's Czech text in English, within quotation marks. However, this term does not appear in Darwin's text, where the only similar phrase is "inherited habit". It is clear that Honzl was not working from Darwin's work directly, but rather drawing on a translation made into some other language (most likely German or Russian).]

usually large size, with interspaces in the opposite jaw for their reception. We may further suspect, notwithstanding that we have no support from analogy, that our semi-human progenitors uncovered their canine teeth when prepared for battle. (Darwin 2009: 264)

Produced under similar circumstances, the movement of individuals repeats in the same manner, becomes a habit, is carried on by generations of offspring - is inherited. What we call a mimetic expression of anger is understood by Darwin as habitual movements preserved by inheritance and made by our ancestors out of elementary necessity, repeated by their descendants under similar or analogous circumstances that resemble these elementary circumstances in some way, even metaphorically. Anger and other kinds of emotional excitement are *signals*, the *residue* of movements that our human ancestors made in a real attack, in defence, while fleeing and so on. The expression of anger and of other emotions is thus a leftover, a throwback, preserved through inheritance, which today seems illogical and pointless; once, however, these expressions found their logic and purpose - and this may still be true today - in the needs of the individual adapting successfully to the circumstances in the surrounding world.

In addition to conserved habits, Darwin also described two other types of mimetic expression: first, expressions that are produced under the direct effect of the nervous system (growing pale or red, crying and so on) and second, expressions that are said to originate on the basis of the general principle that certain feelings are accompanied by movements that are the opposite of those accompanying the opposite feelings. For example, cats *press themselves flat to the ground* before attacking, while they *arch* their backs when they wish to be stroked.

Both of these principles of Darwin's have since been abandoned, but it is useful to recall them in order to show that here too he only took into consideration *spontaneous mimicry*.

Whether Darwin's explanation reflects reality or not - and it is certainly not our purpose to pronounce on this - it is still important for us because it reveals how the science of the individualistic nineteenth century (of which Darwin was a typical representative) examines and systematizes only those mimetic phenomena that are the function of a system inherent in the *individual living organism* when reacting to systematic (or random) changes in external circumstances. (In fact Darwin does not deal with those "external circumstances" to which an individual must react; these are of no scientific interest to him whatsoever. Darwin presupposes them but does not concern himself with them; he does not study how they shape the individual. He focuses *only on the individual in whom* the emotional movements and changes are expressed.)

The systematic nature of the human organism is *impossible to grasp* owing to its diversity and complexity; it will remain as such unless this complexity can be understood as a *unity* of a kind. The systematic nature of external circumstances is one of *chance* – and it will remain such unless this chance is understood as an inherent *necessity* of its kind.

The science of the nineteenth century did not resolve this task of dialectical understanding, and the study of mimicry was no exception. For Darwin, it is only the *spontaneity* of mimetic reaction that serves as a guarantee as to whether a particular mimetic expression is or is not part of that sphere of systematic knowledge that is the proper province of the scientist. The criterion and aim of Darwin's research is to prove by *description* the *agreement* of scientific fact with reality and to find as many proofs of this agreement as possible in the mass of documented facts. For Darwin's scientific explanation of the mimetic phenomenon is an attempt to describe truthfully the history of the phenomenon. For him the truthfulness of the description is a guarantee of its scientific character – that is, of its systematic nature, determined objectively by a living organism.

We are therefore not surprised that Darwin's treatise on mimicry is entitled *The Expression of the Emotions in Man and Animals*. Darwin is not concerned with the specific features of *human* mimetic display, with the specifics that turned it into a mimetic language for social intercourse among people. Instead, Darwin is interested in the *biological organic character of mimicry*. He only studies mimicry that is *common* to both humans and animals. It may be argued it is natural for the biological side of the issue to be the most important for a natural scientist and that all else is secondary for him. Of course – yet for Darwin there is no social background, there is only the individual and his expression. Moreover, we do not take into account that even animal expressions, for instance those indicating anxiety and serving as a warning, have a social function, signalling danger to the family or the herd.

These issues of scientific method and objectives would remain outside our main interest – even though they concern mimicry – were it not possible to use precisely these issues to document the intellectual climate of the second half of the nineteenth century, which was expressed not only in science but also in art.

For artistic work in the theatre in the second half of the nineteenth century as well, *agreement with reality* was the main criterion and a faithful description the most reliable artistic method. For this period as well a *historical description* of human lives meant *understanding* them; this replaced *explaining* them. There is no need here to dwell at length on evidence of the descriptive, "truthful" photographic depiction of reality in the art of the late nineteenth century. Let us only add to this generally familiar matter that this tendency was testimony to *a weakened confidence in the ability of the intellect to systematize in the world of science* and to a weakened confidence in *the ability of the human spirit to bring form to the world of art.* The limitation of scientific research to *bio-history* took place alongside the limitation of artistic work to a focus on *description and truthful depiction.*

It is striking that the orientation of science as seen, for example, in Darwin, leads to the same conclusions as the artistic theories and artistic practice of realist directors at the end of the nineteenth century. Stanislavsky's books (*My Life in Art* and *An Actor Prepares*) give the most comprehensive and best evidence of this. Darwin's bio-historical (rather than biological) interest in the expression of emotions in humans arrives at the same point of view employed by Stanislavsky as the basis for his work and his theories. Where Darwin limits his research into mimicry to spontaneous movements, Stanislavsky too strives for *spontaneity of movement.* His aim is to exclude from acting and from the stage "the mechanical signs of non-existent emotion" (Stanislavski 2008: 254) and to base his method of acting and the art of acting on "the truth of [one's] feelings, mental and physical, the truth of the inner creative fire that is seeking to find expression" (Stanislavski 2008: 261).

The truth of feeling and of the inner creative fire – this is simply another way of saying the spontaneity of the spirit, which wishes to express itself regardless of the forced, mechanically acquired and empty conventions of life and artistic creation. The truth of feeling and experience is Stanislavsky's term for what Darwin calls the spontaneous expression of affective excitement. Where Darwin's focus on affective spontaneity led to the omission, in his research, of expressions produced by the conscious will or formed by social conventions, Stanislavsky's interest in spontaneity in acting led to the exclusion of all conventional mimetic expressions and to the rejection of all methods of expression on the part of the actor that had been acquired externally, without his creative spontaneity. Stanislavsky is suspicious of all the mimetic norms of the craft of acting and is unwilling to accept even those that are indispensable for the art of acting and that form the basis of the theatre. He regards as absurd the very basis of the theatre and theatricality – the fact that an actor does not exist for himself but is here because of the audience, that his speech is not the direct expression of his most subjective feelings but is intended for the audience. Time and time again Stanislavsky analyses the absurdity of the subject, brooding endlessly on this unattainable goal of his profession:

Imagine you have been placed in a high spot in Red Square in front of hundreds of thousands of people. A woman whom, perhaps, you have never met, has been placed next to you. You are ordered to fall madly in love with her in the public gaze so that you will die for her. But you're not up to being a lover. You feel embarrassed. A hundred thousand eyes are fixed on you, expecting you to make them cry, a thousand want to be thrilled by your ideal, selfless, passionate love because they have paid money for it and want you to give them what they have paid for. They, naturally, want to hear everything you are saying and so you have to shout the tender words which, in life, you would whisper looking into a woman's eyes. You have to be seen, understood by everyone and so you have to make moves and gestures that can be seen by those sitting farthest away. Can you think of love, can you even experience the feeling of love in such circumstances? All you do is force, strain and huff and puff, helpless as you are before an impossible task. (Stanislavski 2008: 255-56)

As with Darwin's scientific concerns, in the case of Stanislavsky's artistic concerns there is no mimetic *message*, no need for any mimetic communication, and no need for the actor to communicate with the audience. In this sense we can see the views of Darwin and Stanislavsky as creating an opposition between mimetic message and mimetic expression. Both men examine or are concerned with mimetic *expression*, both also dismiss – or take into account only incidentally and because they are forced in a kind of way to do so by the factual state of things – the mimetic *message*. If the mimetic expression comprises everything that is the spontaneous expression of the individual's inner self, the mimetic message is thought of as mimetic phenomena formed by external conventions and imposed from outside on the individual's inner self for the needs of social contact.

Mimetic expression arising from social contact or directed towards it escaped Darwin's attention. In a similar way, Stanislavsky excluded from the actor's expression those methods of acting that do not originate directly from the inner impulses of the individual actor but are conditioned by the existence of the spectator and the theatre, that is, by the actors' need to be in contact with a community of spectators.

We have shown that the opposition between standardized mimetic movement (determined by certain social conventions serving the purpose of communication between the actor and the audience) and spontaneous mimetic movement (through which the individual manifests himself openly through the direct expression of his inner state, regardless of the social environment) is dealt with by Stanislavsky in favour of spontaneous, non-standardized mimetic movement. Here Stanislavsky is in agreement with the theory of Darwin, whose treatise on mimetic expression in humans and animals is also restricted to spontaneous, socially non-standardized mimetic expressions.

Before we point out the impossibility of resolving such a conception of the opposition of spontaneity and conscious intention, it is useful to note the methodological effect of this view of Stanislavsky's on artistic creation.

Having started with a rejection of routine "craftsmanship", its norms and stereotypical patterns (see Stanislavsky 1921), Stanislavsky turns to *feeling* as the only source of mimetic expression. Experiencing affective excitement is for him the guarantee of spontaneity, and Stanislavsky identifies this with what he terms the *truthfulness* of expression. In the text mentioned above he claims that "a gesture must accompany feeling and not words; *gesture must be born out of feeling...*" (Stanislavsky 1921 – emphasis J. H.). "Be born out of feeling" – note this term "be born", which is intended to bolster the view that a work of art is not *created* but is *born* organically, in a manner similar to the way a flower grows or a bird flies. But to be born out of feeling is too vague a methodological guide for artistic work. Whole chapters of *My Life in Art*, and in fact the entire book, are devoted to the issue of how to find and define a method of artistic work and how to make it comprehensible and accessible to others, when emotion struggles so powerfully not to be constrained by a definition or method.

"I started looking for an alternative physical and mental state that would help, not harm, the creative process. In contrast to the *actor's state* let us agree to call it the *creative state*" (Stanislavski 2008: 256).

It is clear from these few words that Stanislavsky is searching for a path to inspiration that he wishes to make accessible to every actor or – as he argues – to "everyone in the theatre" (Stanislavski 2008: 256). Many pages of the book document this search; Stanislavsky keeps returning to the same question: "How was I to save my work from decline, from spiritual death, from the tyranny of ingrained actor's habits and external schooling? ... I needed, before attempting to be creative, to enter into that spiritual mood in which creative work is alone possible" (Stanislavski 2008: 255).

When it comes to the question of inspiration, Stanislavsky is troubled by several things. The difficulty of finding an answer leads him to revise the widely held view of inspiration in order to define it and fit the conception of inspiration to the particular task at hand – that of finding a method of acting, one based on the spontaneity of emotional experience.

The main issue is the uncontrollable nature of inspiration. "True, sometimes by chance, without knowing the reason why, we had a flash of inspiration... These moments of good fortune happened to me as to other colleagues, *but chance, evidently, is no basis for art*" (Stanislavski 2008: 192 – emphasis J. H.).

Stanislavsky points to two issues here. First, the random nature of inspiration and second, the inability of random inspiration to serve as the basis for art.[2]

---

2   It is interesting that Stanislavsky also tries to avoid the problem by not calling inspiration by its true name. Instead, he always uses synonyms or a general, figurative term. When reading *My Life in Art*, a book whose main topic is in fact the struggle for "inspired acting", we find no use of the word "inspiration". Instead, Stanislavsky talks about "a gift of the gods" (257), "creative intuition"

While the random nature of inspiration is an accepted fact, it is not accepted that random inspiration could not be capable of giving birth to art. The random nature of inspiration does not prevent poets, musicians, painters and other artists from consistently claiming it as the source of their work. The misrepresentation that Stanislavsky introduces here in his explanation of inspiration is undoubtedly caused by the special requirements of acting. Stanislavsky is faced with a fatal antinomy: either inspiration prevails in acting as in the other arts, or acting lacks inspiration – and in that case it cannot be art, just mere craftsmanship. It is no surprise that Stanislavsky avoids this fatal formulation by shifting the meaning of the term "inspiration" to include acting too. Throughout the nineteenth century inspiration maintained its aristocratic stance and garb. If it was not solely possessed by geniuses, it was at least a precious possession of the chosen. It sanctified its priests and rulers, distinguished them from the crowd, gave them the power to speak for everyone or against everyone.

Stanislavsky could not lay claim to the divine inspiration of artists of the nineteenth century, nor could he recommend it to actors as a source or goal. The mysteries of the Dionysia could not become the actor's daily job. He was not interested in inspiration for geniuses and the chosen. He sought creative ecstasy for "everyone in the theatre". And forced by this need, he came up with a daring claim, one that could be called a revolutionary view of inspiration: "... everyone in the theatre, from the genius to the journeyman actor, can achieve the creative state to a greater or lesser degree mysteriously, by intuition" (Stanislavski 2008: 256–57).

It was not only a theoretical tactical necessity that led Stanislavsky to this formulation. The statement also contains some of the insight, some of the experience he had gained by studying genuine artistic work. Dealing himself with the demands of art, both as actor and director, in itself helped him to correct the romantic view of inspiration. His correction is neither complete nor consistent. It goes no further than Stanislavsky's own experience of actual work in the theatre. An active director cannot base his theories on assumptions that contradict his everyday experience. Guided by such experience, Stanislavsky learned to transfer the secrets of inspiration to the realm of the transcendent and not to appeal to the views of the kind of fideism that

---

(192), "the creative state" (258), "the living truth of feelings" (195) and so on, never directly about inspiration.

[Editor's note: Honzl's assertion that Stanislavsky "never" speaks directly about inspiration is mistaken. The standard term for "inspiration" in Russian is *vdokhnoveniye*, a word that is constructed analogously to its Latin-based counterparts in Western European languages (in + spirare – "to breathe into"). This term, in various forms, in fact occurs regularly in Stanislavsky's text. However, it is also true that Stanislavsky frequently chooses other ways to express the concept of inspiration, as illustrated above.]

believes it is celebrating art and inspiration, calling them divine, whereas this is actually a characterization that denigrates individuals because it denies the human origin of artistic creativity. Stanislavsky, as a director engaged in both practice and theory, faces a specific task: to create a methodology of acting as art and seek its real prerequisites. One of them – the main one – is found in the imagination, which Stanislavsky says cannot be denied to "people in the theatre". He considers imagination to be an indispensable condition for artistic creation and the liberation of imagination to be its precondition.

The actor's imagination is connected in a special way with the instrument of his art, his body. In his experiments Stanislavsky keeps finding out that imagination has no power or influence over the actor unless the paths and the means by which it is manifested in the actor are liberated. Imagination does not move a single muscle of the actor's body until the latter is freed from the tension caused by the job of not going beyond a pre-arranged model and until it is prepared to react immediately to every ideomotor nervous stimulus arising in the actor's consciousness on the basis of his imagination "Initially, I merely noticed that *bodily relaxation, the absence of muscular tension,* and the total obedience of the physical apparatus, played an important role in the creative state, in me as well as others" (Stanislavski 2008: 257–58 – emphasis J. H.).

Stanislavsky's methodological discovery is based on the realization that the liberation of the actor's imagination requires liberation of the *body*. However, the body – not only the physics but also the physiology of the body – continues to remain an "instrument" of ideas and feelings, ready and willing to accept every ideomotor stimulus and suppress every mental change related to the imagination or the emotions.

Stanislavsky insists that the mind and the body stand in incompatible opposition to one other. He understands the physical body to be a mechanical set of organs that are subject to mental command. In this sense, Stanislavsky is concerned with "the total obedience of the physical apparatus" (Stanislavski 2008: 257) to the actor's will. Stanislavsky's idea of mental spontaneity is accompanied by the need for a total discipline binding the actor's body. Spontaneity is therefore transformed into the *motor discipline of the body*, governed by volitional intent. The physics and physiology of the body are denied the right to spontaneity; as a result, they cannot be brought to bear positively when it comes to inspiration of movement. We can call this understanding of the actor's spontaneity artistic finalism, for here we have movement being totally, absolutely brought to bear on the actor's artistic expression, which should be the purest expression of the spirit, that is of the artist's ideas.

It is striking that scientists criticize Darwin's view and his explanation of the mimetic expression of impressions as reflecting a similar, but in this case *biological*, finalism. They say that, ultimately, the spontaneous mimetic expression that Darwin explains as the "conserved habit" of a movement that was originally made by prehistoric man as a *purposeful and intentional* form of attack, escape or defence, and that was automatized through heredity – that this spontaneous movement is no longer an example, viewed dimly through associations and heredity, of the *intentional influence of the conscious will on the body*. Further to the criticism of Darwin's view we shall add a quotation from Georges Dumas:

> In assuming the participation of an act of the will, whether obscure or clear, in the origins of so many useful habits … [Darwin] created a comfortable hypothesis according to which, following its own logic, the mechanical expression of emotions appears in the end to have its origin in being *imposed on the body* by the spirit; and in assuming that the usefulness of a habit explains not only its origin but also its transfer by selection in the species, he is linked implicitly to a *finalism* as hypothetical as that of Spencer's. (Dumas 1933: 60 – emphasis J. H.)

The finalism of Darwin and Stanislavsky could only have been created on the basis of an incorrect or at least an incomplete division of expressive movements into the spontaneous and the volitional. This simplified division of movements points all too clearly to a similar simplicity in the opposition of mind and body; we have already said that the kind of finalist contrast between spontaneity and volitional intent as that assumed by Darwin and Stanislavsky does not lead to any real conclusion. The construction created by Darwin's theories and Stanislavsky's theoretical ideas collapses when we point to the fact that spontaneity and volitional intent overlap in habitual and automatic movements, that reflexive and instinctive movements should be added to the division of movements that Darwin and Stanislavsky simplified into a pair of opposites, and that *conscious* and *volitional movements* are only the *fifth* item in this series, whose very existence rules out the two-member schematic opposition of spontaneity and intentionality.

We regard spontaneity as the most characteristic attribute of inspiration. Yet we should not forget that the actor's inspiration is an inspiration of *movement*, inspiration that is manifested in gestures and in facial and vocal mimicry. Let us seek the actor's inspiration in bodily spontaneity and here we show that acting is an art governed by a special kind of inspiration, one that differs from the inspiration for literature, music, painting or sculpture. *It must be acknowledged that all automatized movements, whether instinctive, reflexive, habitual or of any other type, have a decisive influence on the actor's inspiration, and that the part of human existence understood by Stanislavsky as merely the "body", which should obey commands from the mind – that this part of the body has the same regulatory influence on external expression as the conscious mind, and that it also gives "deliberate" commands of a kind, that it is also part of the mind.*

The relaxation or liberation of the body that Stanislavsky calls for would only be truly meaningful if it freed up *bodily* spontaneity, whose automatisms are linked to the mind by complex relations. Stanislavsky, however, does not free the body for this purpose. He relaxes the body so that it can become the obedient instrument of a spontaneity that is completely non-corporeal, that is, of products of the imagination taking shape in the mind with no relation to the mechanics of the body. If Stanislavsky assigns inspiration to the "mind" alone ("mind" in the sense of the old opposition of the body and the soul), the "body" has no choice but to obey.

The relaxation of the body that Stanislavsky's method advocates as an instrument for awakening the actor's inspiration cannot lead to positive outcomes, even though the relaxation and liberation of the body is the true precondition for every instance of spontaneity.

The relaxation of the body called for by Stanislavsky is not a true liberation of the body. It is an absolving of the body that strips it of all activity. It is only the negative side of true liberation, as true liberation must mean freedom of *action*. The origins of the actor's inspiration will not be found unless the body is liberated along with the mind, unless the source of the actor's inspiration is sought in its *activity* (and not just in the activity of the mind).

It is curious that Stanislavsky failed to appreciate the complex nature of the relations between the body and the mind. For acting could be considered the best example and the most suitable application of *muscular* memory, *muscular* spontaneity and hence *muscular* inspiration. Acting, after all, is an expression of the external and the actor's material – his body – takes pride of place in his every expression. Stanislavsky recognized this influence wherever his sense of reality and his feel for specific artistic work revealed it to him. (It was even enough for him, offstage, to assume Stockmann's ways and mannerisms for the feelings that had given rise to them to come alive in his heart [Stanislavski 2008: 217].) Nevertheless, his insights on muscular memory, the influence of muscular feeling on the mind and the influence of physical relaxation on inspiration did not lead him to draw any of the conclusions that offered themselves in this connection. Shaped by the philosophical and scientific views of his age, he only achieved true knowledge by discovering, through the aid of these views, facts that brought him into conflict with them. The fact that "Stockmann's ways and mannerisms" – that is, the gestures and the facial expressions of a specific role, repeated externally – give birth to feelings and emotions with which the movements were once associated, contradicts the all-encompassing power of the mind that Stanislavsky professes. For in this case it was muscular memory and muscular feeling that evoked ideas and emotions in the actor. This is in direct conflict with Stanislavsky's views, for in this case the *movement of the body controls the spirit*, its feelings and emotions. In this connection let us recall Gotthold Ephraim Lessing's theories: he wished to found a system of acting based on muscular memory and on the influence that *motor feelings* have on the mind. In his *Hamburg Dramaturgy* Lessing claims that

> the quick pace; the stamping foot; the raw, now shrieking, now grim tone; the play of eyebrows; the trembling lips; the grinding of teeth, etc. – I repeat, if he imitates just these things that can be mimicked and does so well: then his soul will without question be overtaken by *a dark feeling of anger*, which will then in turn provoke a reaction in the body and bring about those changes that cannot be controlled by our will. (Lessing: par. 6; emphasis J. H.)

And we are reminded here not only of Lessing and Diderot (and his *Paradox of Acting*) but also of the James-Lange hypothesis on the origins of emotions as well as of the modern behaviourists. They claim that organic sensations (the sensations of breathing, the heartbeat, vegetative innervation) are the actual source of emotions. "We do not cry," they argue, "because we are sad, rather we are sad because we cry."

We do not wish to exploit quotations from Lessing or references to Diderot, James and the behaviourists to promote the mechanical and rationalistic view of the eighteenth century and its modern version, nor do we wish to exclude the imagination as a source of inspiration for the actor's movement – in other words, we do not wish to deny the participation of visual and acoustic impressions as sources of inspiration for the actor's movement. But we want to show that Stanislavsky misunderstood the nature of the actor's inspiration when he situated it only in an *imagined consciousness* that evokes impressions through *motor stimuli*. Stanislavsky does not recognize that the precondition for an actor's inspiration is the complex relationship between a whole set of impressions, amongst them *motor muscular impressions*, which are especially important for actors. By "muscular impressions" we mean traces preserved by the muscular memory. These traces are not usually called impressions because they retain their own specific, subconscious character when being evoked.

Stanislavsky, however, completely rejected muscular memory and muscular "impressions". He accuses them of leading over time to a degeneration of the role and of making the role "an empty shell, dust and ashes that had stuck in the mind and in the body, which had nothing to do with genuine art" (Stanislavski 2008: 254). Stanislavsky attributes only negative influences and traits to muscular memory. Through its influence, he had "mechanically created the habit of going through these technical gymnastics" and mindlessly repeated his fixed "habits as a performer" (Stanislavski 2008: 254). An actor who plays the same role on a daily basis for weeks, months or even years and repeats the same movements and words inevitably automatizes his performance to such an extent that he does not need any special mental concentration, let alone inspiration. From the point of view of the actor's mental balance and health this phenomenon must be considered a necessity. Every theorist of the art of acting must take this necessity into account, just as theatre practice does. Rehearsals are nothing but a guide and preparation for the automatization of certain aspects of acting, whether vocal (memorizing the role) or related to gestures and facial expressions.

However, the fact that the actor's performance becomes automatized by repetition is not proof for us that acting should not be an *inspired* art and that it is not suffused with creative élan. If we wish to maintain acting's right to inspiration and to being called an art, the way of thinking about the actor's physical performance and the mental basis of the actor's inspiration must be stripped of the mistaken view that presupposes in the actor's creative act an independent mind shackling and mastering the body, a mistaken view that *links the determined character of the body's physics to the non-determined character of mental inspiration.*

We can only understand the historical function of this mistaken view of the art of acting by looking at the artistic practice from which it arose, which it suited and which it also served. In doing so, we will also show the reasons why Stanislavsky (and the whole "realist" theatre of the end of the nineteenth century) rejected muscular automatism, the fixed habits of actors and all "professional 'craftsmanship'".

Realist acting – that is, the acting of the generation that found its purest expression in the art of Hana Kvapilová[3] – is tied by its theatrical means of expression to automatisms alone. The actor's motor and vocal expression was not and could not be anything else but the most faithful image of the vocal and motor mimicry of real people. The mimicry of the characters on stage had to match the mimicry of their models, who were to be found walking in the streets, labouring in workshops, living in houses and suffering in schools, prisons and hospitals. *Only those motor conventions that life had automatized through continual repetition were allowed on the stage.* These automatisms totally dominated the stage and the actors and for some time this even resulted in free creation on the part of the actor being banished from the stage completely. In fact inspiration was impossible for actors when it came to movement. Acting meant no more than ranking and sorting out vocal automatisms and automatisms of movement, while the question of acting method was not to learn stage movement and stage diction and on the basis of these to discover *new* movements and vocal practices. As against this, Stanislavsky's aim was to reject all theatrical conventions of movement and voice and to replace

---

3   [Editor's note: Hana Kvapilová (1860–1907), widely regarded as the leading Czech actress of her generation, noted for her advanced views and dedication to women's emancipation.]

them with spontaneity of movement and voice, that is with movements and speech that are automatic, unconscious, on the part of everyone when greeting someone, when giving orders, when persuading someone and so forth. But acting technique could not consist in these automatisms – the technique was everyone's property. The actor's problem lay in the *interpretation* of the role, that is the method and intention according to which the automatisms of movement and voice needed to be ordered. It was not, and could never have been, a matter of non-automatized movements and non-conventional vocal expressions. The memoirs, critiques, analyses and theories of the generation of actors and directors to which Kvapilová and Stanislavsky belonged contain no traces or evidence of creative work relating to vocal technique or the technique of movement in acting. It will suffice to go through the literary remains of Hana Kvapilová and her analyses of roles: it is amazing that we can find nothing related specifically to acting, that references to gestures are scarce and that if there are any, they are limited merely to conventional automatisms: "She strokes her [Irena's] cheeks, lost in thought" (Kvapilová 1932: 352); "She stops her ears [and] whistles" and "bursts into tears" (Kvapilová 1932: 353). On the other hand, her notes on studying for a role in Jaroslav Kvapil's *The Clouds* [Oblaka] overflow with terms relating to *psychological moods, feelings, desires* – and our best actress of the generation of the 1890s records them as the *technical terms of acting*:

> Mája Zemanová enters, *stirred by memories*. Meeting Petr, she is a conventional woman of the world, but *her memories resonate with feeling as they talk*. She warms up and *becomes lively* as she gets to know Petr and when she meets Kociánová and the priest. *Within her there bursts into song* all the goodness of a pure-hearted person, freed for a moment from the world of theatre. Its filth vanished utterly when Mája came to the countryside and today, at this moment, in this holiday liberation, there is *within her the strongest, most beautiful joy*. (Kvapilová 1932: 336; emphasis J. H.)

We find the same focus on the mind and the same dismissal of the body, bodily movement and vocal expression in both the great realist actress and the brilliant realistic director. *Mood, emotion* determine acting technique; the body is subordinate to them in all respects. Creative work and inspiration have to do with *deep emotion, experience and suffering* alone. This is what establishes the prerogatives of the artist vis-à-vis the non-artist. Mimicry, bodily movement and vocal expression are not the subjects of technical study, because they are inherent in every ordinary individual; the imitation of voice and gesture is "ingrained" in all people. That is why it is necessary to *live* on the stage – not just to gesture and modulate the voice. If a dramatic character experiences and feels deeply enough, then mimicry will emerge on its own, spontaneously, *automatically*. But it should be added that this will be the mimicry of realist drama and the realist stage. The methodology of realist acting, which, through the voices of its great representatives, declares war on all acting conventions and that sees muscular automatism as the destruction of the art of acting – all this is based on automatisms and conventions.

Why and how is it that realist acting did not recognize this contradiction? Or – how did it recognize it? One tendency that had been present in views on the art of acting since time immemorial took on definitive shape in realist acting. This is the assumption that mimicry – and especially facial and vocal mimicry – is spontaneous and that it mirrors an inner state, that through these expressions one can view and gauge changes in the spirit within. Darwin and Wilhelm Wundt articulated this assumption clearly in the case of scientific research while Richard Wagner's claims can be invoked here in the case of art.

In his work *The Expression of the Emotions in Man and Animals*, Darwin states the following: "The movements of expression give vividness and energy to our spoken words. They reveal the thoughts and intentions of others more truly than do words, which may be falsified" (Darwin 2009: 386). Darwin thus pits *artificial* words, which can be falsified, against *natural*, spontaneous mimicry, which – judging from the opposition – *cannot* be falsified.

In Henri Lichtenberger's *Richard Wagner: Poet and Thinker*, Wagner's views are presented as follows:

> First and foremost the orchestra translates for the ear what the gestures of various characters in the play signify for the eye. As a matter of fact the gesture expresses something that the words cannot convey. A person does not gesture as long as he addresses only the intellect of the person he is speaking with; he limits himself to words alone. If, on the contrary, he wants to affect his feelings, he immediately adds a gesture to the words and makes the gesture express precisely an excess of emotions that cannot be expressed in speech. (Lichtenberger 1898: 241)

For the moment, let us not challenge the claim that speech cannot express the *excess of emotions* that gesture can. Wagner overlooks the fact that speech, too, has its own mimicry and expressive quality reflecting inner emotional states. The trembling of the voice or the degree of intensity, the interruption of the stream of words with laughter or crying, are all very effective methods of vocal mimicry. Let us examine, however, other aspects of Wagner's views. Although there is no specific mention of mimetic spontaneity, it is present implicitly in the opposition between word and gesture, which Wagner interprets as the opposition between intentional reason and spontaneous feeling. If we consider this more closely, it is the same as the opposition between words, "which may be falsified", and mimetic expression, which is sincere because it is an expression of emotional spontaneity. The conscious mind can choose false words; feeling, which controls gestures, is either a natural and truthful trigger for gesture or it is nothing. The actor who is truly mastered by emotion cannot express himself in mimicry other than internally, truthfully, spontaneously – or however else we wish to express the genuine, natural *automatism* of the relationship between emotion and mimicry. The theory and methodology of acting therefore turned its attention to *feeling* and to the methods of evoking it in an actor. For according to this view, feeling automatically resolves all the technical difficulties and problems of mimicry. The expressive automatism of feeling encompasses everything that acting methodology can be based on, it encompasses everything that might be sought as the perfection of the art of acting. "'That means,' I said to myself, 'that you have to feel the role and then everything takes care of itself'" (Stanislavski 2008: 245).

"Communication of feeling" (Stanislavski 2008: 255), "the beauty and excitement of inner truth" (Stanislavski 2008: 254), to "set our innermost feelings ablaze" (Stanislavski 2008: 196), "in the pauses, or the way actors look at each other or in the way they radiate inner feeling" (Stanislavski 2008: 192) – all of these are Stanislavsky's expressions. In his view, the acting system has to teach the candidate first, how to awaken feeling and second, how to make every expression of the body dependent on it. We have already mentioned the liberation and relaxation of the body, which for Stanislavsky is the first technical means of acting coming from within, that is full of feeling. The body, its nervous and muscular systems, liberated and relaxed, must submit to the mind and feeling as its sole master and commander. It must learn to obey every subtle emotional stimulus. The question, however, is how to find the commander – feeling. In *The Aesthetics of Dramatic Art*, Otakar Zich claims that "it is impossible to remember feelings, one can only have them" (Zich 1931: 152). Feelings therefore cannot be "recalled", they have to be *awakened*. Stanislavsky, too, recognizes this psychological fact, which is the core of the problem.

Feelings accompany the perception of reality or accompany the stream of impressions. The reality perceived by the actor is the stage with its set, colleagues with makeup and the faces of the spectators hidden in the dark. This reality can only create anxiety, embarrassment, resistance or derision and irony in the actor. It is possible to laugh at such a false reality or to turn away from it in embarrassment. But if deep feelings inspiring his artistic creation are to develop, the first priority is to free the actor from those feelings that the reality of the stage creates in him most immediately and most strongly.

Stanislavsky recorded the circumstances and various techniques that helped him to rid himself of his fear of the audience and made him forget "that I was onstage":

This new chance discovery led me to another elementary truth which I felt (i.e. understood) deeply: that I felt good and at ease onstage because, apart from muscular release,
the exercises I did in public in focusing attention and relaxing the body distracted my
attention from what was going on beyond the footlights in the auditorium beyond the
black hole. (Stanislavski 2008: 258)

The actor's perception therefore needs to be directed away from external
reality; he needs to be shown first the direction towards his own self, which
comes about when perception focuses on the reality of what one is feeling with
one's body. This concentration on the reality of one's own body is intended to
exclude the perception of external reality, that is to prevent external reality
from influencing the actor's feelings. Owing to this, however, inspirational
feelings are no longer evoked. The feelings raised in concentration are those
of general pleasure or displeasure, arising from the correct or interrupted
course of unconscious vegetative functions or from the smooth course of
conscious muscular, motor functions. For the actor, concentration on emotions of vegetative origin means concentration on a *mood*, whether pleasant or
unpleasant, depending on the overall state of health or illness of the body. This
would make the basic principle of the art of acting unstable, indeterminable,
unpredictable and so variable that it would lack any certainty. Let us recall
that a good mood, as determined by our being in good health, well fed and in
a peaceful state, leads us to enjoy giving ourselves over to *pleasant music*, while
the same music becomes torture if we are ill or hungry or if we are working.
How decisive a factor one's *state* was for realist actors could be observed on
every page of the memoirs and reflections of realist directors and actors. It is
no coincidence that in Stanislavsky's texts the "creative state" is a precondition for acting and the "actor's state" is regarded as its uncreative opposite:
"... naturally, I started looking for an alternative physical and mental state, that
would help, not harm, the creative process. In contrast with the *actor's state*,
let us agree to call it the *creative state*" (Stanislavski 2008: 256). Hana Kvapilová
sees the changeability of mood as the main problem of the art of acting. She
opens her article "Women in Drama" [Žena v umění dramatickém] as follows:

If the actor could merge his being with the being created by the playwright, if he could
utterly deny himself, if he succeeds artistically in interpreting the role, he cannot and
must not claim that the following night he will capture his conception of the role as
perfectly as he did on the first night. Who can be certain that he will create a festive
day instead of a working day, that *he will be just as rich in mood, the mood necessary for
imagining the being*, combined emotionally and physically in just this way? It is a major
event ... if, in the same role played over several consecutive nights, an actor can claim
two identically felt, identically blest moments, two *moods experienced absolutely identically*. (Kvapilová 1932: 227–28; emphasis J. H.)

So we should not be surprised that Margaret in *Faust* changes along with the actress: "I'm looking forward to this evening, though I'm feeling much worse physically than ever. Tonight my timbre will be hidden in a little cloud, it will be murky, and this will take away from Margaret in her first scenes..." (Kvapilová 1932: 365). Nevertheless, the effectiveness of the role does not depend on the actress's mood alone; it is also dependent on the mood of the other actors. This is supported by another remark, this time in reference to *The Three Sisters*: "We had an irritated evening last night, even though the audience was much more decent. My Masha was tart and had new, bitter undertones even in her happiness" (Kvapilová 1932: 370).

In recommending that the actor should pay attention to the feelings of the body for the purpose of stimulating his *creative mood*, Stanislavsky certainly did not want to threaten the actor's certainty, the artistic meaning and intent of his role; he did not want to deliver a dangerous shock to the entire organism of the play and its unity. Yet this threat to certainty and unity follows necessarily from his methodological advice regarding muscular relaxation and concentration on the body's feelings. Stanislavsky's own practice as well as that of his colleagues prove this. But the director saw concentration on the feelings of the body not as something threatening the stability of the artistic whole, its unity and its meaning but rather as a means of ensuring – in his view – the *creative state*, that is a good, positive, encouraging mood that enables the actor's inner images and the feelings associated with them to appear in as favourable a setting as can be offered by the actor's inner self. His assumption is correct insofar as the actor's muscular relaxation and the peaceful state of the body he has consciously induced in himself bring about the innervational harmony of muscular tension and this harmony gives birth to an overall pleasant feeling, a general positive mood, which is a propitious starting point for any physical and mental activity. All this is correct and ingenious. However, the means promoted by Stanislavsky – to concentrate attention on the feelings of the body, by means of which this mood is supposed to enter the consciousness or control the mind – does not guarantee that the actor's mind will become the calm mirror of the surface of a lake, reflecting all the changing play of clouds and mirroring all the configurations of the eternal constellations in the darkness of the night, but rather that it will become the turbulent surface of the actor's subjectivity, for which there are no clouds or stars, only the driving and unstoppable force of his own inner self and his own moods, dependent on the innumerable and uncontrollable influences of his bodily health, unconscious needs and desires, instinctive impulses, elemental attractions or antipathies and the whole uncontrollable basis of his unconscious and subconscious, which lead to what Stanislavsky calls one's own physical feelings. Every work of art, every theatrical production can be shipwrecked on this stormy surface of the actor's subjectivity.

It seems that criticism of the methodological premises of realist acting has led us into a darkness from which there is no escape – that it has brought into play all its negative character and blocked even those routes to creativity on the part of the actor pointed out by the brilliant realist director. However, being in a position from which there is no escape is not the aim of our criticism but rather a characteristic feature of Stanislavsky's method of acting. The theory of this kind of acting must necessarily find itself in a dead end, even with all the new means devised by Stanislavsky, because it adopted a false theoretical assumption, that of the spontaneous mimetic automatism of emotional expression. Our criticism wishes to expose the error of this assumption by pointing to its consequences, which, as we have said, jeopardize the aim of the performance as theatre. We wish to divorce this false assumption from those devices of the technique of acting that were enlisted in its service and we wish to examine their qualities without regard to the erroneous assumption. It is possible for a good technical discovery to be used with a wrong end in mind, and so to fall. It must be uncoupled from this end.

We have already pointed out that muscular relaxation or liberation – which for Stanislavsky is a means by which the body is meant to be prepared for complete obedience to the mind – retains its positive significance only if it does not become fixed on the negative aspect of the process of liberation, but instead develops it further. This means that it does not settle merely for liberating the body from the apposite functions but grants freedom to *its own* functions, which are inherent in it as an organism and through which it can express itself. If this freedom of the functions of the organism of the body is not included among the various preconditions of the technique of acting, its system will be incomplete and will be violated when it comes to its specific device and basic material – that is, the actor's body. On the other hand, the correct formulation of the actor's bodily liberation can also reveal to us the path to the cul-de-sac in which the realist methodology found itself through its use of another device – concentration on the feelings of the body. Variability, uncertainty and the danger of *moods* were the subversive result. Yet Stanislavsky's insight regarding total concentration contains a fruitful core. No performance is possible without intense concentration. However, it is incorrect to concentrate solely on *bodily relaxation* – that is, to an absence of activity and an absence of action. The emotional background that results from such concentration is so little attended by pleasure that it can easily be overcome by any vegetative feelings, which results in a complete change in mood. The only way of excluding the influence of a mood (that is of general physical feeling) on a dramatic performance is by bringing into play more strongly an attendant feeling that is also created by bodily stimuli, by *actions of the body.* Such feeling necessarily suppresses the mood arising from inactivity, excludes its subversive influences and unifies the actor's thinking and feeling, focusing it on the performance and the role.

WORKS CITED

Darwin, Charles (2009), Francis Darwin (ed.), *The Expression of the Emotions in Man and Animals*, Cambridge: Cambridge University Press.

Dumas, Georges (1933) "L'expression des émotions" [The Expression of Emotions] in Dumas and Ombredane (1933), pp. 39-292.

Dumas, Georges and Ombredane, André (1933) *Nouveau traité de psychologie* [A New Treatise on Psychology], vol. 3, Paris: Alcan.

Kvapilová, Hana (1932) *Literární pozůstalost Hany Kvapilové* [The Literary Remains of Hana Kvapilová], Prague: Šolc a Šimáček.

Lessing, Gotthold Ephraim, *Hamburg Dramaturgy*, Essay 3, accessed online at: <http://mcpress.media-commons.org/hamburg/>

Lichtenberger, Henri (1898) *Richard Wagner: Poête et penseur* [Richard Wagner: Poet and Thinker], Paris: Félix Alcan.

Mukařovský, Jan (1970 [1936]) *Aesthetic Function, Norm and Value as Social Facts*, Mark E. Suino (trans.), special issue of *Michigan Slavic Contributions*, vol. 3, Ann Arbor: The University of Michigan Press.

Stanislavsky, Konstantin (1921) "O remesle" [On Craftsmanship], *Kultura teatra*, vol. 5, pp. 10-14; vol. 6, pp. 23-24.

Stanislavski, Konstantin (2008) *My Life in Art*, trans. Jean Benedetti, London: Routledge.

Zich, Otakar (1931) *Estetika dramatického umění: teoretická dramaturgie* [The Aesthetics of Dramatic Art: A Theoretical Dramaturgy], Prague: Melantrich.

A CONTRIBUTION TO THE SEMIOTICS
OF ACTING

JIŘÍ VELTRUSKÝ

[Originally written in English, this was published as Veltruský, Jiří (1976) "Contribution to the Semiotics of Acting" in Matejka, Ladislav (ed.) *Sound, Sign and Meaning: Quinquagenary of the Prague Linguistic Circle*, Ann Arbor: The University of Michigan Press, pp. 553–606.]

Editor's note: This study was translated into Czech by the author and published in 1994 in *Příspěvky k teorii divadla* [Contributions to the Theory of Theatre], Prague: Divadelní ústav, pp. 162–88. Veltruský added a few details to his text, these have been translated into English by the editors and footnoted.

INTRODUCTION

Acting is to be examined here as a component of theatre; other possible aspects, such as film acting, elements of acting in everyday life, and so on, are beyond the scope of the present paper.

The fact that acting is a matter of semiotics has been perfectly obvious for a long time.[1] Yet the semiotic approach has proved particularly difficult in this field. Even the simple concepts worked out in the study of other sign systems tend to become confused here, so that semiotic analyses of details and partial aspects are still mostly anchored in the pre-semiotic, naive view of acting as the impersonation of a character.

The difficulty is mainly due to some of the basic features of acting:

1. Like theatre as a whole, as well as dance and film, acting is an art of both space and time (Zich 1931: 213–14) or, to put it differently, its *signantia* are organized at once in space and in time.

All these arts also use both auditory and visual signs (Zich 1931: 17–19). In this respect, however, theatre differs from film on the one hand and dance on the other. In film, auditory signs may be excluded and replaced by the sort of music that functions not as one of them but as a means of neutralizing their absence (Jakobson 2008 [1933]). In dance, the visual and the auditory signs (music), though linked through the beat, remain largely independent of each

---

1   It was recognized by such pioneers as Charles S. Peirce and Theodor Gomperz.

other (Zich 1931: 22–23), while in acting and theatre the signs belonging to both categories are integrated. It is true that visual signs are excluded from radio plays and auditory signs can be excluded from mime (even in forms of mime that include music, the musical accompaniment can be used merely to neutralize the absence of auditory signs, as in film). But radio plays and mime are perceived against the background of the theatre, which uses both types of signs.

These two characteristics of acting in the theatre seem to be interconnected. In Jakobson's view, an essential trait that distinguishes auditory and visual signs is that only time, never space, acts as a structural factor within the systems of auditory signs whereas the structuration of visual signs always involves space (Jakobson 1971b: 701; 1971e: 340; 1971f: 336). This conception is clearly contradicted by facial and head movements, gestures and bodily movements in general (to the extent that they are signs), which are organized in time to the same degree as in space; this is not a matter of "superinducing the time factor, as in the motion picture" (Jakobson 1971b: 701). Perhaps more thorough study of the signs concerned will explain this apparent contradiction.[2]

2. Human or anthropomorphic beings and their actions and behaviour, which are the *signatum* of acting, are represented by a *signans* of the same nature, namely by human beings and their actions and behaviour (exceptionally animals are represented by animals). Even the concept of similarity in its simplest semiotic sense of resemblance tends, therefore, to give way to the idea of sameness.

3. The material the actor uses is the actor himself – his own body, its properties and abilities, and even, to some extent, his ability to experience and express feelings that are not his own – so that the artist is personally present in his work or product, unlike the writer in his poem, the composer in his symphony or the painter in his picture, even a self-portrait. In this respect, only the reciter, the singer and the dancer are comparable to him because they, too, use only their own abilities as their material. Yet they use just one, or at most a few, of the properties and abilities of their body. Unlike the actor, therefore, they are personally present in their work only to a very limited extent – none of them can be said to become part of it.

---

2 An avenue may have been opened by Jakobsons's concept of "syncretic messages" based on a combination of different sign systems. Among several examples of "traditional syncretism" in ethnic cultures, the following seem to be relevant here: "Bodily visual signs display a propensity toward a combination with auditory sign systems, manual gestures and facial movements function as signs supplementary to verbal utterances or as their substitutes, whereas movements involving legs and the bulk of the body seem to be prevalently and in some ethnic cultures exclusively tied to instrumental music" (Jakobson 1971b: 705).

4. Acting is generally a collective performance. In so far as it merges the work of several artists or at least blurs the borderlines between them, its collective nature conflicts with the actor's personal presence in his work, which tends on the contrary to merge the artist with his own individual work.

5. Whenever the audience perceives the actor's work, he creates it in some measure afresh before their eyes. Rather than just beholding a work of art, the spectators see it in the making – they witness, at least to some extent, the act of its creation. This is also the case of the performing musician who, however, is not personally present in his work – he can only be seen as he produces it with his instrument or with the orchestra he conducts. The reciter, the singer and the dancer, who also, in a certain measure, create in front of the audience, come somewhat closer to the actor. But, as was pointed out, they differ from him by the very limited degree of their personal presence in the work they produce.

6. Not only do the spectators witness the act of creation, they also participate in it because it is either stimulated or hampered, but never unaffected, by their response.

Seen from the angle of other semiotic systems, all these are confusing factors. Yet they are central to the semiotics of acting.

THE SIGNANS

STAGE FIGURE

The first scholar, to my knowledge, who tried to make a clear distinction between the *signans* and the *signatum* in the field of acting was Otakar Zich. Without adopting these semiotic concepts – he was primarily concerned with the psychology of the perceiver – he separated the stage figure from the *dramatis persona* or character represented by that figure.[3] As he formulated it, this distinction needs to be thoroughly revised, especially because the relationships between the actor and the stage figure and between this *signans* and its *signatum* are much more complicated than first appeared. But Zich's identification of the stage figure as distinct from both actor and character remains valid.

As a rule, the stage figure confronts and combines with other stage figures. The figures form a structure within which each has a specific place of

---

3   See Zich 1931: 55–56. The literal translation of Zich's own term, *herecká postava*, would be the "actor's figure", an utterly misleading expression. I chose the somewhat barbarous "stage figure" because in my view it is the only possible term if confusion with the actor on the one hand and with the character on the other is to be avoided.

its own and is connected by all sorts of relations to all the others as well as to each of them separately. Naturally, the respective relations between figure A and figures B, C, D, and so on, differ from each other (a) in quality (they are various combinations of similarity, opposition, complementarity, subordination, and so on) and (b) in intensity (close/loose, direct/indirect, and so on). Any two figures present in a given situation are both complementary and opposed – complementary because the actors produce the stage action jointly and opposed because the action initiated by one is undergone by the other and *vice versa*. All the figures of the same play both differ from and are concerted with each other. If they did not differ enough, they would turn into a sort of chorus. But if they were not concerted, not only the performance as a whole but also individual stage figures would tend to disintegrate.

The opposition between the stage figure as an entity on the one hand and as a mere component of a set of figures on the other is emphasized in "naturalist" theatre,[4] which strives both to make stage figures as different from each other as possible and to put them all on an equal footing, without clear mutual subordinations. By contrast, in the early liturgical theatre of medieval Europe, though the figures are often put on an equal footing, the internal polarity of the figure is weak because they (as distinct from the characters) are little differentiated, often nearly interchangeable. The distinctness and the unity of each figure is sacrificed to its smooth insertion in the whole set of figures. Characteristically, the performers often act in unison, as a sort of chorus, and the figures can even merge, intermittently, with the church choir. In the English folk mumming, too, those figures that are on an equal footing are often more or less interchangeable.

Another means of playing down the opposition is the hierarchy of figures, especially when it is fairly rigid. In the performance of Greek tragedy, the figure at the very top is likely to have appeared as an entity hardly affected by the presence of the others – of course this does not apply to the characters these figures stand for – while those at the bottom appeared more or less as non-entities almost wholly determined by, if not reduced to, their respective relations with the principal figure; this in spite of the fact that the figures in general seem to have looked very much alike.

But the hierarchy may also attenuate the opposition in the opposite manner. The two poles are kept in balance and the conflict between them is reduced when the hierarchical relations are distributed more evenly, so to speak horizontally. For example, the figures may be grouped in parallel

---

4   The quotation marks are used to indicate that wherever the term "naturalism" is applied to theatre in the conventional sense throughout the present paper, it is used for the sake of convenience only. "Naturalism" is hardly an accurate description of the structural characteristics that Stanislavsky's and Nemirovich-Danchenko's typical productions share with Antoine's, with Max Reinhardt's production of Strindberg's *The Pelican*, and so on.

hierarchies instead of all of them being subordinated in different degrees to one single figure. This is how the hierarchy of figures in the French classical tragedy differs from its Greek model. In the *commedia dell'arte*, in which this arrangement seems to have been usual, hierarchy is complemented by an imperative division of functions between the figures. A different conjunction of this type of hierarchy with a clear-cut division of functions exists in Japanese Noh theatre, where stage figures have their own names (not to be confused with the names of the signified characters), which indicate both their rank and their function. At the top is the *shite* or "the one who does, who acts". The *waki* or "the one on the side" is the second figure. Most of the time, the *waki* is the passive spectator of the *shite*'s action. The character represented by the *shite* is often a vision seen by the character represented by the *waki*. Each of them may be accompanied by the *tsure* ("followers") or the *tomo* ("companions"). The *kyógen*, a farcical figure, may occupy the third rank, as far as this figure appears in the Noh play itself (Kyogen farces also alternate with the Noh plays during the performance and in addition short Kyogen "interludes" separate the first part of the Noh play from the second; see Sieffert 1960: 19–20).

When the parts are sung rather than spoken, the figure is integrated into a set of figures more firmly because all the "lines", irrespective of their distribution between the alternating speakers, are subjected to a common rhythm, to the continuity of the melody, and so on. When the parts are danced, these effects of music combine with those produced by the rigorous coordination and common rhythm of the movements. The figure also tends to appear as a mere part of the whole set of figures wherever its quality as an entity is weakened by the subordination of some of its visual components – the colour and shape of the costume, poses, gestures, positioning, and so on – to the pictorial aspect of the scene (as in the Court Theatre of Weimar under Goethe's direction and even more in Meyerhold's "stylized" theatre) or by the subordination of the movements and positioning to the architectural qualities of the three-dimensional stage space (as in the avant-garde theatre of the 1920s and 1930s).

The stage figure as an entity is markedly weakened and its integration into a whole set of figures emphasized in the Japanese Noh theatre. On the one hand, a passage of the text is often sung alternately by the actor creating a leading figure (*shite* or *waki*) alone and jointly with those creating subordinate figures (*tsure* or *tomo*), or alternately by the actor and the chorus. On the other hand, certain passages sung by the chorus are simultaneously mimed by the actor performing the main figure (*shite*).[5] Declamation is also separated

---

5   See the plays reproduced in the second part of Zeami 1960, "A Day of Noh Plays" [Une journée du Nó].

from miming, with a similar effect on the polarity of the stage figure, in some fifteenth century English mummings and disguisings (Wickham 1959: 191–95) and to a certain extent in Vladimir Nemirovich-Danchenko's production of Tolstoy's *Resurrection* (Logan 1968: VIII–IX).

In the performance of the Russian folk tale-teller P. J. Belkov, who enacted all the parts in turn, the polarity takes the form of a sharp contrast between the distinctness of each single figure, underlined by Belkov's acting devices, and the presence of the same actor in all the figures.[6]

The Japanese Kabuki theatre displays a certain tendency to keep the two poles apart by means of its playing areas. On the stage, the figures are confronted and concerted but the leading figures are either alone or accompanied only by subordinate figures on the *hanamichi*, an elevated passageway that runs from the rear of the auditorium to the left side (from the spectator's viewpoint) of the stage. This separation of the two poles is fairly marked although there may be some interplay between the actor on the *hanamichi* and an actor on the stage (Ernst 1956: 92–93 and 102–103).

STAGE ACTION

Stage action as a *signans* must be conceptually separated from the action represented, a *signatum*, like the stage figure from the character. This distinction is crucial, since the *signatum* may be, and often is, represented by other means than by stage action and conversely not every stage action need signify action. In the Greek, the Sanskrit and the French classical drama, for example, vital parts of the represented action are narrated rather than enacted. Stage action that signifies no action whatsoever is fairly frequent in folk theatre – even quite elaborate actions may belong to this category; they may be designed, for example, to emphasize the symbolic value of certain stage objects that bestow a particular dignity on whoever eventually uses them (see Veltruský 1987 [1940]).

Though it is primarily created by acting, stage action does not only consist of what the actors do but can also be carried by changes in lighting or scenery, by music, other sounds not made by actors, and so on.[7] This division of the elements of action between those that are and those that are not produced by the actors is of course not meant in a technical sense. If an actor mimes playing the piano and the sound of a piano are actually produced behind the scenes, there is no reason to interpret this as an action made up of two distinct elements. If in the Japanese Kabuki the assistant arranges the pleats of

---

6   See I. V. Karnaukhova's description as quoted in Bogatyrev 1940: 17–19.
7   See Honzl 2016 [1940]: 130–31; also Veltruský 2016 [1940]: 151–55, on inanimate objects as vehicles of theatrical action; and Scherer 1966: 218–19 and 221–22, on the table and the door as agents.

the actor's costume (Ernst 1956: 107–108; Toita 1970: 102), the pleats are still part of the stage figure. Furthermore, some components of stage action clearly transcend both the actor and the stage figure though they are produced by the actor. Such is the case of sung dialogue, even if it is not accompanied by instrumental music. Because of the unity of the melody, rhythm, and so on, the parts evidently transcend the figures and the musical component of the action is distinct from the rest. Stage action is polarized between those components that become part of the figures and those that do not. As parts of the same action, the two categories are complementary. But they also conflict because the components of each category prevent those of the other from forming a separate structure, as is illustrated by the frictions between the actor or actors on the one hand and the author, stage director, designer, composer or conductor on the other.

In various periods and styles the polarity is thrown into relief – typically in "naturalist" theatre – while others strive to attenuate it, especially by subordinating either group of components to the other. Stage action in *commedia dell'arte* may serve as an example of the predominance of those elements that are integral parts of the figures. In Japanese Noh, on the contrary, the elements that transcend the figures are particularly prominent. Another example of the same tendency is the ubiquity and dominant position of music, combined with various acting procedures, which attenuate the distinctness and unity of every individual figure in the early liturgical theatre of medieval Europe.

POLARITY BETWEEN STAGE FIGURE AND STAGE ACTION

The stage figure is a set of signs, the stage action a progression of signs.

What actually enters the stage figure and stage action respectively are only the *signantia*. Naturally, the relations between the various *signantia* either within the stage figure or within the stage action depend not only on their material qualities but also, and very much, on their respective *signata* and on the specific manner in which the different types of sign involved discharge their semiotic function or, to use Peirce's term, on the specific *semiosis* of each.[8]

It would be tempting to say that both the stage figure and the stage action are made up of the same signs, but that would disregard the complexity of the semiotics of acting. First of all, stage action is jointly produced by several

---

8   Some of the structural relations between the signs of which the stage figure is composed have been discussed in Veltruský 2016 [1941]: 248–61. That paper, however, tended to disregard the possible contradictions and tensions within the structure because it was primarily concerned with the ways in which the text predetermines the other components of theatre and also, of course, the extent to which it does so.

actors, each one of whom contributes something different. Secondly, some of the signs out of which the stage action is composed are exterior to any stage figure. Thirdly, some figures appear to be the objects of action, its instruments or parts of its setting, rather than its subjects.[9]

In other words, there is merely overlapping between the signs respectively used to construct the figure and the action. One of them may predominate. In the avant-garde theatre, which during some three decades reacted against the realism of the late nineteenth and early twentieth century, or in some forms of early medieval theatre, action is clearly dominant; sometimes it tends even to absorb the figures. The same can be said about the Noh theatre. In the performance of the Russian folk tale-teller Belkov, the continuity of the action contrasts with the intermittent appearance of every individual figure. The predominance of the stage action in the early medieval theatre, the Noh, and folk story-telling is also stressed by the occasional insertion of pieces of third-person narrative pertaining to what the actors are doing. In certain theatrically performed folk customs, on the contrary, the action is subordinate and its main function is to help build up the figures.

The two can also be kept so to speak in balance, either by limiting both of them as much as possible to the area of their mutual overlapping (that is, to those signs that they have in common) or, on the contrary, by building each of them up far beyond that area. In the *commedia dell'arte*, for example, each figure and its action tend to be constructed out of a fixed set of signs and those available for the action vary from figure to figure. It is the other way round in "naturalist" theatre. Every figure, whether important or not, includes as many signs as possible irrespective of its action and, at the same time, the action tends to use a great many signs that are external to the figure (off-stage sounds interfering and combining with the actors' action are perhaps the most characteristic example).

To sum up, stage figure and stage action are both opposite and complementary. They are two poles of the *signans*.

COMPONENTS

The signs that form the stage figure fall broadly speaking into two opposite categories, the constant components on the one hand, the variable components on the other (Zich 1931: 142). With some degree of simplification, they can be listed as follows:

---

9   See Veltruský 2016 [1940]: 149; also Scherer 1970: 229 on Flipote, Madame Pernelle's maid in Molière's *Tartuffe*: "To receive a slap in the face is the principal activity of Flipote, who is there only to be slapped in the face."

Constant	Variable
Voice	Delivery
Eyes	Eye-movements
Face and makeup or mask	Play of facial muscles
Head	Head-movements
Body (physical constitution and characteristics)	Gestures
	Posture
Costume [Permanent and recurrent elements of the variable components]	Bodily positions (standing, sitting, lying, kneeling, squatting, hanging, and so on)
	Positions in space (in front/behind, above/below, to the right/to the left, and so on)
	Movements in space
	Extra-linguistic sounds produced by or attributed to the actor

The difference between what is constant and what is variable is relative. None of the constant components is truly invariable. Though some can be more easily modified in the course of the performance than others – the face and the body, for example, tend to be more constant than the costume (Zich 1931: 113), the mask more than the face and the makeup – all are potentially subject to change. This applies even to the mask, which can be not only replaced by another one but also modified by simply removing one of its elements or adding another. The face, too, can be altered at a given point of the performance, either by modifying the makeup or in a more artful fashion, by the actor's tightening or relaxing some of his facial muscles (which may be interpreted by the spectator, for example, as the character's "throwing off" or "putting on" a mask). At the same time, all the variable components have some constant elements – above put in brackets because, unlike the constant components in the narrower sense, they become apparent only gradually and grow stronger as the performance progresses. On the one hand, there are certain more or less permanent features, such as the actor's characteristic fashion of articulating, inflecting the voice, making gestures, standing, walking, and so on; on the other, the characteristic, recurrent voice inflections, inarticulate sounds, gestures, poses, and so on, which the actor often uses as a sort of *leitmotif* (Zich 1931: 114). All the constant components will appear slightly different if any permanent features of the variable components are modified, whether suddenly or little by little.

Nonetheless, the distinction between the variable and the constant components is very important from the semiotic point of view, as a difference pertaining to their respective functions: the variable components are units of the stage action, together with certain other signs that are exterior to the stage figure; the constant components have a triple function, that is, to distinguish every figure from all the others as a separate entity, to unify all the variable components of the same figure and, to some extent, to predetermine them.[10]

The constant components owe their existence largely to the fact that each part is enacted by the same actor throughout (Zich 1931: 45). Yet in some forms of theatre, like the Greek tragedy, the English interludes or the Spanish *comedias*, an actor performs more than one part. At least some of the constant components are then missing or made semiotically irrelevant. The question arises whether some other constant components are accentuated instead or whether the variable components predominate as a result.

The signs that form stage action also fall into two categories, those that become part of the stage figure and those that remain external to it; the first are identical with the variable components of the figure, as already indicated.

As successive units of the action, these signs usually appear not one by one, for example gesture – change of lighting – movement in space – speech – off-stage sound – change in the bodily position and so on, but in clusters, for example: a speech, a facial movement, a gesture and a change of lighting – a change in bodily position, an extra-linguistic sound produced by the actor and a facial movement – a movement in space, a gesture, a head movement and an off-stage sound, and so on. Jakobson's principle that combination works not only in sequence but also in concurrence (1956) is perhaps nowhere more evidently true than in stage action. The extraordinary propensity of acting to use combination in concurrence is of course partly due to its being an art not only of time but also of space.

In some theatrical structures there is a marked tendency to combine many different signs within the same unit of stage action. Some others, on the contrary, seek to eliminate concurrent combination of heterogenous signs as much as possible. The Moscow Art Theatre represents perhaps the most extreme case of the first tendency. In the 1898 production of *Hedda Gabler*, for example, Stanislavsky made Tesman eat his breakfast during the dialogue with Aunt Julle in Act I, conceived by Ibsen as a sequence almost entirely made up of alternating lines of dialogue. A few years later, this device was severely condemned by Meyerhold (Braun 1969: 29), whose own production of the same play in 1906 represents the opposite extreme. The actor's gestures and play of the facial muscles were reduced to the barest minimum. During the entire first dialogue between Hedda and Lövborg, the two actors sat side by side turned towards the auditorium, motionless, looking straight

---

10   Only the first two of these functions have been identified in Veltruský 1941. The third one is nonetheless important. The Kathakali actor of Southern India, for example, is obliged by the costume to stand astride, his weight on the outside edge of the foot (see Southern 1968: 69).

ahead (Braun 1969: 67 and 68). The tendency to limit the concurrence of heterogenous signs within the same unit of action as far as possible can also be found in early medieval theatre.

In their quality of successive elements of the action, the variable components cannot be separated from constant components with which they are intertwined within the stage figure. Consequently, each unit of action that includes in its cluster any sign that is part of a stage figure is also connected with all the constant components of that figure. Therefore, not only is stage action performed by an actor projected into the figure he constructs but the opposite is true as well, namely that the figure as a whole is projected into the action.

Similarly, in their quality as variable components of the stage figure, the actor-produced elements of stage action cannot be separated from the other elements, external to the figure, with which they combine both concurrently and successively within the action. As a result, even those other elements of the action tend to be projected into the figure.

STAGE FIGURE AND ACTOR

It is on the whole true that the figure is created by the actor, but other factors, and other artists, contribute to its shaping as well; at the same time, each actor interferes quite considerably with the construction of all the other figures.

The extent to which a given actor's lines enter the figure he creates is not easy to delineate with precision.[11] But even if only the sounds of the language are taken into account, the impact on the stage figure is far-reaching. In the text itself, the sounds combine into a phonic line that strongly affects the actor's delivery (Veltruský 2016 [1941]). It is true that the phonic line gives the actor considerable leeway; sometimes it may perhaps even be interpreted in different ways as regards its dominant component (Mukařovský 1948: 216–18). The delivery may also in some way run counter to what is implied in the text, creating certain tensions within the stage figure. In no case, however, can the actor simply disregard the phonic line of his speech and mould his delivery freely. This applies even to forms of theatre that allow for a good deal of improvisation. In the *commedia dell'arte* the actors must have drawn a great many of their lines ready-made from the so-called *generici*, collections of verbal formulae, jokes, puns, and so forth, so as not to disconcert each other.

---

11   Zich tried to avoid the difficulty by eliminating the text from the stage figure altogether and attributing it in its entirety to the character, the *signatum*. To achieve this *tour de force*, he resorted to the fiction of the "foreign actor", the actor using a language unknown to the audience (see Zich 1931: 112–15).

The stage and its sets strongly condition the stage action. Even when both the actor and the part remain identical in two successive productions, if one is on a picture-frame stage and the other on a round stage surrounded by the audience from all sides the stage figure will not be the same. Similarly, it will not be the same in the setting of Meyerhold's "stylized" theatre, where the actors have to move and recite on a flat and shallow stage in front of a huge painting, as in his "constructivist" setting, where they are constantly climbing up or down from one platform to another. In realist theatre, they have to perform among many pieces of furniture, of which they must make the fullest possible use. On the Chinese stage, by contrast, there is only a table and a chair, which are not to be touched at all because their various positions indicate whether the action takes place indoors, on a hill, on the city tower, and so on, while the actor uses such props as a whip (which actually stands for the horse itself) or an oar to show that the character is riding or travelling in a boat (Brušák 2016 [1939]). The small size of the stage was one of the basic factors determining acting in the Elizabethan era (see Wickham 1972: 181).[12]

Stage music, though necessarily adapted to the text (see Zich 1931: 304–10; Veltruský 2016 [1941]), strongly affects the actor's voice performance and his movements. The presence of a statue or of several statues on the stage may influence both his posture and the movements of his body, as well as the relationship between the two, and most likely also his gestures. The modern use of stage lighting introduces, among other things, an almost unlimited number of variations into the relations between the posture, gestures and movements on the one hand and the stage space on the other; it also affects acting in the opposite manner to the dim lighting of the playing area in the Kathakali "story play" of Southern India (Southern 1968: 72) or in the French classical theatre (Scherer 1970: 150).

The acting of other actors is yet another vital factor in the construction of the stage figure. As already pointed out, even the simplest features of all the figures confronted at any single moment are concerted. To a certain degree, which varies according to styles and periods, every stage figure is a collective product of all the actors performing the play and every actor participates in the construction of all the figures.

Nonetheless, despite the text, the space, the collective performance and all the other factors that determine and mould the stage figure and condition the actor's performance, the stage figure is still his product. That is so because he uses his own body to construct it and is personally present in his work.

---

12 [Editor's note: Veltruský added this sentence in his translation into Czech.]

REFERENTIAL FUNCTION

COMBINATION OF SIGN SYSTEMS

Acting, like theatre in its entirety, is a distinct semiotic system that uses signs originating from other semiotic systems. This is not a case of the sort Benveniste has in mind when he says that the presence of the same sign in two different systems – the red as a traffic sign and a part of a national flag, the white on that flag and the white of mourning in China – is irrelevant to its sense in either, because the value of any sign is determined only within the system to which it belongs in any given instance (Benveniste 1969). The signs borrowed from other semiotic systems enter acting not as simple perceptible realities but as signs, endowed with the values they have in the systems from which they come – the actor's speech is language, not a mere *flatus vocis*. Yet, at the same time, they also acquire additional semiotic characteristics on stage because acting is a distinct semiotic system.

The combination of sign systems in acting is not the same thing as the participation of various arts in the theatre,[13] though the two are undoubtedly related.

What is involved here can be described as follows. In the messages based on other semiotic systems, signs of the same type refer to things that differ from each other. This is also true of acting: gestures, for example, represent various acts on the part of the characters, the place where these acts occur, the characters' age, mentality and state of mind, and so forth. But in addition, the same thing is referred to, either successively or concurrently, by signs as different as speech, gesture and movement in space.

ACTS, SIGNS AND SIGNS OF SIGNS

In acting, as in any other component of theatre, the two categories of signs distinguished by St Augustine as the *signa* and the *res*, namely those that are nothing but signs and those consisting of realities that can on occasion serve as signs (Jakobson 2008 [1933]), are combined. The actor himself, who is personally present in the stage figure and stage action, is of course a reality of this kind and it is only occasionally – only when he plays – that his physical properties and acts turn into signs; at least some of the accessories belong to

---

13   For a critical examination of the old view of theatre as a synthesis of the arts, which goes as far back, at least, as Richard Wagner's concept of *Gesamtkunstwerk*, see Zich 1931: 32–42; a new formulation of the problem, based on the structural conception of theatre, is proposed by Mukařovský (2016 [1941]).

that category as well. Acting mingles and interconnects the two in so many respects that the very distinction between them often fades.

The actor's practical acts are especially important from this point of view. When he removes a chair, picks up a book or carries a fellow-actor on his back, his act is perceived as a sign, even if he does it in the same way as anybody else. Every element of the figure and action tends to become a sign. The chair, the book and, of course, the fellow-actor are equally perceived as signs, linked by contiguity to the one constituted by the practical act. This act is usually not only perceived but also shaped as a sign, that is, as a *signans* with the character's act as its *signatum*. The actor, indeed, seldom contents himself with merely moving the chair, taking the book or carrying another actor. He rather performs gestures and movements that signify such acts and are sometimes so shaped that these acts would be signified even if their instruments or objects – in our examples, the chair, the book and the fellow-actor – were not there.

Furthermore, the gesture or movement that mimes a practical act lends itself more readily than the act itself to being performed in a way that expresses certain features – strength or weakness, age, momentary physical state, frame of mind, and so on – of the represented character.

There are several reasons why signs are coupled with practical acts: purely practical factors, such as the impossibility of killing a fellow-actor when representing a murder; optical and acoustic distortions of what the actor does or says;[14] theatrical conventions which, for example, require the actor to perform all his gestures or movements in a specific manner, whether or not they have a practical purpose; the ability of such signs to represent certain aspects of the acts that have an expressive value in relation to the character to whom the act is attributed.

When the instruments or objects of the acts are in fact eliminated, the signs produced by the actor are no longer merely coupled with, but actually stand for, the practical acts they mime, so that from simple signs they turn into signs of signs – they represent not only those practical acts but also, through their intermediary, their imaginary instruments or objects.

Acting produces signs of signs in many other cases as well. The human and anthropomorphic beings with their actions and behaviour that are represented by stage figures and actions, are themselves to some extent made up of signs. A face, for example, is habitually taken to reveal a figure's mentality, a gesture is expressive, conative or referential, carriage can hint at the person's physical qualities, mentality, state of mind and intentions. Above

---

14 As much as it might clash with his insistence on "living the part", this aspect was fully recognized by Stanislavsky. See Stanislavski 2008: 102.

all, what the actor says represents the character's speech, which is itself of course made up of signs.

When the actor makes an angry gesture, his purpose is distinctly referential – he seeks to represent a character and the character's emotion, not to express his own. It may be enough to pronounce a simple referential sentence, such as "I am angry," if his lines contain such a sentence. If they do not, he has to convey the same meaning by representing some indication of the character's anger, such as an angry gesture. This indication is itself a sign, and one that is chiefly expressive. Therefore what the actor actually produces to represent such an indication is a sign of a sign; more precisely, it is a (chiefly) referential sign of a (chiefly) expressive sign. Naturally, the same applies when a chiefly conative sign, such as stretching out the arm with the index finger pointing at the door, or a chiefly referential sign, such as a nod to confirm some item of information, is represented. Bogatyrev (2016 [1938]) rightly emphasized that a great many of the signs produced in acting, and in the art of the theatre in general, are actually signs of signs. The capital importance the signs of signs have in acting was fully recognized by the fifteenth-century Japanese actor and playwright Zeami (1960: 98).

In the combination of the sign with a practical act, the same gesture or movement is, as a rule, both the act made by the actor and the sign of the character's act. But emphasis on the semiotic nature of theatrical gestures and movements and on the distinction between the *signans* and the *signatum* may separate the sign from the act. In the Japanese Kabuki, unless the opening or closing of the sliding door has a particular significance, the actor makes only the mimetic gesture while the act itself is left to his "neutrally" costumed assistant (the *kurombo* or the *kôken*; Ernst 1956: 109).

The signs of signs cannot be so divided. The double *semiosis* through which they convey their meaning or meanings proceeds from a single *signans*. The *signans* of the represented sign is therefore the direct *signatum*, and its *signatum* the indirect *signatum*, of the actual sign. Or, in more complicated cases, such as the sign representing both an act and its imaginary instrument or object, the *signans* of the instrument or object is part of the direct *signatum*, the represented act. In any event, the *semiosis* of any sign of a sign proceeds on two planes simultaneously, not in two stages.

The coupling of a practical act with a sign that represents it and the double *semiosis* of the sign of a sign can become fairly apparent where the stage figure and action are markedly stylized. This tends indeed to replace the resemblance between the two aspects of the sign by what Peirce called diagrammatic similarity (Peirce 1932: 157–60), namely a correspondence between their respective division into parts and the relations between these parts. The coupling and the double *semiosis* also come to the fore under the impact of a prominent theatrical convention, which tends both to substitute diagrammatic similarity for resemblance and to supplement similarity by codified contiguity. Signs based on diagrammatic similarity or codified contiguity are less apt to give the impression that the *signans* is the same as the *signatum* – the mimetic gesture or movement as the act it represents, the actual sign as the sign it refers to. But the more acting resorts to "natural"[15] delivery, gestures, movements, and so forth, the more the distinction between the sign and what it stands for – either the practical action or another sign – is blurred and can be overlooked by the audience.

MODE OF SEMIOSIS

Each of the sign systems on which acting draws has its own mode of *semiosis*. When signs belonging to different systems combine within the stage figure and stage action, their respective modes by no means disappear: words still convey their meaning by codified contiguity, makeup by similarity, and so on, it being understood that each mode is merely dominant, not exclusive, in the given sign system (Peirce 1932). At the same time, however, the different types of signs affect each other's way of conveying meaning.

In any event theatrical convention, which is ubiquitous in one form or another, grafts codified contiguity on the signs, which operate either through factual contiguity or through similarity. The share of this additional element varies but it can go so far as to supersede the usual mode of *semiosis*.

Factual contiguity is thus superseded in what is nowadays considered old-fashioned operatic acting. Here, convention governs so firmly that a whole gamut of a character's emotions is represented by just a few gestures and poses, such as the hand on the heart, the "fascist salute", the hand touching the ear, the two arms outstretched with one foot slightly to the fore, and so on (Scotto di Carlo 1973). In Chinese theatre, to signify that the character is telling the spectators some secret that the other characters are not to learn, or voicing some private idea, the actor raises the broad sleeve of his right arm to the level of his face, putting a sort of screen between himself and the other actors, at whom he often also points with his left hand (Brušák 2016 [1939]: 126).

Similarity is superseded by codified contiguity, for example, in the costumes of the *commedia dell'arte*. What really matters in those worn by the

---

15   In its application to the components of the stage figure and action, the term "natural" of course designates merely the striving to shape those signs in such a way as to exploit fully the ability of acting to conceal the difference between similarity and sameness. In other words, "natural" is far from being a descriptive term. The recordings of actors of the past, even when relatively recent, strike the listener as exaggeratedly stylized and those made at the time when "naturalist" theatre triumphed also reveal a considerable degree of stylization – a fact that is less astounding in reality than it appears at first sight. Similarly, every bit of descriptive and pictorial evidence discloses that Garrick's acting, so much praised for being "natural", was utterly stylized in all its aspects.

Zanni in their developed form is not so much their resemblance to servants' dress as that they indicate the wearer's specific function in the whole performance – Brighella will guide and stir up the plot, Harlequin will maintain the rhythm of the stage action (Oreglia 1970: 71 and 58).

The coupling of signs with practical acts and the use of signs of signs are perhaps the most important among the procedures that join together two or more different modes of *semiosis*.

The mimetic sign that is coupled with a practical act represents this act by similarity complemented, if not superseded, by codified contiguity. It also represents it in such a way as to reveal by factual contiguity something about the character to whom the act is imputed. By a different sort of factual contiguity, it points to the instrument or object involved in the act; this is even more pronounced if, instead of being coupled with it, the mimetic sign replaces the act. The sign may also signify some aspects of the instrument or object directly, rather than through the represented act. Marcel Marceau, for example, conjures up a wall by a sequence of gestures that represent the character's touching the wall at different points with his hands, especially with their flat palms and outstretched fingers, sometimes also walking alongside the imaginary wall at the same time; in *The Billposter* he conjures up such a wall between himself and the audience by gestures that represent the character's hands running up and down the wall. In such cases, too, it is by factual contiguity, but of a different sort, that the wall, or any other instrument or object, is signified.

Whatever the mode of *semiosis* of the represented sign, the sign of a sign always relies to some extent on similarity. This makes similarity nearly as ubiquitous as codified contiguity. For instance, a sentence may be pronounced in such a way that it expresses, by factual contiguity, an emotion aroused in the speaker by its contents, but the actor's delivery represents the character's emotional delivery by similarity. To indicate that the character is embarrassed or afraid of being unmasked, the Chinese actor bends the arm at an obtuse angle to his forehead so that the sleeve hangs down over the whole face (Brušák 2016 [1939]: 126). The gesture is not intelligible without the code provided by theatrical convention, yet its similarity to the gesture of hiding one's face is unmistakable.

Speech conveys meanings chiefly by codified contiguity. But as soon as it is pronounced, different sorts of factual contiguity come into play: the delivery brings out or plays down certain words, phrases, puns, rhythms, connections between certain units that are not directly contiguous, the relatedness of the whole line to the first (and second) or the third person, and so forth; on the other hand the voice and the delivery express, to a variable degree, the speaker's sex, age, mentality, emotions, attitude to the subject and to the addressee, and so on. Similarity is grafted on this already complicated *semiosis* when speech is used on stage because it becomes a sign of a sign, an utterance representing the character's utterance. Depending on period, genre and style, similarity of different sorts – resemblance, diagrammatic similarity or any mixture of the two – may be involved here.

Because it is a sign of a sign, theatrical speech can blur or even eliminate the referential function of the represented speech of a character. In some English mummers' plays unintelligible speeches are pronounced (Southern 1968: 50), signifying only that the character speaks but not what he says – the meaning of the represented sign is reduced to what it indicates by factual contiguity. The same device is used in some theatrically performed folk customs in Bohemia (Bogatyrev 1940: 129). The referential function of the represented speech is eliminated in the "artificial language" used in the midst of Latin dialogue in a thirteenth century Nativity play from Rouen (Young 1951: 70); attributed to two of the Magi, the gibberish points to the foreign nationality of the characters. Somewhat comparable is the intermittent insertion of "artificial language" in the speeches of certain figures standing for the devil, the executioner, the angel and occasionally some other characters in Czech and Slovak folk theatre (Bogatyrev 1940: 155–60). In Rutebeuf's *Le miracle de Theophile*, Salatin's conjuring of the devil is also in "artificial language" (1949, verses 160–68); here the referential function of the represented speech gives way to its conative function, again indicated by factual contiguity but of a different kind.

In itself, the fact that similarity, factual contiguity and codified contiguity concur in the *semiosis* is not enough to characterize acting (and theatre in general) as a distinct sign system. All three modes operate in any type of sign. Even in a system so markedly relying on codified contiguity as language, the function of factual contiguity and of similarity is far from negligible (see Jakobson 1971c and 1971d). In the *semiosis* of the pictorial sign, which is often thought to be based on similarity alone, similarity could not in fact work without a basis of contiguity (which allows those elements of similarity that are semiotically relevant to be separated from those that are not; see Veltruský 1973). What really distinguishes acting as a semiotic system is that by combining the signs borrowed from all the other systems it "cross-fertilizes" their respective modes of *semiosis*, so to speak. Here, unlike in the other types of sign, the relations between the three modes are not a matter of one prevailing and being supported by the other two but of all three operating on the same level and even, sometimes, conflicting and competing with each other.

REFERENTIAL POTENTIAL

The referential meanings conveyed by different types of signs differ from each other considerably. Each of these types has its own unique ability to refer to certain kinds and certain aspects of reality and each is different in some other respects. Language, for instance, is inferior to the pictorial sign in indicating colour, the location of objects or people, the distances between them, and so on. A picture is at a disadvantage in comparison to a statue or a building in referring to relations in three-dimensional space and to language in referring to the time sequence, the time flow, and so forth. Music is superior to any other semiotic system in conveying any aspect of the passage of time but is inferior to all of them, except perhaps architecture, in referring to concrete reality.

The mode of *semiosis* also affects the quality of the meanings conveyed. The systems that ordain the signs in time make everything represented appear to some extent as a process because they refer to "things" as well as to processes by means of a succession of signs. By contrast, the systems that ordain the signs in space represent not only static states but also processes by means of a fixed configuration of signs, which has the opposite effect on the meanings they convey. On the other hand, the meanings called forth by similarity have a vividness that those conveyed by contiguity need not have, because they are concrete and situated in the present time of the perceiver; those that are based on factual contiguity are at least related to the perceiver's present time because the *signatum* is at least contiguous in time, if not simultaneous with the *signans*. Codified contiguity explains the flexibility and subtlety that distinguish language; not being tied down to any material correspondence with the *signans*, any meaning can be conveyed in so many ways that it can evolve almost independently of any material support.

Such qualitative *differences* between meanings do not disappear when the signs belonging to different systems come together within the stage figure and stage action and share in the construction of their sense. But these differences are in some sort superseded, or at least attenuated, as a result of all the modes of *semiosis* concurring. Without disappearing, the kind and the quality of meaning proper to one mode tend to merge with those proper to the others.

In this process, what gives each type of sign its unique referential potential may be somewhat curtailed. The free play of meaning that distinguishes language, for example, is no longer quite so free when language is used on stage. As already mentioned, the linguistic meanings conveyed by codified contiguity mix with and are affected by those conveyed by factual contiguity, and they both depend on the similarity and codified contiguity on the basis of which they derive from the actor's voice and delivery. Moreover, they are intertwined with – and sometimes brought out but sometimes overshadowed by – the meanings conveyed by the other components of the stage figure and stage action (gestures, movements, costume, and so on). In forms of theatre that strive to preserve on stage the free play of meanings that can be found in the text, there may be a tendency for acting to use similarity and factual contiguity as an obstacle to be overcome. Gordon Craig's desire to replace the actor by an Übermarionette (1962: 54–95) and Maeterlinck's decision to write for puppets instead of actors are symptomatic in this respect. A kind of compromise is found in the sword dance from Ripon in Yorkshire: all six participants stand in a row speaking as loudly as possible, with no modulation. When "Jack" is killed, the actor who represents him hangs his head. Another actor places his hand on his shoulder and calls for the doctor, leaving it there until Jack comes back to life (Brody 1971: 27).[16] But in other forms of theatre, the injection of similarity and factual contiguity into the *semiosis* of language may act as an enrichment, at least partly because of the additional vividness. As Richard Flecknoe put it in his praise of the Elizabethan actor Richard Burbage: "He had all the parts of an excellent Orator (animating his words with speaking, and Speech with Action)" (Chambers 1951: 370). In other words, the concurrence of different modes of *semiosis* not only somewhat curtails the uniqueness of the referential capacity of every type of sign but also considerably extends this capacity. This is where the "cross-fertilization" of all the modes shows its effects.

For instance, since acting represents human or anthropomorphic beings, much emphasis is naturally put on expressivity. The possibility of conveying whatever expressive meanings are required is considerably widened by the signs of signs, with their double *semiosis* and concurrence of similarity and codified and factual contiguity. A famous seventeenth century Spanish actor who entered reading a letter in silence, held the audience spellbound for a long time by miming a whole sequence of emotions aroused in the character (Rennert 1963: 267). It is reported that when David Garrick wished to entertain his friends, he stood behind a chair and conveyed by his face alone every sort of passion, blending one into the other (Price 1973: 18).[17] A former actor of the Moscow Art Theatre could pronounce the emotionally neutral and elliptical sentence *"Segodnya vecherom"* [This evening] in forty or fifty different ways by diversifying its expressive tint: most of the versions he made of it on a tape recorder, after writing down different situations in which they could be spoken, were understood correctly and assigned to the appropriate circumstances by Moscow listeners (Jakobson 1960: 354–55). In the Kabuki theatre a character's transformation from a sensitive, conscientious priest into a furtive professional thief is conveyed by a pantomime the actor performs while pausing at the most significant spot on the *hanamichi* (Ernst 1956: 99). In the Noh, the madman who is possessed is represented by means of

---

16   [Editor's note: The passage about the Ripon sword dance was added by Veltruský to the Czech translation of the article.]

17   [Editor's note: The sentence about Garrick was added by Veltruský to the Czech translation of the article.]

a stage figure and action that convey both the character and the essence of the being that possesses him; the limits of this double representation seem to be reached when the part is a woman possessed by a warrior or a man possessed by a female spirit (Zeami 1960: 72–73).

The signs produced in acting also convey a great variety of meanings referring to the nature and qualities of the instruments and objects used in the represented action. If, for instance, the lifting of some heavy object is to be signified, its weight may be so to speak depicted by the gesture and the manner in which it is carried out, irrespective of whether the object actually used is heavy or not, or even whether there is any object at all. In a twelfth century mimetic folk dance, Welsh peasants apparently mimed, without any props or accessories, such activities as ploughing, driving oxen with a goad, shoe-making, spinning, weaving, and so on, while, "as if to lighten the labour", each produced "their usual uncouth song" (Giraldus Cambrensis, *Itinerarium Cambriae*, as quoted in Chambers 1903: 189).[18] In Chinese theatre, weaving, sewing, spinning, writing, and so on, are reproduced by mere combinations of gestures and movements, without any props (Brušák 2016 [1939]: 124). In one of his roles, a famous Russian actor of the Imperial Maly Theatre, Sadovsky, suddenly stopped in the middle of a sentence to portray the character feeling in his mouth for a hair from his fur collar, and went on for a long time moving his tongue around and "trying to take the hair out" with his fingers while the sentence he had begun remained unfinished (Stanislavski 1956: 93).[19]

The signs representing an action can also conjure up the place where it is meant to unfold. In the Kabuki theatre, the actor's movement on the bare, undecorated *hanamichi* indicates not only the snow through which the character is walking, the stone over which he has stumbled, the mud-puddle over which he is stepping, and so forth, but also the beating of the ocean waves on the shore where he finds himself (Ernst 1956: 93); the actor's extremely slow exit can convey the impression that the character, an evil magician, is walking on smoke (Ernst 1956: 100). The Chinese actor portrays, through conventional movements and in the absence of the objects concerned, not only the character jumping over obstacles, going up stairs, stepping over a threshold or opening a door but also the nature of these signified things – whether the door is the main gate, an ordinary gate, a plain door and so on (Brušák 2016 [1939]: 123). The movements made by the Spanish actor of the first half of the seventeenth century could represent, sometimes with the help of verbal indications and sometimes without, a space many times bigger than the stage,

---

18   [Editor's note: Chambers (1903) quotes Giraldus' Latin; the whole passage reads: "utrumque quasi laborem mitigando solitas barbarae modulationis voces effere".]

19   [Editor's note: This particular anecdote is omitted from Stanislavski 2008.]

the character's proceeding from a grove to the mountains, wandering in the neighbourhood of a seaport, roaming the streets of a town for a considerable time, and so on (Rennert 1963: 90–91).

The range of meanings a Japanese actor can convey by means of a fan is probably unique: a whip, a dagger, a bottle, a headdress, a lantern, a branch of a pine-tree quivering in the wind, the full moon rising above the mountains are just a few of them (Sieffert 1960: 23; and Ernst 1956: 161).

A sign that signifies the character's behaviour and action can at the same time conjure up animate beings who cause them or at whom they are directed, as well as their behaviour or action. The Indian Kathakali dancer can represent by the movements of his eyes, arms and hands (the face is im-mobile) a bee flying above a lotus flower, alighting and sipping, the flying of another bee above it, the sporting of the two around each other for a mo-ment, then breaking off, parting and flying away (Southern 1968: 70–71). In Meyerhold's production of Ostrovsky's *The Forest*, the comic actor sits down on a step holding a bare fishing rod with no line, then mimes casting the line, catching a fish, taking it off the hook, grabbing for it as it slips out of his hand and falls to the ground and finally putting it away (Tille 1929: 40). The Chinese actor represents a character saddling a horse, mounting, rid-ing at different speeds, dismounting, and so forth; in a scene representing a groom with eight horses, the actor's movements and gestures indicate the qualities of every single one of them – one is beautiful, one bites, one kicks, one is ill, another is old and decrepit and so on (Brušák 2016 [1939]: 124). In his one-man mimetic dance, without accessories or props, the West African pigmy signifies not only an elaborate action on the part of the character – how he strolls through the forest, discovers wild honey in the crack of a rock, makes a fire, tries to climb the rock while holding a torch, slips, falls back and climbs again, smokes out the bees, licks the honey, and so on – but also the insects that interact with the character such as a bee stinging his tongue, then a mounting attack by two, three, ten bees, then a swarm that settles on the sensitive parts of his body (Preuss 1930: 9). In another one-man mimetic dance, the same actor signifies – now alternately, now simultaneously – both the hunter and the elephant he kills, that is, the hunter marching through the forest, the animal appearing and calmly eating (the actor's arm, moving so as to suggest an elephant's trunk, brings imaginary fruit to his mouth), the hunter creeping under the animal's body and piercing it with a poisoned spear, the wounded elephant racing through the undergrowth and suddenly falling, the hunter cutting him to pieces and finally doing a dance of joy and a song of triumph (Preuss 1930: 8–9).

In a Noh play, *Sanemori*, the action of one actor, who represents the ghost of the knight Sanemori, successively conveys the acts of another knight pick-ing up Sanemori's severed head and washing it, the emotion of other knights when they recognize the head and then the previous event, the battle in which Sanemori had heroically fought and been decapitated.[20]

In a cluster of complementary signs, the manner in which each one conveys referential meanings, and the sort of meanings it specifically conveys, may remain under the threshold of the spectator's consciousness, especially when the acting strives to look and sound "natural". But the referential capacity and performance of every sign become much more apparent as soon as the signs belonging to such a cluster are organized in an unusual manner, when the complementary speeches and miming are divided between two different stage figures, or some of the signs belonging to the usual combination are eliminated, as is the case in plays without accessories and props, in radio plays, in mimes, and so on. Even within mime, Decroux – like the Vieux Colombier school of mime – seeks to bring out the semiotic potential of posture and the movements of the whole body by neutralizing the face and restricting the gestures (Decroux 1985: 17, 45, 67, 68). The face is nearly immobilized in the Kathakali as well (Southern 1968: 69–71). Perhaps this is one of the functions of the mask, at least in some of the forms of theatre that use it.

SYNONYMY

This extension of the referential capacity of every sign creates a particular problem of synonymy. Benveniste (1969) emphasizes that there is no "synonymy" between semiotic systems because one cannot "say the same thing" by signs of two different types. On the stage, however, the problem is more complicated. When the same reality is referred to in acting, either successively or simultaneously, by signs so different from each other as speech, gesture and movement in space, none of them denotes it completely; though they all refer to the same thing, each brings out a different meaning or shade of meaning. Yet at the same time, because of the "cross-fertilization" of their respective modes of *semiosis*, the limitations of each are to some extent overcome or negated. While they preserve their own semiotics characteristics, signs of different types can become synonymous in acting.

Like any other originator of a message, the actor has at any single moment of his performance some meaning to convey to the spectator and looks to the most suitable means of doing so. But his problem is particularly complicated. The speaker, for example, makes his choice along a single axis – what Kartsevsky (1929) has called the synonymic series – whereas the actor must choose along two different, and indeed antinomic, axes:

---

20   See the French translation of the play by René Sieffert, reproduced in the second part of Zeami 1960.

1. More or less appropriate means of conveying a given meaning are likely to be found among signs of such different types as language (which may or may not be prescribed by a fixed text), delivery, head movements, gestures, posture, movements in space, costume, and so forth. It is true that the actor is not obliged to choose only one and reject all the others. He can combine some of them, for instance a speech, an inflection of the voice, a gesture and a movement across the stage. But he cannot combine them all, since some of them are physically incompatible and, on the other hand, he tries to avoid what is called hamming and overacting in general (whatever that may mean in any given period or style).

2. It is also likely that the meaning in question can be conveyed by more than one sign belonging to the same type. As regards costume, for example, the actor's throwing off his jacket or rolling up his sleeves can be synonymous. Here, too, the actor may be able to combine several signs rather than fixing his choice on only one, but this does not remove the need to select because he cannot combine all the synonyms available within the same type of sign – for the same reason as he cannot combine all those that appear among signs of different types.

3. The problem of incompatibility faces the actor not only with respect to the synonyms he finds along each of the axes but also with respect to those he finds along both axes simultaneously. To illustrate, let us say that he may be able to combine a speech with a head-movement, any gesture and any movement in space. The choice he makes along one axis narrows down his choice along the other, but he has to choose along both at the same time.

Moreover, just as in language or any other semiotic system, the meaning of two or more synonyms is never quite identical. This, in fact, is even truer in acting than in the other systems of signs because acting uses signs originating from different systems. Their integration in acting makes them potentially synonymous but it does not remove their respective semiotic characteristics, thanks to which each tends to bring out a different meaning or shade of meaning while referring to the same things as the others. Therefore the actor has considerable scope to mould his part through the double choice he has to make between the many synonyms available to him at every point of his performance.

FUNCTIONS PERTAINING TO PARTICIPANTS

THE PARTICIPANTS AND THE TWO PLANES OF THE EVENT

Karl Bühler, who identified the semiotic functions pertaining to the participants with respect to language, derived his conception from Plato's *Cratylus*, where speech is defined as an instrument by which somebody tells somebody else something about things (Bühler 2011 [1934]: 30; 1969: 74). That is the foundation of Bühler's distinction between the relations of the sign to the speaker, to the addressee and to the topic, and between its three semiotic functions: expressive, conative and referential. Like the reference, the expression and the conation are semiotic aspects of the sign (Bühler 2011 [1934]: 35; 1969: 80).

To call "expressive" the function that relates a message to the originator and "conative" the one that relates it to the addressee entails serious risks of misapprehension. On the one hand, phenomena pertaining to meanings and the way in which they are conveyed may be interpreted as psychological problems; on the other hand, the relation between the message and the addressee may appear as just another aspect of its relatedness to the originator. Yet, for lack of more accurate denominations, the traditional terminology cannot be discarded.

The sign functions as an expression inasmuch as it indicates something about its originator, except when the originator himself becomes the topic (in which case it is referential). What it indicates in its expressive function need not be the originator's mentality, state of mind or emotions: it may be anything concerning him, the relation in which he stands to the topic, to the addressee and to the material situation in which he produces the sign and, through any of these, to reality, society or people in general. It may, for instance, indicate his attitude towards, his knowledge or ignorance of, the topic or addressee or the situation, his location in the material situation, and so on. The indications so given by the sign are meanings, expressive meanings. Like its referential meanings, they may more or less correspond to the realities to which they pertain but may also be fictitious.

Benveniste has given an idea of the real extent and importance of the expressive function – a term he does not use – in his analysis of subjectivity in language: the first-person pronoun refers neither to a concept nor to an individual but to the individual act of speech and designates the speaker; also, when certain verbs denoting mental dispositions and operations are used in the first person – *I suppose that...* or *I presume that...* or *I conclude that...* – they do not describe the speaker as performing the mental act in question but imply that he adopts a certain attitude towards what is asserted in the following subordinate clause (Benveniste 1966: 260–66).

The conative function is what relates the sign to the addressee; it should not be mixed up with the philosophical or psychological concept of conation, which relates an act to its originator's striving or volition. What the sign in this capacity calls forth are meanings, in every respect comparable with the referential and the expressive ones; therefore the conative function may but need not actually affect the addressee. At the same time, the manner in which it works is varied and the meanings it creates are of different sorts. Ingarden, for example, speaks of two separate functions relating the sign to the addressee, the communication function and the influencing function (1973), but these are merely two of the many aspects of the conative function.

The functions that relate acting to the participants operate on two planes, one involving the participants in the "acting event", the other participants in the event enacted. In this respect, acting does not differ from verbal communication.[21] But in acting these functions are discharged in a singularly complicated manner:

1. Since acting consists in human beings and their behaviour and actions representing human or anthropomorphic beings and their behaviour and actions, and since the actor is personally present in his work, the difference between the participants in the "acting event" and those in the enacted event tends to fade, to an extent that varies according to styles.
2. On both planes, the participants constantly alternate as originators and addressees.
3. Both functions are variously divided between several distinct participants on both planes:
    (a) As to the "acting event", the actor is not its only originator. The stage director, the designer, the conductor, the choreographer, the playwright, the composer and so on participate in the production of the performance.
    (b) The playwright may, though he need not, appear as the originator of the enacted event, which somewhat undermines the position of the character as the originator of the signified action.
    (c) The spectator shares his position as addressee of the "acting event" with the actor (or actors) who happens to be at the receiving end of the stage action at any given moment. As part of the audience, he also shares this position with the other spectators. Moreover, because the distinction between actor and spectator may be blurred, the spectator may also appear as the originator of the "acting event", either in relation to other spectators or even in relation to the actors.
    (d) With respect to the enacted event, the position of addressee, which different characters assume in alternation, may also be shared by the spectator if the distinction between the two planes fades.

---

21   See Jakobson 1971d: 133, on the distinctions between speech itself and its topic, the narrated matter, and between the event itself and any of its participants, whether "performer" or "undergoer", which results in the separation of four different items: a narrated event, a speech event, a participant of the narrated event and a participant of the speech event (whether addresser or addressee).

EXPRESSIVE FUNCTION

Most of the elements of which stage figures and action are made up are *a priori* expressive. Even off the stage, the face, the voice, the delivery and the bodily behaviour are expressive, whether they are intended to be so or not. Moreover, as components of stage figure and stage action, a great many of them are purposely moulded by the actor, so that what might be called their natural expressivity can be considerably increased; it is a much more complicated affair to diminish their expressivity, if that is what is desired. Theatrical costume, too, can be more expressive than dress in everyday life, while its expressivity can be quite easily diminished where appropriate.

As expressions, human appearance and behaviour are perceived and interpreted directly, without the intermediary of any code; the same seems to be true of animal behaviour (Plessner 1953). That is so because they are primarily connected with what they point to not by convention but by factual contiguity.[22] The expressive meanings of the costume are grasped less directly because what clothes indicate about the people who wear them is very much subject to convention. But some elements of behaviour, too, are strongly fashioned by convention or even governed by a formal code – ritual gestures, expressions of politeness, standardized facial expressions, and so forth (Mukařovský 2016 [1931]: 194). Such signs convey meaning by codified contiguity with more or less identifiable traces of factual contiguity and similarity (Jakobson 1971a: 361). These conventional elements can become individually expressive by a fresh injection of factual contiguity – even so strictly codified a movement as a nod expressing a greeting, approval or consent is often carried out in such a way that it reveals directly, without the help of any code, something about the person who uses it. In the structure of behaviour, there is no clear dividing line between the components that are conventional and those that are not.

The stage figure and stage action stand out, as *signantia*, by their striking reality. The human body that is their material becomes an integral part of them with all its manifold qualities and abilities, irrespective of what is intended and what is not. Even those features of the actor's body that have nothing remarkable about them and the spontaneous physical reactions that accompany intentional acts, such as the flush that comes to his face when he

---

22 If we were to adopt Peirce's classification of signs, they would be considered as indexes. Peirce's distinction between icons, indexes and symbols, operating respectively on the grounds of similarity, of factual contiguity and of codified contiguity, was, however, manifestly conceived with respect to the referential function of the sign. More precisely, in his analyses of *semiosis*, Peirce seems to have disregarded what distinguishes the expressive and the conative functions from the referential, as can be seen for instance from his semiotic description of a driver's calling out "Hi!" to attract the attention of a foot passenger (Peirce 1932: 161–62).

shouts at the top of his voice, tend to be seen as signs; and the absence of an expected reaction of this kind is perceived as a sign as well. Therefore, the two-fold *signans* produced in acting also stands out by its tendency to convey a great quantity and variety of expressive meanings.

These expressive meanings are related primarily to the actor himself. When, for instance, the actor's face tenses during a spectacular leap, the spectator sees how great an effort he is making; when it does not, it shows his virtuosity. Such meanings tend not only to build up a certain image of the action but also to identify him for the audience. He can be recognized by his voice, his size, the proportions of his body, the colour of his hair (unless he wears a wig), his face (often even if he is made up), his way of speaking and moving, and so on. The audience's ability or inability to recognize the identity of the actor is a crucial point in some forms of theatre, for instance in folk theatre (See Chambers 1933: 85–86 and 206–10; Brody 1971: 23–25; Bogatyrev 1940: 111–14; and Veltruský 1987 [1940]). Since they are grasped directly, without the intermediary of a code, all these expressive meanings related to the actor are endowed with a concreteness and vividness that many of the meanings relating to the represented character and event, especially those conveyed by codified contiguity, may not have.

Other expressive meanings belong to the plane of the enacted event and are related to the participants in that event, the signified characters alternately assuming the function of originator. These meanings are conveyed indirectly, by the signs of signs, which have a primarily referential meaning. To the extent that this referential meaning is conveyed by resemblance, however, similarity tends to give way to an impression of sameness and the expressive meaning of the represented sign tends to be attached to the primary sign and related to the actor as much as to the character. Even as a referential sign of an expressive sign, an angry gesture is still a gesture made by the actor and appears as the actor's own expression; the emotions mimed by the seventeenth century Spanish actor as those felt by the character on reading a letter are also perceived as his own. This is one of the cases in which the difference between the participants in the "acting event" and those in the event enacted tends to fade.

To the extent that this interpenetration of the two planes takes place, the expressions related to the actor reflect in their turn on the represented character. It takes many strong conventions, plus the overwhelming predominance of voice and singing over all the other components of the operatic stage figure, plus the attenuation of the referential function every sign undergoes when combined – in a subordinate position – with music, to enable the spectator to discard the soprano's obesity as semiotically irrelevant and not to perceive the love-sick maiden as comic. Another example: it is sometimes considered a fault on the actor's part when his face does not tense during a difficult leap because the extreme effort the character is meant to be making is not shown – the objection being that the actor is more concerned with displaying his own virtuosity than with impersonating the character.

This intertwining of expressive meanings respectively pertaining to the originator of the "acting event" and the originator of the enacted event is bolstered by the actor's endeavour to "live the part". So much emphasis is put upon this approach in some styles that even in his private life the actor to some extent experiences the mentality of the character he is studying or playing. Naturally, however far this may be pushed, the difference between actor and character can never be eliminated because theatrical conventions and the codified contiguity that they generate in the *semiosis* of the signs put definite limits to any effort to merge the two categories of originator. Yet even in periods that do not insist on the actor's "living the part", not all the tears shed on stage are glycerine. There are two reasons for this. First, both the similarity and the factual contiguity between the expressive sign and the attitude or emotion to which it points are links so intimate that mere miming of expressions may cause a sensitive person to experience whatever they express. Second, since the signs out of which the stage figure is constructed are either produced by the actor's body or affect its functioning, even his mind may undergo the impact of their expressive meanings (Zich 1931: 139). Richard Flecknoe's statement that Burbage "was a delightful Proteus, so fully transforming himself into his Part, and putting himself off with his cloathes, as he never (not so much as in the Tyring-house) assum'd himself again until the Play was done" (Chambers 1951: 370), for what it is worth as historical evidence, tends to indicate that "living the part" was not foreign, let alone unknown, to Elizabethan actors. Though by no means universal, this technique is certainly not confined to the periods when it is especially prominent (Honzl 1940).

Other methods strive on the contrary to keep the two sets of expressive meanings apart. This is perfectly clear in the case of those signs of signs that rely more on codified contiguity than on similarity to connect the represented sign with the one by which it is signified. Characteristically, in Chinese theatre the movements and gestures conveying the character's state of mind or his relation to the other characters are the farthest removed from resemblance (Brušák 2016 [1939]). When, for example, the actor moves his right arm slowly up in a circular movement and then quickly down to signify that the character has made a fateful decision (Brušák 2016 [1939]: 124), the expressive meaning relating the gesture to the character is entirely different from that relating it to the actor: one belongs to the psychological sphere, while the other is purely a matter of skill, know-how or virtuosity. In the Japanese Noh, several other procedures concur to the same effect: separation of speech and miming, a character's monologue signified by stage dialogue, a character's movements signified by dance and his speeches by singing, and so forth. It is probably this separation of the actor's and the character's respective expressions that enables the actor to signify the actions and behaviour of more than one character.

Some periods display a marked inclination to play down the expressive function that relates the stage figure and action to the actor. Such is manifestly the case of the Greek tragic theatre, which replaces the face and facial movements by a mask, limits the actor's movements and occasionally substitutes third-person narration for physical action; moreover, the actor's identity becomes somewhat indistinct when he plays two or more parts. The same tendency prevails, though the procedures are entirely different, in the early medieval liturgical plays, where the actor is only slightly differentiated from the spectators, and in some forms of avant-garde theatre, where the actor is perceived so much as an instrument of the stage director that the expressive meanings conveyed by the performance may be more or less deflected from him; that was the essence of Vera Komissarzhevskaya's objection to Meyerhold's methods.[23] The dominance of the writer, too, may lead to the expressive function, which relates the performance to the actor, being toned down. In Nemirovich-Danchenko's production of Tolstoy's *Resurrection*, this was achieved by splitting the performance between a speaking narrator and a miming stage figure (Logan 1968: VIII–IX).

In other periods, styles and genres, it is the expressivity of the signified character that is played down – so much so that in the late sixteenth and early seventeenth century, English actors aroused the enthusiasm of audiences on the Continent, which did not understand their language but admired their gestures and action (Chambers 1923: 343). Something like that can also be observed in opera where, of course, the expressive function stems from the actor's voice and singing rather than from his gestures and movements. Yet the frictions that often take place between opera singers and the conductor suggest that even though the music favours the actor at the expense of the character, it does not always grant him as much primacy among the originators of the performance as he would wish.

---

23 See Gourfinkel 1963: 58; and Tairov 1983: 48–51 (Tairov was an actor in Komissarzhevskaya's theatre when Meyerhold was stage director there). Significantly, Goethe's system as a stage director – which as already mentioned had much in common with Meyerhold's "stylized" theatre – was attacked by certain actors on the same grounds. Karl Reinhold condemned the monotonous uniformity of the figures, charging that the actor representing father and son, old man and young, man and wife spoke and acted alike, while Madame Burgdorf complained in a letter to Goethe that her expression of feeling was forced to bear "the imprint of a borrowed stamp", that her declamation suffered "the fetters of an unaccustomed rhythm", and that she became "a machine moved by alien dictates". See Prudhoe 1973: 92–93.

CONATIVE FUNCTION

One human being calls forth in another a certain degree of empathy, which grows stronger when the face is distinctive enough to suggest some kind of mentality or state of mind, or when a man is observed in action, when his behaviour is in any sense striking, strange, characteristic, and so on. In theatre, the spectator perceives faces, bodies and behaviour that are deliberately shaped; acting is therefore much more apt than ordinary human looks and behaviour to elicit empathy. We are not concerned here with the psychological problems involved in empathy (see Lipps 1903; Zich 1931: 48–49 and 214) but with the fact that this is an outstanding example of the many overlapping ways in which the spectator experiences the conative function of acting.

Another aspect of the same function may be described as arousal.[24] Like empathy, arousal may occur as a direct response, without the intermediary of any code – all sorts of affective responses are due to the psychophysical simulation by the material used and the way it is organized. But arousal may also depend on the spectator's being familiar with the underlying code, as is shown, for example, by the uncalled-for comic effect that the harsh voices of old male actors in female roles have on the Western spectator, unaccustomed to the code of the Noh theatre (Sieffert 1960: 26).

Furthermore, the conative function works through what Ingarden calls the communication function[25] – acting reflects the fact that it is directed at the spectator. The logical counterpart is, to borrow Gombrich's felicitous term (1972a), the "beholder's share" in decoding the message, which may be quite exacting in some cases, especially when the code is somewhat esoteric or radically new.

To the extent that the message is also an action aimed at the addressee, Ingarden (1973) speaks of the influencing function, which could perhaps include the didactic function and the (religious or political) propaganda function as well.

The conative function of acting may also consist in inducing the spectator to participate to some degree physically in the performance.

CONATIVE FUNCTION AND THE "ACTING EVENT"

The conative function works primarily on the plane of the "acting event" where it is directed at the audience. The beautiful and innocent-looking face

---

24   The term "function of arousal" has also been used as a synonym of conative function (see Gombrich 1972b: 82–96).

25   Ingarden's analysis of the semiotic functions performed by speech in theatre is limited to the plane of the enacted event.

moves the spectator even before he has any idea of the character signified, a perilous leap elicits a motor reaction and suspense irrespective of whether it represents the character's leaping over a precipice, throwing himself at a foe, displaying exuberance, and so forth – if indeed it represents anything definite at all – and the Japanese spectator watching the Kabuki stage changes his whole bodily position as soon as a new actor enters the *hanamichi* from the rear of the auditorium.

On the plane of the "acting event", the conative function also affects the actors. This is particularly due to their constantly taking turns with each other as originators and addressees of the performance, which engenders a sort of alternating actor-spectator relation between them. Actors elicit in one another responses of the same kind as in the spectator. That is why the playing of the whole cast suffers and can more or less disintegrate whenever a single one of them performs badly, especially in one of the leading parts, and why an inspired performance by a great actor can carry his fellow-actors – it proves, so to speak, contagious. Like the spectator, the actor is of course exposed to the conative function of the whole performance, not only to what his fellow-actors do; the effect of rhythmic drumming or clapping, of music and of changes of lighting may illustrate this. Among the many elements of the whole event that so affect him, the other actors' performance stands out only because it is likely to discharge its conative function most directly.

Naturally, though it is of the same kind, the impact the conative function has on the actor can hardly ever be quite the same as that on the spectator, since as a rule the actors know the whole play and its production, as well as each other's technique, in greater detail and usually have more insight into the mechanism of acting. But the difference is merely relative and may be attenuated by several factors.

When a fairly limited number of plays is produced again and again and the performance is governed by a strong tradition and convention – as in the Chinese (Brušák 2016 [1939]), the Tibetan (Stein 1961: 248) and the folk theatre (Bogatyrev 1940: 62) – the spectators may be as familiar with the play and with all the procedures and devices that can be used as the actors themselves. The degree to which the spectator is acquainted with the play or the actors or both may vary tremendously within the same audience. Some know the play intimately, others not at all, some have even seen the same performance several times. Some follow the same actor from role to role, others see him for the first time. Some also compare the way different actors play the same part – Hamlet, Othello, le Cid, and so forth.

Improvisation, which is a fairly general feature of acting, engenders some degree of surprise for the actors and obliges them to keep adjusting to each other's innovations. In the Kabuki, improvisation is avoided as much as possible on the stage proper, where several actors perform together, and fully developed on the *hanamichi*, when the actor is alone with his audience (Ernst 1956: 102). On the other hand, while in some forms of theatre, such as the great medieval mysteries in France, there are endless rehearsals for a single performance, certain other forms do without any rehearsing; folk theatre is a case in point. In any case, there is a world of difference between a rehearsal and appearance in front of the audience.

The actor's insight into the mechanism of his fellow-actors' performances also depends on acting methods. It may be considerably weakened, for example, by a strong emphasis on "living the part". After playing Oswald Alving in Ibsen's *Ghosts*, André Antoine notes that starting with the second act he experienced a sensation hitherto unknown to him, a nearly complete loss of his own personality. He could not remember anything, either as regards the audience or the effect of the performance; it took him some time to become himself again after the curtain fell (Antoine 1921: 183). At the opposite extreme there is the *dell'arte* comedian, whose attitude towards his fellow-actors' performance must have been mainly professional.

The actor's exposure to the conative function of the whole performance may be concealed from the audience as much as possible or openly displayed, toned down or stressed. Sometimes it is even feigned: typical examples are the ostensibly strenuous efforts a comedian will make not to burst out laughing when another performs his funny act, and the obligation imposed on minor actors in the nineteenth-century Comédie-Française to spend most of their time on the stage staring at the leading actors in admiration. Insofar as the effect of this function upon the actor is manifest, whether it is genuine or feigned, the actor becomes a mediator between the spectator and the event. He signals, at least in some respects, the reaction the event aims to produce in the spectator. Far from weakening that reaction, the actor's mediation does a great deal to build it up.

CONATIVE FUNCTION AND THE ENACTED EVENT

Conative function also works on the plane of the enacted event where the addressee is not the spectator but the character signified by the stage figure and stage action; in theatre (whether essentially narrative or based on a dramatic text) the characters are represented not only as acting but also as being acted upon and reacting. On this plane, too, the conative function is by no means limited to the effect produced by one character upon another but relates the enacted event in its entirety to the character concerned. In other words, it is as important in *Oedipus Rex* – where the plot arises from gradual discovery rather than action – as in any tragedy of revenge or the *commedia dell'arte*. The signified characters keep alternating, however, as momentary addressees, or undergoers, of the enacted event. The constant shifting of the conative function from one to another tends more or less to reflect that alternation. As a result, the conative effect produced upon the characters by their mutual action may, more often than not, predominate; still, this is not a general rule.

The difference between the plane of the "acting event" and that of the enacted event tends frequently to fade in the actual working of the conative function. The addressee of the "acting event" – that is, the spectator – may feel affected by the signified action in the same sort of manner as the character; for instance, he may experience the didactic function of the enacted story or of a speech addressed by one character to another although, conceptually, it is the characters who should draw the lesson and apply it to themselves; in morality plays like *Everyman* the main character actually stands for the spectator. If the spectator is affected in this way, his response may reflect any aspect of the conative function – empathy, arousal, communication, persuasion, and so on – which will depend on the structural features of acting and on the nature of the signified character's qualities, as well as on the spectator's own qualities, values, views and attitudes. To put it in trivial terms, the spectator may not only identify himself with or keep his distance from the character or even combine the two opposite responses in various proportions, he may also admire, pity, love, hate, despise the character, be frightened, puzzled, attracted by him and so on. And through the mingling and intertwining of different types of responses, an extraordinary degree of intensity can be reached – if that is aimed at by the conative function – so that the spectator may get involved in a sort of silent dialogue with the signified character, arguing with him, imploring him not to take the course of action he is bound to take, and such like.

Since it is an integral part of the conative function to arouse and to elicit empathy, the spectator may feel affected by the enacted event in the same sort of way as both the originator and the undergoer of the signified action. He may, in other words, experience either the savage rage of the strangler or the mortal anguish of his victim or both when such a scene is enacted, just as he may experience either evil stealthiness or helpless fright or both when he witnesses the noiseless unlocking and opening of a door.

The conative meanings of the enacted event stem from a great variety of structural features of acting and staging. A few random examples will illustrate this.

In the last act of Gogol's *The Government Inspector* the actor playing the mayor suddenly turns to the audience in the middle of a long speech to utter the famous "What are you laughing at? You're laughing at yourselves!" In the Moscow Art Theatre, the lights went up at this moment in the auditorium. In *Pazukhin's Death* by Mikhail Saltykov-Shchedrin, one of the characters concludes the play with the words "Vice has been punished and virtue…", rakes the audience with his eyes as if looking for somebody and adds: "Well, where is that virtue?" Again, in the Moscow Art Theatre, the lights went up when the character started looking into the audience (Kouřil 1938: 49–50).

In Georges Duhamel's *The Light*, a blind man stands before an open window and poetically describes the beauty of a mountain lake at sunset, though he has never seen it. In K. H. Hilar's[26] production in the National Theatre of Prague, as soon as the blind man approached the window, the vista turned into sheer darkness, stressed by the sharply lit window-frame. As Charles Vildrac observes, by this procedure "the spectator is invited to put himself in the speaker's place; the spectator too, turns into a blind man in front of this window" (quoted in Mukařovský 2016 [1941]: 73–74).

The Kabuki play *The Loyal Forty-Seven Ronin* uses a procedure so analogous that the question arises whether Hilar was not actually inspired by the Japanese model. The character walks away from the house of his dead master – the actor proceeds to the *hanamichi*. The facade of the house is painted on two flats of equal size hinged together horizontally. When the actor stops at the most important point of the *hanamichi*, the upper flat is folded down over the lower one and on the new surface so revealed appears the facade of the house reduced to half its former size (Ernst 1956: 157). So the increased distance between the character and the house is signified both by the few steps the actor makes on the stage and the *hanamichi* and by the decreased size of the picture. The spectator is induced by this second element, the element of perspective, to see the house and with it the whole signified action through the eyes of the character.

The opposite procedure is more usual in the Kabuki. For example, a character's progress into the house is signified as follows: the actor moves to the rear of the stage and opens two sliding doors before which he stands; this reveals another pair of sliding doors, smaller and only a few inches further than the first; the actor opens this and further pairs, five in all, each one smaller than the previous one and set directly behind it (Ernst 1956: 134). The way the character experiences his own action is entirely disregarded. His moving further away is signified purely from the point of view of the audience and the spectator's possible inclination to share the character's sensations is strongly discouraged.

The chorus in Greek tragedy is a body situated midway between the character and the spectator. The chorus converses with the characters but comments on their activities or reacts to them in the manner of a specta-

---

26 [Editor's note: Karel Hugo Hilar (1885–1935), writer, stage and costume designer, a leading figure of Czech Expressionism. He was the Director of the drama division of the National Theatre in the 1921/1922 season when *Světlo* [The Light] by Duhamel was on the bill (February – April 1921); the production was actually directed by Vojta Novák (1886–1966).]

tor. In the Noh, the character represented by the figure *waki* is the spectator watching the one represented by the figure *shite*, yet at the same time the two characters talk to each other and the first exerts upon the second what Ingarden calls the influencing function.

Conative meanings respectively produced on the two planes may also clash. The structure of the performance may, but need not, tend to avoid this. For example, the comic miserly father could not have been enacted in Moliere's theatre by a heroic-looking young actor using noble gestures, delivery, and so on. However, such a contradiction was not always considered undesirable in the nineteenth century when a tragic Arnolphe, a revolutionary Alceste, and a handsome, seductive and terrible Tartuffe could be seen on the French stage (Coquelin 1968: 40). In the Kyogen farces of the Noh, the gestures and delivery are quasi-hieratic, the joint action of several actors signifying a brawl or a drunkards' scene is choreographed, and so on, so that the comic effect of the farce upon the spectator is due both to the conative function of the enacted event and to its contrast with the conative function of the "acting event" (Sieffert 1960: 30–31). The nineteenth century tragedians' much-decried practice of turning to the audience and stepping to the footlights in order to speak appeared preposterous only when new trends in theatre focused on the enacted event and its conative function, even as regards the effect to be produced on the spectator, and consequently endeavoured to eliminate any clash between the two sets of conative meanings. Characteristically, Antoine's speaking with his back to the audience became a crucial issue in the controversies between those who were in favour of the new trends and those who opposed them, and it appeared as ridiculous to the latter as the Comédie-Française procedure appeared to the former. The actor still turns to the audience in opera, where the practice is considered necessary for technical reasons, though its survival is also due to the fact that in opera the enacted event is strongly overshadowed by the "acting event" and this also reflects on their respective conative functions.

We owe a precious observation about the conative meanings produced on the two planes to Charles Dullin, who served his apprenticeship as an actor in the first decade of this century "in the school of melodrama", as he put it, that is to say in the third-rate troupes playing in the working-class areas of Paris. He observed that to build up his entrance, the actor playing the "third lead" used to stamp loudly, then briskly open the door so as to draw the attention of the spectators and then pause before starting. This made Dullin smile because he had seen Antoine's productions, but, as he points out, it worked for the audience, which often even applauded. When he himself acceded to the "third lead" and eliminated the traditional device "for the sake of truth", he soon discovered that "something was missing". If he was not to resort to the old device to "make his entrance", he had to "find an equivalent of a theatrical nature" (Dullin 1946: 29–30). In other words, the conflict between the two sorts of conative meanings is not eliminated in the interest of those produced on the plane of the enacted event if none are produced on the plane of the "acting event"; rather, this will be conveyed by procedures that do not clash with the enacted event.

The fading of the distinction between the addressee of the "acting event" and the addressee of the enacted event results mainly from two particularities of acting; first, the similarity between the *signans* and the *signatum* tends to give way to an impression of sameness; second, the spectator's share in the conative function relating the enacted event to the character is a counterpart of the actor's share in the conative function relating the "acting event" to the spectator.

To the extent that the enacted event aims at the audience as its addressee, the character may appear as an intermediary between the event and the spectator. In an extreme case, the effect of the enacted event upon the character becomes an image of its effect upon the spectator. This is of course a complete reversal of their respective "roles" on this plane. But the conative effect of the enacted event upon the spectator in considerably strengthened when it is so mediated by the effect the same event has upon the character. In their quest to "strengthen the faith of the uneducated people and the neophytes" (Brinkman 1929: 12) the medieval liturgical plays set out to represent not the Resurrection itself but the Marys' reaction to the announcement of it.

SPECTATORS' ACTIVITY

Though it also depends on social tradition and custom, the behaviour of the audience is primarily a matter of the conative function of acting, of the way it works on the two interlocking planes.

The audience is never quite passive. Its response or lack of it has a considerable influence on the performance. It is of course the actors whom it affects most strongly: the spectator is the primary addressee of the "acting event". But since the "beholder's share" in the decoding of the message is indispensable, the response of the audience impinges on the enacted event, too. For example, a certain type of tragic episode does not yield its full meaning unless it meets with a quite specific kind of tense silence. Or again, a comic character and situation are not funny if the spectators are not amused – that is why it is so difficult to put on *Georges Dandin* nowadays.

The audience is both an assembly of individual spectators and a single body. Every spectator is personally aimed at by the conative function of acting, yet the way he is actually affected also depends very much on the collective response of the audience to which he belongs. The same spectator reacts quite differently when the auditorium is packed than when it is half-empty; the same difference obtains in the cinema, so it cannot be explained away by the enthusiasm or the discouragement of the performers.

In modern times, naive and sophisticated spectators, snobs, young people and old, men and women and many other categories make up an audience that nonetheless reacts collectively. The diversification is much more pronounced in the Elizabethan playhouse, the Spanish *coral* of the seventeenth century, the Tibetan theatre, certain folk performances, and such; the relations between the different categories of the audience are proportionately more explicit – they openly make fun of or revile each other and so on – yet they all equally belong to the same audience. What matters here is that their respective attitudes towards the performance, which are both divergent and complementary, are all somehow determined by the conative function of the performance itself. For instance, historiographers of the Spanish theatre of the sixteenth and seventeenth centuries often take the many contemporary complaints about the ruffianism of the men in the pit too literally and believe that the actors and the other spectators were really afraid of these so-called *mosqueteros*; there is some good evidence to the effect that both playwrights and actors deliberately set out to provoke these men and that had they kept quiet, not only they but the rest of the audience, too, would have enjoyed the performance much less.

Just as there is an actor-spectator relationship between the actors, so there is another actor-spectator relationship within the audience. Both are grafted on the basic relationship between the actual actor and the actual spectator, which they complement and help to build up but with which they can also clash, even to the extent of disrupting the performance. An interesting example of such disruption is mentioned by Antoine. During the performance of a comedy, a well-known critic, rather hostile to the Théâtre Libre, was at one point so overcome by laughter that the whole audience looked at him and laughed with him. And they laughed so long, says Antoine, "that we could no longer regain our self-possession on stage" (1921: 178). By over-reacting to the conative function of acting, this spectator unwittingly "stole the show" from the actors.

Even when the spectators do no more than display their approval or disapproval, their seemingly spontaneous reaction is to some extent guided or even manipulated. The claque is only one device among many. Recalling that at the time when his comedy *The Last Will* was produced by the Imperial Maly Theatre actors used to be acclaimed in the middle of a scene – they came forward and bowed while the other actors waited to resume the action – Nemirovich-Danchenko points out that the playwright "had to know how to write these exits" (1968: 12). In Elizabethan comedy, the spectator was directly addressed by the actors, who asked the audience to applaud, just as they invited it to join in in song or prayer (Bradbrook 1963: 22). The city annals of Seville report that during the performance of a *comedia* on 10 November 1639, a spectator cried out "Bravo, Jacinta!" after a dance executed by Jacinta Herbias, whereupon Antonia Infante, who was playing the lead, called out: "Bravo indeed, and welcome, for she deserves it." The audience divided into those shouting "Bravo, Jacinta, and down with Antonia" and those shouting "Bravo Antonia, and down with Jacinta", and it turned into a brawl that ended with an admirer of Antonia's mortally wounding Jacinta's first well-wisher (Rennert 1963: 127). During the performance of the Russian folk farce *Pakhomushkoi*, the spectators keep encouraging, prompting and criticizing the actors and their text and from time to time invade the playing area to show them how it ought to be done; it is part of the tradition that each village has its own version of the text and its own way of acting and that in every performance there are many people in the audience who have seen or even played different versions.[27]

The conative function may also aim to induce the spectators to participate physically in the actual performance. For instance, certain medieval liturgical plays call on the audience to join in, either by singing certain pieces or by performing certain acts within the playing area. In folk plays about the saints, the audience may enact the behaviour of a congregation. For instance, in the Czech folk play on St. Dorothy, as soon as the first actor enters the door and announces the arrival of the king and Dorothy, the master of the house and his son remove their caps, the women piously join their hands and all put on a devout expression. In the same play, a performer impersonates a spectator.[28] In Elizabethan theatre, the actor may not only perform certain scenes in the pit but also use the "groundlings" as part of the crowd (Bradbrook 1963: 25).

Even the whole performance may be designed to make spectators, or rather the most prominent of them, take an active part. In mumming performed before Henry VI at Hertford on New Year's Eve, six peasants and their wives, represented by two groups of actors, expose their complaints against each other – the peasants are spoken for by the Presenter, the wives by one of their number – and ask the king to arbitrate their quarrels. A third speaker tells them in the king's name to return in a year's time to hear the verdict (Wickham 1959: 204-5). In 1377 the Lord Mayor and the citizens of London visited Richard II dressed as popes, cardinals and African princes carrying gifts; the boy king had to win these gifts from them in a game with loaded dice (Wickham 1959: 197-98).

The spectator's participation in the actual performance may be based on a previous agreement between him and the producer, as was obviously the

---

27 See the report by Sergei Pisarev and Rafael Suslovich (Bogatyrev 1940: 54–55 and 167).
28 See Štěpán Dvořák's transcript and description (Bogatyrev 1940: 219–37).

case when Molière's troupe performed *The Forced Marriage* before Louis XIV and the king himself danced in the third *entrée* after Act II clad in an Egyptian (that is, gypsy) costume.[29]

A different sort of previous agreement seems to govern some spectators' participation in Jhanki ritual theatre performed by travelling professional troupes in North India. Most of the performance consists in the audience's worshipping Sita and Ram, as represented by two child actors, which leads up to a didactic dialogue between the two deities and the concluding chorus sung by the whole assembly. Individual singing, which begins very early in the performance, is one of the many forms of the worship involved here: now and again someone comes forward from the audience, sits down amidst the orchestra to confer with its director, and sooner or later contributes a song. Norvin Hein, to whom we owe a unique description of this ritual theatre, noticed when attending an elaborate Jhanki performance in 1950 that he had seen some of the vocalists among the musicians earning their livelihood by appearances at many local religious meetings. It should be added in this connection that with the exception of its director, who travels with the troupe, the orchestra is hired locally by the host of the evening. In other words, local professionals seem to participate on both sides of the dividing line between the performers and the audience. That, however, by no means implies that the active spectators are simply performers enacting spectators or, to put it differently, that the entire spectators' activity derives from a previous agreement. The task of the local professionals seems to be to give a certain continuity and rhythm to this activity, which in itself is extremely varied, ranging from the infrequent case of a devotee who is in ecstasy dancing before the two child actors to some very devout spectators sitting throughout the performance at the feet of these actors with fixed and happy gaze (which, incidentally, somewhat corresponds to the duty of the minor actors in the nineteenth century Comédie-Française to stare admiringly at the leading actors). Just as the director of the orchestra makes *ad hoc* arrangements with the local vocalists as they come forward, the child actors apparently see to it that the real spectators' action gets properly integrated into the performance – now they accept their attentions with aloof grace, now one of them rewards a devotee who has made a spectacular "entrance" by pulling up the flowing nether garments and baring a foot for the touch of his brow, now the other takes a flower from a nosegay given him by an old woman and returns it to her, made precious by the touch of the divine hand, and so forth. Though only some of them seem to result from a previous agreement, all the activities of the spectators are based on a well-established convention that governs the whole performance.[30]

---

29   See the anonymous scenario, as reproduced in Molière 1956: 882.
30   For a complete description of the Jhanki ritual theatre, see Hein 1972: 19–30.

The dividing lines between the various forms of the spectator's activity are blurred. The transition from mere display of pleasure or displeasure to more active interference with the performance is smooth and so is the transition from such interference to active participation in the actual performance; in a case like the Russian *Pakhomushkoi*, it is hardly possible to tell which is involved. Moreover, any of these activities is partly elicited by the conative function of acting, partly arranged beforehand in one way or another, and the proportion of the two factors varies a good deal.

At the same time, however, the spectators' activity is the least predictable and therefore the most dangerous of all the factors of the performance. To the extent that it depends on this activity, the performance can also be disrupted or even destroyed by it whenever the audience gets out of hand. This is so because the spectators' activity negates the basic correlation between the dramatic space and the audience, which, as Brušák shows, is dialectical: "They are mutually dependent and influence each other but while the dramatic space does this by direct action, the audience does it passively, through its inertia" (Brušák 2016 [1991]: 305).[31] The negation may go very far but as long as it responds to the conative signals produced by the performance it actualizes the basic correlation. As soon as it goes beyond such a response, the correlation is broken and confusion sets in. That may be the reason why the most developed forms of participation by the spectators can usually be found where the performance is strongly governed by a well-established theatrical convention or where the behaviour of the audience is controlled by a close-knit community or both.

NOTES ON THE "SIGNATUM"

Even an incomplete examination of the twofold *signans* and of the referential, the expressive and the conative function gives a fairly clear idea of the complexity of the *signatum* constructed out of the multifarious meanings

---

31   [Editor's note: Veltruský quotes from a draft manuscript version of Brušák's paper, which was only published in English in 1991, fifteen years after the first publication of this study. The reference is to the final wording of this passage, published in this anthology, which reads "The action space and the audience are parts of one totality in which the former is a dynamic, developing component, which is actualized from a latent state and expends itself through its actualization, while the latter is assembled on an *ad hoc* basis and remains static."]

conveyed by the three functions. The picture will appear still more complicated when the other semiotic functions of acting are taken into account.
Only some of the basic features of the *signatum* can be outlined at this stage.

Action as a *signatum* is not simply "represented" in the sense in which
this term is habitually used with reference to acting. It is constructed out of
autonomous meanings that are not necessarily combined in the same way
as the *signantia* that carry them. As already mentioned, action need not be
signified by stage action and conversely stage action need not signify action.
But even where signified action derives from stage action, its inseparable
parts may be conveyed separately, by two or more independent actions. The
speech and the corresponding gestures, and even the practical act and the
sign with which it is coupled, may be kept apart in this way. In such cases,
meanings produced separately, by separate *signantia*, cluster within the
signatum. On the other hand, though the place where the signified action
is meant to unfold is an independent set of meanings, quite distinct from
that action itself, it need not be signified by separate signs, let alone signs
exterior to acting, such as stage sets and scenery. Ocean waves can be signified by the actor's movements, a rising moon by his manipulation of a fan,
a river by his handling of a fishing rod or an oar. Here meanings that arise
in clusters because they derive from the same *signans* become disconnected
within the *signatum*.

Similarly, the stage figure does not simply "represent" – in the usual sense
of the word – a character.

First of all, a figure need not signify any character; such is the case of the
Presenter in the English mumming, of the narrator in Nemirovich-Danchenko's production of *Resurrection*, of the pandit in the North Indian Ramlila, of
the crier, the runner and such like in the Czech folk theatre, of the Expositer
in the miracle play, among many others. What is more, a figure of this kind
may intermittently signify a character, at least faintly; such is the case, to
mention just one example, of the often anonymous Presenter in the English
folk hero-combat who, when one of the two antagonists is killed, may pronounce a lament referring to him as "my son", "my only son", "my only dearly
beloved son", and such like,[32] or whom the other character, the victor, may
address in such terms as: "Oh, Father, Oh, Father, you see what I've done..."
(Brody 1971: 52–53).

Secondly, a figure may signify more than one character, for instance
the hunter and the elephant, the groom and the eight highly individualized
horses, the obsessed man and the being by whom he is obsessed. When Jean

32   As Umberto Eco points out, the first person singular pronoun pronounced by the actor relates
     the speech to the signified character. See Umberto Eco, "Paramétres de la sémiologie théâtrale"
     [Parameters of the Semiotics of Theatre] (qtd. in Helbo 1975: 36).

Cocteau's *The Human Voice* is performed, the only stage figure signifies not only both the abandoned woman and her former lover but also two different images of the woman – the one conveyed to the audience and the one conveyed to her interlocutor.

Thirdly, a character can be signified by more than one figure. The *shite* and his *tsure* usually stand for a single character. The sporadic use of the first person singular by the chorus of Greek tragedy also seems relevant in this context.

Furthermore, even where on the whole each figure stands for a character, a meaning conveyed by a component of one figure may enter into the construction of a character signified by another figure. Ritual prostration may indicate only the kind of character to whom it is addressed and nothing about the one that performs it. In a Czech folk play every figure gives a military salute whenever he or she approaches, or turns away from, the one signifying the king. The meaning of this gesture participates in the construction of the character "king", not of the characters signified by the figures who make it (Veltruský 1987 [1940]). Three figures, however, standing respectively for St. Dorothy, the angel and the devil, do not make the gesture. Its absence has a meaning that is common to the three characters, but it does so only because the gesture is a recurrent component of the other figures.

Finally, a character may comprise meanings that are not conveyed by any stage figure but by signs external to all the figures. In Strindberg's *The Pelican*, as produced by Max Reinhardt, the darkness, the whistling and howling of the wind, the swinging of the open window and the curtains, the stage overcrowded with dark furniture, call forth meanings that compose the chief character jointly with those stemming from the stage figure (Tille 1917: 170–71). In some Czech folk plays, different degrees of dignity are vested in the characters by their standing near or sitting at a table (Veltruský 1987 [1940]). In the Kabuki, the elevated platforms may be used to indicate a character's social superiority (Ernst 1956: 144–45).

The very concept of the character requires a good deal of further elaboration and differentiation. Acting conveys not only referential but also expressive and conative meanings and the three reflect on each other. The expressive and the conative functions relate acting primarily to the actor and the spectator, and the expressive and conative meanings have a vividness that the referential meanings need not have. It is true that as far as the enacted event is concerned these two functions relate to the characters, but even on this plane, their operation involves, respectively, the actor and the spectator. Moreover, as the distinction between the plane of the enacted event and that of the "acting event" tends to fade, so the meanings pertaining to the different categories of participants mingle and combine more or less feely, and these categories may themselves get fairly mixed up. The expressive meanings related to the actor reflect on the character and *vice versa*. Even the distinction between the spectator and the actor is somewhat blurred by the spectator's empathy and by their both undergoing, in a comparable way, the conative function of the "acting event".

As a result, the various meanings conveyed by the stage figure and by such other components of the performance as are relevant in the construction of the character combine in such a way that they build up not only the character but also an image of the actor and an image of the spectator. Naturally, since they are mere meanings, the two images may be related to the reality of the actor and that of the spectator in many different fashions. To fit the *signatum*, an extremely hardworking actor or actress, who rehearses long and carefully before facing the audience and is desperately struggling against poverty, may put across the image of a rascally and insouciant improviser, just as a dissolute drunkard may have a romantic image. Similarly, the image of the spectator may idealize or caricature the spectator as he really is, or anything between the two extremes. The image of the actor, the character and the image of the spectator belong to the same *signatum*, within which they are inextricably intertwined; rather than separate parts, they are its three aspects.

There is no denying the crucial importance of the character. Conceptually, the image of the actor and that of the spectator are complementary to the character. In fact, however, the relative weight of the three is variable.

The acting system that increasingly prevailed in the Comédie-Française towards the end of the last century tended to throw the image of the actor into relief and to make the character appear as a mere part of this image; one old actor considered it more difficult to play a king in melodrama than in tragedy because in the latter his speeches were written by an author of genius (Dullin 1946: 31). It is symptomatic in this respect that Antoine, who sought to place the character in the forefront, charged the actors of the official stages with impersonating their own personality instead of the characters (Antoine 1921: 199). This was of course an overstatement; Coquelin, who was himself an outstanding representative of the Comédie-Française tradition, sharply criticized those actors who went too far in this direction (Coquelin 1968: 28–30).

In medieval morality plays, the character was perhaps constructed chiefly so as to convey a certain image of the spectator.

Pirandello's love for the theatre did not stop him from considering that actors could not help distorting characters though the characters could not do without actors. This contradiction is due to his conception of dramatic literature, according to which the characters are the focal points that determine and organize the entire *signatum* and become so autonomous that the author himself must no longer show his hand, so to speak. Logically, to acquire this measure of autonomy, the characters must leave behind the verbal art to become real or material, yet as they are created by the playwright, the

characters of course do not allow for the image of the actor. Hence Pirandello's dream of "a great actor who can strip himself completely of his own
individuality and enter into that of the character that he is playing" and his
realization that even such trivialities as for instance the actor's face would
still prevent the dream from coming true because makeup is no remedy but
a mere adaptation (Pirandello 1993: 27).

The image of the actor has two different aspects – the actor as an actor
and as a private person – both of which enter the *signatum* in variable proportions. The nineteenth-century technique decried by Antoine emphasizes the
first aspect, but it is a fairly crude example, whereas the Kabuki shows how
subtly an effect of the same nature – semiotically speaking – can be achieved.
For instance, after creating an overbearing woman on the stage properly so
called, the actor left alone on the *hanamichi* at the end suddenly represents
a shy girl, calls the stage assistant to take away the spear he is carrying and
shows himself distraught at the dreadful experience on the stage. When the
stage assistant asks him to perform a *mie* (pose) dating back to the eighteenth
century, he coyly covers his face, saying he could not do it in front of all those
people. After considerable urging, he begs the audience not to laugh at his
ineptness and then finally does it (Ernst 1956: 80–81). Characteristically, when
Dullin saw the Kabuki, he found in it some justification for the melodramatic
actors from whom he had learned his craft and for the devices by which the
"third lead" used to build up his entrance: "His gesture was ridiculous, his
preoccupation that of a ham, yet the spirit of the theatre was there notwithstanding" (Dullin 1946: 30).

The second aspect – the actor as a private person – was apparently stressed
in the Spanish theatre during its great period, as is illustrated for instance by
the complaint made by Lupercio Leonardo de Argensola in 1598, that in a play
by Lope de Vega "the actor who played the part of St. Joseph was living in
concubinage with the woman who represented Our Lady, and this was so notorious that many were scandalized and laughed when they heard the words
in which the most pure Virgin replied to the angel's question: *Quomodo fiet
istud*, and so forth"; another complaint by the same playwright reveals one of
the devices used to call forth the image of the actor as a private person: "... this
same actor who played the part of Joseph reproved the woman in a low voice
because she was looking, as he thought, at a man of whom he was jealous,
calling her by the most vile name that is wont to be applied to evil women"
(Rennert 1963: 261–62).

There are many procedures between these two poles, as for instance when
shipwrights play the building of the Ark, fishermen and mariners Noah and
the Flood, and goldsmiths the coming of the Three Kings with their precious
gifts in the York mystery plays. Another example: in certain forms of the
devotional theatre of Northern India – the Jhanki, the Ramlila – only actors

from the Brahmin caste can take the parts of deities; otherwise the Brahmins in the audience could not bow before them to worship the deities they stand for (Hein 1972: 18 and 72).

As part of the *signatum*, the image of the spectator, too, has different aspects, mainly due to the fact that the spectator faces the performance at once as an individual and as part of the audience (Mounin 1970: 91). At the opening night of Chekhov's *Seagull* in the Moscow Art Theatre, when the curtain went down after Act I, the audience remained plunged in complete silence, so long that the actors were convinced the performance had entirely failed, and then suddenly broke into deafening applause. This unusual collective reaction seems to have been due to the fact that everybody in the audience had perceived his own image arising with growing intensity before his eyes – in Nemirovich-Danchenko's words, "as scene followed scene, the more intimate these people [the characters] became to the spectator, the more perturbing became their fits of anger, half-phrases, silences, the more powerful there rose from the depth of the spectator's soul the perception of his own unhappiness and anguish" (Nemirovich-Danchenko 1968: 187).

A different aspect of the spectator's image comes to the fore when the individual spectator as opposed to the audience is singled out. The actors may reword their lines so as to involve specific spectators or groups of spectators, whether to flatter them or ridicule or castigate them. But an effect of basically the same nature may be obtained by less direct and more sophisticated procedures that tend to integrate the spectator's image more intimately in the whole *signatum*. This is what, in metaphorical terms, the mime Ladislav Fialka[33] describes in his praise of the clown: "He is a clown and so we should not judge him rashly, say in the middle of his act, because he may surprise us at any moment and make the spectators who are watching both him and us burst out laughing. The good thing about clowns and fools is that while they are making themselves ridiculous they suddenly turn the ridicule against us" (Fialka 1972: 30).

Some extremely complicated problems, which cannot yet be studied at this stage, arise in connection with the image of the spectator, especially where the individual spectator perceives his own image in the *signatum*. On the one hand, this implies that the image varies from one spectator to the next and even – since it is so intimately intertwined with the image of the actor and with the character – that the entire *signatum* is variable as well. This variability is not anything like as great as in music, which tends to convey meanings so indeterminate that the same melody may call up thoroughly different meanings in each individual listener's mind. On the

---

33   [Editor's note: Ladislav Fialka (1931–1991), founder of the Czechoslovak school of classical and modern mime.]

other hand, the ability of acting to make the individual spectator perceive his own image in the *signatum* may perhaps one day throw a new light on the old problem of "catharsis" so as to take it at long last out of the area of meaningless metaphors.

Many other problems of the *signatum* must also be left for further study, in particular: the ways in which the signified action as a unified sequence of meanings, endowed with its own sense, is constructed out of single autonomous meanings; the semiotic relationships between the signified action and the characters in the broader sense, comprising the image of the actor, the character and the image of the spectator; the relationship between the three aspects; and the semiotic relationship between the characters in this broader sense, including the sort of image of the spectator that they respectively contain.

WORKS CITED

Antoine, André (1921) *"Mes Souvenirs" sur le Théâtre-libre* ["My Memories" of the Théâtre-libre], Paris: Fayard.

Benveniste, Emile (1966) "De la subjectivité dans le langage" [On Subjectivity in Language] in *Problèmes de linguistique générale* [Problems of General Linguistics], vol. I, Paris: Gallimard: 258–66.

— (1969) "Sémiologie de la langue" [The Semiotics of Language], *Semiotica* vol. 1, no. 2, pp. 127–35.

Bogatyrev, Petr (1940) *Lidové divadlo české a slovenské* [Czech and Slovak Folk Theatre], Prague: Fr. Borový and Národopisná společnost československá.

— (2016 [1938]) "Theatrical Signs", this reader, pp. 99–114.

Bradbrook, M. C (1963) *The Growth and Structure of Elizabethan Comedy*, Harmondsworth: Penguin.

Braun, Edward (ed.) (1969) *Meyerhold on Theatre*, London: Eyre Methuen.

Brinkmann, Hennig (1929) *Zum Ursprung des liturgischen Spieles* [On the Origins of Liturgical Plays], Bonn: F Cohen.

Brody, Alan (1971) *The English Mummers and Their Plays. Traces of Ancient Mystery*, London: Routledge.

Brušák, Karel (2016 [1991]) "Imaginary Action Space in Drama", this reader, pp. 303–19.

— (2016 [1939]) "Signs in the Chinese Theatre", this reader, pp. 115–28.

Bühler, Karl (1969) *Die Axiomatik der Sprachwissenschaften* [The Axiomatics of Linguistics], Frankfurt am Main: Vittorio Klostermann.

— (2011 [1934]) *Theory of Language: The Representational Function of Language*, Amsterdam; Philadelphia: John Benjamins.

Chambers, F. K. (1903) *The Mediaeval Stage*, vol. 1, Oxford: Clarendon Press.

— (1923) *The Elizabethan Stage*, vol. 1, Oxford: Clarendon Press.

— (1933) *The English Folk-Play*, Oxford: Clarendon Press.

— (1951) *The Elizabethan Stage*, vol. 4, 3rd edition, Oxford: Clarendon Press.

Coquelin, Constant (1968) *The Art of the Actor*, London: Allen & Unwin, 1968.

Craig, Edward Gordon (1962) *On the Art of the Theatre*, London: Heinemann.

Decroux, Etienne (1985) *Words on Mime*, trans. Mark Piper, Claremont : Mime Journal.

Dullin, Charles (1946) *Souvenirs et notes de travail d'un acteur* [Memories and Notes of an Actor's Work], Paris: O. Lieutier.

Ernst, Earle (1956) *The Kabuki Theatre*, New York: Oxford University Press.

Fialka, Ladislav (1972) *Knoflík* [The Button], Prague: Divadelní ústav.

Gourfinkel, Nina (ed.) (1963) *Vsévolod Meyerhold. Le Théâtre théâtral* [Vsevolod Meyerhold: The Theatrical Theatre], Paris: Gallimard.

Gombrich, E. H. (1972a) *Art and Illusion. A Study in the Psychology of Pictorial Representation*, London: Phaidon.

— (1972b) "The Visual Image", *Scientific American*, vol. 227, no. 3 (September), pp. 82–96.

Hein, Norvin (1972) *The Miracle Plays of Mathura*, New Haven and London: Yale University Press.

Helbo, André (ed.) (1975) *Sémiologie de la représentation* [The Semiotics of Representation], Brussels: Complexe.

Honzl, Jindřich (1940) "Nad Diderotovým paradoxem o herci" [Looking at Diderot's *Paradox of the Actor*], *Program D 40*, vol. 4, pp. 81–85.

— (2016 [1940]) "The Mobility of the Theatrical Sign", this reader, pp. 129–48.

Ingarden, Roman (1973) *The Literary Work of Art*, trans. George G. Grabowitz, Evanston: Northwestern University Press.

Jakobson, Roman (1956) "Two Aspects of Language and Two Types of Aphasic Disturbances" in Jakobson, Roman and Halle, Morris (eds), *Fundamentals of Language*, The Hague: Mouton, pp. 59–61

— (1960) "Linguistics and Poetics" in Thomas Sebeok (ed.) *Style in Language*, Cambridge, Mass.: Technology Press of M.I.T / New York-London: John Wiley & Sons: 350–77.

— (1971) *Selected Writings*, vol. 2, *Word and Language*, The Hague: Mouton.

— (1971a) "Da i net v mimike" [Yes and No in Facial Expression] in Jakobson (1971): 360–66.

— (1971b) "Language in Relation to Other Communication Systems" in Jakobson (1971): 697–708.

— (1971c) "Quest for the Essence of Language" in Jakobson (1971): 345–59.

— (1971d) "Shifters, Verbal Categories, and the Russian Verb" in Jakobson (1971): 130–47.

— (1971e) "The Relation between Visual and Auditory Signs" in Jakobson (1971): 338–44.

— (1971f) "Visual and Auditory Signs" in Jakobson (1971): 334–37.

— (2008 [1933]) "Is the Film in Decline?" in Szczepanik, Petr and Anděl, Jaroslav (eds), *Cinema All the Time: An Anthology of Czech Film Theory and Criticism,1908–1939*, Prague: National Film Archive, pp. 270–76.

Kartsevsky, Sergei (1929) "Du dualisme asymetrique de signe linguistique" [On the Asymetrical Dualism of the Linguistic Sign], *Travaux du Cercle linguistique de Prague*, vol. 1, pp. 88–93.

Kouřil, Miroslav (1938) *Divadlo práce* [The Theatre of Labour], Prague: Jaroslav Kohoutek.

Lipps, Theodor (1903) Ästhetik: Psychologie des Schönen [Aesthetics: A Psychology of Beauty], vol. I, *Grundlegung der Ästhetik* [Foundations of Aesthetics], Hamburg – Leipzig: Leopold Voss.

Logan, Joshua (1968) "Introduction" in Nemirovich-Danchenko, Vladimir, *My Life in the Russian Theatre*, London: Bles, pp. I–XV.

Molière (1956) *Oeuvres completes* [Complete Works] vol. 1, ed. Maurice Rat, Paris: Bibliotheque de la Pléiade.

Mounin, Georges (1970) "La communication théâtrale" [Theatrical Communication] in *Introduction à la sémiologie* [Introduction to Semiotics], Paris: Editions de Minuit, pp. 87–94.

Mukařovský, Jan (1948) "O recitačním umění" [On the Art of Declamation] in *Kapitoly z české poetiky* [Chapters on Czech Poetics], vol. 1, Prague: Svoboda, pp. 211–21.

— (2016 [1931]) "Attempt at a Structural Analysis of the Actor's Figure", this reader, pp. 192–98.

— (2016 [1941]) "On the Current State of the Theory of Theatre", this reader, pp. 59–75.

Nemirovich-Danchenko, Vladimir (1968) *My Life in the Russian Theatre*, London: Bles.

Oreglia, Giacomo (1970) *The Commedia dell'arte*, London: Methuen.

Peirce, Charles S. (1932) "Speculative Grammar", *Collected Papers*, vol. 2, Charles Hartshorne and Paul Weiss (eds), Cambridge, Mass: Harvard University Press, pp. 129–269.

Pirandello, Luigi (1993 [1908]) "Illustrators, Actors and Translators" (published in 1908), translated by Susan Bassnett, in *Luigi Pirandello in the Theatre: A Documentary Record*, Susan Bassnett and Jennifer Lorch (eds), Philadelphia: Harwood Academic, pp. 23–34.

Plessner, Helmuth (1953) "Die Deutung des mimischen Ausdrucks. Ein Beitrag zur Lehre vom Bewusstsein des anderen Ichs" [The Interpretation of Mimicry. A Contribution to the Theory of the Consciousness of Other Selves] in *Zwischen Philosophie und Gessellschaft* [Between Philosophy and Society], Bern: Francke, pp. 132–79.

Preuss, Konrad Theodor (1930) *Der Unterbau des Dramas* [The Substructure of Drama] in *Zur Geschichte des Dramas* [On the History of Drama], Leipzig and Berlin: B. G. Teubner, pp. 1–88.

Price, Cecil (1973) *Theatre in the Age of Garrick*, Oxford: Blackwell.

Prudhoe, John (1973) *The Theatre of Goethe and Schiller*, Oxford: Blackwell.

Rennert, Hugo Albert (1963) *The Spanish Stage in the Time of Lope de Vega*, New York: Dover.

Rutebeuf (1949) *Le miracle de Théophile* [The Miracle of Theofilus], ed. Grace Frank, Paris: Champion.

Scherer, Jacques (1966) *Les Structures de Tartuffe* [Structures of *Tartuffe*], Paris: SEDES.

— (1970) *La dramaturgie classique en France* [Classical Dramaturgy in France], Paris: Nizet.

Scotto di Carlo, Nicole (1973) "Analyse sémiologique des gestes et mimiques des chanteurs d'opéra" [A Semiotic Analysis of Opera Singers' Gestures and Mimicry], *Semiotica* vol. 9, no. 4, pp. 289–317.

Sebeok, Thomas (ed.) (1960) *Style in Language*, Cambridge, Mass., and London: Technology Press of M.I.T and John Wiley & Sons.

Sieffert, René (1960) "Introduction" in Zeami 1960, pp. 13–58.

Southern, Richard (1968) *The Seven Ages of the Theatre*, London: Faber

Stanislavski, Konstantin (1956) *My Life in Art*, trans. J. J. Robbins, New York: Meridian books.

— (2008) *My Life in Art*, trans. Jean Benedetti, London: Routledge.

Stein, R. A (1961) "Le théâtre au Tibet" [Theatre in Tibet] in Jean Jacquot (ed.) *Les theatres d'Asie* [Theatres of Asia], Paris: Editions du CNRS: 245–54.

Tairov, Alexander (1983) *Notes of a Director*, trans. William Kuhlke, Miami: University of Miami Press

Tille, Václav (1917) *Divadelní vzpomínky* [Memories of the Theatre], Prague, B. Kočí.

— (1929) *Moskva v listopadu* [Moscow in November], Prague: Aventinum.

Toita, Yasuji (1970) *Kabuki. The Popular Theatre of Japan*, trans. Don Kenny, New York: Walker, Tokyo and Kyoto: Weatherhill.

Veltruský, Jiří (1973) "Some Aspects of the Pictorial Sign" in *Semiotics of Art, Prague School*, Matejka, Ladislav and Titunik, J. T. (eds), Cambridge, Mass.: M.I.T. Press: 245–61.

— (1987 [1940]) "Structure in Folk Theatre. Notes Regarding Bogatyrev's Book on Czech and Slovak Folk Theatre", *Poetics Today*, vol. 8, no. 1, pp. 141–61.

— (2016 [1940]) "People and Things in the Theatre", this reader, pp. 147–56.

— (2016 [1941]) "Dramatic Text as a Component of Theatre", this reader, pp. 247–67.

Wickham, Glynne (1959) *Early English Stages 1300–1660*, vol. 1, London: Routledge.

— (1972) *Early English Stages 1300–1660*, vol. 2, part 2, London: Routledge.

Young, Karl (1951) *The Drama of the Medieval Church*, vol. 2, Oxford: Clarendon Press.

Zeami (1960) *La tradition secrète du Nó* [The Secret Tradition of Noh], Paris: Gallimard.

Zich, Otakar (1931) *Estetika dramatického umění: teoretická dramaturgie* [The Aesthetics of Dramatic Art: A Theoretical Dramaturgy], Prague: Melantrich.

VII   ETHNOGRAPHIC ENCROACHMENTS

Questioning the nature of the art of the theatre, the dynamics of its inner structures and the distinctive features of the theatrical sign (as presented in the previous section of the reader) inevitably leads to the issue of the boundaries of the art of the theatre as such. Seminal texts on this theme are assembled in this section. The material they deal with (folk songs, everyday clothing, folk theatre and ritual) demonstrates an interest in phenomena bearing some – to use current terminology – theatrical or performative aspects, phenomena in which the aesthetic function need not be dominant. The authors go even further and propose the opposite – the existence of theatrical features in everyday life.

The concept of dynamic structure is applied here not only to the work of art itself but also to its social context. Hence Petr Bogatyrev and Jiří Veltruský study shifts of the hierarchy of functions in changing social conditions. This approach strongly questions the idea of an elitist, "high" culture as such, because their observations show a transfer (in both directions!) between high and low cultures, elitist and popular cultures, village and town cultures, and so on. This perspective corresponds with the avant-garde theatre practice, which often takes as a source of inspiration phenomena previously neglected as being merely part of popular culture (among them cabaret, the circus, clowning, silent slapstick films and folk theatre traditions).

These texts open a window into a field that in today's humanities might be associated with performance studies, ethnography and cultural studies. Since not all the key texts were available to a wider readership, contemporary research has not always been conscious of these earlier insights, but it is important to acknowledge the pioneering role of the Prague School in this aspect, especially in the figure of Bogatyrev.

FOLK SONG FROM A FUNCTIONAL POINT OF VIEW

PETR BOGATYREV

["La chanson populaire du point de vue fonctionnel" was first published in French in Prague (1936) in *Travaux du Cercle Linguistique de Prague*, vol. 6 (Études dédiées au quatrième Congrès de linguistes), pp. 222–34. The English translation by Yvonne Lock-wood was published in Matejka, Ladislav and Titunik, Irwin R. (eds) (1976) *Semiotics of Art: Prague School Contributions*, Cambridge, Mass.: The M.I.T. Press, pp. 20–32. The Czech translation "Lidová píseň z funkčního hlediska", authorized by Bogatyrev, was published in Kolár, Jaroslav (ed.) (1971) *Souvislosti tvorby. Cesty k struktuře lidové kultury a divadla* [The Context of Creation. In Search of the Structure of Folk Culture and Folk Theatre], Prague: Odeon, pp. 115–25.]

Editor's note: There are several places where the French and Czech versions, both authorized by Bogatyrev, differ; these have been footnoted.

The folk songs quoted in the article employ a simple rhyme scheme. In the interest of conveying the meaning and retaining the original structure of the texts, no attempt has been made to replicate the rhymes.

When we examine the folk songs of various peoples, what draws our attention is their strongly marked functional character. In addition, the functions of song, as in the case of other social facts, form a complete structure. Besides an aesthetic function, song is also a vehicle for various other functions: a magic function, a regional function, a function setting the rhythm of work, a function indicating a singer's age and gender, and so forth. It should be noted that very often the aesthetic function is not the predominant function of a folk song at all.

Similarly, if we study urban songs using the same functional approach, we come to the conclusion that here too the aesthetic function does not always predominate. Let us take as an example the national anthem. Its functions are clearly different from those of, for example, the Russian "romance".[1]

In the anthem the aesthetic function is relegated to second place. The anthem is a sign of a particular state, just like, for example, the national flag. During the performance of the anthem, all the members of the audience who

---

1 [Editorial note (1971): Bogatyrev uses this term to indicate a particular type of sentimental Russian semi-folk song.]

hold the interests of the state in high esteem show their respect for the anthem while at the same time expressing their respect for the state for which it is the sign. The respect expressed for the anthem rises in proportion to the respect shown by the individual or community for the state the national anthem represents. Very little attention is paid to the aesthetic qualities of the anthem. And on the contrary, for enemies of a particular state, hostility toward its anthem grows in proportion to the hatred felt for the state for which it is the sign. And enemies of the anthem, too, pay only scant regard to its aesthetic qualities, which might be considerable.

This is equally true of songs that are a sign of affiliation to some particular political party or other.

Nevertheless, non-aesthetic functions are more frequent in the case of folk songs than in that of urban songs.

Let us first consider the aesthetic function of folk song. An analysis of this function leads to the conclusion that folk song, as compared with the "romance" and urban song, is very diverse in its scope. Let us look at two such examples. A folk song fulfils the function of rhythmic music, that is, music whose predominant characteristics are the tempo and rhythm of dance. In the nineteenth and the beginning of the twentieth century there were very few rhythmic songs among the upper classes. A rhythmic song like this can be performed with or without instrumental accompaniment.[2] For example, *chastushki* and children's songs are often performed without accompaniment. In all these songs, rhythm is predominant, and in certain cases it may overpower the melody and particularly the words of the song.

Very often in such songs – for example in the *chastushki* – not only the words, which often make no sense, but the melodies as well are reduced to a minimum. Among songs that have a special aesthetic function, we include those where the words and dramatic action are inseparable: the latter is carried out during the performance of the song.

What especially distinguishes folk songs from other types of songs is that everyone sings the former together, whereas in the case of the latter there is a growing trend towards a division between the singer and the audience.[3]

I wish to emphasize that I am speaking here of a general tendency. This does not exclude the fact that among the many different genres of folk song there are also cases where one notes a marked difference between the performer and the audience – for example in the performance of *byliny* or of Russian folk songs about heroes. On the other hand, until recently there

---

2 For some time we have seen something analogous in jazz music; the dancing is accompanied by singing, but usually by instrumental music as well.

3 In Russian villages the former manner of interpretation is now vanishing, as pointed out by Z. N. Kupriyanova: "Only in the close family circle does group singing still occur – the men while working at their loom, the women while spinning" (1932: 33).

existed – and in fact still do exist – urban songs marked by group singing, in particular soldiers' songs and student songs performed by members of student societies.

Along with their aesthetic function, folk songs often fulfil the function of historical narratives, which brings them closer to the function of historical works. This was the role of the *chansons de gestes, byliny,* Russian historical songs and South Slav narrative songs. This category also includes songs glorifying the adventures of brigands.

From the functional point of view, broadside ballads and religious broadsides, which are very widespread in Europe, are very interesting. After singing their songs, the itinerant singers then sold the texts to the listeners; in this way the songs spread both in town and through the countryside.[4]

One of the principal functions of the broadside ballads was to inform the rural public about sensational events such as murders, suicides and accidents – like the news items of a daily newspaper. "A Song about a Murder Most Foul" is a Czech example; it begins with the words:

Stop a moment,[5]
Dearest Christians,
What I will briefly tell you
Is no lie —
What took place in London
In the year one thousand eight hundred
And forty-one. (Adámek 1932–1933: 114)

Or there is unhappy love, recounted in "A New Song about Two Lovers Who Died a Cruel Death from a Love Too Sincere" (Adámek 1932–1933: 142).

Czech broadside ballads also communicated news about such things as various kinds of natural disasters. A typical example is "A New Song about the Great Flood in the Capital City, Prague":

Give ear, all you people,
To what I will sing to you,

---

4   Nonetheless, these songs of urban provenance constitute an integral part of the rural repertoire and must be studied as such. Peasants listened attentively to these songs; they played a considerable role in peasant life. For German broadside ballads, see the interesting and richly documented chapter "Studien über den Bänkelgesang" in Naumann 1921: 168–90. In this study, I will cite only Czech broadside ballads.

5   [Editor's note: in this and subsequent similar texts quoted in this article, various forms and patterns of rhyme were used in the original Czech. It was not possible to retain this feature in the English translations without seriously distorting the meaning.]

With trembling I will speak
About Prague in Bohemia
In 1845
On the 30th of March. (Adámek 1932–1933: 143)

Other songs deal with floods in Hungary, Vienna and elsewhere. Moving a little further afield, we find a song entitled "About the Enormous Snowfall in Russia and the Terrible Fire in Moscow, where So Much Snow Fell in this Year of 1838" (Adámek 1932–1933: 145).

Another piece, "A Song about the Potato Harvest", begins in this way:

Let us praise the Lord on high
For His great favour,
For having blessed the potatoes
And brought such abundance last year. (Adámek 1931: 243)

Songs also have topical themes, as in "A New Song, or Farewell to the Banknotes":

How hard life is,
Everyone can believe me,
Now in this world!
How people wailed
When they heard being read out
The decree on paper money —
That the banknotes would be repudiated
And burnt in Vienna. (Adámek 1931: 247)

There are also broadside ballads about the wars with the Turks and the devastation they wrought, and so on. Other broadside ballads express patriotic and Slavophile sentiments.

Comparisons can easily be made between broadside ballads and newspapers. Like newspapers, the songs give the precise year, month and day of the event. They cite the names of the persons involved and the place where the event took place. The comparison can be developed still further: newspapers must relate recent events; the songs, too, take great pride in informing their listeners of the very latest news. Certain editions of broadside ballads and religious songs do not carry a date. The date may be either completely lacking or replaced by the vague indication "printed this year". The publisher of such a song did this deliberately because a song dating from several years earlier would have had no success with buyers keen on getting the latest songs (Adámek 1932–1933: 29).

Today, and even more so in the past, the magical function occupies a prominent place among the various functions of folk song.

The incantation song[6] had, and often still has, the same function as the incantation formula. In the examination of magical songs, as in that of magical acts, we distinguish between those that are *motivated* and those that are *unmotivated*.[7] In the performance of a motivated magical song – like that of a magical rite – the person carrying it out is conscious of performing an incantation while singing the song, of bringing about what is stated in the text of the song by means of natural phenomena through which supernatural beings are controlled.[8]

The incantation song is closely linked to the petitionary song, which expresses a plea rather than an order for a supernatural being to fulfil a particular request.

At the present time, folk song fulfils an *unmotivated* ritual function more frequently than a motivated one. In many cases such an unmotivated song plays approximately the same role as an unmotivated magical act.

Many unmotivated ritual songs are an inseparable part of a ritual act and their absence, like that of other prescribed parts of the rite, deprives it of its power. Peasants, for example, are aware that in a wedding it is obligatory to carry out a particular rite, just as it is to sing a particular song. At the same time, since this is in an unmotivated rite, they are not aware of why the performance of this particular song should produce a favourable result. They are aware only of having to perform this song in a prescribed manner.

For example, a song can be performed in an unknown language. In this case, the singer is completely unaware of the connection between the text and what the singing of the song is meant to obtain from nature or from a supernatural being, but even when the singer is singing in his or her mother tongue, the text may not have any connection with what is meant to be achieved by singing the song.

But not all ritual songs or all rites are carried out solely because they are intended to bring certain favourable results. Sometimes the song and the rite are carried out as a necessary sign of what is appropriate for a ceremony. For example, if at a wedding the rites that are considered by the whole village to be part of the tradition of that region are not carried out and the traditional songs are not sung, this will not result in any misfortune for the newly married couple. But a wedding without the execution of these rites and ritual songs would not be regarded as a "proper" wedding. Just as it is improper, for

---

6   On this subject see Anichkov 1901 and 1903. The author proposes the hypothesis that the original and most ancient form of folk poetry is to be found in such songs (1901: 382).

7   For the difference between motivated and unmotivated magical acts, see Bogatyrev 1929.

8   [Editor's note: The French version (also authorized by Bogatyrev) reads: "…by means of natural phenomena or the supernatural beings that they control".]

example, for a peasant to seat his guests at a table without a tablecloth, so it is improper at a wedding not to carry out all the rites and not to sing all the songs that are appropriate for such a ceremony. So song here is merely a sign indicating that the hosts are fully aware of everything that should be done during the wedding ceremony.

The function of the sign of solemnity resembles closely the preceding function. Songs render the rites more dignified.

The folk song appears as an indicative sign of village wakes and family celebrations. Certain ritual songs are reserved exclusively for specific festivals. Depending on when a song is performed, we may even be able to determine the type of rite; for example, we can say what part of a wedding ceremony the particular rite belongs to.[9]

The aesthetic function is structurally related to all these previous functions.

Let us note that songs that fulfil ritual functions may not always have been linked to a rite from their very origin. It happens that songs are connected to rites for which they were not originally intended – for example, lyrical songs connected at a later date to the wedding ceremony.

Folk song often fulfils the function of regulating work; it marks the rhythm and accelerates productive capacity. On this subject, see Karl Bücher's *Work and Rhythm* [Arbeit und Rythmus] (Bücher 1896), which has attracted the attention of specialists on this question.[10] In this study we are not concerned with the problem of the origin of song from the point of view of its connection with regulating the rhythm of work. But whatever one's views on this question, it must be emphasized that a whole series of songs have played, and continue to play, the role of regulating work.

Let us turn now to the function of the regional sign in songs. Numerous examples could be cited where ritual and non-ritual songs differ according to region. Thus, in one village some particular ritual song will be sung at weddings; in another, sometimes neighbouring, village an entirely different song will be sung on the same occasion. The same is true of songs for circle dances, songs accompanying games, *chastushki* and lyrical songs.

A different repertoire is also the mark of different religious groups. Thus, the repertoire of Catholics is not the same as that of Protestants; Russian Old Believers have a different repertoire from that of the Orthodox; the same can be said for Jews, Moslems and other groups.

However, many songs of a religious nature cannot be considered a sign of a particular confession. Some of these songs – for example, those with

---

9   For details, see the chapter entitled "Das Lied als Zeichen" [The Song as Sign] in Bringemeier 1931: 107–13.

10   See Anichkov 1901: 386–89, where Karl Bücher's theory is corrected and extensively elaborated on.

a biblical content or those having the lives of saints as subject matter – may be linked with songs that fulfil a historical function.

With regard to a sign enabling recognition of a social group, it is first necessary to note the difference between the repertoire of village artisans and that of peasants.

The question of the difference between the repertoires of rich and poor peasants is complex. Wealthy peasants are inclined to break away from their social group and to imitate other classes. The well-to-do peasant, while living his life as a peasant and remaining attached to his milieu, will send his son to study in town, and the latter will introduce changes to the repertoire of his family. It also happens that in a family of wealthy peasants the husband alone will detach himself from his social group in terms of his clothing and his song repertoire, while the wife will remain loyal to the traditions of her social class.

But the opposite is not uncommon either: often it is the wealthy peasants, remaining in the village where they were born, attached to their social class and proud of belonging to it, who preserve the ancient traditional folk songs. The poor peasants, obliged to leave their village in order to seek work elsewhere, become separated from their social milieu, forget their ancient repertoire and learn the songs sung in other villages and in the towns.

As we have stated earlier, a song also indicates who should sing it, whether men or women. Collectors and students of folk songs have often pointed out the differences in male and female repertoires.

Also, *byliny* and Russian historical songs performed by men differ appreciably from similar songs performed by women. This difference is still more marked in lyrical songs. It would be strange, for example, to hear men performing songs intended for women or vice versa. Certain ritual wedding songs are performed by women and others by men. The same differentiation exists in the performance of *chastushki*.

Let us quote here some observations made in contemporary Russian villages.

The transcription and study of songs allows us to establish a distinction in the male and the female repertoire, particularly in the case of old peasants. Wedding songs and songs for circle dances are sung by women. The song "Proshchai zhizn' – radost moia" [Farewell, My Life – My Joy] was transcribed 36 times; on 34 occasions it was sung by women and only twice by men. It is primarily men who know and sing the song "Ekhali soldaty" [The Soldiers Went Riding By]. It was transcribed 11 times – 10 times sung by men and once by a woman. There are also songs common to both sexes. The above demarcation is much less distinct among young people. Songs of the Komsomol [Young Communist League] are sung in equal measure by young men and young women. (Kupriyanova 1932: 34)

With respect to song as a marker indicating the marital status of a woman (married or single), this is especially striking in ritual songs, in particular wedding songs: some songs are performed exclusively by maidens while others are restricted to married women. This is a frequent demarcation: in Slovakia the songs that accompany the springtime rite of the drowning of a straw-stuffed figure representing Death are only performed by maidens.

This demarcation is even more clear-cut in the case of funeral lamentations, which are different for the mother, the daughter and the wife of a deceased man.[11]

It is very easy to find in songs the sign of a performer's age; some are sung from generation to generation by young people, others by adults. Christmas songs usually fit into the first category: these songs have always been sung by boys.

On the other hand, it is necessary to distinguish songs that are only performed nowadays by old men but that may not have always have been restricted in this way. The situation can differ from one generation to another: for example, adults may sing songs that they sang in their youth but that today's young people no longer sing.

Children's songs differ in form and functions from those of adults and are of special interest. We know that these songs are often taken from the adults' repertoire, but they adapt their form to their new functions.

Applying the functional method to the study of folk song also allows us to clarify obscure points in its development – for example, questions about the diffusion of the art song and the "romance" into the folk repertoire and the modifications undergone in transmission. What we were unable to understand in the process of transformation from art song into folk song will be explained if we consider this process from the functional point of view.

As a general rule, we should always keep in mind that the non-aesthetic function plays a much more important role in folk song than in the "romances" sung in the town. This is one of the principal differences between these two genres.

Given the success of certain folk songs, it is necessary to consider both their aesthetic and their non-aesthetic function. We would be committing a major error if we were to seek to explain why a particular song persists in villages on the basis of the functions fulfilled by song and the "romance" type of song among townspeople.

It is quite natural that we forget more quickly than villagers songs that no longer meet our needs but fill other functions; we have at our disposal other

---

11   The same differentiation exists in Russian and Romanian laments. See Barsov 1872 and 1882; Brăiloiu 1932.

social facts that compete more successfully with songs in fulfilling these non-aesthetic functions.

Even if a song that does not meet our aesthetic requirements fulfils its historical function reasonably well, it will not be able to compete for long with historical works of another kind; as a result, the song will be quickly forgotten. If it tells of a sensational event, we will cast it aside and forget it as soon as more sensational news is brought to us by the press. But the situation will be different in a milieu where newspapers and books exist in limited numbers and where song often takes on their functions.

With regard to *byliny* and historical songs, they have undoubtedly served multiple functions, both in the past and at the present time. Their poetic function is reflected in their artistic form, rich in poetic nuances. But at the same time they always fulfilled and continue to fulfil the function of historical narratives. Early in their existence, certain *byliny* seem to have had functions analogous to contemporary newspaper articles dealing with domestic and foreign political topics: they extolled one political faction at a Russian prince's court while attacking another. When they passed from the aristocratic milieu to the peasantry, this function inevitably disappeared. Research employing the functional method in the field of the Slavic and non-Slavic narrative poem will enable us to understand much that has hitherto been inexplicable.

Nevertheless, in order to form some probable hypotheses on the functions of ancient songs, we consider it important from a methodological point of view to first assemble as much material as possible on the functions of modern songs and to establish, as far as possible, the laws by which they are transformed. This would allow us to apply deductions made in the field of modern song to more distant epochs. It goes without saying that we must proceed with great caution when applying findings in the area of modern song to ancient songs; one must never forget that a particular social fact can change its function completely upon entering another social structure, even when its form remains unchanged.

The same song is perceived differently by people who possess a diverse repertoire of songs and by others who only know their local songs. A folk song will be perceived differently by a peasant singer and by, for example, the composer Rimsky-Korsakov, who transcribed the song exactly as the peasant sang it, but who views it against the general background of Russian and European music. This is why one must first determine the position that a given song occupies in the whole repertoire of the performer and the functions that it fulfils. At the same time one must also determine the position the song holds within the whole song repertoire, the whole musical repertoire and, finally, the whole literary repertoire of the particular milieu in question. As we have pointed out several times, the function of folk song is not only aesthetic. When it fulfils the function of a historical narrative, it is essential to take account of the historical knowledge of the singer and his milieu. This allows us to explain how the historical element of the song is understood by the individual and by the entire group, to what degree it is comprehended in a critical manner, and so forth. Again, in order to understand the degree to which certain songs – for example the broadside ballads dealt with above – fulfil the function of newspaper articles, it is necessary to ask how widely distributed newspapers are in a given milieu and how familiar the singer is with them, to know on the one hand how popular newspapers are in the milieu and, on the other, what popularity is enjoyed by chronicles, which are written in a form similar to that of the broadside ballads already referred to. Furthermore, in order to understand the function of folk song as a regional sign, we must take into account movement within the region and the atmosphere of the peasant milieu. In order to grasp the function of song as a sign of social class, it is necessary to understand the composition of the social classes and the nature of the class struggle in the village where the song has been written down.

So it is only when we have a thorough knowledge of all the structures of the cultural, political and economic life of the milieu in question that we are able to comprehend all the functions and the structure of the functions of a song. On the other hand, songs themselves explain many things about the cultural, political and economic structure of this milieu.

I now wish to make a few remarks about the functions of the folk song when it passes from a peasant milieu into the realm of literature. We can trace this evolution in Russia. Up until the eighteenth century, to the best of our knowledge, the difference between the peasant and the aristocratic song repertoire was insignificant. In the eighteenth century folk song was felt to be something exotic in the repertoire of art songs. At that time, in Russian aristocratic circles, folk song's prime function was aesthetic; in addition, it reflected the moral and patriarchal life of the honest peasants.

During the Romantic period, the predominant function of folk song in Russian literary milieus was national. It was a sign of the national vigour of the people. Among the last Romantic Slavophiles, folk song filled the function of a sign of the Slavophile party, representing the Russian and Slav element – in other words, a sign of the Messianic mission of the Russian and Slavic peoples. At the time when he was an enthusiastic Slavophile, Alexander Ostrovsky claimed that "with Terty and Prov we have overturned all the work of Peter."[12] In the literary circle of the Narodniks the predominant function of folk song was revolutionary. For the Narodniks, folk song was the "cri du

---

12 Terty Filippov (1825–1899), a Russian folk song singer, was celebrated in Slavophile circles; Prov Sadovsky (18181–872), a talented actor, who played the roles of Russian character types in dramas and comedies; "the work of Peter" refers to Peter the Great and his Europeanization of Russia.

coeur" of an oppressed people. Among the Symbolists the predominant function of folk song was aesthetic and mystic.

What I have just presented briefly is a broad outline of the predominant functions that folk song has fulfilled in the course of time for different literary schools. In reality the problem is more complex. It is complicated primarily by the fact that in various periods more than one literary school existed and each had its own notion of folk song.[13]

When examining different functions of folk song, we observe that some are expressed simultaneously, in equal or virtually equal proportions, by the words and by the melody. Thus, the regional sign of a song, by which it is differentiated from songs from other regions, is expressed by its particular melody and oral text in equal or virtually equal proportions. Songs as signs of class, specific social groups or different age groups have distinctive features expressed equally by melody and text.

But in certain cases it is the text of the song that is the primary vehicle of its function. This is true, for example, of songs that fulfil the function of news items in newspapers. Such songs are often sung to the melody of older songs that have no connection with the news type of song.

In other cases, on the contrary, a particular function is expressed primarily, and sometimes exclusively, by the melody and rhythm – for example in lullabies. Their predominant function is to calm down and soothe a child through melody and regular rhythm. Hence the content of the texts of these songs is usually rather mediocre. This is understandable because these songs are usually sung to an infant who is not yet able to comprehend the meaning. In cases where there is a more sophisticated text in a lullaby, it undoubtedly plays a secondary role; it is not aimed at the individual to whom the lullaby is sung, that is, the child, but to the person who is singing it and who, while putting the child to sleep, simultaneously experiences an aesthetic pleasure from the fact that the song has interesting words. With some modifications, this also applies to work songs, whose principal function is to produce a rhythm for carrying out work. In this case, too, the words of the song play a secondary role.

One of the urgent tasks of contemporary musicology is the study of the musical form of song in conjunction with its change of function.[14]

The structure of the functions of folk song, like the structure of other social facts, is not fixed but is constantly changing. Functions formerly predominant became secondary and can even disappear completely; sometimes secondary functions come to the fore; at other times new functions appear.

---

13   For the different functions of folk song in various Czech literary schools see Mukařovský 1935.

14   A first effort at this kind of study can be found in an article in Russian (Evald 1934).

The structure of the functions of a song alters owing to changes in the circumstances related to the song. For example, in a work song the predominant function will be to establish and to stress the rhythm of the work. When the same song is sung at a time of rest, the aesthetic function replaces the former function. The evolution of customs and way of life entails modifications in the "world view"; the functions of song adapt to these changes. Thus, a song whose predominant function was that of a motivated incantation will shift its dominant function to that of an unmotivated incantation, and then to one marking the solemnity of the rite. Note that the stages do not always come in this order: they can occur in the opposite direction and sometimes stages can even be skipped.

The functions of a folk song are modified when the song passes from one milieu to another. The scholar should always keep this in mind when studying songs that have passed from aristocratic classes and the urban milieu to the peasantry and vice versa.

We have examined a number of diverse functions that folk song fulfils and has fulfilled. In many respects the functions of song are the same as the functions of other social facts in the village milieu. In particular a number of song functions agree with those of folk costume; both are signs of region, of age, of religion, and so on.

But there are fundamental differences between folk song and folk costume. The latter is not only a sign; it is an object, a thing (see Bogatyrev 2016 [1934]). Folk song (provided that the aesthetic function is understood as a sign of a social fact) is only a sign. From this point of view it will be significantly closer to signs such as speech and various genres of folk literature: tales, legends, proverbs, and so forth.

WORKS CITED

Adámek, Karel V. (1931) "Světské písně jarmareční a poutní" [Secular Broadside Ballads], *Národopisný věstník českoslovanský*, vol. 24, pp. 21–39; pp. 221–52.

— (1932–1933) "Písně jarmareční a poutní" [Broadside Ballads], *Národopisný věstník českoslovanský*, vol. 25–26, pp. 95–146.

Anichkov, Evgenii (1903) "*Vesenniaia obriadovaia pesnia na západe i u slavian*" [Ritual Spring Song in the West and among the Slavs], part 1, *Sbornik otdeleniia Russkogo Jazyka i Slovesnosti*, vol. 74, no. 2.

— (1905) "*Vesenniaia obriadovaia pesnia na západe i u slavian*" [Ritual Spring Song in the West and among the Slavs], part 2, *Sbornik Otdeleniia Russkogo Jazyka i Slovesnosti*, vol. 78, no. 5.

Barsov, E. B. (1872) *Prichitaniia severnogo kraia* [Laments of the Northern Region], vol. 1.

— (1882) *Prichitaniia severnogo kraia* [Laments of the Northern Region], vol. 2.

Bogatyrev, Petr (1929) "Actes magiques, rites et croyances en Russie Subcarpathique" [Magical Acts, Rites and Beliefs in Subcarpathian Ruthenia], *Travaux, Institut d'études slaves*, vol. 11, pp. 22–24.

— (2016 [1934]) "Clothing as Sign", this reader, pp. 441–47.

Brăiloiu, Constantin (1932) "Despre bocetul dela Drăgus" [A Note on the Funeral Lament in the Village of Drăgus], *Archiva pentru ştiinţa şi reforma sociálă – Organ al institutului social român*, vol. 10, pp. 280–359.

Bringemeier, Martha (1931) *Gemeinschaft und Volkslied* [Community and Folk Song], Münster: Aschendorff.

Bücher, Karl (1896) *Arbeit und Rhytmus* [Work and Rhythm], Leipzig: B. G. Teubner.

Evald, Z. V. (1934) "Sotsialnoe pereosmyslenie zhnivnykh pesen belorusskogo Polesia" [Change in Meaning in Harvest Songs of Polesye in White Russia from a Sociological Point of View], *Sovetskaja etnografija*, vol. 5, pp. 17–39.

Kupriyanova, Z. N. (1932) "Pesni derevni Pogromny" [Songs of the Village of Pogromna], *Jazyk i literatura*, vol. 8.

Mukařovský, Jan (1935) "Vítězslav Hálek", *Slovo a slovesnost*, vol. 1, no. 2, pp. 73–87.

Naumann, Hans (1921) "Studien über den Bänkelgesang" [Studies on Ballad Singers], *Primitive Gemeinschaftskultur: Beiträge zur Volkskunde und Mythologie* [Primitive Communal Culture: Contributions to Folklore and Mythology], Jena: E. Diederichs, pp. 168–90.

CLOTHING AS SIGN
THE FUNCTIONAL AND STRUCTURAL
CONCEPT IN ETHNOGRAPHY

PETR BOGATYREV

["Kroj jako znak: funkční a strukturální pojetí v národopisu" was first published in 1936 in *Sloveso a slovesnost*, vol. 2, pp. 43–47. It was translated into English by Yvonne Lockwood and published in 1976 as "Costume as a Sign" in Matejka, Ladislav and Titunik, Irwin R. (eds) *Semiotics of Art: Prague School Contributions*, Cambridge, Mass.: The M.I.T. Press, pp. 13–19.]

Editor's note: The title has been changed from "Costume as a Sign" to "Clothing as Sign". The word *kroj*, which appears in the original Czech title of this article, has two main areas of meaning. The first is a distinctive type of clothing worn by some particular social group (folk costumes) or organization (Scout uniforms). The second meaning (now archaic) is clothes in general (men's clothing). Bogatyrev's *kroj* and other Czech synonyms he employs bridge the gap that exists in English between more limited and generic terms. As his argument is general, dealing as it does with the way clothes signify such things as social status, age, religion, and so on, the most general English word, "clothing" has been chosen as being preferable.

Urban and rural clothing, used in the sense of distinctive types of dress, have many functions: a practical function, an aesthetic function (frequently linked to an erotic function), a magic function. Clothing also functions as an indicator of the age of its wearer, and it has a social and gender function (differentiating married and single people) that is closely linked to a function denoting the sexual morals of its wearer (in Slovakia, for example, a special kind of folk costume indicates an unwed mother). There is also a festive function and functions indicating professions, social status, class, region, nationality, religion, and so forth. At the same time, however, clothing is both a thing and a sign.

Let us first determine the difference between a thing and a sign.[1] We can observe two kinds of objects in the world around us. One kind has no ideological significance – for example natural objects, implements, objects of everyday use. We can make use of them, get to know their structure, learn

---

1   Here I use the word "sign" in a broad sense. Within the term "sign" we could differentiate between signs themselves, symbols and signals. Regarding sign and symbol, see Chizhevsky 1931: 231. For the definition of "sign", see the works of Karl Bühler.

what they are composed of or what role they play in production, and so on, but we do not suppose that a stone or a hammer, for example, is a sign that denotes something else, some kind of other object or other event. However, if we take a stone, paint it white, and then place it between two fields, this is something different. Such a stone takes on a specific meaning: now it will no longer denote merely itself – a stone as part of the natural world – but will acquire a different, new meaning. It will denote something beyond itself: it will become a marker, a signal, that is a sign with a particular and change-able meaning. A sign of what? A sign marking the border that runs between two plots of land. In a similar fashion, when we see an overlapping hammer and sickle (or an image of them) displayed in a prominent place, the ham-mer and sickle are not merely tools or an image of tools, but a symbol of the USSR. What exactly has happened? A material phenomenon has become an ideological phenomenon: a thing has changed into a sign (though it still retains its material nature). Signs are also specific material things, and as we can see, any thing in the world of nature, technology or everyday use can become a sign when it acquires a meaning extending beyond the bounds of its individual existence as a thing of nature or a thing used in production or consumption.[2]

Some objects can be a thing and a sign in equal measure; for example *clothing*, having several functions, is usually a thing and a sign at the same time. This close structural connection of thing and sign in one object is not unique to clothing alone. Take the example of the famous legend about The-seus. Theseus announced that his ship would return with white sails if he was alive and with black sails if he had died. In both cases, the sails would remain things: they would have to satisfy all the requirements of sails with respect to quality, strength, durability of material, suitability of shape, and so on. But besides their existence as sails, they would also be a sign of whether Theseus was dead or alive. So we see from the legend that as a sign the sails had a very clear function, one different from their function as a thing, but besides being a sign they also remained a thing. The same is true of clothing: it always has a practical function and it is always not only a thing but also a sign. Cases where clothing is only a sign are quite rare. Even in the case of a Chinese theatre costume made of paper, whose primary function is to denote that the actor is playing a Chinaman, in addition to being a sign the costume is also a thing covering the actor's body.

If we examine the individual functions of clothing, we again see that they pertain to clothing both *as a thing* and *as a sign*. Of all the functions mentioned above, only the practical and, to a certain degree, the aesthetic functions

---

2   V. N. Voloshinov explains the relationship of thing and sign in this way, drawing on more or less similar examples (1983 [1930]: 45).

pertain to clothing solely as a thing.[3] Many other functions pertain simultaneously to both the clothing itself as well as to other fields that it denotes. For example, the role of Sunday dress is closely linked to the clothing itself – that is, it should be made of expensive material, it should look attractive – but at the same time certain details – including the expensive cloth itself – relate not just to the clothing but also serve to signify that this day is a holiday and not a weekday. The case of the function indicating class is similar. The fact that clothing worn by the rich is made of more expensive fabric relates to the clothing itself but at the same time it also indicates the social class of the wearer. However in this case – let me repeat – the clothing itself also changes as a thing. Let us imagine that we obtain from some village – for example Vajnor in the Bratislava area, where in the past rich peasant women embroidered the sleeves of their clothing in gold and the poor only in silk – the folk costume of a rich peasant woman and that of a poor woman, and that we send these to a second-hand clothes dealer in the city. Even if the dealer were not aware that these two pieces of clothing are signs of the class difference between the two peasant women, he would still appraise the sleeves differently as things. In certain special circumstances, however, an item of clothing that denotes the social status of its wearer may manifest this merely through a sign. A military uniform, for example, displays certain details that denote the rights of the wearer and his rank in the army. When an ordinary soldier sees the uniform of an officer, he knows that he is obliged to obey his command; the quality of the material and the aesthetic value of the uniform are totally irrelevant. But if we take the uniform of a rich soldier, made of better material than an officer's uniform,[4] and send it to a second-hand clothes dealer who knows nothing about military distinctions, he may attach higher value to the ordinary soldier's uniform than to that of an officer. Or if there is no difference in the quality of material, the dealer might assess the uniforms as having equal value, though in the army these two uniforms differ substantially – as signs. In order to understand the social functions of this type of clothing – uniforms – we must learn to understand these signs in the same way that we learn to understand different words in a language. In a similar way, for example, in some places differences in colour denote nationality: in Slovakia Germans wear darker colours than Slovaks. In other areas darker and lighter colours denote a difference in religion between Protestants and Catholics; elsewhere again they denote a difference in age. Just as soldiers learn to distinguish the various insignia on a military uniform, so villagers

---

3   In this I disagree with Voloshinov (1983 [1930]), who attributes an aesthetic function to the sign. Admittedly, the question of whether this function can be attributed to the thing alone or to the sign as well as the thing is not clear, and so we leave it open.

4   [Editor's note: Bogatyrev is referring to a practice in the Imperial Russian army and later whereby those who were able to afford it could, if they wished, have their uniforms privately tailored.]

in a particular region learn from childhood to recognize what differences in the colour of clothing mean.

Some of the functions of clothing mentioned at the beginning derive solely from its properties as a sign. If an unwed mother is supposed to wear certain items of clothing, the neighbours mainly notice whether she is wearing these items and not different ones appropriate for a maiden; in this case it is irrelevant whether these are made of better or worse material, whether they are attractive or not. Moreover, in the process of recognizing this distinctive type of folk dress for unwed mothers, one also has to have a full knowledge of these items of clothing serving as signs, since what in one village denotes an unwed mother can be part of a maiden's costume in another village. Likewise, the regional function of a folk costume is meant to differentiate it from that of another region; it is irrelevant whether the costume from the other region is more practical or more attractive. A folk costume with a gender and social role is designed to show, for example, that a woman is married. And a married woman, though she might consider a maiden's costume more comfortable or more suitable, cannot wear it.

Thus clothing is characterized by an entire structure of functions. Normally – as in the case mentioned above of the sails on Theseus's ship – in addition to a few functions relating to clothes as things (for example a practical function), there are many functions that extend into various other fields. This structure of diverse functions always makes clothing at once a thing and a sign.

Similarly, *language* always fulfils several functions simultaneously. Let us take a concrete example. We ask someone how to get to the railroad station and he tells us. His speech indicates the direction to us, because we understand his words (signs), but at the same time it is also for us a sign that characterizes the speaker himself: while listening to his directions, we note that he is using dialect or slang expressions and on the basis of this can determine where he comes from or his social status. Furthermore, in conversation everyone accommodates himself to whoever he is talking with. Take, for example, the situation in the countryside when someone asks how to get to the railway station. If an eight-year-old child asks the question, the explanation given will be different from that in answer to a question from a local adult, and yet another response will be given to some stranger from the city. In Gogol's *Dead Souls* there is a fine example of how Chichikov, moving in different social circles and continuously meeting people from new and different social and cultural milieus, changes his behaviour and language to suit the setting. Something similar occurs in connection with clothes.

Clothing is far more determined by its wearer than language is by the speaker. From a person's clothes – often against his will – we can determine his social status, his cultural sophistication, his taste and so on more easily than from speech. Yet even clothing – and in this it corresponds with language – is not determined solely by the personality of its wearer. The person wearing an item of clothing is concerned not only that it satisfy his own personal taste but also that it be in keeping with the clothes worn in his surroundings, that it conform to the standards of his milieu. Everyone adapts to his environment both in language and in clothing. Ethnographers know very well that as a rule country people who have returned to their native village from the city stop wearing city clothes and dress in the village style so as not to be rejected by the community, so as not to "stick out". In Subcarpathian Ruthenia, married women wear the folk dress of the village they have married into, where they live with their husband. Even a city dweller very often dresses with a view to how the other people at the gathering he is planning to attend will be dressed. Everyone knows how embarrassed many men are if they are wearing a suit where everyone is in formal dress, and conversely, how unpleasant it is to be the only one at a party in a tailcoat.

I believe that the use of the functional method in ethnography can not only throw a new light on this matter but also expand it. For an ethnographer concerned with the origin and development of the village folk costume, these village folk costumes are the inescapable object of research. If folk costumes disappear from village life, ethnographic fieldwork also comes to an end. The ethnographer is then wholly dependent on museum collections, some of which are more, some less, complete, and which become more and more difficult, and sometimes completely impossible, to complete or verify. A functional analysis of rural dress is another matter. The function of village dress persists even when none of the features of the old folk costume are present any longer and when rural clothing has merged completely with that of the city. For the ethnographer questions then arise as to what functions rural dress has when its appearance and material have changed and when it has become similar to city dress or has completely merged with it. For example, before the Great War galoshes were still very much in style in Russian villages, but the villagers, in particular the young people, did not wear them in bad and muddy weather but on sunny holidays. In the city the primary function of galoshes was to protect one's feet from moisture and mud; in the village, however, the primary function was aesthetic. For example, there is a song that goes as follows:

All the lads look fine in galoshes
but my love, even without galoshes,
is neat and handsome all the time.

So for an ethnographer who employs a historical approach, galoshes are not an object of research when it comes to village folk costume. But for an ethnographer who is focused on the function of costume, galoshes are just as interesting as the lacquered boots or decorated bast shoes of the past, whose primary function, as in the case of galoshes, was aesthetic.

The ethnographer employing a functional method can supply a great deal of information to the sociologist studying contemporary urban dress. On the other hand, the ethnographer must also keep himself informed of the latest findings in sociology.

In this article, which focuses on the functions of clothing and their structure, I would also like to mention some interesting problems arising from the study of functions and their structure in other ethnographic material. Take, for example, village structures. Here we see that in addition to its practical functions a village building has many other functions as well – aesthetic, magic, regional, social, and so on. A building is not only a thing but also a sign. In some regions even at a distance the outward appearance of a building can tell us such things as the nationality and social status of its owner. Implements used for work in the village are also both things and signs. Sometimes in the case of a thing that on the surface seems merely practical, the aesthetic function displaces the practical function, and the thing becomes only a sign. A striking example of this is the rollers of rotary irons, painted and adorned with small mirrors, which it is the custom in some Slovak villages for the grooms to give their brides but which, because of their decoration, cannot actually be used. There are very few village implements whose function is solely practical, that do not have some other function, in particular functions of an aesthetic and regional nature.

Let us move on to *folklore.* Here, too – and especially here – the functional approach to research is opening up new and broader perspectives. The demarcation of folk tales on the basis of form is always imprecise. Collections of folk tales often expand rather broadly to encompass diverse types of tales, for example historical tales, that are very different from fantastic tales, while on the other hand they often omit *byliny,* even those that are no longer sung but only narrated. The classification of the oral folk tradition according to the functions it fulfils in itself sheds new light on folk narrative material. Again, the study of the functions of children's tales, functions both aesthetic and practical (to please the child, and sometimes to lull it to sleep), can reveal a great deal about the form of the tales themselves and lead us to link them more closely to lullabies. On the other hand, a functional study of the narration of tales reveals not only fantastic but also didactic elements. A structural study of the various functions of folk tales then provides much insight for the study of their individual functions as well: for example, many stylistic features of the narration are clarified when we see that the narrative has both aesthetic and didactic functions. In folk songs about customs, to mention another area, one must take note not only of the aesthetic function but also of such other functions as the magical, the regional and the social. An outstanding example of the structural linkage of different functions is that of incantations. Incantations have an aesthetic function, reflected in their wealth of poetic images and tropes, but the suggestive function is also very strongly present, the aim being to exorcise malevolent spirits troubling the sick person, to induce in him a state like that induced by a doctor hypnotizing a patient. The study of proverbs, too, offers the folklorist a great deal of material: in the different periods they pass through proverbs take on different functions. Often they lose their original meaning and take on a new one. What happens to them is similar to what happened to the French expression "*cher ami*" in Russian dialects, where it has become an insult. In a similar fashion the Russian proverb "Ni Bogu svechka, ni chertu kocherga" ("Neither a candle for God nor a poker for the Devil") can lose its religious meaning, and a speaker may well have no inkling that the "poker" is linked to the forces of evil and may think that the proverb merely denotes a person who isn't suited for anything ("neither fish nor fowl").

With these brief comments I only wished to indicate the immense possibilities that a functional and structural approach can offer for research in various fields of ethnography (see Bogatyrev 1935).

WORKS CITED

Bogatyrev, Petr (1935) "Funkčno-štrukturálna metóda a iné metódy etnografie a folkloristiky" [The Functional-Structural Method and Some Other Methods of Ethnography and Folkloristics], *Slovenské pohľady*, vol. 51, no. 10, pp. 550–58.

Chizhevsky, Dmitry (1931) "Etika i logika" [Ethics and Logic], *Nauchnye trudy Russkogo narodnogo universiteta v Prage*, vol. IV, pp. 222–40.

Voloshinov, V. N. (1983 [1930]) "The Word and Its Social Function", trans. Joe Andrew, ed. Ann Shukman, *Bakhtin School Papers* (*Russian Poetics in Translation*, vol. 10), Oxford: RPT Publications, pp. 139–52.

FOLK THEATRE

PETR BOGATYREV

["Lidové divadlo" was first published in Czech in *Program D 37*, vol. 8 (31 March 1937), pp. 188–95.]

Translated by Ivan Kolman

Folk songs, folk dances and all forms of folk creation are an inexhaustible source for modern theatre, they are its vitamins.
From a lecture given by Vsevolod Meyerhold in Prague[1]

Quite understandably modern art gravitates towards folk art, and therefore modern theatre gravitates towards folk theatre. Folk theatre – which arose in a different social environment than artificial theatre, is performed for a different audience and uses different creative means – has created values that our theatre lacks. Whenever the theatre of the so-called upper classes turned to folk theatre in various periods, it always served to stimulate the creation of great works. Think of Stravinsky, Martinů[2] and others just from the recent period. In some cases, regrettably, this borrowing is too simplified, merely mechanical. A folk play is taken, reworked according to the traditions of our theatre and then presented in this form to the audience, often ignoring the most typical artistic elements of folk theatre. To absorb and express Rembrandt's painting methods is something entirely different from just painting people dressed up as they were in the time of Rembrandt. Rembrandt's creative methods can be expressed even in a portrait of a contemporary of ours. Creative borrowing from folk theatre does not necessarily mean including *Bethlehem, St Dorothy*[3] and so on in the repertoire. Folk theatre methods can be employed even when performing a modern play.

Theatre is a structure composed of elements from various arts, but the whole structure is something new, substantially new, which cannot be found

1   [Editor's note: Meyerhold gave a lecture on the modern theatre at the Urania Theatre in Prague on 29 October 1936. The sentence quoted by Bogatyrev can be found in Meyerhold 1936: 72.]

2   [Editor's note: Bohuslav Martinů (1890–1959), Czech composer, who lived and composed in Prague, Paris and elsewhere in Europe and the United States. In his opera *The Plays of Mary* (1935) he draws on medieval and folk texts with a religious theme for the libretto.]

3   [Editor's note: Folk plays telling the story of the birth of Christ, as well as ones based on the life and martyrdom of St Dorothy, enjoyed great popularity in the Czech lands and Slovakia.]

in literature, in the visual arts, in the art of recitation, in choreography or in the other arts whose elements contribute to the theatre performance. Theatre is a unique integral structure whose components are the auditorium and the stage. A change in one element of the theatre performance, just as in any other system, impairs this integrity and results in a change to the whole structure and all its components. The best example of this is puppet theatre. Puppeteers often took plays from the repertoire of the theatre of live actors, but when a puppet took the place of a live actor, it was also necessary to change the text. It suffices to compare the texts of the same plays used for both puppet and live theatre. One could mention a great many examples of a correlation between the actors' acting and the composition of the audience, between the set and the text of the play. We will speak only about this latter correlation. Let us recall what difficulties the realist and the naturalist theatre were forced to overcome with their complicated, cumbersome sets for productions of Shakespeare's tragedies. Because of these sets it was necessary to shorten the texts of these tragedies, which are composed of numerous short scenes. All this explains why we have to study theatre, especially folk theatre, as a coherent structure, without leaving out a single element. Unfortunately, so far nothing has been done, or almost nothing, in the area of the study of folk theatre as a whole, as a coherent structure consisting of numerous elements (the text, set, acting, masks, makeup, and so on). Only *one single account* of a folk theatre production is known in which the script was recorded in such a way as to allow any intelligent director to reconstruct the performance with great precision. This is an account made in the summer of 1926 in the course of an expedition undertaken by the Sociology Committee of the State Institute for the History of Arts in the Soviet Union (Pisarev and Suslovich 1927: 184). Such is the pitiful state of folk theatre studies so far! I will proceed from this account of the Russian folk comedy *Pakhomushka* and I will supplement it with bits and pieces found in accounts of Russian, Czech and Slovak folk productions.

Let us move on to an analysis of the individual elements of a folk theatre production and let us try to find what interesting features this analysis can offer for our contemporary theatre.

Let us start with the main problem of every theatre – the dialectical contradiction of the auditorium and the stage. Throughout its history this problem has been a subject of great interest among all theatre people and it has been dealt with by every theatre movement in a different way. This problem was felt especially acutely in Russia before the revolution at a time of crisis in the theatre. Some theatre practitioners and researchers considered the separation of the theatre from the audience, from the auditorium, the crucial cause of its crisis and they felt it could be solved by bringing the auditorium closer to the stage and vice versa.

However, one of the characteristic features of the folk theatre is this spatial closeness of the audience and the stage.

The intense tempo and the teamwork of the group performing *Pakhomushka* depend not only on the main actors' experience and ability but also on the spectators, who set the direction of the course of the play (and the text) by cheering and prompting. Thus the audience partly replaces the director, who is absent. There is no audience in the true sense of the word in the comedy of *Pakhomushka*. It is a genuine "collective performance". All the people present in the village hall participate in the play so boisterously that their activity goes far beyond the participation of a "spectator" at mass festivities. Anyone who has performed in or seen *Pakhomushka* interrupts the play without hesitation, adding his comments to both the text and the performance. At times those who are present fill the stage space and it is difficult to determine who the characters of the play are. Although the play itself is interrupted by this, the tension does not flag. This goes on until some decisive hand sends them all back to their places. (Pisarev and Suslovich 1927: 184)

It should be said that *Pakhomushka* is a comedy of unrestrained entertainment without any traces of serious action. But as soon as the character of the play changes, the audience's behaviour changes too. Scripts of the *St Dorothy* play in Moravia and Slovakia show that only comic characters, for example the executioner, are allowed to speak to and play with the audience. Similarly, in Czech puppet theatre kings and princesses do not address the audience. It is Kašpárek[4] who acts as a link between the stage and the auditorium.

An original device for linking the stage with the auditorium can be found in eastern Slovakia. Young men from the village present scenes in which they caricature people from the audience. The scenes remain purely theatrical and at the same time they build a bridge between the stage and the auditorium.

A characteristic feature of folk theatre audiences is that they do not hanker after plays with new contents, but watch the same Christmas and Easter plays, *St Dorothy*, and so on, year after year. In Russia these included *Tsar Maximilian*, whose content is very similar to that of *St Dorothy*, and other traditional plays. The spectators watch these plays with extraordinary interest, although they know them more or less by heart. Here lies a basic difference between a spectator at a folk theatre performance and the average member of the audience in our theatre. Many theatregoers sometimes actually beg not to be told the content of the play before the performance because they want to fully experience the whole course of the play and be surprised by the twists and turns of the plot. This is different from the folk theatre audience. We could compare them with those rare theatre lovers who have seen Shake-

---

4   [Editor's note: A popular comic Punch-like figure in the Czech puppet theatre tradition.]

speare's *Hamlet* twenty or thirty times in their lives, know the monologues
and dialogues by heart and remember how a particular scene was played by
famous actors – and then go to see *Hamlet* for the thirty-first time in order
to experience the familiar scenes again. The aesthetic perceptions of such
a theatregoer are similar to those of an actor, who experiences every line,
every monologue, the whole play, again and again. The only difference is that
a theatregoer experiences it passively, an actor actively. A medieval theatregoer, too, probably experienced the same thing when he watched the same
mystery play, whose content he knew from previous performances and from
the Holy Scriptures, with undiminished interest many times. This detailed
knowledge of the content of the play allows the folk theatre audience to take
an active role in the theatre, to sing in the chorus and with the actors or to
participate in the play, as we have seen in the description of *Pakhomushka*.
I believe that actors and theatre people will agree with me that a folk theatre
spectator is more precious than an average visitor to our theatre, who usually
attends each play only once.

Let us move to another major issue of folk theatre – to naturalism and
non-realism in the folk theatre. We will briefly look at this in various forms
of theatrical expression. We will start with the movement of the actors. In
Pakhomushka movement passes through all phases, from pure naturalism to
extreme non-realism. Among the most powerful means of parodying, the
use of comic stock characters should be pointed out. Most of the roles are
of this type. The facial expressions of most of the characters are also exaggerated; however this does not lead to sufficient diversity. As far as the style
of delivery is concerned, the text in *Pakhomushka* is spoken in an ordinary,
slightly histrionic voice, accompanied by individual shouts. Only Pakhomushka forces his voice to a marked degree, the result of having a wood
splinter in his mouth. But it must be stressed that wherever the action requires it, popular *chastushki*, country songs or sacred melodies are sung in
place of speech.

All this refers to the folk play *Pakhomushka*, while in serious plays – Czech
and Slovak folk versions of *St Dorothy*, for example – the text is diversified,
by carols in a Christmas play and sometimes even by prayers delivered by an
angel in Latin.[5]

Of course, all this makes the speech of folk drama very different from
ordinary language. The speech of the devil often contains sentences in nonsense language: this is a sign distinguishing the devil from ordinary mortals.[6]

---

5   See Feifalik 1864, the chapter on "Weihnachtsspiele" [Christmas Plays], variants IV, VI, and VII,
      where an angel sings "Gloria in excelsis Deo".
6   Feifalik 1864, the chapter on "Dorotheenspiele" [St Dorothy Plays], variant XII, where the devil
      begins with "Fixum, fixum, terafixum!".

In one variation of *St Dorothy* the devil is so excited by gaining the king's soul that he twice ends his line with "Hurdy, burdy!" Before St Dorothy's execution the elderly executioner cries out with excitement:

Hopsa, hela, hela,
This work suits this fella! (Feifalik 1864: variant XV)

These nonsense expressions can frequently be found in puppet plays as well, where they are uttered by Kašpárek (Bogatyrev 1923a: 69). In any case, it would be more appropriate to consider folk drama not drama as we understand it but as comic opera or operetta, since the vocal numbers are as important as the spoken parts.

Non-realism can also be seen in the sets and props of the folk theatre or, more precisely, in the way objects are used by the actors in the performance, because there are neither sets nor props in the folk theatre in our sense of the words.

In most cases objects from a peasant household are used. The props include, for example, a chopping block or a washtub, straw, wheels, chairs, a bench, a cane, a poker, sleigh bells, a whip, craftsmens' tools, and so on. There are also objects prepared only for the particular play, for example a cross made of crossed planks, a censer made of a matchbox on a string. Pakhomikha's[7] child is made up of an old coat girded with a belt. (Pisarev and Suslovich 1927: 184)

Even objects of everyday use, which the actor as it were transforms into theatre props, become non-real. Playing with objects in *Pakhomushka* fills almost the entire performance. Of special interest are the moments when, through his acting, the actor's task is to show that the poker has changed into a horse, the bench into a boat, or that the old coat girded with the belt has become a child in his arms. The acting in these moments is exaggerated, but all the characteristic movements are executed carefully, for example pulling in an exaggerated fashion on imaginary reins, cracking the whip, shouting, kicking, and so on. The impression of crossing a lake on the bench, which is meant to represent a boat, is created by making emphatic, careful strokes with a cane.

It is true that in *Pakhomushka*, a purely comic play, this gives the impression of parody and a comic effect is achieved. However, the same non-realism in the set appears in serious plays, for example the Russian folk drama *The Boat*. Several boys sit down in a row behind each other on the floor, moving

---

7   [Editor's note: Pakhomikha is Pakhomushka's wife, whom he marries during the play.]

their arms as if rowing. This is enough for the audience to imagine a boat full of rowers on the stage.

And the most tragic scene in *St Dorothy* is described in the following words: "[The executioner] cuts off St Dorothy's head, that is, they put a crown made of paper on her head and when she kneels down the executioner strikes with the sword and the crown falls to the ground" (Hreblay 1928: 97).

A great deal could be said about the non-realism of costumes in folk drama. Folk drama collectors have paid much attention to the description of costumes. If a costume and makeup are meant to depict a comic figure, then the costumes of folk drama characters somewhat remind us of clowns' costumes. Here is a description of the costumes in *Pakhomushka*:

Pakhomushka puts on a fur coat turned inside out and stuffs under it a big hump made of rags; ragged trousers; shoes or galoshes or felt boots or even bast shoes. He also tries to put something different on each foot and several shabby caps with peaks pointing in various directions on his head. To put on his makeup, Pakhomushka uses charcoal or soot or even a singed cork. He paints his cheeks, eyes, whiskers and chin. He inserts a wood splinter between his front teeth (Pakhomushka's long fang), which changes both his facial expression and his pronunciation. All these accessories are obligatory for Pakhomushka. Everything that Pakhomushka puts on is shabby and he expands his chest to an enormous size with rags. His face is painted with soot. (Pisarev and Suslovich 1927: 184)

But this non-realism in costumes is found not only in comic plays. Here is a description of the *Epiphany Play*. "A prophet: he has a town hat, a blue coat and a kind of stole over the shoulders, trousers and shoes and a Spanish cane. Herod: in a tailcoat, with a crown on his head, sceptre in his hand, tight trousers and shoes" (Feifalik 1864: variant VIII).

And Hreblay describes the devil's costume in *St Dorothy*: "The devil, face blackened with soot, small black horns on his head, a sheepskin over his shoulders, a brush in his hand" (Hreblay 1928: 95).

As we can see, it is not possible here to speak either about naturalism or about preserving the historical accuracy of the costume. The actors' task was to show the exclusive status of Herod and the prophet in comparison with ordinary people. This they achieved through the costumes they used for the characters. Some non-real costumes, like those for angels and devils, are traditional and roughly the same in all Czech and Slovak villages, whereas in other cases the actors have more freedom in creating the costumes. The costumes in the Russian folk play *Tsar Maximilian* are very interesting, since the play is rich in characters and thus provides a wide range of possibilities for costumes.

Let us move on to the question of improvisation in folk drama.

As a matter of principle the text is improvised. Its quality and extent depend entirely on the actors' abilities and mood. In its form the text is usually reminiscent of the jokes of old-timers at village fairs or the sayings repeated by bridesmaids at weddings. In other cases it consists of brief, quite sharp sentences or even single words. *Pakhomushka*, which is found throughout the entire territory investigated, lacks a uniform text, but in almost every village there are actor-specialists for the main parts who have their own texts. If these texts are successful they circulate by word of mouth and become common property. Hence it cannot be claimed that the text is fully improvised during the performance. Improvisation (as in the *commedia dell'arte*) is based on the skilful combination of bits of dialogues and songs within a given scenario. (Pisarev and Suslovich 1927: 184)

In serious plays this improvisation is limited but even there the text is lengthened by making additions and including material from elsewhere. For example in some of its variations *Tsar Maximilian* – basically quite simple, with a content very similar to the Czech and Slovak *St Dorothy* plays – expands to become a long play (cf. inserted passages from Pushkin, analysed in Bogatyrev 1923b: 147). This expansion of the play follows the principles of the revue and the construction of the whole play is similar to that of a revue, where a simple plot is enfolded in a great many varied numbers that are sometimes connected, sometimes very little connected and sometimes not at all connected to the basic plot.

The analysis of folk play texts, too, would provide us with much that is interesting. I will focus here only on some textual features. In folk plays serious or even tragic scenes are often combined with strongly comic ones. For example, the executioner has his most comic bits at the tensest moment in *St Dorothy*, when she is to be executed, and at a similar moment in the Russian play of *Tsar Maximilian*, when Adolph is about to be executed. But what is from our point of view a bizarre linkage between the comic and the tragic does not profane the tragic situation. Such a linkage would not be possible in our theatre, but this principle of our theatre is not a principle in every theatre. In addition to scenes that are filled with deeply dramatic tension, medieval mystery plays, like the folk plays, include comic interludes that sometimes parody the preceding dramatic scenes. Let us recall as well the bizarre connection of the comic and the dramatic in *The Ointment Seller*.[8]

One more feature of folk drama should be mentioned. I have compared folk drama to opera or operetta. If we look carefully at how individual scenes are linked up in folk drama, we can see that this is done through the alternation of various numbers: a monologue is followed by a dialogue and this in

---

8   [Editor's note: This play (the Czech title: *Mastičkář*), also known as *The Apothecary*, comes from the fourteenth century and is the oldest known Czech drama. For a Czech-English bilingual edition by Jarmila F. Veltrusky, see Veltrusky 1985.]

turn by a choral song, then comes another monologue and again a dialogue, then an aria followed by a dance and so on. In this way the construction of folk drama comes closest to that of a revue, with its changing numbers.

It is important to remember that each variant of a folk play is an independent work of art. It follows that every variant must be analysed separately. For example, consider two versions of *St Dorothy*: the first is taken from the Slovak book by Hreblay mentioned above and the second is variant XII from Feifalik's compilation. The first version begins with choral singing about the content of the play and the dramatic performance of the content of the song follows. The latter variant begins with the dramatic performance of St Dorothy's story, after which comes a choral song that retells the story that has just been performed. As these two examples show, variants with the same content may have opposite constructions. Folk theatre, then, recycles in great measure forms known from older forms of theatre and therefore it is an irreplaceable source for theatre historians. Here they can come to understand the practices of older forms of drama correctly and precisely, because they can watch the performances together with the reactions of the audience. And true theatre studies are possible not through the anatomical dissection of individual theatre elements, but through overall research into the entire structure that is theatre.

The Russian folk play *The Horse* deserves special attention because of its original treatment of theatre space. Men painted with soot rush into a room filled with spectators and use whips to disperse them. The audience is pressed up against the walls and so a space is created in which the play can start. Worth noting, too, is the original ending of *Pakhomushka*, ingeniously doing away with a curtain or the stroke of a gong announcing the end of the performance. The main hero, who is angry with his parents, starts beating them with the baby (that is, rags representing the baby). Then he beats a wayfarer and his wife and in the end he starts to beat all those who are present, that is the audience. Everybody runs away, shouting and laughing. In this unconventional way the performance comes to an end.

This short article makes it clear that folk theatre employs many interesting theatre methods that deserve to be studied and creatively reworked for our theatre. However, before systematic research on folk theatre begins, a modest request should be articulated: that at least one variant of a folk play should be recorded in Bohemia, Moravia, Slovakia or Subcarpathian Ruthenia[9] with the same care and precision as in the north of Soviet Russia, where *Pakhomushka* was documented in 1926, so that a director might reconstruct the play according to this record.

---

9   [Editor's note: The four constituent parts of the then Czechoslovakia.]

WORKS CITED

Bogatyrev, Petr (1923a) *Cheshski kukolny i russki narodny teatr* [Czech Puppet and Russian Folk Theatre], Berlin and St Petersburg: Opojaz.

— (1923b) "Stikhotvorenie Pushkina 'Gusar', ego istochniki i ego vliyaniye na narodnoy slovesnost" [Pushkin's poem "The Hussar", Its Sources and Its Influence on the National Literature], Tomashevsky, B. V., Bogatyrev, Petr and Shklovsky, Viktor, *Ocherki po poetike Pushkina* [Essays on Pushkin's Poetics], Berlin: Epokha, pp. 147–95.

Feifalik, Julius (1864) *Volksschauspiele aus Mähren* [Folk Plays from Moravia], Olomouc: Eduard Hölzel.

Hreblay, Anton (1928) *Brezno a jeho okolie* [Brezno and its Surroundings], Turčanský sv. Martin: privately printed.

Meyerhold, V. E. (1936) "Úryvek z přednášky V. E. Mejercholda" [An Excerpt from V. E. Meyerhold's Lecture"], *Program D 37*, vol. 5 (24 November 1936), pp. 69–73.

Pisarev, Sergei and Suslovich, Rafael (1927) "Dosyulnaya igra – komedia *Pakhomushkoi*" [A Dosyulnaya Play – The Comedy of *Pakhomushka*] in *Krestyanskoe iskusstvo SSSR*, vol. 1: *Iskusstvo severa — Zaonezhe* [Christian Art of the USSR, vol. 1: The Art of the North – Zaonezhe Region], Leningrad: Academia, pp. 176–85.

Veltrusky Jarmila F. (trans. and ed.) (1985) *Mastičkář: A Sacred Farce from Medieval Bohemia*, Ann Arbor: The University of Michigan Press.

BROADSIDE BALLADS AND DRAMAS

JIŘÍ VELTRUSKÝ

["Kramářské písně a dramata" was first published in 1941 in Czech in *Slovo a slovesnost*, vol. 7, pp. 98–102.]

Translated by Pavel Drábek

Editor's note: The broadside ballads quoted in the article employ a simple rhyme scheme. In the interest of conveying the meaning and retaining the original structure of the texts, no attempt has been made to replicate the rhymes.

Of all the different branches of folk poetry, broadside ballads have so far received the least attention. Only recently have there appeared two extensive collections of broadside ballads[1] (if we leave aside Miloslav Novotný's 1930 publication, which, as a bibliophile rarity, is completely inaccessible) that attempt to present a clear picture of this form. Yet even a mere two anthologies have sufficed for the broadside ballad to be established as occupying a very distinct literary niche and for a start to be made on defining its character with sufficient clarity to enable it to be distinguished convincingly from both folk poetry as well as "high" poetry. Of course much of the credit for this goes to the two publishers of the collections for their effort to record all the basic types of the broadside ballad; in addition, Robert Smetana and Bedřich Václavek's anthology (1937) contains mostly newer ballads, Novotný's (1940) older ones. Since for the most part broadside ballads were probably performed by singers who accompanied their singing by pointing to illustrative images – in other words, they were performed in a manner passing beyond the usual practice with songs – it will first be necessary to devote attention to their presentation. Only then will it be possible to determine precisely the whole compass of the broadside ballad and its internal differentiation. The mere texts themselves indicate not only that they comprise all three basic literary modes but that there is even the occasional tendency of the ballads towards a curious fragmentary quality that lays stress on illustrations shown to audiences, comparable perhaps to the way in which some passages in dramatic texts call for stage performance.

---

1   Smetana and Václavek 1937; Novotný 1940.

This comparison is not fortuitous: the construction of many, perhaps most, broadside ballads employs specific dramatic devices. For instance, the subject[2] is often handled in a complex manner. The simplest case is when words are given to a particular character (death, a young man in love, a dead man, and so on). The dramatic quality of this technique lies not only in the narrator being replaced by a character but also in narrative past time being replaced by *dramatic* present time. Let me underscore the word "dramatic" to differentiate this time from the time in lyrical poetry, which is also present but does not progress in the way dramatic time does. In the case of the technique in question, however, time is both present and progressive, because characters describe the *course* of their present action, for example in the ballad "In Springtime" (Smetana and Václavek 1937: 80):

> In great haste
> I am searching for the bird ... .

This technique is generally complicated by the standard practice of the poet himself being the subject of the concluding "moral". So it cannot be said that the singer simply represents a certain character in such ballads – but on the other hand, the words of the character are delivered by the singer. An even more complex situation occurs if the character addresses the singer, as in the ballad "Stand on My Highness's Command" (Smetana and Václavek 1937: 41), where the subject is death. This is the final stanza:

> You who are singing this now
> with your listeners,
> take good caution
> for my hand shall thwart you!
> Perhaps even today or tomorrow
> I shall strike my sword at you,
> I know not which way you will go,
> whether to hell or to heaven.

The subject, unified until now, separates into "I" and "you". The explanation for this phenomenon is to be sought in the connection between text and illustration: death, who is speaking here, is only represented by the singer to a certain extent; strictly speaking, the singer is only the vehicle of death's speech, while death's other signs are found in an illustration. This division of the signs of the character between two vehicles is strongly brought to the

---

2   [Editor's note: For Veltruský's use of the term "subject", see his comments in footnote 4 to "Dramatic Text as a Component of Theatre", this reader, p. 261.]

fore: death addresses the singer from the illustration, but through the lips of that very singer.

This also explains the easy transition from narration to the direct speech of characters. Usually this is not indicated in the text, not even through the appropriate punctuation – for example in "Prick up Your Ears" (Smetana and Václavek 1937: 98):

> He learnt of that
> and took great fear,
> right away he thought,
> *where could I run away to.*

Similar smooth transitions can also be found between two neighbouring interchanges in dialogue, as dialogues too tended to be sung straight through by a single singer. However, we also know that two singers often performed together, alternating as they sung. A task of some urgency in the research into broadside ballads is to determine the rules governing this type of alternation. It seems that where the whole ballad is a dialogue between two characters who are indicated before they speak (for example *Young Man: – Maiden: –*) each singer sang one role. This is supported by the fact that even occasional narrative passages are incorporated into lines of direct speech, as in the dialogue "Morning in a Beautiful Alley of Trees" (Smetana and Václavek 1937: 146), where a father speaks to his son, who has not recognized him:

> **Father:** *Calling after him in a muffled voice:*
> Sir, sir, forbear a while ... .

Even clearer evidence is to be found in the same ballad at the moment when the son recognizes his father:

> **Son:** *Here behold, you with tender hearts,*
> *the son prostrate at his kind father's feet.*
> Oh father, father, forgive me my trespasses,
> From love I kiss your grey hair.

It may be concluded from these instances that each of the two singers represented one of the characters; that left no one to deal with lines delivered by the narrator. Importantly, however, the above dialogue does contain such passages: in the narrator's speech the difference between the singer and the character he represents is emphasized because the narrator's speech is the singer's own speech. Also in places where, in dialogues split between two roles, another character appears, this character is not specially indicated.

This is the case, for instance, in "Oh my Only Joy" (Smetana and Václavek 1937: 122), a dialogue between a young man and a maiden:

Young Man: We entrust ourselves with our love
to you, father,
grant us your blessing
for we wish to marry.
I confirm this conjoining in matrimony,
binding it with priestly stole;
live in accordance with God,
this I enjoin upon you.

In the following stanza once again only the young man speaks, and in the stanza after that (the last in the ballad) the singer speaks, without this change being indicated in any way:

Thanks be to Thee, dear God,
for Thy most kind deeds,
for I have asked Thee faithfully
for an unrivalled flower,
I wished for a rose,
For love Thou hast granted it to me,
so that until I die
I may love her with all my heart.

Amen, I sing, and speak to all
of true love
what pain it suffers in its heart
at hindrances,
both sides grieve,
but no one can stop them,
where two hearts are true
and love one another.

The division of the dramatic character between the singer and an illustration is utilized to the full by the broadside theatre.[3] So, for example, in the ballad "Oh Fickle Times" (Novotný 1940: 224), which is delivered by a dying man bidding farewell to the world, not once is the context of the dying man's speech disturbed by the commentary of a narrator or any other character: the

---

3   [Editor's note: "Broadside theatre" and "broadside drama" are terms used by Veltruský to highlight the theatricality of broadside ballads and the performative practice associated with them.]

different status of the singer is blurred rather than emphasized. In addition, those signs of a singer that characterize him as such are weakened in that no attendant audience is ever addressed (not even at the beginning), but rather imaginary characters such as the wife, servants of the dying man and so on. And yet the audience never identifies the singer with the character since an awareness of the distinction between the two was part of the collective consciousness. However, it must be assumed that in this song the bond between the singer and the character was felt very strongly, so the painted illustration of the character was at the same time experienced as a depiction of the singer himself. In other words, the illustration of the dying person was understood as the image of a person in the full flower of life: the Baroque view of life as mere illusion, from the very beginning bearing on its brow the mark of its inevitable decay and doom – this view is expressed here with the utmost possible naturalism, its drastic nature raising what was a commonplace theme of the period to a horrifying vision. Before the very eyes of the audience an ordinary singer of broadside ballads turns into a spectre. It is easy to imagine what horror his words must have evoked:

Sweet music,
I bid you farewell,
no more will you please
my wholesome heart,
once there was merriment
enough in my chateau,
now my body rots in the grave.

My head is already rotting,
where is my glory,
all my joy,
the world's vanity is gone,
like grass I must depart from this world,
and leave everything behind,
I must rot in the ground.

Transitions between the narrator and the characters and between the characters themselves are very frequent. The few examples cited above, which were not intended to include all types, document the division of the character into "I" and "you", the blurring of the border between the speech of the narrator and the direct speech of the characters, the merger of verbal interchanges into the speech of a single character, the creation of a resemblance between the singer and the character, and so on. But all this only pertains to the subject who is speaking. Of equal importance is the way the subject who is being addressed is treated. So in the ballad "Thou, Our Lord Jesus Christ" (Novotný 1940: 174) the strong impression of a dialogue is created at many points through mere changes in the subjects being addressed. Its length precludes the ballad's being quoted in full; here are only two stanzas, each of which is addressed to a different subject – where they adjoin a shift in meaning occurs that is like that between two lines in a dialogue, though the speaker remains the same:

If we entreat,
if we ardently plead with God,
He will avert all evil from us
through those three patron saints.

Oh God, lend us Thine ear,
avert Thy dear wrath from us
for Jesus, Thy Son
and His holy deserts.

This example shows that the dialogic and dramatic qualities of the broadside ballad do not necessarily depend on the division of speech between characters but predominantly on the treatment of the subject, whether the speaking subject or the subject being addressed. Proof of this claim is offered in reverse by the ballad "Oh, Wicked Vizier" (Novotný 1940: 63), consisting exclusively of the direct speech of several characters, each explicitly identified before they speak. And yet the ballad lacks a dialogic character: here the distribution of speech among the characters is only a device for creating a steady rise in dramatic tension, with the speech of each character being one stage: 1. The Grand Vizier; 2. The Grand Vizier's wife with her children and friends; 3. The Turkish army; 4. The Mufti.

The significance of illustrations that were put on display for the semantic construction of the broadside ballad, as has been shown in the analysis of the dramatic character, is also confirmed when an attempt is made to classify the ballads not thematically, as Smetana and Václavek do in their collection, but on the basis of their structure. So for purely lyrical ballads such as "Nobody Knows What Love Is" (Smetana and Václavek 1937: 78) images are, it seems, of relatively little importance; with an increase in action their significance quite naturally grows. However, their proper operational domain is, I believe, drama. Here, too, further differentiation can be made according to their significance: just as every drama with the ambition to be as highly literary a work as possible attempts to capture the whole story and action through linguistic means and – conversely – every drama tending to maximal theatricality disturbs the continuity of the context so that other theatre components may come into play, so among broadside dramas we find a whole range of nuances when it comes to dependence on images. For instance, very often between two lines of dialogue large gaps occur that are filled with action suggested by an illustration. So in the ballad "How Oft Have I Come to See My Love" (Smetana and Václavek 1937: 119) the continuity is broken once when the young man, who was standing under the window, fetches a ladder and climbs up to his beloved, and on another occasion when the maiden rebuffs his confession of love: "Honzíček, I'll whack your hand." Another temporal gap following this line is ended by the young man's words:

I wish you good night, I'll go sleep,
have a sweet dream, my Terinka,
and when we wake up,
then, Terinka, let us share our dreams.

It can be assumed that these and all the other gaps found in this song were filled in by indicating the relevant scenes in illustrations. Apart from this, of course, we also find dramas that contain no substantial gaps in the development of the story line. They are therefore less connected with the images and are more literary – for example "Fare You Well, My Heart's Love, I Take My Leave of You" (Novotný 1940: 190).

Of course any attempt at a more detailed analysis of broadside ballads faces a major hurdle owing to the absence of records of their actual performance. Hence the most pressing task in the study of the broadside ballad – apart from publishing the complete corpus of ballad texts – is that of recording any vestiges of the broadside theatre that may still exist or are at least preserved in the memories of eyewitnesses. Hopefully, the stimulus to action that may have been provided by the two publications mentioned here will have come in time to prevent this important component of artistic creation at the margins from vanishing with scarcely a trace.

WORKS CITED

Novotný, Miloslav (ed.) (1930) *Písničky jarmareční, většinou výpravné a vesměs starodávné* [Broadside Ballads, Mostly Narrative and Often Ancient]. Prague: Erna Janská.

— (ed.) (1940) *Špalíček písniček jarmarečních* [A Collection of Broadside Ballads], Prague: Evropský literární klub.

Smetana, Robert and Václavek, Bedřich (eds) (1937) *České písně kramářské* [Czech Broadside Ballads], Prague: Fr. Borový.

THE EXTRA-AESTHETIC FUNCTION OF FOLK THEATRE

PETR BOGATYREV

["Mimoestetické funkce lidového divadla" was first published in 1940 as a chapter in Bogatyrev's *Lidové divadlo české a slovenské* [Czech and Slovak Folk Theatre], Prague: Fr. Borový, pp. 30–52.]

Translated by Ivan Kolman

A typical feature of the theatre is not only that it has a great many functions but that the aesthetic function often ranks second in the hierarchy of its functions and one of its extra-aesthetic functions becomes its dominant feature.

In the hierarchy of the theatre's functions, just as in the hierarchy of the set of functions of other social facts, functions shift. This shift may be related to a change in the form of the theatre, especially when the number of elements of the different arts that form the structure of theatre increases or decreases. However, the functions can change and shift even when the form itself remains unchanged. Certain theatre genres in today's theatre have their own dominant functions or at least functions that occupy one of the leading places: until recently the extra-aesthetic functions in ballet were of very little significance, while on the other hand the extra-aesthetic functions in drama – for example ethical, social, political – occupy an important place.

Similarly, theatre can be divided into different genres according to various significant extra-aesthetic functions; however, this division only exists for a certain period and for a particular theatre movement and it cannot be transferred to the theatre of other periods and movements. We know, for example, that the dominant function of many oriental ballets is a religious one; recently there have appeared several ballets (by Kurt Jooss and others) with a powerfully expressed, committed social function, and in them this function is in no way weaker than in drama.

We now come to an analysis of the functions of the kind of folk theatre in which these extra-aesthetic functions stand out very strongly, so strongly that we can almost grasp them physically.

Certain dramatic storylines can be found in magic performances that are carried out in accordance with Sir James Frazer's Law of Similarity. Let me give an example. On the Porechsky and Krasninsky districts in the Smolensk Governorate a complex ceremony takes place in spring on St George's Day when the herds of cows are turned out to pasture for the first time. The ceremony ends as follows:

A dish is prepared from the eggs and bacon that the cowherd and his helpers have received from the housewife. When the meal is ready the cowherd appoints which of his helpers will be a hare, a blind man, a lame man, a lock and a trough. He places them around the herd and takes the meal that has been prepared and first goes to the hare and asks him "Hare, hare, is aspen bitter?" The hare answers "Bitter." "God grant that our cattle too will be bitter to wild beasts." Then he asks the blind man "Blind man, blind man, can you see?" The blind man answers "No, I can't." "God grant that the wild beasts too will be unable to see our herds." Then he approaches the lame man "Lame man, lame man, will you make it?" "No, I won't." "God grant that the wild beasts too will be unable to make it to our herds." Then he asks the lock "Lock, lock, will you unlock yourself?" "No, I won't." "God grant that the wild beasts too will not open their jaws for our herds." Finally he approaches the trough "Trough, trough, will you fall over?" "No, I won't." "God grant that the beasts too will not fall upon our herds." The cowherd walks around the herd this way three times. Then all the performers sit down and eat the meal. (Dobrovski 1908: 151)

Another example of a magic performance is one carried out on Christmas Eve in Subcarpathian Ruthenia: "The boys and young people in the household roll about in straw strewn on the trampled floor of the room in order to be rewarded with sacks of oats and potatoes as big as themselves" (Bogatyrev 1929: 49; see also Stránská 1931: 58).

These magic actions in accordance with the Law of Similarity are accompanied by imitation of the sounds made by the animals that are represented. Another example from Subcarpathian Ruthenia: "On Christmas Eve a sheaf is brought home and a child hides under it; it moos like a cow, neighs like a horse, bleats like a lamb so that these animals will be fertile" (Bogatyrev 1929: 45).

Primitive properties are often used during these magic action-dramas.

So we have various elements of the theatre in these magic actions: transformation into another person or even a thing, dialogue, imitation of the voices of animals that are being represented, imitative performances and sometimes theatre costumes, masks and so on. However, the dominant function is always that of *magic*, although there is often an *aesthetic* function as well; on occasion the latter will shift into first place, thus demoting the magic function to second place.

Many Czech and Slovak folk plays, even though they have a dominant aesthetic function, are connected with primitive folk faith. For example, the custom by which the Three Kings go from door to door is connected with the following superstition:

Boys dressed up as the Three Kings write the letters K+M+B[1] on the door into the main room of the cottage as they sing their well-known carol. Then they pass the chalk to the housewife and she goes into the entrance corridor of the cottage and makes three crosses on the outside door. She then comes back to the main room, hands the chalk back to the boys and adds a few small coins to help them out on their long journey to Bethlehem. Three days later the housewife goes early in the morning, before sunrise, and wipes out the three crosses so that her hens will lay well throughout the following year. (Linhart 1892: 506)

A document from the mid-eighteenth century recorded by Ullmann[2] provides evidence that when schoolboys went from door to door on St. Gregory's Day the housewives shooed them out with a broomstick; this was thought to drive fleas and other vermin from the house (Zíbrt 1910b: 19 and 1889: 66).

The drastic custom of hurling a billy goat down from a height is connected with several folk superstitions (clarification of its origin is an interesting question in itself. this custom can be compared to the ceremonial killing of a bear). From the point of view of theatre this custom is interesting because of the parodic speech that is delivered before the billy goat is thrown down. The oldest references to this ceremony "were preserved in records about an old Czech folk treatment that attributed to the blood of a billy goat thrown down from St James's tower a particularly magic and effective power" (Zíbrt 1911: 36). This superstition survived until recently. In various places the blood of a billy goat thrown down on St James's Day was preserved as a remedy for various afflictions.

In Pelhřimov, for pricks and cuts; in Mrákotín near Skuč, for epilepsy or pricks. In Sebranice people added the dried blood of a billy goat that had been hurled down from a height to a mixture that was burned to produce smoke used in treating individuals who had been startled; the aim was to prevent the shock from having any ill effects on their health. (Zíbrt 1911: 69–71)

Some ceremonial dramatic scenes are often on the borderline between entertainment and a religious action. For example the visit of St Nicholas leaves a sacral or semi-sacral impression on older children even though they know that it is only a man in disguise and not the saint himself. A similar experience, partaking of both pure entertainment and fear and with a certain religious aspect, has been recorded in Slovakia in connection with the occasion when Lucy goes from door to door visiting adults. The tales that spread

1   [Editor's note: The traditional names of the Three Kings (the wise men or magi who attended the birth of Christ), Kaspar, Melchior and Balthazar.]
2   [Editor's note: We were not able to identify this person.]

about St Lucy going from house to house strengthen the religious function of this folk theatrical action: on the one hand they heighten its mysteriousness while on the other this mysterious theatrical action itself has reinforced and helped spread the legends about visits from St Lucy. Here are two such tales:

At the upper end of the small section of the village of Bošáca at Pekárovec there lived a hard-working shoemaker who often sewed deep into the night. And he was sewing at night on the Feast of St Lucy (13 December) when something outside knocked on his window and cried "Shoemaker, are you sewing?" "I am," answered the shoemaker. "Make me slippers before I come back," said Lucy (Death), because it was her. "Show me your foot," said the shoemaker, "so that I know what size slippers I should make." And Lucy put her foot through the window, it was a goose's foot, and said: "Hurry up with your sewing so that the slippers are ready before I return: otherwise you'll be in a bad way!" And she left. The shoemaker took a piece of rough paper and smartly cut out the slippers from it, sewed the pieces together and put the slippers outside the window. Lucy returned shortly and when she saw the finished slippers she put them on, started stamping and jumping about in them and cried out excitedly: "Oh! How well I can jump! And how well they fit. Shoemaker, somebody gave you good advice, that you worked so quickly!" And as she had come, she left.

That same night Lucy continued walking around the village and she saw a woman spinning. She stopped by the window and called inside: "Are you spinning, woman?" "I am," answered the frightened woman. Lucy put a basket full of empty spindles on the window and said "Spin all these spindles before I come back or else you'll be in a bad way!" and she disappeared. The woman opened the window, took the basket with spindles inside and she smartly spun one thread on each spindle and put them all in the basket and put it back outside the window. Before long Lucy came back to the window, found all the spun spindles in the basket and said: "Whoever advised you, advised you well; you're lucky you've spun all the spindles!" and she took the basket with the spindles and disappeared. (Holuby 1897: 146)

Stories about Lucy wandering from door to door are similar to those about Perchta:[3]

There are various stories about going from door to door with Perchta - for example, it is said that some people went "with Perchta" from Čertyně to Záluží. However, along the way another Perchta, much more terrifying, approached them. The people were frightened and fled back home. But the spectre followed them. When they had locked

---

3   [Editor's note: A female spirit found in the folklore of many countries in Central Europe. She was said to roam the countryside at midwinter, being especially active between Christmas Day and Epiphany.]

themselves inside, the spectre disappeared, leaving the stamp of a horseshoe on the door. It is said that until recently this was still visible. (Zíbrt 1910a: 55)

It is interesting that superstitions and customs that promote economic prosperity were connected with the comic figure of a bear as part of the exuberant gaiety of Carnival customs. "Bits and pieces torn from the bear (pea straw, straw) are supposed to have their own special powers, for example to help ensure that poultry is productive: housewives put them in goose nests" (Zíbrt 1910a: 92). František Bartoš describes going from door to door with a bear in Moravia in the following way:

> Most frequently they go "with a bear", that is, a young farm hand in disguise, completely covered in pea straw, dragging a long straw tail and with a bell between his legs. When they come to a house the bear dances round twice in a circle with the homeowner's daughter "for hemp and flax". Were they not to dance with the bear in some house, they would harvest no hemp or flax. The housewife tears off a bit of pea straw from the bear for her goose nests "so that goslings will tumble about". (Bartoš 1892: 31)

During Carnival in the Klatovy region "they disguise a man as a bear, covering him with long rye and wheat straw. He has a tall conical cap on his head. Housewives dancing with him make a wish for the grass and corn to grow as tall as the man" (Zíbrt 1910a: 97–98).

According to folk superstition, other bits of the costumes worn by Carnival revellers also have beneficial effects:

> These days [in Vrbčany] ... men and women go round disguised as a Jew and a Jewess, sometimes even as a bear; they run around the village green shouting at everybody, offering snuff even to children and collecting doughnuts. Housewives tear pea straw off the bear or a bit of rag from the Jew and put them under the geese so they will lay well. (Sixta 1893: 71)

We have already mentioned that folk theatre performances are connected with folk superstitions and folk medicine.

It is clear that folk plays based on subjects taken from the Gospels and the Bible and the lives of the saints have both an aesthetic and a religious function for the audience and the actors alike. The expert on the Slovak folk play *Bethlehem*, Štefan Krčméry, who himself played one of the parts in the play when he was a child, says that "a spark of the liturgy can be felt in the actors' performance" (Krčméry 1934: 107). The religious function is strengthened within the framework of the Christian religion in theatre performances such as *Bethlehem*, *The Three Kings*, and so on, through these performances being only one element in a whole system of folk ceremonies, a system that also includes the singing of carols of a religious nature, prayers read at home at this time of year and finally going to church, where the villagers are addressed in a different form with regard to the subject that folk actors present in *Bethlehem* and *The Three Kings*. And the performance of the play about St Dorothy on her feast day undoubtedly strengthens the religious function of this folk play as well.

Performances of rustic plays[4] on themes from the Gospels and the Bible, Christmas and Easter plays, and so on, were in a way merely an extension of the services in the church.

> In France folk performances started with a religious service in the church; then the procession of actors proceeded from the church to the place where the play was to take place. Such economy was also in evidence in Bohemia. Since the plays were performed on Sunday afternoon, even the blessing was over and done with at one o'clock; where there was no church, no church service took place. (Menčík 1895: IX)

Sometimes performances were accompanied by the sound of church bells. "As Jesus was dying on the cross, the church bells in Bozkov were tolling Vespers, which heightened the impression of the play to a marked degree" (Menčík 1895: XII). We also know that the church lent priests' vestments to the actors as costumes. "Church garments were lent to important people; this was the case in Lastiboř and Bozkov, where the Jewish high priests and Jesus were dressed in dalmatics and copes" (Menčík 1895: XI).

The actors in productions like these recognized their religious function, which is confirmed by their donating the money collected in the course of these performances to religious ends. We have the following testimony concerning this:

> Some monuments that were built from the proceedings of the plays still remind us of them. In Držkov the Stations of the Cross for the local church and the Holy Sepulchre were procured in this way, and thanks to amateur actors in Lastiboř an iron cross near Jílové was erected. In 1820, when Josef Kramář was parish priest, the cemetery Chapel of the Holy Cross was built in Božkov. (Menčík 1895: IX)

In addition to a religious function, the folk plays also have a ceremonial function. In some cases folk plays, like folk traditions, have both religious and ceremonial functions. In other cases the religious function fades away and

---

4 [Editor's note: A general term for plays originating in the Baroque period (the seventeenth and particularly the eighteenth centuries) in the Czech countryside. They were performed by village amateurs and dealt mostly with religious themes. The Czech history of theatre of this period uses a term that translates as "neighbours' folk theatre".]

only the ceremonial function remains. In some cases the presentation of folk plays and folk traditions is preserved only so as not to disrupt a ceremony. Thus, for example, villagers often no longer believe that by not performing dramatic scenes at a wedding some harm could come to them. Nevertheless these performances are considered necessary in order for the wedding to follow all the rules required by public opinion. I once watched a Subcarpathian Ruthenian farmer before the arrival of carollers and after they left. While the children waited impatiently for their arrival and looked out impatiently from the window for the carollers to finally come to their house, the farmer tried to remain calm, but even so it was obvious how proud he was that the carollers were also coming to him, a respectable landowner. The arrival of the carollers was an inseparable part of the festive ceremony for him. This ceremonial function is similar to that of attending a concert of outstanding musicians for people from a certain group for whom the aesthetic function of going to a concert is not dominant: they have to go because it is appropriate, it is required by the behavioural rules of their social class.

Let us now analyse the issue of the regional function of folk plays. All ethnographic phenomena can be divided into active communal phenomena and passive communal phenomena. The former include phenomena and especially forms of expression created by the community itself. This is the case, for example, of folk embroideries in Subcarpathian Ruthenia, which are made by all the members of the community, in this case its female members. A girl or a woman who is unable to embroider would feel embarrassed in front of the entire village. Active communal phenomena also include various widely practised customs and ceremonies. Every woman must know all the customs and ceremonies that should be carried out by a woman in the six-week period immediately following childbirth. Active communal phenomena also include commonly found ceremonial songs as well as *kolomyiki* and *chastushki*,[5] which are sung by all the young people.

Passive communal phenomena in a village include phenomena that are widespread but are not performed by the rural community itself. These include, for example, the paintings on glass that decorated every rural household but that had in fact been made by certain craftsmen who sometimes did not even belong to the community or that had simply been bought from traders at a fair. Russian fantastic tales should also be included here and, for example, *byliny*, which were only told by some folk artists in a particular village, as well as songs – especially Russian and Ukrainian religious songs – that were sung by singers from elsewhere.

---

5   [Editor's note: The *kolomyika* is a fast-paced folk dance with humorous rhymed verses, traditionally popular in Ukraine. *Chastushki* are songs composed of humorous rhyming couplets, widespread in Russia and often sung to be danced to.]

Active communal phenomena have a clearly expressed regional function and indeed tend to strengthen it. In the case of passive communal phenomena this function is weak. The degree to which the regional function is apparent is directly dependent on the degree to which a community is active in creating ethnographic phenomena. Take song, for example. Very widespread minor musical forms such as *kolomyiky, chastushki* and others that are sung by the entire rural community have a strongly expressed regional function. Songs of this kind are composed everywhere, praising their own village and mocking the neighbouring village. On the contrary, narrative songs, for example Russian *byliny* as they developed in the eighteenth and nineteenth centuries, recount events affecting all of Russia, without any mention of a native village. Therefore it is more correct to categorize narrative songs not according to villages but according to schools, singers and their followers, because, for example, singers of religious songs often travelled from place to place and thus it is not possible to talk about the regionality of these songs at all.

Magic-dramatic actions are in most cases actively communal, whether they are performed by the entire rural community together or by each member of the community separately at home – for example dramatic scenes during wedding ceremonies, where the bride's father, the matchmaker, bridesmaids and even the bridegroom and the bride perform as actors. The regional function is clearly expressed in all these dramatic acts: the community in each village, each region, regards certain details as their *own* in contrast to other details that are found in weddings in neighbouring villages or regions.

Another type of folk play is passively communal – plays like *St Dorothy*, *Bethlehem* and plays performed by schoolchildren on the feast days of St Gregory and St Blaise, which were mostly plays performed by a few people, village amateurs, and which were passively received by the other villagers as the audience. The guiding spirits behind these plays were individual farmers or teachers in the villages. Hence much of the original "editing" of these plays can be linked to specific individuals, so it is better to categorize the plays according to artistic schools rather than regions, just as we distinguish various versions of puppet plays according to puppeteer families. But of course local actors in each region added to and developed plays from elsewhere and so gave them local features.

Rustic plays are even more passively communal but even these include a higher degree of collective participation than with contemporary theatre plays, since the audience participates in every folk production much more actively than is the case in today's theatre. And in fact in most cases one can only speak of some degree of passivity with regard to communal facts. Like factory products, they often change in each village and thus acquire an at least slightly active communal quality (for example folk costumes sewn of factory-made fabrics are different in each region). Likewise every village changes numerous plays from elsewhere in its own way, thus bringing them closer to active communal facts.

Folk plays are also differentiated according to the age of the actors: some are only performed by children, others by young people and others solely by adults. *Bethlehem* in the Czech lands and Slovakia is usually performed by children, the ceremony of "little queens"[6] and others by young women, scenes at weddings usually by married adults. In some places only women play the role of Lucy. And so certain spheres of folk dramatic art are a sign of the age and sex of the performers, so that participation in a particular performance has the function of marking the actor's age and sex.

With the shifting of a folk performance – just as with other customs – from adults towards children and so on, its function and form also change. Thus the ride of the kings,[7] which is performed by adolescent males, was often dangerous and "it is said that for this reason officials, village councils and priests sought to abolish this custom"; however, for boys it became a typical children's game, with the appropriate transformation of a switch into a live horse, and so on:

> As the young men set out with the king, the schoolboys chased after the king round the village on willow switches, following the example of their elders. Using knives, they cut out decorations on the willow switches, which they called horses, beautified them with nosegays at the top end and attached bridles. Then they mounted the horses – that is, they stuck the switches between their legs and held the bridles at the upper end. They too elected a king... In front of the house, one of the king's attendants recited a short rhyme that was slightly different from that of the young men. (Zíbrt 1910c: 12)

We must also look at the satirical function of folk theatre, which involves making fun of some of the people in the village. This function often blends with the social function when, for example, actors direct the sharp edge of their mockery at their superiors or when actors from poorer strata ridicule the rich farmers and vice versa (we will look at the social function later). However, satire in folk plays is often present without any social bias.

In the following chapter on the relationship between the stage and the audience we will present excerpts from the Russian play *Barin*, recorded by N. E. Onchukov. He describes the court scene from the play: "The court is a satire on the local way of life and manners, sometimes very unkind, sometimes cruel" (Onchukov 1911: 115). For example, the Tenant Farmer makes a comic rhymed

---

6   [Editor's note: A Whitsuntide custom carried out by girls and young women (the "little queens").]
7   [Editor's note: In this ancient Whitsun festival, a colourful mounted procession of young men passes through the village, stopping at each house to chant humorous rhymes.]

response in which – in addition to "a hundred rubles" – he asks Barin for "Michalko Talishchykh's nose, / Our Kozharikha's tail". Onchukov comments: "Actors 'come down' on villagers who are distinguished by their defects or mistakes. For example, in Nizhmozer they say: 'Kuricha's goitre, Ulkina's fore-head, Akhonka's wooden cottage, Matreshka's … big nose, a bridge could be built across the Nizhema River'" (Onchukov 1911: 116).

To fully understand the actors' allusions we have to know the community in which the performance is taking place – its way of life, interests, past events, and so on. When Ivan Aksakov was describing how the Russian folk play *Tsar Maxmilian* was performed by soldiers, he came to a parodic scene where a doctor and a bonesetter are treating Adolf, who has already been executed, and made the comment that "the actors were probably making fun of somebody" (Aksakov 1892: 221–22). It was probably quite clear to everyone in the audience who the soldiers were taking off, and only the "gentleman" (Aksakov) was unaware of the target of their mirth.

Here are several examples from Plampač's speech in the Czech play *Ochoz krále a králky* [The King and Queen Go from House to House]:

I'll start at Adámek's place:[8]
he's got a lot of miserable calves,
one with no tail, a second all pale,
a third can barely raise its tail…

Thus he goes from house to house…

When I continue to the next house,
I must say, to their embarrassment:
Drda sold his horses,
weeping for them the whole week,
his wife sold the cows,
because she had no grass for them.
Their son squandered away the oxen,
because he said he had no water for them,
their daughter sold the sows,
because she had nothing for them.

This old blacksmith
Doesn't lack anything.

---

8   [Editor's note: in this and subsequent similar texts quoted in this article, various forms of rhyme were used in the original Czech. It was not possible to retain this feature in the English translations without seriously distorting the meaning.]

And what would he lack,
when he has steel, iron?
But his wife
Hasn't turned out well.
When her husband isn't at home,
What's the blacksmith's wife doing,
when he's away?
She's sitting on the bench,
calling out to young men:
Boys, come on over to our house,
my husband is away.

The girls at the Pleskals' are cursed,
because of all the gossip.
An oleaster is growing under their window,
the oldest daughter is still in the cradle.[9] (Zíbrt 1910c: 24–26)

Onchukov's words, quoted above, concerning the "satire on the local way of life and manners, sometimes very unkind, sometimes cruel" could apply equally well to this Czech village play.

[...]

V. N. Kharuzina gives an interesting example of the satirical function in the Arizona tribe of the Hopi. Among others things, Jesse Walter Fewkes observed this special clown act among the Hopi:

> During one of the breaks in a sacred dance two clowns appeared: the first had his face painted black, the second was decked out as an American woman. With great success they imitated White visitors who had come to an Indian reservation because of an interest in their rituals. One of the clowns was holding a scrap of paper and a pencil and pretended to write something, probably parodying Fewkes. (Kharuzina 1927: 60)

We now come to one of the most important questions in the folk theatre – the social function of folk drama performances.

The entire body of folk literature can be divided into two groups. The first group includes those forms of expression whose social function is apparent from the content of the work itself. For example, a proverb may condemn the injustice of the rich vis-à-vis the serfs. The second group includes works whose content is asocial. As an example, take an anecdote about a clever thief who deceives a feeble-minded lord. This is only the outline of a story and it is up to the narrator how he wishes to fill it in. One narrator will make it a story

---

9   [Editor's note: The point of the comments in the last stanza is that the family is desperately poor.]

about the victory of the oppressed over the oppressor: of the poor thief over the rich lord and exploiter. Another narrator will present the clever thief as an immoral character and the lord as a victim of deception, a character that arouses sympathy.

As an example of social protest against poverty and especially against taxes in folk theatre, let us look at the narration of the shepherd Valenta in the pastoral play[10] *The Three Kings,* who describes his dream in the following way:

But after a short while
I had a very pleasant dream:
A golden stream gushed forth,
rejuvenating the whole world,
for everything had changed into gold,
even the humble mud.
And that tattered pallet of mine
all darned with patches
seemed to shine with gold
and to be striped with gold.
My pouch seemed full,
full of ducats,
which filled me with great joy,
and I kept thinking
that those oppressive seizures of property
those odious land taxes
would come to an end at Carnival,
excise taxes, the army's fines, would cease.
But when I wake up in the morning,
I look from one corner to another, all's empty;
soldiers are battering at the door,
once again they'll torture me for my pouch. (Feifalik 1864: 46)

However, in folk theatre it is rare to find the social function clearly expressed in the content of the play itself. The majority of folk plays must be assigned to the second group, that of asocial plays. The majority of texts only hint at social satire, poking fun at the village councillors or the rich. Every actor can soften these hints or, on the other hand, sharpen them – it is enough, for example, just to wink or to make an obvious gesture.

---

10   [Editor's note: Czech pastoral plays date from the seventeenth and eighteenth centuries. They tell the nativity story, often with the shepherds in leading roles, and were performed in villages by the local people.]

And here we must again express regret that, because there is a lack of precise records of folk performances among Czechs and Slovaks, we are forced to limit ourselves to merely posing the question of the extent to which the social function is expressed in each play. However, we have no possibility of exploring this in detail. I repeat: each performance of any particular play is a unique manifestation of art that differs from the previous and subsequent performances of the same piece. And therefore these performances must be recorded and described again and again.

The social bias of a folk performance depends on the composition of the audience. For example, if most of the audience is made up of poor folk, the actor, backed by them, can mock the rich much more sharply; if the audience is only made up of the rich, the actor, wishing to be successful, may avoid mockery entirely. Current and future researchers have the rewarding task of studying the social function of folk theatre productions in great detail, something that was almost completely neglected by researchers in the past. The social function is in evidence particularly sharply in the theatre. The best testimony to this is the fact that plays performed in the theatre are censored much more strictly than those that are only published. This is natural: in a play the actor addresses social protest to a group, while when a book is read the author speaks to only the one reader.

Czech puppeteers also expressed clearly marked social views in their performances and for this reason they were harassed by the Austrian government.

When satire in the theatre directs mockery – through, for example, speech, acting, an actor's clothes, and so on – against another nationality or against the inhabitants of other regions, thus indirectly praising the superiority of the nation or the inhabitants of the region that the actors and the audience are part of, it has a national or regional function: to extol its own nation or region at the expense of other nations or regions.

In folk productions this function can be found, for example, in scenes that make fun of the Jews (cf. Czech and Slovak Christmas and Carnival folk plays and many plays in the Czech puppet theatre repertoire).

We can observe the same function in the plays of so-called primitive tribes.

Suddenly the spectators' attention was turned elsewhere: six people in rags came out of the forest behind the house. Their bodies were covered with ragged matting, and they had dirty caps on their heads made of rattan or sewn from mangy fur. They were carrying old baskets, wooden lances and very long quivers similar to the bamboo troughs used by the Kayan people for feeding their sows. Looking around timidly in all directions, they moved forward cautiously. The crowd of spectators stepped back to make place for them and welcomed them with merriment and banter. Nieuwenhuis says that the point of the scene would have been entirely incomprehensible to them [as outsiders] if the Kayan had not told them that when disguising themselves during the rice sowing season they make fun of various people and situations. In this case they were laughing at the neighbouring Punan tribe's way of life in the forest. They are actually afraid of the Punan tribe, but their way of life makes them a target of ridicule. (Kharuzina 1928: 24, with reference to Nieuwenhuis 1904: 329)

Sometimes this function (to extol one's own nation at the expense of another nation) verges on a different function: to show the virtues of one's own class by mocking those who belong to a different class. It is well known that villagers often laugh at "renegades" from their class who have left the rural community, gone abroad to look for work and become quasi-respectable and are forgetting their mother tongue or their dialect. The character of the "bristle dealer" in the folk custom of going from door to door with Perchta has this function indicating social status.

The bristle dealer is the last in the procession (with Perchta). He is dressed like a "toff", and has a green hat on his head. He has a pack basket on his back, used for collecting doughnuts, bits of roast meat and so on. When he comes to a house he asks for bristles: "Haf you got any bristles?" or "Vould you like to buy any vitevashing brushes?" He is imitating bricklayers and similar people who go "to Austria" to earn money and then mispronounce the Czech language. (Janás 1895: 56–57)

Now let us move on to the economic function of folk plays. This function, which has been – and still is – of such great significance in the history of art, is often passed over in embarrassed silence by the experts. However, this function had and continues to have a great impact on both artists' productivity and the form of the works they create. For example, so many works of art have been curtailed in some way just so they could be completed and the artist be paid. Yet the influence and the pressure of this extra-aesthetic function has not always been at the expense of the artist's creativity and the value of his work, and has in fact often been beneficial. Both the art of the folk theatre as well as other folklore performances are suitable means for observing all the positive and negative influences that this function has on both the aesthetic and the extra-aesthetic impact of the work as well as on its form.

Here we should particularly mention passages in plays and dramatic scenes in which the actors turn to the audience and ask for material contributions. Comic characters were usually chosen for this role. The devil closes the Slovak play about St Dorothy with the following words: "My dear town councillors, we have sung the song, give us a ducat or two, the Lord will bless you for the whole year, and if you don't give us anything, the devil will take it all from you" (Rybák 1904: 246). Voceďálek's[11] play *Moses* ends this way:

Fool. Whoever likes to listen to a play,
Please come next Sunday.
If it rains, we won't put on anything,
If the weather is fine, don't forget – you know what – mo-mo-money. (Mikovec 1855: 837)

At the end of a puppet performance Kašpárek[12] collects money. "In the final scene, Kašpárek (in Nýr's[13] version) begs for alms: 'I have eight children and Granny's the ninth – every day she needs four ounces of tobacco for her conk because...'" (Veselý 1910: 146). However, even respectable characters, for example Theophilus in the play about St Dorothy or the angel in the Christmas play, often beg for money for the actors (Feifalik 1864: 92 and 232). In rustic theatre productions "the devil or the fool along with the main character, that is the king or the high priest, stood by the gate and collected money" at the entrance to the theatre. "However, nimble boys climbed over a board fence and got in for free. The devil usually made sure nobody slipped through to the seats" (Mikovec 1855: 812).

In plays about kings, Plampač had words of praise for those who made generous donations to the king and the other actors and critical words for those who gave little or nothing. However, there might be many nuances here, depending on how pleased the actors were by the audience's generosity or how angry at its miserliness.

In the puppet theatre, when the collection was poor the performance was shortened:

Some puppeteers have a shortened version, especially when there are few spectators. If a forest was needed, Pelant[14] stuck a notably small tree, a branch, at the front of the stage, so that at once the action was taking place in "a dark, thick forest", even though there was open countryside in the background; at least the members of the Vršovec family[15] on the stage satisfied themselves as to the impassability of the surrounding thickets... This puppeteer was very easygoing, and so when for example Prince Oldřich was having lunch at a poor charcoal-burner's – something that is truly quite uncom-

---

11   [Editor's note: František Voceďálek (1762–1843), an active figure, as actor, director and playwright, in the amateur rustic theatre of northeastern Bohemia.]
12   [Editor's note: A popular comic Punch-like figure in the Czech puppet theatre tradition.]
13   [Editor's note: A Czech puppeteer, active in the late 19th and early 20th centuries.]
14   [Editor's note: A Czech puppeteer, active in the late 19th and early 20th centuries.]
15   [Editor's note: The Vršovec family, one of the three most powerful clans in early medieval Bohemia. The whole extended family and their retainers (about 3,000 in all) were massacred by the ruling Přemyslid dynasty in 1108.]

mon – the unusual nature of the occasion was conveyed visually by a stove in the left corner hanging upside down from the ceiling with pots on it (their lids also upside down), and in the right corner clock chains stretching upwards from the floor, their weights pointing to the ceiling, defying the law of gravity. (Veselý 1910: 137)

As we see here, the poor collection resulted in a change not only to the text but also to the stage set. In recent years even the repertoire of puppet plays has changed because of the fear of poor earnings:

The farmer as he appears in this play (*Farmer Dopita, or the Burning Down of Belgrade Castle, and also Věnceslav and Adleta, otherwise Kurando and Špádolíno*) – that is as a comic character – is said not to be appreciated by today's rich farmers. Apparently – and this I have been told by all the commercial puppeteers – they feel offended by this play. And the same is true of *Mr Franc from the Chateau*. So for business reasons professional puppeteers seldom put these plays on today, not wanting to get into trouble... Similarly, they leave out Jews from other, old plays because Jews who visit the puppet theatre feel offended, as do shoemakers, although they are not so sensitive because thanks to Baťa[16] they are on the verge of extinction... What will be allowed to put on, then? (Veselý 1927: 421)

Everything I have mentioned in connection with the economic function of the folk theatre can be found in our theatre. However, it does not manifest itself in such an overt form as in the folk theatre: actors in our theatre do not beg the audience for financial support from the stage. Our theatre people could say a great deal about the extent to which concern for making a good profit influences the repertoire even in our best theatres. So far we have focused on the positive and negative influences of the economic function on the aesthetic role of the folk theatre. However, the economic function also influences other extra-aesthetic functions of theatre plays, primarily the social function. This is proved by Plampač's speech, in which he praised or defamed his fellow citizens not according to their merits in the social life of the community but according to how much they gave the actors. As we have seen, for the sake of their earnings puppeteers abandon even quite innocent plays that some perceive as containing socially biased attacks, for example when a stupid farmer appears.

All this is entirely understandable. In the complex structure that is the theatre, the change of a single function, indeed even no more than the form of a play, may entail a rapid change in other functions as well.

---

16 [Editor's note: Tomáš Baťa (1876–1932), Czech entrepreneur, whose highly successful footwear factories produced low-cost shoes that resulted in many local shoemakers being put out of business.]

WORKS CITED

Aksakov, Ivan Sergeyevich (1892) *Ivan Sergeyevich Aksakov v jego pismakh* [Ivan Sergeyevich Aksakov in His Writings] I/3, Moscow: M. G. Volchaninov.

Bartoš, František (1892) *Moravský lid* [The Moravian People], Telč: Emil Šolc.

Bogatyrev, Petr (1929) Actes magiques, rites et croyances en Russie Subcarpathique [Magical Acts, Rites and Beliefs in Subcarpathian Ruthenia], Paris: Honore Champion.

Dobrovski, V (1908) "'Egorev den' v Smolenskoi gubernii", ["Yegor's Day" in the Smolensk Governorate], *Zhivaia Starina*, vol. 17, pp. 150–54, no. 2.

Feifalik, Julius (1864) "Dreikönigsspiel aus Rossitz" [The Three Kings Play from Rosice] in *Volksschauspiele aus Mähren* [Folk Plays from Moravia], Olomouc: Ed. Hölzel, pp. 40–73.

Holuby, Jozef Ľudovít (1897) "Drobné poviestky z Bošáckej doliny" [Minor Tales from the Bošáca Valley], *Český lid*, vol. 6, p. 146.

Janás, V. (1895) "Chození s 'perchtou'" [Going from Door to Door with "Perchta"], *Český lid*, vol. 4, pp. 55–57.

Kharuzina, V. N. (1927) "Primitivnye formy dramaticheskogo iskusstva" [Primitive Forms of Dramatic Art], *Etnografiia*, vol. 2.

— (1928) "Primitivnye formy dramaticheskogo iskusstva" [Primitive Forms of Dramatic Art], *Etnografiia*, vol. 3, pp. 22–43

Krčméry, Štefan (1934) "O slovenskom chodeni s Betlehemom" [Going from Door to Door with Bethlehem in Slovakia], *Sborník Matice Slovenskej*, pp. 11–12 and 85–110.

Linhart, Karel (1892) "Trhová Kamenice" [The Town of Trhová Kamenice], *Český lid*, vol. 1, p. 506.

Menčík, Ferdinand (1895) *Vánoční hry* [Christmas Plays], Holešov: F. Menčík.

Mikovec, Ferdinand Břetislav (1855) "Stopy selského či sousedského divadla v Čechách" [Traces of Rustic Theatre in Bohemia], *Lumír*, vol. 5, pp. 809–13.

Nieuwenhuis, Anton Willem (1904) *Quer durch Borneo* [Across Borneo], Leiden: E. J. Brill.

Onchukov, Nikolai Evgenevich (1911) *Severnye narodnye dramy* [Northern National Dramas], St Petersburg: A. S. Suvorin.

Rybák, Miloslav (1904) "Slovenská hra o sv. Dorotě" [A Slovak Play about St Dorothy], *Český lid*, vol. 13, pp. 193–96.

Sixta, Václav (1893) "Vrbčany" [The Village of Vrbčany], *Český lid*, vol. 2, p. 71.

Stránská, Drahomíra (1931) "Lidové obyčeje hospodářské" ["Folk Farming Traditions"], *Národní věstník českoslovanských*, vol. 24, pp. 41–91.

Veselý, Jindřich (1910) "O loutkách a loutkářích" [On Puppets and Puppeteers], *Národopisný věstník českoslovanský*, vol. 5, pp. 121–46.

— (1927) *Komedie a hry podle starých rukopisů, loutkářských tradic a Matěje Kopeckého* [Comedies and Dramas According to Ancient Manuscripts, Puppeteer Traditions and Matěj Kopecký], vol. 1, Prague: A. Štorch syn.

Zíbrt, Čeněk (1889) *Staročeské výroční obyčeje, pověry, slavnosti a zábavy prostonárodní pokud o nich vypravují písemné památky až po náš věk: příspěvek ke kulturním dějinám českým* [Old Czech Annual Customs, Superstitions, Festivals and Popular Entertainments as Evidenced by Written Records Down to Our Times: A Contribution to Czech Cultural History], Prague: J. R. Vilímek.

— (1910a) *Veselé chvíle v životě lidu českého, vol. II: Masopust držíme* [Merry Moments in the Life of the Czech People, vol. II: Keeping Carnival], Prague: F. Šimáček.

— (1910b) *Veselé chvíle v životě lidu českého, vol. III: Smrt nesem ze vsi - pomlázka s čepejří: obchůzky a zábavy na Blažeje, Dorotku, Řehoře, v postě a na pomlázku* [Merry Moments in the Life of the Czech People, vol. III: Carrying Death out of the Village - A Willow Switch with a Topknot: Going from Door to Door and Entertainments on St Blaise's Day, St Dorothy's Day, St Gregory's Day, during Lent and at Easter.] Prague: F. Šimáček.

— (1910c) *Veselé chvíle v životě lidu českého, vol. IV: Králové a královničky: jízda, honění, stínání, koupání králů na letnice, králky, královničky, král ptačí* [Merry Moments in the Life of the Czech

People, vol. IV: Kings and Little Queens: the Ride, Chasing, Beheading and Bathing of the Kings at Whitsuntide, Queens, Little Queens, the Bird King], Prague: F. Šimáček.

— (1911) *Veselé chvíle v životě lidu českého, vol. VIII: Na tom našem dvoře: obřady a zábavy při slavnostní odpravě kohouta, housera, kačera, beránka, kozla a vepřka* [Merry Moments in the Life of the Czech People, vol. VIII: In Our Farmyard: Rituals and Entertainments during the Ceremonial Dispatching of Cocks, Ganders, Drakes, Rams, Billy Goats and Hogs], Prague: F. Šimáček.

RITUAL AND THEATRE

JINDŘICH HONZL

["Obřad a divadlo" was published in Czech in instalments as a series of articles with varying titles in *Otázky divadla a filmu*, vol. 1 (1945-1946), pp. 44-50, 117-23, 159-69, 234-42, 315-23; vol. 2 (1946-1947), pp. 74-81. Its translation into English by John Burbank was published as "Ritual and Theater" in Steiner, Peter (ed.) (1982) *The Prague School: Selected Writings, 1929-1946*, Austin: University of Texas Press, pp. 135-73.]

Editor's note: Here we present only the first two of the original instalments, which contain conceptual issues crucial to the study of theatre. The remaining four are increasingly marked by contemporary political and ideological dogmas, reflecting the rise of the Communist Party in Czechoslovakia. Honzl, at the time a convinced Communist and later a member of the Party, shifted in his text from a semiotic analysis of theatrical elements to ideological statements about rituals in society.

Ritual and theatre share two fundamental similarities: they are *actions*, and they are *signifying* (symbolic) actions.

This correspondence has resulted in the two being identified with each other, judged to have had a common source and asked to have a common goal. The religious character of primitive theatricality cannot be denied. But what activity of the human spirit among primitive peoples does not have a religious character? In their beginnings mathematics and medicine, geometry and astronomy were all an inseparable part of the religious complex of primitive ideas of the world and man. But this religious origin has not prevented these sciences from defending their autonomy, first gained at the time of the Renaissance in Europe, more and more vigorously. It is also clear to scientists that they cannot discover a new complexity on the illusive basis of religious views. But for many artists and theoreticians the fact that the theatre was a *religious ritual* at the beginning of its development suffices to prove that the true goal of this development is the *theatre-temple*.

Let us look at one example of this identification of theatre and ritual action in an artist who represents a historical turning point for nineteenth-century German theatre, Richard Wagner. His theories arose as the flower of the German Romanticism of the revolutionary year 1848, a romanticism of a kind that had its religiously inspired precursors in the poets Novalis, Clemens Brentano and others. Wagner's theories about the Greek theatre try to prove the social significance of theatre by revealing its *religious character*: "Such a day of tragedies was [in Athens] a festival of the god ... the poet was its high priest" (Wagner 1892 [1849]: 33). Wagner accordingly longed to renew the social significance of theatre; he made of it a unique religious ceremony (*Festspiel*) and drew on religious and mythical materials. After the old Germanic myth of the Rhine ring he chose a medieval Christian myth, the legend of Parsifal. *Parsifal*, Wagner's last work, transforms an opera performance into a religious act by introducing a liturgical motif – the Catholic mass – onto the opera stage.

Wagner's romanticism associated theatre with society (and with the state) through the medium of religion. He thereby modified the classical orientation of Schiller (1810: 243–57), who associated theatre with society and the state through morality. A true Romantic, Wagner replaced the moral examples of Schiller's classicism with religious symbols. The development of the German theatre from Schiller to Wagner is therefore a progression from the severity and rationality of an ethical norm to the multiplicity of meaning, and irrationality, of a religious norm. Wagner's theatre touches the sphere of emotions much more deeply than Schiller was able to do, rejuvenating itself with all the atavisms religious magic arouses in its participants through the *symbolic nature* of its action. The multiple meanings of Wagner's theatrical symbol, taken over from religious rituals and myths, touches the spectator's heart much more intensely and instinctually than the one-sidedness of Schiller's moral imperative, which springs from the noble, rational fitness of the relations binding the individual to the state.

Wagner's more profound appeal does not prevent us, however, from calling attention to the retrogressive nature of his theatricality, which substitutes religious symbolism for purely theatrical symbolism.

Neither Wagner nor the theorists who followed in his steps and his epigones could legitimately invoke an example to illustrate the liturgical nature of the ancient Greek theatre. The leading component giving meaning to this theatre comprised the *citizen* and the *state*. The first consideration not only of the dramas of Aeschylus and Sophocles but also of Aristophanes' comedies was the polity and its welfare. This can be documented on the basis of both their themes and their artistic devices. Let us recall the theme of Aeschylus' *Oresteia*: it is the myth of the origin of the *state's highest court of law*, as we would refer to it today. It follows from the way Aeschylus elaborated this myth that the state's claim prevails over religion and the gods, for in the *Oresteia* even *the oldest goddesses of revenge* had to *submit* to the argument for the necessity of establishing the Areopagus. And they had not only to submit but also to change from punishing furies (Erinyes) into beneficent goddesses of welfare and happiness (Eumenides).

Even a theme like that of Sophocles' *Oedipus*, which admittedly is an example of a wholly individual dramatic fate, acquires a universal and civic interest by virtue of the fact that Sophocles combines the fate of an individual with the interest of the state.

Thus Oedipus is told at the beginning of the tragedy:

> Noblest of men, restore
> Life to your city! Think how all men call you
> Liberator for your triumph long ago;
> Ah, when your years of kingship are remembered
> Let them not say We rose, but later fell –
> Keep the State from going down in the storm!
> Once, years ago, with happy augury,
> You brought us fortune; be the same again! (Sophocles 1949: 5)

If Sophocles considers the matter of the state's welfare (the entire polity suffers for the unpunished act) the initial impulse behind the tragedy, the gods' affairs are subordinate to the polity, and Apollo's Delphic oracle and her interpreter Tiresias are concerned only with the welfare of the polity. Thus Oedipus compels Tiresias to interpret the oracle with the argument:

> **Oedipus**. What you say is ungracious and unhelpful
> To your native country. Do not refuse to speak.
> ...
> What! You do know something, and will not tell us?
> You would betray us all and wreck the State?
> ...
> Why,
> Who would not feel as I do? Who could endure
> Your arrogance toward the city?
> **Tiresias**. ... Never speak again to these men or to me:
> You yourself are the pollution of this country. (17–18)

The dominance of a matter of state over a religious matter is manifested here in the fact that the divine prophecy and the priest's interpretation *serve* (literally, as a servant serves a master who gives him orders) the welfare of the polity, which is the supreme and ultimate value. This would immediately be clearer to us if we transferred such a dialogue to the domain of, for example, the medieval theatre, where the celebration of divine glory and power was the supreme aim.

Not only do the theatre and the drama attest to this supremacy of the state over religion, but so does the Greek social organization itself.

Officials, not priests, represented the state [the totality of the citizenry] before a god. The priests were experts who carried out the ceremonies of the cult or individuals who offered advice when they were being performed, but *not mediators between the people and the gods*. They performed the prescribed rituals, but they did not determine them; *the state itself established the cults and, if need arose, changed them*. (Novotný 1925: 4 – italics J. H.)

One cannot accordingly assert that a "day of tragedies … was a festival of the god" in the sense that the religious ritual aspect prevailed over that of the state. In the present study, therefore, we do not draw on ancient examples – although ancient examples could be transposed to the ritual actions of other periods and countries if we took into account their common essence – because religion was not the leading component in either Greek polities or the Roman Empire.

On the other hand, we choose frequent examples from primitive peoples, whose social life was undifferentiated but all of whose thought and action was organized by collective *religious* notions. According to these notions, the forces that govern every natural process and every human act are religiously interpreted invisible forces. Even a sense of responsibility for an act and an awareness of it, which individuals possessed in the Classical period, are completely lacking in primitive peoples, who see in everything – even in their own acts – only the functioning of invisible forces of which man is the unconscious and involuntary instrument. There is, then, no change that members of primitive societies would not have interpreted religiously.

If we subject the religious actions of primitive peoples and Christian ritual (especially Catholic ritual) to frequent comparisons, it is not because we equate the two modes of religious action. But the ritual actions of medieval Christianity are manifestations forming part of a social structure in which religious consciousness was also *the leading component*. Medieval society was organized religiously. This assertion does not require extensive proof. But if someone were nevertheless to pursue the point, then consider medieval art and theatre, the Passion plays (the mysteries), the miracles and the moralities, about which it can be said that they were *components* of ritual actions just as it could be asserted that the days of Greek theatre were a component of a state cult.

What we are speaking of here is *theatricality*, which is a *common* property of Greek tragedies and medieval mysteries and which distinguishes the tragedies and mysteries from both religious and state cults. We maintain that theatricality is so independent of both these spheres that it can itself become the *leading* component of social organization. And for this too we can find historical examples. Such social structures as the Court of Louis XIV are examples of the theatrical organization of social life. The term "the Sun

King" is a theatrical allegorization of the ruler's functions. It is in keeping with the allegorical processions, ballets and plays that symbolized his actions (state weddings, victories, inductions, and the like) and that linked up into a continuous series of acts called "life at Court". The history of that period has preserved for us the memory of the participation of the royal prince in one ballet or another rather than in some diplomatic or military enterprise. Being part of the Court was conditioned by a mastery of all the rules of the "refinement" of morals and the spirit.

Social reality – political and military – was not admitted here except as a spirited or witty mode of conversation. And a politician or a soldier would have failed disgracefully, even though his business were supremely important in itself, if he had not known how to present it as an example of a spirited idea, a witty or humorous situation, or a brilliant rhetorical form.

In this period even the most dramatic state action – battles and warfare – acquired the form of a theatrical scene. The pre-battle dialogue between commanders, each granting the other the right to fire the first shot, became famous.

So the theatre of that period was – and this was certainly a peculiar relationship – a *component* of a higher theatrical structure: an event at the Court. A performance by Molière was a component of a Court feast that itself was a state act. Félibien gives an account of a "Feste de Versailles" at which one component was various scenes from Molière.

> The king, who at the insistence of his allies and at the request of all Europe granted us peace, showed signs of unprecedented restraint and kindness even after his greatest victories; he did not think otherwise than how he *could accommodate himself to the interests of his kingdom, when ... he decided to perform a feast in the garden at Versailles. ...* For that purpose, wishing to present a comedy after lunch and after the comedy a banquet, which was to be succeeded by a ballet and fireworks, he looked for people whom he considered the most talented for this affair. (Félibien 1668: 3–4 – italics J. H.)

In his function as poet and playwright, Molière was an *official* at the Court of Louis XIV. In the Athenian state theatrical ceremonies, the welfare of the polity was the first consideration. At Versailles theatrical beauty and the grace and charm of costume, movement, gesture and word, in which the king and the nobility excelled, were of primary importance.

The autonomy of the mode of thinking and feeling that we call theatrical and its specificity vis-a-vis modes of religious, political and philosophical thinking are thus documented by the history of its development. The point of this development can be nothing other than the crystallization of this theatrical mode of thinking and feeling to such a degree of purity and clarity as to make it possible – precisely because of this crystalline clarity – to bring about

harmony in the mutual relationship of all the basic modes of human representation, emotion and intention, a harmony that will guarantee the flexible
stability of their relations as well as their free development.

We are therefore interested in the facts of social and individual consciousness. These are the facts of mental life. But in interpreting them, we
constantly draw attention to the fact that the phenomena of social and individual consciousness that we are examining are realities through which
a society or an individual realizes its needs, among them self-fulfilment in the
material domain and self-awareness in the mental domain. For man, the need
to satisfy his hunger and to love are inseparably associated with his need and
yearning to understand and experience the world, for this is his human lot.

As an introduction to an analysis of the religious mode of thought and
action, let me cite a statement by Alfred Loisy, whose entire life's work on
the history of religion proves that "the essence of religion is religious action"
(a sacred act, a sacrifice) and that

> no religion can do without it if it does not want to commit suicide. Just as there is no
> sacred act without faith in the *real* presence of a god in it, there is no religion without
> sacred acts. ...
>
> A sacrifice cannot be limited to a simple gift even in the most primitive cults, nor
> can a sacrifice become, if it is not to vanish completely, merely a simple symbolic ges-
> ture even in the most spiritual religions. ... Effective ritual action has remained the
> essence of religious development right through to the Christian sacraments. (Loisy
> 1931: 123)

Loisy defines a ritual action as follows: a religious sacrifice is

> a ritual action – the destruction of a physical object, alive or deemed to contain life –
> whereby one thought to influence invisible forces, whether to escape their blow, when
> they were assumed to be harmful or dangerous, or to encourage their work, to render
> them satisfaction and homage, to enter into communication or even into communion
> with them... (Loisy 1920: 5)[1]

It is therefore evident that the efficacy of a ritual action stems from its
influence on the polar opposites of the egoistic instinct, on its positive and
negative aspects. The instinct of self-preservation manifests itself here both
as self-realization and as self-denial (behaving with humility before an invisible force and raising oneself to equality with or in some cases imposing
one's own will on the invisible power). With respect to the external world, the
egoistic instinct during a ritual action asserts itself negatively as a destruc-

---

1   [Editor's note: This section is italicized in the French original.]

tive instinct (the destruction of a living object) and positively as an effort to
identify oneself with a force that is not one's own, to expand one's self. The
approval of a social collective endows these egoistic, instinctive actions with
a special power. The purpose of a ritual act is the gratification of basic human
needs (with primitive peoples just as with civilized Christians it concerns
crops, success in the hunt, a victory, health, and the like), indispensable and
accessible to all individuals as parts of the social whole.

A sacred act (a ritual sacrifice) is therefore precisely the means through
which a religion strives to, and believes it can, control and change the world
in accordance with its adherents' longings. Religion believes that through
sacrifice one can impose human will on God, that through it one can rise to
divine power, one can become – as Catholics put it – a participant in divine
grace.

An invisible force, a transcendent God, cannot be present in the physical
world other than *symbolically*. The symbol is the main and only means for
primitive peoples and believers to adapt the world to their understanding and
their will, and to participate actively in changing it. Symbolism is thus the
basic feature of every religious interpretation of the world and every ritual
act. A religious interpretation is a special case of a sign-based interpretation
of reality, and a religious act is a special case of an action that functions as
a sign. We have said that the ritual action's nature as a sign makes it analogous
to a theatrical action. For this reason the confusion of a religious symbol with
a theatrical sign recurs again and again, and Richard Wagner's old error generates new confusion among his imitators and among eclectics, especially in
Germany.[2] Theatre movements for which the symbolic nature of the theatre
has been a basic concern have been particularly subject to such confusion
among their religiously oriented adherents – Paul Claudel, Henri Ghéon and

---

2   See Geissler 1926, particularly K. Preisendanz, "Vom antiken Schauspieler" [On the Actor in An-
      tiquity], and Richard Benz, "Schauspielkunst und kultische Sprechkunst" [Theatre Art and the
      Art of Religious Speaking], from which I quote the following:
      "The art of the religious speaker is an absolute art like the art of the actor, who also awakens
      a worthless theatrical piece to a suggestive semblance of life and celebrates his greatest triumphs
      in creating something that the poet has not created. For this reason the art of the speaker en-
      compasses a world that is greater and more enduring than the brief hour of the illusive reality of
      a dubious piece that only gives rise to new questions and new debates: the world of values, which
      is established not as a question but as a myth of the spirit, as a material and super-material hint
      of the metaphysical truth, in which we participate directly in its living presence... Thus the path
      leads to the stage of the future through the pulpit of the poetic word, which will ultimately be
      taken seriously and religiously... For the speaker ... there must emerge a new stage alongside
      today's theatres, a stage that will reinstate the old German style of the mysteries and speak to
      us, and thus we shall find a model for the drama of the present and the future that is directed
      beyond ordinary speech as well as an image of reality, that is directed beyond a theatre play and
      closet drama to the higher unity of the true *Gesamtkunstwerk*, realizing the truthful word and the
      truthful image." (9–10)

others. In Russia, symbolism (Vyacheslav Ivanov and others) has generated theories about transforming the theatre into a temple. A late flowering of Catholic theatrical symbolism in this country is František Pujman's little book *The Mother Tongue Set to Music*.[3] Those who believe that the essence of ritual action is theatrical or who think that theatrical action must be a sacred act establish confused and regressive goals for the theatre, which must be rejected in the interest of *genuine* development.

In a similar fashion, Lucien Lévy-Bruhl, the author of *Primitive Mentality* and *How Natives Think*, confuses the relationship between theatricality and religious ritualism when he quotes from George Catlin's *North American Indians* a description of a ritual dance performed by the Indians during a buffalo hunt. Lévy-Bruhl is carried away by the vivid character of the dance synopsis and says about this ritual act of the Indians: "It is a kind of drama, or rather pantomime, representing the prey and describing the fate that awaits him at the hands of the Indians" (Lévy-Bruhl 1966: 202). The mistaken identification of a ritual action with a theatrical play arises here through a (perhaps intentional) substitution of perspective. For the Indians, believing in totems and in the mystical forces controlling animals as well as people, the dance is a *ritual* act. To a European, who does not believe in totems and who also sometimes knows nothing about them (and the scholar studying the mental functions of Indians should not be such a European), the dance can appear to be a non-utilitarian activity that is an end in itself and that unfolds solely from the aesthetic pleasure of the dance movements.

About ten or fifteen Mandans at a time join in the dance, each one with the skin of the buffalo's head (or mask) with the horns on, and in his hand his favourite bow or lance, with which he is used to slay the buffalo... These dances have sometimes been continued for two or three weeks without stopping an instant, until the joyful moment when buffaloes make their appearance... [They represent the capture and the killing of the buffalo.][4] When an Indian becomes fatigued of the exercise, he signifies it by bending quite forward, and sinking his body towards the ground; when another draws a bow upon him and hits him with a blunt arrow, and he falls like a buffalo, is seized by the bystanders, who drag him out of the ring by the heels, brandishing their knives about him; and having gone through the motions of skinning and cutting him up, they let him off, and his place is at once supplied by another, who dances into the ring with his mask on; and by this taking of places, the scene is easily kept up night and day, until the desired effect, that of making "buffalo come", has been produced. (Lévy-Bruhl 1966: 201–202)

---

3   [Editor's note: František Pujman (1889–1961), a prolific Czech theatre and opera director.]
4   [Editor's note: This sentence is Lévy-Bruhl's bridging of a passage in Catlin he omitted.]

Lévy-Bruhl's evaluation of the dance rite and Catlin's description come from non-participating spectators who do not share any of the Indians' totemic notions. They can therefore speak of *drama* or *pantomime*, regard the dance as an *imitation* of movements made when hunting and talk about a man with a dance mask who *represents* a buffalo. As spectators they avail themselves of theatrical terms for their description. A Chinese person who has been raised on the Chinese theatre and who does not know any of the collective notions on which Catholic ritual is based could speak in just such theatrical terms and from the perspective of a spectator about the Catholic mass performed in a church.

A spectator can understand the meaning of such actions as a hunt, a fight with an enemy, the healing of a sick person, and so on, anywhere and anytime. The Indian dance or the Catholic mass is then transposed in the mind of the non-participating observer into a domain in which religious acts can be understood as *representing, imitating, indicating* those actions whose meaning is evident to everyone, actions that gratify basic human needs. This is the domain of theatrical images and metaphors. The dance is thus understood as an *imitation* of a buffalo hunt; the mass is perceived as the *image* of an event that brings succour and benefit to believers. Such an interpretation, however, is *non-religious*, transferring the modes of theatrical perception into the thought and action of the believers.

To believers and primitive peoples, whose thinking is governed by the same collective ideas, the Catholic mass is not an image of the Lord's last supper but the *actual* sacrifice of Christ, the sacrifice of his *actual* body and blood. And to the Indians the dance is not an image of a buffalo hunt but the hunt itself or at least an important and indispensable part of the hunt. The Catholic Church has always defended and continues to defend the dogma of Christ's *actual* presence in the bread and the wine because it was and is aware of the basis on which every religious faith rests and because it was and is aware of the catastrophic consequences for the Church of admitting the mere figurative presence of Christ in the bread and the wine. The atavistic basis of the Catholic rite is its strength and the source of its deep-rooted indestructibility. The Catholic mass resembles every ritual action of Indians, Australian aborigines, African natives and primitive Asiatic tribes in that *a symbolic ritual act is taken as reality*, that the participant believes that by eating and drinking (by destroying – that is, sacrificing) the bread and the wine, the communicant merges with the actual Christ and actually rises to a state of divine grace, just as the Indian believes that he will prevail over and catch a buffalo through his dance.

The symbolic nature of a ritual act is based on a special way of consciously interpreting a symbol (the dance is a hunt, the mass is part of a triumph, a successful undertaking or recovery from an illness) with the aim and purpose of satisfying social needs and attaining values equally necessary to everyone. So a ritual act is not an image or a metaphor or an allegory of an actual act (an actual hunt, Christ's actual sacrifice), but neither is it associated with an actual act causally, in the sense that it is *not taken as the cause for the success* of the actual hunt, battle, cure, and so forth. A successful hunt is not the *result* or the *consequence* of the dance performed before the hunt, but rather *its success lies precisely in the dance*, an inseparable part of every successful hunt. The dance is not the cause of the fact that a buffalo has been killed – for a buffalo could have been killed elsewhere without ritual preparations – but a buffalo can only be prey for the hunt if it has been killed in a ritual hunt. Otherwise its killing would not be a success but, on the contrary, a danger for the primitive tribe. Nor is the success of the victory the vanquishing of the foe itself; its success lies in the fact that a *divine* victory was achieved. For this interpretation of a triumph we are, of course, assuming an army of believers – soldiers on medieval campaigns against nonbelievers and heretics, soldiers for whom offensive military action was seen as participation in the propagation of the Christian faith; or we are assuming the Hussite and Taborite believers, for whom the defeat of Sigismund was participation in the victory "of the chalice over the whore of Babylon".[5]

The inability of an ordinary civilized person to identify a symbol with reality, to identify the bread and the wine with Christ – or the dance with the buffalo hunt – implies his inability to think and act religiously. Religions that lack or deny symbolic ritual are deprived of the major support on which their power rests; they are deprived of the possibility of "communion with God". The inaccessibility of God necessarily entails for the believer the impossibility of intervening in reality through a religious act, that is an act that identifies the believer's will with the divine will. Primitive religions achieve a correspondence between the will of man and the will of higher, invisible powers by winning over these powers through sacrifices – or by threatening them with punishments. (The pain caused to a fetish because a nail is driven into its body – into the body of a wooden figure – compels the fetish to comply with the black man's wish.) Not even higher religions – as Alfred Loisy demonstrates – can deprive themselves of sacrifice as a means for obtaining God's approval of a human aim. However, *uncertainty* about the course of an

---

5   [Editor's note: Hussites, followers of the teachings of John Huss (Jan Hus, c. 1370–1415), a reformer of the Church from Bohemia, burnt at the stake in 1415. Taborites, a radical faction of the Hussite movement, based in the town of Tábor, where they raised a substantial military force that played a major role in the resistance to the crusades launched by the Catholic Church. Sigismund of Luxemburg (1368–1437), Holy Roman Emperor (1433–1437) and King of Bohemia (1419–1437), adversary of the Hussite movement; in the Czech national mythology, he is considered a traitor to the nation. The chalice is the symbol of the reformist church, standing for the partaking of the blood of Christ by all participants in Holy Communion, not only the priest as in the Catholic Mass.]

event, *dissatisfaction and disagreement* with the common impulses driving people and the things of this world, is always the precondition behind every religious act. The only religions that activate people are those that presuppose a *disparity* between the real impulses driving people and things and a longing that this drive does not satisfy. The world of religion is the world of human longing. This is a world that religion shares with many other modes of human thought and action. But a *religious* resolution of this disparity entails overcoming it through a religious act, that is an act identifying human will with the divine will. In fact human will (provoked by the needs of hunger, love, health, self-fulfilment, and so on) has real preconditions and goals. The divine will is the same longing projected outwardly, objectified in the physical world through a *religious symbol*. The symbol is the means through which man realizes his longing by separating it from himself, by isolating it, by objectifying it in external reality (in some object or event); it thereby becomes a sacred object or event.

WORKS CITED

Félibien, André (1668) *Relation de la feste de Versailles du 18 juillet 1668* [A Narrative of the Versailles Feast on 18 July 1668], Paris: Pierre le Petit.

Geissler, Ewald (ed.) (1926) *Der Schauspieler* [The Actor], Berlin: Bühnenvolksbundverlag.

Lévy-Bruhl, Lucien (1966) *How Natives Think*, trans. Lillian A. Claire, New York: Washington Square Press.

Loisy, Alfred (1920) *Essai historique sur le Sacrifice* [A Historical Essay on Sacrifice], Paris: E. Nourry.

— (1931) "Considérations sur l'histoire des religions" [Considerations on the History of Religions] in Dandieu, Arnaud (ed.) *Anthologie des philosophes français contemporains* [Anthology of Contemporary French Philosophers], Paris: Editions du Sagittaire, pp. 123–35.

Novotný, František (1925) *Antické státy a náboženství* [Ancient Greek States and Religions], Prague: L. K. Žižka.

Schiller, Friedrich (1810) "Die Schaubühne als eine moralische Anstalt betrachtet" [The Theatre Considered as a Moral Institution], *Friedrich Schillers sämtliche Werke* [The Complete Works of Friedrich Schiller], vol. 16, Vienna, pp. 243–57.

Sophocles (1949) *Oedipus Rex*, trans. Dudley Fitts and Robert Fitzgerald, in *The Oedipus Cycle: An English Version*, New York: Harcourt, Brace & World, pp. 1–81.

Wagner, Richard (1892 [1849]) "Art and Revolution", trans. William Ashton Ellis, in *Richard Wagner's Prose Works. Vol. I. The Art-work of the Future etc.*, London: Kegan Paul, Trench, Trübner & co., pp. 21–68.

The texts in this section deal with issues treated in previous sections and open new perspectives, especially in terms of attention to the specific social contexts of the art of the theatre.

E. F. Burian's short treatment of film in the theatre reflects the deep interest of an avant-garde artist in using new media such as photography and film on stage. What relates it to the context of Prague School thinking is Burian's way of posing the question: his aim is to pin down the specific function of film and photography in the theatre structure. Burian's second short text, on the stage metaphor, represents an unconventional approach to theatre as a medium. Even though Burian as a theatre director could never go so far, it is striking how he conceives of a theatre performance as a multi-media event. He viewed the complicated structure of signs not only as communicating meaning, but also as initiating an intense experience on the part of the audience. To use today's terminology, Burian was well aware of the performative power of theatre.

Jiří Veltruský's text "Theatre in the Corridor" (1939) is the only analysis we have of a performance (in the strict sense of the word) in which the terminology of the Prague School is applied to a contemporary theatre production. At the same time, it is an attempt to elaborate in great detail the problem of the relation between various layers of signs in theatre, to specify features of acting in avant-garde theatre (the text was written almost simultaneously with his "People and Things in the Theatre" (this reader, pp. 147–56), so the two texts can be viewed as complementary), and also to discuss the social relevance of such artistic experiments.

An awareness of the social role of theatre is also clear in Jan Mukařovský's "On the Artistic Situation of the Contemporary Czech Theatre" (1946). This essay forms part of an extensive discussion that began during World War II at illegal seminars and meetings (members of the Prague School who remained in the country often took part in activities of this kind). These discussions focussed on planning a new approach to organizing theatre culture after the war. A number of models for a non-commercial, state-supported system were worked out. After 1945, the issue was widely discussed in the media and became caught up in the post-war political changes. The issue was settled with the Communist *coup d'état* in February 1948: soon after, a state-supported but at the same time completely state-controlled system was introduced (though the first signs of this tendency were already evident in 1945).

In this heated discussion, Mukařovský takes a completely neutral position. He uses a structuralist approach as a means of describing the development of the Czech theatre in order to show its current condition, and rather than proposing solutions tries to grasp the artistic problems of the period.

THE FUNCTION OF PHOTOGRAPHY AND FILM IN THE THEATRE

E. F. BURIAN

[First delivered as a public lecture at a debate about contemporary theatre in the building of the Mánes Fine Artists' Society in Prague on 3 April 1936, and published in 1936
as "Divadelník E. F. Burian o fotografii" [The Theatre Practitioner E. F. Burian on Pho-
tography], České slovo, vol. 28, no. 106 (6 May 1936), p. 12. Burian included a version
of the text in his 1936 pamphlet Zaměřte jeviště [Sweep the Stage], Prague: O. Jirsák,
pp. 29–30. This translation is based on the text found in the 1981 collection E. F. Burian
a jeho program poetického divadla [E. F. Burian and His Programme of the Poetic Theatre],
Prague: Divadelní ústav, where it appears under the title "Divadelní funkce fotografie
a filmu", which has been preserved.]

Translated by Eva Daníčková

Photography is of great technical significance for the modern theatre. This
is not just because it can be used for sets based on the use of projection;
that would only scratch the surface of its possibilities. The main reason
is that photography's whole perspective on things, the world and people
has caused an accelerated revolution in the development of theatre. If we
substitute the eye of the director for the lens, then the stage, the actor and
the set become what for the photographer is not only the shot but also the
chemical procedure of developing the film and the technique of enlarging
detail. In the same way light, which until recently still served as a tool of
illusion for theatre practitioners, changes under the photographic eye of the
director into a spatial matter and assumes the same function as in modern
photography. But we must not forget that what we find so clearly expressed
in today's photography was already present in the paintings of the old masters. And not only in the paintings but in architecture and in sculpture. For
Rembrandt, for example, light and shadow is the leading principle. It was not
by accident that Classical sculptures were situated so as to face the light, and
the placement of Greek columns created its own special plastic light. From
an analytical point of view, the black and white in modern photography is
merely something similar to the painter's use of grey tones. And it is typical
of the modern theatre that it approaches photography through the old masters. However, what theatre adopts from photography is not its naturalistic
tendency. Denaturalized detail, the realistic photogram and, most importantly, a broad scale of light and dark tones are the main elements that the

theatre has adopted from photography for its creative purposes. Today the function of slide projection in the theatre has more to do with spatial than illustrative or static effects. A detail appropriately projected onto new material reveals the future of plastic optics. The photomontage, too, has great value for the theatre, as does film projection. Today, when all the arts are interacting and influencing each other, it is difficult to distinguish what film has adopted from theatre and what theatre has adopted from film. Unity of plot, which was the main limiting factor of the old theatre, fell from favour when the first illusion of the old theatre fell. When Ernst Lubitsch writes that 3D film is in no danger of copying theatre because film technology is diametrically different from the technology of the theatre owing to the ability of the former to change the scene of action, he is mistaken, since the logic he employs when discussing film scenery has long since ceased to be applicable to the theatre. If we are to speak about a liberated scene of action at all, then let us speak about it in connection with the theatre, especially since in the historical past, in ancient Greece just as in the age Shakespeare and at other times, the imagination of theatre practitioners and the audiences functioned in such a way that it was transported from one place to another at the mere mention of a change of place, without the action on the stage coming to a halt. The main virtue of film for the modern theatre has been to facilitate the maximum possible narrative drive and to help theatre to free itself from the shackles of the old illusion. But the projection of a film on stage cannot have the naturalistic character that we see in almost all of today's films. The projection of a film on stage is a spatial, non-illustrative and non-naturalistic matter. It is for its detail that the modern stage values film most. Piscator's mistaken earlier practice, when he complemented the stage set with moving film images, has long since ceased to be capable of raising astonishment in the audience. Detail alone makes theatrical montage possible, most of all the kind of detail that is capable of raising the dramatic conflict to monstrous dimensions and that makes accessible to the audience what cannot be perceived by the naked eye. The same applies to static photography. But the whole of stage technology must be viewed in the same way a filmmaker or a photographer views the technology of film or of photography. The lights must pick out detail, rarely the whole stage. The set must be neither naturalistic nor illusionist. The actors' costumes must be designed in a way that does not clash with the projection. The plot must flow smoothly, almost like in film montage. In short, everything that functions in the theatre must emerge from the image and the musicality of film footage in relation to the photographic shot.

THE STAGE METAPHOR

E. F. BURIAN

[Written in Czech as "Jevištní metafora" in 1937, this was first published in Burian, E. F. (1938) *Pražská dramaturgie 1937* [The Prague Dramaturgy 1937], Prague: privately printed.]

Translated by Eva Daníčková

A stage metaphor is anything that, emanating from the stage, evokes the idea of something different from what it really is. A stage metaphor uses one reality to hide another and vice versa. Through one reality it evokes the idea of another reality in the spectator's imagination. This imagined reality is often very different from or the complete opposite of the reality that is being performed. The stage metaphor was born with the first light that was not content to be simply a lamp or a spotlight but wanted to evoke the image of moonlight or sunshine in the spectator's imagination. A visible spotlight with a green filter that is used to light an actor delivering a monologue about moonlight is in effect an old illusionist metaphor, stripped bare and purified. The old stage language, in which delight at the view of a forest was expressed in front of a backdrop showing painted trees, was already to a certain extent a metaphor. Let us do away with this stage and its painted backdrop showing a forest and speak this same monologue on a bare stage delimited by a beam of light and we will arrive at a simple, modern stage metaphor. But if we add a fluttering veil lit by a pale blue light, the monologue about the view of the forest becomes a heightened metaphor. Already in the past opera composers composed stage storms, with chromatic passages for the strings, lightning for the piccolo and thunder for the tympani. This hidden employment of a sound metaphor would become evident to us as a reality quite simply if we placed the orchestra on stage and revealed what was going on behind the scenes, with one stagehand turning the handle of the rain machine, another working the wind machine and a third pulling the rope of the thunder machine. It would become a clear metaphor if the sound of the orchestra was projected through speakers in the auditorium and from several projection screens placed on stage hugely magnified rain drops appeared to be falling in the direction of the audience. The stage floor would be covered in silver mesh, its reflection caught in mirrors and directed at the audience. The rhythm of the whole stage would have to correspond with the rhythm and the tone of the orchestra. The audience might well flee from the auditorium, afraid of getting wet or being struck by lightning.

THEATRE IN THE CORRIDOR
E. F. BURIAN'S PRODUCTION OF *ALLADINE AND PALOMIDES*

JIŘÍ VELTRUSKÝ

[Originally written in Czech as "Divadlo na chodbě" [Theatre in the Corridor] in 1939, it was translated and reworked by the author and published under the present full title in 1979 in *The Drama Review: TDR*, vol. 23, no. 4, Private Performance Issue, pp. 67–80. See below for further details. The Czech version was published in (1994) *Příspěvky k teorii divadla* [Contributions to the Theory of the Theatre], Prague: Divadelní ústav, pp. 237–48.]

Editor's note: Veltruský wrote an introduction to the article when it was published in *The Drama Review: TDR* in 1979 in which he explained its origin and development. He also outlined the historical and theoretical contexts of his text, both in 1939 and 1979. As the information provided is highly valuable to those with a limited knowledge of the Czech cultural context, we have decided to include his introduction along with the actual article.

INTRODUCTION

"Theatre in the Corridor" was written, in Czech, in December 1939; this explains why the first paragraph sounds rather anachronistic. It has remained unpublished for nearly forty years. This was my third attempt to write a theoretical paper, after "Man and Object in the Theatre", published in 1940[1] and "Mácha's Conception of the World", published the same year.[2]

My approach followed the general theory of the Prague Linguistic Circle, focusing on the concepts of structure and sign. But I was much more influenced by the Prague School's poetics, linguistic and general aesthetics than by its sporadic studies about the theatre, which I found somewhat loose in their reasoning. As regards the strictly reasoned treatise *The Aesthetics of Dramatic Art* by Otakar Zich (1931), I was still at that time unable to see its full value because it disregarded the avant-garde theatre, in which I had been directly involved during the few previous years. (As I did not yet realize, political circumstances had already put an end to my ephemeral theatrical activities.)

---

1   [Editor's note: Published in this reader as "People and Things in the Theatre", pp. 147–56.]
2   [Editor's note: Veltruský, Jiří (1940) "Básníkův poměr k světu a skutečnosti" [The Poet's Relationship to the World and Reality], in *Věčný Mácha* [The Eternal Mácha], Prague: Čin, pp. 98–122.]

One of the problems I sought to clarify in this paper was the relationship between puppet theatre and theatre with live actors. The same problem had given rise to "Man and Object in the Theatre", although in the final version it disappeared. I am still trying to clarify it (see my (1977) "Puppets for Adults", *Sub-Stance*, no. 18–19, pp. 105–11), though I had the opportunity meanwhile to work out my ideas about acting more thoroughly ("Contribution to the Semiotics of Acting").[3]

Since this was only my third theoretical paper in the strict sense of the word, and the second concerning the theatre, it is hardly surprising that some of the concepts owed more to instinct than to reasoning, despite my objections to the loose reasoning of the other Prague theoreticians of the theatre. When I reread the article, I was quite surprised to notice that at the time I considered that the reason why the activation of the audience attenuated the distribution of the action between the stage and the adjacent "offstage" areas was, quite simply, that the imaginary action space was transferred into the auditorium. This is the view I hold at present. But I had obviously forgotten all about it several months later when in a major study ("Notes Regarding Bogatyrev's Book on Czech and Slovak Folk Theatre", 1940, unpublished[4]) I vainly speculated about the reason why offstage action seems to be incompatible with the activation of the spectator. No doubt the insight I had forgotten was not mine. Most likely I got if from Karel Brušák's article on the imaginary action space, published a year or two earlier in the programme of E. F. Burian's theatre; unfortunately neither Brušák nor I have managed to find a copy of his article to check.[5]

Finally, I want to add that František Deák was right when he pointed out that one of the weak spots of the Prague School theory of theatre was that it did not produce analyses of specific productions or of the work of specific artists (Deák 1976). The present paper dealing with a specific production may help to explain this weakness. It was written for a review specializing in literature; it was never published for the silly reason that before it was finished I had quarrelled with the editor about an entirely different matter. We did try to work out a new theory of theatre, back in Prague, but we had no *Drama Review*.

The proscenium stage is coming under increasing attack from avant-garde directors. Yet they can seldom express their hostility toward this conventional form in their actual work, because new theatres with other forms of playing areas have not been built. Whatever arguments he may put forward against it in his theoretical or programmatic writings, the stage director has to use the proscenium stage in his productions. The various projects for a theatre of

---

3   [Editor's note: Published in this reader as "A Contribution to the Semiotics of Acting", pp. 376–424.]

4   [Editor's note: Published only later in English as Veltruský, Jiří (1987) "Structure in Folk Theater. Notes Regarding Bogatyrev's Book on Czech and Slovak Folk Theater", *Poetics Today*, vol. 8, no. 1, pp. 141–61.]

5   [Editor's note: For Brušák's paper, see this reader, pp. 303–19.]

a new type remain on paper because only a miracle could produce the money needed to carry them out; this has also happened to E. F. Burian and Miroslav Kouřil's important project for the Theatre of Labour (Kouřil and Burian 1938).

The first serious attempt ever made in Prague to organize the theatrical space in a radically new manner took place in a corridor: on 14 December 1939, E. F. Burian staged Maurice Maeterlinck's *Alladine and Palomides* in the corridor of his theatre D 40, and the performance was repeated on 15 and 16 December. The actors played on the floorboards of the corridor, in front of a wall with doors, and they were surrounded on three sides by the spectators, who stood on the same floorboards and marked the limits of the playing area. Each of the five acts was performed at a different place in the corridor, but the playing area remained unchanged during any one act, irrespective of the division of Acts II and III into scenes with different locales; between the acts, ushers showed the audience where it was to move next. For technical reasons only 120 spectators could be admitted to each performance. So this important production was seen by 360 people in all.

This bold experiment did not provide a viable solution to Burian's problems with theatrical space; a professional company cannot live on performances for such a small audience. But this was not makeshift. The exiguity of the playing area and the close proximity between the spectators and actors were important factors of the dramatic structure.

In relation to Burian's previous work (see Deák 1976) this production constitutes a sort of milestone. It sums up the basic tendencies of his conception of the theatre and brings them to a culmination point. This statement is not meant as a value judgment. The present paper is a theoretical study, not criticism, and the formulations or conclusions it contains have no normative implications with respect to artistic creation. Theory can clarify, not sit in judgment. Moreover, theoretical concepts are abstractions that cannot be substituted for concrete facts; these never exist in such a pure form.

* * *

However they are staged, Maeterlinck's plays invariably affect the performance very strongly by their own structure. This is particularly noticeable in the case of the plays the author designated "little plays for puppets", one of which is *Alladine and Palomides*. In Burian's production, the poetic unity of the play was somewhat attenuated by the insertion of short versified prologues by Vladimír Holan,[6] recited before each of the five acts. Moreover, Burian disregarded most of the author's stage directions, especially those concern-

---

6   [Editor's note: Vladimír Holan (1905–1980), Czech poet and translator. He was the editor of the journal *Program D 40*, published by Burian's Theatre D, for a year.]

ing the sets and the distribution of the action between the playing area and the imaginary action space. Even so, the performance strongly reflected the structure of the play. And though it was done by live actors, it definitely had some features more characteristic of puppet theatre.

The difference between puppet theatre and theatre with live actors centres on, but is by no means limited to, the stage figures. And it is not merely a technical difference (the human body as opposed to wood, cloth and such like) but a structural one. A puppet that represents a character has only those features of a real person that are needed for the given dramatic situation; all the components of a puppet are intentional signs. By contrast, the stage figure created by an actor is shaped not only by artistic intention but also by physiological necessity. The movements of the facial muscles, for instance, are controlled both by the semiotic and by the physiological functions: the actor's wrinkled brow looks very much the same whether it signifies the character's wrath or results from an excessive strain on the actor's vocal cords. Yet the audience perceives all the elements of the stage figure as signs The stage figure created by a live actor is therefore made up from a greater number of signs than are needed for a given dramatic situation. It oscillates between being a sign, that is, a reality standing for another reality, and being a reality in its own right. That is why the stage figure stands out among the components of the theatre. The other components (sets, costumes, props, and so on) are pure signs, just like puppets. They remain, so to speak, under the threshold of awareness, so that they acquire their meaning through the intermediary of the actor. The stage figure created by the actor unites all the signs. In puppet theatre this unifying function is assumed by the vocal performance, the only element of the live person that here enters into the stage figure.

It does not follow from this structural difference that the two forms of theatre are strictly delimited. On the contrary, they are connected with one another by a constantly changing dynamic relation, a relation in the nature of dialectical antinomy. There exists a whole range of phenomena that lie between them. The theatre with live actors often strives to come closer to puppet theatre and vice versa. The use of masks, for example, eliminates from the stage figure not only the intentional movements of the facial muscles but also the unintentional ones, which particularly affects its semiotic nature. The same effect is obtained in the case of the simplified and selective movements and gestures usually described as stylized, because such movements and gestures are designed to eliminate automatic bodily reflexes. Yet another example: when the dramatic action is relegated to the imaginary action space and is signified to the audience by offstage speeches, everything turns into pure immaterial meaning except the actor's vocal performance, which stands out as in the puppet theatre.

The imaginary action is particularly important in Maeterlinck's conception of the theatre. Most of the physical action is removed from the spectator's field of vision and signified by speeches alone, uttered either by the characters offstage (such as the voices of the dying Alladine and Palomides in the last act) or by the characters on the stage referring to offstage action (Alladine and Ablamore's dialogue in the first act, commenting on Palomides' approach before he appears on the stage). In addition, certain crucial segments of the plot are presented in narrative form in the course of the dialogue. These literary procedures restrain the actors' movement. Meyerhold's staging of Maeterlinck, which translated this tendency into theatrical performance in the strictest possible way, largely immobilized the actors and drastically reduced the depth of the stage (Honzl 1928: 13).

In this way Maeterlinck seeks to adapt all of his theatre to the intrinsic structure of the puppet theatre. But he goes beyond even the puppet theatre in his effort to eliminate the elements of reality. By giving his text very pronounced rhythmic and melodic contours, he obliges the actor to emphasize rhythm and intonation so much that the other components of his vocal performance are to a large extent neutralized. This engenders a peculiar "stage speech" that is made up of a limited number of features, much less than appear in colloquial speech, and is common to all the stage figures. In any given situation the sound structure of the speeches of all Maeterlinck's stage figures consists only of such signs as are actually needed. Stage figures of this kind do not differ much from each other; in fact, the same characters reappear, with only minor changes though under different names, in several plays. The verbal component, or text, becomes the dominant[7] of the kind of theatre that is implied in the plays, and all the other components of the theatrical structure are subordinated to it.

Václav Tille, who was an unusually perceptive theatre critic, said about Maeterlinck's dialogues that they

are nothing but a tiresome philosophical treatise: they have neither plot nor moods, the characters that voice them apparently dissect their own hearts to the last tremor but in truth have no internal life whatsoever, they are mere spokesmen of certain opinions about certain feelings which they themselves do not manifest in an individual way. Their questions and answers, the utterances they address to each other, do not produce in their hearts any effect that would manifest itself by a real individual reaction. One clearly sees the puppeteer who expresses his view in a circumstantial monologue and merely changes the voice as he moves the puppets. (Tille 1910: 158–59)

---

7   [Editor's note: "The dominant" is Jakobson's term. Veltruský uses the more intuitively comprehensible "dominant component" in his 1939 manuscript.]

* * *

In Burian's production, the action unfolds on a bare playing area that holds nothing but a few indispensable functional objects, such as a chair on which an actor is to sit. Only the word and the lighting localize the action represented and conjure up the scenery. For example, the prologue to Act I indicates "A wild spot in the gardens" (Maeterlinck 1890: 15), while in Act III, Scene 3, turning on a white floodlight means that Ablamore has opened the shutters. As soon as it is mentioned that the action takes place on a drawbridge, the polished parquet on which the actors – as well as the spectators – are standing turns into the rough beams of the bridge; or, more exactly, it represents the beams. When a few moments later the dialogue implies that the characters are in a room, the same parquet represents the floor of a room in the palace (Act III, Scene 2).

The extremely complicated semiotic process that results from the absence of stage sets is particularly impressive in Act IV, situated in "vast subterranean grottoes" (41), because here references to the scenery constitute one of the axes of the dialogue, and a drastic transformation of the scenery, to which the dialogue alludes only indirectly, accompanies the reversal of the situation. Here is how this transformation is described in the stage direction: "... a light that streams into the cavern with ever more resistless abundance, revealing little by little the wretchedness of the grotto that had seemed so marvellous to them; the miraculous lake becomes dull and sinister; the light fades out of the stones in the rocks, and the ardent roses are seen to be nothing but fungus and decaying matter" (51). In Burian's production nothing of the sort happens on the bare playing area. The transformation of the characters' surroundings is only hinted at very obliquely by Palomides' line, "This is another light...," followed after a brief silence by his question, "Where are we?" and Alladine's answer: "And yet I do love you, Palomides..." (51).

The same themes reappear in Act V when the extraordinary dialogue between the voices of the dying Alladine and Palomides is coming to its end:

The Voice of Palomides. You are thinking of something that you will not tell me...
The Voice of Alladine. They were not jewels...
The Voice of Palomides. And the flowers were not real...

...

The Voice of Alladine. It was the light that had no pity... (60)

This reappearance of the theme emphasizes the elusiveness of the hidden meaning of what happened in Act IV. In Burian's treatment this effect intended by the play is considerably strengthened. Moreover, the elimination of all stage sets indicating the scenery furthers Maeterlinck's endeavour to "dematerialize" the theatre and impose on the performance a structure in

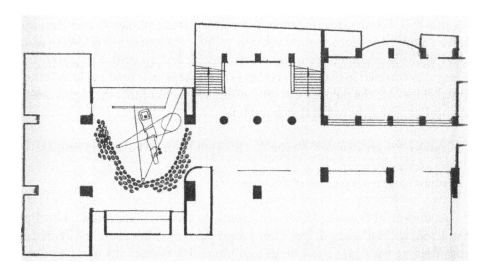

Fig. 1a, 1b: Ground plan of the foyer with disposition of playing area, lights, actors and spectators for Act 1. The placement of the three actors corresponds to the situation in the photo – Zdeněk Podlipný (Ablamore), Vladimír Šmeral (Palomides) and Jiřina Stránská (Alladine) during the dialogue of Alladine and Palomides toward the end of Act I.

which all the components are subordinated to an uninterrupted flow and interplay of meanings as loosely linked to the material sign-vehicles as possible, so as to shift freely between different levels of meaning.

Furthermore, with the method adopted by Burian in this production, the scene can change very fast without causing any interruptions. As already indicated, the playing area remains unchanged during each act even though Acts II and III are composed of scenes separated from each other both in space and in time.

In Act II, Scene 1, for instance, the playing area represents an interior, as Ablamore's questions to Alladine imply: "What is it in the park? Were you looking at the avenue of fountains that unfolds before your windows?" In Scene 2, performed in the same area, only a few steps over to one side, it is the drawbridge over the palace moat. The audience learns of this through a brief opening exchange between the characters:

Palomides: You are going out, Alladine? – I have just returned; I have been hunting... There has been a shower...
Alladine: I have never yet crossed this bridge. (24)

At the end of Scene 2, Ablamore approaches them, takes Alladine by the hand and, without a word, leads her away. The two actors playing Ablamore and Alladine walk just a few steps and immediately start the opening dialogue of Scene 3. The few steps are enough to bring the characters into a room in the palace; moreover, during this short movement of theirs the plot leaps several days ahead, because the characters talk in the past tense about what happened after the encounter on the drawbridge.

The few steps that form the transition from one scene to the next mean a long walk from the drawbridge to an apartment and their duration means the elapse of several days. There is no attempt to make the sign resemble the reality it stands for. On the contrary, the disparity between them is brought out by the choice of a single sign (walking a few steps) to convey two different meanings (the journey to the room and the passage of several days) which, moreover, are incompatible with one another.

The tension created in this way between the sign and what it represents focuses the spectator's attention on the fact that the action he perceives is not a real action but a play or, to put it differently, that the action represented is only a progression of immaterial meanings. This has been emphasized in advance by the prologue, which contains the following lines (literal translation by J. V.):

What good is the comb of reality
When phantoms, charms and dark myths
Have dishevelled our petty peace of mind

...

And we play, we play, we play, we play.

* * *

The tension between the sign and the reality it stands for, which stems primarily from the fact that a bare playing area is made to represent specific

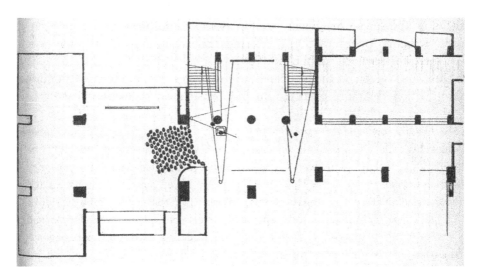

Fig. 2a, 2b: Ground plan of the foyer with disposition for Act II. The placing of the two actors by the column nearest to the spectators corresponds to the situation shown in the photo – Jiřina Stránská (Alladine) and Zdeněk Podlipný (Ablamore), seated in a chair, in Act II, Scene 1.

and frequently changing scenery, is constantly recreated and brought out by other means as well. Some of them are due to the staging in the narrow sense, some to the text of the play and some to the method of acting (which is, of course, also determined in the last resort by the staging).

When in Act I Ablamore says "Be careful; your horse has frightened Alladine's lamb. It will run away" (19), this means that two beings are interacting although the spectator sees no such interaction on the stage, nor even any horse or lamb. The interaction and the agents are pure meanings.

The same semiotic status – that of a pure meaning whose link to reality is elusive – is given, in the play itself, to the action of Alladine and Palomides about which Ablamore speaks in the past tense in Act II, Scene 3:

> See, Alladine, my hands are not trembling, and my heart beats as tranquilly as that of a sleeping child, and indeed my voice has never been raised in anger. I do not blame Palomides, though his conduct may well seem unpardonable. And as for you, why should I blame you? You obey laws that you know not of; nor could you have acted otherwise. I shall say not a word of all that took place, but a few days ago, by the side of the castle moat, or of what the sudden death of the lamb might have revealed to me, had I chosen to believe in omens. But last night I witnessed the kiss you exchanged beneath the windows of Astolaine's room. At that moment I happened to be with her. The one great dread of her soul is lest she disturb the happiness of those about her by a tear, or even a quiver of the eyelid, and thus I never shall know whether she also beheld that miserable kiss. But I do know how deeply she can suffer. I shall ask nothing of you that you cannot confess to me; all I wish you to tell me is whether you obeyed some secret plan when you followed Palomides underneath the window where you must have seen us. Answer me fearlessly; you know I have already forgiven. (26–27)

The tenuousness of the link between the meaning so evoked and the reality is underscored in the ensuing dialogue, where Alladine denies that she kissed Palomides.

In this way the dramatic present and the narrative past are superimposed on each other. Sometimes even the future is injected, as in Act III, Scene 2:

> **Palomides**. Tomorrow all will be ready. We must not wait any longer. He is wandering like a madman through the palace corridors; I met him but a short time ago. He looked at me, but said nothing; I passed on, but, when I turned round, I saw that he was laughing to himself and flourishing a bunch of keys. When he saw that I was watching him, he nodded, and smiled, and tried to look friendly. He must be nursing some secret scheme – we are in the hands of a master whose reason is tottering. Tomorrow we shall be far away. Out yonder there are wonderful countries that are more like your own. Astolaine has already prepared for our flight and for that of my sisters...
> **Alladine**. What did she say?
> **Palomides**. Nothing, nothing... We shall be on the sea for days, then days of forest and afterwards we shall come to the lakes and mountains that surround my father's castle; and you will see how different they are from everything here, where the sky is like the roof of a cavern and the black trees are done to death by the storms ... Ours is a sky beneath which none are afraid; our forests are full of life, and with us the flowers never close...
> **Alladine**. Did she cry? (33–34)

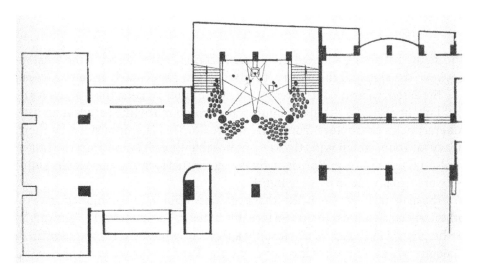

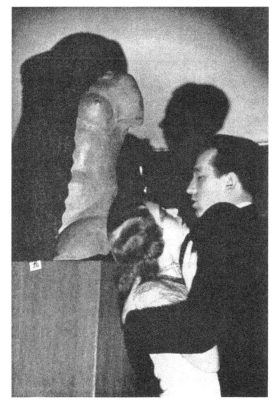

Fig. 3a, 3b: Ground plan of the foyer with disposition for Act III. This act is performed in the same part of the foyer as Act II but the dramatic space is quite different because the position of the spectators, the delimitation of the playing area and the lights have been changed. In the photo Jiřina Stránská (Alladine) and Vladimír Šmeral (Palomides) in Act III, Scene 2. Unlike the chair, which is a stage object, the sculptures are exhibits in the foyer. Their positions are indicated by small rectangles (above). During Act II they were cut off from the spectators' view by the columns and the light.

All the time dimensions so evoked, whether future, past or present, are immaterial meanings that are in constant tension with the real time experienced as present by the spectator.

* * *

The method of acting adopted in this production keeps recreating the tension between the sign and the reality it represents in particularly involved ways.

The actors wear modern dress – the men dinner jackets, the women neutral long dresses. So the stage figures look much more like actors than like Maeterlinck's characters from a dream world. This is emphasized by their heavy makeup, which is particularly noticeable since it is contrary to a fairly well-established convention, namely that actors performing close to the audience are usually made up very lightly.

The makeup here is so heavy that at certain moments, in conjunction with other aspects, it almost turns the face into a mask. The most striking example is the physician in Act V, whose only speech provides the subsequent final dialogue with yet another level of meaning. The actor's face is covered with a uniform, heavy coat of white and remains deliberately expressionless when he turns it directly towards a nearby spotlight as he declaims this pivotal speech. This is an extreme case. But the tendency to use heavy makeup and, at the same time, to restrain the play of the facial muscles is general. The face of the stage figure is thus perceived not as the face of the character enacted but as a sign. Insofar as the movements of the facial muscles are not eliminated altogether, they are so inexpressive and so indeterminate semantically that the spectator guesses their meaning only with the help of the words.

The same principle governs the gestures and other movements. In Act III, Scene 3, the actor playing Ablamore sits down and his head drops to his chest. The combination of the two movements has no straight resemblance to any ordinary behaviour. It is endowed with definite meaning only when Astolaine says: "He has fallen asleep on the bench" (36). A little later in the same scene Palomides says he will take away from Ablamore his three golden keys. The actor kneels down, stretches out his hands to bring them close to Ablamore's empty hands, pauses a few seconds, then pulls them back and says: "I have the keys" (38). Without the words the spectator would have no idea what these gestures signify. In Act II, Scene 1, Ablamore asks Alladine "Not well? You are falling…" (23) while the actress remains completely immobile. Somewhat earlier in the same scene Ablamore says "Oh how pale you look! Are you ill?" (21). Nothing in the behaviour of the actress playing Alladine corresponds to this speech.

When the movements made by the actor are perceived as not necessarily representing the character's movements but rather as intentionally constructed signs whose meaning depends on their combination with other, especially verbal, signs, the same movement can convey several incongruous meanings. The case of a few steps at the end of Act II, Scene 2, which signify at the same time Ablamore's leading Alladine from the drawbridge to a room inside the palace and the passing of several days, has already been mentioned in another connection. But a movement carried out by one actor can also signify two opposite and complementary movements attributed to two different characters. In Act I, Ablamore and Alladine sit on a bench; the wall is behind their backs. Suddenly the actress playing Alladine turns right. The action develops as follows (the notes in square brackets are not Maeterlinck's stage directions but describe Burian's staging):

Ablamore. What is it? Why look you out yonder?
Alladine. Someone has passed by, on the road.
Albamore [*looking in the same direction as Alladine*]. I heard nothing...
Alladine. I tell you someone is coming... There he is! [*She points in the direction in which they are looking.*] Do not hold my hand; I am not frightened... He has not seen us...
Ablamore. Who would dare to come here?... If I were not sure... I believe it is Palomides... He is betrothed to Astolaine... See, he raises his head... Is it you, Palomides?
Palomides [*enters by the door in the wall behind them*]. Yes, my father... [*approaches them from behind, from the left side, while they continue to look to the right*] if I may already call you by that name... I have come here before the day and before the hour... (17)

Figure 4: Zdeněk Podlipný (Ablamore) and Jiřina Stránská (Alladine) during Ablamore's opening monologue in Act I. In the background is a lattice screening a wall with a door.

The actors playing Alladine and Ablamore turn in the same direction in which the actor playing Palomides is going to walk, instead of facing him as he approaches. They do so one after the other, which underscores the importance of this motion. The direction in which they turn signifies the direction of Palomides' own movement, while their other motions, interpreted by the speeches they utter, signify that Alladine and Ablamore are watching him coming.

The possibility of having a single actor produce signs that represent the behaviour of two different dramatic characters has been exploited by Burian before, especially in his distinctive ways of shaping the dialogue. Perhaps the most striking example of this procedure can be found in his production of his own montage of folk poetry, dance and music entitled *War* (it opened on 22 January 1935). Here the same actress recites a dialogue between a girl and boy (Srbová 1937: 224) borrowed from a folk song (literal translation J. V.):

You are late, my dear lad,
You are late coming home,
You have horses in the stable,
They are neighing with hunger,
When will you go and feed them?
Give them, my dear lass,
Give them a bit of hay,
So that they may feed
And not wait for me,
Since I'm not at home.

Such acting methods tend to disrupt the unity of the stage figures. The different signs produced by the same actor or of which he is the vehicle are separated and redistributed between new configurations that no longer coincide with individual actors.

This corresponds to Burian's efforts to model the theatrical performance on that of an orchestra. He tries in all his work as a stage director to subordinate all the components of the theatre to an overall rhythmical organization of the performance (see Burian 1939). To achieve this effect he imposes a strong rhythm on everything, be it the speech, the actors' movements, the successive colour combinations, the ceaseless movement of the lights, the broadening and narrowing down of the constantly shifting action space and so on. Characteristically, the architect who of all Burian's associates has most consistently participated in his efforts to fit the stage to this conception of the dramatic art makes the following statement: "All... elements form an orchestra of instruments through which the stage director performs the score of his own orchestration of the author's literary work, the play" (Kouřil and

Burian 1938: 40). And Burian himself states "The stage director works with the material, consisting of the actors, in such a way as to transform it in order to achieve stage unity" (Burian 1930: 15).

The tendency to disrupt the unity of the stage figure so as to strengthen the integration of its various elements in the broader unity of the whole performance also manifests itself in Burian's frequent use of spotlights to single out details such as the face, the hands, a specific gesture, and separate them from the rest of the stage figure as independent signs.

This production of *Alladine and Palomides* takes to an extreme certain structural features of Burian's theatre. In particular, his work has never before produced such a degree of dissociation, and indeed of discrepancy, between the dialogue and the physical action. So it is all the more remarkable that in the same production he exercised considerable restraint over his inclination to assimilate the stage speech to music by imposing upon it a measurable rhythm, separating the syllables like musical notes and organizing the rise and fall of the pitch of the voices into definite intervals. In some previous productions, especially that of Alfred de Musset's *The Moods of Marianne* (which opened on 12 April 1939), this assimilation went so far as to border on caricature. In *Alladine and Palomides*, too, the sound structure of the dialogue is dominated by rhythm and melody; but here it is the rhythm and melody of speech, as distinct from music, that has prevailed. No doubt the restraint exercised by Burian in this respect is due to the fact that the two sound features are extremely prominent in the organization of Maeterlinck's own language (even in translation).

* * *

To sum up, the thoroughgoing reorganization of the theatrical space that Burian undertook in his staging of *Alladine and Palomides* is not a matter of space alone. It is intimately connected with the way all the other components of the performance are shaped. The theatrical implications of the play itself constitute a very important factor, much more than is usually the case in Burian's productions; in other words, he does not take nearly as many liberties with the play as he usually does. Obviously this is because Maeterlinck has anticipated many of the basic features of the theatrical structure Burian seeks to achieve.

Some of these aspects of Maeterlinck's drama have already been mentioned, in particular the assimilation of the live actors to puppets, the prominent rhythmic and melodic contour of the language, the author's monologue constantly perceptible behind the dialogue among the characters, a monologue directly addressed to the audience. The mingling of the past, the future and the present time in the dialogue also falls into this category.

Fig. 5: Vladimír Šmeral (Palomides) and Marie Burešová (Astolaine) in Act II, Scene 4

The injection of narrative elements attenuates the interaction of the characters, which unfolds in the spectator's present time. But by this very token the dramatic principle takes a different form in Maeterlinck's dialogue, that of a constant though ceaselessly changing tension between the system of values created by the work of theatrical art and the system of values accepted by the community represented by the audience. The dialogue and mutual action between the subjects represented on the stage recedes and is superseded by another, hidden, dialogue between the artist and the public. In performance, the playwright surrenders this privileged position to the stage director.

In the last analysis, Burian's reorganization of the theatrical space seeks to include the auditorium in the dramatic space; that is, in the dynamic, constantly changing set of relations and tensions deriving from the stage action. This considerably attenuates another tension, that between the stage and the imaginary acting space conventionally situated offstage (behind, on the sides, above, and so on). Though this tension is one of the outstanding features of Maeterlinck's conception of the theatre, Burian's staging aimed to reduce it as much as possible. To this effect, the stage director rather systematically modified the distribution of the action between the playing area and this conventional imaginary acting space. That was perhaps his most radical departure from the theatrical implications of the play.

The way he did it is best illustrated by his handling of Palomide's arrival in Act I. Maeterlinck divided this action into two phases, the first situated in the imaginary action space conjured up by Alladine and Ablamore's reaction and comment, the second starting with the entrance of the actor playing Palomides. In Burian's staging, as already described, the division into the two phases is maintained but the offstage scene, as far as it was conjured up by the two actors present on the stage, is cancelled as soon as the third makes his entrance because he moves in, not opposite to, the direction in which they have turned. So it becomes apparent that a decisive element of the supposed offstage action, the side from which Palomides is coming, has been signified on the stage directly, rather than metonymically. Perhaps not all the spectators analyse the apparent clash between the spatial aspects of the actors' movements in this precise way; but even if they do not, the clash itself is strong enough to dislocate any idea they may have about what the invisible areas adjacent to the playing area represent.

The effort to include the auditorium in the dramatic space can be pursued even when the proscenium stage is used. But this type of stage can only be adapted to this effect in a limited way. Yet this effort has deeply marked Burian's whole work as a stage director.

In the thinking of many avant-garde directors, the extension of the dramatic space into the auditorium is synonymous with the activation of the audience. Burian is one of them. The project of the Theatre of Labour has been expressly conceived in order to make it possible to activate the audience. There are some good reasons for this way of conceiving the problem that the most varied forms of avant-garde (and not only avant-garde) forms of theatre are facing at present. In "high-culture" theatre there has long been an extremely strong tradition of strictly separating the stage from the auditorium, and this tradition is still very much alive. On the other hand, no attempt to activate the audience in the strict sense of the spectators' actively participating in or interfering with the actors' performance can get anywhere unless the auditorium is encompassed by the dramatic space; so the effort to enlarge the dramatic space in this way is an integral part of the current attempts to activate the audience. Nonetheless, in the light of the history of the theatre on the one hand and of the diversity of the avant-garde theatre on the other, the whole concept of activating the audience needs some differentiation.

In this respect it should be pointed out that for Burian, as he himself put it, "the activation of the spectators does not mean: the spectators are to act. It means only: the spectators sitting in the auditorium are to be staged in the same way as the different parts of the playing area" (Kouřil and Burian 1938: 8).

WORKS CITED

Burian, E. F. (1930) "Dynamické divadlo" [Dynamic Theatre], *Nová scéna*, vol. 1, no. 1, pp. 13–18.
— (1939) "Příspěvek k problému jevištní mluvy" [A Contribution to the Issue of Stage Speech], *Slovo a slovesnost*, vol. 5, no. 1, pp. 24–32.
Deák, František (1976) "Structuralism in Theatre: The Prague School Contribution", *The Drama Review: TDR*, vol. 20, no. 1, pp. 89–94.
Honzl, Jindřich (1928) *Moderní ruské divadlo* [Modern Russian Theatre], Prague: Odeon.
Kouřil, Miroslav and Burian, E. F. (1938) *Divadlo práce: studie divadelního prostoru* [The Theatre of Labour: A Study of Theatre Space], Prague: J. Kohoutek.
Maeterlinck, Maurice (1890) *Alladine and Palomides*, trans. Alfred Sutro, in *Three Little Dramas*, London: Duckworth & Co., pp. 13–61.
Srbová, Olga (1937) "Postava v novém dramatu" [The Character in the New Drama], *Slovo a slovesnost*, vol. 3, no. 5, pp. 221–26.
Tille, Václav (1910) *Maurice Maeterlinck: analytická studie* [Maurice Maeterlinck: An Analytical Study], Prague: J. Otto.
Zich, Otakar (1931) *Estetika dramatického umění: teoretická dramaturgie* [The Aesthetics of Dramatic Art: A Theoretical Dramaturgy], Prague: Melantrich.

ON THE ARTISTIC SITUATION
OF THE CONTEMPORARY CZECH THEATRE

JAN MUKAŘOVSKÝ

[Originally written for the *Yearbook* of the National Theatre in Prague for 1945, it was published in Czech as "K umělecké situaci dnešního českého divadla" in 1946 in *Otázky divadla a filmu*, vol. 1, no. 2, pp. 61–75. The English translation by Michael L. Quinn was published in 1995 as "On the Artistic Situation of the Contemporary Czech Theatre (1945)", *Theatre Survey*, vol. 36, no. 1, pp. 65–75.]

I

The world tempest that has now subsided has left its mark on all areas of artistic creation. Everywhere that Fascism reached it disturbed the inner coherence of things, their mutual relationships, in order to create a formless, passive mixture, incapable of taking the initiative. When it came to art, Fascism trumpeted the term "degenerate art" (*entartete Kunst*) and declared a war of annihilation against it. In actual practice, however, the particular artistic methods that had been created by the modern art that was blacklisted remained intact: it was only that those methods could not create a system, that they could not be used to express any specifically focused artistic intention that, owing precisely to its being conscious, might have created a breach in the totality of violence. Naturally this state of affairs endangered not only the coherence of the internal components of the artistic structure but also the systematic nature of the functional organization of individuals and institutions serving art. Art schools and artistic movements vanished or were at the very least disrupted. In many instances the affiliation of artists with particular associations and societies became more a matter of external circumstances than of artistic decision, and so on.

Quantity replaced quality as the criterion: the sign of the artistic development of theatres became the number of theatre buildings and the size of theatre audiences. Art exhibitions – sometimes entitled "The Artists, for the Nation", sometimes "The Nation, for the Artists"[1] – welcomed materials that

---

1   [Editor's note: Mukařovský here makes an ironic paraphrase of the inscription "The Nation, for Itself" [*Národ sobě*], situated above the curtain in the auditorium of the Czech National Theatre. The curtain and its portal were created by Vojtěch Hynais (1854–1925) in 1883. The inscription re-

were extremely heterogeneous artistically with open arms, but nevertheless they were able to fill large numbers of exhibition halls everywhere. Legions of books of lyric poetry were published, but in many cases it was enough to read a single poem in a single one of them to learn all one needed to know about dozens of similar collections, and so on. During the occupation *any* artistic expression was welcomed gratefully because the hierarchy of functions had shifted and art's major task was to offer comfort and help people forget, a role that in normal times is one of its least important.

But once the occupation was crushed there immediately arose the need to renew the internal and external order in all artistic matters, and the uncertain state brought to art by Fascism and its accompanying phenomena became clear. The demands placed on art today are great. To build a new relationship between man and reality, between the society and cultural creation, to create a new set of relations between the individual and society and, in connection with this, a new understanding of the human character – these are the most pressing tasks. But they can only be fulfilled by an art that evinces not only a certain level of skill (something not lacking today, having been inherited from the period of artistic experimentation) but also the ability to use this skill for a certain purpose, systematically and with a precise awareness of the impact of each of these artistic methods and their relationship to the general purpose of the work, an art that is conscious of artistic problems and consistent in solving them. Only an art that acts in this way can attain fundamentally new results, extending beyond its own sphere, able to change the appearance and significance of things and of relations between people. A great deal, of course, can be achieved by spontaneous evolution alone, without conscious intervention; for example, the appearance on the scene of a young generation that brought with it a certain artistic orientation could create straightaway a whole network of shared views and disagreements among creative artists generally, including even those who are not part of it, and thereby rekindle a demand for fully thought out artistic assumptions and conclusions. However, it would not be right to wait until today's problems are solved this way, as the automatic result of development. It is necessary to repeatedly try to anticipate it, even though it is clear in advance that all such reflections may well be disproven by the very next events. But not even then would these be absolutely superfluous, since the main task of all such prospective reflections is to point to pressing questions, not to mentor the unforeseeable variety of reality. Such is also the modest task of this study. As every art has its own special features determined by the material that it works with, our study takes as its object only

flects the belief that the National Theatre was built from the financial contributions of ordinary people of the nation at the time of the National Revival.]

a single art, the theatre. Perhaps – after appropriate changes – the conclusions we arrive at will be applicable at least in part to the current situation in other arts.

II

What is the state of today's theatre – and today's Czech theatre in particular – in terms of the differentiation of theatrical life and with regard to the artistic structure of the stage work? As far as differentiation is concerned, we can hardly speak in this country of distinct movements; the fact that the only thing in evidence is a few strong personalities supports rather than disproves our assertion, since a personality speaks only for itself. However, this rather monotonous seascape does have two shores – one that receives official support,[2] and the other that used to be called the avant-garde – but this is only a relic of the complicated tensions that once animated the world of the theatre. For that matter, the boundary today between what is official and what is avant-garde is rather hard to distinguish; sometimes the only differentiation is which storehouse of scenic conventions is drawn upon, and how consistently this is done. Sometimes even this difference is absent.

The structure of the stage work is in an equally poorly defined state. The external expression of this indistinctness is an uncertainty as to the leading authority figure in the theatre. Until recently this was the director, who changed playwrights' texts at will and who insisted on the right to determine every single nuance of the actor's voice and gestures in line with his own overall conception. Today his rule is coming to an end, though there has not been any sudden change; in most cases the director's ambition has become that of giving final shape to the ideas implanted in the text by the playwright rather than forcing the play to reflect his own ideas. However, any path back to a solely "reproductive" understanding of theatre – which maintained, for example, that "in the art of acting, style is primarily the product of a literary current, of which it becomes an onstage instrument" (Schmoranz 1930: 9) – is blocked once and for all. The autonomy of the stage devices has been so thoroughly revealed and their independent semantic capacity has become

---

2   [Editor's note: Mukařovský works with the term "official theatre", which is regarded in the Czech context as a label for the kind of theatre that conforms to the general taste and as such receives public funding. Artistically, it is usually understood as being non-experimental, mainstream theatre. This can be compared with Honzl's term "stone theatre", which builds on the fact that mainstream theatre often takes place in theatre buildings whose structures are made of stone, producing theatre marked by a rather "petrified", that is, non-progressive, aesthetic approach. In his discussion further below, Mukařovský's argument is based on an objective distinction between such "official" theatre and another kind of theatre: progressive, experimental, that is, "avant-garde" theatre in the narrow sense of the word.]

so apparent that the playwright can no longer regain his position as the dominant force in the theatre. So the director has abandoned his sovereignty without being shouldered aside by anyone else. This has led to an unstable situation, one that demands resolution.

Of course the question of the chief authority figure with regard to stage activity involves the structure of the theatre as an art – not the whole of the structure, however, but rather a certain part of it: the subject from whom the work arises. But when we regard the theatrical structure as a whole and in its parts, as a dynamic unity of vocal, gestural, spatial and other components, the situation does not strike us as any more certain. If we are to comprehend the true likeness of the current state of the theatrical structure, it will be necessary to look briefly at the not so distant past.

In the past it was clear that the spectators in the theatre had before them actors and a set – actors on the set or, more precisely, within the set, but nevertheless two clearly differentiated worlds, the world of people and the world of things, a living world and an inanimate world. The focus of attention was on the living beings, while things were secondary, creating no more than the setting or at most supplying instruments for the action. This clear duality facilitated the task of the actor as well as that of the spectator. The actor was only responsible for his performance, or at most for ensemble playing. The spectator only concentrated on the actors moving about on the set, and especially on the protagonist. Such was the case during more than two-thirds of the nineteenth century. The first step toward disturbing this state of affairs came with the impressionist theatre, which enabled the stage design to express the "mood" and so play a role in establishing the point of the action. In this way the setting moved towards closer interaction with the actor. An even closer union of these two worlds took place on the stylized stage, where there was an attempt to make the actors a direct part of the setting, to force onto the human body geometrical contours, through which inanimate things are indicated, to limit the actors' mobility, and so on. But not even then did the sphere of living beings interpenetrate with the sphere of things on stage. This could only happen when the actor's appearance and the set were broken down into their individual components. So it was no longer a question of the living actor and the inanimate set standing as opposites to one another but rather, for example, of a voice and light, with each of these components capable of being further divided, not only theoretically but in practice.

This loosening of the structure could be seen clearly for the first time in the expressionist theatre in the form of an excessive and, from the standpoint of theme, unmotivated emphasis on some individual components at the expense of others. In Czech expressionist theatre, for example, this was the case of vocal intensity in declamation, as can be seen in Honzl's remark that "vocal intensity and its changes in Hilar's[3] expressionism are not a measure of emotional excitement, but rather a way of stitching together the dialogue, which Hilar composes as an encounter of dynamic contrasts through which the characters take on sharper contours" (Honzl 1937: 187). The continuation of this process leads to a state where the various components, which had hitherto been felt to be indivisibly linked, break away from one another. This happens, for example, when the spectator gets to know what a particular dramatic character is saying not from his spoken words but from a sign projected on the backdrop, while the actor carries out the appropriate movements. Individual components become independent, break loose from their normal connections, and, as is natural in this situation, the borderline between living beings and inanimate things is definitively breached. Things and beings are broken down into individual components that in themselves are neither alive nor inanimate and they can enter into any kind of relation. From case to case the vehicle of the action, and thus the "actor", may become any of the components:

> We have freed the concept of "stage" from its being limited to architecture and we can also free the concept of "actor" from the limitation that regards the actor as a human being who represents a character. If the only thing that matters is the representation of the character by something else, then not only can a person be an actor, but also a figure of wood (a puppet), a machine (for example, the mechanical theatre of El Lissitzky, Oskar Schlemmer and Friedrich Kiesler) or a thing (for example, the theatre advertising of Belgian purchasing cooperatives, where a bolt of material, a spider's leg, a coffee grinder and the like were all characters)... But once [Zich] has relieved us of the limitation that restricted the stage to architecture, then all the other elements of the theatre performance jostle their way forward to freedom. The character, heretofore closely associated with the human actor, is liberated, the playwright's message, hitherto the *word*, is liberated, other devices are liberated. Much to our amazement, we discover that the stage space need not always be a space, but that sound can be a stage, music can be an event, scenery can be a message. (Honzl 2016 [1940]: 130–31)

So it is now not the actor-person who occupies the foreground in the theatre but rather the non-material yet supremely real dramatic action itself, which can take possession of anything on stage to serve as its temporary vehicle. Light serves as a powerful agent of movement, which can be found in all components of the set. It shapes the stage space, highlights the actors (or on the contrary enables them to vanish), adds the finishing touch to their costumes, creates the set via projections and finally, drawing the spectators'

---

3   [Editor's note: Karel Hugo Hilar (1885–1935), theatre director, dramaturge and critic, one of the pioneers of Expressionism in the Czech context.]

attention to changes in colour and intensity, wandering about the stage in the form of the beam of a spotlight, actually assumes the role of the vehicle of the action. The result of the radical change thus experienced by the theatre is that the traditional composition of the stage components upon which the theatre has hitherto been built is broken down, that the components are no longer fixed in a relationship of permanent subordination and domination but are instead, in principle, equal and parallel. At any moment one of them can dominate the others, or in the blink of an eye shift into the background. Surprise follows surprise; some detail of the director's conception often becomes more important for the spectator than a play's overall line of action. Aristotle's theory of unity of action, with the tension gradually reaching a climax and after that steeply declining, gives way to a completely different concept. The play becomes an uninterrupted flow of partial tensions, each of which reaches an independent resolution and does not enter into relation with those before and after. The domination of the director reaches its peak: everything that is present and that happens on the stage is in his hands, with no limitations. In his eyes, the actor is no more than a stage object, since the director himself decides who or what, at any given moment of the play, will carry the scenic action and who or what will be the passive object of that action. Since even the individual components of the actor's performance are mutually independent, sovereign power over decision-making falls to the director, who decides on every quiver of the actor's voice, every nuance of gesture, the tiniest movement. The reason why a certain timbre, a certain intonation, a certain rhythmic pattern, a certain gesture should be used at some particular point in the play is no longer rooted in the way the actor interprets the character he is playing but rather in the overarching interplay of everything that is on the stage at a given moment, which is solely in the hands of the director, who alone determines the complex motivation behind it. If in its development the theatre has ever become a house of magic, it is now. But this kind of dynamics can only be fully alive and fully in movement for a relatively short period of time; of necessity, surprise soon becomes a habit and loses its effectiveness. As soon as the spectators lose the conviction that they are witnessing something extraordinary and impossible, the unexpected becomes the expected, and the only real surprise would be if the usual surprise did not occur.

The result of this radical change experienced by the theatre in recent decades is that the traditional hierarchy of components, as mentioned above, has been disturbed. But this disturbance, which in the beginning was a dynamic process, later became a permanent state, one that it is very difficult to find a way out of. There is no system here that is based on a positive structural principle against which it would be possible to construct, in dialectical fashion, another principle, but rather a collection of components incapable of forming a coherent structure. Connected with this there is also the unusual situation that was mentioned above: namely, that the contemporary theatre lacks a central authority figure around whom the others might group.

The playwright, who once filled this role, has been irreversibly deprived of supremacy owing to the theatre's becoming independent of literature. The actor, who became the ruler – or at least the co-ruler – of the theatre in the era of Realism and Naturalism, has been reduced to individual components of voice, gesture, facial expression, and so on. The director, who is still nominally in charge, is losing the courage to exercise authority in all its ramifications. It is of course questionable whether at today's level of development it is possible for the theatre to be in the hands of a single authority figure who would himself represent the subject from whom the work arises, or whether the next step will be for this subject to become a real dialectical synthesis of several agents. This will be discussed in the following section.

This reflection on the structure of the stage work has thus led us to the very core of the current theatre crisis, which is the disintegration of the theatrical structure. However, it is not possible to end this diagnosis without an explanatory comment. For it would not be correct to draw even the suggestion of a negative conclusion concerning the development of the modern theatre from the preceding reflection. It is necessary to stress that it is exactly this detailed analysis of the theatrical structure in its individual components, the verification of the semantic capacity of each of them and the revelation of their complicated correlation, that constitutes a new basis of the theatre for the future. No matter how the theatrical structure is re-organized, it will still be more dynamic than it was in the past thanks to what happened to it between the two World Wars.

Besides the kind of theatre that stands at the forefront of development, there is, however, another type, one that has so far been mentioned only briefly in this piece but that nevertheless plays a significant role in the current situation of the theatre – one so significant that without explaining it our diagnosis of the situation would be only half complete. This is the theatre that is labelled "official". Thus far all we have said about it is that the boundary between the official and the avant-garde theatre is not exactly precise – at least not in this country. We know that during World War I and its immediate aftermath the official theatre, thanks to Hilar, was at the very centre of the whirlwind of development for a certain time. Even though the avant-garde soon had its own centre of gravity elsewhere, the "official" theatre and the avant-garde remained linked, at least in terms of mutual imitation. In this, the official theatre broke with the principle of rigorous traditionalism that is usually associated with its very concept. It abandoned the traditional artistic basis that the Czech theatre had built up step by step, beginning with the Provisional Theatre,[4] where – as Jan Bartoš (1937) has demonstrated – the foundation was laid by Josef Jiří Kolár, a tradition that continued and culminated in the National Theatre with Eduard Vojan and Hana Kvapilová.[5] This tradition, which, as embodied in its greatest representatives, Kolár and Vojan, led to the strict adherence to a specific style, was now pushed into the background by eclecticism.[6]

The necessary result of eclecticism, however, is a tendency toward cliché, towards stereotyped declamation, facial expressions, and so on; a technique develops for the smooth coordination of heterogeneous artistic methods. Uncertainty also arises regarding the central authority figure in the theatre. Until the end of Vojan's era, this function was clearly held by the actor; in the contemporary situation the actor is neither pushed radically into the background nor placed obviously in the foreground. Nor is there any firmly articulated hierarchy in the construction of the dramatic character. A strong emphasis on declamation has survived in the official theatre, evidently as an inheritance from Expressionism, but it has lost the extreme expressionist deformations that were the artistic justification for this forcible highlighting of declamation at the expense of the other components. In today's situation this unjustified foregrounding of declamation is to a large extent a formalist convention. The only criterion for declamation has become that it be "neat and tidy" (correct pronunciation included); the relation between declamation and the other components, especially facial expression and gesture, has led to the passive dependence of those components on declamation; gesture and facial expression show a tendency towards becoming no more than a concomitant illustration of the word. The relationship between the components of the theatrical structure is unclear in other ways, too: thus the stage design often determines the meaning of the play along its own lines, restricting the action; here, too, one can usually detect a hangover from Expressionism.

There is, however, no doubt that even with its structure in this state the official theatre was able to achieve outstanding individual successes. Nor does the analysis just presented wish to be a criticism of practice: its only aim is to determine whether the artistic structure of the contemporary official theatre is a consistent, firmly crystallized – though conservative – system that could become a model and a starting point in the renewal of the coherence and hierarchization of the components of the theatre's artistic

---

4 [Editor's note: In operation from 1862–1883, predecessor of the Czech National Theatre.]
5 [Editor's note: Josef Jiří Kolár (1812–1896), writer and translator, as well as director and actor, famous for his Romantic interpretations of heroes and villains; Eduard Vojan (1853–1920), actor, a leading personality of the school of psychological-realistic acting; Hana Kvapilová (1860–1907), actress at the National Theatre in Prague, famous for her interpretation of roles in works by Ibsen, Chekhov and contemporary Czech playwrights.]
6 For this side of Kolár see Bartoš 1937: 109; for Vojan see Honzl 1937: 185.

structure. And clearly our analysis shows that the answer to this question is negative. Has the theatre, then, any possibility of escape from the structural uncertainty in which it finds itself? And is it at all desirable that it strive to do so? Should not the structural indeterminacy of the theatre be regarded simply as the state that we are faced with, which has to be taken into account and which, through further development, will almost automatically undergo reinforcement in the future? The next section attempts to answer these questions.

III

When we speak of an endeavour that might lead today's theatre structure out of the state of uncertainty in which it finds itself, it might seem that we are speaking about a conscious intervention into the objective development of the theatre, a development that is independent of the individual will. Efforts along these lines are indeed frequent, as seen in manifestoes of artistic movements, reviews and critical writing, and so on. As a rule these are expressions of developmental tendencies intrinsic to the developing structure itself; the subject of these efforts, or of the disagreements among the different parties involved, is the direction that the future development of the structure should take. Often such an attempt, strongly affected by the objective situation, undergoes a development that leads to a completely different result than the one originally intended. This too is proof of the extent to which the forward movement of the development is stronger than the will of an individual. But we are not concerned here with concrete guidelines for the future development of the theatre, which means we are not interested in any intervention into the composition of its structure. It is clear that in the immediate future the development of the theatre will be affected both by its inherent laws and – more strongly than ever before – by the development of society and of all the other branches of culture. To predict the direction and strength of those interventions would be a risky undertaking. But what is important is now, with these crucial influences in play, for the structure of the theatre to create a genuine whole, able to react to the needs of the times with all its components simultaneously and not just with some of them, for example the verbal aspect.

The preceding sections have shown that the structure of today's theatre has been significantly loosened, such that it is ill-prepared for the tasks it is facing today. What has to be improved is quite clear. Above all there is the matter of the central authority figure in the theatre. The question as to whether, in the immediate future, this will still be the director or some other individual – as the history of the theatre testifies, no one is excluded from the list of candidates, since there was even a time during the Baroque era when this role was played by the stage artist[7] – is, however, interesting, even though it is not of direct concern here. As we have indicated above, in the future the single leading authority figure could be replaced by a dialectical tension between all the agents that are components of the creative subject of the theatrical work. However, the actor – no matter whether he takes a leading or subordinate position or perhaps one that is equal to the others – remains the most basic, most absolutely essential of all the agents that take part in theatrical creation. Any of the others can be missing, and in the history of the theatre there is plenty of evidence to show that in earlier times one or another of them was not present in theatre work (no director in the current sense of the word) or vanished for some time (the playwright in *commedia dell'arte*). But there is no theatre without the actor, that is without a human actor or at least a sign that stands for the actor (a puppet, shadow, or whatever). If in the modern theatre, as mentioned before, a prop, a light, and so on, sometimes become an actor, they do so only temporarily, for a moment, inside a play carried by human actors; by taking on the function of a human actor, these things in fact draw attention to him. The two beams of light that wander about the empty stage at the beginning of Burian's production of *Romeo and Juliet*[8] are followed by the audience in a state of tension because they are seeking, and for a long time are unable to find, the actors. The flashing lights on the empty stage in Burian's production of *The Barber of Seville*[9] constituted an action because they signified a popular uprising offstage; without this significance, they would have been a mere lighting effect, no more than a component of the stage space.

No matter how the configuration of agents in theatrical creation changes, the actor will always remain the crystallizing axis. The unification of the overall structure of the stage work depends on him, on the unity of his own artistic structure. The only source for the consolidation of the theatrical structure is the actor. In today's conception of the theatre, as established through the struggle of modern experimental theatre, all components of the theatre are felt as a coherent context, and there is therefore no danger that any reinforcement of the theatrical structure, if it starts with the actor, will end with him. We are once again faced with the problems of the avant-garde theatre of the recent period, but this time our task is to point out not which part of its legacy must be overcome, but rather what aspect of it is a historic and permanently valid breakthrough. For never again will the actor be alone

---

7   See Miroslav Kouřil's preface to Furtenbach (1944: 5–7).

8   [Editor's note: The production *Romeo a Julie, sen jednoho vězně* [Romeo and Juliet, A Prisoner's Dream] premiered at the D 46 on 13 September 1945. Burian transferred his experience when imprisoned during WWII to this adaptation, which is set in a concentration camp where the dying prisoner remembers passages from Shakespeare's play.]

9   [Editor's note: *The Barber of Seville* premiered at the D 37 on 22 September 1936.]

on stage, cut off by some precise dividing line from its inanimate parts. Today the animation of objects on stage, their transformation into vehicles of dramatic action, is losing its experimental character and is on the way toward becoming an integral part of theatrical convention, of the standing repertoire of theatrical techniques. If the personality of the actor is again united, of necessity this reinforcement also affects the remotest components of the stage structure, especially when the spectator is a contemporary, a member of an incredibly complex and organized civilization, who encounters mutual dependence between phenomena that are very remote from one another every moment in his everyday life. As for the position of the actor with regard to the other agents in the theatre, which was dealt with above, it is also necessary to point out that the actor, just as he occupies the central position among the components present on stage, is to a considerable degree centrally positioned in relation to those other agents as well. If the playwright dominates the theatre, he degrades the actor to being a reproductive artist; if the director, he makes the actor an instrument for his purposes; if the designer, he treats him as part of the stage design. On the other hand the actor, even if he has the dominant position, relies on all the others to an equal extent, does not deprive any of them of active participation in the creation of the work. For the modern actor, the director in particular is the indispensable personification of the links interconnecting the entire stage with everything on it. For that matter, there exists, independently of passing trends, a certain type of director, commonly referred to as an "actors' director", which does not mean that he was originally a trained actor, but rather someone who, in doing his own specific job, takes his starting point from the actors, lays on them the obligation to do their utmost by drawing on their own capacities and working in their own way. And is this not the least fortuitous resolution of the polarity between the actor and director?

In the preceding section we attempted to show how the actor paid for the recent development of the theatre: the avant-garde theatre broke him down into individuated components, and the official theatre actually transformed him into a collection of clichés. However, it is absolutely necessary for the actor to once again view himself as a unity and for him to be perceived as such by the spectator. So, for example, it is necessary for a correlation to be reestablished between the gesture and the word. By "correlation" we certainly do not mean harmony: we pointed out earlier that this automatic, uninterrupted harmony between word and gesture in fact gives the impression of an absence of correlation. This effect occurs because an automatically observed unity, in which attention is never drawn to the independence of the components being connected, is perceived as an undifferentiated alloy, and not as a unity of several discrete things. The sensation of unity, then, does not arise where the spectator fails to sense the principle of unity as a force holding different things in a union. Nor does it arise where the components always, consistently, diverge from one another. Both – conflict and harmony – are necessary for the result to be a unification perceived as a process, and not as a lifeless fact. As we are speaking of word and gesture, let us mention Stanislavsky's artistic system as an exemplary case. It is well-known – and described with an admirable capacity for emotional understanding in Tille's study of Stanislavsky in *Memories of the Theatre* – how Stanislavsky "took advantage of his knowledge that in real life gestures, facial expressions and people's actions are not a logical consequence of the spoken word, just as words are not a consequence of external impulses" (Tille 1917: 199). In other words, Stanislavsky managed to make artistic use of the lack of coordination between gesture, facial expression and the spoken word.

The second thing needed for the successful resolution of today's uncertainty in the theatre is to make use of the rich variability of the individual structural components. One can hardly deny, even though it has rarely been stated openly, that beginning with Expressionism the theatre – both avantgarde and official – started simplifying the devices employed in acting. The actor's voice, gestures and movement on stage came to be viewed as wholes, deliberately shaped in such a way that some of the components reached extremes that continued unvaryingly for whole stretches of the action. This led to a tendency towards caricature, so typical in contemporary theatre, as well as an inclination toward hackneyed vocal tricks and facial expressions, which for that matter is closely connected to caricature. However, the disadvantage is that vocal and facial stereotypes, which force the voice and the muscles into sustained, extreme tension, prevent the alternating use and varying combination of vocal and facial components. When, for example, the timbre of the voice reaches an extreme, flexible changes of intonation become impossible, and vice versa.

Detailed analysis of this phenomenon would be illuminating, but our sole critical concern at the moment is to indicate the necessity of once again allowing – from the point of view of artists face to face with the public – a revision of the entire repertoire of possibilities available to the art of acting, no matter which direction the development of the theatre takes in future. Is a concrete example necessary? Here is a quotation from a study of Eduard Vojan: "Vojan disclosed his voice from scene to scene, as if he were raising before it countless curtains or veils, constantly revealing new tones and intensities... He distributed his moments of whispering and of speaking loudly with precision, and only roared, releasing the full force of his voice, at two or three points in the play" (Honzl 1937: 185). This specific example expresses clearly what we mean: absolute mastery of the wealth of vocal components. We are actually returning to the point where we were at a while ago when we stated that a renewal of the dynamic interconnection of components is the main requirement for the reconstruction of the theatrical structure. For if we have in mind correlation as a process and not as static continuity, we inevitably arrive at the requirement that a collection of components that is united must be differentiated as delicately as possible, since it is precisely in this way that the effort of sustaining equilibrium in it gains heightened artistic effect.

We have already stressed that we are not concerned with promoting any artistic movement, but rather with pointing out the necessary prerequisites of any future development. However, the examples we have given – first the system of Stanislavsky and second Eduard Vojan – might lead to the assumption that what we have in mind is the renewal of stage realism. But that would be wrong. Realism, as it reached its peak on the stage at the turn of the century, was only possible – like any other historical formation – in the context of certain concrete artistic, cultural and social conditions, and is therefore not repeatable. Any attempt at its renewal would necessarily lead to second-rate imitation, a phenomenon scarcely to be desired, and scarcely productive. The aim of Realism was to create the illusion of reality, yet even so contemporaries, commenting on the performances of the Moscow Art Theatre and of Vojan, were already conscious that "reality on stage is something terribly relative" (Schmoranz 1930: 55–56) and that the entire purpose of authentic realist acting "went against realistic improvisation, spontaneity, easiness and unconstraint" (Honzl 1937: 185). Creating an illusion of reality is already a certain kind of unequivocal artistic intention, and we have stated repeatedly that the appropriateness of any particular artistic intention for the contemporary moment is a question that we do not wish to examine.

However, we do not reject the word "reality" if it is meant not in the sense of a demand for an external model to which the performance should be accommodated or that it should evoke, but rather in the sense of the multifarious variety, the inexhaustible wealth of different forms, of the very devices that the theatre and especially the art of acting have at their disposal. Only when the theatre allows the spectator to experience the full force and diversity of voice, facial expression, gesture and so on will there arise in the spectator's mind a sense of the full relevance of acting and of the theatre. For it is precisely this inexhaustible wealth of different forms that characterizes reality in the deepest sense of the word, material reality existing before any human intention and independent of it. How to arrive at such a reality in the theatre can only be decided by the artists, and then not through theoretical deliberation but rather through the praxis of their creative activity.

At the end it is necessary to add that any profiling of the theatre that is functional, and not purely artistic, could become the basis for further development in the near future: a tendentious theatre, a theatre of "entertainment", and so on could prove itself, since in the past they were able to create striking artistic works. There is only one condition: that such a functional profiling take on an intensity that will enable it to animate the *entire* stage structure, *all* its components, and not only some of them, for example the theme of the text. But first this structure must be built anew, the correlation and the differentiation of its components renewed. The purpose of this study has been to point toward this necessity.

WORKS CITED

Bartoš, Jan (1937) *Prozatímní divadlo a jeho činohra* [The Provisional Theatre and its Dramas], Prague: Sbor pro zřízení druhého Národního divadla.

Furtenbach, Joseph (1944) *Prospektiva: základy kukátkového divadelního prostoru* [Perspective: The Basis of the Proscenium Arch Theatre Space], trans. Jaroslav Pokorný, Prague: Ústav pro učebné pomůcky průmyslových a odborných škol.

Honzl, Jindřich (1937) "Slovo na jevišti a ve filmu" [The Word on the Stage and in Film] in *Sláva a bída divadel: režisérův zápisník* [The Glory and the Misery of Theatres: A Director's Notebook], Prague: Družstevní práce, pp. 178–207.

— (2016 [1940]) "The Mobility of the Theatrical Sign", this reader, pp. 129–16

Schmoranz, Gustav (1930) *Eduard Vojan*, Prague: Alois Srdce.

Tille, Václav (1917) *Divadelní vzpomínky* [Memories of the Theatre], Prague: B. Kočí.

PRAGUE SCHOOL THEATRE THEORY AND ITS CONTEXTS (AFTERWORD)

BY PAVEL DRÁBEK WITH MARTIN BERNÁTEK, ANDREA JOCHMANOVÁ AND EVA ŠLAISOVÁ

"There is only one thing you must not forget – these twenty years were immensely beautiful.
Remind everyone of how much work we managed to do."
The poet Jaroslav Seifert, bidding farewell to Roman Jakobson
in Prague in April 1939 (cited in Toman 1995: 2)

THE PRAGUE LINGUISTIC CIRCLE AND ITS MISSION[1]

The Prague Linguistic Circle (PLC) was established in 1926 with the vision that scholarship should become engaged in the practical problems of the modern world. This diverse community of intellectuals, artists and practitioners exercised what would later come to be known as "critical theory" and integrated practice and theory organically.

In 1935, the Prague Linguistic Circle (PLC) launched its journal *Slovo a slovesnost* (The Word and Verbal Art); in the introduction to the first issue (Havránek et al. 1935), the founding members Bohuslav Havránek (1893–1978), Roman Jakobson (1896–1982), Vilém Mathesius (1882–1945), Jan Mukařovský (1891–1975) and Bohumil Trnka (1895–1984) outlined the programme of the journal – almost a manifesto of their initiative. It is worth citing at length:

The *scholarship* of today requires the detailed development of a terminology that would be both accurate and flexible, whose terms would have an internationally uniform meaning. The functions of language keep differentiating more and more. It suffices, for instance, to consider how many new tasks are required of language in today's journalism, which is constantly developing and continues to grow in importance: the very technology of newspapers, the problem of rapid and easy reading, issues of having an effective impact on the reader and other specific purposes. With the development of technical means language has found its way into novel, unprecedented situations: *in radio*, we have the word as a mere sound devoid of visual phenomena; *in sound film*, there are undreamed-of possibilities for combining speech and visual impressions. The language of *fiction* departs more than ever before from a unified canon: linguistic criticism must not employ one single standard to assess a Surrealist poem gravitating towards a dream, the language of James Joyce or Vladislav Vančura, in which several layers are interwoven polyphonically, Louis-Ferdinand Céline's or Jaroslav Hašek's rich use of colloquial speech, or the prose of classical realism, sticking anxiously to the generally valid literary norm. By no means the last source of new tasks is the astonishingly rich *translation activity*; it is enough to look at the statistics for translations in the areas of fiction,

1   We would like to express many thanks to peer readers and editors of this essay, namely Veronika Ambros and Yana Meerzon; also, David Drozd's contributions have been much welcome. Special thanks go to Don Sparling; his unique dedication and his expertise in all aspects of Czech, his historical expertise and his refined feeling for language have profoundly helped the essay's final shape.

journalism and specialized literature to realize the great linguistic influence translations have. [...]

Our scholarship must not look on passively when it comes to solving the current
tasks outlined above. Once and for all Czech linguistics, too, must overcome its temporary dissociation from present-day culture and enter directly into its service; it must
take the initiative in dealing with contemporary issues of linguistic culture. However,
the fragmented efforts of individual philologists will not do; the urgency of the tasks
calls for a collective, organized coordination of scholarly forces. Nor will the separate
activity of philologists themselves suffice; what is needed is the close collaboration of
linguists with teachers and lawyers, with philosophers and psychologists, with psychiatrists and phoniatrists, with historians and theorists of literature and the arts
generally, with specialists in sociology, history, geography and folklore. But what is
needed above all is cooperation with the practitioners of linguistic culture, with writers
and translators, with theatre, film and radio artists and technicians, with educational
specialists well as with administrative and technical professionals who have practical
experience in questions of terminology.

This is the programme and the path for *Slovo a slovesnost*. (Havránek 1935: 3-4)

The programme outlined above makes several crucial statements. At its
centre is modern language and its uses, and it is through a critical study of
language that modern reality is reflected in its novel complexities and the
innovations of the Modernist age.

Slovo a slovesnost became the main platform of the PLC in the Czech
language. In addition a number of significant articles also appeared in
German-language periodicals published in Czechoslovakia, in particular the
daily *Prager Presse* and the journals *Slavische Rundschau, Germanoslavica* and
Prager Rundschau. Publishing in German played a crucial role in making the
PLC's research findings available to an international readership. The *Prager
Presse*, for instance, had over 2,000 subscribers outside Czechoslovakia in 1937
and was also on sale publicly alongside the rest of the daily press (Bernátek
2016: 10).[2]

The programme formulated by Havránek not only clarifies the concept
of language and linguistics within which the writers operate but also sees
scholarship and intellectual efforts as a *social and cultural need* – a public issue
that needs addressing. Scholarship is an instrument of public activity and
engaging in it is what later became known as critical theory in action. This
appeal for active, engaged and committed public intellectuals was a crucial
contribution of one of the PLC founders, the linguist and pioneer of Czech

---

2   Martin Bernátek is the editor of a supplement to *Theatralia* vol. 19, no. 1, dedicated to the German-
     language publishing platforms of the PLC. He has also compiled a bibliography of texts published
     on the PLC between the two World Wars (Bernátek 2016).

Fig. 1: Cover of the *Prager Presse*, a daily newspaper founded in March 1921 by the news section of the Czechoslovak Ministry of Foreign Affairs. In 1922, the state-owned publishing house Orbis became its publisher. The journal promoted the official policies of the Czechoslovak state (it continued to be supported financially by the Ministry of Foreign Affairs). The *Prager Presse* ceased publication in the wake of the Munich Agreement of September 1938, which marked the collapse of the political conception of the Czechoslovak state promoted by President Tomáš Garrique Masaryk and his successor as second Czechoslovak President, Edvard Beneš. The last issue of the *Prager Presse* appeared on 31 December 1938.

Fig. 2: Cover of *Slovo a slovesnost* (design Jiří Kan), published by the Prague Linguistic Circle from 1935. This issue dates from 20 September 1941. On the cover there is a propaganda piece entitled "The Reich is Winning on All Fronts in Europe"; this appeared just as the armies of the Third Reich were poised to launch the disastrous Battle of Moscow. The issue includes, among other articles, Jiří Veltruský's "Dramatic Text as a Component of Theatre".

English studies Vilém Mathesius. In his 1925 booklet *Cultural Activism: English Parallels to Czech Life* (Mathesius 1925), Mathesius articulated his belief "in rationally organized work and in the active involvement of intellectuals in public affairs" (Toman 1995: 3). This impulse harmonized with the activism of the Russian intellectuals who joined in the initiative and their Cubo-Futurist leanings. For scholarship to be a valid part of the society it needs to be practised hand in hand with public servants, artists, technicians and administrators – the very practitioners who come into immediate contact with the active life of the society and its problems. In this sense, for research and scholarship to be effective it has to be *embodied* and realized in practice; this gives it full momentum and the power to influence public wellbeing. This approach counters the negatives of the monastic tradition of the academia that secludes itself from everyday life and assumes a *faux* elitist stance of knowledge and superiority. Prague School intellectuals practised their scholarship in direct contact with cultural workers, not only by contributing to theatre programme notes and to newspapers with analyses of new work but also by being practitioners themselves. For instance, Jindřich Honzl (1894–1953), Jiří Frejka (1904–1952) and Emil František Burian (1904–1959) were members of the PLC as well as being the leading Czech avant-garde stage directors of the day. Their participation was far from symbolic: when the Czech universities were closed by the Nazi occupiers on 17 November 1939, Burian's acting school, which operated at his Theatre D 41, organized public lectures that in many ways substituted for academic activities (see Drozd 2016: 100, n. 25). Of great significance was the active participation of three leading Czech intellectuals and artists: the critic František Xaver Šalda (1867–1937), the writer and dramaturge Karel Čapek (1890–1938) and the avant-garde poet Vítězslav Nezval (1900–1958) were all influential public personalities and their contribution to the PLC in the 1930s played an important role in bridging academic activities and the public sphere.

The range of topics and disciplines covered by Prague School theory is indicative of its energy as well as its reach – from performance and theatre theory and film theory, through theatre phenomenology, theatre semiotics, drama analysis, adaptation and dramatization, theoretical scenography, costume studies and theatre proxemics, the structural analysis of acting and folk theatre (folk plays, ballads, puppet theatre), to media studies and theatre sociology.

The wide range of interests and the avant-garde subversion of traditional art forms and modes of criticism can be approached in many ways as an anticipation of a much later phenomenon: Prague School theatre theory amounted to a version of Performance Studies *avant la lettre*.

The links between Prague and other metropolises as well as the active contributions of the PLC's affiliated linguists Nikolai Sergeyevich Trubetskoy

Fig. 3: Cover of Petr Bogatyrev's *Czech and Slovak Folk Theatre*, 1940. The neo-classical design by František Muzika forms a contrast to the Modernist design of *Slovo a slovesnost*. The traditional appearance is due to motifs such as the stylised flower, common in folk design, the improvised theatre curtain (even though the folk theatre productions discussed by Bogatyrev very rarely used any kind of curtain) and the use of Gothic script. At the time the book was published, Bogatyrev had already left Prague and returned to Moscow.

(1890–1938), based in Vienna, Boris Tomashevsky (1890–1957) of the Art History Institute in Moscow and Sergei Osipovich Kartsevsky (1884–1955) of Zurich, gave the PLC an international reach. After the outbreak of World War II, when several of the key members went into wider diaspora, the activities of the PLC extended even further.

When Honzl wrote his renowned "The Mobility of the Theatrical Sign" (1940) and presented it as a lecture in the PLC series, he had already had a successful and rich career in the arts. Not only had he contributed to the Devětsil (literally *nine forces*) movement, which created a new synergy for the avant-garde artists working in the spheres of the "Nine Muses" (art disciplines), but he had also established and was stage director of the era-defining avant-garde Liberated Theatre (Osvobozené divadlo) and had made three feature films – not to mention his other activities in leading theatres throughout the country and his publications on Soviet theatre. Honzl's essay is written with an acute awareness of the practical theatre and with all his abundant experience with experimental performative forms. While Honzl's legacy survives more in his theoretical and pedagogical work, despite his prolific activities as theatre director and occasionally as film director, the core of the work of

Teige-Mrkvička

Fig. 4: Karel Teige and Otakar Mrkvička: "Liberated Theatre", photomontage, 1926. An example of Teige's Modernist typographical style. In includes photos from some of the Liberated Theatre's early productions: Georges Ribemont-Dessaignes's *The Mute Canary*, directed by Jindřich Honzl (top right and centre left); a reworked version of Molière's *Georges Dandin* entitled *Cirkus Dandin* (The Dandin Circus), directed by Jiří Frejka (centre right); and Frejka's adaptation of Aristophanes' comedy *The Women Celebrating the Thesmophoria* (bottom left).

his two companions and contemporaries, the directors E. F. Burian and Jiří Frejka, lay predominantly in innovative theatre practice, which was underpinned by theoretical reflections. All three of them were influenced by the Russian theatre avant-garde, in particular the work of Vsevolod Meyerhold and Alexander Tairov.

Burian came to the theatre as an accomplished and acclaimed composer and musician and his authorial style, developed fully in his Theatre D, bore witness to this artistic background. In his programme of the *theatre of synthesis (syntetické divadlo)*, he undermined the established relations between

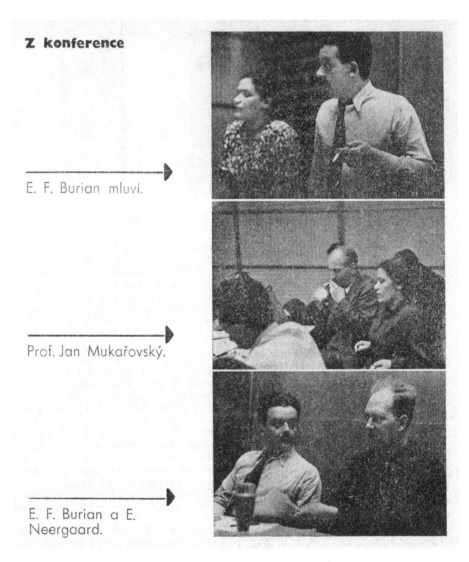

Fig. 5: Jan Mukařovský (with E. F. Burian on the left, in white shirt) at an international conference on the avant-garde theatre organized by Theatre D in Prague in May 1937. The conference was accompanied by a presentation of the theatre's work and an exhibition of avant-garde art, which included publications of the Prague Linguistic Circle. At the conference Mukařovský delivered a paper on stage dialogue; Petr Bogatyrev, one of the other participants, spoke on folk theatre. The captions reads: "from the conference", "E. F. Burian speaking", "prof. Jan Mukařovský" and "E. F. Burian and E. Neergaard".

individual components of the art form and approached them in a dynamic way. The organizing principle of the theatre was the inherent musicality of movement, space, sounds and words. Rather than imposing a musical logic onto the form, Burian developed the elements present in the material itself. Jan Mukařovský identified this feature in an essay for an almanach of Burian's Theatre D and contextualized it with the operatic experiments of Leoš Janáček (1854–1928):

> Burian transposes a musical rhythm into his stage action, an accurately measurable time sequence; through that he controls the entire stage business – enunciation, mimicry and the substance of the scenes. He even treats pauses in the dialogue and the action as musical rests. [...] The normative tasks in Burian's theatre are also exercised by other musical features, in particular the melody. There are moments in Burian's direction of the dialogues that resemble Janáček's method of speech melodies (*nápěvky mluvy*), only applied here in reverse order: the intonational schema of an act of speech is given voice directly as a musical motif transferred into the spoken word. Burian constructs the links between individual lines in the dialogue and between individual onstage actions

Fig. 6: Members of the Liberated Theatre company toast Vsevolod Meyerhold following a performance of *Nebe na zemi* [Heaven on Earth], 1936. Meyerhold (centre) is flanked on the left by the actors František Filipovský and Jan Werich and on the right by the actor Jiří Voskovec and the director Jindřich Honzl (Werich and Voskovec stand out in their distinctive clown garb). During his visit to Prague, Meyerhold also met with E. F. Burian and his company.

and reactions with a fluidity corresponding to the progression of musical motifs in a continuous musical stream. (Jan Mukařovský, cited in Srba 1971: 40)

This approach was in keeping with the innovative experimentation of the theatre avant-garde, as testified to by Meyerhold himself on his visit to Prague in October–November 1936. On watching Burian's production of *The Barber of Seville*, he observed in a journal interview "E. F. Burian is close to me as a stage director: he composes his production like a musician, which I consider the only truthful method of theatre art" (Meyerhold, cited in Srba 1971: 40).

Burian's musical experimentations developed into a novel genre of recitation he called Voiceband, which anticipated later developments in music theatre (see Adámek 2010).

In a similarly *actualized* fashion, Burian's theatre productions refreshed the roles and functions of individual components of the art form, from words and sounds, through acting, to other scenographic elements: stage sets, costumes, masks, props and accessories as well as film projection and lighting, implemented in collaboration with Miroslav Kouřil, Jiří Novotný and Josef Raban (Srba 1971: 48). The use of film projection is worth emphasizing: the footage was often employed as a contrast to the words or the onstage action, almost like a polyphonic theme complementing the action (for a detailed discussion focusing on Burian's production of *Onegin* see Srba 1971: 48–61). The sum total of these innovative practices was far from technological – they were used to achieve greater subjectivity of the art form through a heightened sense of metaphor and emotional appeal.

Burian's collaboration with the stage designer Miroslav Kouřil (1911–1984) was of great importance. Together, in 1936, they developed a scenographic system they called theatregraph (Císař 2010: 315; Burian 2002: 51) that allowed them to explore the potential of light design and projection in creating a scenographic space. It was "a new theatre form in which acting moves fluently from the stage onto film, splitting actors' activities, speeding up the tempo and rhythm of the storytelling, allowing for a new type of stage-film montage and a range of tools for artistic expression" (Miroslav Kouřil; cited in Císař 2010: 315). In the 1950s this principle was further developed by Kouřil, Josef Svoboda (1920–2002) and Alfréd Radok (1914–1976) and gave rise to the phenomenal Laterna Magica (Stehlíková 2011).

One of the PLC members who bridged the gap between theory and artistic practice was the stage director Jiří Frejka. The culmination of his theatre work came in collaboration with the stage designer František Tröster (1904–1968) in the National Theatre in Prague in the late 1930s. This era coincided with his activities in the Prague Linguistic Circle and his analytical, theoretical work can be shown to have played a key role in the novelty of his theatre practice –

a style he called "hyperbolic realism", dominated by the "psychologization" (*zpsychičtění*) of the performance space (Frejka 1936: 84). In 1929, Frejka published a book entitled *Člověk, který se stal hercem* (How People Become Actors; Frejka 1929), the first comprehensive study of theatre acting in Czech, predating Otakar Zich's *The Aesthetics of Dramatic Art* (1931), Ferdinand Pujman's *Herecké tvarosloví* (The Actor's Grammar, 1931), and the later Prague School writings on acting (Hyvnar 2008: 107).

Frejka and Tröster emphasized the role of the actor in the creation of drama – a stance that was unique in the context of the avant-garde, which regarded the actor as a mere instrument of an artistic vision. In this approach Frejka and Tröster anticipated later developments in theatre aesthetics (Miholová 2011: 7). In his work with the actor, Frejka abandoned the conventional, "old-style" character work of analysing the literary mental world of the character in favour of an intuitive, emotional and psychological embodiment of the persona.

> It is beside the point that the character of Richard III is written with a certain moral edge and it matters in fact very little that he is characterized as a monstrous type greedy for power. The most important thing for the actor [...] is the character's most subjective side, the ceaseless flipping between being an ambitious aristocrat and a sweet courtier; what matters more is [...] a thorough immersion in his emotions, sentiments and affects. (Frejka 1929: 34; cited in Miholová 2011: 8).

In this context, Frejka shows the clear influence of Meyerhold's system, for example when he makes this summarization: "It is more appropriate to give the average actor his role while explaining at the same time how it is to be interpreted and describing its biomechanical realization" (Frejka 1929: 96–97; cited and discussed in Miholová 2011: 8–9). Despite this decisive and directive approach as formulated in his 1929 treatise, Frejka's work with actors was much more subtle. Actors' memoires reveal that Frejka's approach was very mild and suggestive rather than imperative; actors often believed they had arrived at a particular interpretation by themselves, although Frejka's own script shows that all of the details had been prepared in advance (Miholová 2011: 68–69). Frejka was an analytical creator, harnessing his intuitive and emotional approach with rational principles; his theories were inspired by the psychology of William James, the associationist psychology of Théodule Ribot and the German irrationalist philosophy of Richard Miller-Freienfels (Hyvnar 2008: 108). It was typical of Frejka to combine such theoretical inspiration with his practical theatre work.

This unique synergy between theory and practice – the ultimate forte of the Prague School writing – was succinctly formulated in a poem written by

Vítězslav Nezval in his collection *Zpáteční lístek* (Return Ticket, 1933); in his "Dopis Mukařovskému" (Letter to Mukařovský), Nezval apostrophizes Jan Mukařovský, one of the key theorists of the Prague School:

Letter to Mukařovský

We walk hand in hand with the scholars
Poetry is no longer created by saints
The age of the *passionale* is past
Throw the flagelant's whip away

...

[The poet] has fantasy instead of feelings
Like a shoemaker he returns to the last
This last is human speech

My friend, come after work today
And explain to the poets and the bees
What honey is and how I make it

...

(translated by Thomas G. Winner; Winner 2015: 159)

Avant-garde artists experimenting with forms, genres and language as well as with scientific discoveries and new social and cultural realities welcomed this partnership with theorists who shared their creative energy, cultural ambitions and political outlook – many were enthusiastic Communists, at a time before the noble ideas of Communism degenerated into ideological atrocities. The PLC's activities formed a heterogenous community that, for a decade or so, kept its finger on the pulse of the age – a "republic of scholars", as Jindřich Toman has called it (Toman 1995: 6 and 103-33). These activities also wove together a number of traditions and tendencies and culminated in a lucky conjunction. The first generation of the Prague Linguistic Circle brought forth a group of younger scholars who in turn had a lasting influence in their respective disciplines. To name a few, the theatre theorist Jiří Veltruský (1919-1994), the now little-known but very important theatre, film and radio scholar and critic Olga Srbová (1914-1987), the Classical scholar and translator Julie Nováková (1909-1991), the literary scholars René Wellek (1903-1995), author of the influential *A Theory of Literature* (1942; with Austin Warren), Vojtěch Jirát (1902-1945) and Felix Vodička (1909-1974), the literary and translation scholars Karel Horálek (1908-1992) and Vladimír Skalička (1909-1991). Their texts bear witness to this rare constellation and offer a critical apparatus that interacted effectively with theatremakers of its time; like any good theoretical writing, it has also proved potent enough to appeal outside the original context in which in was created.

The present study contextualizes Prague School theory by examining the historical, political, cultural, artistic and philosophical setting in which the Prague Linguistic Circle operated and to which its members contributed. It presents the Prague School as an intellectual initiative at the heart of the Central European avant-garde movement and reassesses the body of theoretical writings with a view to its continuing critical value, which originated in its close links with the artistic and cultural practice of its time.

THE PRAGUE SCHOOL AT THE HEART
OF THE AVANT-GARDE

The Prague School appeared within the context of the international avant-garde movement
and may be justly perceived as one of its major intellectual achievements

The main period of Prague School activities coincides with the zenith of the Euro-American avant-garde movement – an era bursting with artistic, intellectual and scientific activities, fascinated by inventions, progress and the potential of the human. The heightened intellectual and artistic energy that pulsed through the Western world in the decades following the Treaty of Versailles was nourished by a belief in a new and modern mission for humanity. Intellectuals and artists finally sensed a genuine opportunity to break away from the old days, which came to be identified with the retrograde policies of the losers in the Great War, the countries of the Central Powers: Germany, Austria-Hungary, the Ottoman Empire and Bulgaria. The cultural and ideological leaders were the self-proclaimed harbingers of modernity, broadly coinciding with the leading states of the winning Allied Powers – France, Great Britain, Italy, the United States – and the newly-emerged Soviet Union. The new political allegiances had a profound impact on the traditional links between countries and their cultures. The map of the world after the post-war negotiations reflected the greatest single change in political arrangements in all of history (see McNeill and McNeill 2003: 288–95). Advancing in the name of modernity and riding on a wave of enthusiasm for the unbounded potential of human achievement, the interwar years were marked by a remarkable intellectual and artistic boom.

In the arts, the Modernist project had been proliferating in a series of avant-garde movements – Abstraction, Expressionism, Constructivism, Dada, Futurism, Cubism, Cubo-Futurism, Surrealism and Functionalism. It would be too much of a simplification to interpret these as *mere* products of the sweeping cultural change around the time of the Great War: the artistic and intellectual sophistication, the ambitions and the achievements of each individual artist in these many movements are far too complex to be reduced to a common denominator. However, in most cases the political bedrock of these movements was embedded in radical ideologies, whether Anarchism, Communism or Fascism, all of which retained an appeal to aspiring public intellectuals and "affectuals"[3] – that is, at a time before Communism and Fascism had degenerated and resorted to mass murder and manifold other atrocities. A number of artists and intellectuals subscribed to these ideologies, became their champions and sympathisers and sometimes even became involved as politicians, abandoning the arts for politics. With a belief in a better and brighter future – a hope often fuelled by a rhetorical acceptance of the necessary sacrifice – the era's agitation stemmed from synergies between the ideational (idealistic, ideological) and the political momentum. A close interconnection between the two spheres – the arts and politics – was perhaps never as intense as in the 1920s and 1930s. Instances of leading Modernist artists becoming affiliated with radical ideologies – whether the notorious cases of Ezra Pound's and T. S. Eliot's involvement with Fascism or Luigi Pirandello's support of and from Mussolini – are only too common. Conversely, ideologists made ample use of the arts for their personal and political ends, one striking example being Benito Mussolini's ambition, in the culminating years of his political career (1928–1939), to become a successful dramatist (see De Benedictis 2014: 113).

The avant-garde's infatuation with radical ideologies was perceived as cognate with the colossal progress in technology and the ongoing cultural shift. Writing in 1929, Walter Benjamin in his essay "Surrealism" interpreted the new artistic movement as the culmination of a long trajectory aimed at attaining a modern type of freedom, hand in hand with the revolutionary, ideological spirit of his day.

Various avant-garde movements were not just intellectual and artistic endeavours but were imbued with the ambition to achieve a new, more just world order. These endeavours were fuelled by unprecedented freedom of thought and the potential for change that came with it: ideas were given the opportunity to be implemented and were seen to be improving the life of humanity on a mass scale. The cataclysm of the Great War served in many ways as a trumpet call and trigger for these changes, with modernity, progress and the visionary ideas of the avant-garde as the ultimate driving forces for the eventual solution to all grievances and sufferings of the past. This assertion is far from being a rhetorical flourish: the leading Russian theorist and critic Viktor Shklovsky, writing about the arts during the famine-ridden horrors of the blockade of Petersburg between 1919 and 1921, made the dramaturgical powers of war and its uncanny ability to innovate techniques and means of expression tantalizingly explicit:

---

3   Ladislav Kováč coined the concept of the *affectual* as follows: "These are people with a strong emotional drive to seek a universal explanation of the world, to be strongly bound to the explanation and to vigorously impose their ideas upon others, usually by means of the mass media" (Kováč 2002: 13). See also Kováč 2007: 62.

Fig. 7: Karel Teige: collage, 1941. One of the many collages created by this art critic, leading theoretician of Czech avant-garde art and Surrealist artist.

If you take hold of a samovar by its stubby legs, you can use it to pound nails, but that is not its primary function.

I saw war. With my own hands I stoked stoves with pieces of a piano in Stanislavov and made bonfires out of rugs and fed the flames with vegetable oil while trapped in the mountains of Kurdistan. Right now I'm stoking a stove with books. I know the laws of war and I understand that in its own way it reorganizes things, such as reducing a man to 180 pounds of human flesh, or using a rug as surrogate for a fuse. (Shklovsky 2005: 25)

In the 1920s and 1930s, European theatre found itself confronted with novel challenges commensurate with the greatness of the cultural moment. Not only did the First World War bring the unprecedented trauma of the Lost Generation, which had a profound impact on culture and society, but there was also the new popular and democratic medium of film, first silent and later (from 1927) sound. The theatre had to respond to these impulses and redefine its cultural role. Simultaneously, the heightened nationalism of all aspects of public life in the 1920s and 1930s influenced the formerly much more international cultural sphere and created divisions and borders that had not been there previously. Avant-garde artists – often international and leftist in their outlook and ambitions, and forming a small minority on the artistic scene – found themselves even more in opposition to mainstream culture, which was commonly nationalist, middle-class and realist in its aesthetics (cf. Bruce McConachie in Zarrilli et al. 2010: 323). Nevertheless, it is the legacy of the avant-garde with its idealistic vision that has survived until the present and that has retained much of its relevance and topicality.

THE NEW MULTICULTURAL STATE
OF CZECHOSLOVAKIA

*The political and historical backdrop to the Prague School played a significant role.
The new democratic state of Czechoslovakia was based on modern principles
and its ideologies were conducive to the PLC's theoretical project.*

The new state of Czechoslovakia was set up on the ruins of the Austro-Hungarian Empire on 28 October 1918. This unprecedented practical arrangement for a new state that had been worked out by Czech and Slovak politicians – rather oddly, with the support of immigrant communities in the United States – was riding the wave of pan-Slavism, a nineteenth-century movement of Slavic intellectuals and artists with a strong belief in the shared roots and values of all Slavic peoples.[4] Czechoslovakia was a short-lived cohabitation of several cultures, combining Czechs (themselves subdivided into Bohemians, Moravians and Silesians), Slovaks and Carpathian Ruthenians, with significant numbers of Germans, Hungarians, Jews and Poles. The belief was that Czechoslovakia would be a modern, multi-ethnic republic based on democratic and anti-clerical principles. The conglomerate state was created in order to be large enough to compete with the big players on the political and economic map. A boost in confidence – especially in the Czech lands, which played the dominat role vis-à-vis the underdeveloped Slovakia and Carpathian Ruthenia – came with the fact that the intellectuals promoting the new state became leading political figures of the new establishment.

Such was the case of Tomáš Garrigue Masaryk (1850–1937), a former professor of aesthetics and philosophy and public intellectual who played a key role in public affairs, most notably in his opposition to the anti-semitic prosecution of Leopold Hilsner for the alleged ritual murder of a young Czech woman, and his role in the exposure of the fake medieval Czech Zelená Hora and Dvůr Králové manuscripts, which were defended uncritically by Czech nationalists as they appeared to validate Czech claims to a cultural antiquity that would

---

4   See for instance Mary Heimann's critical history *Czechoslovakia: The State that Failed* (Heimann 2009). See also Peter Demetz's *Prague in Danger: The Years of German Occupation, 1939-45* (Demetz 2008) and the introductory chapter to Kevin McDermott's *Communist Czechoslovakia, 1945-89: A Political and Social History* (McDermott 2015).

antedate that of the Germans. Together with other politicians, Masaryk lobbied Woodrow Wilson's government in the United States for support of a new state that would be created after the eventual dissolution of the Austro-Hungarian Empire. When the state was officially established, Masaryk became its first President and also the emblem of the new era – in later years this period came to be referred to as the First Republic or Masaryk's Czechoslovakia. Another key figure in the wartime negotiations was Milan Rastislav Štefánik (1880–1919), an enterprising young Slovak who had studied in Prague as an astronomer and who subsequently became a general in the French Army. On 4 May 1919, on a flight from Italy to the Slovak capital, Bratislava, Štefánik's aircraft crashed and the new Slovak leader died in the catastrophe. This single event had a far-reaching impact on Czech-Slovak relations and the emancipation of the Slovak nation within Czechoslovakia.

The new state brought new perspectives and opened up new intellectual horizons:

> The establishment of the new state [of Czechoslovakia in 1918] freed Czech intellectuals from a one-sided preoccupation with national self-determination and, on the other hand, diffused the predominant cultural orientation toward the German-speaking world. The cultural policy of the new republic was succinctly expressed in Masaryk's metaphor of "opening the windows to the world". (Steiner 1982: 197)

Nonetheless, Czechoslovakia was also a dream come true for many Czech and Slovak nationalists. The Czechs had been subsumed within the Habsburg Empire since the sixteenth century. A Slovak kingdom or state was almost beyond history; the last independent Slovak state formation dated back to Pribina's principality in the early ninth century and had acquired mythological dimensions. It was therefore with a sense of nationalist and patriotic elation among Czechs and Slovaks that Czechoslovakia came into existence and became a projection of many ambitions. Set up as a parliamentary democracy, Czechoslovakia intentionally played down the traditional regional association of the Catholic Church with the state, with *democracy* almost becoming an ecumenical state religion, bridging the many denominations present in Czechoslovakia. This is more than a rhetorical phrase; as a liberal intellectual, Masaryk was well aware of the cultural role of religion and religious belief in the new state and made plans for the establishment of a Czechoslovak Church that would combine the country's humanistic heritage with the positives of Christian culture. The Czechoslovak Church, founded in 1920 (renamed the Czechoslovak Hussite Church in 1971), advocated a return to the primitive church and the true core of Christianity. It attracted significant numbers of followers and pursued a modern version of the Reformation, breaking away from the Catholic Church, which was regarded as not only problematic and retrograde but politically tainted owing to its role as the state-endorsed religion of the Austro-Hungarian Empire. Popular discontent with the Catholic Church as the bulwark of the old empire spilled over into a peculiar event that took place on 3 November 1918, only six days after Czechoslovakia had been proclaimed. An enraged mob of Prague citizens tore down the Column of the Immaculate Virgin Mary in the Old Town Square, a monument erected in 1648. This outbreak was indicative of popular Czech sentiment against the Austrian regime, symbolized and mediated by the Catholic Church. However, despite a significant Protestant minority, the great majority of Slovaks were deeply Catholic, while most Carpathian Ruthenians belonged to the Uniate (Greek Catholic) Church. As a result of the forceful efforts of the Counter-Reformation in the seventeenth century, the Czech lands were predominantly Catholic, though for many this had become a matter of social practice rather than deep faith. Ideologically linked with the new Czechoslovak state, the new Czechoslovak Church was intended as an ecumenical religious movement that would supersede the old denominations that had been compromised to a great extent by clerics and their subservience to the old regime.

Despite the enthusiasm and creative and civic energies, Czechoslovakia went through a crisis of identity in its first decade. The initial impulse soon tired and it became increasingly clear that a negative definition of Czechoslovakia – as the modern vanquisher of the decadent Austro-Hungarian Empire – was insufficient. Calls for a pan-Slavic identity were also soon exhausted: other independent Slavic countries had also come into existence (Poland, Yugoslavia) and many regarded the new Soviet Union with deep suspicion. Any definition of what it meant to be Czechoslovak had to negotiate a tension between the Germanic states, with their traditional cultural, political and geographic links, and those that were Slavic. The contentions over territorial boundaries with Poland in parts of Silesia (in the Těšín/Cz-eszyn region) had a military nature; similarly, the sovereignty of Carpathian Ruthenia was only settled with the signing of the Treaty of St Germain in September 1919. So the relations with other Slavic states (with the exception of Yugoslavia) were far from conducive to embracing the nineteenth-century dream of pan-Slavism.

The Slavic definition of Czechoslovakia was also problematic for at least one more significant reason. The new state comprised not only ethnic Czechs and Slovaks (65.5%) but also a large number of ethnic Germans (23.4%) – considerably outnumbering the Slovaks, who made up 14.5% – Hungarians (5.6%), a range of eastern Slav ethnics, including Russians, Ukranians and Carpathian Ruthenians (3.5%), a culturally and economically significant minority of Jews (1.4%) and, in the Ostrava region, a minority of Poles (0.6%), as the results of the census of 1921 show (Tóth et al 2012: 625–7). From this perspective of a multiethnic and multicultural state, a simple definition of what it meant to be a citizen of the new Czechoslovakia was impossible. The most significant ethnic group outside Czechs and Slovaks – regarded officially, owing to an artificially created national designation, as *Czechoslovaks* – were Germans, whose roots in the Czech lands went back more than 700 years. Not only did they form almost a fourth of the population, but until quite recently they had played a major, at times a dominant, role in many institutions and public life thanks to their privileged position under the Austrian regime. By the early twentieth century the relations between Czechs and Germans had reached a point of permanent tension and while there were attempts at a mutual rapprochement, many of the bilingual cities and towns operated in a parallel mode, a telling example being the case of the German and the Czech theatre life in Prague, documented in detail by Jitka Ludvová (2012). The tension later deteriorated with the radicalizing influence of Nazi Germany and Nazi propaganda, culminating not only in World War II but also in the brutal expulsion of the vast majority of German-speaking inhabitants in 1945.

The situation was further complicated by the cultural heritage of the Slovak ethnicity. After centuries of cultural, economic and ethnic oppression, Slovakia lacked a clear self-definition of its own identity; the system of education and culture was non-functional and it was severly underdeveloped economically. Many Slovak intellectuals had studied at Austrian, German, Hungarian and Czech universities but had never been given a full opportunity to develop Slovak culture in their homeland. It was only after the establishment of Czechoslovakia that a belated process of Slovak national emancipation took place, modelled on that of Czech culture – a fact that would also cause further crises of identity and tensions, influencing politics for the better part of the century to come. Bratislava was pronounced the capital of the Slovak nation for its size and its relative development rather than as a natural capital; until then, national aspirations had been directed towards the city of Martin, the seat of the influential Slovak Foundation (Matica slovenská, established in 1863 on the basis of an idea reaching back to the 1820s); later claims were made that the Slovak capital should be transferred either to Banská Bystrica or to the eastern Slovak city of Košice. Slovak as a language was codified on the Czech model; the two languages are so closely related that several intellectuals in the First Republic considered Slovak a mere popular dialect of Czech and indirectly denied its right to self-assertion. Despite this charged situation, Slovak emancipated itself as a fully fledged nationality – with the seminal help of Czech teachers, artists, intellectuals and industrialists who helped build the infrastructures of modern Slovakia, from the network of schools, grammar schools and universities, through theatres, musical institutions and museums to industry. When the Slovak National Theatre was established in Bratislava in 1920, the first several seasons were offered in the Czech language before a repertoire in Slovak was created through translation and new writing. Czech ensembles were associated with the important municipal theatres of Bratislava and Košice until 1939, when the Fascist Slovak Republic abolished them. The First Republic was the time of the emancipation of Slovaks as a nationality; this process further complicated an understanding of what it meant to be a Czechoslovak in the new multi- and quasi-ethnic state.

In addition to this multiethnic and multicultural state, the region and its population bore a significant heritage not only as a crossroads of cultures but also as the site of turbulent histories, a characteristic that was further confirmed in the upcoming century. Bohemia, Moravia, Silesia and to a lesser extent Slovakia and Carpathian Ruthenia as well had witnessed many political systems and regimes over the centuries, most of them accompanied by feuds, persecutions and wars. A lasting trauma, which can also be sensed in the above-mentioned symbolic aggression towards the forceful Counter-Reformation – the destruction of the Marian column in Prague – was the Thirty Years' War. Although seemingly historically distant and politically inconsequential in the long run, this protracted conflict has only recently been recognized as "Europe's Tragedy" (Wilson 2009; for the cultural impact see pages 812–20), a cataclysmic breaking point in European history with a lasting impact on Central European culture. During the period from 1618 to 1648 around 5 million people died (through either violence or illness) in the Holy Roman Empire alone – a shocking 20 percent of the Empire's population (Wilson 2009: 787). This trauma lived on and formed a significant element in cultural identity. It was also with this legacy in mind that the newly established Czechoslovakian Republic – based on the principles of modern parliamentary democracy, stripped of clerical and aristocratic power structures – was welcomed with great hopes, as the first instance of the people's self-determination and civic freedom.

It is within this intellectual and cultural context – permeated by scepticism towards old institutions and establishments – that the Prague Linguistic Circle was established. Although the political and ideological resonances of the initiative have never been in the forefront of reassessments of the Prague School, the historical and political realities played a significant role in its unique features, as will be shown later. The hopes with which the Czechoslovak state was welcomed were commensurate with the intellectual and artistic ambitions of the Prague Linguistic Circle as articulated in their programme in *Slovo a slovesnost*. It was a unique moment in history, one that mandated and lent plausibility to ambitious projects fuelled by a will to change.

CONTROVERSIES AND IDEOLOGIES SURROUNDING THE MODERN CZECH LANGUAGE

Among the key concerns of the new state of Czechoslovakia was the Czech language. The academic and cultural influences after the First World War and the uncomfortable legacy of German/Austrian culture were significant aspects of linguistic endeavours.

In the context of Czechoslovakia, the cultural, political, historical and social dependence on Austria (or Hungary) and Germany could not be ignored – institutions continued to exist, social habits and customs survived and ethnic continuity played a decisive role. The positive aspect of the troubled historical and cultural legacy was the receptivity and adaptability of the Czechoslovaks. Bohemia and Moravia in particular, as Austria's industrial powerhouses, were characterized by a progressive and dynamic spirit. The establishment of the new state was characterized by attempts to redirect these energies towards the progressive powers, the winners of the Great War, and to replace the Germanic influence with the cultivated influence of France, Britain and the United States. In this context, the study of the modern Czech language became an issue of heightened political and cultural significance.

The Prague School often found itself in opposition to the traditionalist scholarship practised in Czechoslovakia, provoking its opponents with its near-iconoclastic, avant-garde approach to knowledge.[5] Nowhere was this perhaps more visible than in the study of language, which became the crucial critical instrument for analysing and understanding cultural, artistic and intellectual practices. The Prague Linguistic Circle (PLC) was established as a community that agreed to study language by means of a novel, near-scientific methodology – the functional-structural method. It activities were not only academic but had a public outreach: the PLC organized several public lectures on the standard modern language and had a significant influence on the shape of modern Czech. However, its approach often clashed with the established ways of Czech linguistics.

---

5   This passage develops a paper presented at the Prague Semiotic Stage Revisited international symposium, convened by David Drozd, the opening event of the Czech Structuralist Thought on Theatre project. The symposium was hosted by the Department of Theatre Studies, Faculty of Arts, Masaryk University, Brno from 27–29 June 2011. The paper was published in Drábek 2012b.

The first decade of Czechoslovakia's existence was a time when English and French became academic fields of study throughout the Western world. The Czech linguists around Josef Zubatý and the journal *Naše řeč* (Our Language) took explicit inspiration from the French system of state exams, systematically building a sense of nationality among the people through the use of literature (cf. Terry Eagleton's discussion of New Criticism in his chapter on "The Rise of English" in *Literary Theory*; Eagleton 1983: 17ff.). *Naše řeč* published René Lote's account of the French practice (Lote 1920) and referred again to it as crucial and inspirational several years later on the occasion of the tenth anniversary of the establishment of Czechoslovakia (Zubatý 1927: 30). The young academic Otakar Vočadlo, later an influential and authoritative English professor and Shakespeare scholar, in his 1924 radical, pamphlet-like treatise entitled *V zajetí babylonském: německé vlivy u nás* (In Babylonian Captivity: German Influences in Our Country), advocated what he termed "cultural hygiene" (Vočadlo 1926: 7), and called for adopting British cultural and political influences as opposed to what he considered the negative, pathological German and Austrian impact on Czechoslovak culture. These concerns hearken back to the 1895 treatises of Tomáš Garrigue Masaryk, *Česká otázka* (The Czech Question) and *Naše nynější krise* (Our Current Crisis). In the latter book, Masaryk admonishes his readers, somewhat obliquely, "For practical and intellectual reasons we shall learn world languages, especially English, French, Russian" (Masaryk 1895: 425).

Although the French-English influence was predominant, it was far from universal; there was a group of people who recognized the hypocrisy of this stance and the shortsightedness of aligning oneself too closely with a particular powerful player.

What is of crucial importance in this context is the ongoing debate over cultural influences, nationalism and literary and linguistic studies. In 1922, Václav Ertl, in the language-purist journal *Naše řeč*, discussed the need for a state-funded institute for the cultivation of the language, arguing that

> Caring for the mother tongue is not only a matter of love and respect for the language, in which a voluntary association may well be of assistance; first and foremost, if it is not to degenerate into dilettante purism or a race to prosecute foreign words, which was eventually the fate of such organizations as the German *Sprachvereine*, it is a scholarly task. (Ertl 1922: 978)

These intellectual efforts formed a crucial background for the birth of the Prague Linguistic Circle.

The disagreement between the nationalist and essentially conservative intelligentsia on the one hand and the more progressive intellectuals on the other came to an open clash in a deeply embarrasing episode in 1933. This event also encapsulated some of the controversies that marked the intellectual and cultural life of the first Czechoslovak Republic. The by then renowned linguist Roman Jakobson applied for his *habilitation* (associate professorship) at the Faculty of Arts of Masaryk University in Brno. Jakobson had lived in Czechoslovakia since 1920 and had contributed significantly to Czech cultural life and to Czech scholarship, not only with his 1923 monograph on Czech verse (first published in Russian as *O cheshskom stikhe*, Jakobson 1923; and later in Czech, Jakobson 1926), but also with his research on Euroasian language systems, his musicological contribution on early sacred songs (Jakobson 1929) and – far from least – his seminal role in establishing the Prague Linguistic Circle in 1926. In 2005, Tomáš Glanc edited the documents accompanying Jakobson's 1933 habilitation (Glanc 2005). For two of Brno's leading professors, Jakobson was not to be tolerated. One of them was Antonín Beer (editor-in-chief of *Naše věda* (Our Scholarship)) and the other František Chudoba, the founder of the English Department in Brno and a leading Czech Shakespeare scholar. These two language purists did their best to block Jakobson's career, employing every means at their disposal, from protesting against his academic and scholarly expertise, through thinly veiled xenophobic attacks on his reputation as a foreign scholar, to spreading doubts about his date of birth, his primary education, the validity of the list indicating previous employment and the legality of his stay in the country, insinuations about his surreptitious agendas and rumours of his employment in the intelligence service.[6] The motives behind these libels were simple: Jakobson was a harsh critic of language purism as practised by Beer's journal *Naše věda* and a dangerous rival.

The study that provoked the Brno professors most was Jakobson's 1932 essay "O dnešním brusičství českém" (On Today's Czech Language Purism, Jakobson 1932), in which he criticized the policies of *Naše řeč* and its attempts to rid the Czech language of all unwelcome Germanisms. The word *brusičství* (glass-grinding or polishing) was not in fact Jakobson's invention; as quoted above, in his 1922 article Václav Ertl had had called for a "scientific" (that is,

---

6   On this point and on Jakobson's complicated position among the "White émigrés" – anti-Bolshevik Russians fleeing the Soviet Union – see Jakobson's letters to Elsa Triolet. In a letter of 14 November 1920, written only four months after his arrival in Czechoslovakia, he says: "[I]n September I was strongly attacked here for my participation in the [Soviet] Red Cross Mission. The newspapers were crying out about 'the boa constrictor, grasping in its tenacious embrace our local professors' (this is me), and so on; the professors vascillated whether I was a bandit or a scholar or an illegal mongrel; in the cabaret they were singing little songs about me – all of this was not very witty. The situation was complex, but it seems to me that my fate is to tightrope-walk in inconceivable situations. As a result I left work (without tears or cursing), and embarked on university scholarship and so on" (Jakobson 1996: 117). Jakobson's teacher Nikolai Durnovo, upon his return from Czechoslovakia to Soviet Russia in 1933, was sentenced to ten years' imprisonment in the gulag and eventually executed in 1937 on the basis of his alleged "Fascist" contacts, who included Roman Jakobson and Nikolai Trubetskoy (Mach 2012: 38).

scholarly) treatment of language that must not "degenerate into dilettante purism [*diletantské brusičství*] or a race to prosecute foreign words". It seems to have been this article that Jakobson was alluding to when he criticized the "pseudoscientific methods and objectives of such out-and-out purism" (Jakobson 1932: 116). With disarming consistency Jakobson concludes that this linguistic policy is dubious and hardly valid. Rather than calling it *nationalistic*, he opts for "a more appropriate term" for it, which is "racism. Germanisms are, on principle, prosecuted only because of their parentage, no matter how distant" (Jakobson 1932: 119). Besides, Jakobson mercilessly points out the contextual implications of such racism. It ignores the fact that "the Czech intelligentsia of the nineteenth century was bilingual, writing in German almost equally well as in Czech" (Jakobson 1932: 96) and that the "inherited Germanisms of standard Czech are part of the same cultural heritage of the past as, for instance, the close connection of Czech Romanticism to German Romanticism or the link between the ideology of the Czech national revival and German philosophy" (Jakobson 1932: 117). Such a scholarly exposé was a bitter pill to swallow for people like Beer and Chudoba, who would later, for instance, reproach the future renowned literary scholar René Wellek for daring to have critical ambitions in a Czech context when he had been born in Vienna (in this way also hinting obliquely at Wellek's Jewish origin).

This conflict illustrates not only two opposing sides of the intellectual life of the 1920s, the nationalist scholars and the more progressive intellectuals. It also illustrates different practices of scholarship. While the internationalist Jakobson argued by examples from all over Europe, calling for a *functional* analysis of phenomena - drawing on the mode of their existence and effectiveness; how they operate and assert themselves - the followers of *Naše řeč* derived their authority from other sources, mostly from adhering to conservative traditions, established institutions and schools of thought, and primitive patriotism and xenophobia. Jiří Haller, one of the language purists whom Jakobson criticized most, voiced it explicitly: "By what right does *Naše řeč* pretend to be the arbiter of language? It is simple: by the right of experts" (quoted in Jakobson 1932: 88). Against this superficial arrogance of *experts* who argue *ad hominem* (whether to confirm their own greatness or to denigrate their opponent, when the occasion serves), the new *functional* approach - embodied by the Prague Linguistic Circle - was a breath of fresh air. They argued strictly *ad rem*, analysing *phenomena* as they are, without preferences for, or prejudice against, political, historical or social contexts.

This approach to knowledge served not only as the epistemology of the Prague School but also as the principle constituting the new Czechoslovakia. With some licence the Prague Linguistic Circle could be perceived as an ideological academy of sciences of the new republic - not only because the Prague Structuralists were supporters of T. G. Masaryk's and Edvard Beneš's policies but more importantly because the *functional-structural* method that the PLC codified in its statute is cognate with the constitutive ideologies behind the modern Czechoslovak identity. These ideologies were characterized by a *functional* approach: to be a citizen of Czechoslovakia meant to *embody* the *inherent* and *inherited* qualities one possesses and deploys here and now, rather than identifying oneself through historical and cultural memory as a member of a nation. This new identity was characterized by *activism* and *agency* – a potential that is actively realized (cf. the above-mentioned treatise on cultural activism by Vilém Mathesius) – rather than by the assertion of an inherited right and status.

THE FUNCTIONAL-STRUCTURAL METHOD

> *The PLC's functional-structural method was a specific epistomological tool
> that developed influences of the earlier Russian Formalism
> and influenced later versions of Structuralism.*

Theoretical writings very often try to be terminologically normative in order to *consolidate*, define or in some other way fix their object, be it a thing or a process.[7] Many theories tend towards a nomenclature, a terminological matrix that defines the object's form, significance and pragmatics. Conceptually, these efforts result in a hermetic and near-nominalist world, of which a typical representative would be recent semiotics (or semiology) with its elaborate structures of relations and all but cabalistic universe of names (see Elam 1980). Names, terms and concepts define the nature of knowledge to the extent that they are constitutive of reality and we understand reality through the prism of these concepts (cf. the Sapir-Whorf hypothesis of language as the power constitutive of cognition). The *functional-structuralist* method of the PLC operated out of a completely different concept of theory, characterized by a fascination with the instability of conceptual knowledge and the void beyond it. With a view to the long history of philosophy, this approach could be called *realist* (as opposed to *nominalist*), focusing on real-life phenomena themselves *a priori* of their naming – studying their functions and operations in the pre-conceptual (or non-conceptual) reality and prioritizing these realities over the conventionalized nomenclatures. As opposed to late twentieth-century theatre semiotics, which is fundamentally *nominalist*, the early Prague School theories were closer to the *realist* approach – focusing on ontological gestures or dialectical relationships between individual phenomena.

The Prague School is most often referred to as "Prague Structuralists" – a shorthand common as early as the 1930s. However, this does only partial justice to the epistemological core of their theories, stressing as it does the *structural* (nominal) as opposed to the *functional* and dynamic. In view of the customary use of the term *structuralism* when designating the theorists and

---

7   An earlier version of this section was presented at the Prague Semiotic Stage Revisited II international symposium, Masaryk University, Brno, 20–22 May 2013. It was published in Drábek 2014.

their approach, a historical qualification must be made. The statutes of the Prague Linguistic Circle imposed strict rules on its members; one of them was ideological loyalty, a commitment to "develop linguistics on a functional-structuralist basis" (*pěstovat lingvistiku na základě funkčně strukturálním*; for a formulation of the Circle's aims, see the Introduction to the first issue of *Slovo a slovesnost* (1935)).[8] The compound is highly significant and out of the two components it is the *functional* that is rightly prioritized. These theorists were not intent on building a structure (or a nominal system). Nor was it their aim to analyse the existing structures of meaning, as was the case of the postwar Structuralists in the United States, France and Italy. It is the *function* of a phenomenon – be it a word, a statement, a gesture or some other semantic initiative – that creates structures of meaning and imposes a hierarchy of related components.

The concept of *functionality* or *function* – in many ways the more significant half of the *functional-structuralist* method – is key to the Prague School. As has been mentioned above, the *function* (or actual operation) of a particular thing *defines and creates a certain structure* or *a hierarchy of relations* (*usouvztažněnost*); this hierarchy/structure is not only created but keeps changing dynamically depending on the function and the actual existence of the phenomenon. Another key term of the Prague School, *aktualisace*, is closely related to this notion. It has been translated variously as *foregrounding*, *highlighting* and *actualization*.[9] An informed definition and discussion of the term and its relation to the Russian Formalist *ostranenie* (остранение, estrangement, or making it strange) and the Brechtian notion of *Verfremdung*, is provided by Veronika Ambros in her essay "Prague's Experimental Stage: Laboratory of Theatre and Semiotics" (Ambros 2008; see also Meerzon 2012). *Aktualisace* in its essence names the novelty, freshness and non-routine use of a certain expressive tool. Etymologically, the term was derived from the French *actuel* – that is, not only *topical* but also *contemporary, up to date, actual, real, current* – in other words that which is taking place only just now. That is to say, the term *aktualisace* gives a name to the fact of meaning as an activity or an event, and thematizes, by the same token, the very act of the communication. In this sense, the critical term disregards the existing semantic structures, focusing on the signifying and semantic processes that are presently underway.

The close relationship between *aktualisace* and *functionality* (*funkčnost*) was outlined by Roman Jakobson (see Zelenka 1993). It is also worth noting that the later PLC linguists Josef Vachek and Jan Firbas translate their

---

8   The by-laws (statutes) of the PLC are published in Toman 1995: Appendix, pp. 263–7.
9   For a detailed discussion of the concept of *aktualisace* and the numerous misconceptions and confusions around it, see Šlaisová 2012.

key critical term *aktuální členění větné* (literally, the *actual structuring of the sentence*) as *functional sentence perspective*, thus drawing on the relationship between the two terms and indirectly proclaiming them as near synonyms. Their very translation is in itself an instance of *aktualisace* in that it explains functionally what the term *aktuální* signifies here: the ontological gesture here is the *perspective of immediate functionality*, not a terminological hypostasis. Similarly, the term *členění* (structuring, ordering or arrangement) has been translated into English as *perspective* – as if a static structure (i.e. a given hierarchy) has been reduced to a mere *perspective*, a *point of view*, an *aspect* or a *visual projection*. From a translation perspective this is an imprecise, unfaithful rendering. At the same time, it is a prominent instance of a *functional-structural* approach to meaning and its verbal formulation.

This *functional-structural ontological trick* to disregard things nominally but rather approach them functionally is, inherently, an ideological act. By means of this dialectic tool it is possible to dismantle any power structures and discourses and get at their very foundation: from the basic semiotic core of culture to state establishments, this tool is capable of cancelling the existing structures and replacing the nomenclature perspective with a perspective of functionality – the role, its effectiveness and its objective.[10] This subversiveness is present only latently in the generation of the PLC; however, a few decades later, in the United States and in France, it is this subversive potential that becomes a declared anti-establishment stance of critical theory, represented by Roland Barthes, Michel Foucault and their followers, the self-declared *deconstructivists* (or *post-structuralists*) Jacques Derrida, Paul de Man and Julia Kristeva. This post-1945 generation developed the political and ideological potential of the functional-structural method, mediated by Roman Jakobson in particular through his contacts with Claude Lévi-Strauss and other theorists of the postwar Structuralist movement.[11] While this generation worked with Ferdinand de Saussure's concept of the sign, the PLC approach differed substantially from the Swiss linguist's doctrine. Roman Jakobson had received and read a copy of de Saussure's *Course in General Linguistics* from Albert Sechehaye, who had published the volume with Charles Bally in 1916 on the basis of their notes from de Saussure's lectures. However, it was only after Jakobson's arrival in New York in 1942 that he started negotiating the divide between de Saussure and his own conceptual system.[12]

---

10   Though this may seem adventurous and even conspiratorial from a linguistic point of view, it corresponded to the personal style of Roman Jakobson and the cunning tricks he played with the police and his playful coquetry with being a secret agent and a subversive factor, as Miloš Zelenka has pointed out (Zelenka 2012).

11   For details of this influence, see Bradford 1994: 80–94.

12   In his *Dialogues*, he recounts his teaching on a course in New York in 1942: "I took as my starting point the doctrine of Ferdinand de Saussure as it appears in a version of his *Course in General*

However, the same ontological gesture – of a *functional-structural* redefinition or *actualization* – can be traced in the political and ideological agenda of the early Czechoslovakia and in the intellectual discussions about the significance and justification of its peculiar composite national identity. Cultural and national identity had to be defined anew – not on the basis of existing institutions, let alone their nomenclature, but rather on the basis of their *functionality* and *effectiveness* in the new conditions. It is worth noting that Masaryk, Czechoslovak President and ideologist, was a patron of the Prague Linguistic Circle, financing its activities behind the scenes.[13] A certain affinity between the *functional-structural* method and the state-forming processes of the newly established Czechoslovakia is apparent. In 1920, for instance, Czechoslovakia replaced the previous Austrian arrangement of administrative units (hetmanships; *hejtmanství*) with units inspired by the French *départements*. The first priority in the new state was the reconstruction of a functional political and economic infrastructure: the imperative was to replace the well-trodden paths of the Austro-Hungarian regime and its channels of power on the level of both fact and nomenclature. These processes were to sever the actual events from links to political traditions, something analogous to the ontological approach of the *functional-structural* method: disrupting all dependence on established structures, whether linguistic, institutional and political in the public sphere or mimetic, realist, positivist or Young Grammarians in the sphere of critical theory. Such was the central ontological gesture of the Prague School – a characteristic that places it in a close relationship with European Modernism and avant-garde movements, with their opposition to conventions and traditions.

Russian Formalists – Viktor Shklovsky in particular – came up with an ontological gesture centred around the notion of *estrangement*, or *making it strange* (остраннение) as the pivot of artistic creation. Closely connected with the radical movement of Futurism, *ostranenie* broke away from a conventional or conformist way of perceiving reality: pulling out an object from its habitual, everyday use, art presents it differently, with a change, with a *new* set of eyes. That was the revolutionary sentiment of the artists and intelligentsia of the First World War – breaking away from the decadent and

---

Linguistics …. The question at hand was to specify those aspects of de Saussure's teaching that were shared by my views and those that separated us from each other. First and foremost there proved to be a considerable break with the Genevan precepts even in their two fundamentals, namely the arbitrariness of the linguistic sign and the rigid insistence on the linearity of the verbal form. Our entire phonological analysis, with its systematization of minimal phonological elements, clearly illustrated this fact. It was perfectly logical to base an exposition of the new approach precisely on an explication of these essential divergencies" (Jakobson and Pomorska 1980: 41).

13   It is also noteworthy that the PLC's journal *Slovo a slovesnost* never published personal news; however, an obituary on Masaryk appeared there in 1937.

degenerate world of conventions and societies with an absolute (and often uncritical) belief in progress, modernity and scientific innovation, even at the cost of sacrifices. As Peter Steiner has pointed out, "the Prague structural-ists rejected [Shklovsky]'s radically formalist ideas about art because these ideas seemed a return to the passé nineteenth-century trend of Herbartian formalism" (Steiner 1982: 181).[14]

While *making it strange* has a close relationship to the ontological gesture of the Prague School – to the *functional-structural* method and the notion of *actualization* – there is a crucial difference between them. Shklovsky's Futurist-inspired concept *estranges* or *alienates* everyday objects and imbues them with a new, poetic and artistic life; for Shklovsky, a poet sees things dif-ferently, without understanding its function, as if for the first time: "Change in art is not the result of changes in daily life. Change in art results from old forms becoming petrified, the endless passage of things from tactile percep-tion to habitualized recognition" (Shklovsky 2005: 56).

In several of his essays, Shklovsky analyses examples of artistic vision that truly estranges, or is estranged from, everyday reality. But there it stops: there is no functionality beyond the alienated vision. In contrast to this, the Prague School method *actualizes* everyday objects, revisiting and redefining them in relation to their actual function and within the new structures that this function establishes. This is the crucial difference between Russian For-malism and the Prague School: the former was principally a revolutionary, Futurist movement, the latter a constitutive or formative one.

---

14   For a detailed discussion of Russian Formalism and Prague Structuralism see Peter Steiner's brilliant essay "The Roots of Structuralist Esthetics" (Steiner 1982). A meticulous new edition in Czech has been made by Ondřej Sládek (Sládek 2014a: 34–87).

THE ROLE OF THEATRE IN CZECHOSLOVAK LIFE

The PLC members had an avid interest and were active participants in the theatre of the time, benefitting from the cultural momentum and general theatricality of Czechoslovak society.

The Czech lands, with Prague at its heart, were conducive to the rise of the Prague School as an influential intellectual and philosophical generation for a variety of reasons in addition to the democratic, liberal and forward-looking state project of Czechoslovakia. One of the key catalysts of the Prague School initiative was the Czech theatre tradition, which played a central role in Czech culture. Since the late eighteenth century, theatre had been a constitutive force of modern European civilization: cities as industrial and commercial centres emancipated and presented themselves through it. Municipal stages were established as essential parts of all cities and as the heart of their social and cultural lives. As the research of Margita Havlíčková, Sylva Pracná and Jiří Štefanides has shown, municipal theatres in the region not only served the purposes of entertainment and public education, in line with Schiller's concept of theatre as a moral institution, but were also charged multicultural spaces of the burgeoning public sphere (Havlíčková et al 2010; see also Havlíčková 2013 and Štefanides et al 2011–2013; for a modern theory of the theatrical public sphere, see Balme 2014).

Even more can be claimed: public theatre is not only an important social instrument presenting and representing images of reality, it is also a laboratory of sorts, modelling possible worlds, behaviours and systems. Any theatre play presents a hypothetical "what if" situation – a proposition that is acted out with its possible consequences and developments. In so doing, theatre as a knowledge laboratory invents, presents and tests models – not as theoretical concepts, but as embodied onstage realities. This role of the theatre is almost universal. In the Czech lands, this agency was heightened by the longstanding disenfranchisement of the culture: in a remarkable way, theatre became a surrogate space for political and social ambitions. Perhaps the most telling instance is that of the Czech National Theatre in Prague. The idea of a national theatre long predated its actual establishment (in 1868): manifestations of a national sentiment had long been realized through theatre, from the early Czech-language performances of the Patriotic Theatre

(Vlastenské divadlo) of the 1780s and 1790s through to the Shakespearean celebrations of 1864 (Drábek 2016). When the Austrian Empire made its peace with Hungary in the Compromise (*Ausgleich*) of 1867, the Czech nation considered this a direct insult – a deliberate effort to demean the industrial, political and social achievements of the empire's strongest economy. A period quip had it that while Budapest built its magisterial Houses of Parliament on the banks of the Danube, Prague erected the Czech National Theatre on the banks of the Vltava.

The same historical moment of Czech cultural and national emancipation witnessed another significant event: the founding of the Sokol movement by Miroslav Tyrš in 1862. The Sokol were modelled loosely on the German *Turner* movement, early nineteenth-century gymnastic clubs that also had a nationalist political agenda. The Czech Sokol movement, however, also had far-reaching cultural ambitions. It was not only a mass gymnastics union; unlike the German *Turnervereine*, the Czech Sokols were committed to the classical Greek concept of *kalokuyulhlu* (the union of physical fitness and mental well-being) and embraced the arts as a crucial aspect of physical and spiritual growth. The Sokols were trained as an unarmed military – to be ready for the moment when the nation became a state and needed armed forces. However, their events and functions were crucially connected with the arts and the theatre – from the establishment of Sokol theatre companies (putting on both live performances and puppet shows) to thematic displays that re-enacted historical events in collaboration with leading Czech theatre practitioners. This was the case, for instance, at the 6th All-Sokol Festival in Prague in 1912, where "Marathon, or Classical Greek Scenes from the Year 490 Before Christ" represented this historical event from Classical Greece. Directed by the head of the Czech National Theatre, Jaroslav Kvapil (1868–1950), performed by 1,000 actors/gymnasts in historical costumes, the event was seen by approximately 80,000 spectators (Frýbertová 2012: 70, 75). These activities educated whole generations across all age groups. The Sokol, with its elaborate structure and aesthetic and ethical codes, also created a significant counterculture that was truly national and also, effectively, subversive vis-à-vis the Austro-Hungarian Empire. The Sokols' performative practices originated in theatre culture and developed it further in the new mode of public mass performances.

Czech theatre as a surrogate space and a laboratory for political life was an integral part of the culture, in the nineteenth and early twentieth centuries as well as later. Many of those involved politically with the new Czechoslovak state were recruited from within the theatre. During World War I, Jaroslav Kvapil, an influential artist and leader of a whole generation, was a member of the anti-Austrian underground organization called the *Maffie*. The *Maffie* was headed by the future Czechoslovak President

Tomáš Garrigue Masaryk and his Foreign Minister and Presidential successor Edvard Beneš (1884–1948) and coordinated by the later Presidential Chancellor Přemysl Šámal (Demetz 2008: 71). Other artists, among them the opera diva Emmy Destinn/Ema Destinnova, were involved as agents and messengers. Theatre served as effective cover. When Czechoslovakia was established, Kvapil became a member of the Czechoslovak Parliament. Similarly, the leading theatre critic Jindřich Vodák (1867–1940) was called to serve at the Ministry of Education and National Enlightenment and later served as a Minister-Counsellor, and the famous writer and dramatist Alois Jirásek (1851–1930) was one of the leaders who proclaimed Czechoslovak independence on 28 October 1918; he later became a Member of Parliament and Senator. In this way the new regime was co-constituted by personalities from the arts, and the theatre in particular.[15]

In addition to the political dimensions of Czech theatrical life, theatre as a tool of learning and knowledge had always been deeply embedded in the culture. Ever since the end of the nineteenth century community life had gradually been moving away from life in the parish, a setting that had become increasingly contested given the role of the Catholic Church in the Austrian Empire. It was amateur theatre (and choral singing in the more religious regions) that became the true heart of cultural and social life in villages, towns and cities. Even today Czech amateur theatre remains a phenomenon of great significance and popularity. It is worth noting that Europe's oldest amateur theatre festival was set up in Czechoslovakia, in 1931; ever since, Jiráskův Hronov (Jirásek's Hronov, named after Alois Jirásek, a native of the small town of Hronov) has been a national event, supported by a number of regional offshoots as well as by other affiliated festivals of amateur theatre. Several regional amateur companies collaborated with leading Czech actors: they would often produce plays that were in the repertoire at the National Theatre in Prague and invite the main actor for a guest appearance.[16] Amateur

---

15   It is worth observing that theatre retained its significant role throughout the twentieth century: the so-called Velvet Revolution of 1989 started in the theatre, with actors and directors joining the strike launched by the students in the wake of their peaceful demonstration of 17 November 1989, which was violently attacked by police forces. Theatres became the venues for public meetings and the process culminated in the election of the dramatist Václav Havel as President, flanked by a number of new politicians recruited from the theatre. This phenomenon has continued to the present day, with a number of key ministerial and parliamentary posts being held by former Czech and Slovak actors and theatre practitioners (for example the dramatist Milan Uhde, the dramaturges Milan Lukeš, Pavel Dostál and Martin Porubjak, the actors Vítězslav Jandák, Martin Štěpánek, Martin Stropnický and others).

16   There are many examples of this practice. An indicative case study – which stands out from the common practice only in its ambition and size – is presented by Eva Stehlíková: in the small village of Heřmaň (532 inhabitants), the local amateur company Heyduk implemented an innovative dramaturgy between 1920 and 1937, putting on between 120 and 200 theatre productions. In 1936, Václav Krška (later to become a leading film director) prepared what turned out to be

theatre has also taken the place of acting schools: it is not uncommon (though less and less so) for a Czech professional actor to have only been trained in an amateur theatre company, or for an amateur theatre company to attain professional status.[17]

The significance of theatre as a cultural phenomenon has also been strongly rooted in puppet theatre.[18] Originally a popular travelling entertainment that developed from early modern performative practices, puppetry played an important cultural role in the Czech-speaking countryside of the late eighteenth and nineteenth centuries. With the arrival of the twentieth century, traditional puppetry began to be perceived as an obsolete form and its popularity diminished rapidly, only to be replaced by a wave of interest in modern puppet theatre in social clubs and in families. This trend, boosted by a generation of avant-garde practitioners and the form's popular advocates, grew into a national phenomenon that complemented amateur theatre. Leading visual artists designed modern puppets and stage sets for commercial firms, who turned out thousands of copies of these toy theatres. Throughout the twentieth century, it was common for every family to have its own small puppet theatre, for children to play with and for parents to perform stories and educative tales.[19] By promoting these imaginative activities in the amateur sphere, puppet theatre engendered whole generations of theatre practitioners and thinkers and served as a channel for expressing creative ambitions.[20] The importance of amateur puppet theatre in Czech culture cannot be overstated – for most Czech children it is through puppets, and at a very early age to boot, that they first encounter the theatre and its power.

Given the centrality of theatre in Czech culture and the historically and politically favourable moment created by the establishment of the new, liberal Czechoslovak state, the emphasis that the Prague School theorists laid

---

the first open-air, almost site-specific production of a Classical Greek play: Sophocles' *Oedipus Rex*, with around 150 performers. The main part was played by Eduard Kohout, the soloist of the National Theatre, who had acted in Karel Hugo Hilar's famous production of 1932 (for details see Stehlíková 2010).

17   This was true not only of some of the leading actors of the past but also, more recently, of leading Czech studio theatres, among them the Goose on a String (Husa na provázku, Brno) and the HaDi Theatre (originally Prostějov, later Brno), which began as an amateur ensemble and evolved over time into a professional company (HaDi).

18   For a comprehensive treatment of the phenomenon of Czech puppet theatre, see Billing and Drábek (2015).

19   For the phenomenon of Czech family puppet theatres, see the research of Jaroslav Blecha (Blecha 2011) and Marie Jirásková and Pavel Jirásek's essay in Billing and Drábek (2015). For the early twentieth-century movement called the Puppetry Renaissance, see Martin Bernátek's essay in Billing and Drábek (2015). In 2016, Czech and Slovak puppetry was inscribed on the UNESCO's Representative List of the Intangible Cultural Heritage of Humanity.

20   Pavel Kohout, a leading Czech playwright of the late twentieth century, is only one among many who have recognized their debt to their early experiences with family puppet theatre.

on the dramatic art is not surprising. The cultural role of theatre – something unique in the international context – allowed the theories to be taken
not as critical commentaries on an agreeable pastime but rather as theoretical attempts at tackling a highly complex art form that had profound and
direct repercussions in the formation of the everyday reality of Czechoslovakia as a newly modelled culture and an experiment in social and political
interaction.

ARTISTIC EXPERIMENTS OF THE CZECH AVANT-GARDE

The PLC was a community of scholars as well as artists and its close relations with the Czech avant-garde were marked by a significant mutual influence.

The new state of Czechoslovakia fuelled artistic experiments and allowed the free expression of ambitions in a wide range of interests. In October 1920 an artistic group called Devětsil (literally *nine forces*, a playful name for the butterbur, used in traditional folk medicine) was formed in Prague, bringing together initially fifteen personalities from different artistic disciplines, suggestive of the classical Nine Muses. The Devětsil organized lectures, poetry evenings and theatre performances, stressing the proletariat, anti-bourgeois nature of their art. The group's aesthetic direction was later termed *Poetism* – a new movement inspired by Dada but abandoning its mechanical randomness in favour of a poetic vision of the world. The artists associated with the group, led by the "father" of the Czechoslovak avant-garde Karel Teige (1900–1951), were often recruited from Marxist intellectuals and sympathizers. In February 1921 a rival initiative emerged in Brno under the name of the Literary Group (*Literární skupina*), led by František Götz (1894–1974); it was based on the principles of Expressionism. Both groups had a significant and lasting influence on the theatre, Götz becoming the dramaturge of the National Theatre Prague and Jindřich Honzl of the Devětsil developing into a leading avant-garde director of the Liberated Theatre; he also served as a director and dramaturge in the Brno theatre.

It is significant that from the very early years of the new cultural and political situation theatre was approached as a synthesis of various arts and inspiration flowed freely between individual artistic disciplines. This was an organic change in the traditional theatre trades, and it was not uncommon for an artist established in one discipline to reach success and recognition in other spheres. Jindřich Honzl (1894–1953) was originally a secondary-school teacher of physics and mathematics. In the 1920s he established himself as a specialist in modern Russian and Soviet theatre with visionary publications such as his 1922 essay "Nestavte divadla" (Don't Build Theatres) and his books/manifestoes *Roztočené jeviště: úvahy o novém divadle* (The Whirling Stage: Reflections on the New Theatre, 1925), *Vznik ruského moderního divadla* (The Rise

Fig. 8: Cover of Jindřich Honzl's first book, *Roztočené jeviště* [The Whirling Stage], 1925. The graphic design, by Karel Teige, makes use of a photomontage created by the leading Czech Surrealists Toyen and Jindřich Štyrský.

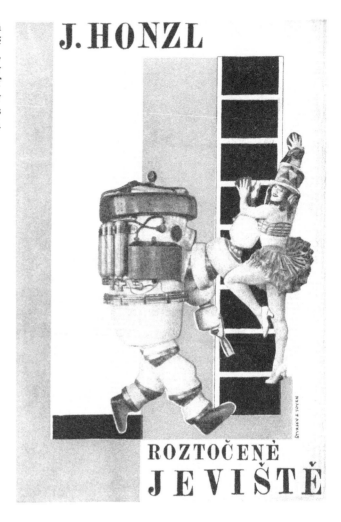

of Modern Russian Theatre, 1927) and *Moderní ruské divadlo* (Modern Russian Theatre, 1928). Profoundly influenced by Konstantin Stanislavsky, Vsevolod Meyerhold and Alexander Tairov as well as by the Russian avant-garde film techniques of the collage and montage as promoted by Sergei Eisenstein, Honzl presented his views on modern acting styles, the expectations for stagecraft as well as other aspects of aesthetics and ideology.

In 1926, along with his younger peers, the stage director Jiří Frejka and the composer, musician and later stage director E. F. Burian, Honzl founded the Liberated Theatre as a theatre section of the Devětsil. Their activity began in February 1926 with the revived production of Jiří Frejka's *Circus Dandin* (of May 1925) – a playful variation on Molière's *George Dandin*. In April 1927 the Liberated Theatre hosted a guest performance by a comedy cabaret called *Vest Pocket Revue* (1927) by Jiří Voskovec (1905–1981) and Jan Werich (1905–1980).

Fig. 9: Ivan Goll's *Methuselah*, directed by Jindřich Honzl, at the Liberated Theatre, 1927. This early production by the Liberated Theatre used Meyerhold's technique of biomechanics.

The tremendous success of this show led Honzl to invite the Voskovec and Werich duo to join the Liberated Theatre, later directing some of their productions, including the film version of their *Pudr a benzín* (Powder and Petrol, 1931). Voskovec and Werich became the legendary V+W – a phenomenal theatre enterprise of the late 1920s and the 1930s. With their jazz-inspired composer Jaroslav Ježek (1906–1942), who contributed music to their songs and shows, they created a defining era of Czech theatre history and hold a "completely unique position in the context of European avant-garde theatre" (Císař 2010: 263; see also Burian 2002: 20–39). In their era as well as somewhat in their style, they were peers of Brecht and Weill and their avant-

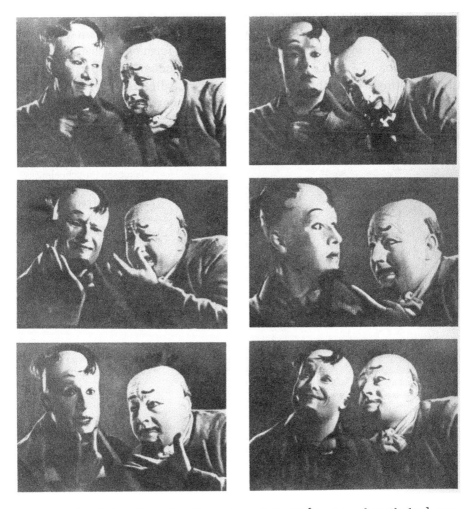

Fig. 10: A series of photos from the anti-war drama *Osel a stín* [The Ass and His Shadow], 1933, capturing the rich play of facial expressions of Jiří Voskovec and Jan Werich, who both wrote and acted in the plays in which they appeared.

garde experiments. The Liberated Theatre soon became completely identified with V+W. Burian and Frejka left the company in 1927 and Honzl took up the position of stage director and dramaturge in Brno, handing over the reins to V+W as actor-managers. It is noteworthy that the Liberated Theatre continued to interact with the Prague Linguistic Circle. The publication marking the tenth anniversary of the Liberated Theatre in 1937 contained an essay in appreciation of V+W's art by Roman Jakobson entitled "An open letter from Roman Jakobson to Jiří Voskovec and Jan Werich on the Epistemology and Semantics of Fun" (Jakobson 1987 [1937]).

Another prime example of the variability and synthetic nature of the Czechoslovak avant-garde was the multi-talented E. F. Burian. Like Honzl, he was a member of the Devětsil group. He made his career as an actor, singer and opera composer (Spurná 2014), writing four full-length avant-garde operas before turning his hand to an experimental form of musical recitation called Voiceband – a jazz-inspired precursor to modern group rap – and to stage directing. With another leading avant-garde director, Jiří Frejka (1904–1952), he left the Devětsil and the Liberated Theatre after disagreements with the impulsive Honzl and established an experimental theatre company called

Fig. 11: Adolf Hoffmeister: "Jakobson the schoolmaster examining his pupils", 1933. Period caricature of Roman Jakobson and the Liberated Theatre actors Jiří Voskovec and Jan Werich, an illustration for a proposed monograph on V + W's popular songs that Jakobson was writing but never actually completed.

Profesor Jakobson zkouší žáky.

Fig.12: Photo from Burian's production of *The Barber of Seville*, set by Miroslav Kouřil, 1937.

Fig. 13: The director Jiří Frejka with a model of the set for his production of Vladislav Vančura's *Jezero Ukereve* [Lake Ukereve] at the National Theatre, 1936.

Divadlo Dada (1927). Burian then worked as a stage director in Olomouc in 1930 and later transferred to Brno before establishing what became another leading theatre company in Prague in 1933 – the D 34 (see also Jarka M. Burian's chapter dedicated to EFB; Burian 2002: 40–58).

Burian also experimented with different theatre traditions, combining the more conventional staging of playscripts with an avid interest in the dramatization of other texts (see Mukařovský's essay "Dialogue and Monologue" in this reader, pp. 220–46) and in folklore, staging folk poetry and folk plays such as the folk play of *St Dorothy*, the lurid all-female farce *Salička* and the *Begging Bacchus*, which comprised his 1939 *First Folk Suite*. His production of *Manon Lescaut* (1940), a poetic adaptation by Vítězslav Nezval of the 1731 romance by Abbé Prévost, became a defining moment in Czechoslovak culture during the Protectorate regime (Demetz 2008: 153).

On leaving the Liberated Theatre, Jiří Frejka set up the Modern Studio (*Moderní studio*) in 1929, proposing to pursue an a-political Dada programme of voiceband and poetical productions, discovering new playwrights and synthesizing artistic efforts in theatre form. The programme was influenced by the poetics of Jean Cocteau, for instance his 1924 ballet version of *Romeo and Juliet* with music by Igor Stravinsky. For the Modern Studio's production of *Romeo and Juliet* in 1929 Miloš Hlávka, the company's dramaturge, radically cut the play's text with a view to creating fast-paced, mime-based scenes. The production raised some controversy but helped to establish the unique style of the company. Soon after, Frejka left the Modern Studio after Karel Hugo Hilar invited him to join the National Theatre as a stage director. This started a fruitful era and, very importantly, Frejka's collaboration with the stage designer František Tröster. In 1934 he staged an adaptation of Aristophanes' *The Birds*, co-written with the satirist Václav Lacina; the production unwittingly became a political act, as it resonated harshly with the Nazis' recent accession to power in Germany. In the following year, Frejka's production of Lope de Vega's *Fuente Ovejuna* (staged as *Vzbouření na vsi* (The Village Rebellion)) capitalized on its political dimension. A similarly decisive moment was Frejka's and Tröster's production of Shakespeare's *Julius Caesar* in 1936 (Miholová 2011).

All three leading avant-garde theatre directors of the 1930s – Honzl, Frejka and Burian – were also active as theorists and contributed to the seminars of the Prague Linguistic Circle. In fact they had contributed to the debate about modern theatre even before the PLC was established: Burian, for instance, theorized his practice in a series of essays dedicated to stage space, the stage metaphor and musical rhythm (*Polydynamika*, 1925), and the use of photography and film in the theatre (see the essays by Burian in this reader, pp. 284–89, 497–500). Frejka contributed with a series of reflections, for instance in his very brief early essay "Cesta moderního jevištního myšlení" (The

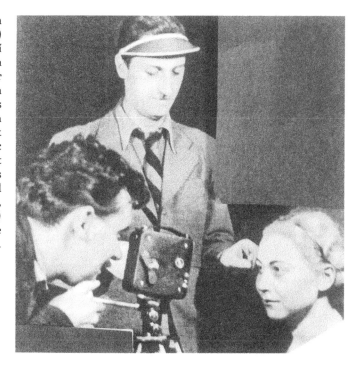

Fig. 14: E. F. Burian (looking into the camera) and the cameraman Jiří Lehovec shooting a film sequence with the dancer Anna Fischlová. Burian used the material for his own stage adaptation of the poet Karel Hynek Mácha's Romantic classic *Máj* [May], produced at Theatre D 35, 1935. Burian's production combined voiceband declamation, dance, film (and photo) projection and the live action of actors on stage.

Progress of Modern Stage Thinking), which calls for "an ecstatic theatre, full of amusing analogies, funny and unburdened by literature" (Frejka 1926). In his 1929 treatise *Člověk, který se stal hercem* (How People Become Actors), Frejka argues that "the aim of the stage is not to imitate life; that is the purpose of life itself." Due to its entertaining role, the theatre is a place where

> we want to encounter something new, an art that will entertain and please us, capture our imagination and drag us out of thoughts about everyday work and worries, and will teach us how to look at the world. (Frejka 1929)

Honzl, Burian and Frejka continued to publish essays on theatre practice throughout the 1930s and, to a lesser extent, in the 1940s. Very significantly, their activities inspired other Prague School theorists – in particular Petr Bogatyrev, Roman Jakobson, Jan Mukařovský and Jiří Veltruský – and triggered groundbreaking contributions to theatre theory based on an organic synergy with innovative theatre practice.

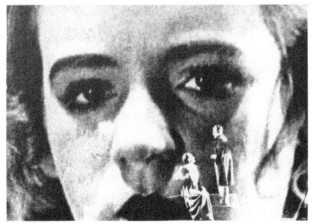

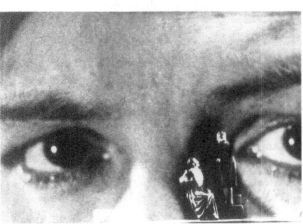

Fig. 15: E. F. Burian's production of his own adaptation of Frank Wedekind's *Spring Awakening* at Theatre D 36, 1936. The photographs depict one of the closing scenes of the production. On the stage the actors playing the parents of the protagonist, Melchior, are discussing his supposed moral lapse with no empathy whatsoever. A film projection first shows the faces of the three main teenage characters in the play. Then the film cuts to the face of the dead Wendla, who is in fact the victim of insensitive upbringing at the hands of her parents. The image zooms in slowly to a detail of her reproachful young eyes, contrasting with the total absence of emotion in the dialogue of the parents present on stage. In this way Burian employs a montage technique to contrast filmic detail with live acting.

Fig. 16: A scene from a production of Vladislav Vančura's *Učitel a žák* [The Teacher and the Pupil] directed by Jindřich Honzl at the National Theatre Studio, Prague, 1945. The set, which was based on the use of slides, was designed by the Surrealist painter Toyen. Honzl later remarked: "Toyen understood very well that only stages filled with real things or evoking quite real things in our imagination have the capacity to be poetic. This is why she abandoned all abstract stage constructions of surfaces, the abstract use of colours and lights, and replaced them with [...] photomontages, which replace each other through projection so easily and so imaginatively that they best suit the movement of the dramatic thought."

THE PRAGUE SCHOOL AND THE CINEMA

Members of the PLC were among the first film theorists
and helped emancipate the new medium as a serious subject of study.

Alongside theatre, Prague School scholars also reflected theoretically on cinema. Film became a recurring source of inspiration, resulting in one of the earliest systematic critical theories of the medium. On the one hand, Prague School film theory explores film's dependence on the older arts (especially theatre and literature), approaching film from an intermedial perspective. On the other hand, the writings attempt to establish film as an "autonomous art" with its own "material" and "laws" (Jakobson 1976 [1933]: 145). In addition, film also provided the opportunity for a convenient case study to test their theories.

Jan Mukařovský's 1931 essay "An Attempt at a Structural Analysis of an Actor's Figure" (this reader, pp. 192–98) analyses Charlie Chaplin's performance in *City Lights* (1931). It is the first definition of the term *structure* in connection with a dramatic art form, demonstrating its validity by analysing Chaplin's acting style. Like language and literature, Mukařovský perceived Chaplin's figure as a structure consisting of actualized and automatized elements. Chaplin's gestures, posture and facial expressions are considered as the actualized components (that is, the dominant ones), while his movements represent subordinated ones. Mukařovský's study is worth comparing with two studies of Chaplin by Petr Bogatyrev ("Chaplin and *The Kid*" and "Chaplin, the Fake Count", 1923, both in this reader, pp. 175–84 and 185–91); the comparison suggests a shift from Bogatyrev's formalism to Mukařovský's pre-semiotic structuralism. Bogatyrev deals with the problem of how Chaplin transforms literary and theatrical principles into film. Like Viktor Shklovsky, Bogatyrev talks about several devices and principles of construction, including contrasts, retardation and parallelism, upon which Chaplin builds his comedies. The aesthetic qualities of Chaplin's persona and acting are identified through a structural analysis that is closely related to Shklovsky's notion of *estrangement (ostranenie)*. In their essays, Mukařovský and Bogatyrev show the potential of their respective concepts *aktualisace* and *ostranenie*, which were originally devised for the study of language and

Fig. 17: Cover of Karel Teige's *A World of Laughter*, 1928. One of the manifestos of the Czech avant-garde, the book is subtitled "On Humour, Clowns and Dadaists".

KAREL TEIGE:

SVĚT, KTERÝ SE SMĚJE

Odeon   1928

literature, and apply them to film. By implication, they show their potential for other arts too.

Another significant contribution of Bogatyrev's studies of film is the notion of film's dependence on other arts, to be specific on the techniques of literature and theatre. This was later elaborated by Mukařovský, Yury Tynyanov, Roman Jakobson and Bogatyrev himself. A decade later, in 1933, Mukařovský in his essay "K estetice filmu" (A Note on the Aesthetics of Film) and Jakobson in his "Úpadek filmu?" ("Is Cinema in Decline?") also accept that film draws on techniques of other arts, namely literature, the visual arts and theatre; however, in their essays they shift the terminology further when they observe that certain devices are deployed in relation to aesthetic norms and their violation – that is, they serve the purpose of *actualization*. Jakobson makes the claim that film, in a mutual relationship with older arts, "creates its own norms, its own laws, and then confidently rejects them" (Jakobson 1976 [1933]: 145). In other words, Jakobson is saying that even though film borrows from other arts it is an autonomous art and its development should be discussed primarily on its own, independent of other arts.

A similar view is expressed in Bogatyrev's study "Disneyova *Sněhurka*" (Disney's *Snow White*, 1938); Bogatyrev reformulates Jakobson's argument in the language of semiotics. At the same time there is a significant difference between their studies. In 1933, Jakobson tried to establish the laws of filmic art – at that time still unfixed and insufficiently defined – while six years later, when Bogatyrev was writing, the position of film as an independent art was more or less taken for granted.

As in the case of folklore and exotic art, film theory was formulated and reformulated along with the development of the Prague School, moving from formalism (Bogatyrev 1923) through pre-semiotic structuralism (Mukařovský 1931) to the semiotic theory of film (Jakobson 1933 and Bogatyrev 1938). Although Prague School film theory is based on popular film (mainly the films of Chaplin), it is equally valid for cinematic art in general and some of the work also for the theatre (Elam 1980, Ambros 2012). Moreover, by comparing film with other arts, Prague School writing also represents an important contribution to the theory of intermediality, or to use Mukařovský's terms, the "comparative semiotics of the arts" (Mukařovský 1982a [1940]).

In the study of new media, of great significance was the Prague School's radio theory, an activity connected especially with Olga Srbová (1914–1987), who made a name for herself in the 1930s and early 1940s as an influential theatre critic. Her rich output features not only original texts on actors and acting and on the theory of drama – for examples her 1937 essay on the significance of *didascalia* (stage directions in play texts) – but also several essays dedicated to the theory of the radio. In an article in 1941 Srbová theorizes the difference between the dramatic illusion in the theatre and that in the radio, a point succinctly summarized by Eva Stehlíková:

> While the theatre spectator sees a stage set representing a forest (and knows all the time that these are merely decorations), when listening to the radio (just like when reading a novel) the listener "does not imagine a canvas and colours, but a real forest; this is no longer a system of theatrical signs but the real thing" (Srbová 1941: 18).[21] The

---

21 In 1941 Srbová published an extensive study dedicated to the radio, entitled *Rozhlas a slovesnost* (The Radio and Verbal Art), originally published as part of a series of articles in *Slovo a slovesnost* (Praha: Vyšehrad, 1941). The reference in Stehlíková is made to this study.

theatre spectator becomes a direct witness of the action, while the radio illusion is more intense than the theatrical, literary and even filmic illusion. (Stehlíková 2016: 186)

Srbová also pioneered theoretical reflections on audience participation in the theatre and in the radio, distinguishing between the role of the recipient of a theatre performance or a concert within the public sphere as opposed to that of the solitary listener beside the radio set, who exists in an intimate space (Stehlíková 2016: 186). After World War II, Srbová gave up her theoretical work and had a successful and influential career in the radio – a theorist turned practitioner.

THE PRAGUE SCHOOL AND THE PUPPET THEATRE

Another significant context of the Prague School is the international rise
of interest in puppets, known as the Puppetry Renaissance,
culminating in the establishment of the UNIMA in Prague in 1929.
The puppet theatre was a fruitful stimulus for critical reflection.

In 1911, the world's oldest puppet theatre association was established in Prague – Český svaz přátel loutkového divadla (The Czech Union of Friends of the Puppet Theatre). A year later the historian, puppet collector and puppetry enthusiast Jindřich Veselý (1885–1939), a leading personality of the era, founded a new journal entitled *Český loutkář* (The Czech Puppeteer), shortened in 1914 to simply *Loutkář* (The Puppeteer); still appearing, it is the world's longest-running periodical dedicated to puppetry. These initiatives were the culmination of a wide range of activities by cultural societies and clubs. The rise of mass interest in puppet theatre was an international phenomenon: from Oscar Wilde's musings on the puppet, through the well-known writing of Edward Gordon Craig (1872–1966) and his inspiring correspondence with the Hungarian theatre artist Sándor Hevesi (1873–1939),[22] to developments in Germany and Austria.[23] As early as 1858 Josef Leonard "Papa" Schmid (1822–1912) established the Munich Puppet Theatre (Münchner Marionettentheater), later followed by Paul Brann (1873–1955) in his Munich Artists' Puppet Theatre (Marionettentheater der Münchner Künstler); the well-known puppeteer Ivo Puhonny (1876–1940) was the founder of the influential Artistic Puppet Theatre in Baden Baden (Baden-Badener Künstler-Marionettentheater); artistic experiments with puppets were also undertaken by Richard Teschner (1879–1948) in his Viennese workshop theatre and elsewhere (Bernátek 2015: 145–6). Psychologists and psychiatrists showed an equally enthusiastic interest in puppets: Ernst Jentsch (1867–1919) wrote a famous essay, "On the Psychology of the Uncanny" (Zur Psychologie des Unheimlichen, 1906), and Sigmund Freud contributed to the debate with his 1919 essay "The Uncanny" (Das Unheimliche), both significant contributions to an understanding of

---

22   See Székely 1991. (Thanks to Gabriella Reuss of Péter Pazmány University for drawing my attention to this source. – P. Drábek)

23   For a discussion of Craig's puppet theory, see Shershow 1995: 193ff.

the puppet and of how the mind perceives its mysterious quality (see Bell 2014). In the Czech lands, the international phenomenon of family puppet theatre (or toy theatres) led to significant developments in the visual arts: it was mainly through the initiative of Jindřich Veselý that leading painters and stage designers were commissioned to design sets for serial production. The widespread fascination with puppets permeated nearly all strata of the society, from leisure activities, through education to the influence it had on the new medium of the cinema (Bernátek 2015). This phenomenon soon came to be known as the Puppetry Renaissance – *"eine Renaissance des Puppenspiels"*, as Paul Rilla called it in 1914. Alongside the thousands of new amateur puppet theatre makers appearing across Europe, a number of professional associations were established – Nos marionettes, founded by Gaston Cony in France (1917); a German association of puppet theatres established in 1921; and the British organization The Puppet and Model Theatre Guild (1925). The indefatigable Veselý launched and curated a number of puppetry exhibitions and managed to popularize puppetry widely. It therefore came as no surprise when, in May 1929, during an international puppet theatre exhibi-

Fig. 18: Puppets by traditional Czech puppeteers, from Petr Bogatyrev's *Czech and Slovak Folk Theatre*.

tion in Prague organized by the Masarykův lidovýchovný ústav (the Masaryk Educational Institute), the International Puppetry Association (UNIMA – Union internationale de la marionette) was founded, with Prague as its seat and *Loutkář* becoming its official publication platform in the opening years. Veselý was elected the UNIMA's first President (Billing and Drábek 2015: 5).

The Czech puppetry renaissance may only be tangentially relevant to the Prague School theory. However, its impact on Czech culture was far-reaching. Not only did it establish a widespread respect for puppet theatre, an art form that had often been mocked as negligible, obsolete and infantile; it also activated other artistic disciplines. Theatre with live performers was confronted with the popularity of the puppet theatre and was forced to respond to it at least as much as it did to the popular medium of the cinema. Playwrights were stimulated to write for puppet theatre – an equally international phenomenon, thanks to Maurice Maeterlinck's influential plays for puppets as well as Craig's own (incomplete) cycle of puppet plays called *Drama for Fools* (1914–1921). On a more national level, a number of new plays were written with a particular educational purpose. Puppetry was an important catalyst for the visual arts. The fact that leading visual artists designed for the puppet theatre and that these often avant-garde stage designs found their way into families and were absorbed by the public *as an everyday reality*, had an unprecedented impact on openness and tolerance towards modernity and progressive ideas. Alongside the cinema, puppetry significantly influenced architecture and a discipline that we would call now creative technologies. Hand in hand with the new visual media (cinema being only one of them), a number of multifunction "theatres" were build in the early decades of the century to accommodate film screenings as well as various live performance art forms. Many of these construction projects necessitated innovative technological solutions and led to the development of new performance technologies.[24] In this way, avant-garde artists became household names and phenomena – a crucial factor in paving the way for the Prague School's avant-garde theories. It is also no coincidence that the two founding texts anticipating the Prague School's theatre theory – and by extension theatre theory as such – were two essays on puppet theatre published in 1923 and written in Czechoslovakia: Otakar Zich's "Puppet Theatre" and a study by Petr Bogatyrev entitled "Czech Puppet Theatre and Russian Folk Theatre".[25] Both appeared almost a decade before the PLC's members published their first

---

24   For more details of the relation between the cinema and puppet theatre, see Bernátek 2015. Martin Bernátek is also working on a project dedicated to media change and innovations in theatre architecture.

25   Zich's essay was first published in English in Billing and Drábek (2015: 505–13); Bogatyrev's essay first appeared in English in *TDR/The Drama Review*, vol. 43, no. 3 (T163; Fall 1999): pp. 97–114.

texts on theatre and, of course, were responding to the phenomenal success of the Puppetry Renaissance.[26]

---

26   Bogatyrev was a leading member of the PLC. Otakar Zich (who died in 1934) expressed his appreciation of and support for the functional-structural method of the Prague Linguistic Circle in an interview in 1933 (Novák 1933: 467–8). Zich attended some of the PLC lectures, and in 1933 even gave one himself, on poetic rhythm. Although he did not become a formal member, perhaps owing to his early death, his 1931 book *The Aesthetics of Dramatic Art* was regarded as foundational by the PLC theatre theorists.

THE PRAGUE SCHOOL, FOLKLORE AND MODERN ETHNOGRAPHY

Among the interests of Prague School theorists were folklore and popular phenomena. Petr Bogatyrev was the leading proponent of research in this area as well as of a modern concept of ethnography. His interest in the theatrical aspects of folklore culminated in a number of theatre projects with E. F. Burian's Theatre D.

Another significant context that provided a productive intellectual confluence in the 1920s was the study of folklore and culture. Both Russian and Czech scholars had an avid interest in ethnography, not only as a continuation of the Romantic vogue for pure, folk art but also as a modern scholarly endeavour to understand the cultural specifics of individual nations. Czech ethnography had played a significant role in the emancipation of modern Czech culture; collecting folklore was part of the nationalist agenda of consolidating this culture's specific features. The leading figure of the period, the ethnographer Čeněk Zíbrt (1864–1932), became the first editor of the influential journal *Český lid* (The Czech People, established in 1891). *Český lid* published a vast amount of material on folklore and it played a key role in the understanding of folk theatre, among other areas. The Czech variant of the Puppetry Renaissance was substantially connected with these ethnographic endeavours: the first large exhibition of traditional Czech puppetry, which can be taken as the very start of the movement, took place as part of the *Národopisná výstava českoslovanská* (Czechoslavic Ethnographic Exhibition) in Prague in 1895 (Bernátek 2015: 135).[27] Another crucial figure in Czech ethnography was Václav Tille (1867–1937), a co-founder of the journal *Národopisný věstník českoslovanský* (The Czechoslavic Ethnographic Journal, established in 1906). Tille, who taught at Charles University, had a decisive influence on a whole generation of literary theorists and translators, many of whom became leading figures of the Prague School. These included René Wellek, for whom Tille was an inspirational figure along with the PLC founder Vilém Mathesius,

---

[27] Čeněk Zíbrt was a Professor of cultural history and it was probably his influence and that of Arnošt Vilém Kraus (1859–1943), a Professor of German, that led Jindřich Veselý to his interest in traditional folk puppeteers. Kraus published a critical edition of the traditional puppet play of *Johannes Doktor Faust* in 1904. This was most likely the impetus behind Veselý's decision to write his dissertation on *Čeští loutkáři a* Faust (Czech Puppeteers and *Faust*, 1909).

and the poet, translator and dramaturge Otokar Fischer (1883–1938).[28] Czech ethnographic research was far from retrospective: it was an active tool for articulating the popular culture. The above-mentioned phenomena of amateur theatre and puppet theatre should be perceived as ethnographic realities as much as cultural trends.

Peter Bogatyrev and Roman Jakobson had been active in folklore studies long before coming to Czechoslovakia. It is less known that Nikolai Trubetzkoy shared their interest and training in ethnography. Both Jakobson and Trubetskoy studied with Vladimir Vladimirovich Bogdanov (1868–1949), the leading Russian ethnographer at the turn of the century (Jakobson and Pomorska 1980: 2–3). When Jakobson started his university studies in Moscow in 1914, he joined the older students Bogatyrev and Nikolai Feofanovich Yakovlev (1892–1974); under the supervision of Nikolai Ivanovich Narskiy and Vsevolod Fyodorovich Miller they were "pushed [...] to collect and study Russian folklore" (3).[29] Jakobson recollects his ethnographic beginnings: "It is worth noting that in our collective research and recording of popular works, we always insisted on working in an area close to the capital – in the districts of the old government of Moscow, that of Vereja, for example" (Jakobson and Pomorska 1980: 4).

In 1919 Bogatyrev and Jakobson worked together in writing "Programma po sobiranii svedeniiu o narodnom teatre" (A Programme for the Study of Folk Theatre); however, the text was published in Petrograd in 1923 without Jakobson's name after Bogatyrev compromised the methodological framework they had developed (Jakobson and Pomorska 1980: 15). After they moved to Czechoslovakia, their ethnographic interests continued and cannot be divorced from their other critical endeavours – as in their co-authored article "K problematike razmezhevaniia folkloristiki i literaturovedeniia" (On the Boundary between Studies of Folklore and Literature, 1931). Bogatyrev grew to become a leading figure in Czechoslovak folklore studies and Jakobson, too, made significant contributions to the discipline, for example in their jointly written 1929 essay "Die Folklore als eine besondere Form des Schaffens" (Folklore as a Special Form of Creativity).[30] These two folkloristic essays were immediate applications of contemporary linguistic and literary theories. Following closely on Yury Tynyanov and Jakobson's "Problems in the Study of Literature and Language" (Tynyanov and Jakobson 1978 [1928]) and the

---

28   For the decisive influence of Václav Tille and Otokar Fischer on the avant-garde generation of translators of the 1920s and 1930s, see Drábek 2012a: 158, 161–64.

29   For the folkloric strand in Jakobson's work see also Chapter 2 in Toman 1995.

30   Galit Hasan-Rokem highlighted the significance of this text in her paper "Roman Jakobson's 'Die Folklore als eine besondere Form des Schaffens' [Folklore as a Special Form of Creativity] (1929) in a disciplinary-historical perspective", delivered at the Prague Semiotic Stage Revisited II international symposium in Brno in May 2013.

"Theses" of the Prague Linguistic Circle (1929), they make use of the same terminology and propose the same approach; as such they can also be perceived
as transitional studies between Russian Formalism and Prague Structuralism (Kaplan 1984: 232). In their approach, folklore was not a cultural fetish
collected and conserved by patriots but a crucial *formative* force that was
ceaselesly active in constructing the society and the nation – a construct that
Benedict Anderson would, half a century later, term *imagined communities*
(Anderson 1983). This force comprised not only traditional folklore but also
modern myths, gossip and superstitions. As Jakobson points out, while in
Czechoslovakia in the 1920s and 1930s

> Bogatyrev insisted on the importance of collecting the superstitions that had currency
> among various professions. He published his observations on the superstitions pro-
> fessed by actors and sportsmen, and planned to deal with the superstitions of the left-
> and right-wing members of the Czech Parliament. (Jakobson and Pomorska 1980: 17)

Bogatyrev's "Herecké pověry" (Actors' Superstitions), co-written with
Vladimír Ryba, was published in 1927; this text presents a range of contemporary beliefs and customs current among professional actors that were
practised to make the profession more bearable – to cope with the stress and
risks of theatre performances or to bond with the troupe and the audiences.
It is important to note that both Jakobson and Bogatyrev were analysing the
society and folklore of their immediate surroundings rather than distant and
somewhat idealized (or somehow "authentic") ethnic groups. This is perfectly
in line with a key feature of their version of *cultural activism*: connecting
elements and aspects that are conventionally left separate as having no relationship.[31] This fundamental *modus operandi* is as valid in their studies of
contemporary Moscow folklore and professional superstitions as it is in their
analyses of the latest Disney animated films (Bogatyrev's 1938 essay on Disney's *Snow White*), their examination of the humour of leading avant-garde
comedians (Jakobson's 1937 analytical essay on Voskovec and Werich's "epis-
tomology and semantics of fun") or complex arguments on the relationship
between phonology and semantics in poetry. The Prague Linguistic Circle
never abandoned the ethnographic aspect of their work, and they participated in international academic platforms where they presented their method
and work, for example at the 1st International Congress of Anthropological
and Ethnological Sciences in London in 1934. Taken from this perspective,
the PLC's functional-structural method was in essence *ethnographic* in an

---

31   Though never a member of the PLC, Václav Tille shared a number of their features, among them
     a vital, avant-garde energy aimed at embracing and grappling critically with all that was new. As
     early as 1908 he wrote a study on the cinema entitled "Kinéma" (see Szczepanik and Anděl 2008).

avant-garde way in that it analysed phenomena of contemporary society. As Jaroslav Kolár has observed, when it came to Bogatyrev's three main thematic fields – ethnography, literary folklore and theatre – his work underwent "a methodological development that was common to all three" (Kolár 1971: 181). It is not an exaggeration to state that these analytical *quasi-ethnographic* forays were forerunners of what is known nowadays as *cultural studies*.

The ethnographic strand of Prague School theatre theory came full circle in E. F. Burian's work with Theatre D in the late 1930s, when he created two productions based on folk plays and customs, *První lidová suita* and *Druhá lidová suita* (The First and Second Folk Suites, 1938 and 1939). Burian and Bogatyrev collaborated on these two theatre productions; Bogatyrev's role was

Fig. 19: E. F. Burian: *Vojna* [War], 1935. From a production by Burian based on a montage of folk poetry, dances and customs that was also inspired by Bogatyrev's ethnographic research.

to contribute with a number of essays to the Theatre D's cultural journal (*Program D 39*), such as his "Lidové divadlo" (Folk Theatre, *Program D 39*: 1938–1939: 151–57). Veronika Ambros presents this collaboration as "an excellent example of such a synergy" between Russian ethnography and Czech avant-garde theatre, realized under the direct influence of the Prague Linguistic Circle (Ambros 2004).[32]

---

32   Of great importance was also Burian's 1940 opera *Maryša*, based on Alois and Vilém Mrštík's 1894 drama of the same name and profoundly influenced by Moravian folklore (Spurná 2014: 123–49).

THE PRAGUE SCHOOL'S ETHNOGRAPHIC THEORY AND THE THEATRE

The Prague School's inclusive ethnographic theory had its applications in theatre theory, including theories of intercultural theatre.

Petr Bogatyrev's ground-breaking contribution to ethnography and the study of popular cultures started with his application of linguistic and literary theories to folklore and popular phenomena. In turn, his studies of folklore and popular cultures influenced the texts of Jan Mukařovský, Jiří Veltruský and other Prague School scholars as well as contemporary avant-garde theatre practice. From the outset, Bogatyrev and Jakobson criticized the nineteenth-century ethnographic approach of exploring folklore phenomena genetically and heuristically, culminating in Hans Naumann's theory that proposed the idea that phenomena from higher strata of society are transferred mechanically or noncreatively to lower strata. Bogatyrev and Jakobson opposed this classist and condescending model and proposed a structural and functional approach to explain the fundamental features and principles of folklore.

Two studies published in 1929 and 1931 – "Folklore as a Special Form of Creativity" and "On the Boundary between Studies of Folklore and Literature", respectively – as well as Bogatyrev's later texts are heavily influenced by Saussurian linguistics in that that they utilize the concepts of *langue* and *parole* (that is, language as a general code and language in particular use); synchronic and diachronic research; and concepts of the centre and the periphery linked with productive and non-productive elements. Bogatyrev and Jakobson transpose these linguistic concepts and deploy them in the realm of folklore and ethnography. In accordance with Saussure and hand in hand with late Russian Formalism and Prague Structuralism, Bogatyrev and Jakobson perceive folklore as a structure of components and functions; these are organized hierarchically and keep evolving over time. Referring to Yury Tynyanov, Bogatyrev understands the evolution or transformation of a system not as a "sudden and complete renovation or the replacement of formal elements, but rather the new function of these formal elements," resulting in diverse "functional systems" (Tynyanov 1978: 77). In a parallel to the formation and development of language through the novel use of words, phrases or grammar, folklore and popular culture make innovative and functional use of existing elements, realized through a particular deployment at a given moment. Functionalism occupies a central position in Bogatyrev's theories of folk phenomena such as folk song, costume, theatre and architecture. He observes that each phenomenon fulfils several aesthetic as well as extra-aesthetic functions – for example magic, gender, erotic, moral, religious – and these are organized into a hierarchy. The hierarchy of functions changes as a phenomenon moves in time and/or space, an example being the cultural phenomenon of the Christmas tree (as he pointed out in his 1932 essay on "The Christmas Tree in Eastern Slovakia"; see Jakobson 1985: 295–96).

Bogatyrev's functionalism was directed primarily against Hans Naumann's theory of the *Gesunkenes Kulturgut* (submerged or sunken cultural value). According to Naumann, the folk or "primitives" (as Naumann refers to lower strata) do not produce, but only reproduce; folk culture does not create but only appropriates high-brow art. Bogatyrev (and Jakobson) agreed with Naumann that folk art appropriates high art, but with a proviso:

> What is fundamental to the science of folklore is not the origin and existence of the sources outside of folklore, but the function of appropriation, the selection and the transformation of the appropriated material. ... The transformation of a work belonging to so-called high art into the so-called primitive is, likewise, a creative act. Creativity expresses itself here not only in the selection of the works appropriated but also in their adaptation to other customs and demands. (Bogatyrev and Jakobson 1982 [1929]: 40)

Echoing Mukařovský, Bogatyrev perceives transfers from "high" art to "low" art as a creative act governed by a dialectical struggle between two different norms (Bogatyrev 1971 [1936]). Bogatyrev also raises a second major objection to Naumann's theory, pointing to the fact that high-brow art also borrows from folk and "primitive" art – giving telling examples from the work of Pushkin, Picasso, Stravinsky and Meyerhold. Given this mutual dependence of high-brow and low-brow art, Bogatyrev argues that one cannot talk of the *sinking* of art from high to low, but rather of the "constant interpenetration of so-called high art and popular [or folk] art" (Bogatyrev 1940: 22).

Bogatyrev's polemics with Naumann inspired Mukařovský in his theory of aesthetic norms. Like Bogatyrev, Mukařovský argues that a norm that has sunk to the lower strata of society can be elevated to the centre of aesthetic activity and again become a "topical (actualized) and fresh norm"; for this reason, Mukařovský suggests the notion of the *circulation* (*koloběh*) of aesthetic norms (Mukařovský 1970 [1936]: 51).

In the late 1930s the language of semiotics appeared in Bogatyrev's work. He published several texts on the semiotic character of folk phenomena;

Fig. 20: Performance of a St Dorothy folk play in its original setting in Slovakia.

more precisely, he fused the functional and semiotic approaches. This can be seen in essays published in this reader: "Clothing as Sign: The Functional and Structural Concept in Ethnography" (also known as "Costume as a Sign", 1936), "A Contribution to the Study of Theatrical Signs" (1937) and "Theatrical Signs" (also known as "Semiotics in the Folk Theatre", 1938). His contribution to the Prague School theory were related to his writings on material signs, particularly his distinction between the thing and the sign. According to Bogatyrev, a thing is an object that does not have any "ideological function" and does not stand for something else, while a sign is an object that refers to something outside of it; a sign is not only a "material phenomenon" but also an "ideological" one (Bogatyrev 2016 [1936]: 442). There are also –

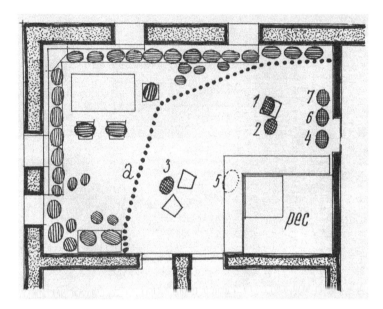

Fig. 21: Schematic drawing of the main room of a cottage when *St Dorothy* is being performed.
a – the imaginary forestage (the division between the "stage" and the "auditorium"); 1 – King
Africius; 2 – Doufil, his Secretary (in another recorded version this character is called Teofil)
3 – St Dorothy; 4 –Angel; 5 – Devil; 6 and 7 – Executioners. In the lower right, *pec* indicates
a built-in stove taking up the whole corner of the room. The devil (number 5) peeks out from
beneath the bench running round the edge of the stove.

Fig. 22: From Burian's production of the St Dorothy play as part of his *Folk Suite*, 1948.

he argues – objects that are things and signs simultaneously, such as folk costumes. These objects fulfil several functions. Some of them are related to the costume-sign, such as particular parts or colours of a folk costume whose function is to mark a woman's marital status, social status, a particular nationality or specific religion. Other functions of the folk costume are practical and aesthetic and relate only to the costume-thing – for example to cover the body, protect it from cold, keep it dry, and so forth (Bogatyrev 2016 [1936]: 445–46).

In "Theatrical Signs", Bogatyrev further develops his classification of material signs in relationship to theatre. He argues that a costume or a house that exist as a thing and a sign in a folk environment are transformed when they appear on the stage and become a sign of a sign. By this, Bogatyrev means that a theatrical costume, since it is a sign, signifies something else – the nationality or financial standing or some other aspect of the stage figure – for instance a rich Chinese person (Bogatyrev 2016 [1938]: 99). In addition to a sign of a sign, Bogatyrev distinguishes a sign of a thing. The sign of a thing refers to the thing itself, as it does not have any "ideological" function. Bogatyrev provides the example of "the actor playing the role of a hungry person can indicate that he is eating bread *sui generis*, and not bread as a sign of, for example, poverty" (Bogatyrev 2016 [1938]: 100). Regardless of the distinction between a sign of a sign and a sign of a thing, Bogatyrev's crucial observation is that both things and people, when they appear on the stage, become signs. Keir Elam has claimed that Bogatyrev "undertook to chart the elementary principles of theatrical semiosis" and ended in what "was to become virtually a manifesto for the Prague Circle" and their theories of drama and theatre (Elam 1980: 5).

Bogatyrev's interest in folklore and ethnography has had a lasting impact on semiotics as a transdisciplinary epistemology, from linguistics and aesthetics to critical and cultural theories. In the hands of Bogatyrev and under the influence of Mukařovský's linguistics and aesthetics, folklore studies departed from their traditional interest in fairy tales, legends and myths (collecting, classifying and comparing different folk forms) towards an analysis of material culture. Summing up the influence of Bogatyrev and Jakobson on ethnography, Charles D. Kaplan has asserted that they instigated

a movement from folklore to folkstyle. Bogatyrev, more than Jakobson, radically shifted his interest by concentrating on the active expression of diverse structures and functions – the "general function" that composed a particular people's folkstyle. (Kaplan 1988: 234)

Despite Bogatyrev's dominant position in this field, several significant studies on folklore were also published by Veltruský, Mukařovský and Jakobson. A characteristic feature of many of their studies – dedicated to puppet theatre, broadside ballads and other popular phenomena – is the transitional position between folklore and high art, most importantly theatre. Describing the principles of folk theatre, song or costume, Prague School theorists arrived at a number of general principles of theatre and its functions; in this way their studies of folklore represent a significant contribution to theatre semiotics and theory in general. Beyond interwar Czechoslovakia, Roman Jakobson played a seminal role as a mediator in that he brought the theories of the Prague School to the attention of two famous anthropologists, Franz Boas and Claude Lévi-Strauss, during his work in the United States in the mid-1940s (Kaplan 1988: 230).

A related sphere of interest of Prague School theorists was exotic cultures – African, Asian, Pacific and Native American. Avant-garde artists and theorists responded to the late nineteenth and early twentieth century wave of Orientalism. Leading Czech artists incorporated the influence of exotic cultures in their works, among them the visual artists Emil Filla, Toyen and Jindřich Štyrský; the theatremakers Jiří Frejka, Jiří Voskovec and Jan Werich; and the poets Vítězslav Nezval and Konstantin Biebl.

Just as artists found inspiration in non-European cultures, Prague School theorists turned to various forms of Asian theatre as suitable material to demonstrate their theses. The poet and literary scholar Karel Brušák (1913–2004) contributed with two interrelated essays published in 1939 and dedicated to Chinese theatre, "Signs in the Chinese Theatre" (this reader, pp. 115–28) and "The Chinese Theatre", which have been hailed as "the first outstanding scholarly work[s] in this area" in the former Czechoslovakia, with Prague School structuralism being applied to Oriental theatre (Havlíčková Kysová 2012: 90). Brušák takes over Mukařovský's concept of the work of art as a language-like structure of components and approaches Chinese theatre semiotically as "a complicated and precise system of signs carrying a large and categorically diverse range of meanings" (Brušák 2016 [1939]: 115). Signs in the Chinese theatre are highly "codified" (Brušák 2016 [1939]: 125) and their meaning is only comprehensible to spectators familiar with the sign system. In accordance with a general interest in the synchronic approach, Brušák focuses on an analysis of the basic elements – the signs out of which the theatrical structure is composed. Following Zich's distinction, he divides them into acoustic elements – such as dialogues, music and sounds – and visual elements, which include costume, mask-like makeup, theatre properties, movements, gestures and facial expression. Discussing these particular elements, their meaning and the relationships between them, Brušák arrives at the conclusion that, in contrast to Western theatre, Chinese theatre does not strive for innovations or actualization of the structure, but "depends on the maintenance of virtually inviolate lexicons" (Brušák 2016 [1939]: 127). As such, he presents an

Fig. 23: Studio photo of Jiří Frejka's production of Miloš Hlávka's *Paní studánka* [Lady of the Spring] at the National Theatre in Prague, 1937. Hlávka's play was an original work based on the English adaptation of a traditional Chinese play by Shich-I Hsiung entitled *Lady Precious Stream*. The production took place at the same time as Karel Brušák was working on his first version of "Signs in the Chinese Theatre".

analogous view to that of Bogatyrev in relation to folk theatre, which mostly sticks to the norm rather than changing it in individual manifestations.

Brušák's theories inspired other members of the Prague Linguistic Circle. In 1940, Jindřich Honzl and Jiří Veltruský presented and published two papers that deal with Asian theatre. However, in contrast to Brušák, neither Honzl nor Veltruský offers a systematic study of the form: Asian theatre – along with folk theatre, modern Russian theatre and Czech theatre – merely serves as a case study to exemplify the topic in question. Jindřich Honzl refers to Japanese theatre in his 1940 essay "The Mobility of the Theatrical Sign". Its main thesis is that signs in the theatre – such as the actor, text, props and light – are not fixed: theirs is a changeable nature. Consequently, a dramatic character does not have to be presented by a human being but may also be presented by means of sound or a piece of wood (a puppet); conversely, a theatrical prop can be represented by a real object, an actor's gesture or a sound or through other means. In other words, the material component of the sign – that is, the "vehicle" of the meaning – may vary in nature and may change several times during a performance (Havlíčková Kysová 2012: 94): a character may appear as an actor, as a shadow or a projection, as an offstage sound or through the action of other actors (for instance speaking to the character over the phone), to name a few possibilities. To demonstrate this mobility (or dynamics) of the theatrical sign – a feature considered a fundamental principle of theatrical semiosis – Honzl uses an example from Japanese Kabuki theatre.

References to Asian theatrical forms can also be found in Jiři Veltruský's essay "People and Things in the Theatre" (1940). Like Brušák and Honzl, Veltruský applies Prague structuralist theory to Asian theatre. In his essay he argues that one cannot strictly take people in the theatre as the active elements on stage and objects (things) in the theatre as the passive elements. Using examples from Japanese and Chinese theatres, Veltruský shows that things can take the role of active elements, while people can take the role of passive ones. According to Veltruský, there is no strict boundary between objects and subjects in the theatre as people and things are potentially both. He posits a tension or a "dialectic antinomy" between them (Veltruský 2016 [1940]: 155). Asian theatrical forms and Prague School theories continued to appeal to Veltruský in later decades (Havlíčková Kysová 2012: 94–5). In his book *An Approach to the Semiotics of Theatre* (published posthumously as Veltruský 2012), Veltruský draws on a rich array of examples from Asian drama. In combination, the early texts and the later revisitings create an organic whole and contribute to general theatre theory as well as to the theory of Asian theatre in particular. Moreover, texts from around 1940 played a significant role in introducing a geographically distant theatre practice to Czech society and mediated an alternative aesthetic for Czech theatremakers.

THE PRAGUE LINGUISTIC CIRCLE AND FORMALISM(S)

The functional-structural method had its roots in Russian Formalism as well as in earlier Czech Formalism. Its originality firmly establishes it as an autonomous critical school.

Sometimes the Prague School is presented as a mere transfer of the ideas of Russian Formalists or as representing a transitional form between two more advanced theories, Russian Formalism and the Western Structuralism of the 1960s. The crucial ontological distinction between Russian Formalism and the Prague School has been formulated above – the difference between an essentially revolutionary, radicalized theory practised hand in hand with Cubo-Futurism and a theory that is constitutive and constructive, existing in harmony with the cultural efforts of the avant-garde oriented, pluralistic state of Czechoslovakia. The relationship between Russian Formalism and Prague Structuralism has been discussed in detail in a number of works. While Victor Erlich (1965) perceives the Prague Linguistic Circle as a mere continuation of the Moscow Linguistic Circle and St Petersburg's OPOJAZ, other critics firmly establish the uniqueness and originality of the Prague School, among them František Galán (1985), Jurij Striedter (1989; chapter 2, "From Formalism to Structuralism", 83–119) and – very significantly – Peter Steiner (1982), who details the contribution of Russian Formalism to Czech Structuralist thought but also pays meticulous attention to other traditions that culminated in the Prague Linguistic Circle. In Steiner's balanced and well-argued account, German philosophy, early phenomenology and the Czech aesthetic tradition (Durdík, Hostinský and Zich) have comparable weight in the evolution of the new school. Zich was among the first to point out the originality of the Prague School method and its independence of the earlier Czech Formalist school (Novák 1933: 467). The meeting point of the Russian and the Czech schools may be exemplified in Roman Jakobson and Yury Tynyanov's "Problems in the Study of Literature and Language" (Tynyanov and Jakobson 1928); this essay summarizes the achievements of Formalism and proposes the next steps, which were further developed by the Prague Structuralists (Broekman 1974: 45). The development of Prague Structuralism from Russian Formalism was not only a continuation but also a negation and reassessment of several concepts, among them the immanence and autonomy of art, poetic language and poetic function, the dominant, system, mutation of system and *ostranenie* (Veltruský 1981: 121).

Both schools were concerned with the question of immanence (materiality) and the utonomy of art. In contrast to the methods of the nineteenth century, which tended to explain literature with reference to psychology, philosophy, economy and biography, Formalists perceived literature (and art, by extension) as a separate branch governed by its own principles of functioning and having a specific object of study (Jakobson 1973: 62). They focused on the examination of these inner laws, considering how literature is made or what makes literature literature, apart from the external factors. The perception of literature as immanent was questioned in the final stage of Formalism by Tynyanov and Jakobson (1928), who claimed that literature is an autonomous domain but cannot be isolated from its social contexts: changes in the literary system (in styles of writing or in literary styles and movements) cannot be explained by "the immanent law of its history alone" (Veltruský 1981: 121; Winner 1979: 4). It is worth noticing the development in the Czechoslovak theory. For example, in 1923 the leading Prague School literary theorist Jan Mukařovský wrote a study on the Czech Romantic poet Karel Hynek Mácha. While he called this essay of 1923 "formalist" and advocated the independence of literature and its self-driven evolution (autonomy), in 1934 he published a similar analysis of poetry entitled "Polák's *The Sublime of Nature*" – and this employed a "structuralist" approach. The essay departed from pure Formalism and, to paraphrase Mukařovský's later words, emphasized the relationship of a literary work to its society and other arts (Mukařovský 1970 [1936]: 94–96). The autonomy of art versus its dependence on society was a popular topic in the Prague School; it was considered in relation not only to Russian Formalism but also to the philosophies of Immanuel Kant, Johann Gottfried Herder, Karl Marx and Georg Wilhelm Friedrich Hegel.

A significant methodological approach that Russian Formalists shared with the Prague School was the analysis of phenomena through a critical study of language. Linguistics as a critical and theoretical study of language played a key role in emancipating literature and other arts as independent scholarly disciplines. Formalists observed that the material of literature is language, and thus linguistics made an apt "tool for study of verbal art" (Steiner 1982: 198). As a result of this view, linguistic principles were applied to literature and poetics was perceived as a branch of linguistics (Eichenbaum 1978: 8). From the very beginning, however, the Formalists and Structuralists were aware of the difference between the use of language within and outside literature and aimed at distinguishing poetic language from non-poetic language, a project carried out by the Russian theorists Lev Yakubinsky, Viktor Shklovsky and Roman Jakobson and the Czech theorists Jan Mukařovský and Bohuslav Havránek. They demonstrated that poetic language was specific and served different functions than practical language. The first to distinguish poetic and non-poetic language according to their functions was Lev Yakubinsky, in an essay of 1916. He claimed that "the purpose of practical language is to transmit practical pieces of information, while in poetic language, practical purposes move to the background and attention is paid to formal components of language as autonomous values" (Eichenbaum 1978: 9).

This was further elaborated by Jakobson, who claimed that poetic language is not characterized by the sole existence of the poetic function but by the prevalence of the poetic over others, such as the emotive and the practical (Steiner 1982: 199). He perceived these functions as hierarchically organized, with the poetic function in the dominant position.

A year after Yakubinsky, Shklovsky presented his view on the difference between poetic and everyday language in his celebrated essay "Art as Technique" (1917), which became the cornerstone of Russian Formalism. Like Yakubinsky and Jakobson, Shklovsky claimed that what makes literature literature is its form; by that he meant a form that is unusual, new or deautomatized:

> The technique of art is to make objects "unfamiliar", to make forms difficult, to increase the difficulty and length of perception because the process of perception is an aesthetic end in itself and must be prolonged. Art is a way of experiencing the artfulness of an object: the object is not important... (Shklovsky 1965: 3)

Such a "palpable" form is established through various defamiliarizing or estranging devices such as plot structure, rhythm, expression, word play and imagery; the form organizes non-aesthetic material and transforms it into an aesthetic object.

Drawing on Shklovsky's concept of *ostranenie* (defamiliarization or estrangement) and Yakubinsky's and Jakobson's concept of the hierarchical organization of functions, Tynyanov developed his notion of a work of art as a system of interrelated and interacting elements that are organized hierarchically and fulfil certain functions ("On Literary Evolution", 1927). Tynyanov's notion refined Shklovsky's approach to literature as a "material" and a "technique", and offered a more complex perception of a work of art, one that incorporated literary evolution. Evolution, which Tynyanov defined as the "mutation of a system", was perceived as a change in the hierarchy of elements and/or functions; this change occurs when a system becomes automatized (Tynyanov 1978: 67).

Jan Mukařovský's first definitions of structure – in his 1931 essay on Charlie Chaplin's acting in *City Lights*, called "An Attempt at a Structural Analysis of an Actor's Figure" (2016 [1931]), and his 1932 study "Standard Language and Poetic Language" – resemble Tynyanov's to a large extent. Mukařovský replaces the term *system* with *structure*; Tynyanov's *deautomatized* elements are replaced by *actualized*; and *evolution* is not defined as the mutation of a system but as *aktualizace* (actualization or foregrounding) of a structure. According to Mukařovský, "a work of art [is] a structure ... a system of components aesthetically deautomatized and organized into a complete hierarchy that is unified by the prevalence of one component over the others" (Mukařovský 2016 [1931]: 192; Mukařovský 1964: 19–20). The component highest in the hierarchy – the most actualized one – is the dominant, which "sets in motion, and gives direction to, the relationship of all other components" (Mukařovský 1964: 20). The actualized and automatized elements of the work of art as a structure are in dialectical tension. Their coexistence makes the work of art a dynamic unity characterized by "harmony and disharmony, convergence and divergence" (Mukařovský 1964: 21). Convergence is caused by a trend toward the dominant (the most actualized elements) and divergence by the resistance of automatized elements, such as standard language and/or an older aesthetic norm.

This definition of a work of art as a structure of individual components that bring into play conventional (automatized) and innovative (actualized) elements allowed for an analysis that was both *synchronic* – studying art in its present moment, as a social act with its own sets of values – and *diachronic*, taking into account its place within cultural history and development and within the particular art form and its genre. At the same time, this formulation reflects the way in which early Prague Structuralism, while evolving alongside the final stage of Russian Formalism and drawing on its concepts, in the end moved beyond them.

THE PRAGUE SCHOOL AND HUSSERL'S PHENOMENOLOGY

> *For a long time Prague School theory was mistakenly considered a development*
> *of linguistic structuralism originating with de Saussure. However,*
> *the influence of Edmund Husserl's phenomenology was more prominent;*
> *the PLC closely followed Husserl's philosophy.*

The phenomenology of Edmund Husserl (1859–1938), a native of the Moravian town of Prostějov, represents another significant source of inspiration for the Prague School. Elmar Holenstein identified the links between Husserl's philosophy and the Prague School theories of Jan Mukařovský and Roman Jakobson. He considered them so significant that he referred to Prague Structuralism as "phenomenologic structuralism" and "a branch of the phenomonological movement" (Holenstein 1977; Holenstein 1979; and Holenstein 2005). Three fundamental areas of thematic correspondence can be distinguished between Husserl and the Prague Structuralists: anti-psychologism, the idea of a pure universal grammar or doctrine of forms, and the doctrine of signification (Holenstein 2005). But there are also other points of contact between Husserl's philosophy and Prague Structuralist theories. According to Josef Vojvodík, Mukařovský and Husserl shared an interest in things as objects, an interest that was also fostered by the concerns of the avant-garde movements (Vojvodík 2011). Květoslav Chvatík asserts that Mukařovský came close to Husserl's philosophy in his aim to overcome "historical relativism and to focus on the anthropological constant" (Chvatík 1970: 140). In parallel to Husserl's concept of the sign, the Prague Structuralists focused on the distinction between a work of art as an aesthetic object and as a thing. They also theorized the questions of meaning, intentionality and unintentionality in art as well as the role of the perceiver in artistic communication, and suggested the impossibility of separating the perception from the perceived object (Holenstein 2005, Mathauser 2005, Vojvodík 2011).

Husserl's anti-psychologism and the search for fundamental laws are linked with his concepts of phenomenological and eidetic (form-related) reductions. These are attitudes that aim at revealing the invariant (the essence) of an object by abstracting from everything that is accidental, particular and circumstantial, and from everything that has been associated with the studied phenomenon, and focusing only on its necessary, essential form, which contains its defining feature (Holenstein 2005: 33; Mathauser 2005: 164). Husserl – like Jakobson and Mukařovský – did not reject psychology as a whole, only the methods and forms of late nineteenth-century psychology, which reduced one science to another (Holenstein 2005: 19). Jakobson and Mukařovský were critical of psychology primarily for its reduction of literary works of art to no more than expressions of the author's *psyche*. According to Husserl as well as the Russian Formalists and the Prague Structuralists, each scientific discipline should be studied separately as an autonomous branch with its objects of inquiry and one should aim to reveal the essence of a studied phenomenon, the invariable elements or universal principles upon which it operates (Holenstein 2005: 23). These principles, to which Jakobson alludes in his study on aphasia, were defined by Husserl as "relations of foundations". The search for the "relations of foundations" was a key aim of the Prague Structuralists and it is linked with their concept of structure defined as relationships of elements and functions, as has been discussed above.

For the Prague School, an analysis of the founding principles of a structure was impossible without the question of meaning. Each element in a structure has a meaning that contributes to the overall significance of a word, an utterance or a work of art as a whole (Mukařovský 1966 [1946]: 111). In relation to meaning, the Prague School – and Mukařovský in particular – departed from Ferdinand de Saussure's two-part model of sign (*signifier–signified*) and inclined toward the three-part model proposed by Husserl (and later developed by Roman Ingarden). This phenomenological three-part model extended the concept of the sign to the *referential* or *intentional object* and thus offered a more complex conception of the construction of meaning. The referential object is not a fixed component of the sign but joins the signifier and signified "in a communication situation, when a speaker communicates his thought about a referential object to a hearer" (Schmid 2012: 117); in other words, the referential object is established in the intentional act of linking the sign with the intended significance (its *denotatum*).

In accordance with Husserl, Mukařovský defines meaning as the *intentional object*, "which a word/utterance establishes as a bridge between the sign and transcendental reality" (Volek 2004: 40), and he applies it to a work of art. As has been discussed above, Mukařovský perceives a work of art as an artefact, an aesthetic object as well as a relationship to reality (Mukařovský 1976 [1936]: 9). As a word, an aesthetic object does not have a fixed meaning, but it is established in the process of literary communication. In other words, depending on the perceiver, an aesthetic object differs over time; in various periods it is related to different transcendental realities and perceived against the backdrop of different social norms. With this in view, as Husserl suggests, it is impossible to extract an object of inquiry from the activity of the perceiving subject, who intentionally focuses on it and co-creates its meaning (Schmid 2012).

The three-part model is particularly important in discussing works of art, for instance in the case of metaphors or symbols. In poetic language, a word and its meaning (the signifier and the signified) are the vehicle for conveying the tenor of the metaphor – for example, the word *frown* conveys a different intended significance if used in connection with the sky. In the theatre an object and its common function or use – for instance a *chair* – will convey a different intended meaning when used as a horse or referred to as a mountain top. Depending on the *function* it is put to, the onstage object will vary in significance. While such a distinction is in line with Husserl's three-part model and with the Prague School's theory of the onstage sign – in the theories of Jindřich Honzl and Jiří Veltruský – the Saussurean two-part model (*signifier–signified*) does not enable this analytical approach. In the arts, the more complex model is vital. An example to illustrate this could be taken from a classical scene, from Richard B. Sheridan's play *The Rivals* (1775). The most famous character is Mrs Malaprop, who notoriously misuses long foreign words – a phenomenon that become known as *malapropism*. Mrs Malaprop, for instance, says of her niece:

> O, there's nothing to be hoped for from her! she's as headstrong as an *allegory* on the banks of Nile. (*The Rivals*, Act 3 Scene 3)

Instead of saying *alligator*, Mrs Malaprop muddles the sentence. Her intended meaning is clear; however, her whole character as a theatrical work of art turns around the fact that she does say *allegory*. The interplay of the words she says and her intended meaning are, on another level, the artistic intention of the play as a whole, and we are well aware of this as spectators and enjoy this intellectual titillation. We reconsider and reinterpret what we perceive with a view to different *frames* of reference and significance – *framing* being another crucial phenomenological concept. Even more could be argued: the uncertainty principle that comes into play – the fact that we cannot take everything we see and hear for granted but need to question it, test it and respond to it creatively (that is, with openness and mental activity) – is one of the key components of the theatre and of the arts as such.

Mukařovský elaborates on the idea of intentionality in his article "Intentionality and Unintentionality in Art" (1978 [1943]). In brief, when one perceives a work of art, s/he strives to understand it as a semantic whole. In the process of perception, there are parts that, according to the perceiving subjects, contribute to the semantic unification of a work of art and those that resist it. Mukařovský calls the former intentional and the latter unintentional. Intentionality in art is then defined as semantic unification of a work of art, while unintentionality is the denial of this unification. Mukařovský believes that the parts that the perceiver considers to be intentional cause the work to be perceived as a sign, while the unintentional parts are perceived as reality (Mukařovský 1978 [1943]: 128). During the perception of a work of art, the perceiver oscillates between impressions of intentionality and un-intentionality. As a result, the perceiver takes the work of art as a whole for a sign – "a self-referential sign lacking the unequivocal relation to society" (Mukařovský 1978 [1943]: 106); at the same time it is also an experiential fact that "immediately affect[s] man's mental life" (128). This complex rela-tion between the intentional in art (the artistic sign) and the unintentional (the unintended interventions of reality) form the basic dialectic – the two "fundamental antinomies" of art (128). This conceptual framework directly infuenced the thinking of several PLC scholars and became a key contribu-tion of Husserl's phenomenology to Prague School theory.

THE PRAGUE SCHOOL AND INGARDEN'S AESTHETICS

Roman Ingarden's aesthetics provided the Prague School with a defining theoretical impulse.

The Prague School theory also incorporated the influence of the Polish phenomenologist Roman Ingarden (1893–1970), who was a student of Edmund Husserl. This influence is most visible in reception aesthetics as developed by Felix Vodička. In his study "The Concretization of the Literary Work" (1941), which is regarded as the starting point of the Prague School's reception theory (Doležel 1988; Galán 1982; Striedter 1989), Vodička adopts and reworks Ingarden's concept of literary concretization: from individual concretization during an act of reading or when experiencing a work of art to a historical one, comprising the cultural awareness and reception of a particular aesthetic object. The concept of *concretization* captures the moment when a work of art is received and experienced by the recipient – in a concrete situation and in confrontation with a concrete mind set. This concretization is both *individual* (the recipient draws on his or her own individual knowledge and experiences for the interpretation) and *cultural* and *historical* (the circumstances of the reception go beyond the individual and interact with larger frames of reference).

Like the members of the Prague School, Ingarden did not understand a work of art (focusing predominantly on literary works) as the reflection of an author's *psyche* but as a structure, "a fixed textual entity" that acquires meaning during the process of perception (Meerzon 2012: 130; Pešat 1999: 142, Striedter 1989: 124). According to Ingarden, a work of art consists of four formal layers: the strata of (1) linguistic sound formations, (2) meaning units, (3) represented objects and (4) schematized aspects "through which the objects are represented in the work" (Vodička 1982: 109). These four aspects are in many ways parallel to the extended Bühler-Mukařovský model of functions. Ingarden's four layers – especially those of represented objects and schematized aspects – contain *places of indeterminacy* that are filled in by the reader in the process of reception. Since each reader fills in different places of indeterminacy and in a different way, a work of art – or as Mukařovský liked to call it the "thing" – is realized and exists in the form of various personalized *aesthetic objects*.

Vodička incorporated Ingarden's theory of concretization into the Prague School theories, in particular Mukařovský's theories of the sign and of aesthetic norm and value. This enabled Vodička to confront and criticize Ingarden's theory and refine it. Following Mukařovský, who discusses the relationship between the perceived object and the perceiving subject in his seminal studies *Aesthetic Function, Norm and Value as Social Facts* (1970 [1936]), "Art as Semiotic Fact" (1976 [1936]) and "Intentionality and Unintentionlality in Art" (1978 [1943]), Vodička emphasized that an aesthetic object cannot be rooted solely in an individual interpretation or "consciousness". The work of art surpasses individuality; "its place is in the consciousness of the whole collective" (Mukařovský 1976 [1936]: 3) and it acquires its meaning and aesthetic value only "in relationship to literary conventions of a certain period" (Vodička 1982: 110). Vodička's conclusions mirror and rework those of Ingarden, stating that "reception is influenced by the contemporary norm, which results in a work being perceived similarly by all members of a community regardless of the individual differences of the perceivers" (Pešat 1999: 144).

No aesthetic norm is universal, unchanging and/or eternal; it is constantly being redefined: "an older norm is violated by a newly created norm", posits Mukařovský (Mukařovský 1970 [1936]: 33) and "every work becomes a potentially endless series of concretized aesthetic objects" (Galán 1976: 465). Mukařovský's and Vodička's position regarding the norm's changeability and the impossibility of a universal concretization stood in direct opposition to Ingarden, who asserted that it is possible to activate all parts and create a universal, timeless concretization. Effectively, the Prague School relativized Ingarden's universal claims and emphasized the particularity of concrete moments and the significance of accidentals for the concrete interpretation. Vodička stressed that a work of art does does not become part of the literary tradition automatically: it enters its literary tradition only through concretizations that have been generally accepted by the community, whether via critics, literary canons, education or simply general popularity (Vodička 1982: 112).

A crucial difference thus arises between the understanding of concretization in Ingarden and in Vodička. Though the concepts of both are based on the perception of a work of art by a perceiver, they are oriented differently. In the case of Ingarden, the perceiver's concretization stems from the particular qualities of the work of art that are brought to realization in the reader's mind; Vodička, in contrast, emphasizes that the perceiver's concretization is affected by external factors – the "conditions of perception". The work of art is understood and interpretively realized by means of the changing aesthetic norms; particular concretizations reflect external circumstances as much as inner, inherent qualities (Galán 1984: 154).

KARL BÜHLER'S LANGUAGE THEORY

The PLC incorporated the language theory of the Vienna-based Karl Bühler into their critical thinking. In so doing, the influence of psychological investigation enriched their method and effectively combined phenomenology with psychology.

Another significant influence on the Prague School was the German psychologist and linguist Karl Bühler (1879-1963). His main contribution to Prague School theory was in the area of the function of language, or language in communication (*parole*), and his influence was far from marginal. Bühler's theory was integrally incorporated in Prague School theatre theory (see Veltruský's essay on Bühler, Veltruský MS; and Drozd 2016: 106). The Prague School's model of literary and aesthetic communication was based on Bühler's *Organonmodel*, a schema of communication linking the verbal sign with the sender, the recipient and the referent – that is, the objects talked about (Doležel 1990: 150). Bühler showed that understanding the nature of the sign in terms of its relationship to the referent is not sufficient; one also has to take into consideration the originator of the message (the sender) as well as its addressee (the recipient) (Galán 1984: 71-2, Veltruský MS). From this model, Bühler derived three basic functions, each focused on one of the three components: (1) the expressive function (*Ausdruck*), which perceives the "speech event" with a view to the sender; (2) the connative function (*Appel*), which approaches it in relation to the recipient; and (3) the referential function (*Darstellung*), which considers the "speech event" with a view to the message, the referent. The expressive function of the sign realizes the intention of the speaker, including his or her unique view as an individual. The connative function is the appeal that sign has towards the addressee and realizes the effect the communication is to have on him or her. The referential function communicates something about reality, provides information that is passed from the speaker to the addressee. According to Bühler, these three functions are hierarchically organized, with one of them dominating the utterance. While most utterances are dominated by the referential function, "in certain type of utterances the connative or expressive function moves into the foreground" (Doležel 1990: 150). At the same time, none of the three functions is completely excluded during any communication.

Bühler's model of communication was appropriated by the Prague School and further developed. Among the first who reconsidered it was Jan Mukařovský, in his essay "Poetic Denomination and Aesthetic Function of Language" (1938). Mukařovský claims that Bühler's scheme applies to standard language, which is object-oriented, while for poetic language the *Organonmodel* must be revised. With regard to literature it is necessary to take into account a fourth function: the aesthetic function. The characteristic feature of the aesthetic function is that it is oriented towards the sign itself: it turns the signs through which communication occurs into artefacts and these verbal artefacts are in themselves one of the key purposes of artistic communication. In so doing, Mukařovský used Bühler's model to refine the Russian Formalist notion of estrangement (*ostranenie*). He argued that the aesthetic function

> is in opposition to all the others: it renders the structure of the linguistic sign the centre of attention, whereas the first three functions were oriented toward extra-linguistic factors and toward goals transcending the linguistic sign. (Mukařovský, quoted in Doležel 1990: 150)

This self-referentiality of the aesthetic function, however, does not mean that art is a self-centered or self-contained aesthetic game. On the contrary, it is crucially linked with its society, reality and human activities (Doležel 1990: 151). In the early 1940s, Mukařovský and his student Felix Vodička created the concept of the expressive function pertaining to the creator (Mukařovský, "The Poet", 1941) and complemented it with the connative function pertaining to the recipient of a work of art (Vodička, "The Concretization of the Literary Work", 1941).

In 1960, Jakobson revisited the refined model in his essay "Closing Statements: Linguistics and Poetics" and offered another modification, based on Bühler's and Mukařovský's functions of linguistic and literary communication. Jakobson's refined model, which adds another two functions, is more famous than Mukařovský's earlier model. In addition to the (1) *expressive*, (2) *connative*, (3) *referential* and (4) *poetic* (or *aesthetic*) functions, Jakobson elaborates another two elements – the channel of the communication itself and the code in which the communication occurs. His added (5) *phatic* function concerns the consensual act of communication, which needs to be established before other functions come into play and is maintained throughout: people meeting and asking "ritual" questions (such as "How are you?", "Hi there, are you all right?" or "Ahem, may I ask you something?") that serve no other purposes than opening the channel of communication, "tuning up" with the interlocutor, getting used to his or her voice and mood. Finally, Jakobson also adds (6) the *metalingual* (also known as *reflexive* or *metalinguistic*) function; this function realizes the actual type of language, dialect, jargon – or simply the code – that is used in the communication (see Jakobson 1960).

PRAGUE SCHOOL THEATRE THEORY AND OTAKAR ZICH

Otakar Zich (1879–1934) expressed his admiration for the theoretical activities of the Prague Linguistic Circle. Although his involvement with them was only partial, his was perhaps the most significant single influence on Prague School theatre theory.

As has been shown, the traditions existing in Czech and Central European cultures were crucial for the development of the Prague School. They prepared the ground for and played a seminal role in the acceptance of foreign trends and the formation of the School's own distinctive theories (Mukařovský 1982a [1940]: 82; Steiner 1982: 184–98; Striedter 1989: 85; Sus 1968). Among the traditions that made a crucial contribution to the Prague School were Czech Hegelianism and its later extension in the spirit of Marxism, and Herbartian aesthetics and its derivatives in the older Czech Formalism. The advocates of Hegel fostered questions about the relation between art and society, while the proponents of Herbart – sometimes referred to as forming the Czech school of formal aesthetics – were concerned with formal issues and the question of immanent qualities in the work of art (Striedter 1989: 84–86; Sus 1968). This Czech Formalist school shared a number of perspectives with the Russian Formalists, although both schools developed independently of one another. The older Czech Formalist school is represented by the names of its leading proponents, the aestheticians Josef Durdík (1837–1902) and Otakar Hostinský (1847–1910) and their student Otakar Zich; Zich played a direct and decisive role in the formation of Prague School theories of the theatre. Peter Steiner has provided a detailed discussion of the Czech Formalists and the ground they prepared for the reception of Russian Formalism, itemizing the concepts fostered by Durdík and further developed by Hostinský and Zich (Steiner 1982: 184–98; see also Sus 1968: 293–94). Otakar Zich continued in the tradition set by his teachers but transformed it significantly by the inclusion of an aesthetics that was profoundly informed by Gestalt psychology and its related mind-oriented semantics. These were of decisive importance for the Prague School (Sus 1968: 293).

Otakar Zich's interests were wide-ranging, both as a theorist and as a practitioner. Despite his premature death at the age of 55, Zich's left a lasting legacy in aesthetics, literary theory, musicology, theatre studies and the history of the opera. In 1910, Zich published his first comprehensive aesthetic theory in his book *Estetické vnímání hudby: Psychologický rozbor na podkladě experimentálním* (The Aesthetic Perception of Music: A Psychological Analysis on an Experimental Basis), shortly followed by "K psychologii uměleckého tvoření: Metodologická úvaha" (Towards a Psychology of Artistic Creation: A Methodological Essay, 1911). In these works, Zich combined the Czech-German formalist tradition with the psychology of perception, a feature that was both novel and iconoclastic, given the Formalists' scepticism and objections towards psychology as a scientific discipline. In the following decade, Zich's interest shifted towards the aesthetics of literature – *O typech básnických* (On Poetic Types, 1917–1918) – and other arts. During his activities at the newly established Masaryk University in Brno (1919–1923), Zich began to outline his aesthetic theory of the dramatic arts; the prolegomena are published in this reader as "Principles of Theoretical Dramaturgy" [2016: 34–58]. In 1923 he also published a seminal essay on puppet theatre theory, "Loutkové divadlo" (Puppet Theatre; Zich 2015). It is also worth observing that he dedicated a study to the aesthetic aspects of the Sokol movement, *Sokolstvo z hlediska estetického* (The Sokols from an Aesthetic Perspective, 1920). His theoretical work culminated in the publication of his monumental *Estetika dramatického umění* (The Aesthetics of Dramatic Art, 1931). Simultaneously, Zich was prolific as a composer of classical music in the late Romantic tradition. His oeuvre includes three operas, two of which – *Vina* (Guilt, 1911–1915; for a new edition see Zich 2014), based on Jaroslav Hilbert's play of the same name, and *Preciézky* (The Affected Ladies, 1922–1924), based on Molière's *Les Précieuses ridicules* – were awarded the State Prize, in 1923 and 1927 respectively. After Zich's death, Jan Mukařovský took over the Chair of Aesthetics at Charles University University that he had founded (Sládek 2015: 60).

In several ways Otakar Zich's revision of the earlier Formalist tradition is parallel to the developments of Russian Formalism. Zich was critical of the domestic tradition for its overestimation of the thematic components of a poetic work of art and its underestimation of the work's formal aspects. Unlike the radical, Cubo-Futurist Russian school, which tipped the scales towards an almost exclusive study of the immanent form, Zich never broke away from semantics and the significance of meaning in relation to form. In 1917, a year after Lev Yakubinsky published his study on the difference between poetic and practical language, which established form as a value *sui generis* and perceived literature as an immanent system, Zich began to publish his study *On Poetic Types* (1917–1918). Zich also categorized literature, in this case poetry, according to the formal elements, but did not eliminate formal analysis from the question of meaning (Sus 1968: 298). In addition, Zich tried to establish a relationship between the psychology of the creator and the structure of a poem; in so doing he moved beyond the immanent understanding of literature. However, in contrast to nineteenth-century psychological approaches, which reduced literature to expressions of the author's *psyche,* Zich fused the psychology of artistic creation with the typology of the objective features of a poetic structure and created a "psychopoetic" poetic approach (Sus 1968: 298).

Analysing the artistic structure was a characteristic feature of Zich's aesthetics, one that brought him close to the later structuralist school. Departing from pure Herbartism, which perceived the structure of a work of art as static, Zich viewed a work of art as a dynamic whole characterized by a constant tension between its individual elements and components (Mukařovský 1982b [1934]: 286). Moreover, he argued that the aesthetic whole cannot be described by the enumeration of its parts as it is more than their sum; upon entering the whole, particular parts (such as tones in music or visual arts in the theatre) gain features that they do not have on their own and become subject to the logic of the work of art as a whole (Steiner 1982: 191) – a concept that Zich took from Gestalt psychology and applied to his aesthetics. After a book-length study outlining a theory of the aesthetic perception of music (1910), Zich synthesized his previous critical endeavours and theoretical concepts in his *opus magnum,* which was dedicated to the theatre. Entitled *The Aesthetics of Dramatic Art: A Theoretical Dramaturgy* (1931), the work is viewed as the cornerstone of the semiotic theory of the arts (Keir Elam, Ivo Osolsobě). Zich presents the theatre as a synthesis of auditory, visual and tactile elements, a feature that distinguishes it from the other arts, which are based on only one or (at best) two senses, such as paintings (visual elements), music (auditory elements) or sculpture (visual and tactile elements). Zich provides a detailed analysis of visual, auditory and tactile components such as the dramatic text, the dramatic figure, onstage action, stage music, theatrical space and stage design (Zich 1931: 22–23). These were later elaborated by Prague School theorists in their writings on theatre and drama, as represented in this reader.

Zich's groundbreaking concept is simple. Without using the sign in a strictly semiotic way, Zich differentiates between what we perceive through our senses and what we imagine: for example, watching an actor on stage is a visual, auditory and tactile perception, which we interpret in our imagination as a fictional character. Theatre is created through the interaction of these two. On the one hand, an actor creates the onstage figure (or actor's figure; *herecká postava*) through concrete action (gestures, expressions, mimicry, words, and so on); Zich calls the product of this creative effort the *technical image (významová představa technická)* as it is created through technique (or *techné*) in a material world but guided by an underlying meaning (the semantic concept or idea). On the other hand, this *technical image* is also what the spectator perceives, then transforming it through imagination into a *symbolic image* or *imaginary concept (významová představa obrazová)* and into a *dramatic character* (*dramatická osoba*), which is the fictional character of the play. So, for instance, an actor takes on the role of Hamlet and plays it in a particular way, creating the *technical image*: a portrayal of Hamlet's behaviour, action, diction and words through a particular technique. What is created by the actor is the *stage figure*, which the spectators watch, try to understand – through interpretation, rational and emotional reflection, self-projection and emphathy – and in so doing create the *dramatic character*: Hamlet, the fictional prince of Denmark. So while the stage figure is the product of the actor's effort, the dramatic character is the product of the spectator's imagination. Zich's distinction between the stage figure and the dramatic character is crucial: the stage figure uses specific codes (for instance, Shakespeare's English or a translation into another language), while the dramatic character exists in the imaginary world of "Denmark" with its fictional rules and codes. The triad *actor–stage figure–dramatic character* is a seminal and truly revolutionary contribution to theatre theory (see Quinn 1988 and Quinn 1995).

In his theory, Zich pays equal attention to form and its perceptible components as well as to mind-created meaning. Zich understands this meaning as "our image [or idea] (*naše představa*), which we add to formal elements during the process of perception", and he refers to it as the *semantic image* (*významová představa*) (Zich 1931: 52; Mukařovský 1982b; Sus 1992). Distinguishing between the sensory and the mental parts of the perception of a phenomenon, Zich refers to the concept of the sign as the sensory aspect (the sign-vehicle of the communication) and its meaning or referent as the mental image (the semantic concept) evoked by it (Steiner 1982: 194–95).

Another feature of Zich's aesthetics that anticipated Prague School concepts was his concept of the aesthetic norm and value, which he refers to as aesthetic and artistic evaluation. Zich does not perceive norms as static; they are constantly in the process of development; he calls this the *plasticity* of norms. At the same time, they are binding within a given society, in a given time and place (Steiner 1982: 192), and they play a crucial role in the evaluation of any aesthetic phenomena: all "products of conscious human activity [aesthetic and non-aesthetic] require for their evaluation the background of an appropriate norm" (Steiner 1982: 191). The relationship between norm and value, perceived (in opposition to Kant) as something relative and interconnected, was taken up by Prague School theorists, in particular Jan Mukařovský and Felix Vodička in the 1930s and 1940s, and developed towards a more general aesthetic theory.

Although Zich was never a member of the Prague Linguistic Circle, and owing to his early death was precluded from participating in its debates, many of his key concepts were of fundamental importance for the Prague School, especially the issues of form and meaning, norm and value, structure and the actor triad (*actor–figure–character*). Mukařovský considered

Zich a "structural aesthetician" (Mukařovský 1982b [1934]) and Ivo Osolsobě called him a semiotician *avant-la-lettre*: although Zich did not use semiotic and structuralist terminology he "*de facto* practised the semiotic agenda" (Osolsobě 2002 [1981]: 216). Zich's *The Aesthetics of Dramatic Art* was a point of departure that both inspired and provoked many Prague School theorists, above all Jiří Veltruský, who specialized in theatre theory and both developed and critiqued Zich's concepts. Taken all in all, Otakar Zich is the founding figure of theatre theory and his influence on the Prague School and later theatre thinkers was decisive.

HEGELIAN AND MARXIST DIALECTICS

In the work of Jan Mukařovský and his student Jiří Veltruský, the theories of the Prague Linguistic Circle were profoundly influenced by dialectical thinking.

Apart from the traditions of Czech Herbartism and Russian Formalism, the Prague School was also – through them as well as directly – influenced by the traditions of Hegelianism and Marxism and their emphasis on the connections between art and society/reality. The first of the Prague School theorists to elaborate on this crucial relationship was Jan Mukařovský in his two 1934 studies "Polák's *The Sublime of Nature*" and "Art as a Semiotic Fact", the latter originally a conference paper delivered at the 8th World Congress of Philosophy in Prague. It was the former essay, however, that resonated most with contemporary Marxist theorists, among them the literature and theatre critic Kurt Konrad, who perceived it as "an evolutionary step of Structuralism toward a dialectic-materialistic exploration of literature" (quoted in Chvatík 1966: 352) and lauded Mukařovský's departure from Formalism towards an interest in the link between art and society. Similarly, the influential Communist critic and ethnographer Bedřich Václavek expressed the need for a synthesis of the "Marxist sociology of literature and structuralist poetics as a fruitful approach to the study and understanding of art and society and the relationship between them" (Chvatík 1966: 352). In the 1930s the relationship between Marxists and the Prague School was not marked by tension – as it would be after 1945 or as it had been between Soviet Marxists and the Russian Formalists in the 1920s. On the contrary, the democratic and open intellectual and artistic milieu of interwar Czechoslovakia allowed for a productive methodological dialogue between movements (Galán 1985: 62; Striedter 1989: 115–6). Besides, several Prague School thinkers had Marxist or Communist sympathies and perceived their theoretical research as being in line with materialist dialectics. Such was the case of Mukařovský and Jindřich Honzl, whose political ardour after 1945 (and even more so after 1948) led to a renunciation of or scepticism towards their interwar structuralist views. In the 1930s, however, the benefits of the critical dialogue were mutual. Mukařovský's views on the relationship between art and society were influenced by the debates with Marxists as well as by the theories of de Saussure and the French sociologist Émile Durkheim. Conversely, Václavek's folklore studies were informed by structuralist aesthetics, as is evident in his study *O lidové písni a slovesnosti* (On Folk Songs and Verbal Art; published posthumously in 1963). In a number of his seminal essays included in this reader, Jiří Veltruský elaborated on Mukařovský's dialectical theory, such as when he argued that the dynamics (mobility) of the theatrical sign has to be approached dialectically, against a background of something stable: the root of the dynamics lies in the tension between material and immaterial signs (for a detailed discussion see Drozd 2016).

The most fruitful concept taken on by the Prague School thinkers from Hegelian and Marxist philosophy was *dialectics*, a notion that started to appear in their texts in the 1930s (Toman 2011: 197) and "became a characteristic feature of all the works produced in the Prague Linguistic Circle" (Mukařovský, quoted in Steiner 1982: 200). It was in Jan Mukařovský's structuralist aesthetics that dialectical antinomies became the fundamental principle of existence and development of any artistic and extra-artistic phenomenon. A dialectical relationship was taken for an essential feature of any structure since its components are never in static harmony but are constantly in tension, renegotiating their mutual relations. It is only through these antinomies underlying the permanent process of the *actualization* and renegotiation of relations between individual components and elements that any structure evolves and is given form in a work of art. In other words, experiencing a work of art requires the recipient to interpret and understand the relations of the work's individual components – for example, understanding how music and various noises contribute to the performance or how changes in light interact with the dramatic action: while there are moments where light does not play a significant role, at others it may be crucial in the realization of the theatre performance. That is to say, the individual components are in permanent flux and the work of art is understood only through a negotiation of the dialectical relations between them; it is this dialectical process that constitutes the structure of a work of art in any given moment.

Hegelian and Marxist dialectics fostered other types of antinomies that resonated with the theories of the Prague Linguistic Circle. These included the antinomies of the artist's expression and the objective sign; of the work of art as an autonomous sign and as an informative sign; and of the work of art as an aesthetic structure and as an artefact in its social contexts. Other dual concepts included theories such the aesthetic function and non-aesthetic functions; intentionality and non-intentionality; the active subject and the passive object in the theatre; and folk (or popular) culture and urban culture. Dialectics was understood as the opposite of mechanical or static conception of art as represented, for example, by Viktor Shklovsky's concept of estrangement (*ostranenie*), by the more static antinomies of de Saussure, of Herbatian formalism and the opposition between high and low culture as proposed by

the ethnographer Hans Naumann's theory of the *Gesunkenes Kulturgut,* so
ardently opposed by Petr Bogatyrev and Jakobson (see above and Bogatyrev
1971 [1936]). Structuralist dialectics as practised by Mukařovský as well as
Jakobson and others was the fundamental principle linking the internal contradictions of phenomena and setting everything into motion (Striedter 1989:
115–7; Galán 1985: 52; Steiner 1982: 200; Toman 1995: 171–6).

CONCLUSION

An overview of critical work on Prague School theatre theorists and practitioners.

What remains is to give a brief overview of the broad and detailed research of many scholars and academics who have recently published on individual problems, trends or theorists of Prague School provenience. To name a few. Martina Musilová has done extensive research into the work of Jindřich Honzl from both the interwar and postwar periods, studying how he was inspired by Soviet theatre and discussing his political, artistic and teaching activities (Musilová 2015). Eva Stehlíková has brought to light the structuralist activities of theatre and film scholar Olga Srbová, who was a leading female critic of the 1930s and 1940s before abandoning her scholarly career (Stehlíková 2016). Helena Spurná has published a monograph dedicated to E. F. Burian's operas (Spurná 2014), developing the critical legacy of theatre historians Adolf Scherl and Bořivoj Srba. Kateřina Miholová has made a detailed analysis of Jiří Frejka's 1936 production of Shakespeare's *Julius Caesar* with František Tröster's scenography; in an interactive reconstruction realized with Jiří Vrzba, Miholová brings original insights into Frejka's directorial style of the late 1930s with a special view to Frejka's and Tröster's concepts of the dramatic space and scenography (Miholová 2011). The literary scholar Ondřej Sládek has published extensively on the Prague School and its literary theories; of particular interest are his meticulous academic biography of Jan Mukařovský (Sládek 2015) and an article on Mukařovský's relations to the theatre (Sládek 2014b). David Drozd has done extensive research into the life and work of Jiří Veltruský, whose academic activities were cut short in February 1948 when, as a vocal critic of the Communist Party and the author of a Social Democratic sponsored translation of Marx's *Capital* that challenged the official Communist version, he was forced to escape from Czechoslovakia. Although Veltruský returned to theatre theory in the late 1970s and 1980s (for instance Veltruský 1977 and the posthumously published Veltruský 2012), most of his working life was spent as an activist in the international trade union movement. Drozd has shown that Veltruský was expected, as Mukařovský's assistant in the Department of Aesthetics at Charles University, to devote his attention to theatre theory; his sudden exile left this position vacant (Drozd 2016). Herta Schmid has published extensively on Czech Structuralism. Particularly relevant is her essay "Jiří Veltruský Revisited" (Schmid 2014), a discussion of Veltruský's theory of dramatic literature, contextualized with the theories of Karl Bühler, Yury Tynyanov, Edmund Husserl, Jan Mukařovský and Roman Ingarden. Šárka Havlíčková Kysová and Barbora Diego Rivera Příhodová have published on the theoretical legacy of Miroslav Kouřil, also addressing his highly problematic role in postwar theatre life (Havlíčková Kysová and Příhodová 2012).

Comprehensive research into the Prague School precursor Otakar Zich was carried out by an earlier generation of theorists. Oleg Sus published an extensive critical introduction to his German edition of *The Aesthetics of Dramatic Art* in 1977; Ivo Osolsobě and Miroslav Procházka produced a monumental critical edition of Zich's *oeuvre* in 1986. Jaroslav Kolár collected and edited a range of essays by Petr Bogatyrev that was published in 1971, highlighting his contribution to a number of academic disciplines. However, a recent reassessment is missing, while other theorists have not yet received a systematic treatment at all – for a variety of reasons, often closely connected with the troubled history of the Czechoslovak intelligentsia in the twentieth century. Comprehensive studies of Petr Bogatyrev, Karel Brušák and Jiří Frejka and E. F. Burian as theatre theorists are still waiting to be made.

FURTHER READING

The critical heritage of the Prague School has been the subject of a number of publications. Michael Quinn's 1995 monograph *The Semiotic Stage: Prague School Theater Theory* marked a key moment in the critical revision of the original writings. Quinn's untimely death left his large project incomplete; in more senses than one, our own project is a completion of his unfinished initiative. Petr Szcepanik and Jaroslav Anděl's 2008 anthology *Cinema All the Time* was in many ways an inspiration for this reader and provides a fascinating selection of texts on Czech film theory, both pre-dating the Prague School (such as Václav Tille's 1908 essay "Kinéma") and post-dating it.

A significant and original continuation of the Prague School tradition is the Tartu School, sometimes known as the Tartu-Moscow Semiotic School, which was established by Yuri Lotman (1922–1993) in 1964 at the University of Tartu, Estonia. Its journal *Trudy po znakovym sistemam* (Questions of Sign Systems) was influential in developing the heritage of Russian Formalism and Prague Structuralism in the direction of a coherent semiotics of culture.

As part of the semiotic wave of the 1970s and 1980s, four significant books of Prague School criticism were published – Mark E. Suino's translation of Jan Mukařovský's seminal 1936 study *Aesthetic Function, Norm and Value as Social Facts* (Mukařovský 1970) and three anthologies: Ladislav Matejka and Irwin R. Titunik's *Semiotics of Art: Prague School Contributions* (Matejka and Titunik 1976); Paul Garvin's *A Prague School Reader on Esthetics, Literary Structure, and Style* (Garvin 1982); and Peter Steiner's *The Prague School: Selected Writings, 1929–1949* (Steiner 1982). Some of the essays published in these anthologies have been revised and re-published in this reader. These publications have been very influential despite the oversemiotization of some of the terminology.[33]

Steiner's anthology included his seminal study on "The Roots of Structuralist Esthetics" (Steiner 1982). This essay is a comprehensive and meticulous discussion of the complex origins of Prague School theory, with inspiration from the Russian Formalist school as well as Central European traditions. This is an excellent starting point for anyone interested in pursuing a critical

---

33 For the sake of completeness, František Deák's reassessment of the Prague School's legacy in the theatre (Deák 1976) must be mentioned.

study of the theoretical system. Three other publications are of particular relevance here. Jurij Striedter's *Literary Structure, Evolution, and Value: Russian Formalism and Czech Structuralism Reconsidered* (Striedter 1989) is a detailed study of the relationship between the two schools in question, setting right the earlier and rather problematic discussion by Victor Erlich. Jindřich Toman's *The Magic of a Common Language: Jakobson, Mathesius, Trubetzkoy, and the Prague Linguistic Circle* (Toman 1995) is a fascinating and even deeply moving account of the great work and profound humanity that not only made the Prague Linguistic Circle possible but also transformed it into the great movement it was. This is an excellent starting point for anyone interested in the history and context of the short-lived community of artists and academics. Thomas Winner's posthumously published *The Czech Avant-Garde Literary Movement between the World Wars* (Winner 2015) focuses on the literary side of the same era and presents leading literary figures who interacted with, provoked and let themselves be provoked in turn by the Prague School theorists and their ideas.

Richard Bradford's *Roman Jakobson: Life, Language, Art* (Bradford 1994) is a useful starting point for an understanding of one of the leading figures of the Prague School, although its purpose is more narrowly focused on literary art and the contexts of literary and cultural theory. Ondřej Sládek's academic biography *Jan Mukařovský: Life and Work* (Sládek 2015) is a detailed account of its subject; unfortunately it is only available (to date) in Czech. Jiří Veltruský's comprehensive theatre theory, modestly entitled *An Approach to the Semiotics of Theatre* (Veltruský 2012), is the much belated lifework of the leading Prague School theatre theorist. Published two decades after Veltruský's death thanks to the perseverance of his wife Jarmila F. Veltrusky and Tomáš Hoskovec, the book has the potential to become a key text in modern theatre theory.

Readers interested in the history of Czech theatre should start with Jan Císař's compact account in *The History of Czech Theatre: A Survey* (Císař 2010); though the book understates its importance and apologizes for not going into too many details, it is a reliable and rigorous account of the long tradition of Czech theatre. Jarka M. Burian provides an introduction with two books. His *Modern Czech Theatre: Reflector and Conscience of a Nation* (Burian 2000) focuses predominantly on the middle of the twentieth century, specifically from the 1920s to the 1980s. This is a passionate account with a few inaccuracies, but useful as an introduction to the crucial period when Czech theatre was in the spotlight of the world's attention. Burian's sequel, entitled *Leading Creators of Twentieth-Century Czech Theatre* (Burian 2002), treats the expressionist director Karel Hugo Hilar, the Liberated Theatre of Voskovec and Werich, the avant-garde director E. F. Burian, the director and co-creator of the Laterna Magica Alfréd Radok, the postwar directors Otomar Krejča, Jan Grossman, Miroslav Macháček and Evald Schorm, the playwright Václav

Havel and the internationally pre-eminent innovator and stage designer Josef Svoboda as well as other Czech stage designers. The individual chapters give good starting points for further critical study of these key figures. Two richly illustrated special issues of the *Theatralia* journal, edited by Christian M. Billing and Pavel Drábek, are devoted to *Czech Stage Art and Stage Design* (Billing and Drábek 2011) and *Czech Puppet Theatre in Global Contexts* (Billing and Drábek 2015); both cover a wide range of historical, theoretical and contextual aspects of the themes in question.

Readers interested in the contexts of Czech culture and history are recommended to read Jan Bažant, Nina Bažantová and Frances Starn's *The Czech Reader: History, Culture, Politics* (Bažant). This large anthology includes texts documenting Czech culture and history that range from the medieval period, through the Reformation down to the modern age. Brian S. Locke's *Opera and Ideology in Prague: Polemics and Practice at the National Theater 1900-1938* (Locke 2006) not only provides detailed analyses of key operatic works of the the early twentieth century, including those by Otakar Zich, but also brings an informed critical overview of the entire Czech cultural scene. Derek Sayer's impressive *Prague, Capital of the Twentieth Century: A Surrealist History* (Sayer 2013) is a true labour of love, the biography of a city that was a crossroads of immense artistic, cultural and intellectual endeavour from the early twentieth century to shortly after World War II. Sayer shows Prague as the unsung gem of the Surrealist movement. His earlier book *The Coasts of Bohemia: A Czech History* (Sayer 1998) is a deeply enjoyable account of the history as well as the art and culture of the Czech lands. Both books include many illustrations and are a fascinating read for anyone with a love of the arts. Mikuláš Teich's *Bohemia in History* (Teich 1998) is an original collection of essays by a range of authors from different disciplines, covering a period from prehistory until the late 1990s. Mary Heimann's *Czechoslovakia: The State That Failed* (Heimann 2009) is a modern critical history of Czechoslovakia (1918-1993), focusing on the politics and ideology of the state in the tumultous context of twentieth-century Europe. Heimann's book may be provocative but it is a refreshing and non-nationalist portrait of Czechoslovakia as a political project. Kevin McDermott's *Communist Czechoslovakia, 1945-89: A Political and Social History* (McDermott 2015) covers Czechoslovakia's four Communist decades, critically revisiting historical and archival materials and providing a modern and sympathetic history of this troubled period in the life of the country. Although only a short chapter is devoted to the interwar years that overlapped with the activities of the Prague Linguistic Circle, it is a useful companion to the period that prevented further developments of the intellectual and artistic freedom and creativity that flourished in the 1920s and 1930s. McDermott's book may be read as a coda to the cultural and political contexts of the Prague School.

WORKS CITED

Adámek, Jiří (2010) *Théâtre musical: Divadlo poutané hudbou* [Théâtre musical: theatre bound by music], Prague: AMU.

Ambros, Veronika (2004) "A Suitcase Full of Manuscripts: Petr Bogatyrev and his legacy", a book review of L. P. Solntseva (ed.) (2002) *Petr Grigorevich Bogatyrev: Vospominaniia. Dokumenty. Statii* [Petr Grigorevich Bogatyrev: Memoirs, Documents, Articles], St Petersburg: Aleteia, in *Toronto Slavic Quarterly*, vol. 9. Available at <http://sites.utoronto.ca/tsq/09/ambros09.shtml>.

— (2008) "'Prague's Experimental Stage: Laboratory of Theatre and Semiotics", *Semiotica*, vol. 168. no. 1, pp. 45–65.

— (2012) "Puppets, Statues, Men, Objects and the Prague School", *Theatralia*, vol. 15, no. 2, pp. 74–88.

Anderson, Benedict (1983) *Imagined Communities: Reflections on the Origin and Spread of Nationalism*, London: Verso.

Balme, Christopher (2014) *The Theatrical Public Sphere*, Cambridge: Cambridge University Press.

Bažant, Jan et al. (eds) (2010) *The Czech Reader: History, Culture, Politics*, Durham and London: Duke University Press.

Bell, John (2014) "Playing with the Eternal Uncanny: The Persistent Life of Lifeless Objects" in Dassia N. Posner, Claudia Orenstein and John Bell (eds) *The Routledge Companion to Puppetry and Material Performance*, Abingdon and New York: Routledge, pp. 43–52.

Benjamin, Walter (1929) "Surrealism", translated by Edmund Jephcott, in Walter Benjamin, *Selected Writings*, vol. 2, part 1, 1927–1930, Michael W. Jennings, Howard Eiland and Gary Smith (eds), Cambridge, Mass., and London: Harvard University Press, pp. 207–21.

Bernátek, Martin (2015) "The Renaissance of Czech Puppetry and the Cinema" in Billing and Drábek (2015), pp. 135–67.

— (2016) "Projekty spolupráce, formy propagace: Pražský lingvistický kroužek a německojazyčný tisk v meziválečném Československu" [Collaboration Projects and Forms of Promotion: the Prague Linguistic Circle and the German-Language Press in Interwar Czechoslovakia], *Theatralia*, vol. 19, no. 1 (Supplementum), pp. 7–34.

Billing, Christian M. and Drábek, Pavel (eds) (2011) *Czech Stage Art and Stage Design*, a special issue of *Theatralia*, vol. 14, no. 1.

— (eds) (2015) *Czech Puppet Theatre in Global Contexts*, a special issue of *Theatralia*, vol. 18, no. 2.

Blecha, Jaroslav (2011) "The History of Scenographic Influence of Czech Family Marionette Theatre" in Billing and Drábek (2011), pp. 114–46.

Bogatyrev, Petr (2016 [1936]) "Clothing as a Sign (The Functional and Structural Concept in Ethnography) ", this reader, pp. 441–47.

— (2016 [1938]) "Theatrical Signs", this reader, pp. 99–114.

— (1940) *Lidové divadlo české a slovenské* [Czech and Slovak Folk Theatre], Prague: Fr. Borový and Národopisná společnost českoslovanská.

— (1971 [1936]) "Několik poznámek o vztazích mezi folklorem a vysokým uměním" [Several Notes on the Relationship between Folklore and High Art] in Jaroslav Kolár (ed.) *Souvislosti tvorby: Cesty ke struktuře lidové kultury a divadla* [The Contexts of Creation: In Search of the Structure of Folk Culture and Theatre], Prague: Odeon, pp. 94–97.

Bogatyrev, Petr and Roman Jakobson (1982 [1929]) "Folklore as a Special Form of Creativity" in Peter Steiner (ed.) *The Prague School: Selected Writings, 1929–1949*, Austin: University of Texas Press, pp. 32–46.

Bradford, Richard (1994) *Roman Jakobson: Life, Language, Art*, London and New York: Routledge.

Broekman, Jan M. (1974) *Structuralism: Moscow - Prague - Paris*, Dordrecht and Boston: D. Reidek Publishing Company.

Brušák, Karel (2016 [1939]) "Signs in the Chinese Theatre", this reader, pp. 115–28.

Burian, Jarka M. (2000) *Modern Czech Theatre: Reflector and Conscience of a Nation*, Iowa City: University of Iowa Press.

— (2002) *Leading Creators of Twentieth-Century Czech Theatre*, London and New York: Routledge.

Chvatík, Květoslav (1966) "Estetika Jana Mukařovského" [Jan Mukařovský's Aesthetics] in Jan Mukařovský, *Studie z estetiky* [Studies in Aesthetics], edited by Felix Vodička and Květoslav Chvatík, Prague: Odeon, pp. 339–63.

— (1970) *Strukturalismus a avantgarda* [Structuralism and the Avant-garde], Prague: Československý spisovatel.

Císař, Jan (2010) *The History of Czech Theatre: A Survey*, Prague: NAMU.

Deák, František (1976) "Structuralism in Theatre", *The Drama Review*, vol. 20, no. 4, pp. 83–94.

De Benedictis, Michele (2014) "Crossing the Rubicon in Fascist Italy: Mussolini and Theatrical Caesarism from Shakespeare's *Julius Caesar*" in Keith Gregor (ed.) *Shakespeare and Tyranny: Regimes of Reading in Europe and Beyond*, Newcastle: Cambridge Scholars Publishing, pp. 105–26.

Demetz, Peter (2008) *Prague in Danger: The Years of German Occupation, 1939–45: Memories and History, Terror and Resistance, Theater and Jazz, Film and Poetry, Politics and War*, New York: Farrar, Straus and Giroux.

de Toro, Fernando (1990) Introduction to Jiří Veltruský, *El drama como literatura* (Drama as Literature), translated by Milena Grass, Buenos Aires: Editorial Galerna.

— (2012) "The Legacy of the Linguistic Circle of Prague", *Theatralia*, vol. 15, no. 2, pp. 24–36.

Doležel, Lubomír (1988) "Literary Transduction: Prague School Approach" in Yishai Tobin (ed.) *The Prague School and its Legacy in Linguistics, Literature, Semiotics, Folklore and the Arts*, Philadelphia: John Benjamins, pp. 165–76.

— (1990) *Occidental Poetics. Tradition and Progress*, Lincoln and London: University Nebraska Press.

Drábek, Pavel (2012a) *České pokusy o Shakespeara* [Czech Attempts at Shakespeare], Brno: Větrné mlýny.

— (2012b) "Launching a Structuralist Assembly: Convening the Scattered Structures", *Theatralia*, vol. 15, no. 2, pp. 13–23.

— (2014) "Functional Reformulations: Prague School and Intralingual Translation", *Theatralia*, no. 17, no. 2, pp. 81–95.

— (2016) "Shakespearean Tragedy in Eastern Europe", chapter 49 of Michael Neill and David Schalkwyk (eds) *The Oxford Handbook of Shakespearean Tragedy*, Oxford: Oxford University Press, forthcoming.

Drozd, David (2016) "Od propozic k systému? aneb 'Historisovati' Jiřího Veltruského..." [From Propositions to a System? or "Historicizing" Jiří Veltruský...], *Theatralia*, vol. 19, no. 1, pp. 86–128.

Eagleton, Terry (1983) *Literary Theory: An Introduction*, Oxford: Blackwell.

Eichenbaum, Boris M. [Ejxenbaum] (1978) "The Theory of the Formal Method", translated by Irwin R. Titunik, in Ladislav Matějka and Krystyna Pomorska (eds) (1978) *Readings in Russian Poetics. Formalist and Structuralist Views*, Ann Arbor: Michigan Slavic Publications, pp. 3–37.

Elam, Keir (1980) *The Semiotics of Theatre and Drama*, London and New York: Routledge, 2nd edition published in 2002.

Erlich, Victor (1965) *Russian Formalism: History – Doctrine*, The Hague and Paris: Mouton.

Ertl, Václav (1922) "Ústav pro jazyk československý" [An Institute for the Czechoslovak Language], *Naše řeč*, vol. 6, no. 4, pp. 97–112.

Frejka, Jiří (1926) "Cesta moderního jevištního myšlení" [The Progress of Modern Stage Thinking], *Pásmo*, vol. 2, no. 8 (10 April), pp. 87.

— (1929) "*Člověk, který se stal hercem*" [How People Become Actors], Prague: Melantrich.

— (1936) "O novém jevištním realismu" [On the New Stage Realism], *Život*, vol. 15, pp. 75–84.

Frýbertová, Tereza (2012) "Sokolská sletová scéna Marathón z roku 1912" [Marathón (1912): a group outing organized by the Sokol movement], *Theatralia*, vol. 15, no. 1, pp. 65–81.

Galán, František William (1982) "Reception History" in Miroslav Červenka, Peter Steiner and Ronald Vroon (eds) *The Structure of the Literary Process: Studies Dedicated to the Memory of Felix Vodička*, Amsterdam: John Benjamins, pp. 161–86.

— (1984) *Historic Structures: the Prague School Project, 1928–1946*, Austin: University of Texas Press.

Garvin, Paul L. (ed.) (1982) *A Prague School Reader on Esthetics, Literary Structure, and Style*, Washington, D.C.: Georgetown University Press.

Glanc, Tomáš (ed.) (2005) *Roman Jakobson: Formalistická škola a dnešní literární věda ruská* [Roman Jakobson: The Formalist School and Contemporary Russian Literary Criticism], Prague: Academia.

Havlíčková, Margita (2013) *Berufstheater in Brünn 1668–1733* [Professional Theatre in Brno 1668–1733], Brno: Munipress.

Havlíčková, Margita, Sylva Pracná and Jiří Štefanides (2010) "Německojazyčná městská divadla na Moravě a ve Slezku (1733–1944)" [German-Language Municipal Theatres in Moravia and Silesia (1733–1944)], *Theatralia*, vol. 13, no. 1, pp. 47–71.

Havlíčková Kysová, Šárka (2012) "'Asian' Theatre Sign: Its Potential and Its Limits in the History of the Czech Structuralist Thought", *Theatralia*, vol. 15, no. 2, pp. 89–99.

Havlíčková Kysová, Šárka and Příhodová, Barbora (2012) "Miroslav Kouřil's Theory of Scenography in the Archive Materials: A Research Report", *Theatralia*, vol. 15, no. 2, pp. 227–31.

— (2012) *Prague Semiotic Stage Revisited*, a special issue of *Theatralia*, vol. 15, no. 2.

Havránek, Bohuslav et al. (1935) "Úvod" [Introduction], co-authored by Bohuslav Havránek, Roman Jakobson, Vilém Mathesius, Jan Mukařovský, Bohumil Trnka. *Slovo a slovesnost*, vol. 1, no. 1, pp. 1–7.

Heimann, Mary (2009) *Czechoslovakia: The State That Failed*, New Haven: Yale University Press.

Holenstein, Elmar (1977) *Roman Jakobson's Approach to Language: Phenomenological Structuralism*, Bloomington: Indiana University Press.

— (1979) "Prague Structuralism – A Branch of the Phenomonological Movement" in John Odmark (ed.) *The Language, Literature and Meaning. Volume I: Problems of Literary Theory*, Amsterdam: John Benjamins, pp. 71–99.

— (2005) "Jakobson and Husserl: a contribution to the genealogy of structuralism" in Rudolf Bernet, Donn Welton and Gina Zavota (eds) *Edmund Husserl: The Web of Meaning: Language, Noema, and Subjectivity and Intersubjectivity*, London and New York: Routledge, pp. 11–48.

Hyvnar, Jan (2008) *O českém dramatickém herectví 20. století* [On Twentieth-century Czech Dramatic Acting], Prague: KANT.

Jakobson, Roman (1923) *O cheshskom stiche: preimushchestvenno v sopostavlenii s russkim* [On Czech Verse: Predominantly in Relation to the Russian], Berlin: OPOJAZ-MLK.

— (1926) *Základy českého verše* [The Principles of Czech Verse], Prague: Odeon.

— (1929) *Nejstarší české písně duchovní* [The Earliest Czech Sacred Songs], Prague: Ladislav Kuncíř.

— (1932) "O dnešním brusičství českém" [On Today's Czech Language Purism] in Bohuslav Havránek and Miloš Weingart (eds) *Spisovná čeština a jazyková kultura* [Standard Czech and Language Culture], Prague: Melantrich, pp. 85–122.

— (1960) "Closing Statements: Linguistics and Poetics" in Thomas A. Sebeok (ed.) *Style in Language*, Cambridge, Mass.: M.I.T. Press, pp. 350–77.

— (1976 [1933]) "Is Cinema in Decline?" in Matějka and Titunik (1976), pp. 145–52.

— (1985) "Petr Bogatyrev", *Selected Writings: Volume VII: Contributions to Comparative Mythology. Studies in Linguistics and Philology, 1972–1982*, Berlin and New York: Mouton, pp. 293–302.

— (1987 [1937]) "An Open Letter from Roman Jakobson to Jiří Voskovec and Jan Werich on the Epistemology and Semantics of Fun" in Michael L. Quinn, "Jakobson and the Liberated Theatre", *Stanford Slavic Studies*, vol. 1, pp. 153–62; reprinted in Roman Jakobson (1971) *Studies in Verbal Art*, Ann Arbor: Michigan Slavic Contributions; and also in Jakobson's *Selected Writings*.

— (1996) *My Futurist Years*, New York: Marsilio Publishers.

Jakobson, Roman and Pomorska, Krystyna (1980) *Dialogues*, Cambridge: Cambridge University Press.

Kaplan, Charles G. (1988) "From Folklore to Folkstyle: The Prague Circle's Contribution to Ethnoinquiries" in Yishai Tobin (ed.) *The Prague School and its Legacy in Linguistics, Literature, Semiotics, Folklore and the Arts*, Philadelphia: John Benjamins, pp. 227–44.

Kolár, Jaroslav (1971) "Československá léta Petra Bogatyreva" [Petr Bogatyrev's Czechoslovak Years] in Petr Bogatyrev, *Souvislosti tvorby: Cesty ke struktuře lidové kultury a divadla* [The Contexts of Creation: In Search of the Structure of Folk Culture and Theatre], edited by Jaroslav Kolár, Prague: Odeon, pp. 171–82.

Kováč, Ladislav (2002) "Natural History of Communism", *Central European Political Science Review*, vol. 3, no. 8, pp. 74–110, pp. 111–64. This essay is available in two parts at < http://www.biocenter.sk/lkpublics_files/C-11.pdf > and< http://www.biocenter.sk/lkpublics_files/C-12.pdf >.

— (2007) *Prírodopis komunizmu: Anatómia jednej utópie* [The Natural History of Communism: The Anatomy of a Utopia]. Bratislava: Kalligram.

Locke, Brian S. (2006) *Opera and Ideology in Prague: Polemics and Practice at the National Theater 1900–1938*, Rochester: University of Rochester Press.

Lote, René (1920) "Vyučování jazyku mateřskému ve Francii" [Teaching the Mother Tongue in France], *Naše řeč*, vol. 4, no. 6–7, pp. 161–68.

Ludvová, Jitka (2012) *Až k hořkému konci: Pražské německé divadlo 1845–1945* [To the Bitter End: Prague German Theatre 1845–1945], Prague: Institut umění – Divadelní ústav and Academia.

Mach, Jaroslav (2012) *Ruští intelektuálové v emigraci a jejich institucionální základna v Praze (na modelu Ruské svobodné univerzity a přidružených institucí, 1923–1945)* [Russian intellectuals and their institutional base in Prague (on the model of the Russian Free University and its affiliated institutions, 1923–1945)], PhD thesis, Brno: Masaryk University, Faculty of Arts, available at <http://is.muni.cz/th/18830/ff_d/>.

Macura, Vladimír (1998) *Český sen* [The Czech Dream], Prague: Nadace Lidových novin.

Masaryk, Tomáš Garrigue (1895) *Česká otázka* [The Czech Question], Prague: Čin.

Matejka, Ladislav and Titunik, Irwin R. (eds) (1976) *Semiotics of Art: Prague School Contributions*, Cambridge, Mass.: M.I.T. Press.

Mathauser, Zdeněk (2005) "Strukturalismus – fenomenologie – avantgarda" [Structuralism – Phenomenology – Avant-garde], *Slovo a slovesnost*, vol. 66, no. 3, pp. 163–75.

Mathesius, Vilém (1925) *Kulturní aktivismus: Anglické paralely k českému životu* [Cultural Activism: English Parallels to Czech Life], Prague: Gustav Voleský.

McDermott, Kevin (2015) *Communist Czechoslovakia, 1945–89: A Political and Social History*, London: Palgrave Macmillan.

McNeill, J. R. and McNeill, William H. (2003) *The Human Web: A Bird's-Eye View of World History*, New York and London: W. W. Norton & Company.

Meerzon, Yana (2012) "Concretization-Transduction-Adaptation: On Prague School Legacy in Theatre Studies Today", *Theatralia*, vol. 15, no. 2, pp. 125–53.

Miholová, Kateřina (2011) *Julius Caesar: Shakespeare – Frejka – Tröster: 1936*, Prague: Augias.

Mukařovský, Jan (1964 [1932]) "Standard Language and Poetic Language" in Garvin (1982), pp. 17–30.

— (1966 [1946]) "O strukturalismu" [On Structuralism] in *Studie z estetiky* [Studies in Aesthetics], edited by Felix Vodička and Květoslav Chvatík, Prague: Odeon, pp. 109–16.

— (1970 [1936]) *Aesthetic Function, Norm and Value as Social Facts*, translated by Mark E. Suino, Ann Arbor: University of Michigan Press.

— (1976 [1936]) "Art as Semiotic Fact" in Ladislav Matejka and Irwin R. Titunik (eds) *Semiotics of Art. Prague School Contributions*, Cambridge, Mass.: M.I.T. Press, pp. 3–9.

— (1978 [1943]) "Intentionality and Unintentionality in Art" in John Burbank and Peter Steiner (eds) *Structure, Sign and Function*, New Haven and London: Yale University Press, pp. 891–28.

— (1982a [1940]) "Structuralism in Esthetics and in Literary Studies" in Peter Steiner (ed.) *The Prague School: Selected Writings, 1929–1946*, Austin: University of Texas Press, pp. 65–82.

— (1982b [1934]) "Otakar Zich" in *Studie z poetiky* [Studies in Poetics], Prague: Odeon, pp. 328–32.

— (2016 [1931]) "An Attempt at a Structural Analysis of an Actor's Figure (Chaplin in *City Lights*)", this reader, pp. 192–98.

Musilová, Martina (2015) "Avantgardní sňatek umění a politiky: Vliv ideologie na teoretické texty Jindřicha Honzla" [An Avant-Garde Marriage of Art and Politics: The Influence of Ideology on the Theoretical Texts of Jindřich Honzl], *Divadelní revue*, vol. 26, no. 3, pp. 27–49.

Novák, Bohumil (1933) "Rozhovor s Otakarem Zichem" ⌊An Interview with Otakar Zich⌋, *Cin*, vol. 4, pp. 465-69.

Osolsobě, Ivo (2002 [1981]) "Semiotika semiotika Otakara Zicha" [The Semiotics of the Semiotician Otakar Zich] in *Ostenze, hra, jazyk* [Ostension, Performance, Language], Brno: Host, pp. 213-38.

Pešat, Zdeněk (1999) "Artefact, Aesthetic Object and Concretization" in Vladimír Macura and Herta Schmid (eds) *Jan Mukařovský*, Prague: Ústav pro českou literaturu, pp. 142-47.

Quinn, Michael L. (1988) "The Prague School Concept of the Stage Figure" in Irmengard Rauch and Gerald Carr (eds) *The Semiotic Bridge: Trends from California*, The Hague: Mouton de Gruyter, pp. 75-85.

— (1995) *The Semiotic Stage: Prague School Theater Theory*, New York and Berlin: Peter Lang.

Sayer, Derek (2013) *Prague, Capital of the Twentieth Century: A Surrealist History*, Princeton and Oxford: Princeton University Press.

Schmid, Herta (2012) "The Concept of Sign, its Origin and Influence on Mukařovský's Structuralism", *Theatralia*, vol. 15, no. 2, pp. 112-24.

— (2014) "Jiří Veltruský Revisited", *Theatralia*, vol. 17, no. 2, pp. 96-110.

Shershow, Scott Cutler (1995) *Puppets and "Popular" Culture*, Ithaca and London: Cornell University Press.

Shklovsky, Viktor (1965) "Art as Technique" in Lee T. Lemon and Marion J. Reiss (eds) *Russian Formalist Criticism: Four Essays*, Lincoln: University of Nebraska Press, pp. 3-24.

— (2005) *Knight's Move*, translated and edited by Richard Sheldon, London: Dalkey Archive Press.

Sládek, Ondřej (ed.) (2014a) *Český strukturalismus v diskusi* [Czech Structuralism in Discussion], Brno: Host.

— (2014b) "Jan Mukařovský and Theatre", *Theatralia*, vol. 17, no. 2, pp. 122-36.

— (2015) *Jan Mukařovský: Život a dílo* [Jan Mukařovský: Life and Work], Brno: Host.

Šlaisová, Eva (2012) "'Aktualisace' in English Scholarly Literature: Interpretation, Ignorance, and Misunderstanding", *Theatralia*, vol. 15, no. 2, pp. 154-67.

Spurná, Helena (2014) *Emil František Burian a jeho cesty za operou* [Emil František Burian and His Path to Opera], Prague: KLP - Koniasch Latin Press.

Srba, Bořivoj (1971) *Poetické divadlo E. F. Buriana* [E. F. Burian's Poetical Theatre], Prague: SPN.

Štefanides, Jiří, Havlíčková, Margita and Pracná, Sylva (2011-2013) *Německojazyčné divadlo na Moravě a ve Slezsku / Deutschsprachiges Theater in Mähren und Schlesien* [German-Language Theatre in Moravia and Silesia], 3 volumes, Olomouc: Palacký University.

Stehlíková, Eva (2010) "Divadelní vesnice, aneb, První plenérové představení řecké tragédie v Čechách" [A theatrical village, or The first open-air production of Greek tragedy in the Czech lands], *Theatralia*, vol. 13, no. 1, pp. 72-83.

— (2011) "The Laterna Magika of Josef Svoboda and Alfréd Radok", *Theatralia*, vol. 14, no. 1, pp. 173-91.

— (2016) "Strukturalistická stopa Olgy Srbové" [The Structuralist Imprint of Olga Srbová], *Theatralia*, vol. 19, no. 1, pp. 181-200.

Steiner, Peter (1982) "The Roots of Structuralist Esthetics" in Peter Steiner (ed.) *The Prague School: Selected Writings, 1929-1949*, Austin: University of Texas Press, pp. 174-219.

Striedter, Jurij (1989) *Literary Structure, Evolution, and Value: Russian Formalism and Czech Structuralism Reconsidered*, Cambridge, Mass., and London: Harvard University Press.

Sus, Oleg (1968) "Typologie tzv. slovanského formalismu a problémy přechodu od formálních škol ke strukturalismu" [The Typology of the So-Called Slavic Formalism and Issues of the Transition from the Formalist Schools to Structuralism] in *Československé přednášky pro VI. mezinárodní sjezd slavistů v Praze* [Czechoslovak Papers at the 6th International Congress of Slavic Studies in Prague], Prague: Nakladatelství ČSAV.

— (1992) *Geneze sémantiky hudby a básnictví v moderní české estetice: Dvě studie o Otakaru Zichovi* [The Birth of the Semantics of Music and Poetry in Modern Czech Aesthetics: Two Studies of Otakar Zich], Brno: Masaryk University Press.

Szczepanik, Petr and Anděl, Jaroslav (eds) (2008) *Cinema All the Time. An Anthology of Czech Film Theory and Criticism, 1908-1939*, Ann Arbor: University of Michigan Press.

Székely, György (ed.) (1991) *The Correspondence of Edward Gordon Craig and Sándor Hevesi (1908-1933) / Edward Gordon Craig és Hevesi Sándor levelezése (1908-1933)*, translation, introduction and epilogue by György Székely, Budapest: Hungarian Theatre Institute and Museum. Available at <http://library.hungaricana.hu/en/view/SZAK_SZIN_Sk_1991_Craig_es_Hevesi_levelezese/>.

Teich, Mikuláš (ed.) (1998) *Bohemia in History*, Cambridge: Cambridge University Press.

Toman, Jindřich (1995) *The Magic of a Common Language: Jakobson, Mathesius, Trubetzkoy, and the Prague Linguistic Circle*, Cambridge, Mass.: M.I.T. Press.

Tóth, Andrej, Novotný, Lukáš and Stehlík, Michal (2012) *Národnostní menšiny v Československu 1918-1938. Od státu národního ke státu národnostnímu?* [National Minorities in Czechoslovakia 19181-938. From a National State to a State of Nationalities?], Prague: Charles University.

Třeštík, Dušan (1999) *Mysliti dějiny* [To Think History], Prague and Litomyšl: Ladislav Horáček - Paseka.

Tynyanov, Yury (1978 [1927]) "On Literary Evolution" in Ladislav Matějka and Krystyna Pomorska (eds) *Readings in Russian Poetics. Formalist and Structuralist View*, Ann Arbor: Michigan Slavic Publications, pp. 79-81.

Tynyanov, Yury and Roman Jakobson (1978 [1928]) "Problems in the Study of Literature and Language" in Ladislav Matějka and Krystyna Pomorska (eds) *Readings in Russian Poetics. Formalist and Structuralist View*, Ann Arbor: Michigan Slavic Publications, pp. 66-78.

Veltrusky, Jiří (1977) *Drama as Literature*, Lisse: Peter de Ridder Press.

— (1981) "Jan Mukařovský's Structural Poetics and Aesthetics", *Poetics Today*, vol. 2, no. 16, pp. 117-57.

— (MS) (undated) "Bühler's Organon Model and the Semiotics of Art", unpublished manuscript. A copy is deposited in the Arts and Theatre Institute Prague (Institut umění - Divadelní ústav Praha).

— (2012) *An Approach to the Semiotics of Theatre*, Travaux du Cercle linguistique de Prague, nouvelle série, vol. 6, edited by Jarmila F. Veltrusky and Tomáš Hoskovec, Brno: Masaryk University Press.

— (2016 [1940]) "People and Things in the Theatre", this reader, pp. 147-56.

Vočadlo, Otakar (1924) *V zajetí babylonském: německé vlivy na nás* [In Babylonian Captivity: German Influences in the Czech Lands], Prague: Nové Čechy.

Vodička, Felix (1982 [1941]) "The Concretization of the Literary Work" in Garvin (1982), pp. 103-34.

Vojvodík, Josef (2011) "Structuralism, Phenomenology and Czech Avant-garde" in Petr A. Bílek, Josef Vojvodík and Jan Wiendl (eds) *A Glossary of Catchwords of the Czech Avant-garde: Conceptions of Aesthetics and the Changing Faces of Art 1908-1958*, Prague: Charles University Press, pp. 361-78.

Volek, Emil (2004) *Znak, funkce, hodnota* [Sign, Function, Value], Prague and Litomyšl: Paseka.

Wilson, Peter H. (2009) *The Thirty Years War: Europe's Tragedy*, Cambridge, Mass.: Harvard University Press.

Winner, Thomas G. (2015) *The Czech Avant-garde Literary Movement Between the World Wars*, edited by Ondřej Sládek and Michael Heim, New York: Peter Lang.

Zarrilli Phillip B., McConachie, Bruce, Williams, Gary Jay and Fisher Sorgenfrei, Carol (2010) *Theatre Histories: An Introduction*, 2nd edition, edited by Gary Jay Williams, New York and London: Routledge.

Zelenka, Miloš (1993) "K otázkám metodologické transformace ruského formalismu a českého strukturalismu (R. Jakobson a meziválečné Československo)" [On the Questions of the Methodological Transformation of Russian Formalism and Czech Structuralism (R. Jakobson and the Interwar Czechoslovakia)], *Romboid*, vol. 28, no. 8, pp. 50-59.

— (2012) "Roman Jakobson mezi ruským formalismem a českým strukturalismem" [Roman Jakobson between Russian Formalism and Czech Structuralism], a lecture delivered at the Faculty of Arts, Masaryk University, on 23 April 2012.

Zich, Otakar (1931) *Estetika dramatického umění: teoretická dramaturgie* [The Aesthetics of Dramatic Art: A Theoretical Dramaturgy], Prague: Melantrich.
— (2014) *Vina: Opera in Three Acts*, edited by Brian S. Locke, Middleton, Wisc.: A-R Editions.
— (2015 [1923]) "Puppet Theatre" in Billing and Drábek (2015), pp. 505–13.
— (2016) "Principles of Theoretical Dramaturgy", this reader, pp. 34–58.
Zubatý, Josef (1927) "Na prahu druhého desítiletí II" [On the Threshold of the Second Decade II], *Naše řeč*, vol. 11, no. 2, pp. 25–31.

BIOGRAPHIES OF AUTHORS PRESENTED IN THE READER

These biographies present only the most important information about the authors. Many other details about their activities in the Prague Linguistic Circle and Czech avant-garde theatre (or both) can be found in the Aferword.

PETR GRIGORIEVICH BOGATYREV
(29 JANUARY 1893, SARATOV – 18 AUGUST 1971, MOSCOW)

Bogatyrev was enrolled in Slavic studies and ethnography at Moscow University, graduating in 1918. In 1915 he participated in the establishment of the Moscow Linguistic Circle. From 1921 Bogatyrev acted as a translator for Soviet diplomats in Prague, and in 1926 he joined the Prague Linguistic Circle. In 1936, after submitting his habilitation thesis, entitled *Polaznik u južnych Slavjan, Madjar, Slovakov, Poljakov i Ukrajincev* (The "polaznik" Figure among the Southern Slavs, Hungarians, Slovaks, Poles and Ukrainians), at Comenius University in Bratislava, Bogatyrev became an Associate Professor there, remaining at the university until 1939. In 1940 he was forced to return to the USSR, where he taught at Moscow University, later becoming head of the Institute of Ethnography and, in 1964, a full Professor.

Bogatyrev was engaged in a broad range of research activities that took in philology, literary studies, ethnography and theatre studies. His research included folk theatre and Slavic folklore. In particular, he studied folklore phenomena in Sub-Carpathian Ruthenia, elsewhere in Czechoslovakia and in other Slav regions. In his work he focused on the structural and semantic aspects of folk creativity. After his return to the USSR, he started translating and publishing Czech literature, thus introducing it to the Russian milieu.

Bogatyrev was a prolific author, publishing a great many short articles in a variety of fields. His key books are Cheshskii kukolnyi i ruskii narodnyi teatr (Czech Puppet and Russian Folk Theatre, 1923; together with Roman Jakobson); *Actes magiques, rites et croyances en Russie Subcarpathique* (Magical Actions, Rituals and Beliefs in Sub-Carpathian Ruthenia, 1929) and *Lidové divadlo české a slovenské* (Czech and Slovak Folk Theatre, 1940). The most extensive collections of his work available at the present time are *Souvislosti tvorby. Cesty k struktuře lidové kultury a divadla* (The Context of Creation: In Search of the Structure of Folk Culture and Folk Theatre, 1971) and, in German, *Funktional-strukturale Ethnographie in Europa: Texte aus den 1920er und*

1930er Jahren zu Brauchtum, Folklore, Theater und Film (Funcional-Structural Ethnography in Europe: Texts from the 1920s and 1930s on Customs, Folklore, Theatre and Film, 2011).

KAREL BRUŠÁK

(2 JULY 1913, PRAGUE – 3 JUNE 2004, LONDON)

After three years of studying medicine, Brušák changed over to art history and aesthetics, graduating in 1938 from Charles University. Brušák was introduced to structuralism by his teacher Jan Mukařovský. This led to the publication in 1939 of his article "Znaky v čínském divadle" ("Signs in the Chinese Theatre"). A second article, "Imaginary Action Space in Drama", though probably begun around 1939, was only published in 1991.

After the Munich Agreement in 1938, Brušák left Czechoslovakia and moved to Paris. There he studied at the Sorbonne, taught at the National School of Living Oriental Languages (ENLOV) and worked at the ethnographically-focused Museum of Man. In 1940, following the Nazi occupation, Brušák fled to Great Britain, where he became a member of the Home Guard, among other things manning an anti-aircraft gun. In the 1940s he worked in the Press Department of the Czechoslovak Government-in-Exile. From 1941 he was employed as an editor for the Czechoslovak division of the BBC's Overseas Service. In addition to producing a variety of programmes on art and culture, he was also the author and director of a number of radio plays and satirical political reviews.

In 1948 Brušák obtained British citizenship. During the 1950s he studied Czech and French at the University of London, graduating in 1959. From 1962 until the 1990s he taught Czech and Slovak literatures and comparative literature at the University of Cambridge. He was the teacher of a whole generation of scholars in the field of Czech studies, among them Robert Pynsent and James Naughton.

Throughout his career he published articles on cultural topics in exile periodicals (*Čechoslovák, Obzor, The Central European Observer*). He contributed articles to journals published by the School of Slavonic and Eastern European Studies in London and to *The Year's Work in Modern Language Studies*. Many of his texts remained unpublished during his lifetime, only becoming available later in the posthumous collection *Básnické a prozaické dílo* (Poetry and Prose, 2009).

EMIL FRANTIŠEK BURIAN

(11 JUNE 1904, PLZEŇ – 9 AUGUST 1959, PRAGUE)

Burian studied at the Prague Conservatory until 1924 and then continued in J. B. Foerster's master class in composition, from which he graduated in 1927. Between 1925 and 1929 Burian worked in several avant-garde theatres (The

Liberated Theatre, Theatre Dada and The Modern Studio), first as a musician and later as an actor. He was also a member of the left-wing oriented artistic movement Devětsil. In 1927 Burian established the Voiceband, a group of actors presenting poetry in the form of musically organized recitation.

In 1933 he founded Theatre D in Prague; this enabled him to bring to the stage his own concept of theatre. After Theatre D was closed by the Gestapo in 1941, Burian was arrested; he spent the rest of the war in concentration camps at Terezín, Dachau and Neuengamme. In 1945 and 1946 Burian was in charge of three theatres in Brno as well as the Karlín Operetta Theatre in Prague; later he concentrated solely on reopening Theatre D. Burian also worked as a reporter for Czechoslovak Radio, as an editor for the periodical *Kulturní politika* (Cultural Policy) and as a Czechoslovak Communist Party deputy in the National Assembly.

Burian's productions at Theatre D are regarded not only as the peak of his work as a director but also as the most representative examples of the Czech interwar avant-garde theatre. Burian's work is characterized by its distinctive stage poetics, marked by many metaphors, expressive musicality and the adaptation of texts. He staged non-dramatic texts (narrative literature, montages of poems, folk texts) as well as adaptations of classical plays. As director, he was the main creative force of the whole production, often responsible for the music, visual components, dramaturgical adaptation and direction of the productions. Together with the stage designer Miroslav Kouřil he introduced what they termed theatregraph, a stage form combining projected images with the action of the performer.

In addition to his work in the theatre, he was a film director and composed film, opera and stage music. During his career, Burian was active as a publicist and was the author of theoretical essays on theatre and artistic manifestos.

JIŘÍ FREJKA
(6 APRIL 1904, ÚTĚCHOVICE U PELHŘIMOVA – 27 OCTOBER 1952, PRAGUE)
After Frejka left off his studies at the Prague Conservatory he turned to the study of aesthetics at Charles University in Prague, where he graduated in 1929. During his studies, Frejka was greatly influenced by his teacher Otakar Zich. In 1925, together with Jindřich Honzl, he founded the Osvobozené divadlo (The Liberated Theatre). In 1927 he left it and established (in cooperation with E. F. Burian) Theatre Dada, later renamed the Modern Studio. Between 1930 and 1945 he was a director at the National Theatre in Prague. While working there, he combined his avant-garde conception of theatre with the traditional approach of this rather conservative institution.

In 1946 he was named Dean of the newly established Theatre Faculty of the Academy of Arts (AMU) in Prague; in 1948–49 he served as Rector of AMU.

In 1945 he was named Artistic Director of the Municipal Theatres of Prague and Director of the Vinohrady Theatre in Prague. From 1950–52 he was head of the Karlín Operetta Theatre in Prague. In 1952 Frejka committed suicide, being unable to withstand the political pressures following the Communist coup d'état in 1948.

Frejka's early theatre work was inspired by Russian Constructivism and Czech Poetism. In his work, he often put emphasis on poetic expression and theatricality in the stage action. He created a distinctive directorial style employing many metaphors and marked by lyricism. He also paid special attention to the development of modern acting and its methods (and later the training of actors). His books dealing with theatre theory are numerous, the most important being *Člověk, který se stal hercem* (How People Became Actors, 1929), *Smích a divadelní maska* (Laughter and the Theatrical Mask, 1942), *Jevištní řeč a verš tragédie* (Stage Speech and the Verse of Tragedy, 1944) and *Železná doba divadla* (The Iron Age of the Theatre, 1945).

JINDŘICH HONZL

(14 MAY 1894, HUMPOLEC – 20 APRIL 1953, PRAGUE)

Honzl studied at the College of Education in Prague, subsequently (1914–1927) teaching chemistry and physics at a number of upper primary schools. It was during this period that he started participating in amateur left-wing theatres. In 1920 Honzl and Josef Zora founded the Dědrasbor (short for Dělnický dramatický sbor – Workers' Dramatic Company). This amateur proletarian declamatory group functioned until 1922. Another amateur group that Honzl joined was the Blue Blouse (1926–1927). From 1920 he was a member of Devětsil, an association of left-wing avant-garde artists. In 1925, together with Jiří Frejka, Honzl founded the Osvobozené divadlo (The Liberated Theatre), where he directed many productions, especially plays by Jiří Voskovec and Jan Werich.

Beginning in 1929 Honzl tried to work for traditional theatres subsidized by the state or municipalities – the National Theatre in Brno, then the National Theatre in Prague as well as the Municipal Theatre in Plzeň – but with limited success. During World War II he had few opportunities to work publicly owing to his outspoken Communist and anti-fascist views, with the result that he directed only a few productions with the semi-professional Theatre for 99. At this time, however, he dedicated much energy to the theory of theatre; it was during this period that he published his key texts, among them "Pohyb divadelního znaku" ("The Mobility of the Theatrical Sign").

After World War II Honzl held many leading positions in theatre management and academia. He worked as a director at the National Theatre in Prague (till 1951) and for two years (1946–1948) ran its experimental Studio A; from 1948–1950 he was head of the National Theatre's drama section. In 1946 he was named Professor of theatre studies at Charles University in Prague. In 1951–1952 he was also head of the Department of Theatre Studies and Dramaturgy at DAMU (the Theatre Faculty of the Academy of Performing Arts in Prague).

In 1945 he founded the journal *Otázky divadla a filmu* (Issues in the Theatre and Film), which published theoretical articles as well as topical texts on the theatre (often with clear support for Communist-favoured positions). He was also Editor-in-Chief of the journal *Sovětské divadlo* (Soviet Theatre).

Honzl made many dramatizations and adaptations of the classical pieces of world theatre and montages of poetry. Occasionally he worked in film: *Pudr a benzín* (Powder and Petrol, 1931), *Peníze nebo život* (Your Money or Your Life, 1932), *Dobrý vedoucí* (A Good Boss, 1939).

He published articles on the Russian and French theatre avant-garde and on the theory of theatre in many periodicals. The most representative selections of his work are the volumes *K novému významu umění* (On the New Significance of Art, 1956) and *Základy praxe moderního divadla)* (The Foundations of Modern Theatre Practice, 1963).

MIROSLAV KOUŘIL
(15 OCTOBER 1911, JAROMĚŘ – 29 SEPTEMBER 1984, PRAGUE)

Kouřil began engineering studies at the Higher Technical School in Prague and then went on to study architecture at the Czech Technical University in Prague (1930–1935). From 1935 he was the chief stage designer in E. F. Burian's avant-garde Theatre D. After the enforced closure of Theatre D in 1941, he found employment in the Municipal Theatres of Prague, where he stayed until 1943.

After World War II he became a Communist Party official and participated in creating a system for the political control of Czech theatres, one that started to function fully after the Communist putsch in 1948. He went on to become a member of the Theatre Dramaturgical Council under the Ministry of Information. Between 1947 and 1952, Kouřil worked as the director of the Cultural Department of the Central Committee of the Czechoslovak Communist Party. In 1957 he returned to his stage design work and at the same time began to publish theoretical works concerning stage design, for example *O malém jevišti* (The Small Stage, 1955). From 1957–1963 he was head of the National Theatre's Stage Design Lab. In 1963 he founded the Scenographic Institute in Prague, where he remained as head until 1974. In 1971, he became a Professor at the Faculty of Arts of Charles University. Finally, from 1962–1980 he taught at DAMU (the Theatre Faculty of the Academy of Performing Arts in Prague) and at VŠMU (the Academy of Performing Arts in Bratislava).

He and E. F. Burian created theatregraph, a stage form based on a combination of the acting of the performers and projected images. Kouřil was of central importance for the institutionalization of Czech stage design and for publishing policy in this field, in particular through the series of publications entitled *Knihovna divadelního prostoru* (The Theatrical Space Series), *Prolegomena scénografické encyklopedie* (Prolegomena to a Scenographic Encyclopaedia) and the journals *Interscaena* and *Acta scaenographica*.

JAN MUKAŘOVSKÝ
(11 NOVEMBER 1891, PÍSEK – 8 FEBRUARY 1975, PRAGUE)

Mukařovský studied Czech and French as well as aesthetics at Charles University in Prague from 1910–1915. After his graduation he taught at grammar schools in Plzeň and Prague until 1934. In 1922 he defended his doctorate *Příspěvek k estetice českého verše* (A Contribution to the Aesthetics of Czech Verse). In 1929 he became an Associate Professor at Charles University, teaching aesthetics (his habilitation thesis was *Máchův Máj. Estetická studie* (Mácha's *May*: An Aesthetic Study)). Following the death of Otakar Zich he became head of the Aesthetics Seminar in 1937 and in 1945 a full Professor. Alongside this, had had also been teaching from 1931–1937 at Comenius University in Bratislava.

After 1945 he held many positions at Charles University – most notably Rector (1948–1953) and Chair of its Department of Czech and Slovak Literature and of Literary Studies (1950–1956) – and at the Czech Academy of Sciences, where he was head of the Institute of Czech Literature from 1952–62.

From 1926 on, Mukařovský was a member of the Prague Linguistics Circle, where, with his wide-ranging scholarly background, he was a key figure. His specializations included literary studies, general aesthetics, philology, semiotics and theatre studies. After 1948, in the face of the negative stance of Communist-orientated cultural policies vis-à-vis avant-garde art and structuralist theory, he abjured his previous structuralist views in the article "Ke kritice strukturalismu v naší literární vědě" (Towards a Critique of Structuralism in Our Literary Criticism, 1951). After the liberalization of the political situation in the 1960s, he made a partial return to his earlier positions.

Mukařovský's work has appeared in many publications. In English the most important volumes, translated and edited by John Burbank and Peter Steiner, are *On Poetic Language* (1976), *The Word and Verbal Art: Selected Essays* (1977) and *Structure, Sign and Function: Selected Essays* (1978).

JIŘÍ VELTRUSKÝ
(5 JUNE 1919, PRAGUE – 31 MAY 1994, PARIS)

Veltruský studied aesthetics and sociology at Charles University in Prague from 1939–1941, when all Czech universities were closed by the Nazis. In 1941 he became a member of the Prague Linguistic Circle and published his first studies on theatre theory, among them "Člověk a předmět v divadle" (People and Things in the Theatre, 1939) and "Dramatický tekst jako součást divadla"

("Dramatic Text as a Component of Theatre", 1941). During World War II he was active with the outlawed trade unions and at the end of war he took an active role in the May 1945 uprising in Prague.

From 1945-1948 Veltruský was an assistant to Jan Mukařovský in the Aesthetics Seminar at Charles University; he finished his studies formally by defending his thesis on *Drama jako básnické dílo* (published in 1977 as *Drama as Literature*). He was also very active in the Social Democratic press, criticizing the Stalinist tendencies of the Communist Party.

Immediately following the Communist coup d'état in 1948 Veltruský emigrated to Paris, where he lived until his death. Under the pseudonym Paul Barton he continued writing socio-political analyses of the situation in the Eastern European bloc for radio and various Socialist journals. In the 1960s he worked for the International Confederation of Free Trade Unions (ICFTU). From the 1970s on Veltruský returned to writing theoretical articles, focusing predominantly on aesthetics, theatre studies and semiotics.

English versions of Veltruský's texts on theatre can be found in a number of publications, starting with *Semiotics of Art: Prague School Contributions* (1976). The reconstructed manuscript of *An Approach to the Semiotics of Theatre* was published posthumously in 2012; it includes his complete bibliography.

OTAKAR ZICH
(25 MARCH 1879, MĚSTEC KRÁLOVÉ – 9 JULY 1934, OUBĚNICE)

Zich studied mathematics and physics at Charles University from 1897-1901. During his studies he also attended T. G. Masaryk's lectures on philosophy and sociology as well as lectures on psychology, aesthetics and music history given by the prominent Czech aesthetician Otakar Hostinský. From 1903-1911 Zich worked as a teacher in several secondary schools in Domažlice and Prague. His interest in traditional Czech folk music dates from this period. In 1911, after publishing his *Estetické vnímání hudby* (The Aesthetic Perception of Music), he was appointed an Associate Professor at Charles University.

In 1919, with the establishment of Masaryk University in Brno, he was named Professor of Philosophy and became Chair of the Department of Philosophy there. His lectures dealt mainly with psychology and aesthetics. In 1924 Zich was named Professor of Aesthetics at Charles University in Prague, where he re-established the Department of Aesthetics. Besides his scholarly work, he composed music. Among his musical compositions were three operas: *Malířský nápad* (The Painter's Idea, 1908), *Vina* (Guilt,1915) and *Preciézky* [The Affected Ladies, 1924]. All of these operas were staged at the Czech National Theatre.

His *Estetika dramatického umění: teoretická dramaturgie* (The Aesthetics of Dramatic Art: A Theoretical Dramaturgy, 1931) became the foundational text for Czech theatre studies. Thanks to its innovative, complex and systematic approach to theatre as "dramatic art" (Zich's term), this work has continued to be drawn on by the majority of Czech theatre scholars. Although *The Aesthetics of Dramatic Art* was published five years after the foundation of the Prague Linguistic Circle, Zich's thinking was closely connected to earlier methodological approaches. Hence he is generally regarded as the link between earlier Czech aesthetic formalism and the structuralism of the Prague Linguistic Circle.

In addition to his works on music theory, other equally important works treat the aesthetics of specific arts and the psychology of perception: "K psychologii uměleckého tvoření" (On the Psychology of Artistic Creation, 1911), "Hodnocení esthetické a umělecké" (Aesthetic and Artistic Evaluation, 1917), *O typech básnických* (On Poetic Types, 1918) and "Estetická příprava mysli" (The Aesthetic Preparation of Mind, 1921).

At the present time the only texts of Zich's that are available in English are "Puppet Theatre" (2015 [1923]), "Hodnocení esthetické a umělecké" ("Aesthetic and Artistic Evaluation" (2009, 2010 [1917]) and "Principles of Theoretical Dramaturgy" (2016 [1997]).

INDEX

Printed and bound by CPI Group (UK) Ltd, Croydon, CR0 4YY

09/06/2025

14685715-0001